Social Cognition in Middle Childhood and Adolescence

Social Cognition in Middle Childhood and Adolescence

Integrating the Personal, Social, and Educational Lives of Young People

S. L. Bosacki

WILEY Blackwell

Registered Office
John Wiley & Sons, Ltd, The Atrium, Southern Gate, Chichester, West Sussex, PO19 8SQ, UK

Editorial Offices
350 Main Street, Malden, MA 02148-5020, USA
9600 Garsington Road, Oxford, OX4 2DQ, UK
The Atrium, Southern Gate, Chichester, West Sussex, PO19 8SQ, UK

For details of our global editorial offices, for customer services, and for information about how to apply for permission to reuse the copyright material in this book please see our website at www.wiley.com/wiley-blackwell.

Library of Congress Cataloging-in-Publication Data

Names: Bosacki, Sandra Leanne, author.
Title: Social cognition in middle childhood and adolescence : integrating the personal, social, and educational lives of young people / Sandra Bosacki.
Description: Chichester, UK ; Malden, MA : John Wiley & Sons, 2016. |
    Includes bibliographical references and index.
Identifiers: LCCN 2016014405| ISBN 9781118937952 (cloth) | ISBN 9781118937969 (pbk.)
Subjects: LCSH: Interpersonal relations in adolescence. | Interpersonal relations in children. |
    Self in adolescence. | Self in children. | Social perception in children.
Classification: LCC BF724.3.I58 B67 2016 | DDC 155.5/182–dc23
LC record available at https://lccn.loc.gov/2016014405

A catalogue record for this book is available from the British Library.

Cover image: ivan604/Gettyimages

Set in 10/13pt Minion by SPi Global, Pondicherry, India

Printed in Singapore by C.O.S. Printers Pte Ltd

1   2016

In memory of my beloved late Mother, Ludmilla (Lucia) Olga Bosacki (née Szul)
who left us suddenly on February 28th, 2015. I exist because of her love.

Her love taught me to share, help, and love others.

Contents

Preface   ix
Acknowledgments   xi

Introduction   1

Part I   Foundations   13

1   Social Cognitive Abilities and School Experiences of Young People:
    Theory and Evidence   15

2   Developmental Social Cognition and Research Methodologies   34

Part II   Social Cognitive Educational
and Developmental Research: Self   55

3   The Cognitive Self: Language and Executive Functions   57

4   The Emotional Self: Self-Development and Emotional Regulation   82

5   The Moral Self: Morality, Spirituality, and Self-Development   109

Part III   Social Cognitive Educational
and Developmental Research: Social   133

6   Peer Relationships   135

7   Family Relationships   157

8   Gender and Culture   188

Part IV   Ecologies of Social Cognitive Development   223

9   Digital Worlds and Social Media   225

10 Social Cognition and Behavioral and Emotional Challenges   248

Part V   Future Questions and Implications for Practice: Helping Young People to Move Forward   277

11   Developmental Social Cognitive Pedagogy   279

12   Beyond Social Cognition   307

Conclusion: Closing Thoughts and New Questions   324
Index   328

Preface

As a developmentalist, I often see myself as a "developmentalist detective." A kind of cautious, careful, meticulous and persistent researcher and explorer who is always searching to solve various puzzles of life. Why does this happen? Why did she feel that way? Why did he say that and what did he mean? Why did I say that? Why did I do that? Such personal questions have guided my thinking and provided my main motivation to dedicate my life to the exploration of why people do what they do and what are some of the reasons behind their actions—mostly involving their inner worlds.

As a child I often wished I could read others' minds and I was always so grateful that no one could read mine. One of my main goals as a child and adolescent was to portray a mask of neutrality (always aiming for perfection), that would in no way provide clues as to what I was truly feeling in my heart and soul. I was too sensitive. My experiences as a youth have also motivated me to focus on the time period of middle childhood and early adolescence in my areas of research and teaching. Surprisingly, until the past decade, this age range of emerging adolescents or children approximately between the ages of 8 to 12 are often skipped over in the majority of developmental textbooks and research.

Although much work has now been done and continues to be done on this age range, there still remain large gaps in the literature and numerous unknowns or "puzzles"—a main impetus for this book. As an educator and scholar, I aim to provide a valuable source of critically reviewed research and suggestions for new directions regarding the area of social cognition in youth. That is, how do emerging adolescents make sense of their personal and social, moral, and educational worlds during the transition from late childhood to early adolescent years?

In sum—it is my aim as a developmental interventionist to provide you with an interesting and innovative read regarding cutting-edge research on the personal and social worlds of young people during late childhood and early adolescence. I hope this book inspires readers to continue to read critically like a detective—always asking what are the missing pieces of the puzzle, where do they fit, how, and why. I encourage you to keep searching and never give up—and I invite you to join me on this journey through the "missing years" of youth. I hope you enjoy the adventure! I did, and continue to do so.

S. L. Bosacki, Hamilton, Ontario, January 20, 2015

Acknowledgments

I owe a debt of gratitude to Brock University for providing a rich opportunity to learn from some of the finest scholars in education. I appreciated the timely response and constant support from my editor, Darren Reed. I thank Helen Kemp, Gunalan Lakshmipathy, Manish Luthra, Neil Manley, Karen Shield, Olivia Wells, Liz Wingett, and the Wiley production team for their time in responding to my questions, and for helping me with the manuscript during the production process. I thank my parents and sister for their patience, tolerance, and humor while I devoted my time and energy to this project.

I wish to thank the schools within which I have conducted my past research studies on adolescents' thoughts and emotions over the years. I thank Fiona Blaikie and David Siegel, deans of the Faculty of Education, Brock University; Renee Kuchapski and Mary-Louise Vanderlee from the Department of Graduate and Undergraduate Studies in Education, Brock University, for their support of the book preparation process; and the Faculty of Education for their financial support of my communication with Wiley.

The conceptualization of this book was supported, in part, by funding from the Spencer Foundation, Research and Development Fund, Faculty of Education, Brock University, Internal SSHRC Grants, Brock University, and the Social Sciences and Humanities Research Council of Canada.

Introduction

"You're thinking about something, my dear, and that makes you forget to talk. I can't tell you just now what the moral of that is, but I shall remember in a bit." (Carroll, 1865/1984; p. 105)

Overview

The aim of this chapter is to provide the reader with a broad overview of the field of developmental social cognition, and a rationale for this book. In doing so, I touch upon some of the key issues that I will address in more depth later in the text. To provide the reader with a sense of what is to follow, in the closing section of this chapter I provide a concise overview of the structure and content of the book.

Rationale for the book

In general, this book focuses on some of the main questions of the personal, social, and educational lives of children as they approach adolescence. That is, how can we help young people grow emotionally and socially during the transition from later childhood to early adolescence? How can we encourage them to develop adaptive skills that will help them navigate their identity and relationships through the turbulent transition from approximately ages 7 or 8 to 12 or 13? Why is this important? What are the key issues and implications for children's emotional health and educational lives? That is, how can educators and researchers draw on developmental theory and research to integrate the

Social Cognition in Middle Childhood and Adolescence: Integrating the Personal, Social, and Educational Lives of Young People, First Edition. S. L. Bosacki.
© 2016 John Wiley & Sons, Ltd. Published 2016 by John Wiley & Sons, Ltd.

emotional, cognitive, and social worlds of the child into the classroom, and develop innovative strategies for progressive educational practice?

Given the growth in research on developmental social cognition and emotion regulation, it is surprising that the majority of research in learning and development continues to focus largely on cognitive aspects. Challenging this dominant view, the proposed book discusses theoretical, empirical, and intervention issues relating to *emotional* and *social* aspects of emerging adolescents' educational experiences that may contribute to their broader emotional health and relationships. Drawing largely upon the social cognitive research field of Theory of Mind (ToM) or the ability to "read" others' mental states within the context of social action that allows us to grasp multiple perspectives and thus communicate effectively, I will explore young people's ability to understand or make meaning of human thoughts and feelings, and how such "psychological understanding" relates to their sense of self, peer relations, and sociocommunicative competence within the school setting.

Drawing on examples from recent research and findings from longitudinal studies on children's social cognition, the book will integrate emotional and social accounts of development during childhood and the transition to adolescence. In particular, this book will focus on the ambiguities and challenges young people experience as they navigate the uncharted waters of personal identity and relationships. The book will build on and move beyond traditional cognitive-developmental representations of how children and adolescents learn.

Specifically, the text will provide a critical analysis of cutting-edge empirical evidence from psychological studies, and then translate these research findings into practical suggestions for progressive education. The overriding aim of this book is to foster the growth of new ideas in developmental and educational psychology. Most importantly, this book aims to encourage innovative, forward-thinking strategies that will help young people to develop healthy minds and relationships in the classroom, community, and beyond.

Research has shown that the ability to make sense of the signs and symbols evident in human communication may influence children's self-conceptions and their social interactions in childhood and adolescence. The book will investigate which aspects of these experiences foster the growth of psychological understanding. That is, it will explore how young people understand mind, emotion, and spirit and use this ability to help them navigate their personal identity and relationships with the classroom. This book aims to bridge the gap between theory and practice within the fields of human development and education through a critical review of the literature from the perspective of a researcher and a practitioner.

In particular, this book will critically analyze empirical research evidence concerning aspects of adolescents' social and emotional worlds, including psychological understanding, self-conceptions, and peer relations, and then explore implications for educational practice. Unlike some books that focus either on theory and research or on education, this book seeks to integrate the two, encouraging educators and researchers to critically engage the two disciplines in an ongoing discourse. By combining research findings with real-world applications, the book aims to be of empirical, inspirational, and practical value to readers.

As one of the few existing books that examines social and emotional development during later childhood and early adolescence from a dual perspective of both research and practice, this book is targeted at a wide variety of researchers and educators that range from youth workers to academics. In particular, as the book explores the developmentally appropriate needs of the "whole young person" in education, I hope that the topic will interest "developmental interventionists." Given that the topics of cognition, spirituality, emotion, and education are of interest to educators across the globe, this book also aims to reflect the international scope of social cognitive developmental research.

What Is Social Cognition?

Social cognition research finds that most children between 5 and 8 years develop: (a) an understanding of self-conscious or complex emotions (e.g., pride, embarrassment); (b) complex self-understandings of people as psychological beings; (c) ideas about the nature of the divine, the concept of faith, and the meaning of prayer (Coles, 1990; Fowler, 1981); and (d) an understanding of ambiguity within social and personal contexts. Based on this research and our previous work, this book explores how children in late childhood and early adolescence use their understandings of mind to navigate their identity and relationships during the elementary to secondary school transition.

Why Is There So Little Research on Later Childhood and Early Adolescence?

Since the turn of the 21st century, the age-old debate of traditional, cognitive, and academic-focused versus more student-centered progressive education that recognizes the socioemotional and ethical aspects of learning (Malti & Krettenauer, 2013; Siegel, 2013) continues to remain somewhat contentious. Although there is a broad consensus among parents, educators, school administrators, academics, and community leaders that suggests schools need to help young people become productive, globally aware, and emotionally well citizens, at the same time there remains a group that suggests the main goal of education is to promote cognitive development and academic success. That is, although the majority of researchers and educators agree that young people need to learn how to share responsibility for nurturing social-emotional learning, character development, social engagement, and emotional health (Hughes & Devine, 2015; Neff, 2011), the disciplines of research and education have, until fairly recently, been focused on the cognitive aspects of learning.

Thus, many educators continue to face difficult choices about priorities between academic and socioemotional goals, and continue to be subjected to increasing pressure from policymakers regarding academic achievement (Goldstein & Winner, 2012). Given this demand, schools around the world have become highly demanding environments, and middle schools in particular may be vulnerable. That is, given that the middle-school grades include the student population that involves older children and emerging adolescents, past research suggests that this particular population has been associated with substantial academic and social stress and psychoemotional challenges among young adolescents (Siegel, 2013; Tough, 2012; Twenge, 2006, 2011; World Health Organization, 1999).

Past research shows that *juvenile transition*, or the transition between later childhood and early adolescence, involves simultaneous changes in school environments, social interactions, and academic expectations, and it coincides with other biological and social and emotional changes associated with the transition from childhood to adolescence (Del Giudice, 2014). Past research from an evolutionary developmental approach claims that the transition encompasses all the major domains of behavior—from learning and self-regulation to attachment and sexuality. Moreover, this juvenile transition has been considered to represent a switch point in the development of life history strategies, which according to Del Giudice (2014) are coordinate suites of physiological, morphological, and behavioral traits that partly determine how organisms allocate their resources to key biological activities such as reproduction, growth, mating, and parenting. In particular, this approach claims that gonadarche and adrenarche are endocrinological events during which the adrenal glands are awakened, usually between the ages of 6 to 8 years when the adrenal glands begin to secrete increasing amounts of androgens, mainly dehydroepiandrosterone (DHEA).

According to this evolutionary developmental research, adrenal androgens have a relatively minor influence on a child's physical development, but more of a powerful influence on brain functioning, which has implications for social and cognitive development. According to recent research on pubertal changes in young children (Del Giudice, Angeleri, & Manera, 2009; Greenspan & Deardorff, 2014), gonadarche and adrenarche provide the foundation for the further hormonal changes in early adolescence (e.g., pubarche followed by menarche), and also coordinates the expression of individual differences in life history strategies through the integration of individual genetic variation with a child's social experiences and physical environment throughout infancy and early childhood (Belsky, Steinberg, & Draper, 1991). Similarly, the concept of differential or vantage susceptibility has also gained popularity and may help to explain why some children are framed as particularly sensitive (orchids) versus hardy (dandelions) to environmental context (Belsky & Pluess, 2009; Dobbs, 2009).

Despite this biomedical evolutionary developmental research on middle childhood and early adolescence, little is known about how the role of the environment, particularly the school environment and the transitions throughout grade school to later secondary school, plays a role in development (Greenspan & Deardorff, 2014). That is, how do environmental and biological and hormonal changes affect young people's social cognitive and emotional development during late childhood and early adolescence, including their abilities to cope adaptively with the physical, social, and emotional changes. Thus, building on these past studies, this book will discuss individual and developmental differences in the ways that older children and young adolescents develop within the social cognitive realm.

Understanding of the mind may grow from a foundation of understanding of emotions and develop in part through social relationships (Dunn, 2002). Few studies have examined these links beyond early childhood (Miller, 2012), and even fewer have explored emerging adolescents' understanding of social-emotional issues within the psychosocial context, and its role in understanding others' inner lives (Lopez, Driscoll, & Kistner, 2009; Siegel, 2013). Given the important role that mental state discourse plays in emotional, cognitive, spiritual, and social competence within the classroom (Amsterlaw, Lagatutta, & Meltzoff, 2009; de Rosnay & Hughes, 2006; de Rosnay, Fink, Begeer, Slaughter, & Peterson, 2014; Hughes, 2011), and the need to understand how the emerging adolescent mind and emotion connect (Damon, 2008; Larson, 2011; Siegel, 2013), this book addresses a much needed area of study. More specifically, this book is one of the first to unpack which aspects of these discourses foster the growth of understanding mind, spirit, and emotion within late childhood and early adolescence. To provide a snapshot of the social cognitive landscape of young people, the following sections provide a brief outline of the theoretical and empirical foundations for the book.

What Can We Learn from Research on Social Cognition in Late Childhood and Early Adolescence?

Research on the understanding of mind, spirit, emotion, and morals

The development of the ability to represent and reason from second-order beliefs (two or more mental states) has received little attention during the childhood to adolescence transition. Surprisingly, given that this developmental transition affects our social-emotional experiences and our social cognitive abilities, little research explores how social communication depends mainly on what people believe about other people's beliefs during this developmental time (Hughes, 2011). For example, second-order or interpretive reasoning is important for children's and youths' ability to understand speech acts such as lies, jokes, sarcasm, and irony, as well as gestures (Filippova & Astington, 2008; Goldin-Meadow, 2014; O'Reilly, Peterson, & Wellman, 2014), moral and spiritual beliefs (Bosacki, 2013), and self-representational display rules (Banerjee, Watling, & Caputi, 2011). Such complex reasoning and its related skills continue to develop throughout the adolescent years until adulthood.

Research suggests that emerging adolescents' sense of identity may influence their developing sense of self, particularly ethnicity and gender (Lopez et al., 2009). Given that higher order social reasoning may help adolescents understand the ambiguous nature of personal and social silences (Bosacki, 2013), this book also explores how higher order reasoning may also play a fundamental role in adolescents' understanding of moral and spiritual beliefs, self-conscious moral emotions (e.g., embarrassment, pride), their sense of self and other persons, and social interactions. Recent evidence suggests that emotional understanding continues to develop during early adolescence and beyond, particularly the understanding of complex and ambiguous emotions (Lagatutta, 2014; Pons, Lawson, Harris, & de Rosnay, 2003; Pons, Harris, & de Rosnay, 2004). In contrast to simple emotions (e.g., happiness, sadness), to understand complex sociomoral emotions, children must hold in mind two separate pieces of information: other people's beliefs and societal norms (Saarni, 1999).

Older children and young adolescents may imagine how others judge their actions, and may self-evaluate their behavior against internalized or self-imposed behavioral standards. Thus, the moral imperatives derived from spiritual beliefs (e.g., honesty, beneficence) may also impact emerging adolescents' attitudes and behaviors that could lead to positive or negative self-adjustment. Although complex emotion understanding hinges partly on cognitive abilities such as second-order sociomoral reasoning and self-evaluation, to date no studies have investigated the links between these social and emotional abilities during the transition to adolescence (Larson, 2011). Accordingly, this book aims to discuss the emergence and development of mental state processing that may help young people to navigate the complex and ambiguous self-development and social relationship challenges across the transition from elementary school to high school.

Research on identity and relationships

Despite the theoretical connection linking ToM understanding and self-perceptions, including a sense of a spiritual self (Wellman, 2014), few studies have investigated the links among ToM, self-perceptions, and social interactions directly, especially developmentally across older childhood and adolescence (Wellman, 2014). In relation to ToM, no studies have looked at verbal or graphical self-representations, or other aspects of the self-system such as self-evaluation or self-agency, and self-compassion and care (Bruner, 1996; Neff, 2011; Neff & Germer, 2013). Although research supports positive links between emotional understanding and self-concept (Selman, 1980; Siegel, 2013), spirituality, positive emotional regulation and coping skills, and resilience (Aldwin, Park, Jeong, & Nath, 2014; Neff, 2011; Ream & Savin-Williams, 2003), some studies suggest that relations among ToM, self, and social and emotional competencies may not be uniformly positive (Bosacki, Bialecka-Pikul, & Spzak, 2015; Hughes, 2011).

These contradictory findings have inspired the examination of the complex connection between understanding of others' inner lives and self. Although social interactions and the understanding of complex emotions require second-order reasoning, these areas have been studied separately in the past. Despite the increasing number of studies on ToM and children's friendships and peer interactions, the majority of studies focus on young children (Bosacki, 2013; Miller, 2012; Walker, 2005), with a growing number of studies on older children and emerging adolescents (Banerjee, Watling, & Caputi, 2011; Bosacki, 2013; Bosacki & Astington, 1999; Devine & Hughes, 2013; Fink, Begeer, Hunt, & de Rosnay, 2014; Fink, Begeer, Peterson, Slaughter, & de Rosnay, 2015; Hughes & Devine, 2015).

Although past results suggest that a sophisticated ToM may be linked to greater social competence, it remains unclear as to what kind of role friendships and peer networks play. Yet, the extent to which moral and spiritual competence plays a role remains unexplored. This book extends the exploration of the associations of ToM, self-development, and social relationships during ambiguous or new social situations during the elementary to secondary school transition.

Research on diversity and social cognitive development

Although gender and cultural identity and gender-role orientation may influence young people's ability to understand the mental, emotional, social, moral, and spiritual lives of others, despite investigations of gender differences in sociocognition (Bilewicz, Mikolajczak, Kumagai, & Castano, 2010; Hyde, 2014), results remain contradictory and inconclusive. While some studies show girls to possess higher levels of ToM understanding and emotion understanding (Bosacki & Astington, 1999; Bosacki, 2013; Bosacki & Moore, 2004), others show boys to possess higher levels of emotion understanding, or no gender differences at all (Bosacki, 2015). Differences have also been found across cultures regarding ToM and self-concept in which Canadian youth were found to focus on the role of self in ToM, whereas Polish youth focused on the role of the other (Bosacki, 2013). In sum, more research is needed in the area of gender and cultural diversity within the area of social cognitive development.

What Are the Educational Implications of this Research?

The unique contribution of this book is that it will systematically discuss and analyze how older children and early adolescents learn to understand more about others' thoughts and emotions and how they influence the way they think and feel about themselves and how they relate to others. More specifically, to discuss the emerging field of social cognition that explores ToM, self, and social relations across later childhood and early adolescence, this book will outline past and current research in this area and the implications for educational practice.

The ability to use ToM to help relate mental states to behaviors in others provides a framework to help explain and predict others' behaviors (Hughes, 2011; Wellman, 2014). Given the complex and ambiguous nature of the social and self experiences of older children and early adolescents in the school, interventions that strengthen ToM may serve as a valuable method to help youth develop sensitivity to social information and to develop control and a sense of responsibility over their personal and social lives. This ability to reason about the connections among mind, world, and behavior is important given the difficulties that some young people face when transitioning from elementary to secondary school.

Theoretically, this book illustrates the bidirectional patterns between intra- and interpersonal features of psychological understanding concurrently and longitudinally, and provides the most comprehensive discussion regarding psychological understanding in older children and early adolescents. Practically, the results will help to build positive youth developmental intervention programs and curricula that encourage the use of mental state talk to promote adolescents' sociocognitive and emotional competencies. Such abilities are also referred to as life history strategies or skills such as self-regulation and the development of supportive and caring relationships (Del Giudice, 2014).

This book will further the discourse on the psychological and social lives of young people (Bosacki, 2008; Goleman, 1995; Nelson, Henseler, & Plesa, 2000), and provide implications for practice. For example, some recommendations for practice discussed later in the book (see Chapter 11), include an empirically based framework for an integrated, developmentally appropriate curriculum aimed to foster inter- and intrapersonal competencies through critical enquiry and dialogue. Overall, this book aims to help educators to design and apply timely interventions to enhance emerging adolescents' emotional health and well-being over the course of school transitions.

The ability to understand mind, spirit, and emotion in school is foundational to older children and young adolescents' educational experiences, yet few have studied the influence of understanding mind in school success beyond the age of 7 or 8 (Bosacki, 2013; Devine & Hughes, 2013). Regarding academic competence, research suggests that ToM is associated with the production of stories and general language ability (Hughes, 2011). In addition, research suggests that children's ToM facilitates children's ability to self-monitor their cognitive process and engage in reflexive thinking and develop positive peer relations (Fink et al., 2014; Hughes, 2011).

Taken together, these claims suggest that understanding of mind is linked to higher-order thinking or more advanced mental state reasoning (Hughes, 2011). That is, emerging adolescents who possess high levels of psychological understanding may be more likely to think about their own and others' thinking and engage in critical philosophical enquiry and shared dialogue during the school day (Bruner, 1996). Given that teaching, learning, and relationships play a key role in understanding mind and self-development (Bruner, 1996), this book will explore how emerging adolescents' discourse about inner states including private speech, understanding of mind, spirit, and emotion play a role in the transition from elementary to secondary school (Siegel, 2013).

As I will explain within this book, programs that focus on social-emotional learning (SEL) have become increasingly popular across the globe over the past few decades (Humphrey, 2013). For example, the Roots of Empathy program in Canada is a universal social-emotional learning (SEL) elementary school (K-8) program that promotes specific skills such as empathy, compassion, and self-regulation with the aid of real-life examples, as caregivers and infants visit the classroom and lessons are worked on with the children in the classroom (Gordon, 2005; Schonert-Reichl, Smith, Zaidman-Zait, & Hertzman, 2012). Additional examples include various mindfulness programs (Schonert-Reichl et al., 2015), and recent neuroscience and educational programs (Pincham et al., 2014).

Such programs focus on a preventative approach that helps young people to acquire skills to assist them to develop healthy relationships with self and others, such as coping strategies and resilience. Although evaluative research findings of these programs as to how they improve learners' social-emotional competencies are mixed and are ongoing (Humphrey, 2013), the majority of past evaluations suggest that the majority of the programs are more helpful than harmful in young learners' social and emotional development.

The Structure of this Book

This book is divided into five main sections consisting of 12 chapters. Specifically, the book begins with an Introduction, followed by five conceptually organized sections, or "parts," that frame the 12 chapters on social cognitive development. The book ends with a conclusion. Each of the five "parts" represent a conceptual organizer containing two or three chapters that provide in-depth analysis of relevant topics on social cognitive development in late childhood and early adolescence. In the following paragraphs, I will outline the five organizing sections and their corresponding chapters.

Part I focuses on the conceptual foundations of social cognitive developmental research within later childhood and early adolescence. Part I contains two chapters, with the first chapter providing a critical overview of developmental and educational frameworks that aim to explain young people's social and emotional growth. In particular, Chapter 1 focuses on the definitions and theories of social cognition, and the social cognitive abilities and school experiences of youth. Chapter 2 highlights the importance of developmental research methods within the field of social cognition.

Parts II and III provide a critical overview of developmental social, cognitive research on the social cognition of self and others. The focus of Part II is the self, and each chapter focuses on various aspects of the self in terms of cognition (Chapter 3), emotionality (Chapter 4), and morality (Chapter 5). Part III details past research on young people's social worlds that involve their relationships with peers (Chapter 6), family (Chapter 7), and issues of diversity such as gender and culture (Chapter 8).

Part IV explores how youth apply their social cognitive abilities to diverse social ecologies. Chapter 9 focuses on the importance of the digital world and social media navigation and habits. Chapter 10 highlights the social cognition research on the various behavioral and emotional challenges experienced by young people.

Part V focuses on future questions and implications for practice that aim to help young people to move forward toward a healthy and balanced life. This section will address key future questions for researchers and practitioners that include queries such as: "How do we work with youth to promote a wise and caring critical adolescent listener within the global cultural mosaic?" and "How can we help emerging adolescents to develop a healthy sense of self and relationships?," and finally, "How can we help young people to cope in healthy ways with growing diversity and technology?"

Chapter 11 expands on the connections between social cognitive developmental research and pedagogy, and includes social and emotional learning programs that promote emotional and social learning. Chapter 12 introduces topics that move beyond the category of social cognition through the exploration of nascent but promising areas of research. For example, Chapter 12 outlines research on young people's understanding of the complex moral emotions for self and other including compassion, gratitude, remorse, among others, and emotional sensitivities and internalizing challenges such as unsociability, and social anxiety. Finally, Chapter 12 concludes with a section on future research topics that are in need of further investigation.

Although I have only touched upon a selection of the fundamental issues that will be explored in the ensuing chapters, I hope that this brief introduction has convinced you of the need for a critical appraisal of the field of developmental social cognition. The organization of the text aims to provide a comprehensive coverage of the fundamental issues that pertain to social cognitive development during late childhood and early adolescence.

References

Aldwin, C. M., Park, C. L., Jeong, Y.-J., & Nath, R. (2014). Differing pathways between religiousness, spirituality, and health: A self-regulation perspective. *Psychology of Religion and Spirituality*, 6(1), 9–21.

Amsterlaw, J., Lagatutta, K., & Meltzoff, A. (2009). Young children's reasoning about the effects of emotional and physiological states on academic performance. *Child Development*, 80, 15–133.

Banerjee, R., Watling, D., & Caputi, M. (2011). Peer relations and the understanding of faux pas: Longitudinal evidence for bidirectional associations. *Child Development*, 82, 1887–1905. doi:10.1111/j.1467-8624.2011.01669.x

Belsky, J., & Pluess, M. (2009). Beyond diathesis stress: Differential susceptibility to environmental influences. *Psychological Bulletin*, 135, 885–908.

Belsky, J., Steinberg, L., & Draper, P. (1991). Childhood experience, interpersonal development, and reproductive strategy: An evolutionary theory of socialization. *Child Development*, 62, 647–670. doi:10.1111/j.1467-8624.1991.tb01558

Bilewicz, M., Mikolajczak, M., Kumagai, T., & Castano, E. (2010). Which emotions are uniquely human? Understanding of emotion words across three cultures. In B. Bokus (Ed.), *Studies in the psychology of language and communication* (pp. 275–285). Warsaw, Poland: Matrix.

Bosacki, S. (2005). *Culture of classroom silence.* New York, NY: Peter Lang.

Bosacki, S. (2008). *Children's emotional lives: Sensitive shadows in the classroom.* New York, NY: Peter Lang.

Bosacki, S. (2013). Theory of mind understanding and conversational patterns in early adolescence. *Journal of Genetic Psychology, 174,* 170–191.

Bosacki, S. (2015). Children's theory of mind, self-perceptions, and peer relations: A longitudinal study. *Infant and Child Development, 24,* 175–188. doi: 10.1002/icd.1878

Bosacki, S. L., & Astington, J. W. (1999). Theory of mind in preadolescence: Relations between social understanding and social competence. *Social Development, 8,* 237–255.

Bosacki, S., Bialecka-Pikul, M., & Spzak, M. (2015). Theory of mind and self-concept in Canadian and Polish Youth. *International Journal of Youth and Adolescence, 20*(4), 457–469. doi:10.1080/02673843.2013.804423

Bosacki, S., & Moore, C. (2004). Preschoolers' understanding of simple and complex emotions: Links with gender and language. *Sex Roles: A Journal of Research, 50,* 659–675.

Bruner, J. (1996). *The culture of education.* Cambridge, MA: Harvard University Press.

Coles, R. (1990). *The spiritual life of children.* Boston, MA: Houghton Mifflin.

Damon, W. (2008). *The path to purpose: How young people find their calling in life.* New York, NY: Simon & Schuster.

de Rosnay, M., Fink, E., Begeer, S., Slaughter, V., & Peterson, C. (2014). Talking theory of mind talk: Young school-aged children's everyday conversation and understanding of mind and emotion. *Journal of Child Language, 4,* 1179–1193.

de Rosnay, M., & Hughes, C. (2006). Conversation and theory of mind: Do children talk their way to socio-cognitive understanding? *British Journal of Developmental Psychology, 24,* 7–37.

Del Giudice, M. (2014). Middle childhood: An evolutionary-developmental synthesis. *Child Development Perspectives, 4,* 193–2000.

Del Giudice, M., Angeleri, R., & Manera, V. (2009). The juvenile transition: A developmental switch point in human life history. *Developmental Review, 29,* 1–31. doi:10.1016/j.dr.2008.09.001

Devine, R., & Hughes, C. (2013). Silent films and strange stories: Theory of mind, gender, and social experiences in middle childhood. *Child Development, 84,* 989–1003.

Dobbs, D. (2009). Orchid children. *The Atlantic, 1,* 51–60.

Dunn, J. (2002). Mindreading, emotion understanding, and relationships. In W. W. Hartup & R. K. Silbereisen (Eds.), *Growing points in developmental science: An introduction* (pp. 167–176). New York, NY: Psychology Press.

Filippova, E., & Astington, J. W. (2008). Further development in social reasoning revealed in discourse irony understanding. *Child Development, 79,* 126–138.

Fink, E., Begeer, S., Hunt, C., & de Rosnay, P. (2014). False-belief understanding and social preference over the first 2 years of school: A longitudinal study. *Child Development, 85,* 2389–2403.

Fink, E., Begeer, S., Peterson, C., Slaughter, V., & de Rosnay, P. (2015). Friendlessness and theory of mind: A prospective longitudinal study. *British Journal of Developmental Psychology, 33*(1), 1–17.

Fowler, J. (1981). *Stages of faith: The psychology of human development and the quest for meaning.* New York, NY: Harper & Row.

Goldin-Meadow, S. (2014). How gesture works to change our minds. *Trends in Neuroscience and Education, 3,* 4–6.

Goldstein, T., & Winner, E. (2012). Empathy and theory of mind. *Journal of Cognition and Development, 13*(1), 19-37.

Goleman, D. (1995). *Emotional intelligence.* New York, NY: Bantam Books.

Gordon, M. (Ed.). (2005). *The roots of empathy: Changing the world child by child*. Toronto, ON, Canada: Thomas Allen.

Greenspan, L., & Deardorff, J. (2014). *The new puberty: How to navigate early development in today's girls*. New York, NY: Rodale.

Hughes, C. (2011) *Social understanding and social lives: From toddlerhood through to the transition to school*. New York, NY: Psychology Press.

Hughes, C., & Devine, R. T. (2015). A social perspective on theory of mind. In M. E. Lamb (Ed.), *Handbook of child psychology and developmental science (volume III): Socioemotional processes* (pp. 564–609). Hoboken, NJ: Wiley.

Humphrey, N. (2013). *Social-emotional learning: A critical appraisal*. London, England: Sage.

Hyde, J. (2014). Gender similarities and differences. *Annual Review of Psychology, 65*, 373–398.

Lagatutta, K. (2014). Linking past, present, and future: Child ability to connect mental states and emotions. *Child Development Perspectives, 8*, 90–95.

Larson, R. (2011). Positive development in a disorderly world. *Journal of Research in Adolescence, 21*, 317. doi:10.1111/j.1532-7795.2010.00707.x

Lopez, C. M., Driscoll, K. A., & Kistner, J. A. (2009). Sex differences and response styles: Subtypes of rumination and associations with depressive symptoms. *Journal of Clinical Child and Adolescent Psychology, 38*, 27–35. doi:10.1080/15374410802575412

Malti, T., & Krettenauer, T. (2013). The relation of moral emotion attributions to prosocial and antisocial behaviour: A meta-analysis. *Child Development, 84*(2), 397–412.

Miller, S. (2012) *Theory of mind: Beyond the preschool years*. New York, NY: Psychology Press.

Neff, K. D. (2011). Self-compassion, self-esteem, and well-being. *Social and Personality Psychological Compass, 5*, 1–12. doi:10.111 1/j.1751-9004.2010.00330

Neff, K., & Germer, G. (2013). A pilot study and randomized controlled trial of the Mindful Self-Compassion Program. *Journal of Clinical Psychology, 69*, 28–44.

Nelson, K., Henseler, S., & Plesa, D. (2000). Entering a community of minds: Theory of mind from a feminist standpoint. In P. Miller & E. Scholnick (Eds.), *Toward a feminist developmental psychology* (pp. 61–83). New York, NY: Routledge.

O'Reilly, K., Peterson, C., & Wellman, H. (2014). Sarcasm and advanced theory of mind understanding in children and adults with prelingual deafness. *Developmental Psychology, 50*(7), 1862–1877.

Pincham, H., Matejko, A., Obersteiner, A., Killikelly, C., Abrahao, K., Benavides-Varela, S., … Vuillier, L. (2014). Forging a new path for educational neuroscience: An international young-researcher perspective on combining neuroscience and educational practices. *Trends in Neuroscience and Education, 3*, 28–31.

Pons, F., Harris, P. L., & de Rosnay, M. (2004). Emotion comprehension between 3 and 11 years: Developmental periods and hierarchical organization. *European Journal of Developmental Psychology, 2*(1), 127–152.

Pons, F., Lawson, J., Harris, P. L., & de Rosnay, M. (2003). Individual differences in children's emotion understanding: Effects of age and language. *Scandinavian Journal of Psychology, 44*, 347–411.

Ream, G., & Savin-Williams, R. (2003). Religious development in adolescence. In G. Adams, & M. Berzonsky (Eds.), *Blackwell handbook of adolescence* (pp. 51–59). Malden, MA: Blackwell.

Saarni, C. (1999). *The development of emotional competence*. New York, NY: Guilford.

Schonert-Reichl, K., Lawlor, M. Abbott, D., Thomson, K., Oberlander, T., & Diamond. A. (2015). Enhancing cognitive and social–emotional development through a simple-to-administer mindfulness-based school program for elementary school children: A randomized controlled trial. *Developmental Psychology, 51*, 52–66.

Schonert-Reichl, K., Smith, V., Zaidman-Zait, A., & Hertzman, C. (2012). Promoting children's prosocial behaviors in school: Impact of the "Roots of Empathy" program on the social and emotional competence of school-aged children. *School Mental Health, 4*, 1–21. doi: 10.1007/s12310-011-9064-7

Selman, R. L. (1980). *The growth of interpersonal understanding: Developmental and clinical analyses*, New York, NY: Academic Press

Siegel, D. (2013). *Brainstorm: The power and purpose of the teenage brain*. New York, NY: Jeremy Tarcher/Penguin.

Tough, P. (2012) *How children succeed: Grit, curiosity, and the hidden power of character*. New York, NY: Houghton Mifflin Harcourt.

Twenge, J. (2006). *Generation me: Why today's young Americans are more confident, assertive, entitled—and more miserable than ever before*. New York, NY: Free Press.

Twenge, J. (2011). Narcissism and culture. In W. K. Campbell & J. D. Miller (Eds.), *The handbook of narcissism and narcissistic personality disorder* (pp. 202–209). Hoboken, NJ: Wiley.

Walker, S. (2005). Gender differences in the relationship between young children's peer-related social competence and individual differences in theory of mind. *The Journal of Genetic Psychology: Research and Theory on Human Development, 166*(3), 297–312. doi:10.3200/GNTP.166.3.297-312

Wellman, H. (2014). *Making minds: How theory of mind develops*. Oxford, England: Oxford University Press.

World Health Organization (1999). *WHO Statistical Information System*. Geneva, Switzerland: Author.

Part I

Foundations

"...such beautiful, sacred memory, preserved from childhood, is perhaps the best education." (Dostoevsky, 1990/1880, p. 774)

Section Overview

Based upon the assumption that children's capacity to think about themselves and others both influences, and is influenced by, their social interactions and peer relationships (Wellman, 2014), I will discuss theoretical and empirical literature that supports plausible correlates of social cognitive development including (a) self-cognitions and emotions, and (b) social interactions and peer relationships. This book also addresses the need to examine gender and culture in the links among higher-order social reasoning, emotionality, spirituality, and social behavior. Within the context of a relational and developmental theoretical approach, the next two chapters will describe research studies on social cognition in late childhood and early adolescence. Chapter 1 provides a critical overview of developmental and educational frameworks that aim to explain social and emotional growth in young people. Building on theory and conceptual foundations, Chapter 2 will focus on research methods used to study advanced social cognitive skills such as Theory of Mind (ToM) in late childhood and early adolescence.

Social Cognition in Middle Childhood and Adolescence: Integrating the Personal, Social, and Educational Lives of Young People, First Edition. S. L. Bosacki.
© 2016 John Wiley & Sons, Ltd. Published 2016 by John Wiley & Sons, Ltd.

1

Social Cognitive Abilities and School Experiences of Young People
Theory and Evidence

"... *education is a leading out what is already there in the pupil's soul.*" (Spark, 1962/2009, p. 36)

Introduction

This chapter provides a critical overview of developmental and educational theoretical frameworks that aim to explain social and emotional growth in young people. In addition, I will address the recent applied neurocognitive research's interest in the transition between middle childhood and adolescence, and how this guides empirical research and neuroeducational programs.

Research

The maturation of social cognitive research

In the quarter-century that followed the first wave of developmental social cognitive science of the 1970s and 1980s, human resilience science has expanded and matured, becoming more global and multidisciplinary in scope. Advances in the measurement of genes and biological processes have also boosted research on the neurobiology of resilience. Models, methods, and findings have become more dynamic and more nuanced with a focus on multiple levels of analysis. And finally, as international and multicultural social cognitive research has gained traction, global perspectives on resilience have emerged and stimulated

Social Cognition in Middle Childhood and Adolescence: Integrating the Personal, Social, and Educational Lives of Young People, First Edition. S. L. Bosacki.
© 2016 John Wiley & Sons, Ltd. Published 2016 by John Wiley & Sons, Ltd.

the need to constantly review and refine developmental theory and research methods. Key changes are highlighted in the next section.

Resilience and social cognitive research in developmental science has deep roots in research and theory in child development, clinical sciences, and the study of individual differences (Luthar, Barkin, & Crossman, 2013; Masten, 2014a, 2014b). The history of research on resilience is closely tied to the history of developmental psychopathology (see Masten, 2014a; Moffitt, 2006), and the relational developmental systems theory (RDST) and evolutionary developmental systems theory that infuses this integrative approach to understanding variations in human adaptation over the life course (Del Giudice, 2014; Lerner, Lerner, Von Eye, Bowers, & Lewin-Bizan, 2011; Mueller, 2014; Overton, 2013).

Over the decades since the science on resilience in children began, the conceptualization of the construct grew more dynamic and reflected a broader systems transformation in developmental science (Lerner et al., 2011; Mueller, 2014; Zelazo & Lyons, 2012). This relational developmental systems framework (RDST; Overton, 2013) integrated ideas from developmental systems theory (Lerner et al., 2005), ecological-developmental systems theory (Bronfenbrenner & Morris, 2006; Del Giudice, 2014), family systems theory (Bretherton, 2010), biological systems (Kim & Sasaki, 2014), and developmental psychopathology (Cicchetti, Toth, & Handley, 2015; West-Eberhard, 2003). Contemporary systems models assume that many systems interact or "co-act" to shape the course of development, across levels of function, from the molecular to the macro levels of physical and sociocultural ecologies.

The resilience of an individual over the course of development depends on the function of complex adaptive systems that remain in constant interaction and transformation. As a result, the resilience of a person remains fluid and dynamic and enables an individual to remain flexible within, and adapt to, multiple interacting systems and contexts. Many of the widely observed protective factors for individual resilience in children reflect adaptive systems shaped by biological and cultural evolution (Del Giudice, 2014; Masten, 2014a, 2014b).

Research has suggested that protective factors that strengthen one's emotional resilience include the development of close and secure attachment relationships, reward systems and mastery motivation, intelligence and executive functions, and forms of cultural belief systems and traditions including religion (Masten, 2014a, 2014b). Each of these adaptive systems are considered at various levels of analysis from multiple disciplinary perspectives, including anthropology, biology, ecology, economics, psychology, and sociology. Thus, overall, multilevel dynamics or processes that link levels of function within and across systems hold considerable interest in resilience theory.

For example, there remains great interest in the processes by which adversity is biologically embedded and mitigated (Kim & Sasaki, 2014); researchers are interested in how violence at the community level influences family function and thus may cascade to affect children (Main & Solomon, 1990). Other resilience researchers explore how good parenting influences the development of executive function skills in children at the neural and behavioral levels (e.g., Masten, 2014a).

In addition, research on environmental or ecological disasters underscore the interdependence of individual, family, and community systems, as well as biological, physical, and ecological systems across levels (Masten, 2014b). Large-scale catastrophic life events like the 2006 hurricane in the United States, or the 2011 tsunami in Japan, challenge or may impair many adaptive systems simultaneously across large areas and groups of people. Consequently, recovery and growth can take some time, and adequate preparation for disasters usually requires an integrated perspective with consideration of multiple, interdependent systems.

Why emerging adolescence?   Recently, the academic discourse of middle to late childhood and early adolescence has become increasingly complex and multivoiced (Blakemore & Mills, 2014; Del Giudice, 2014; Siegel, 2013). The assumptions that underlie the developmental period known as emerging adolescence help shape teaching practices, curricular decisions, and social roles. However, such discourse has the potential to construct "terministic screens" that may homogenize students, and may render many of their behaviors invisible to school personnel and researchers. As Burke (1990) explains, terministic screens work like multicolored photographic lenses to filter attention toward and away from a version of reality: "Even if any given terminology is a reflection of reality, by its very nature as a terminology it must be a selection of reality; and to this extent it must function also as a deflection of reality" (p. 1035).

   Researchers have suggested that in addition to biological and physical changes such as adrenarche (Del Giudice, Angeleri, & Manera, 2009; Geary, 2010), students' gender stereotypic beliefs may also help explain gender differences in academic self-belief (Bosacki, 2015) and peer relations (Hughes & Devine, 2015). However, given the complexity of the social world of older children and emerging adolescents, research on why girls and boys may view self-confidence and competencies in multiple contexts through different lens remains sparse (Rose & Rudolph, 2006). For example, recent findings suggest that stereotypic gender-role and cultural expectations may influence emerging adolescents' developing sense of self and their social relations. Furthermore, the lack of attention on sociocultural issues in developmental social cognitive science advocates the need for the exploration of sociocultural influences such as race, ethnicity, and gender (Hyde, 2014). In Chapter 8 I will discuss the role of gender and culture in social cognitive development among emerging adolescents.

Why is social cognitive development in emerging adolescence special?   Over the past decade, psychoeducational research has come to envision older children and adolescents as interpretive psychologists who depend upon a mentalistic construal of reality to make sense of their social world (Blakemore & Mills, 2014; Bruner, 1996). This psychocultural approach to education provides a new framework in which to investigate the phenomenon of adolescents' social understanding or social cognition, including studies that explore: "theories of mind" (Astington, 1993; Byom & Mutlu, 2013), various aspects of the "self" (Harter, 1999; Marshall, Parker, Ciarrochi, & Heaven, 2014), and how these areas of social reasoning are connected to social behavior. Although there is a growing body of evidence to show that a positive link exists between social cognitive thought and social action (Hughes, 2011; Laible, McGinley, Carlo, Augustine, & Murphy, 2014), few studies have examined such a link in children beyond the early school-age years (Devine & Hughes, 2013). Given these past findings with younger children, it can be expected that such links may also exist between social cognitive thought and behavior among emerging adolescents.

Despite the fact that the school is a complex social institution that provides a data-rich environment in which to explore how young adolescents' make sense of their social world, little is known about the role that social cognitive processes play in self-development and social relations within the school context (Eccles & Roeser, 2003; Hughes, 2011). Given that schools are formal organizations and have their own characteristics (values, activities, rituals, norms), the school as a culture can have an influence on all aspects of adolescents' development. As Bruner (1996) states, viewed as a "culture," schools can create an atmosphere or climate that can either promote or impede self-expression, cognitive and emotional growth, and self-compassion.

A psychocultural and relational developmental systems approach to social understanding focuses on emerging adolescents' ability to recognize themselves and other people as psychological beings. It can draw on various social cognitive and epistemological theories and research (Selman, 1980; Tomasello, 2014a, 2014b), and may shed some light on the wealth of findings from psychosocial studies that show a significant drop in self-worth and an increase in reflection and self-conscious emotions approximately between the ages of 10 to 12 (Harter, 1999; Rochat, 2009). Similarly, there is substantial evidence of declines in academic motivation, attachment to school, and academic achievement across the emerging adolescence years (approximately ages 10 to 13 or 14) (Eccles & Roeser, 2003; Simmons & Blyth, 1987). Such developments can have a direct influence on adolescents' inner world, and how they choose to express themselves. In other words, schools have an important impact on how adolescents choose to "voice" their thoughts and avoid being silent.

Given the complexities surrounding the emerging adolescent experience (both personal and social), the adolescent personal fable has often been discussed in negative terms because of its potentially self-harmful consequences. That is, some risk-taking older children and adolescents may believe that they are immune to social and emotional problems experienced by others (Blakemore & Mills, 2014; Elkind, 1967; Finy, Bresin, Korol, & Verona, 2014). As a result, they may tend to disregard natural physical limitations, sometimes even the permanence of death. Moreover, such beliefs of infallibility may lead to the engagement of risk-taking behaviors (e.g., driving while inebriated or texting, engagement in extreme risk sports).

The personal fable, however, may also have protective value against suicidal, self-harming, and depressive behavior. For example, Cole (1989) found that adolescents who endorsed optimistic views of the future and life-affirming values were less likely to resort to suicidal thoughts or behavior. Cole hypothesized that adolescents who have a strong sense of their own invulnerability, and who do not see themselves as possible targets for silencing, nor feel the need to silence their own voices, will likely see themselves as capable of effectively coping with life challenges. Thus, Cole supports the idea that aspects of the adolescent personal fable may act as a buffer against suicidal thoughts and behavior (Larson, 2011).

In contrast, sometimes impulsivity, fueled by the belief of invincibility and coupled with a failure to recognize one's own limitation, has the potential to lead the young person who feels alienated from parent, family, and peers. Such impulsive tendencies may also lead the youth to develop self-critical, punitive, and cruel thoughts and perhaps attempt self-harmful behaviors such as suicide (Nock, Prinstein, & Sterba, 2009). For example, the report on adolescent suicide formulated by the Group for the Advancement of

Psychiatry (1996) suggested that the changes that characterize late childhood and early adolescence may leave some young people at risk.

A heightened sense of self-consciousness, fluctuating levels of self-esteem and incoherent, unstable sense of self, and a degree of impulsivity may set the stage for the development of future social and emotional difficulties such as conduct and impulse challenges (Del Giudice et al., 2009), and anxiety and internalizing or self-harm tendencies (Brinthaupt, Hein, & Kramer, 2009). The developmental characteristics may place particular youth at a heightened risk for an inappropriate response to stress under the most optimal or ideal circumstances. (Larson, 2011; Rose, 2014; Siegel, 2013). Even a relatively minor perceived loss or rejection or disappointment in oneself has the potential to trigger self-destructive urges and thoughts, which can lead to self-silencing, self-alienation, and self-harm (Callan, Kay, & Dawtry, 2014).

Later childhood and early adolescence is also a special time when many youth establish a degree of autonomy from their family and take significant steps in personal identity formation. At the same time, peer relationships become increasingly important. Family and peers may have positive and negative consequences for a young person's private speech and experiences of social silences. In the cases where emerging adolescents do not feel comfortable to voice their own opinions, they may distance themselves from their friends and families.

Also, given North America's relatively age-stratified society, emerging adolescents and their peers may interact within a social milieu that may not be a positive source of support (Blakemore & Mills, 2014; Robbins, 1998). Thus, emerging adolescents may feel that their personal voice is silenced and not valued by their family or peers, which, in turn, may lead to greater self-silencing, and consequent social and emotional challenges such as depression, self-harming behavior, or aggressive and impulsive behaviors (Del Giudice, 2014; Larson, 2011; Nock, 2009; Nock et al., 2009).

Social cognitive research: Theory of mind

Over the past decade, social cognitive research has increasingly come to envision the child as an interpretative psychologist (Astington & Olson, 1995; Tomasello, 2014a). That is, this research approach views the child as an intersubjective theorist (Bruner, 1996); one who depends on a mentalistic construal of reality to make sense of the social world. Based on the collective works of various social constructivists (Gergen & Walhrus, 2001; Tomasello, 2014b; see Harter, 1999 for review), and symbolic-interactionists (Mead, 1934; see Bruner, 1996), such an approach proposes that children come to understand or make meaning from their experiences guided by the tenets of relativism, constructivism, narrative and self-agency. Moreover, the Vygotskian notion that cognitive growth stems from social interaction is congruent with humanistic and psychobiological-cultural approaches to development (Bruner, 1996; Rochat, 2009).

Also referred to as a psychocultural or social ecological developmental approach (Bronfenbrenner & Morris, 2006; Sternberg, 2014; Tomasello, 2014a), this approach draws on various theories that assume children create and then rely on both emotional and cognitive structures to make sense of the world (Del Giudice et al., 2009; Piaget,

1967/1929; Rochat, 2009). Such an integrative approach may assist researchers to answer the increasingly common question of how children come to make meaning from their social experiences and eventually become "socio-emotionally literate" or socially intelligent (Goleman, 1995). Thus, the larger question becomes which conceptual framework can provide a unifying developmental theory that emphasizes the interactions among thought, emotion, and action in emerging adolescents?

In search of such a theory, developmental social scientists continue to investigate the social cognitive underpinnings of young people's ability to understand the social and personal world. The main goal of such research is to find a theory that will assist in their exploration of how children acquire the knowledge that others are thinking and feeling beings. Accordingly, over the past three decades, many researchers have approached the area of social cognition from what is referred to as a "Theory of Mind" (ToM) perspective. This unique way of viewing social understanding has also been referred to as folk psychology, commonsense psychology, or belief-desire reasoning (Apperly, 2012; Bjorklund & Ellis, 2014; Byom & Mutlu, 2014).

A ToM perspective on social cognitive development is unique in that it is founded on the premise that all humans are folk or commonsense psychologists. That is, humans understand social information by means of ascribing mental states to others and thinking that overt behavior is governed by these states. This ability to "read" others' minds, and to predict how people will act in social situations, focuses on the understanding of mental states such as beliefs, desires, and intentions (Devine & Hughes, 2014; Hughes, 2011; Ruffman, 2014).

More specifically, to understand social behavior, children must first understand mental representation. That is, they must understand that there is a difference between thoughts in the mind and things in the world (Astington, 1993). The inference of mental states from people's actions enables children learn to understand that minds are active and contain mental states that can bring about events in the world. Thus, the same world can be experienced in different ways by different people. Each person may have a distinctive belief about reality.

A ToM approach to social cognition claims that a largely implicit conceptual framework with intentional elements allows us to understand, explain, and predict our own and other people's behavior and mental states (Blakemore & Mills, 2014; Ruffman, 2014). Consistent with this view is the assumption that this mentalizing ability allows children to make sense of social behavior by ascribing desires and intentions to others' actions for the specific purpose of regulating their interactions with others (Tomasello, 2014a). Moreover, research suggests that the ability to recognize, represent, and understand others' thoughts and emotions in early childhood provides the social cognitive foundation for the later development of social and emotional competency (Rochat, 2009).

Interestingly, although the interest in the development of folk psychology has been paralleled by an interest in the social cognitive processes of the adolescent (Larson, 2011; Siegel, 2013), the two research areas have failed to connect. Perhaps the greatest impediment that has prevented researchers from adapting a ToM approach to social cognitive development beyond early childhood has been the lack of conceptual and methodological agreement among ToM theorists. Examples of some of the ongoing conceptual debates include the argument of how exactly a "Theory of Mind" develops beyond preschool, and what exactly *are* the processes or systems that develop (Apperly, 2012; Devine & Hughes, 2014)?

Although ToM research could enrich investigations of social cognition in older children and adolescence, particularly in the areas of self-concept (Wellman, 2014), perspective-taking (both affective and cognitive) (Hughes, 2011), and person perception (Bosacki & Astington, 1999), the two research areas (ToM and developmental social cognitive research including social information-processing; Dodge, 1986), have now started to collaborate and build on each other's findings (Ibanez et al., 2013; Lagattuta, 2014; Lagattuta, Nucci, & Bosacki, 2010).

Given that ToM understanding, or the ability to "read" others' mental states within the context of social action, can also be referred to as psychological understanding (Bruner, 1996) this ability enables children to understand multiple perspectives and to communicate with others (Nelson, Henseler, & Plesa, 2000). Recent research in children's ToM shows that, by age 5, children begin to understand that people have desires that lead them to actions, and that these actions are based on beliefs. Beyond the age of 5, however, little is known about the links between psychological understanding and social experience (Lagattuta, 2014).

Given that children who possess an advanced psychological understanding are more likely to think about their own and others' thinking during the school day, such an ability has important educational implications (Pincham et al., 2014). For example, recent research shows that this ability to make a meaningful story out of people's thoughts and actions plays a role in self-regulated learning and language competence such as storytelling. Moreover, research has shown that the ability to "read others," or to make sense of the signs and symbols evident in human communication, has an influence on children's self-conceptions and their social interactions.

Emerging adolescents' theories of mind: A case for complexity

Despite the claim that late childhood and early adolescence is a pivotal time in many areas of social cognitive development including cognitive reflexivity (Piaget, 1929), self-concept formation (e.g., Erikson, 1968; Harter, 1999), and interpersonal relations (e.g., Rosenberg, 1965; Selman, 1980), a relational developmental systems approach to help explain the links among these social cognitive areas remains to be taken. This inquiry promotes a better understanding of the two main tasks of later childhood and adolescence which are: (1) the intrapersonal task of constructing a coherent psychosocial identity (Erikson, 1968; Larson, 2011), and (2) the interpersonal task of understanding the multiple and contradictory intentions of others, allowing judgments to be made in an uncertain and ambiguous world (Bosacki, 2012). Thus, drawing on various social cognitive (Selman, 1980) and epistemological theories and research (Wellman, 2014), a folk psychological approach to social cognition may help to illustrate the linkages among the understanding of mental states in others, self-concept, and social relations.

Past research studies have focused mainly on the aspect of children's ToM development which involves their recognition of false belief (Wimmer & Perner, 1983). Around 4 years of age, children understand that people act on their representation of the world, even in situations where it misrepresents the real situation. That is, at this age children can represent and reason from people's first-order beliefs (one mental state): X believes p. From as young as age 5 or 6, children are able to represent and reason from second-order beliefs (two or more mental states): X believes that Y believes that P (Perner & Wimmer, 1985). As mentioned earlier, compared to first-order ToM, the development of second-order understanding has received little attention in the literature. This is surprising, given that much of our social interaction depends on what people believe about other people's beliefs and emotions (Astington, 1993).

The importance of second-order reasoning has been shown to be related to children's ability to understand speech acts such as lies and jokes (Fu, Xiao, Killen, & Lee, 2014), and in their ability to understand self-representational display rules (Banerjee & Yuill, 1999). Although research on ToM and social and self-competence remains in its infancy, there are some research findings that suggest that such higher-order reasoning is also fundamental to children's understanding of complex emotions, their self-concept, and social interactions.

For example, in some of our past research with early adolescent learners, we found that a more sophisticated ToM ability was positively related to social competence for boys only. In contrast, for girls, the link between ToM and social competence was moderated by self-perceptions (Bosacki, 2000; Bosacki & Astington, 1999). More specifically, if girls scored relatively high on the ToM measure (i.e., possessed a sophisticated ToM understanding), and also reported a relatively negative sense of self, compared to boys they received relatively low social competence ratings from their teachers and peers. Thus, how girls felt about themselves influenced the connection between their ToM ability, or their ability to "read other" in social situations, and how their teachers and peers viewed them within a social context.

Many social cognitive (e.g., Bruner, 1996; Harter, 1999; Selman, 1980; Tomasello, 2014b), and ToM theorists (e.g., Astington, 1993; Miller, 2009; Wellman, 2014) agree that the ability to understand self and others within the context of social relations develops in complexity throughout one's lifetime. However, how this growth comes about and what it consists of remains debatable (Byom & Mutlu, 2013). Recently, various authors have emphasized that to better understand the concept of a general, overarching Theory of Mind, one must map out or chart the components that create an adult or mature Theory of Mind (Apperly, 2011; Apperly, Samson, & Humphreys, 2009; Hughes, 2011). Although a few attempts to apply the ToM approach to social understanding have been expanded to the early adolescent years (e.g., Chandler, 1987; Miller, 2012), the majority of literature written on later childhood and adolescent social cognition remains mainly within the field of social or social cognitive psychology.

Furthermore, the idea that effective communication is dependent upon both the attribution of mental states to ourselves and others and the maintenance of a positive self-concept remains relatively unexplored in older children and adolescents (Rochat, 2009). Thus by focusing on the understanding of, and the coordination with, the perspective of others, a ToM approach to social cognitive development in the preadolescent may help to illustrate the relations between social understanding (theory of other minds and emotions), intrapersonal understanding (theory of one's own mind and emotions), and social relations (Tomasello, 2014a).

Social cognitive (Bruner, 1996; Pinker, 2007; Tomasello, 2014b) and ToM theorists (Wellman, 2014) have recognized the significant role that higher-order mental states play in social interactions. Both groups of researchers contend that complex, reflexive reasoning skills are a prerequisite for the ability to understand self and others within the context of social relations. However, the mechanisms and processes surrounding how this reasoning ability develops, or what it consists of, lack consensus (Miller, 2012). Despite the potential to shed light on the complex workings of the adolescent mind, the two research paradigms of ToM and social cognition have only recently started to connect beyond the early school-age years (Devine & Hughes, 2013).

To date, the majority of social cognitive research remains largely fragmented, as studies of advanced ToM often remain in isolation and disconnected from other social cognitive abilities (Bosco, Gabbatore, & Tirassa, 2014; Byom & Mutlu, 2013; Lagattuta et al., 2015). Likewise, social cognitive studies on attribution and perspective or role-taking (both of self and other) (e.g., Selman, 1980, 1989), person perception (e.g., Bosacki & Astington, 1999), and empathetic sensitivity and emotional regulation rarely explore or cite possibly related ToM research (e.g., Hollenstein & Lougheed, 2013). Similarly, the realm of social cognitive research has generally failed to integrate the mainly cognitive studies of higher-order mental processes with developmental research on older children and adolescents (e.g., Pinker, 2007).

For example, studies have shown that the emergence of relativist thought, or the process of becoming a reflective knower (Chandler, 1987), co-occurs with the ability to understand the meaning of promising (Maas, 2008; Miller, 2012); social commitment (Malti & Krettenauer, 2013); sarcasm, irony, and gesture (Filippova & Astington, 2008; Goldin-Meadow, 2014; O'Reilly, Peterson, & Wellman, 2014); self-conscious emotions such as shame and guilt (Rochat, 2009); and metacognitive and metalinguistic verbs (verbs that represent mental states) (Astington & Olson, 1995; Pinker, 2007). Moreover, despite the increasing interest in the development of an advanced constructivist ToM beyond middle childhood (Devine & Hughes, 2013), at the time of this writing, there have been no studies that have attempted to either conceptualize or systematically empirically study the workings of the emergent adolescent mind as a dynamic, multifaceted network of cognitive and affective components that may serve as a template for self and other understanding.

Furthermore, this book defines social cognitive development in later childhood and early adolescence within a critical analysis of psychosocial studies that show a significant drop in self-worth (Harter, 1999; Larson, 2011), and an increase in self-consciousness (Rochat, 2009; Simmons & Blyth, 1987) between the ages of approximately 8 and 13 years. Given that some social cognitive theories claim that links may exist between the development of relativistic and self-conscious thought and the human tendency to experience generic self-doubt and fear of rejection (implying a decrease in self-worth) (Rochat, 2009), more research is needed on social cognitive development and emotional experiences of emerging adolescents. Moreover, despite the recent popularity of cultural psychology and cultural neuroscience (Bruner, 1996; Kim & Sasaki, 2014), a large gap continues to exist in the ToM literature concerning sociocultural issues such as gender, culture, and socioeconomic status (Hughes, 2011).

The need for an integrative, multilateral theory to explain an advanced ToM is supported by the assertion that the period of late childhood and emerging adolescence (approximately 8–13 years) is the second period of individuation that involves a developmental "shift-point" (Blakemore & Mills, 2014; Blos, 1979; Del Giudice, 2014; West-Eberhard, 2003). That is, when a developmental shift occurs, a regulatory mechanism may help to alter all areas of development. Within this shift, the fusion of interpersonal and intrapersonal understanding enables the young person to continue to develop a sense of identity and attachments with others (Del Giudice, 2014; Erikson, 1968).

The majority of past literature on social cognition has assumed that self and person perceptions develop in parallel (Tomasello, 2014a). That is, self and other concepts arise simultaneously from social interactions, develop in the same fashion, and share the same features. Alternatively, in agreement with other social cognitive theorists (Hughes, 2011), a ToM approach to social cognition may provide an avenue to investigate the dynamic relations between these two processes.

Drawing on various theories of social cognitive processes, particularly that of attribution theory (e.g., Killen & Smetana, 2012), conceptual role-taking (Piaget, 1929; Selman, 1980), folk psychology and the conceptual formulation of social understanding in adolescence (Miller, 2012), empathy (e.g., Harris, 1989; Lonigro, Laghi, Baicco, & Baumgartner, 2014), and person perception, ToM research provides a framework to help investigate the connections between understanding of self and other and social interaction. Given the philosophical foundations of folk psychology and the conceptual formulation of social understanding in adolescence, researchers have yet to describe how this understanding influences self-concept and social relations in emerging adolescence. Such a framework will provide the opportunity to study the influences of a developing ToM on older children and early adolescents' construals of other people, the self, and the reasons behind social behavior.

Similarly, ToM as an ability to co-construct or narrate one's social reality may also provide a framework in which to investigate the consequences of the process of becoming "perspectival." That is, how does the process of becoming a constructivist epistemologist influence one's social and emotional development (Tomasello, 2014b). For example, some social cognitive developmentalists suggest that as children enter adolescence they move from a dichotomous "true/false" view of knowledge and mind to a more constructivist or "degrees of certainty" view (Blakemore & Mills, 2014; Larson, 2011). This view of development has just begun to incorporate aspects of social-emotional and cultural competence (Blakemore & Mills, 2014). It is therefore important to investigate traditionally researched areas of social cognitive understanding from the perspective offered by ToM theorists.

Chandler (1987) proposed that a collaborative approach toward understanding the adolescent's mind may help to illustrate the social cognitive and emotional processes that occur during early adolescence, when a shift from a realistic to a constructivistic epistemology occurs (e.g., Lalonde & Chandler, 1995). More specifically, Chandler suggested that the investigation of conceptual role-taking, empathetic sensitivity, and person perception may provide a clearer picture of how emerging adolescents infer mental states in others. That is, the examination of these three constructs within the context of relationships may help to explain the complex social cognitive processes underlying social understanding during emerging adolescence. Accordingly, the following section provides a brief overview of research findings in each of the three social cognitive constructs.

Conceptual role-taking   As already noted by various ToM and social cognitive researchers (Astington, 1993; Flavell & Miller, 1998; Harris, 1989; Hughes, 2011), research on young people's understanding of mind is reminiscent of the notion of social role-taking or perspective-taking that took place almost 50 years ago (e.g., Flavell & Miller, 1998). However, the majority of studies performed during the 1960s and 1970s involved preschool and early grade school children. Although an attempt was made by cognitive developmentalists to investigate perspective-taking and ego development in older children, the majority of the studies involved older adolescents and adults and often failed to investigate social-cultural factors such as gender and culture-related variables (Hyde, 2014).

For example, an account of how children learn to differentiate self from other is offered by Selman's (1980) model of interpersonal understanding. Selman's theory explains how we learn to coordinate their perspective with others and thus develop role-playing skills. According to Selman's five-stage theory, children gradually progress from an egocentric stage to learning how to appreciate that others also have perspectives and that these may be different from their own.

Selman's model states that emerging adolescents (i.e., 10- to 13-year-olds) learn to understand multiple perspectives simultaneously. Within this third person or mutual perspectives stage, the emerging adolescent abstracts the self from an interactive situation and views the perspectives of each person involved in the interaction. That is, the individual viewpoint can be reflected upon from that of another person. However, Selman's (1980) model has been criticized for an overemphasis on the structure of various stages that closely resemble Piagetian stages of cognitive development (Schaffer, 1996).

Theory of Mind research also readdresses the development of young people's egocentrism (Chandler, 1987; Elkind, 1967; Rochat, 2009). One example from past literature refers to adolescents' failure to differentiate between their own thoughts and those of others as the imaginary audience syndrome. Similarly, as mentioned earlier, overdifferentiation between adolescents' own thoughts and the thoughts of others is known as the personal fable. From a ToM perspective, young people who experience this egocentrism may find it challenging to understand how others think, feel, and have different perspectives. That is, since some youth may find it difficult to take the roles or perspectives of another person, they may also have difficulty trying to imagine themselves in "another person's shoes"—either cognitively or emotionally. Such results imply that the links between mental reasoning for self and other are complex and suggest the need for further investigation in older children and adolescents (Ibanez et al., 2013).

Drawing on past conceptual role-taking research, a ToM approach to social cognition integrates the multiple cognitive abilities that one utilizes to make sense of human behavior. A ToM approach also enables examination of the complexity of social understanding by investigating the different aspects of perspective-taking such as understanding others' thoughts and emotions. In contrast to past perspective-taking research that assumed thought caused emotion and behavior, a ToM approach to social cognition illustrates the complex transactional relations between cognition and emotion.

In addition, within a ToM framework, researchers explore and delineate the dynamic interplay among cognitive abilities, emotional, social, and moral action. Theory of Mind research may thus provide an integrative and dynamic overarching conceptual framework that guides research on social cognitive, emotional, moral, and spiritual competencies (Apperly, 2012; Hughes, 2011; Miller, 2009). Outlined below are various social cognitive components of ToM research that may help educators and researchers to further explore the complex interplay among the ToM-related variables.

Empathetic sensitivity   Research suggests that young children's initial emotional understanding provides the foundation for the later development of empathy (ability to recognize emotions in others) and prosocial behavior (Paulus, 2014). Relatedly, a ToM approach to emotional understanding assumes that to achieve effective social relations youth must interpret and understand both the thoughts and feelings of self and other. According to Killen and Smetana (2013), empathy contains both affective and cognitive components, and is related to one's ability to interact with others in relationships. Although some ToM researchers are starting to show an interest in the role that empathetic sensitivity plays in the understanding of minds (Ensor, Devine, Mark, & Hughes, 2014; Hughes, 2011; Ibanez et al., 2013; Wellman, 2014), more ToM research is needed on the role empathetic sensitivity plays in adolescents' social understanding within various cultural backgrounds and across varying levels of developmental ability.

Past research shows that the majority of typically developing young people understand multiple internal states and relate them to each other in a coherent fashion (Harris, 1989). Studies have also shown that most children as they approach adolescence begin to develop the ability to understand that another person or themselves may have conflicting emotions and/or hide emotions from others (Harris, 1989). As I will explain further in Chapters 4 and 5, related research on the more complex, or self-conscious, emotions shows that most children gradually learn how to understand complex emotions, or that one can have conflicting emotions throughout late childhood and emerging adolescence (Harter, 1999).

Furthermore, the importance of empathy and self-regulation in social cognitive development is supported by research from two relatively independent, although related, areas. ToM research has shown that, in addition to cognitive understanding, emotional understanding plays an independently significant role in school-aged children's social interactions (Bosacki, 2015; Hughes, 2011). Similarly, social cognitive studies of empathy in early adolescence have generally found that empathetic responding is positively related to popularity or peer acceptance (Bosacki, 2000; Hughes, 2011), to peer competence (e.g., Deci & Ryan, 2013; Wellman, 2014), and delayed self-gratification or self-control and regulation (Mischel, 2014). Thus, to achieve a fuller understanding of an emerging adolescent's ToM, the two research areas need to connect in more comprehensive and coherent ways. I will elaborate on the role emotions play in young people's identity development and social cognitive experiences such as self-regulation later on in the book.

Person perception   Although research on person perception stems from diverse theoretical and methodological perspectives (Blakemore & Mills, 2014), the basic assumption is that social interactions are influenced by one's conceptualization of others. That is, our social experiences shape our perceptions of others (Mead, 1934). In general, research has shown that children's understanding of the behavior and personality of others progresses along a developmental continuum (Schaffer, 1996). This continuum reflects a shift from viewing others in terms of concrete, observable characteristics (e.g., "She is tall"), to an increased understanding of others in terms of abstract, psychological characteristics (e.g., "He is more worried than his brother"). During early adolescence, research has also shown that there is an increase in the use of psychological comparisons and categories reflecting consistent traits, interests and abilities, and beliefs (Hughes, 2011).

Although studies of person perception and related studies of gender stereotyping have occurred independently of ToM research, the ability to attribute or ascribe gender-role stereotypes relates to the general rubric of trait attribution and thus suggests indirect implications for ToM research (Flavell & Miller, 1998; Hyde, 2014). This ascription of gender-role stereotypes can be viewed as a heuristic device that enables girls and boys to understand their own and others' intentions and beliefs (Hyde, 2014). Consequently, the representations of these social roles may help shape evaluative perceptions about the self and other that, in turn, could be used to guide social interactions.

The explanatory or predictive use of trait terms and gender roles shares some of the concepts that are associated with ToM research as they illustrate how people create implicit personality theories to predict or explain others' behavior. Although person perception and trait attribution research continues to grow, the area continues to be neglected by ToM researchers (Hughes, 2011). In general, research gleaned from social cognitive psychology has shown that emerging adolescents may interpret each other's behaviors based on gender-role stereotypic attributes such as associating greater sociability and emotionality with girls (Hyde, 2014), and greater instrumentality and autonomy with boys (Fine, 2010).

Such findings provide support for various feminist epistemological theories that claim females' conceptions of self and others are more psychologically oriented, or rooted in a connection with, and relatedness to, others. In contrast, such theories suggests that most males often define themselves and others in terms of behaviors or accomplishments (Hyde, 2014). Such gender-related difference findings also support the evolutionary developmental approach that claims the adrenal gland and the commencement of anarche plays a significant role in gender-related differences during later childhood (Bjorklund & Ellis, 2014; Del Giudice, 2014). Thus, a ToM approach to development could help to investigate the specific processes that enable emerging adolescents to create gender-typed implicit personality theories and why this occurs. The role of gender in social cognition will be further explained in Chapter 8 when I discuss the development of young people's social cognition within the larger culture of gender and ethnicity.

Applications: So What?

Despite the increasing recognition that schools play a crucial role in the overall development of emerging adolescents, researchers have just begun to explore the extent to which school experiences affect the social cognitive life of the adolescent. That is, to what extent does school life affect the adolescents' ToM, emotional competencies, self-beliefs and regulation, and the ability to make behavioral choices, such as decision-making? Although a growing number of researchers explore peer and teacher–student relationships, most have mainly focused on the impact of schools on cognitive rather than social, moral, and emotional outcomes. As noted by many scholars, the need for a transdisciplinary and developmental psychocultural approach to the study of social cognitive development within a school context during emerging adolescent has increased over the past decade (Sternberg, 2014).

As researchers in educational, psychology, sociology, anthropology, and other fields tend to work independently of one another, the utilization of a variety of different methodologies creates a challenge for educators and researchers to build a coherent body of knowledge about the social cognitive development of the emerging adolescent. In the following chapter and in the remainder of this book, through the lens of an integrated, multidisciplinary, and psychocultural approach, I will outline multiple ways in which researchers and educators might consider how various aspects of the school experience may influence the emerging adolescent's sense of self, and social cognitive experiences. I will also suggest some strategies that educators can perhaps integrate into their classrooms to promote the development of social cognitive abilities, and ways to develop caring and supportive relationships and a sense of positive self-worth.

Future Questions and Summary

As discussed in this first chapter, the developmental relational systems approach to social cognitive development has implications for multidisciplinary, holistic, therapeutic, and educational programs that draw on other cultures for their sources of expertise. An integrated, transformational learning model that connects education to therapy could provide a useful foundation within which holistic educational and therapeutic programs can be developed. Research findings from the areas of developmental evolutionary cognitive science and positive psychology (Donaldson, Dollwet, & Rao, 2015), with a focus on resilience and compassion, could be used to help create inclusive, developmentally appropriate educational and clinical programs.

For example, as I will describe further throughout this book, to promote interpersonal and intrapersonal competencies among youth, findings from applied developmental cognitive science research could help to create a developmentally appropriate curriculum. The next chapter will explore various research methodologies to help researchers and educators to measure and evaluate developmental social cognition in emerging adolescence.

References

Apperly, I. A. (2011). *Mindreaders: The cognitive basis of theory of mind.* Hove, England: Psychology Press.

Apperly, I. A. (2012). What is "theory of mind"? Concepts, cognitive processes and individual differences. *Quarterly Journal of Experimental Psychology, 65,* 825–839. doi: 10.1080/17470218.2012.676055

Apperly, I. A., Samson, D., & Humphreys, G. W. (2009). Studies of adults can inform accounts of theory of mind development. *Developmental Psychology, 45,* 190–201. doi:10.1037/a0014098

Astington, J. (1993). *The child's discovery of the mind.* Cambridge, MA: Harvard University Press.

Astington, J., & Olson, D. (1995). The cognitive revolution in children's understanding of mind. *Human Development, 38,* 179–189.

Banerjee, R., & Yuill, N. (1999). Children's understanding of self-presentational display rules: Associations with mental-state understanding. *British Journal of Developmental Psychology, 17,* 111–124.

Bjorklund, D., & Ellis, B. (2014). Children, childhood and development in evolutionary perspective. *Developmental Review, 34,* 225–264.

Blakemore, S.-J., & Mills, K. (2014). Is adolescence a sensitive period for sociocultural processing. *Annual Review of Psychology, 65,* 187–207.

Blos, J. (1979). *The adolescent passage: Developmental issues.* New York, NY: International Universities Press.

Bosacki, S. (2000). Theory of mind and self-concept in preadolescents: Links with gender and language. *Journal of Educational Psychology, 92,* 709–717.

Bosacki, S. (2012). *Culture of ambiguity: Implications for self and social understanding in adolescence.* Boston, MA: Sense Publishers.

Bosacki, S. (2015). Children's theory of mind, self-perceptions, and peer relations: A longitudinal study. *Infant and Child Development, 24,* 175–188. doi:10.1002/icd.1878

Bosacki, S. L., & Astington, J. W. (1999). Theory of mind in preadolescence: Relations between social understanding and social competence. *Social Development, 8,* 237–255.

Bosco, F. M., Gabbatore, I., & Tirassa, M. (2014). A broad assessment of theory of mind in adolescence: The complexity of mindreading. *Consciousness and Cognition, 24*(1), 84–97. doi:10.1016/j.concog.2014.01.003

Bretherton, I. (2010). Fathers in attachment theory and research: A review. *Early Child Development and Care, 180*(1–2), 9–23.

Brinthaupt, T. M., Hein, M. B., & Kramer, T. E. (2009). The self talk scale: Development, factor analysis and validation. *Journal of Personality Assessment, 91,* 82–92. doi:10.1080/00223890802484498

Bronfenbrenner, U., & Morris, P. (2006). The bioecological model of human development. In R. M. Lerner (Ed.), *Handbook of child psychology: Vol. 43. Theoretical models of human development* (pp. 793–828). Hoboken, NJ: Wiley.

Bruner, J. (1996). *The culture of education.* Cambridge, MA: Harvard University Press.

Burke, K. (1990). Language and symbolic action. In P. Bizzell & B. Herzberg (Eds.), *The rhetorical tradition: Reading from classical times to the present* (pp. 1034–1041). Boston, MA: Bedford Books of Martin's Press.

Byom L., & Mutlu. B. (2013). Theory of mind: mechanisms, methods, and new directions. *Frontiers in Human Neuroscience, 7,* 413.

Callan, M., Kay, A., & Dawtry, R. (2014). Making sense of misfortune: Deservingness, self-esteem, and patterns. *Journal of Personality and Social Psychology, 107,* 142–162.

Chandler, M. (1987). The Othello effect. Essay on the emergence and the eclipse of skeptical doubt. *Human Development, 30,* 137–159.

Cicchetti, D., Toth, S. L., & Handley, E. D. (2015). Genetic moderation of interpersonal psychotherapy efficacy for low-income mothers with major depressive disorder: Implications for differential susceptibility. *Development and Psychopathology, 27,* 19–35.

Cole, D. (1989). Validation of the reasons for living inventory in general and delinquent adolescent samples. *Journal of Abnormal Child Psychology, 17,* 13–27.

Deci, E., & Ryan, R. (2013). The importance of autonomy for development and well-being. In B. Sokol, M. Grouzet, & U. Muller (Eds.), *Self-regulation and autonomy: Social and developmental dimensions of human conduct* (pp. 19–46). New York, NY: Cambridge University Press.

Del Giudice, M. (2014). Middle childhood: An evolutionary-developmental synthesis. *Child Development Perspectives, 4,* 193–200.

Del Giudice, M., Angeleri, R., & Manera, V. (2009). The juvenile transition: A developmental switch point in human life history. *Developmental Review, 29*, 1–31. doi:10.1016/j.dr.2008.09.001

Devine, R., & Hughes, C. (2013). Silent films and strange stories: Theory of mind, gender, and social experiences in middle childhood. *Child Development, 84*, 989–1003.

Devine, R., & Hughes, C. (2014). Relations between false belief understanding and executive function in early childhood: A meta-analysis. *Child Development, 85*, 1777–1794.

Dodge, K. A. (1986). A social information processing model of social competence in children. In M. Perlmutter (Ed.), *Minnesota symposium on child psychology* (Vol. 18, pp. 77– 125). Hillsdale, NJ: Erlbaum.

Donaldson, S., Dollwet, M., & Rao, M. (2015). Happiness, excellence, and optimal human functioning revisited: Examining the peer-reviewed literature linked to positive psychology. *The Journal of Positive Psychology, 10*, 185–195.

Dostoevsky, F. (1990/1880). *The brothers Karamazov* (R. Pevear & L. Volokhonsky Trans.). New York, NY: Farrar, Straus and Giroux.

Eccles, J., & Roeser, R. (2003). Schools as developmental contexts. In G. Adams & M. Berzonsky (Eds.), *Blackwell handbook of adolescence* (pp. 129–148). Malden, MA: Blackwell.

Elkind, D. (1967). Egocentrism in adolescence. *Child Development, 38*, 1025–1034. doi:10.2307/1127100

Ensor, R., Devine, R., Mark, A., & Hughes, C. (2014). Cognitive references to 2-year-olds predict theory of mind at ages 6 and 10. *Child Development, 85*, 1222–1235.

Erikson, E. (1968). *Identity, youth, and crisis.* New York, NY: Norton.

Filippova, E., & Astington, J. W. (2008). Further development in social reasoning revealed in discourse irony understanding. *Child Development, 79*, 126–138.

Fine, C. (2010). *Delusions of gender: How our minds, gender, and neurosexism create difference.* New York, NY: Norton.

Finy, M., Bresin, K., Korol, D., & Verona, E. (2014). Impulsivity, risk-taking, and cortisol reactivity as a function of psychosocial stress and personality in adolescents. *Development and Psychopathology, 26*, 1093–1111.

Flavell, J., & Miller, P. (1998). Social cognition. In D. Kuhn & R. Siegler (Eds.), *Handbook of child psychology: Vol 2. Cognition, perception and languagedevelopment* (5th ed., pp. 851–898). New York, NY: Wiley.

Fu, G., Xiao, W. S., Killen, M., & Lee, K. (2014). Moral judgment and its relation to second-order theory of mind. *Developmental Psychology, 50*, 2085–2092.

Geary, D. C. (2010). *Male, female: The evolution of human sex differences.* Washington, DC: American Psychological Association.

Gergen, K., & Walhrus, L. (2001). *Social construction in context.* London, England: Sage.

Goldin-Meadow, S. (2014). How gesture works to change our minds. *Trends in Neuroscience and Education, 3*, 4–6.

Goleman, D. (1995). *Emotional intelligence.* New York, NY: Bantam Books.

Group for the Advancement of Psychiatry, Committee on Adolescents (1996). *Adolescent suicide* (Report No. 140). Washington, DC: American Psychiatric Press.

Harris, P. (1989). *Children and emotion: The development of psychological understanding.* Cambridge, England: Blackwell.

Harter, S. (1999). *The construction of the self: A developmental perspective.* New York, NY: Guilford.

Hollenstein, T., & Lougheed, J. P. (2013). Beyond storm and stress: Typicality, transactions, timing, and temperament to account for adolescent change. *American Psychologist, 68*(6), 444–454. doi: 10.1037/a0033586

Hughes, C. (2011) *Social understanding and social lives: From toddlerhood through to the transition to school.* New York, NY: Psychology Press.

Hughes, C., & Devine, R. T. (2015). A social perspective on theory of mind. In M. E. Lamb (Ed.), *Handbook of child psychology and developmental science (volume III): Socioemotional processes* (pp. 564–609). Hoboken, NJ: Wiley.

Hyde, J. (2014). Gender similarities and differences. *Annual Review of Psychology, 65,* 373–398.

Ibanez, A., Huepe, D., Gemp, R., Gutierrez, V., Riveria-Rei, A., & Toledo, M. (2013). Empathy, sex and fluid intelligence. *Personality and Individual Differences, 54,* 616–621.

Killen, M., & Smetana, J. (Eds.). (2013). *Handbook of moral development.* Mahwah, NJ: Erlbaum.

Kim, H., & Sasaki, J. (2014). Cultural neuroscience: Biology of the mind in cultural contexts. *Annual Review of Psychology, 65,* 487–514.

Lagattuta, K. (2014). Linking past, present, and future: Child ability to connect mental states and emotions. *Child Development Perspectives, 8,* 90–95.

Lagattuta, K. H., Kramer, H. J., Kennedy, K., Hjortsvang, K., Goldfarb, D., & Tashjian, S. (2015). Beyond Sally's missing marble: Further development in children's understanding of mind and emotion in middle childhood. *Advances in Child Development and Behavior, 1*(48). doi:10.1016/bs.acdb. 2014.11.005

Lagattuta, K. H., Nucci, L., & Bosacki, S. L. (2010). Bridging theory of mind and the personal domain: Children's reasoning about resistance to parental control. *Child Development, 81,* 616–635. doi:10. 1111/ j.1467-8624.2009.01419.x

Laible, D., McGinley, M., Carlo, G., Augustine, M., & Murphy, T. (2014). Does engaging in prosocial behavior make children see the world through rose-colored glasses? *Developmental Psychology, 50,* 872–880.

Lalonde, C., & Chandler, M. (1995). False belief understanding goes to school: On the social-emotional consequences of coming early or late to a first theory of mind. *Cognition and Emotion, 9,* 167–185.

Larson, R. (2011). Positive development in a disorderly world. *Journal of Research in Adolescence, 21,* 317. doi:10.1111/j.1532-7795. 2010.00707.x

Lerner, R. M., Lerner, J. V., Almerigi, J. B., Theokas, C., Phelps, E., Gestsdottir, S., … von Eye, A. (2005). Positive youth development, participation in community youth development programs, and community contributions of fifth-grade adolescents: Findings from the first wave of the 4-H Study of Positive Youth Development. *Journal of Early Adolescence, 25*(1), 17–71.

Lerner, R. M., Lerner, J. V., Von Eye, A., Bowers, E. P., & Lewin-Bizan, S. (2011). Individual and contextual bases of thriving in adolescence: A view of the issues. *Journal of Adolescence, 34*(6), 1107–1114.

Lonigro, A., Laghi, F., Baicco, R., & Baumgartner, E. (2014). Mind reading skills and empathy: Evidence or nice and nasty ToM behaviours in school-aged children. *Journal of Child and Family Studies, 23,* 581–590.

Luthar, S., Barkin, S., & Crossman, E. (2013). "I can, therefore I must": Fragility in the upper middle classes. *Development and Psychopathology, 4,* 1529–1549.

Maas, F. K. (2008). Children's understanding of promising, lying, and false belief. *Journal of General Psychology, 135,* 301–322. doi:10.3200/ GENP.135.3.301-322

Main, M., & Solomon, J. (1990). Procedures for identifying infants as disorganized/disoriented during the Ainsworth Strange Situation. In M. T. Greenberg, D. Cicchetti, & E. M. Cummings (Eds.), *Attachment in the preschool years: Theory, research, and intervention* (pp. 121–160). Chicago, IL: University of Chicago Press

Malti, T., & Krettenauer, T. (2013). The relation of moral emotion attributions to prosocial and antisocial behaviour: A meta-analysis. *Child Development, 84*(2), 397–412.

Marshall, S., Parker, P., Ciarrochi, J., & Heaven, P. (2014). Is self-esteem a cause or consequence of social support: A 4-year longitudinal study. *Child Development, 85,* 1275–1291.

Masten, A. (2014a). Global perspectives on resilience in children and youth. *Child Development, 85,* 6–20.

Masten, A. (2014b). *Ordinary magic: Resilience in development.* New York, NY: Guilford.

Mead, G. (1934). *Mind, self, and society.* Chicago, IL: University of Chicago Press.

Miller, S. (2009). Children's understanding of second-order mental states. *Psychological Bulletin, 135*(5), 749–773. doi:10.1037/a0016854

Miller, S. A. (2012). *Theory of mind: Beyond the preschool years.* New York, NY: Psychology Press.

Mischel, W. (2014). *The marshmallow test: Mastering self-control.* New York, NY: Little, Brown.

Moffitt, T. (2006). Life-course persistent versus adolescent-limited antisocial behaviors. In D. Cicchetti and D. Cohen (Eds.), *Developmental psychopathology* (Vol. III, pp. 57–98). New York, NY: Wiley.

Mueller, M. (2014). Is human-animal interaction (HAI) linked to positive youth development? Initial answers. *Applied Developmental Science, 18,* 5–16.

Nelson, K., Henseler, S., & Plesa, D. (2000). Entering a community of minds: Theory of mind from a feminist standpoint. In P. Miller & E. Scholnick (Eds.), *Toward a feminist developmental psychology* (pp. 61–83). New York, NY: Routledge.

Nock, M. K. (2009). Why do people hurt themselves? New insights into the nature of functions of self-injury. *Current Directions in Psychological Science, 18,* 78–83. doi:10.1111/j.1467-8721.2009.01613.x

Nock, M. K., Prinstein, M. J., & Sterba, S. K. (2009). Revealing the form and function of self-injurious thoughts and behaviors: A real-time ecological assessment study among adolescents and young adults. *Journal of Abnormal Psychology, 118,* 816–827. doi:10.1037/a0016948

O'Reilly, K., Peterson, C., & Wellman, H. (2014). Sarcasm and advanced theory of mind understanding in children and adults with prelingual deafness. *Developmental Psychology, 50*(7), 1862–1877.

Overton, W. F. (2013). A new paradigm for developmental science: Relationism and relational-developmental systems. *Applied Developmental Science, 17,* 94–107. doi:10.1080/10888691.2013.778717

Paulus, M. (2014). The emergence of prososical behavior: Why do infants and toddlers help, comfort, and share? *Child Development Perspectives, 8,* 77–81.

Perner, J., & Wimmer, H. (1985). "John thinks that Mary thinks that…": Attribution of second-order beliefs by 5- to 10-year-old children. *Journal of Experimental Child Psychology, 39,* 437–471. doi:10.1016/0022-0965(85)90051-7

Piaget, J. (1967/1929). *The child's conception of the world.* London, England: Routledge & Kegan Paul.

Pincham, H., Matejko, A., Obersteiner, A., Killikelly, C., Abrahao, K., Benavides-Varela, S., … Vuillier, L. (2014). Forging a new path for educational neuroscience: An international young-researcher perspective on combining neuroscience and educational practices. *Trends in Neuroscience and Education, 3,* 28–31.

Pinker, S. (2007). *The stuff of thought: Language as a window into human nature.* New York, NY: Viking.

Robbins, P. (1998). *Adolescent suicide.* Jefferson, NC: McFarland.

Rochat, P. (2009). *Others in mind: Social origins of self-consciousness.* Cambridge, MA: Cambridge University Press.

Rose, R. (2014). Self-guided multimedia stress management and resilience training. *Journal of Positive Psychology, 9,* 489–493.

Rose, A., & Rudolph, K. (2006). A review of sex differences in peer relationship processes: Potential tradeoffs for the emotional and behavioral development of girls and boys. *Psychological Bulletin, 132,* 98–131.

Rosenberg, M. (1965). *Society and the adolescent self-image.* Princeton, NJ: Princeton University Press.

Ruffman, T. (2014). To belief or not belief. *Developmental Review, 34,* 265–293.

Schaffer, R. (1996). *Social development.* Oxford, England: Blackwell.

Selman, R. L. (1980). *The growth of interpersonal understanding: Developmental and clinical analyses,* New York, NY: Academic Press.

Siegel, D. (2013). *Brainstorm: The power and purpose of the teenage brain.* New York, NY: Jeremy Tarcher/Penguin.

Simmons, E., & Blyth, D. (1987). *Moving into adolescence: The impact of pubertal change and the school context*. Hawthorn, NY: Aldine de Gruyter.

Spark, M. (1962/2009). *The prime of Miss Jean Brodie*. New York, NY: Harper Collins.

Sternberg, R. (2014). The development of adaptive competence: Why cultural psychology is necessary and not just nice. *Developmental Review, 34*, 208–224.

Tomasello, M. (2014a). *A natural history of human thinking*. Cambridge, MA: Harvard University Press.

Tomasello, M. (2014b). The ultra-social animal. *European Journal of Social Psychology, 44*, 187–194.

Wellman, H. (2014). *Making minds: How theory of mind develops*. Oxford, England: Oxford University Press.

West-Eberhard, M. J. (2003). *Developmental plasticity and evolution*. New York, NY: Oxford University Press.

Wimmer, H., & Perner, J. (1983). Beliefs about beliefs: Representation and constraining function of wrong beliefs in young children's understanding of deception. *Cognition, 13*, 103–128. doi:10.1016/0010- 0277(83)90004-5

Zelazo, P., & Lyons, K. (2012). The potential benefits of mindfulness training in early childhood: A developmental social cognitive neuroscience perspective. *Child Development Perspectives, 6*(2), 154–160.

2

Developmental Social Cognition and Research Methodologies

"The idea is a seed; the method is the earth furnishing the conditions in which it may develop, flourish and give the best fruit according to its nature … The method itself gives birth to nothing." (Claude Bernard, 1865, cited in Hyman, 1963, p. 3)

Introduction

This chapter provides a critical overview of social cognitive developmental research methodologies that researchers use to help explain social cognitive growth in young people. That is, this chapter highlights the importance of developmental research methods in the area of social cognition. In this chapter I will discuss questions such as how do you measure Theory of Mind (ToM), self-worth, and well-being in youth? In addition to social cognitive constructs, I will also discuss measurement of outcomes of educational programs. Subsequently, this chapter will also explore the question of how you measure emotional and moral aspects of social cognitive learning within educational programs that include social-emotional learning (SEL), social-emotional and character development (SECD), youth positive development (YPD), mindfulness, and compassion (self and other).

Social Cognition in Middle Childhood and Adolescence: Integrating the Personal, Social, and Educational Lives of Young People, First Edition. S. L. Bosacki.
© 2016 John Wiley & Sons, Ltd. Published 2016 by John Wiley & Sons, Ltd.

Research

The measurement of social cognition

Online and nonverbal tasks of advanced Theory of Mind   Previously developed tasks conceptualize false-belief understanding and ToM in many ways, though, to date, no single task explicitly captures the multiple factors at play in social cognitive reasoning such as developmental changes in children's implicit and explicit ToM understanding (see Ruffman, 2014). Beyond early childhood, to assess ToM in older children, commonly used tasks such as strange stories (Happé, 1995), faux pas vignettes (Banerjee & Watling, 2005; Banerjee, Watling, & Caputi, 2011), and the Reading the Mind's Eye Task (Baron-Cohen, 2002) rely on specific social knowledge, such as socially scripted narratives and social conventional emotion expression.

For example, to respond to questions based on the strange stories or faux pas vignettes, children need to rely on social scripts about how people typically behave (e.g., a girl lying to her mother in saying the dog broke the lamp). In these vignettes, children consider well-rehearsed, conventional social events. However, the extent to which these vignettes require active social cognition, as compared to a task that presents a novel social scenario, has not yet been investigated. There is a need for a measure that purposively investigates the interpretation of emotions and nonverbal behaviors such as gestures and what is sometimes referred to as an implicit ToM (see Goldin-Meadow, 2014 for a review of gestures and social cognitive development; Ruffman, 2014), as well as a more explicit ToM that involves social scripts when reasoning about the young person's mental world.

Another factor at play in ToM development is language (verbal and nonverbal), as research demonstrates that ToM reasoning within childhood has been found to be associated with language (Milligan, Astington, & Dack, 2007). For example, several training studies have implicated language development and metamemory as a key factor in false-belief understanding (Lecce, Bianco, Demichelli, & Cavallini, 2014). The findings indicate that language and memory support the conceptual shift in understanding that occurs as children come to succeed at false-belief tasks.

Research also suggests that, in older children, ToM ability continues to be related to language competence and metamemory such as declarative metamemory (Bosacki, 2000, 2013; Lecce, Caputi, & Pagnin, 2015). Recent findings implicate verbal abstract reasoning ability in the prediction of performance on Happé's (1995) advanced ToM task of strange stories (Hughes, 2011). Future tasks will need to address language and metamemory specifically, as past research suggests language competence and metamemory may serve as an influential factor when individuals learn how to reason about their social world (Lecce et al., 2015).

To minimize the influence of language, some researchers use online (Apperly, 2012) and spatial visual ToM tasks, including photos of eyes as in Baron-Cohen's Reading the Mind's Eye Task (RMET; Baron-Cohen, 2003). Recently, Ibanez et al. (2013) explored the influence of gender on ToM and fluid intelligence (FI) in which the RMET measured advanced ToM. As Ibanez et al. (2013) explained, they selected the RMET to measure ToM from a pool of more than 30 available paradigms for several reasons.

Ibanez et al. claimed that RMET was one of the most widely used ToM tasks in both normal and clinical samples and was easy to apply and to respond to. This task indexed one of the most fundamental ToM processes, which includes the explicit ability to report emotional inference of others' feeling and thoughts. Although other ToM processes are important, many researchers agree that this is a core component of mentalizing (Baron-Cohen, 2002). RMET has received validation with scales used with individuals diagnosed with autism and Asperger's Syndrome (Baron-Cohen, 2002; Rueda, Fernandez-Berrocal, & Baron-Cohen, 2015), and does not require explicit verbal report, which may indirectly affect ToM performance (see Milligan et al., 2007).

The RMET is currently considered an equivalent to a second-order ToM task and requires similar or higher ToM demands as other post-first-order tests (Miller, 2009). RMET presents a strong correlation with the faux pas test, which is considered a higher level ToM test (Banerjee & Watling, 2005; Banerjee et al., 2011; Torralva, Roca, Gleichgerrcht, Bekinschtein, & Manes, 2009). Conversely, RMET, compared to other ToM tasks (strange stories, Theory of Mind Inventory (TOMI; Hutchins, Prelock, & Bonanzinga, 2012), or faux pas), is less affected by language and does not require an explicit verbal report. Moreover, in a nonclinical population (and contrary to classic tasks such as strange stories or faux pas), no relations have been found between RMET and executive functions (Ahmed & Miller, 2011).

Overall, RMET is a widely used and validated task correlating with higher order ToM tasks and indexing core basic mentalistic processes instead of other processes (such as executive functions and language). Nevertheless, as many researchers emphasize, ToM is a complex construct involving different subcomponents (Ensor, Devine, Mark, & Hughes, 2014; Ibanez et al., 2013; Korkmaz, 2011; Lagattuta, 2014), and future research should include a battery of basic (RMET) and more linguistically complex tasks (e.g., strange stories, faux pas). In addition, future studies will need to incorporate a variety of perspectives beyond young people's self-report of ToM ability such as teacher and parent assessments of ToM development in youth (Tahiroglu et al., 2014).

To date, most studies on social cognition including social perspective-taking and social behavior in adolescence have employed "offline" measures, such as questions about cartoon characters and vignettes (Bosacki & Astington, 1999; Byom & Mutlu, 2013; Devine & Hughes, 2013; Smith & Rose, 2011). These approaches have yielded valuable insights into perspective-taking, but have been somewhat unable to capture its dynamic and interactive aspect. There is now an increasing acknowledgment of the importance of the participatory aspects of social cognition during social interaction (Wellman, 2014). For example, some researchers explore perspective-taking through the use of an online communication paradigm in which participants use their conceptual competence for mentalizing to take another person's perspective into account (Apperly, 2012).

In this paradigm, participants view a 4 × 4 set of shelves consisting of slots that contain different objects. Most of these objects are visible to the participant and a person standing on the other side of the shelves. However, some objects are only visible to the participant. The person on the other side of the shelves (i.e., the "director") instructs the participant to move certain objects to different slots. To select the correct objects, participants have to consider the director's perspective, rather than using their own egocentric viewpoint, which seems to be the default in human judgment (Apperly, 2012).

Social perspective-taking tasks have frequently been referred to as a measure of ToM usage in online social interactions (Apperly, 2012; Apperly, Samson, & Humphreys, 2009; Dumontheil, Hillebrandt, Apperly, & Blakemore, 2012; Smith & Rose, 2011). However, researchers continue to debate the question of to what degree the task actually measures perspective-taking, as compared to visual-spatial manipulation. In contrast, there are some arguments in favor of perspective-taking. First, good performance on the perspective-taking task relies on a translocation of the egocentric viewpoint from the self to the other. As such, the task employs the same underlying logic as false-belief paradigms, which dissociate the knowledge of the self and that of the other to assess the ability to take others' perspectives.

Second, recent neuroimaging research has shown that social brain regions, as compared to brain regions typically activated during visual-spatial tasks, are activated during the "director" condition of the tasks (Dumontheil, Apperly, & Blakemore, 2010). However, Dumontheil et al. claim that it is invalid to make concrete deductions about psychological mechanisms underlying a task from brain imaging data. This evidence is supportive of ToM, rather than visuo-spatial processing, as the underlying mechanism of perspective-taking in the current paradigm. Yet future studies should investigate this issue further by including additional measures of ToM and visual-spatial measures.

Another line of research has employed exchange paradigms from game theory, such as the trust game, for the online investigation of social mechanisms that cannot be captured with questionnaires or observation (Belli, Rogers, & Lau, 2012; Evans & Krueger, 2011; Van den Bos, Van Dijk, Westenberg, Rombout, & Crone, 2011; Van den Bos, Westenberg, Van Dijk, & Crone, 2010). In the trust game the first player (the investor) is given an initial endowment from the experimenter (Berg, Dickhaut, & McCabe, 1995). The investor can share any part of that amount with the second player (the trustee). The shared amount is multiplied and, after having received the money, the trustee decides whether to honor the investor's trust (i.e., send part of the money back) or to behave in an untrustworthy manner (i.e., keep all or most of it). For the trustee, the highest earnings are obtained by keeping the money. Thus, sharing money in the first place requires the investor to trust in the benevolence of the trustee.

Also, a higher initially shared amount signals prosocial intentions toward the trustee. The financial repayment of the trustee is a proxy of trustworthiness. Decision-making in repeated trust games requires perspective-taking skills of varying complexity. On the one hand, it is important to predict the moves and intentions of the game partner. In contrast, is also crucial to understand how the game partner perceives and interprets one's own moves.

Initial evidence for an important role of perspective-taking within adolescent social interactions in the context of social behavior has been demonstrated by Van den Bos et al.'s (2011) trust game study. More specifically, Van den Bos et al. (2011) studied young people between 12 and 22 years in the role of the trustee. Interestingly, there were no age-related changes in reciprocity toward the investor. However, with increasing age, adolescents became increasingly sensitive to the perspective of the investor, as indicated by an increased reciprocity when the investor took a higher risk during trusting decisions.

In a related study, Fett et al. (2014) studied changes in social cognition and social behavior from childhood to adulthood by exploring the links between perspective-taking and social processes involving reciprocity and trust in 13- to 18-year-olds. In their study, participants completed two trust cooperative games and an online perspective-taking task, and found that those with a high perspective-taking tendency demonstrated greater trust toward others and trust during cooperative interactions. Although high and low perspective-takers adapted their trust levels in response to unfair behavior, high perspective-takers reduced their trust more drastically and showed more malevolent and less benevolent reciprocity strategies (i.e., the tendency to return the trustee's trustworthiness tit-for-tat) when they were treated unfairly by their counterpart.

Fett et al.'s (2014) findings suggested that a higher perspective-taking tendency in adolescence may be associated with specific mechanisms of trust and reciprocity, as opposed to undifferentiated increases in positive social behavior toward others. Such a finding could be explained by the further investigation of how people interpret when we think someone has treated us unfairly. That is, what role do cognitive and emotional abilities and the quality of our relationships (family, friend, acquaintance, stranger), play in our interpretation of unfair treatment? Furthermore, future longitudinal research could explore how ToM links to cognitive and emotional aspects of trust, promises, and reciprocity, as well as revenge or retribution.

To further explore the relation between perspective-taking and social behavior, in a series of experimental studies with adults, Epley, Caruso, and Bazerman (2006) found that the competitive or cooperative nature of the social interaction was an important moderator of the impact of perspective-taking on adults' social behavior. In cooperative interactions, perspective-taking reduced egocentric behavior, whereas in competitive circumstances perspective-taking appeared to highlight self-interested motives. Such findings suggest a potentially changing and complex association between the increasing tendency to take others' perspectives into account and social behavior, which may change from childhood to adulthood. Given that few studies explore the association between perspective-taking and complex social and moral behavior in older children and adolescents, we will return to this issue in Chapters 4 to 6 when we explore the role of moral and emotional reasoning in peer relations. In the next section we will explore ToM measures appropriate for older children and adolescents.

Advanced Theory of Mind text and audiovisual-based measure development   ToM evolves early in human development (Miller, 2009; Ruffman, 2014). ToM precursors such as joint attention appear early on (arising at 3 months; Wellman, 2014), and are sometimes referred to as illustrating that infants show the beginning stages of ToM or implicit ToM before language is developed. More specifically, children at 3 years or earlier provide mentalistic explanations for behavior in terms of a ToM (Wellman, 2014). Thus, the first-order ToM (e.g., inferring the thoughts and emotions of another person to explain their behavior) is fully achieved at 4–5 years old.

The second-order ToM (one person's (A's) belief about another person's (B's) mental state) is achieved at 5–6 years old (Korkmaz, 2011; Miller, 2009). The inference of complex emotions and thoughts of other persons from the eye regions is considered an equivalent to second-order ToM (Miller, 2009). Following this development, more complex ToM inferences are accomplished at 7–9 and the full ToM achievement is achieved during young adolescence (10–11 years; Miller, 2009).

More complex interactions of ToM and pragmatic language processes (e.g., figurative language) have been found to appear later in the development although the evidence is scarce (Miller, 2009). Most of the research has been performed in children and young adolescents; and differences among children, adolescents, and adults are now well known (Korkmaz, 2011). Thus, late childhood and early adolescence provides an optimal developmental period to test ToM individual differences due to the continuous development of mentalizing skills (Ibanez et al., 2013). In addition, results can be more generalizable to other reports of similar mental reasoning tasks.

Although most researchers agree that basic or first-order false-belief or ToM reasoning is achieved by most children in preschool, the nature of mental state reasoning beyond preschool has not been firmly established (Lagatutta, 2014). It is generally accepted that children are competent on the most widely used measure of advanced ToM, the second-order false-belief task (Perner & Wimmer, 1985), by 5 or 6 years of age (Miller, 2009). However, research suggests that ToM continues to develop and children gain insight into others' thoughts and emotions as they transition to adolescence (Bosco, Gabbatore, & Tirassa, 2014; Miller, 2009). Observationally, we know that children and adolescents become more sophisticated in their social reasoning as they age. Furthermore, ToM functioning has been linked to the medial prefrontal cortex, a region of the brain that has been found to increase in activation from childhood to adulthood (Coricelli et al., 2005; Garcia & Scherfe, 2015; Wellman, 2014).

Several tasks developed over the past few decades are currently used to assess mental state understanding in typically developing older children and adults. The most commonly used advanced ToM tasks include second-order false-belief tasks (Astington, Pelletier, & Homer, 2002), interpretive ambiguous figure and "droodle" tasks (Hughes, 2011; Lalonde & Chandler, 1995), strange stories (Happé, 1994), faux pas vignettes (Banerjee & Watling, 2005; Banerjee et al., 2011), and the Reading the Mind in the Eyes Task (RMET) (Baron-Cohen, Wheelwright, Hill, Raste, & Plumb, 2001).

However, past research indicates that a major confound to date in this research is the arbitrary and artificial nature of the stimuli used, which casts doubt upon the link between ToM and the understanding of social situations and related social competencies (Mathersul et al., 2013; Ruffman, 2014). For example, first- and second-order false-belief tasks, recognition of faux pas (social blunders), and the strange stories task (nonliteral expressions) are all abstract *text-based* measures of mentalizing judgments and inferences, and their relationship to everyday functioning is unclear. As already mentioned, online, animated tasks such as the triangles or point-light motion displays (Marchetti, Castelli, Sanvito, & Massaro, 2014) may improve ecological validity but remain abstract relative to the demands of complex and ambiguous everyday social interaction.

Regarding one of the most commonly used tests of advanced ToM, the RMET mentioned above, which requires participants to select a descriptor for the mental state of a person based on a photo of the eye region alone (Baron-Cohen, 2003; Baron-Cohen et al., 2001), some researchers ask if it is actually a measure of ToM (Garcia & Scherf, 2015), or rather a measure of complex emotion recognition. That is, performance on this task is not correlated to some tests of advanced ToM (Garcia & Scherf, 2015), and performance in autism spectrum disorders (ASDs) is mixed, as some studies have demonstrated impaired performance (Baron-Cohen et al., 2001), whereas others have found intact performance (Baron-Cohen, 2003).

According to Mathersul et al. (2013), audiovisual vignettes of indirect speech acts may provide closer correlates to real-life situations than either faces showing static emotional expressions or prose passages describing social blunders. One newly developed measure is The Awareness of Social Inference Test (TASIT; McDonald, Flanagan, & Rollins, 2002) in which video vignettes are used to display conversational exchanges to assess basic emotion recognition, and the ability to understand more subtle emotions, speaker beliefs and intentions, as well as counterfactual remarks such as deception and sarcasm. This test has been used mainly within the traumatic brain injury population (McDonald & Flanagan, 2004), and more recently in schizophrenia (Brune, 2005; Garcia & Scherfe, 2015), and dementia (Torralva et al., 2009).

TASIT performance has been found to be associated with more conventional, text-based ToM tasks and static emotion recognition as the task is sensitive to clinical conditions and also predictive of real-world function (McDonald, Flanagan, Martin, & Saunders, 2004). TASIT is designed to assess a person's understanding of the speaker's beliefs (first-order ToM), intentions (i.e., what the speaker thinks or wants the other person to think: second-order ToM), and emotions and pragmatic meaning in both sincere, straightforward interactions and counterfactual/indirect speech that involves sarcasm and deception. For example, the scenario can portray a situation where the speaker says one thing but knows and means otherwise (sarcasm), or alternatively makes a statement that has a meaning to be believed (false statement), while knowing otherwise (deception and lies). As Mathersul et al. (2013) and others suggest, researchers may use the TASIT to investigate ToM in older children and adults as well as high-functioning adults with ASDs as an ecologically valid test focused on everyday conversational interactions.

Regarding the task's limitations, TASIT has a forced choice response format and is thus not a direct representation of real-world situations. However, this is a difficulty inherent in quantitative research in general. Furthermore, TASIT demonstrates significant correlations with social problem-solving and emotion recognition and has been found to be predictive of real-world difficulties with social interactions (McDonald et al., 2004). Nevertheless, to build on the ecological validity of TASIT, future research could investigate freely generated responses to video vignettes depicting conversational exchanges.

Similar to Mathersul et al.'s use of TASIT, Devine and Hughes (2013) recently developed a narrative, visual task—although the films were silent. That is, the black and white films show a series of silent ambiguous social situations enacted by characters on the screen. The silent films task consists of five short film clips (mean length = 25.4 s) adapted from Harold Lloyd's classic 1923 silent comedy, *Safety Last*. Such silent movie scenes leave the viewer free to interpret the scenario in multiple ways, with no set "correct" response. Participants' responses were coded using a graded scheme developed for many of the narrative-style advanced ToM tasks that assess cognitive complexity and mental state understanding (Bosacki, 2013; Happé, 1994). For example, full understanding (2 points) was awarded if a participant provided a mentalistic explanation; partial understanding (1 point) was awarded if a participant provided a correct response that fell short of a fully mentalistic explanation; and an item was considered failed (0 points) if the participant provided an irrelevant or factually incorrect response.

Devine and Hughes (2013) found that, among 8- to 13-year-olds, children's scores on two advanced ToM tasks (silent films and strange stories) were strongly intercorrelated. Such relations provide evidence of convergent validity for the silent films task. Devine and Hughes in their analysis also found that all items from the silent films and strange stories tasks could be combined to form a single ToM latent factor. Unlike other widely used tasks (e.g., Baron-Cohen's RMET task), both the silent films and strange stories were specifically developed to index an individual's use of their understanding of beliefs to explain behavior. Despite the two tasks different content and modalities of administration, Devine and Hughes (2013) found that participants were consistent in using their understanding of beliefs to answer the questions.

Such a finding may suggest that during middle childhood and the approach to adolescence (approximately ages 8 to 13 years), children may differ in meaningful and consistent ways in their use of ToM. Although Devine and Hughes's (2013) study provides evidence of the convergent validity of the silent films task, researchers need to continue to investigate the discriminant validity to show that both tasks (silent films and strange stories) measure a distinct construct (Rust & Golombok, 2009). The relation exhibited between the strange stories and silent films tasks may have reflected shared demands on participants' ability to comprehend meaning rather than to understand mental states. Future development of the silent films task could include the inclusion of control questions that do not require mental state inferences, and the examination of performance on these control questions in relation to social competence outcomes. Furthermore, the validity of the strange stories and silent films tasks could be strengthened by longitudinal evidence that suggests young children's performance on classic first- and second-order false-belief tests predicts later performance on the same advanced ToM tasks during adolescence and adulthood.

Summary of advanced Theory of Mind tasks

The tasks listed above operationalize advanced ToM in a variety of ways, including the ability to predict beliefs based on false beliefs, to predict beliefs based on multiple valid beliefs, to recognize specific mental states, to recognize how collectively held social culture beliefs operate, and to read expressions of emotions or thoughts in the eyes. These tasks differ considerably in the type of social knowledge they require, as well as in the cognitive task demands they present. These tasks form a loosely associated set of measures, assessing a constellation of skills that fall under the umbrella of social cognitive ability (Hayward, 2011).

Despite the fact that ToM reasoning is widely considered to be a developing phenomenon, research has yet to delineate how ToM reasoning changes over the life span. Many of the various tasks currently available to assess ToM beyond preschool are not sensitive enough to identify to developmental changes (Garcia & Scherf, 2015; Hayward, 2011; Ruffman, 2014), as well as cultural differences in older children (Bjorklund & Ellis, 2014; Bosacki, Bialecka-Pikul, & Spzak, 2015; Shahaeian, Nielsen, Peterson, & Slaughter, 2014). The use of dichotomous and pass-or-fail measures of ToM reasoning may result in tools that lack the sensitivity necessary to capture variation due to development in older childhood, adolescence, and adulthood. Moving forward, it seems of particular importance to develop tasks that capture variation in ToM reasoning in typically developing older children, adolescents, and adults, as well as in atypical (clinical) populations (Calero, Salles, Semelman, & Sigman, 2013; Ibanez et al., 2013; Mathersul et al., 2013).

Additional measures of social cognitive reasoning

Emotional regulation (ER)   In addition to ToM, another important skill that fits within the framework of social cognition involves the ability to be aware of and regulate, or manage, one's emotional states and related behaviors (ER). This complex social cognitive ability entails the ability to use one's understanding of one's emotional states to help guide appropriate emotion-related behaviors during social interactions (Thompson, 2011). For example, if a child claimed to be aware and understand that she was feeling angry, but at the same time engaged in harmful actions toward either the self or others, such behaviors could suggest that the child has self-regulation or emotional management challenges. Thus, ER includes the ability to apply one's self-knowledge of one's internal state or the ability to adjust and cope emotionally with one's actions or behaviors in adaptable ways.

Past literature suggests that some of the most common way to assess ER in older children and adolescence is through self-reported use of specific ER strategies (e.g., coping styles, suppression, and reappraisal; Thompson, 2011). From the relatively limited research on adolescent ER, a variety of strategies have been associated with both individual and developmental differences in socioemotional functioning (Aldao & Nolen-Hoeksma, 2010). Some of the most commonly identified ER strategies include suppression and reappraisal of emotions; tolerating, concealing, adjusting; effortful control; avoidance, rumination, perseveration, and distraction (Brose, Schmiedek, Koval, & Kuppens, 2015). In addition, in contrast to developmentally fixed traits, temperament or emotional tendencies represent a summary of current emotional response tendencies that facilitate effective coping skills and regulation (Laceulle, Nederhof, Karreman, Ormel, & van Aken, 2012); emotional awareness and acceptance of emotions.

Such a combination may represent the various ways that young people can manage and regulate their emotional experiences. It is likely that ER development progresses from less mature (e.g., suppression, concealing), to more mature (e.g., reappraisal, awareness) ER processes (Siegel, 2013; Thompson, 2011), but this has yet to be tested across the full range of strategies or in this age range. Moreover, the degree of use of any particular strategy may be less important than having a repertoire of emotional regulation and coping strategies that can be adaptively deployed to navigate specific social situations. Overall, given that research needs to focus on intra- and interindividual differences in young people's ER strategies, further studies on the developmental trajectories, as well as individual differences regarding types of emotion, are necessary to create a comprehensive picture of adaptive social cognitive development and emotional well-being (Thompson, 2011).

Applications: So What?

The social and educational benefits of researching social cognitive development across the transition to adolescence, through extensive knowledge mobilization, are far reaching. Empirical research findings can help to assist programs that aim to better inform youth, families, and educators about the nature of social cognitive development growth and change across the transition to adolescence. That is, research focused on the typicality of social cognitive development may help to alleviate the negative perceptions and social impact that some youth might create by reducing misunderstanding about their experience through delineating what is normative at this age.

Empirical results and conclusions disseminated to the general public on advanced ToM measures will increase discourse among adolescents, parents, educators, community programs, and other professionals who work with youth. For example, results of social cognitive research on older children and adolescents may serve to better inform the recent educational trend in North America to teach "software strategies" of emotion regulation as a way of improving academic success and overall well-being. In the following section, I will describe empirical results that translate into a variety of evidence-based approaches to enhance social, cognitive, and emotion regulation skills in youth for the betterment of all society.

Measurement Issues of Social-Emotional Learning (SEL) and Social-Emotional Character Development (SECD)

As Humphrey et al.'s (2011) systematic review suggested, there is a need for a critical, systematic review of measures of social and emotional skills for youth. The growing attention to this area in recent years has resulted in the development of a large number of measures to aid in the assessment of children and young people (Merrell & Gueldner, 2010). These measures vary on a number of variables relating to implementation characteristics and psychometric properties. The methodology of their review followed the general principles of systematic reviewing, such as systematic search of databases, the adoption of predetermined set of inclusion and exclusion criteria, and a multistage filtering process. The review process resulted in the retention of 12 measures of social-emotional learning (SEL) and social-emotional character development (SECD), which were presented and discussed in relation to key issues in this area, including difficulties with the underlying theory and frameworks for social and emotional skills, inconsistent terminology, the scope and distinctiveness of available measures, and more practical issues such as the type of respondent, location, and purpose of measurement.

Background: Why develop a measure of SECD?

Conceptualizations of SECD emphasize social and emotional skills that promote youth's positive adaptation and well-being, including self-management, self-awareness, social awareness, relationship skills, and responsible decision-making. Such skills help youth to manage their emotions, thoughts, and behaviors, their relationships, and their work effectively and ethically (Zins, Weissberg, Wang, & Walberg, 2004). These types of skills help to prepare youth for success in adulthood by teaching them to be good communicators, cooperative members of a team, effective leaders, and caring, concerned members of their communities (Denham, 1998; Denham et al., 2014; Greenberg et al., 2003).

In addition, the development of one's own personal qualities, capacities, talents, and skills are also viewed as demonstrations of exemplary character. That is, a person with good character and virtues consciously acts in accordance with principles that are valued by society, so that the person makes decisions that reflect, not only the quality of the person, but are also good for others and society (Elias, 2009; Lerner et al., 2005; Linkins, Niemiec, Gillham, & Mayerson, 2015; Park & Peterson, 2006).

Discussions of SECD also emphasize the extent to which youth demonstrate respect for rules and expectations for appropriate behavior and, by implication, adult authority figures (e.g., teachers and parents), with studies indicating that such behavior may differ considerably across home and school settings (Morris, Silk, & Steinberg, 2007; Ruffman, 2014). Conceptualizations of SECD also include references to broader, meta- or second-order manifestations of these constructs—that may reflect a youth's overarching motivation and ability to act in several interrelated ways that are consistent with social-emotional learning and good character and virtues (Denham et al., 2014; Malti & Krettenauer, 2013; Park & Peterson, 2006).

Despite the broad base of interest in programs that focus on SECD within schools and other settings, comprehensive approaches to assess the behaviors and skills underlying these constructs remain in early stages of development (for reviews see Humphrey et al., 2011; Wigelsworth, Humphrey, Kalambouka, & Lendrum, 2010). Although scales that assess skills and behaviors in areas similar to those highlighted above demonstrate relatively robust psychometric properties, several concerns merit attention.

First, there remains a lack of measures for middle school and early adolescent populations, especially those that use self-report paper-pencil measures (Bosacki, 2013; Hughes & Devine, 2015). It may be difficult to assess constructs relevant to SECD in a valid manner without directly assessing the personal knowledge that children have of their own behaviors, associated attitudes, and motivations.

Second, the skills and behaviors associated with SECD may manifest themselves differently as children mature, and contexts such as home, school, and peer groups exert varying degrees of influence on their development (Denham, 1998). Given the importance of the early years for social cognitive development, surprisingly few studies have examined the psychometric properties of instruments used to measure constructs relevant to SECD as children mature and develop.

Third, only a few studies have used factor analysis to investigate the structural validity of instruments that measure the distinct SECD skills and behaviors (Humphrey et al., 2011). With notable exceptions regarding the 5Cs Model of Positive Youth Development (Bowers et al., 2010; Donaldson, Dollwet, & Rao, 2015), possible higher order hierarchical or second-order factor structures that might reflect broader SECD constructs have not been considered. Finally, reports of SECD instruments offer little evidence for their validity (Durlak, Weissberg, Dymnicki, Taylor, & Schellinger, 2011; Humphrey et al., 2011).

For example, future research needs to demonstrate the validity of SECD instruments by showing associations with theoretical constructs and supporting past studies on SECD (Humphrey et al., 2011), and more work needs to be done to connect to youth involvement research (Rose-Krasnor, 2009). Moreover, reports of validity evidenced by student gender and cultural background are lacking and would be informative to help examine how SECD programs affect young people's learning within culturally diverse contexts (Lu, Su, & Wang, 2008; Sternberg, 2014). As an example of a newly developed comprehensive measure of SECD, the section below describes research related to the validation of the SECDS.

The Social-Emotional and Character Development Scale (SECDS), was developed within the context of an ongoing program of research on the Positive Action (*PA*) program (Allred, 2014). As Allred described, the *PA* program is based on theories of self-concept/esteem, learning, behavior, and school ecology and includes classroom, school-wide climate, and family components. The program was designed to improve the abilities of children and adolescents to develop positive prosocial interactions with peers including: the practice of honesty with self and others, self-improvement and self-management or regulation, demonstration of self-control in terms of respect for rules and expectations for appropriate behavior in school and home contexts. These skills and behaviors, in turn, were intended collectively to strengthen overall SECD. In addition, these competencies and actions aimed to contribute to the prevention of problem behaviors (e.g., violence, substance abuse), and the promotion of positive outcomes including emotional/mental and physical health and school performance.

The SECDS assesses each of the overlapping facets of social-emotional learning and character including prosocial behavior, honesty, self-development, self-control, and respect for rules and expectations for appropriate behavior both at school and in the home. Allred (2014) conceptualized these different facets of skill and behavior as being subsumed under a more global construct of overall SECD. The SECDS uses a self-report format and was designed for use with children as young as third grade. The SECD scale uses a self-report to contribute an instrument to the literature that would be of value both in the evaluation of SEL/SECD/YPD programs (Mueller, 2014), and to help further the discourse on the development and etiology of elementary school-age children's character and social-emotional skills.

Data for this study were gleaned from a longitudinal evaluation of the *PA* program in 14 culturally diverse K-6 and K-8 schools in the Chicago Public. Ji et al.'s (2006) study results provided encouraging initial support for the SECDS as an instrument that measures elementary school children's social-emotional skills and character. The findings support the instrument's multidimensional and hierarchical factor structure as they were broadly consistent with prior conceptualizations of SEL and SECD (Denham et al., 2012; Park & Peterson, 2006). Moreover, the findings proved to be consistent across waves of assessment that began at a relatively young age (Grade 3) and spanned over three years. Thus, the overall total SECDS score and individual scales aligned with this factor structure, and demonstrated evidence of reliability and validity, both for the sample as a whole, and for gender and racial/ethnic groups.

The SECDS measure was also found to be sensitive to change in that it specifically demonstrated the effectiveness of the *PA* program to change the targeted social-emotional skills and character. Ji et al.'s (2006) study also demonstrated that, consistent with relational developmental systems theory (RDST; Overton, 2013), changes in SECDS were considered the proximal manifestations of character. That is, such aspects of a youth's character mediated the effects of the *PA* program on more distal manifestations of character, namely negative behaviors (substance use), emotional/mental health, and positive health-related behaviors (hygiene and healthy food and exercise).

Thus, past research suggests that it was possible to measure a latent construct that was related to character, virtues, and social-emotional skills. In addition, the study illustrated that the SECDS scores on the resulting scale were related to multiple social cultural factors and sensitive to change due to exposure to the *PA* program. Finally, the results suggested that changes in SECD were related to changes in more distal manifestations of SECD in ways predicted by social cognitive theory and RDST (Mueller, 2014; Overton, 2013).

Methodological issues: Cautions regarding the study of social cognition in youth

As discussed in Chapter 1, the concept of social cognitive development in youth is complex, ambiguous, and applied to different academic disciplines including psychology, education, sociology, anthropology, psycholinguistics, and others. Given this complexity, within this book I argue that a psychocultural and relational developmental systems approach to social cognitive development may provide the researcher and educator with an inclusive lens to explore emerging adolescents' personal, social, and educational lives.

Moreover, the approach taken within this book promotes the notion "that in order to participate in any social world, people must incorporate cultural models, meanings, and practices into their basis psychological processes" (Fiske, Kitayama, Markus, & Nisbett, 1998, pp. 915–916). Given that cultural and social ecological psychology suggest contextualism may serve as a general explanatory framework or a metatheory (Bjorklund & Ellis, 2014; Bronfenbrenner & Morris, 2006; Sternberg, 2014), young people's social behavior should be understood within the social, cultural, and historical context. Thus, a developmental, trans-cultural explanatory framework may help researchers and educators to make sense of their students' social cognitive development within culturally and economically diverse contexts.

Regarding research ethics, many researchers suggest that respectful research must be a main priority for the examination of social cognition in youth, and value must be given to young people's communicative skills (nonverbal and verbal). Regarding interpretivist research approaches such as ethnographic research, implications of reflexivity in interpretation are also important. A sensitive researcher–participant rapport that facilitates conversation about emotional and social experiences is necessary to develop a trusting, reciprocal relationship. As researchers within the educational and psychological context suggest (Sternberg, 2014), research on topics that hold personal relevance and sensitivity, such as one's identity and peer relational experiences, needs to be conducted in a respectful and cautious manner in order to actively respect the rights and views of participants.

Regarding researcher reflexivity, and the issues surrounding the insider/outsider dilemmas of the researcher, as interpretivist researchers, developmentalists are responsible for addressing their subjectivity and personal biases in their research. Researchers must also remain cautious in the sense that they will need to "tame their own subjectivity" (Peshkin, 1988), if they intend to provide authentic interpretations of young people's self-stories. As Wolcott (1985) warns, ethnographic sensitivity entails an attentive, empathic listening not only during interviews, but also during the review of video and audio recordings and associated transcripts.

Tilley (1998) asserts that the notion of respectful research needs to be applied to situations in which researchers work with young people, as they remain a vulnerable population. Thus, future mixed method, transcultural longitudinal studies will help to enrich the current research landscape on emerging adolescents' social cognitive development. Studies over time and cultures will help to illustrate the possible influences age, gender, and ethnicity may have on emerging adolescents' social cognitive abilities.

Future Questions

Given the complex and multidimensional nature of social cognitive abilities, future research with youth will need to incorporate multiple measures, as well as multiple informants of social cognitive competencies including parents, teachers, coaches, and so on (Sternberg, 2014; Tahiroglu et al., 2014). For example, given the role the language plays in ToM and other social cognitive abilities, the combination of narrative, interview-style tasks (e.g., strange stories: Happé, 1994; socially ambiguous stories: SAS, e.g., Bosacki, 2015; Hayward, 2011), with visual measures such as RMET and the silent film task (Baron-Cohen, 2003; Devine & Hughes, 2013), and computer-assisted tasks will help researchers to assess complex social cognitive abilities such as ToM and inhibitory control, among others, in a more accurate and comprehensive way. Furthermore, given the range of ages and abilities across later childhood and adolescence, each of the tasks and methods used will need to be developmentally appropriate. In addition, given the need for further transcultural research, measures will need to be translated to be culturally relevant as well as gender sensitive (Bosacki, 2015).

In addition to longitudinal, transcultural research, measures adapted from brain imagery tools (functional Magnetic Resonance Imaging; fMRI), developmental endocrinology, and neuroimaging research will also be useful as added measures to explore social cognitive development in youth (Bjorklund & Ellis, 2014; Del Giudice, 2014; Sternberg, 2014). The use of such neuroscience and sociobiological measures in combination with offline (e.g., narratives, films), and online tasks (e.g., computer games) will help researchers and educators to investigate the processes involved in young people's neurodevelopment during engagement with ToM and related tasks. Future research needs to continue to investigate these ToM abilities in terms of social relationships such as family and friendships. Such research will clarify how the brain and mind work within relationships in terms of emotional and social reasoning, problem-solving, decision-making, and so on.

In sum, researchers have only just started to explore how emerging adolescents' social cognition and sense of identity develops across time and cultural contexts. Multidisciplinary, transcultural, and mixed-method longitudinal studies could provide fruitful investigations into the development of social cognitive abilities, and how this plays a role in emerging adolescents' developing sense of self and understanding of others. Further systematic research is also needed to explore the role of social cognitive processes within young people's personal, social, and educational worlds.

Summary

Overall, this chapter critically summarized social cognitive developmental research method-ologies to help assess social cognitive growth in emerging adolescents. More specifically, it focused on the role developmental research methods play in the area of social cognition, and discussed evaluative study findings of social-emotional and cognitive educational programs for youth. Various measures of emotional and moral aspects of social cognitive learning such as social-emotional learning (SEL), social-emotional and character development (SECD), youth positive development (YPD), mindfulness and compassion (self and other) were outlined, and implications for future practice and research were discussed. As the remainder of this book will show, such research techniques may help researchers to further explore the complex factors involved in youth's social cognitive development.

References

Ahmed, F. S., & Stephen Miller, L. (2011). Executive function mechanisms of theory of mind. *Journal of Autism and Developmental Disorders, 41*(5), 667–678.

Aldao, A., & Nolen-Hoeksema, S. (2010). Specificity of cognitive emotion regulation strategies: A transdiagnostic examination. *Behavioral Research and Therapy, 48*(10), 974–983. doi:10.1016/j.brat.2010.06.002

Allred, C. G. (2014). *Effects of a social-emotional and character development (SECD) program on character and distal manifestations of character such as positive and negative health behaviors, emotional/mental health, and academics.* Paper presented at Can Virtue Be Measured? The Second Annual Conference of the Jubilee Centre for Character and Values, University of Birmingham, Oriel College, University of Oxford, England.

Apperly, I. A. (2012). What is "Theory of Mind"? Concepts, cognitive processes and individual differences. *The Quarterly Journal of Experimental Psychology, 65*, 825–839. doi: 10.1080/17470218.2012.676055

Apperly, I. A., Samson, D., & Humphreys, G. W. (2009). Studies of adults can inform accounts of theory of mind development. *Developmental Psychology, 45*, 190–201.

Astington, J. W., Pelletier, J., & Homer, B. (2002). Theory of mind and epistemological development: The relation between children's second-order false belief understanding and their ability to reason about evidence. *New Ideas in Psychology. Special Issue: Folk Epistemology, 20*(2–3), 131–144. doi:10.1016/S0732-118X(02)00005-3

Banerjee, R., & Watling, D. (2005). Children's understanding of faux pas: Associations with peer relations. *Hellenic Journal of Psychology, 2*, 27–45.

Banerjee, R., Watling, D., & Caputi, M. (2011). Peer relations and the understanding of faux pas: Longitudinal evidence for bidirectional associations. *Child Development, 82*, 1887–1905. doi:10.1111/j.1467-8624.2011.01669.x

Baron-Cohen, S. (2002). The extreme male brain theory of autism. *Trends in Cognitive Sciences, 6*, 248–254.

Baron-Cohen, S. (2003). *The essential difference.* London, England: Penguin.

Baron-Cohen, S., Wheelwright, S., Hill, J., Raste, Y., & Plumb, I. (2001). The "Reading the Mind in the Eyes" test revised version. *Journal of Child Psychology and Psychiatry, 42*(2), 241–251.

Belli, S. R., Rogers, R. D., & Lau, J. Y. F. (2012). Adult and adolescent social reciprocity: Experimental data from the trust game. *Journal of Adolescence, 35*(5), 1341–1349.

Berg, J., Dickhaut, J., & McCabe, K. (1995). Trust, reciprocity and social history. *Games and Economic Behavior, 10*, 122–142.

Bjorklund, D., & Ellis, B. (2014). Children, childhood and development in evolutionary perspective. *Developmental Review, 34,* 225–264.

Bosacki, S. (2000). Theory of mind and self-concept in preadolescents: Links with gender and language. *Journal of Educational Psychology, 92,* 709–717.

Bosacki, S. (2013). Theory of mind understanding and conversational patterns in early adolescence. *Journal of Genetic Psychology, 174,* 170–191.

Bosacki, S. (2015). Children's theory of mind, self-perceptions, and peer relations: A longitudinal study. *Infant and Child Development, 24,* 175–188. doi:0.1002/icd.1878

Bosacki, S. L., & Astington, J. W. (1999). Theory of mind in preadolescence: Relations between social understanding and social competence. *Social Development, 8,* 237–255.

Bosacki, S., Bialecka-Pikul, M., & Spzak, M. (2015). Theory of mind and self-concept in Canadian and Polish youth. *International Journal of Youth and Adolescence, 20*(4), 457–469. doi:10.1080/02673843.2013.804423

Bosco, F. M., Gabbatore, I., & Tirassa, M. (2014). A broad assessment of theory of mind in adolescence: The complexity of mindreading. *Consciousness and Cognition, 24*(1), 84–97. doi:10.1016/j.concog.2014.01.003

Bowers, E. P., Li, Y., Kiely, M. K., Brittian, A., Lerner, J. V., & Lerner, R. M. (2010). The five Cs model of positive youth development: A longitudinal analysis of confirmatory factor structure and measurement invariance. *Journal of Youth and Adolescence, 39*(7), 720–735.

Bronfenbrenner, U., & Morris, P. (2006). The bioecological model of human development. In R. M. Lerner (Ed.), *Handbook of child psychology: Vol. 43. Theoretical models of human development* (pp. 793–828). Hoboken, NJ: Wiley.

Brose, A., Schmiedek, F., Koval, P., & Kuppens, P. (2015). Emotional inertia contributes to depressive symptoms beyone perseverative thinking. *Cognition and Emotion, 29,* 527–538.

Brüne, M. (2005). "Theory of mind" in schizophrenia: A review of the literature. *Schizophrenia Bulletin, 31*(1), 21–42.

Byom L., & Mutlu. B. (2013). Theory of mind: Mechanisms, methods, and new directions. *Frontiers in Human Neuroscience, 7,* 413.

Calero, C., Salles, A., Semelman, M., & Sigman, M. (2013). Age and gender dependent development of theory of mind in 6- to 8-years old children. *Frontiers in Human Neuroscience, 7*(281), 1–6. doi:10.3389/fnhum.2013.00281

Coricelli, G., Critchley, H. D., Joffily, M., O'Doherty, J. D., Sirigu, A., & Dolan, R. J. (2005). Regret and its avoidance: A neuroimaging study of choice behavior. *Nature Neuroscience, 8,* 1255–1262. doi:10.1038/nn1514

Denham. S. (1998). *Emotional development in young children.* New York, NY: Guilford.

Denham, S., Bassett, H., Way, E., Kalb, S., Warren-Khot, H., & Zinsser, K. (2014). "How would you feel? What would you do?" Development and underpinnings of preschoolers' social information processing. *Journal of Research in Childhood Education, 28,* 128–202.

Denham, S., Bassett, H., Way, E., Mincic, M., Zinsser, K., & Graling, K. (2012). Preschoolers' emotion knowledge: Self-regulatory foundations, and predictions of early school success. *Cognition and Emotion, 26,* 667–679.

Devine, R., & Hughes, C. (2013). Silent films and strange stories: Theory of mind, gender, and social experiences in middle childhood. *Child Development, 84,* 989–1003.

Donaldson, S., Dollwet, M., & Rao, M. (2015). Happiness, excellence, and optimal human functioning revisited: Examining the peer-reviewed literature linked to positive psychology. *The Journal of Positive Psychology, 10,* 185–195.

Dumontheil, I., Apperly, I. A., & Blakemore, S. J. (2010). Online usage of theory of mind continues to develop in late adolescence. *Developmental Science, 13*(2), 331–338.

Dumontheil, I., Hillebrandt, H., Apperly, I. A., & Blakemore, S.-J. (2012). Developmental differences in the control of action selection by social information. *Journal of Cognitive Neuroscience, 24*(10), 2080–2095. http://dx.doi.org/10.1162/jocn_a_00268

Durlak, J. A., Weissberg, R. P., Dymnicki, A. B., Taylor, R. D., & Schellinger, K. B. (2011). The impact of enhancing students' social and emotional learning: A meta-analysis of school-based universal interventions. *Child Development, 82*(1), 405–432.

Elias, M. (2009). Social-emotional and character development and academics as a dual focus of educational policy. *Educational Policy, 23*(6), 831–846.

Ensor, R., Devine, R., Mark, A., & Hughes, C. (2014). Cognitive references to 2-year-olds predict theory of mind at ages 6 and 10. *Child Development, 85*, 1222–1235.

Epley, N., Caruso, E., & Bazerman, M. H. (2006). When perspective-taking increases taking: Reactive egoism in social interaction. *Journal of Personality and Social Psychology, 91*(5), 872–889.

Evans, A. M., & Krueger, J. I. (2011). Elements of trust: Risk and perspective-taking. *Journal of Experimental Social Psychology, 47*(1), 171–177.

Fett, K., Shergill, S., Gromann, P., Dumontheil, L., Blakemore, S., Yakub, F., & Krabbendam, L. (2014). Trust and social reciprocity in adolescence – A matter of perspective taking. *Journal of Adolescence, 37*, 175–184.

Fiske, A., Kitayama, S., Markus, H., & Nisbett, R. (1998). The cultural matrix of social psychology. In D. Gilbert, A. Fiske, & G. Lindzey (Eds.), *The handbook for social psychology* (Vol. 2, pp. 915–981). New York, NY: McGraw Hill.

Garcia, N., & Scherfe, S. (2015). Emerging sensitivity to socially complex situations: A unique role for adolescence? *Child Development Perspectives, 9*, 84-90.

Goldin-Meadow, S. (2014). How gesture works to change our minds. *Trends in Neuroscience and Education, 3*, 4–6.

Greenberg, M. T., Weissberg, R. P., O Brien, M. U., Zins, J. E., Fredericks, L., Resnik, H., &

Elias, M. J. (2003). Enhancing school-based prevention and youth development through coordinated social, emotional, and academic learning. *American Psychologist, 58*(6/7), 466–474.

Happé, F. G. (1994). An advanced test of theory of mind: Understanding of story characters' thoughts and feelings by able autistic, mentally handicapped, and normal children and adults. *Journal of Autism and Developmental Disorders, 24*(2), 129–154. doi: 10.1007/BF02172093

Happé, F. (1995). The role of age and verbal ability in the theory of mind task performance of subjects with autism. *Child Development, 66*, 843–855.

Hayward, E. O. (2011). Measurement of advanced theory of mind in school-age children: Investigating the validity of a unified construct. Doctoral Dissertation

Hughes, C. (2011). *Social understanding and social lives: From toddlerhood through to the transition to school.* New York, NY: Psychology Press.

Hughes, C., & Devine, R. T. (2015). A social perspective on theory of mind. In M. E. Lamb (Ed.), *Handbook of child psychology and developmental science: Vol. III. Socioemotional processes* (pp. 564–609). Hoboken, NJ: Wiley.

Humphrey, N., Kalambouka, A., Wigelsworth, M., Lendrum, A., Deighton, J., & Wolpert, M. (2011). Measures of social and emotional skills for children and young people: A systematic review. *Educational and Psychological Measurement, 71*(4), 617–637.

Hutchins, T., Prelock, P., & Bonanzinga, L. (2012). Psychometric evaluation of the theory of mind Inventory (ToMI): A study of typically developing children with autism spectrum disorder. *Journal of Autism Development Disorders, 42*, 377–341. doi:10.1007/s10803-011-1244-7

Hyman, R. (1963). *The nature of psychological inquiry.* Englewood Cliffs, NJ: Prentice-Hall.

Ibanez, A., Huepe, D., Gemp, R., Gutierrez, V., Riveria-Rei, A., & Toledo, M. (2013). Empathy, sex and fluid intelligence. *Personality and Individual Differences, 54*, 616–621.

Ji, P., Flay, B. R., DuBois, D. L., Brechling, V., Day, J., & Cantillon, D. (2006). Consent form return rates for third-grade urban elementary students. *American Journal of Health Behavior, 30*(5), 467–474.

Korkmaz, B. (2011). Theory of mind and neuro-developmental disorders of childhood. *Pediatric Research, 69*(5 Pt 2), 101R–108R.

Laceulle, O. M., Nederhof, E., Karreman, A., Ormel, J., & van Aken, M. A. G. (2012). Stressful events and temperament change during early and middle adolescence: The TRAILS study. *European Journal of Personality, 26*(3), 276–284. doi:10.1002/per.832

Lagattuta, K. (2014). Linking past, present, and future: Child ability to connect mental states and emotions. *Child Development Perspectives, 8*, 90–95.

Lalonde, C., & Chandler, M. (1995). False belief understanding goes to school: On the social-emotional consequences of coming early or late to a first theory of mind. *Cognition and Emotion, 9*, 167–185.

Lecce, S., Bianco, F., Demichelli, P., & Cavallini, E. (2014). Training preschoolers on first-order false belief understanding: Transfer on advanced ToM skills and metamemory. *Child Development, 85*, 2404–2418.

Lecce, S., Caputi, M., & Pagnin, E. (2015). False-belief understanding at age 5 predicts beliefs about learning in year 3 of primary school. *European Journal of Developmental Psychology, 12*, 40–53.

Lerner, R. M., Lerner, J. V., Almerigi, J. B., Theokas, C., Phelps, E., Gestsdottir, S., … von Eye, A. (2005). Positive youth development, participation in community youth development programs, and community contributions of fifth-grade adolescents: Findings from the first wave of the 4-H Study of Positive Youth Development. *Journal of Early Adolescence, 25*(1), 17–71.

Linkins, M., Niemiec, R., Gillham, J., & Mayerson, J. (2015). Through the lens of strength: A framework for educating the heart. *The Journal of Positive Psychology, 10*, 64–68.

Lu, H., Su, Y., & Wang, Q. (2008). Talking about others facilitates theory of mind in Chinese preschoolers. *Developmental Psychology, 44*(6), 1726–1736. doi:10.1037/a0013074

Malti, T., & Krettenauer, T. (2013). The relation of moral emotion attributions to prosocial and antisocial behavior: A meta-analysis, *Child Development, 84*, 397–412.

Marchetti, A., Castelli, I., Sanvito, L., & Massaro, D. (2014). Is a bird in the hand worth two in the future? Intertemporal choice, attachment and theory of mind in school-aged children. *Frontiers in Psychology, 5*, 483–493.

Mathersul, D., McDonald, S., & Rushby, J. (2013). Understanding advanced theory of mind and empathy in high-functioning adults with autism spectrum disorder. *Journal of Clinical Experimental Neuropsychology, 35*, 655–668.

McDonald, S., & Flanagan, S. (2004). Social perception deficits after traumatic brain injury: Interaction between emotion recognition, mentalizing ability, and social communication. *Neuropsychology, 18*, 572–579. doi:10.1037/0894-4105.18.3.572

McDonald, S., Flanagan, S., Martin, I., & Saunders, C. (2004). The ecological validity of TASIT: A test of social perception. *Neuropsychological Rehabilitation, 14*, 285–302. doi:10.1080/09602010343000237

McDonald, S., Flanagan, S., & Rollins, J. (2002). *The Awareness of Social Inference Test*. Sydney, Australia: Harcourt Assessment.

Merrell, K., & Gueldner, B. A. (2010). *Social and emotional learning in the classroom: Promoting mental health and academic success*. London, England: Guilford.

Miller, S. (2009). Children's understanding of second-order mental states. *Psychological Bulletin, 135*(5), 749–773. doi:10.1037/a0016854

Milligan, K., Astington, J. W., & Dack, L. A. (2007). Language and theory of mind: Meta-analysis of the relation between language ability and false-belief understanding. *Child Development, 78*(2), 622–646. doi:10.1111/j.1467-8624.2007.01018.x

Morris, A. S., Silk, J. S., & Steinberg, L. (2007). The role of the family context in the development of emotion regulation. *Social Development, 16,* 361–388. doi:10.1111/j.1467-9507.2007.00389.x

Mueller, M. (2014). Is human-animal interaction (HAI) linked to positive youth development? Initial answers. *Applied Developmental Science, 18,* 5–16.

Overton, W. F. (2013). A new paradigm for developmental science: Relationism and relational-developmental systems. *Applied Developmental Science, 17,* 94–107. doi:10.1080/10888691.2013.778717

Park, N., & Peterson, C. (2006). Moral competence and character strengths among adolescents: The development and validation of the Values in Action Inventory of Strengths for Youth. *Journal of Adolescence, 29,* 891–909. doi:10.1016/j.adolescence.2006.04.011

Perner, J., & Wimmer, H. (1985). "John thinks that Mary thinks that…": Attribution of second-order beliefs by 5- to 10-year-old children. *Journal of Experimental Child Psychology, 39,* 437–471. doi:10.1016/0022-0965(85)90051-7

Peshkin, A. (1988). In search of subjectivity—one's own. *Educational Researcher, 14,* 17–22.

Rose-Krasnor, L. (2009). Future directions in youth involvement research. *Social Development, 18,* 497–509.

Rueda, P., Fernandez-Berrocal, P., & Baron-Cohen, S. (2015). Dissociation between cognitive and affective empathy in youth with Asperger Syndrome. *European Journal of Developmental Psychology, 12,* 85–98.

Ruffman, T. (2014). To belief or not belief. *Developmental Review, 34,* 265–293.

Rust, J., & Golombok, S. (2009). *Modern psychometrics: The science of psychological assessment.* London, England: Routledge.

Shahaeian, A., Nielsen, M., Peterson, C. C., & Slaughter, V. (2014). Cultural and family influences on children's theory of mind development: A comparison of Australian and Iranian school-age children. *Journal of Cross-Cultural Psychology, 45,* 555–568. doi:10.1177/0022022113513921

Siegel, D. (2013). *Brainstorm: The power and purpose of the teenage brain.* New York, NY: Jeremy Tarcher/Penguin.

Smith, R., & Rose, A. (2011). The "cost of caring" in youths' friendships: Considering associations among social perspective taking, co-rumination, and empathetic distress. *Developmental Psychology, 47*(6), 1792–1803.

Sternberg, R. (2014). The development of adaptive competence: Why cultural psychology is necessary and not just nice. *Developmental Review, 34,* 208–224.

Tahiroglu, D., Carlson, S. Olofson, E., Moses, L., Mahy, C., & Sabbagh, M. (2014). The children's social understanding scale: Construction and validation of a parent-report measure for assessing individual differences in children's theories of mind. *Developmental Psychology, 50,* 2485–2497.

Thompson, R. (2011). Methods and measures in developmental emotions research: Some assembly required. *Journal of Experimental Child Psychology, 119,* 275–285.

Tilley, S. (1998). Conducting respectful research: A critique of practice. *Canadian Journal of Education, 23,* 316–328.

Torralva, T., Roca, M., Gleichgerrcht, E., Bekinschtein, T., & Manes, F. (2009). A neuropsychological battery to detect specific executive and social cognitive impairments in early frontotemporal dementia. *Brain, 132*(5), 1299–1309.

Van den Bos, W., Van Dijk, E., Westenberg, H., Rombout, S. A. R. B., & Crone, E. A. (2011). Changing brains, changing perspectives: The neurocognitive development of reciprocity. *Psychological Science, 22*(1), 60–70.

Van den Bos, W., Westenberg, M., Van Dijk, E., & Crone, E. A. (2010). Development of trust and reciprocity in adolescence. *Cognitive Development, 25,* 90–102.

Wellman, H. (2014). *Making minds: How theory of mind develops.* Oxford, England: Oxford University Press.

Wigelsworth, M., Humphrey, N., Kalambouka, A., & Lendrum, A. (2010). A review of key issues in the measurement of children's social and emotional skills. *Educational Psychology in Practice, 26*(2), 173–186.

Wolcott, H. (1985). On ethnographic intent. *Educational Administration Quarterly, 21,* 187–203.

Zins, J. E., Weissberg, R. P., Wang, M. C., & Walberg, H. J. (2004). *Building academic success on social and emotional learning: What does the research say?* New York, NY: Teachers College Press.

Part II

Social Cognitive Educational and Developmental Research
Self

"We become luminous to ourselves only when we know what is not ourselves." (Schall, 2001, p. 11)

Section Overview

In Part II, the focus is on the self, and each chapter focuses on various aspects of the self in terms of cognition (Chapter 3), emotionality (Chapter 4), and morality (Chapter 5).

More specifically, this section will provide a critical overview of state-of-the-art research that explores the personal world and self-development of the young person including cognitive skills, emotions, morality, and spirituality. Given the importance of the development of the self-concept throughout childhood and adolescence (Marshall, Parker, Ciarrochi, & Heaven, 2014), the next three chapters will focus on various aspects of the self that may influence the way in which youth think about, feel, and interact with the world.

3

The Cognitive Self
Language and Executive Functions

"All the same," said the Scarecrow, "I shall ask for brains instead of a heart; for a fool would not know what to do with a heart if he had one." (Baum, 1984/1900, p. 47)

Introduction

Focusing on self-development, Chapter 3 builds on the two previous chapters by incorporating theory and research regarding the cognitive self. Specifically, this chapter will explore the role of cognitive abilities in self-development.

The period of transition between childhood and adolescence is often defined as the period between the onset of puberty and the achievement of relative self-sufficiency (Del Giudice, 2014; Greenspan & Deardorff, 2014). The beginning of adolescence is largely defined as a neurobiological event, whereas the end of adolescence is often defined within the social cultural context. Although behavioral changes and improvements in social cognitive skills in adolescence have been reported for millennia (Blakemore & Mills, 2014), with the recent advent of brain-imaging technologies, researchers are gaining new knowledge about developmental changes that occur during late childhood and early adolescence (Casey, Getz, & Galvan, 2008; Del Giudice, 2014). This chapter highlights research on social cognitive development during emerging adolescence when there is a heightened sensitivity to biosociocultural signals in one's body and environment.

More specifically, this chapter will focus on neurobiological and social contextual factors that might influence the development of social cognition and behavior during later childhood and adolescence. This chapter integrates research across neuroscience and psychology within the framework that suggests emerging adolescents' health and

Social Cognition in Middle Childhood and Adolescence: Integrating the Personal, Social, and Educational Lives of Young People, First Edition. S. L. Bosacki.

well-being are developed in part through interactions between biological factors and social interactions (Call et al., 2002). The chapter ends with a discussion of potential implications of empirical research on emerging adolescence for the school context.

Research

As part of a growing focus on developmental-evolutionary relational systems approaches to psychology (Bjorklund & Ellis, 2014; Del Giudice, 2014; Overton, 2013; Sternberg, 2014), Tomasello (2014a) discusses an evolutionary-psychological perspective to explain the development of social cognition in humans. Drawing from his work in comparative psychology with primates, Tomasello discusses the shared intentionality hypothesis. Specifically, he cites work by cultural theorists (Hegel, Vygotsky, Bakhtin), and the social infrastructurists (Mead, Piaget, Wittgenstein) who claim that human thinking is individual improvisation enmeshed in a sociocultural context.

Tomasello builds on his 1999 book, *The Cultural Origins of Human Cognition*, which discussed what made human cognition unique to explore the question of what makes the human thinking process unique. He claims that, compared to a process of social transmission, human culture is a process of social coordination. In particular, he explores the shared intentionality hypothesis that claims three main components of thinking distinguished humans from primates: cognitive representation, inference, and self-monitoring. To survive and thrive, these abilities transformed twice during evolution as humans first needed to coordinate their behaviors in collaborative or cultural activities, and then to coordinate their intentional states through cooperative communication or conventional language.

However, before one begins to share intentionality, one must first develop individual intentionality. Drawing on the philosophical belief-desire model of rational action, a goal or desire coupled with an epistemic relation to the world (e.g., a belief based on an understanding of the causal or intentional structure of the situation) creates an intention to act in a particular way. Such a flexible, self-regulated, and cognitive way of acting is referred to as individual intentionality. This self-regulation model allows thinking to occur when a person attempts to solve a problem and to meet a goal by imagining what would happen if she tried different actions in a situation, or if different external forces entered the situation before actually acting (Bjorklund & Ellis, 2014; Tomasello, 2014b). This imagining of a future scenario is considered to represent an "offline" simulation of potential perceptual experiences.

Thus, to think before acting in this way, as a prerequisite, an individual must possess the following three cognitive skills: (1) the ability to cognitively represent experiences to oneself "offline," (2) the ability to simulate or make inferences that causally transform these representations, intentionally, and/or logically, and (3) the ability to self-monitor and evaluate how these simulated experiences might lead to specific behavioral outcomes—and thus, to make thoughtful behavioral decisions (Ruffman, 2014; Tomasello, 2014b). Furthermore, according to Tomasello (2014b), the success or failure of a particular behavioral decision reveals the underlying processes of representation, simulation, and self-monitoring.

Regarding the social construction of cognitions, for social communicative actions to occur, some unique cognitive tools are necessary. The skills for joint attention and shared intentionality, which first emerge around 8 to 12 months, fulfill this need. These skills enable young children to engage with adults in social communicative ways. As Mead (1934) emphasized, most typically developing infants demonstrate a need to establish joint attention and common ground about a situation in which they are currently engaged with mature family members. Such intentionally communicative actions ensure that children have the opportunity to share and develop their cognitions with others, and this ability continues to develop as children mature through childhood and adolescence.

Language and social cognitive development in emerging adolescence

Tomasello (2014b) claims that Mead, Piaget, and Wittgenstein are social infrastructure theorists who proposed that language and culture represented humans' ultrasocial ways of connecting with the world in a cognitive sense. The past two decades of research supports this focus on cooperative communication by showing that nonhuman primates have sophisticated cognitive abilities, and prelinguistic and linguistic infants are capable of engaging with others in ways that primates cannot—mainly joint attention and cooperative communication. These findings suggest that in contrast to culture theorists such as Hegel, Vygotsky, and Bakhtin, who claimed that human thinking derived from sociality, culture, and language, humans' thinking derived from deeper and more primate forms of individual problem-solving abilities and uniquely human social engagement. This kind of objective, reflective, and normative thinking is also connected to the process of mental recursion as illustrated through the use of embedded language such as that used in Theory of Mind (ToM) and mental time travel or future-oriented thinking (Corbalis, 2011).

Many researchers who focus on psycholinguistics also support this view that private and inner speech help to drive the development of conscious awareness and communicative competence across childhood and into adolescence (Winsler, 2009). That is, our ability to communicate effectively with others in social situations is mainly dependent upon our ability to engage in private mental speech. In particular, our ability to develop private speech that is reflective and recursive is intricately related to a sense of collective or shared intentionality.

As mentioned throughout this book, social cognition encompasses various cognitive skills involved in the interpretation and navigation of social information, including emotion cognition, ToM, and personal and social problem- solving (Marton, Abramoff, & Rosenzweig, 2005). Competent language ensures that a child can attribute meaning to social information to mentally represent the emotions, intentions, and needs of the self and other during social interactions (Lockl & Schneider, 2007; Ruffman, 2014). Although research has consistently shown the importance of language for social cognition (Marton et al, 2005; Milligan, Astington, & Dack, 2007), limited research exists on the role language plays in emerging adolescents' social cognitive abilities such as social and personal problem-solving. That is, the ability of a young person to learn how to make rational decisions involves complex mental reasoning skills that incorporate emotion cognition, self-regulation, and inter- as well as intrapersonal perspective-taking.

For example, researchers have started to build on Selman's (1980) theory of social cognitive development, and take into consideration the developmental relational systems and evolutionary approach (Overton, 2013; Tomasello, 2014b), as well as the sociocultural perspectives of Vygotsky (1986/1934) and Goffman (1959, 1981). Regarding the various dimensions of language competencies, semantic and syntactic language have been shown to be important for social perspective-taking and moral reasoning during childhood (Lockl & Schneider, 2007; Milligan et al., 2007). Semantic language allows us to form mental representations of events, and the thoughts and feelings of others, which are invisible and abstract. These mental representations form the basis of our understanding of different social perspectives, which is crucial for social problem-solving.

Astington and Baird (2005) have argued, however, that, compared to semantic language, syntactic language may play a more significant role in the development of young people's social perspective-taking. For example, sentential complements, which consist of a main clause and a subordinate clause that allows for the integration of intentions and desires, have been shown to facilitate social perspective-taking in young children (Tomasello, 2014a). Moreover, past research shows that, compared to other aspects of language (e.g., general language, general syntax, semantics, and vocabulary), sentential complement knowledge has been found to be more highly correlated (although not significantly) with young people's social perspective-taking (Milligan et al., 2007).

Regarding developmental changes, the majority of the research that has investigated the relation between language and ToM and social perspective-taking has focused on children under the age of 5 years (Marton et al., 2005; Miller, 2009; Milligan et al., 2007). Fewer studies address language and social perspective-taking into later childhood and early adolescence, although recent evidence suggests that various language competences continue to play a significant role in ToM and social reasoning (Bosacki, 2013; Filippova & Astington, 2008; Hughes, 2011; Milligan et al., 2007; Rutherford et al., 2012).

Despite past research on children's understanding of thoughts and emotions, very little is known about how older children's and adolescents' ToM has the potential to shape and emotionally color their conversations with their family and friends (Bosacki, 2013). Past research suggests children who possess high levels of ToM, or provide advanced psychological explanations, are more likely to "think about their own and others' thinking" and engage in critical philosophical enquiry and shared dialogue during the school day (Bosacki, 2008; Hughes, 2011). Thus, given that the process of teaching and learning is crucial to self and ToM understanding (Bruner, 1996), researchers need to further explore how young people's ToM plays a role in their perceptions of their school experiences with their peers and teachers within the middle school and secondary or high school years.

Although some researchers have started to investigate individual differences in ToM and children's views of themselves and their school experiences with teachers and peers (Bosacki, 2015; Fink, Begeer, Hunt, & de Rosnay, 2014; Leeves & Banerjee, 2014), this area remains in need of further exploration (Hughes, 2011). A recent study on ToM and young adolescents' social conversations showed that longitudinal associations existed between young people's perceptions of their peer and family conversations, ToM understanding, and how they thought and felt about themselves and others during the late elementary school years (Bosacki, 2013). More specifically, results showed significant positive relations between positive perceptions or the number of positive emotion words of conversational patterns and ToM understanding for boys only. That is, boys who were more likely to perceive experiences of talking and listening with their friends and family as positive emotional experiences were also more likely to score relatively higher on the ToM task.

In addition, we also found that children who received a relatively high ToM score also used a relatively high number of mental states verbs, particularly emotion talk, in their interviews. Interestingly, we also found that most children were more likely to prefer listening to talking during social conversations, whereas the majority of children reported mixed feelings or ambiguous emotions during experiences of silence. The results of this study suggest differential gendered patterns in family and peer conversations and ToM and thus warrant further investigation (Bosacki, 2013). Such findings may encourage further longitudinal study of the links between young people's ToM and metacognitive abilities including self-regulation and reflective private speech within family relationships and friendships.

Development of theory of mind, self-knowledge, and private speech

The investigation of self-development within the framework of ToM also provides an opportunity to explore the role language (social and private) plays in self-conception. Although the notion that language and the cultural context influences the individuation process is not new (Bakhtin, 1981; Tomasello, 2014b; Vygotsky, 1978), Bakhtin's claim that the "selfing process" takes place within the context of relationships, such as the ongoing dialogue between self and others, has gained popularity within psycholinguistic and episte-mological research circles. In particular, research has focused on the concept of "voice," that is, the changing social nature of the selfing process is expressed in "voice," or the articula-tion of one's subjective experience (Harter, Waters, Whitesell, & Kastelic, 1997).

Furthermore, many researchers claim that the development of this voice and/or self may become differentiated according to gender and cultural experiences during late childhood and early adolescence (Bjorklund & Ellis, 2014; Hyde, 2014). The fact that the self is developed within, and by complex social interaction and experiences of language, suggests that self-conception entails one's ability to speak (and listen) to oneself and to others.

Regarding self-talk or private speech, this self-oriented language refers to overtly vocalized speech that is not addressed to anyone other than the speaker (Berk, 1986). According to Vygotsky's (1986/1934) social cultural developmental theory, private speech plays an important role in the development of higher cognitive processes such as planning, self-regulation, and the forecasting and management of emotions (Van Dijk, Van Dillen, Seip, & Rotteveel, 2012). In particular, Vygotsky argued that private speech helps the child to regulate ongoing cognitive activity.

This type of self-regulatory speech is assumed to be an intermediate step between external social tools for behavioral and emotional regulation and the silent verbal thought, defined as inner speech (Berk & Winsler 1995; Lee, 2011). From this perspective, Vygotsky hypothesized that private speech would show a curvilinear developmental pattern, peaking in the early school years and then decreasing as regulation becomes increasingly internal-ized between the ages of approximately 7 to 10 years (Winsler, 2009).

In Vygotsky's (1986/1934) theory of cognitive development, private speech is pro-duced by the progressive functional differentiation of language, from communicative to self-regulatory functions (Bjorklund & Ellis, 2014; Lee, McDonough, & Bird, 2014). That is, private speech first develops with minimal functional differentiation between speech for others and speech for oneself. Research suggests that this lack of differentiation may continue for some time but then disappear with development. Thus, sometime during late childhood, children gradually learn how to differentiate between two functions: social communicative speech oriented to others and internal self-oriented speech directed at the self. At this point in development, researchers claim that private speech disappears or "goes underground" and is transformed into inner speech (Vygotsky 1986/1934).

Empirically, most of Vygotsky's hypothesis about private speech in child development has been supported by the studies gleaned from the past three decades (Winsler, 2009). Private speech has been observed as early as 23–25 months of age (Sanchez, Alarcon, & De la Mata, 2009), and as late as 17 years (Winsler, 2009). In general, children's use of private speech increases with age, peaks around 4 or 5 years old, and gradually becomes more abbreviated until it is internalized around the age of 7 or 8 years (Berk, 1986). Private speech gradually develops and becomes useful to emerging adolescents and adults as a tool for self-regulation and emotional forecasting and management (Lee et al., 2014; Van Dijk et al., 2012).

For example, Winsler (2009) has shown that 10–30% of children aged from 11 to 17 spontaneously used fully overt self-talk during a cognitive task. Duncan and Cheyne (1999) administered a self-report questionnaire to 1,132 university undergraduate students and found high levels of reported self-verbalization for the regulation of various cognitive processes. Furthermore, Duncan and Cheyne (2001) observed private speech in young adults while working on tasks of varying cognitive difficulty. Similar to research findings on children, young adults' private speech was sensitive to experimental manipulations, and thus suggests contextual and functional similarities across age.

Although the majority of research on private speech development remains in the field of early childhood, during the past decade an increasing amount of research has studied the development of private speech and related social cognitive factors in older children and adolescence as well as adults (Sanchez et al., 2009). For example, during the past decade, a small but growing number of studies have shown that private speech appears to develop and follow similar patterns to childhood private speech throughout adolescence and into adulthood (Duncan & Tarulli, 2009). More specifically, although private speech contains more mental state terms in adults, across all ages research shows that private speech appears to serve as a normative form of verbal mediation beyond childhood and into adulthood. For instance, as mentioned earlier, the task difficulty effect that reflects that the amount of private speech increases according to the cognitive difficulty of task completion occurs in most children as well as adults (Duncan & Cheyne, 2001; Lee et al., 2014).

Although research shows that private speech occurs in childhood throughout adolescence and into adulthood, Duncan, Smith, McLaren, and Scott (2001) found that across three groups of participants (young children, late childhood, and young adults), the rates of private speech significantly decreased according to age only when the participants knew that their private speech would be recorded. That is, the amount of private speech did not significantly differ across the three age groups when the participants were not being video-taped. According to Duncan et al. (2001) such a finding may suggest that as children develop they become more aware of the social stigma of private speech vocalization or "talking to oneself out loud." As Duncan and Tarulli (2009) note, given that talking to oneself is commonly socially stigmatized across various cultures, and that the transition to adolescence typically involves an increase in self-consciousness (Hyde, 2014), it may be difficult to research private speech, ToM, and moral emotions in emerging adolescents.

Research on adults' private speech shows that overt self-verbalization continues to play a mediational role in problem-solving and self-regulatory processes during adulthood (Lee et al., 2014; Sanchez et al., 2009). Further research shows that private or internalized speech may become explicit after becoming internalized when adults need to complete novel or difficult tasks. Although some studies exist on adult second-language learners and athletes (Alarcon-Rubio, Sanchez-Medina, & Winsler, 2013; Conroy & Metzler, 2004), the role of self-talk in terms of self-harming or self-helping behaviors remains mixed and inconclusive. For example, some studies have found positive relations between the frequency of emotional private speech and internalizing problems such as anxiety, depression, and obsessive-compulsive behaviors among older adolescents and adults (Brinthaupt, Hein, & Kramer, 2009; Kendall & Hollon, 1989; Khodayarifard, Brinthaupt, Zardkhaneh, & Azar, 2014).

Given the complex relations between private speech and social cognitive abilities such as emotional regulation, more research is needed on how youth perceive and feel about their experiences of self-talk and private speech. Few studies explore the prosody or the emotional component or tone of private speech and self-talk. For example, how do children talk to themselves—with what kind of rhythm or pattern, and with a loving and compassionate or cruel and punishing voice? Moreover, how do the rhythm and emotional tone of private speech develop throughout late childhood and early adolescence (Bronson, 2000)? Such research may help researchers to understand the developmental process of private speech in terms of Vygotsky's general cultural–historical framework and his claim that human psychological processes become verbally mediated (Lee et al., 2014).

Moreover, an increase in the study of private speech may help researchers to understand the self-regulatory functions of language in young people (Bjorklund & Ellis, 2014; Kinnucan & Kuebli, 2013). For example, recent research in older children and adults has found a positive relation between self-reported private speech and integrative self-knowledge and regulation (Khodayarifard et al., 2014; Morin, 2005). Given the importance of self-knowledge in the emerging adolescent's social cognitive development, the sections below will describe research findings that may help to explain how youth develop a cognitive sense of self.

Self-conception and self-understanding   In addition to the aforementioned advanced social cognitive processes, social cognitive research also includes the role of self-cognitions such as the development of self-perceptions and understanding self-concept development. In particular, a growing number of studies have started to explore how these self-focused cognitive processes are relevant to social learning (Leeves & Banerjee, 2014; Wellman, 2014). Increasingly, research with children claims that the developmental processes involved in intra- and interpersonal understanding appear to be intricately interwoven (Bosacki, 2012; Hughes, 2011; Ruffman, 2014), and support the view that self and other perception derives from social experience (Mead, 1934).

Similar to ToM research, since the field's conception, the study of the self has included the challenge of internal theoretical conflict (Bridges, 1925; James, 1890; Mead, 1934). Such theoretical conflict has perhaps led to its continued popularity within various social science disciplines, especially in psychology (Rochat, 2009) and philosophy (Nagel, 1986; Wellman, 2014). Conceptually, the "theory" of the self shares the greatest affinity to ToM research given that it emphasizes the individual's construction of the self, and deals with one's feelings and beliefs directed toward oneself (Damon & Hart, 1988; Harter, 1999; Ruffman, 2014).

In addition, since the 1960s, self-concept research has moved from the monolithic conception of self (Rosenberg, 1965), to one that is multidimensional (Harter, 1999) and hierarchical in nature (Marshall et al., 2014). This notion of the dialogical or "omnibus" self suggests that the self is a dynamic, multilayered entity that reconceptualizes itself as a combination of cognitive abilities, and emotional and social experiences (Bruner, 1996; Orth & Robins, 2014).

From a developmental perspective, a young person's self-concept becomes increasingly differentiated with age, and gradually shifts from the physical and active self in early childhood to the psychological and social self in early adolescence (Damon & Hart, 1988; Harter, 1999). During later childhood and early adolescence, the concept of the self moves from physical to mental terms as it increases in complexity and abstractness. Many researchers have noticed the similarities in children's understanding of self and other, that person and self-perceptions progress along a developmental continuum from concrete, physicalistic, and situation-specific views of the self to abstract, psychological, and trait-like self-definition (Schaffer, 1996).

Accordingly, as mentioned earlier, a growing number of social cognitive researchers have begun to investigate how children and adolescents come to understand the complex experience of their own individuality, and how this differs from their understanding of others (Blakemore & Mills, 2014). For instance, studies have found that social cognitive competencies may differ according to whether or not they are applied to the self or other. For example, it may be possible to have a sophisticated conceptual and positive sense of self, but a less well developed conceptual understanding, and negative view toward other people, or vice versa (Damon & Hart, 1988; Neff, 2011).

An ongoing debate among identity researchers involves the question of how to integrate the cognitive, moral, and affective aspects of the structure of self (Marshall et al., 2014). The majority of researchers in the past have defined one's cognitive representation of self in mainly affective terms. That is, such research claims that "self-esteem" assesses how negatively or positively one feels about one's selfhood (e.g., Marshall et al., 2014; Orth & Robins, 2014; Rosenberg, 1965). However, as described earlier, recent research with young people now focuses on the more cognitive aspects of the self through the investigation of self-evaluative justifications (Baumeister, Campbell, Krueger, & Vohs, 2003; Chaplin & Norton, 2015; Marshall et al., 2014; Neff, 2011). That is, to what extent do young people help to create their conceptual sense of self, and how do youth learn to evaluate their worthiness as individuals and learn to think and feel about themselves as good and worthy human beings?

As Damon and Hart (1988, p. 14) claim, the question that asks "how much" understanding a person has fails to explain how the self is understood. Subsequently, researchers have started to incorporate qualitative (e.g., interview) and quantitative (e.g., self-report questionnaire) methods to obtain a clearer picture of the conceptual system of self-conception. That is, what are the cognitive underpinnings of self-understanding that encompass the thoughts, attitudes, and beliefs about oneself that distinguish self from others (Damon & Hart, 1988)? Moreover, given a dynamic, multidimensional approach to self-concept, many researchers continue to question whether or not the structure of the self-concept is equivalent across diverse cultures and gender orientations (Fine, 2010; Harter et al., 1997; Hyde, 2014).

Within the research domain of ToM, the concept of the self has been increasingly mentioned, particularly regarding the issue of whether or not mental states are equally ascribed to both the self and other (Barresi & Moore, 1995; Bosacki, Bialecka-Pikul, & Spzak, 2015). As I've mentioned throughout this book, the connections between the research fields of ToM and developmental social cognition require ongoing attention and strengthening. The former mainly focus on infants and preschool children, whereas the latter offers a range of research studies on the relation between self-concept and social development in emerging adolescents.

Thus, the study of self-concept development from a ToM perspective may help to unpack the complex relations between theories of mind and theories of selves. A fuller, more complex model of social understanding, including the role of self-talk in self-knowledge development (Khodayarifard et al., 2014; Morin, 2005), may shed some light on the various research questions concerning self-concept during emerging adolescence. For example, a more complete model of social and self-understanding could help to explain findings of recent studies that have shown that self-consciousness (Rochat, 2009), social anxiety (Coplan & Rubin, 2010; Leeves & Banerjee, 2014), and loneliness (Goossens & Marcoen, 1999) may also increase in tandem with social cognitive competencies including the frequency of private speech.

To support this view, some of our recent research with Canadian youth has found that sophisticated or advanced ToM understanding may perhaps have intrapersonal and interpersonal costs and benefits (Bosacki, 2013). In particular, we found negative relations between young adolescent females' sense of global self-worth and their ToM. Such a finding suggests that, although more advanced ToM skills may enable youth to understand others' thoughts and feelings, young adolescent females may begin to imagine that others are thinking negatively or critically about them, which may lead to feelings of low self-worth and self-doubt (Bosacki, 2008; Hughes, 2011).

In addition, regarding interpersonal relations, we found significant positive relations between children's ToM at approximately 6 years of age, and their teacher ratings of anxious/fearful behavior at approximately 8 years of age. This finding suggests that the ability to understand others' thoughts and emotions may have implications for social and peer behavior later in later childhood. For example, children with a highly advanced emotional understanding ability may use this ability to either help (e.g., befriend someone), or harm others (e.g., excluding a peer from a group by developing a friendship with someone else) (Bosacki, 2015; Devine & Hughes, 2013).

In addition, this social cognitive model could also be used to test the various theories of ToM development by comparing self and other interpretations. For instance, ToM theory theorists would expect self- and other-understanding to develop in tandem (e.g., Barresi & Moore, 1996), whereas the ToM simulation theorist would expect self-understanding to develop before other-understanding (e.g., Harris, 1989). Alternatively, given that a sense of self is derived in part through social interactions (e.g., Mead, 1934; Ruffman, 2014; Tomasello, 2014a), a social relational systemic constructivist ToM theorist could perhaps predict that other-understanding would develop before self-understanding. In any case, given inconsistent and sparse research findings, the study of the development of self-formation and ToM within emerging adolescence continues to remain an elusive puzzle.

Past ToM research studies have found significant correlations between the understanding of mental states in self and other (Bosacki, 2015; Ruffman, 2014). Such findings support the theory-theory hypothesis that claims children use the same conceptual system to reason about their own and other people's second-order mental states. Alternatively, there are a few social cognitive, cross-cultural (Vinden, 1999), and ToM preschool studies that provide support for the social relational constructivist claim that one needs to understand the concept of "other" to understand the self (Banerjee & Yuill, 1999; Mink, Henning, & Aschersleben, 2014; Verschueren, Buyck, & Marooen, 2001).

Due to these conflicting findings, a collaborative effort between social cognitive researchers and ToM theorists is needed to investigate emerging adolescents' self- and other-understanding from a ToM perspective. That is, methods gleaned from the more general research area of social cognition, and the more focused research area of mental state understanding may help researchers to take a ToM approach to social cognition and provide ideas for future research. For example, despite the theoretical connection between ToM understanding and self-concept (Wellman, 2014), few studies investigate this link directly (Banerjee & Yuill, 1999; Bosacki et al., 2015). Furthermore, in relation to ToM, few studies have looked at various self-representations such as verbal and graphical, or other aspects of the self-system such as self-evaluation or self-agency (Bruner, 1996).

Although the majority of research supports a positive link between social perspective-taking and self-concept (Selman, 1980), some investigators claim that self-perception correlates of ToM and emotion understanding may not be uniformly positive (Dunn, 2002; Hughes, 2011). That is, although there is evidence to suggest that high levels of children's ToM may be positively associated with higher academic achievement and constructivist learning beliefs (Lecce, Caputi, & Pagnin, 2015), research has also found that higher ToM scores are also related to greater sensitivity to teacher criticism, and possibly lower self-esteem (Bosacki, 2008; Lecce, Caputi, & Hughes, 2011; Lecce, Caputi, & Pagnin, 2014). In addition, studies have shown that children and adults with advanced levels of ToM may experience diminished self-concept and emotional problems, given the amount of time they spend on self-reflection and imagining what others think of them (Bosacki, 2015; Chaplin & Norton, 2015). Also, given the finding that children who scored high on second-order ToM tasks were also able to better understand self-presentation rules (Banerjee & Yuill, 1999), perhaps children who are adept at reading social cues are adept at pretending to be who they think people want them to be.

Overall, such explorations of the links between psychological understanding and self will help to illuminate the complex connections between understanding oneself and others.

Taken together, ToM studies that have shown links between adolescents' cognitive abilities and self-concept support the contention that high psychological mindedness may have deleterious consequences such as a negative self-concept (Bosacki, 2008, 2014, 2015; Hughes, 2011). Thus, such findings suggest that social and emotional correlates of interpersonal understanding or "psychological mindedness" need to be further examined in emerging adolescents (Hughes, 2011).

Social cognitive development within social context during emerging adolescence

Past research has proposed that adolescence is a time of particular social and cultural sensitivity (Choudhury, 2010; Fiske et al., 1998; Kim & Sasaki, 2014), and that the impact of puberty on the brain makes adolescents particularly sensitive to their social environments (Greenspan & Deardorff, 2014). Until recently, there was a shortage of studies on social cognitive abilities within the social context after childhood, as it was usually assumed that these abilities were already mature by mid-childhood in typically developing children. Most paradigms have been designed to investigate social cognition (in particular, ToM) in young children and have thus resulted in ceiling effects after mid-childhood (Apperly, 2012).

Most emerging adolescents experience a period of social reorienting where the opinions of peers become more important than those of family members (Larson, 2011). Past research shows that, during the ages of approximately 10 to 18 years, youth become increasingly sensitive to the evaluations and exclusionary behaviors of their peers in that peer judgments affect their feelings of social or personal worth (Bosacki, 2013; O'Brien & Bierman, 1988; Sebastian et al., 2010). Such studies suggest that the increase in children's abilities to form abstract representations, as well as an increase in motivation for peer acceptance, might account for the influence of peers on self-evaluations in emerging adolescence. Thus, it appears that the need to be accepted by one's peers, and avoidance of social rejection, is particularly acute during the transition from later childhood to adolescence and might drive particular social behavior in young people.

One of the first studies to investigate neurotypical changes in social cognitive behavior in adolescence showed the ability to integrate the perspectives and intentions of others during fairness judgements continued to improve (Guroglu, van den Bos, & Crone, 2009). Guroglu et al's findings suggested that the rewarding nature of peer relationships during adolescence may influence social decision-making processes. A related study, with participants aged 7 to 27 years, on their ability to take the perspective of another person during tasks that involved decision-making demonstrated that online social cognitive skills improved across adolescence (Dumontheil, Apperly, & Blakemore, 2010). In particular, Dumontheil et al's paradigm adapted a referential communication task in which participants were instructed to move objects around a set of shelves by a director, who could not see some of the objects that the participants could see.

Past research has shown that most adults frequently make mistakes in this type of trial, in which the participant needs to take into the account the director's perspective to guide decisions (Keysar, Barr, Balin, & Brauner, 2000; Keysar, Lin, & Barr, 2003). Dumontheil et al. (2010) included a control condition in which the director was absent, and participants followed a nonsocial rule (e.g., "ignore objects with a grey background") when following (otherwise) the same instructions as in the director condition.

Although in both conditions accuracy improved until mid-adolescence, accuracy in the director condition continued to improve after mid-adolescence. These results suggest that the ability to use another's perspective to guide decisions continues to develop beyond the abilities within the control condition (e.g., working memory, response inhibition). This improvement may have been due to the increased motivation to take account of another's perspective, as well as an improved integration of social cognition and cognitive control systems (Dumontheil et al., 2010). Introspective awareness of one's performance on a perceptual task has also been shown to improve across adolescence, following a trajectory similar to mentalization (Siegel, 2013). Thus, the finding that self-awareness increases during adolescence might have implications for how adolescents integrate their own self-judgments with peer evaluations.

Research on the social brain network during emerging adolescence

Some researchers claim that social cognition plays a fundamental role in the survival and reproductive fitness of various primate species that have brain regions specialized for social cognitive processes (Mills, Lalonde, Clasen, Giedd, & Blakemore, 2014). Although this idea remains contentious, there exists a network of brain regions consistently involved in social cognitive processes (Wellman, 2014). For example, ToM, or the process of mental state attribution, has been associated with a network of brain regions including the dorsal medial prefrontal cortex (dmPFC), temporoparietal junction (TPJ), posterior superior temporal sulcus (pSTS), and anterior temporal cortex (ATC). This set of regions is sometimes referred to as the social brain network, and has been found to show gender and age differences during adolescence (Mills et al., 2014).

As mentioned in the previous chapter, some mentalizing tasks that recruit these regions use stimuli such as cartoon stories (Hughes, 2011; Wellman, 2014), animated shapes, and written stories designed to elicit the representation of mental states (Bosacki, 2013; Mahy, Moses, & Pfeifer, 2014). Although the co-activation of these regions has been demonstrated in many social cognitive neuroimaging experiments (Tomasello, 2014b), the individual contributions of these anatomically distinct regions to social cognitive processes remains an open question for future research.

Some of the strongest evidence that suggest links between the mentalizing brain network and adaptations to the social environment comes from primate studies. In macaques, the size of an individual's social group is associated with both the structure and function of homologous brain areas involved in social cognition (Tomasello, 1999; Wellman, 2014). For example, macaques housed in more complex social environments had greater gray matter volume in the temporal cortex and rostral prefrontal cortex, and higher ranking male macaques had greater gray matter volume in similar regions after controlling for network size, weight, and age (Dunbar, 2013). These studies support in part the idea of the existence of a mentalizing brain network and the possibility that this network may exist in nonhuman primates (Tomasello, 2014a).

Executive functions and theory of mind research

Cognitive abilities such as processing speed, voluntary response suppression, delay discounting, future planning, and emotional forecasting or emotional time travel, working memory, and metamemory all mature during the transition from childhood to adolescence (Lecce et al., 2015; Van Dijk et al., 2012). Executive functions, or the set of cognitive processes that control, regulate, and manage other cognitive processes, have been found to have a reciprocal relation with social cognitive processing during adolescence. For example, developmental neuroimaging studies show correlations between the protracted development of the orbitofrontal cortex and maturing emotional, cognitive, and behavioral abilities during adolescence, such as manipulating multiple items in the mind (Siegel, 2013), suppressing reflexive behavior (Mahy, Moses et al., 2014), decision-making and relational reasoning (Coricelli et al., 2005; Dumontheil et al., 2010), future planning, and delay discounting (Mahy, Vetter et al., 2014).

Successful emotion regulation in early adolescence (10 to 13 years) may be influenced by the adolescent's sensitivity to rejection as well as situational factors of the emotional stimuli. Compared with older adolescents and adults (14 to 23 years), young adolescents found it harder to regulate their emotions when presented with social affective stimuli compared to nonsocial affective stimuli (Siegel, 2013). The ability to consider future consequences of actions continues to improve across adolescence (Crone & Dahl, 2012), which might impact how adolescents interact in social situations. Young (12 to 14 years) and older adolescents (16 to 18 years) showed heart rate slowing after erring on a task-switching task, which might indicate an increased ability to monitor performance.

The ability to monitor one's performance in social situations likely affects the overall success of the interaction. Developmental fMRI studies suggest that distinct neural systems develop at different rates across childhood and adolescence. Such age-related changes in regions involved in feedback processing may underlie behavioral differences in flexible performance adjustment (Kim & Sasaki, 2014). A qualitative shift in neural recruitment during feedback-based learning has been found in early adolescence and may reflect the influence of negative feedback on behavioral adjustment (Siegel, 2013). The changes in feedback processing in emerging adolescence have implications for successful social communication. However, further studies are needed to use integrative tasks to test directly the influence of executive functions on social cognition into middle childhood and adolescence (Devine & Hughes, 2014).

Cognitive self across time and emotion

Similarly, studies on the role of cognitive process in self-development have also examined children's emerging causal understanding about separate components: mind and decision, decision and emotion, life history and mind, and mind and emotion. These studies confirm surprising strengths in preschoolers' knowledge combined with significant development between 3 and 10 years of age and between childhood and adulthood. As children grow older, they understand better when and how past experience alters minds (Lagattuta, Sayfan, & Harvey, 2013). Children may understand better that minds may cause, augment, reduce, or change emotions, even without altering the objective situation (Lagattuta, 2014). Most children may also develop an understanding that emotions have the potential to impair or enhance thinking and problem solving. Such knowledge is especially important for the school context and will be discussed in more detail later in this chapter (Amsterlaw, Lagattuta, & Meltzoff, 2009).

Moreover, between 4 and 10 years of age, most typically developing children become more adept at reasoning about how conflicts between different mental states (e.g., between desires and knowledge of rules; between desires and awareness of others' needs) affect decisions and emotions in morally relevant situations (Lagattuta, Nucci, & Bosacki, 2010; Lagattuta & Weller, 2014). Many of these studies further confirm that children develop earlier, more sophisticated insights in the context of negative as opposed to positive thoughts and emotions. The role of social emotions in self-perceptions and cognitive processes will be further explored in the next two chapters that consider the emotional and moral self.

Past research on the cognitive self has also identified additional sources of variability in children's and adults' reasoning about the coherence of experience, mind, and emotion across time. Such a combination is also referred to as mental time traveling, which is essential for adaptive social functioning (Suddendorf & Corballis, 2007). For example, 4- to 10-year-olds and adults with greater working memory and inhibitory control exhibit more advanced reasoning about the impact of past experience on people's interpretations of ambiguous events (Lagattuta et al., 2010). In addition, 4- to 10-year-olds who can better seriate events by future likelihood better understand future uncertainty in their judgments about people's thoughts, emotions, and decisions in ambiguous situations (Lagattuta, 2014).

Related research has also shown that 4- to 10-year-olds and adults who focus more on negative versus positive past event information expect people to think, feel, and act more pessimistically. Thus, despite age-related regularities in children's concepts about life history, emotion, and mind, young people differ in ways that may have implications for their social functioning and mental health.

Applications: So What?

Historically, the notion that self-regulation plays an important role in the classroom and influences learning has been of interest since the late 1800s, as James (1890) stated that school-work includes "a large mass of material that must be dull and unexciting" (pp. 104–105). In particular, the notion that inherited traits or genetics may play a role in learning is illustrated in James's comment that, "Some of us are naturally scatter brained, and others follow easily a train of connected thoughts without temptation to swerve aside to other subjects" (p. 112). Thus, research from over a century ago suggests that there may be a dispositional or temperamental advantage in the capacity for learning and that sustained attention is beneficial to learners and teachers of youth.

In the decades that followed James's (1890) work, the researchers who developed the concept of intelligence and how it could be tested also supported the claim that self-regulation plays a role in academic performance (Kim & Sasaki, 2014). In contrast to these early claims that temperament and genetics played a role in social learning (Lane et al., 2013), throughout the majority of the twentieth century, research on genetics and academic achievement was scarce. However, within the past decade, the topic of self-regulation and classroom learning has emerged as a cutting-edge topic—much studied by developmental, social, and applied neurocognitivists (Carlson, 2011).

Later childhood and early adolescence represents a period of brain development during which environmental experiences—including teaching—can and do profoundly shape the developing brain. If early childhood is seen as a major opportunity—or a sensitive period—for teaching, so too might later childhood and emerging adolescence. It is only recently that teenagers have been routinely educated in developed countries (Masten, 2014). In many countries a large proportion of teenagers have no access to secondary school education. And yet the adolescent brain is malleable and adaptable—this is an excellent opportunity for learning and creativity.

In particular, risk-taking within an educational context is a vital skill that enables progress and creativity. Given that research shows that as children approach adolescence their propensity for risk-taking may increase (Finy, Bresin, Korol, & Verona, 2014; Steinberg, 2011), through the use of appropriate teaching strategies, such heightened risk-taking in this age group could possibly be harnessed for learning and creativity.

A prevailing view in developmental cognitive research is that some behaviors and emotions are desirable (e.g., long-term planning and emotional time travel), whereas other behaviors are undesirable (e.g., risk-taking). Although long-term planning, reflective, and future-oriented thinking and affective forecasting can help many individuals attain high-quality and stable adult lives (Wilson & Gilbert, 2005), other external factors may prevent individuals from attaining this goal despite their using long-term planning (Kahneman, 2011). In various contexts, taking a risk might actually be more likely to help the learner to obtain a preferred learning outcome.

The neurocognitive development research described earlier in this chapter emphasizes the role of contextual cues that may influence child and adolescent cognitive development and related behaviors. In contrast to viewing risk-taking behaviors as isolated variables, an integrative model that integrates social and cultural environmental cues might enhance our understanding of emerging adolescents' cognitive development and behaviors and improve interventions. Such self-harming behaviors may also be influenced by poor impulse control, self-consciousness, and so forth, and may reflect brain changes. Thus, such learning exceptionalities provide a valuable opportunity for social and emotional learning (Bjork & Pardini, 2015; Sternberg, 2014).

For example, given the well-documented finding that the act of practicing a behavior will help to strengthen the brain circuits that control or regulate that behavior (Kahneman, 2011), educators need to provide learners with opportunities to practice strategies such as planning, predicting the consequences of a decision, balancing risks and rewards, and self-regulation in terms of positive self-talk. Although some teachers and parents may find themselves challenged when young adolescents strive for greater freedom and autonomy, adults need to respond by providing opportunities for self-regulation. Assignments that require young people to think ahead or predict, make a plan, practice, and then reflect on their actions may stimulate the maturation of brain systems that enable more mature self-regulation.

Substantial empirical evidence suggests that learners' ability to regulate attentional, behavioral, and emotional impulses provides the foundation for academic success. That is, learning, the effective application of skills and knowledge within the school context depends partly upon the capacity to inhibit dominant impulses to execute subdominant but superior actions. Such a capacity overlaps with the temperament or personality trait of conscientiousness. Growing evidence of the benefits of self-regulation for success in school has motivated several school-based interventions targeting school culture or climate, classroom curriculum and environment, metacognitive strategies, and aerobic exercise and play. Several of these efforts have been shown to have measurable effects on behavior and academic performance, including improvements in report cards and standardized tests as well as high school and university completion.

As Blakemore and Mills (2014) suggest, later childhood and early adolescence is an opportune time to learn new skills and develop an identity. Research on brain development suggests that later childhood and adolescence might represent a period of relatively high neural sensitivity and plasticity, particularly in brain regions involved in executive function and social cognition. The research on the brain basis of social development in adolescence might have implications for "when to teach what" and could inform curriculum design and teaching practice aimed to ensure that classroom activities exploit periods of neural plasticity that facilitate maximal learning.

As I have discussed elsewhere (Bosacki, 2008, 2012), drawing on SEL (social and emotional learning) and mindfulness programs, programs for emerging adolescents could adapt an approach that involves the routine of taking time to predict, plan, practice, and reflect (PPPR), in addition to also developing cognitive flexibility and openmindedness. Such a metacognitive and mindful approach to learning may help teachers to instruct learners to develop self-regulated learning strategies, self-knowledge, and cognitive flexibility (Sternberg, 2014; Tan & Martin, 2012).

Most importantly, building on the private speech research (e.g., Alarcon-Rubio et al., 2013), self-regulation programs need to focus on the promotion of developing positive private speech (PPS) that promotes self-management and reinforcement—not self-criticism. The main goal of such programs focus on helping students to learn strategies to "silence their negative voice" and retain a caring and kind friendly voice who speaks *with* you as opposed to *at* you, and provides encouragement, unconditional love, and support. Such holistic learning programs that focus on radical acceptance and mindfulness within the classroom are further discussed in Chapter 11 on developmental pedagogy.

As mentioned earlier, one example of a classroom strategy that can be implemented in the later elementary and secondary school classroom is the development of positive emotional self-talk as used in cognitive behavioral therapy studies and research with athletes (Conroy & Metzler, 2004; Khodayarifard et al., 2014; Marsh & Perry, 2005). Such programs incorporate the promotion of kind and encouraging private speech and self-regulatory behaviors. These programs may help youth to develop positive feelings of worth and value through activities such as role-playing, self-narrated conversations, and videotaping oneself performing a challenging task such as teaching a self-management lesson to a group of learners, solving a difficult puzzle. Further educational suggestions to develop a positive and coherent integrated sense of self will be outlined in Chapter 11 on developmental pedagogy.

Another example of research applications to classroom practice is recent work on the development of the mind's neurobiology within the larger cultural context such as a school or neighborhood (Kim & Sasaki, 2014). In particular, cultural neuroscientists study how neurobiological processes may guide social behaviors, Such research findings provide some understanding of how the meanings shared by cultural experiences trigger a neurobiological, psychological, and behavioral chain of events, and how these events may be coordinated and maintained within a person.

Future directions include research on cognitive development that moves beyond current methodological issues that have limited a causal understanding of the interplay of culture and genes (Bronson, 2000). Both are factors that are difficult to study in a true experiment, at least among humans, and thus the field has inherent uncertainty about the causal roles of these factors. Kim and Sasaki (2014) encourage researchers to borrow from the methods of cultural psychology and cultural neuroscience to increase confidence in the causal role of cultural and biological factors. Such an integrative approach to development and education will also be discussed in Chapter 8 within the context of how sociocultural factors such as class, ethnicity, and gender play a role in social cognitive development.

Culture and cognition in the classroom: Educational programs

Walter Mischel and colleagues who developed the seminal Marshmallow Test for delayed self-gratification (Mischel, 2014) and many others (Kidd, Palmeri, & Aslin, 2013) ask: How can educators work with youth to ensure that they develop a sense of self-control or regulation? Given that these self-cognitions are partially contingent upon context (e.g., self-controlled in classroom, impulsive with friends) (Roeder et al., 2014), how can we develop programs with youth to promote consistency in self-control and self-regulated behaviors? This question is one of interest to many applied social cognitivists and neuroscientists who aim to work with educators focused on developing self-regulation and academic competence in emerging adolescents.

The creation of an effective educational program that develops self-regulation must find a balance between either an overemphasis on control and self-regulated learning, or an approach that is more lenient in terms of self-responsibility and focuses on contextual cues and external motivators and support. Such extremes from both perspectives—either over- or under-control—may have deleterious outcomes for the well-being and academic success of the emerging adolescent (de Ridder, Lensvelt-Mulders, Finkenhauer, Stok, & Baumeister, 2012; Kohn, 2008).

In response to the increase in research on self-regulation and learning over the past two decades, many school-based interventions have recently been developed—with the majority aiming to promote self-regulation and academic success (Bronson, 2000; Lee et al., 2014). Past research on program evaluation shows that classrooms that offer strong emotional and instructional support to promote attention and self-regulation can help boost academic performance (Seligman, 2011). In addition, programs that focus on teaching metacognitive strategies such as goal-setting, planning, and affective forecasting can also improve self-regulatory competence and academic achievement. For example, a technique first developed for adults regarding the strategy of mental contrasting with implementation intentions

(MCII) has also been found to help grade school students with their learning—especially report card grades and school attendance (Duckworth & Carlson, 2013).

According to Humphrey (2013), SEL taxonomies include various compositions of the intervention itself. That is, he distinguishes between programs that include primarily a single component between programs that involve multiple components. He suggests that research on SEL programs have identified three common components: a taught curriculum, school environment or culture, and parents and the wider community. Regarding a taught curriculum, this would most likely take the form of a series of teacher-guided lessons, and activities designed to help children develop the social and emotional skills outlined earlier in this chapter. The school environment would typically include activity in a range of areas including revisions to school policies and rules focused on the improvement of school's ethos/climate. Such policies and rules would aim to ensure that, as an institution, the school would more closely embody the values embedded in SEL. Finally, programs that involve parents and the wider community would incorporate a particular focus on broadening the reach of SEL beyond the immediate school environment. This could include parenting support and community projects with partners such as afterschool programs (e.g., YWCA, YMCA).

Research on these programs suggests that there remains a lack of balance among programs that focus on one or some component of these factors. For example, recent research showed that multicomponent programs comprised only approximately one-quarter of the research evidence base (Durlak, Weissberg, Dymnicki, Taylor, & Schellinger, 2011; Wigelsworth, Humphrey, Kalambouka, & Lendrum, 2010), and that the majority of universal SEL programs focus on the academic curriculum that included few references to current research on social-emotional development.

Similar to the dimensions of SEL programs, future social cognitive learning (SCL) programs will need to consider how prescriptive they plan to be in following the programs. Prescriptive programs (such as the Second Step program in the United States) are usually curriculum-based, and typically provide very detailed manuals that instruct school staff in the appropriate method to follow delivery in a step-by-step fashion. In contrast, flexible approaches to SEL, such as the SEAL secondary school programs in England, emphasize choice, local ownership, and goodness of fit with the local context. Further, some programs contain a balanced approach that includes an inherent structure that has a degree of flexibility. That is, such a program (e.g., KidsMatter program in Australia) would encourage teachers to implement the programs, but at the same time, allow them to develop their own materials (curriculum content and assessment), and/or supplement with other alternative activities.

In addition to these dimensions, SCL programs may also differ in their choice of the modality of the intervention. For example, some programs may wish to focus on behavioral strategies, whereas others may focus more on cognitive as compared to social skills. Other programs may focus more on the social and emotional aspect of learning and less on the cognitive and behavioral. In sum, current and future SCL programs need to continue to increase their flexibility in their implementation process and perhaps be instructed by a set of diverse, transdisciplinary instructors. Such programs may call to a need for further evaluative research studies to explore the influence of these programs on young people's social cognitive development.

Future Questions

Future questions include the exploration of a balanced approach that combines social cognitive ability with emotional health in young people's learning experiences (Denham et al., 2014). In addition, given the increasing prevalence of educational technologies within young people's learning contexts, a key question for future social cognitive developmentalists may be to explore the role of technology in the development of young people's social cognition and identity.

More specifically, researchers need to explore what motivates young people's media choices and how do their technological habits influence their social cognitive development? For instance, why do some young people choose to engage in computer-mediated communication as opposed to face-to-face learning activities, and how does this preference influence their social cognitive development? What role does the family and peer group play in young people's engagement with the media and how does this influence their social cognitive reasoning? I will return to such questions in more depth in Chapter 9 when the role of technology in social cognitive development is further discussed.

Summary

Moving forward, researchers should investigate individual differences in how children's perceptions of self and their life experiences contribute to biases in expectations about how life events, mind, and emotion cohere from past to present to future. That is, different children may formulate different theories about these interrelations based on how these connections played out in their daily lives. For example, how do children learn to imagine the extent to which people should expect others who harmed them in the past to harm again them in the future, or how worried or fearful one should feel thinking about negative future possibilities? We also need to explore further how children's reflections on, and insights about, mental time travel affect their social relationships, decision-making, and emotional health. Finally, given past evidence that a main function of episodic memory is to imagine or simulate future what-ifs (Schacter, Addis, & Buckner, 2007), future neuroscience research needs to study the interplay between young people's emotional experiences of mental time travel, and their emerging abilities to contemplate and reason about their past.

This chapter discussed research that describes emerging adolescence as a period of biological and social transition. Neuroimaging and behavioral studies in humans and neuroanatomical and behavioral studies in animals have demonstrated that the social brain and social cognition undergo a profound period of development in adolescence. As such, adolescence represents a sensitive period for the processing and acquisition of sociocultural knowledge. In the next chapter, the role of emotions and emotional regulation will be further discussed in terms of the developing self-concept and overall emotional well-being.

References

Alarcon-Rubio, A., Sanchez-Medina, J., & Winsler, A. (2013). Private speech in illiterate adults: Cognitive functions, task difficulty, and literacy. *Journal of Adult Development, 20*, 100–111.

Amsterlaw, J., Lagatutta, K., & Meltzoff, A. (2009). Young children's reasoning about the effects of emotional and physiological states on academic performance. *Child Development, 80*, 15–133.

Apperly, I. A. (2012). What is "theory of mind"? Concepts, cognitive processes and individual differences. *Quarterly Journal of Experimental Psychology, 65*, 825–839. doi:10.1080/174702 18.2012.676055

Astington, J. W., & Baird, J. (2005). *Why language matters for theory of mind.* New York, NY: Oxford University Press.

Bakhtin, M. (1981). *The dialogic imagination.* (C. Emerson & M. Holquist Trans.) Austin, TX: University of Texas Press.

Banerjee, R., & Yuill, N. (1999). Children's understanding of self-presentational display rules: Associations with mental-state understanding. *British Journal of Developmental Psychology, 17*, 111–124.

Barresi, J., & Moore, C. (1995). Intentional relations and social understanding. *Behavioral and Brain Sciences, 18*, 256–279.

Baum, F. (1984/1900). *The wonderful wizard of Oz.* New York, NY: Penguin Putnam.

Baumeister, R., Campbell, J., Krueger, J., & Vohs, V. (2003). Does high self-esteem cause better performance, interpersonal success happiness, or health? *Psychological Science in the Public Interest, 4*, 1–44.

Berk, L. E. (1986). Relationship of elementary school children's private speech to behavioral accompaniment to task, attention, and task performance. *Developmental Psychology, 22*(5), 671–680.

Berk, L. E., & Winsler, A. (1995). *Scaffolding children's learning: Vygotsky and early childhood education.* Washington, DC: National Association for Education of Young Children.

Bjork, J., & Pardini, D. (2015). Who are those risk-taking adolescents? Individual differences in developmental neuroimaging. *Developmental Cognitive Neuroscience, 11*, 56–64.

Bjorklund, D., & Ellis, B. (2014). Children, childhood and development in evolutionary perspective. *Developmental Review, 34*, 225–264.

Blakemore, S.-J., & Mills, K. (2014). Is adolescence a sensitive period for sociocultural processing? *Annual Review of Psychology, 65*, 187–207.

Bosacki, S. (2008). *Children's emotional lives: Sensitive shadows in the classroom.* New York, NY: Peter Lang.

Bosacki, S. (2012). Socioemotional competence, self-perceptions, and receptive vocabulary in shy Canadian children. *International Electronic Journal of Elementary Education, 4*(3), 573–591.

Bosacki, S. (2013). Theory of mind understanding and conversational patterns in early adolescence. *Journal of Genetic Psychology, 174*, 170–191.

Bosacki, S. (2015). Children's *theory of mind*, self-perceptions, and peer relations: A longitudinal study. *Infant and Child Development, 24*, 175–188. doi:10.1002/icd.1878

Bosacki, S., Bialecka-Pikul, M., & Spzak, M. (2015). Theory of mind and self-concept in Canadian and Polish youth. *International Journal of Youth and Adolescence, 20*(4), 457–469. doi:10.1080/02673843.2013.804423

Bridges, J. (1925). A reconciliation of current theories of emotion. *The Journal of Abnormal Psychology and Social Psychology, 19*, 333–340.

Brinthaupt, T. M., Hein, M. B., & Kramer, T. E. (2009). The self talk scale: Development, factor analysis and validation. *Journal of Personality Assessment, 91*, 82–92. doi:10.1080/00223890802484498

Bronson, M. (2000). *Self-regulation in early childhood: Nature and nurture.* New York, NY: Guilford.

Bruner, J. (1996). *The culture of education.* Cambridge, MA: Harvard University Press.

Call, K., Riedel, A., Hein, K., McLoyd, V., Petersen, A., & Kipke, M. (2002). Adolescent health and well-being in the twenty-first century: A global perspective. *Journal of Research in Adolescence, 12,* 69–98.

Carlson, S. (2011). Introduction to the special issue: Executive function. *Journal of Experimental Child Psychology, 108,* 411–413.

Casey, B., Getz, S., & Galvan, A. (2008). The adolescent brain. *Developmental Review, 28,* 62–77.

Chaplin, L, & Norton, M. (2015). Why we think we can't dance: Theory of mind and children's desire to perform. *Child Development, 86,* 651–658.

Conroy, D. E., & Metzler, J. N. (2004). Patterns of self-talk associated with different forms of competitive anxiety. *Journal of Sport and Exercise Psychology, 26,* 69–89.

Coplan, R. J., & Rubin, K. H. (2010). Social withdrawal and shyness in childhood: History theories, definitions, and assessments. In R. Coplan & K. Rubin (Eds.), *The development of shyness and social withdrawal* (pp. 3–20). New York, NY: Guilford.

Corbalis, M. (2011). *The recursive mind.* Princeton, NJ: Princeton University Press.

Coricelli, G., Critchley, H. D., Joffily, M., O'Doherty, J. D., Sirigu, A., & Dolan, R. J. (2005). Regret and its avoidance: A neuroimaging study of choice behavior. *Nature Neuroscience, 8,* 1255–1262. doi:10.1038/nn1514

Crone, E. A., & Dahl, R. E. (2012). Understanding adolescence as a period of social-affective engagement and goal flexibility. *Nature Reviews Neuroscience, 13,* 636–650. doi:10.1038/nrn3313

Damon, W., & Hart, D. (1988). *Self-understanding in childhood and adolescence.* New York, NY: Cambridge University Press.

Del Giudice, M. (2014). Middle childhood: An evolutionary-developmental synthesis. *Child Development Perspectives, 4,* 193–200.

de Ridder, D., Lensvelt-Mulders, D., Finkenhauer, C., Stok, F., & Baumeister, R. (2012). Taking stock out of self-control: A meta-analysis of how trait self-control relates to a wide range of behaviors. *Personality and Social Psychology Review, 16,* 76–99.

Denham. S., Bassett, H., Way, E., Kalb, S., Warren-Khot, H., & Zinsser, K. (2014). "How would you feel? What would you do?" Development and underpinnings of preschoolers' social information processing. *Journal of Research in Childhood Education, 28,* 128–202.

Devine, R., & Hughes, C. (2013). Silent films and strange stories: Theory of mind, gender, and social experiences in middle childhood. *Child Development, 84,* 989–1003.

Devine, R., & Hughes, C. (2014). Relations between false belief understanding and executive function in early childhood: A meta-analysis. *Child Development, 85,* 1777–1794.

Duckworth, A., & Carlson, S. (2013). Self-regulation and school success. In B. Sokol, M. Grouzet, & U. Muller (Eds.), *Self-regulation and autonomy: Social and developmental dimensions of human conduct* (pp. 208–230). New York, NY: Cambridge University Press.

Dumontheil, I., Apperly, I. A., & Blakemore, S. J. (2010). Online usage of theory of mind continues to develop in late adolescence. *Developmental Science, 13*(2), 331–338.

Dunbar, R. (2013). An evolutionary basis for social cognition. In M. Legerstee, D. Haley, & M. Bortstein (Eds.), *The infant mind: Origins of the social brain* (pp. 3–18). London, England: Guilford.

Duncan, R. M., & Cheyne, J. A. (1999). Incidence and functions of self-report private speech in young adults: A self-verbalization questionnaire. *Canadian Journal of Behavioral Science, 31,* 133–136. doi:10.1037/h0087081

Duncan, R., & Cheyne, J. (2001). Private speech in young adults: Task difficulty, self-recognition, and psychological predication. *Cognitive Development, 16,* 889–906.

Duncan, R., Smith, A., McLaren, T., & Scott, J. (2001). *The effect of awareness of audiovisual recording on private speech: A cross-sectional experimental study.* Poster presented at the biennial meeting of the Society for Research in Child Development, Minneapolis, MN.

Duncan, R., & Tarulli, D. (2009). On the persistence of private speech: Empirical and theoretical considerations. In A. Winsler, C. Fernyhough, & I. Montero (Eds.), *Private speech, executive functioning, and the development of verbal self-regulation* (pp. 176–187). New York, NY: Cambridge University Press.

Dunn, J. (2002). Mindreading, emotion understanding, and relationships. In W. W. Hartup & R. K. Silbereisen (Eds.), *Growing points in developmental science: An introduction* (pp. 167–176). New York, NY: Psychology Press.

Durlak, J. A., Weissberg, R. P., Dymnicki, A. B., Taylor, R. D., & Schellinger, K. B. (2011). The impact of enhancing students' social and emotional learning: A meta-analysis of school-based universal interventions. *Child Development, 82*(1), 405–432.

Filippova, E., & Astington, J. W. (2008). Further development in social reasoning revealed in discourse irony understanding. *Child Development, 79,* 126–138.

Fine, C. (2010). *Delusions of gender: How our minds, gender, and neurosexism create difference.* New York, NY: Norton.

Fink, E., Begeer, S., Hunt, C., & de Rosnay, P. (2014). False-belief understanding and social preference over the first 2 years of school: A longitudinal study. *Child Development, 85,* 2389–2403.

Finy, M., Bresin, K., Korol, D., & Verona, E. (2014). Impulsivity, risk-taking, and cortisol reactivity as a function of psychosocial stress and personality in adolescents. *Development and Psychopathology, 26,* 1093–1111.

Fiske, A., Kitayama, S., Markus, H., & Nisbett, R. (1998). The cultural matrix of social psychology. In D. Gilbert, A. Fiske, & G. Lindzey (Eds.), *The handbook for social psychology* (Vol. 2, pp. 915–981). New York, NY: McGraw Hill.

Goffman, I. (1959). *The presentation of self in everyday life.* New York, NY: Doubleday.

Goffman, I. (1981). *Forms of speech.* New York, NY: Doubleday.

Goossens, L., & Marcoen, A. (1999). Adolescent loneliness, self-reflection, and identity: From individual differences to developmental processes. In K. J. Rotenberg & S. Hymel (Eds.), *Loneliness in childhood and adolescence* (pp. 225–243). New York, NY: Cambridge University Press.

Greenspan, L., & Deardorff, J. (2014). *The new puberty: How to navigate early development in today's girls.* New York, NY: Rodale.

Guroglu, B., van den Bos, W., & Crone, E. (2009). Fairness considerations: Increasing understanding of intentionality during adolescence. *Journal of Experimental Child Psychology, 104,* 398–409.

Harris, P. (1989). *Children and emotion: The development of psychological understanding.* Oxford, England: Blackwell.

Harter, S. (1999). *The construction of the self: A developmental perspective.* New York, NY: Guilford.

Harter, S., Waters, P., Whitesell, N., & Kastelic, D. (1997). *Predictors of level of voice among high school females and males: Relational context, support, and gender orientation.* Paper presented at the biennial meeting of the Society for Research in Child Development, Washington, DC.

Hughes, C. (2011). *Social understanding and social lives: From toddlerhood through to the transition to school.* New York, NY: Psychology Press.

Humphrey, N. (2013). *Social-emotional learning: A critical appraisal.* London, England: Sage.

Hyde, J. (2014). Gender similarities and differences. *Annual Review of Psychology, 65,* 373–398.

James, W. (1890). *Principles of psychology* (Vol. 1). New York, NY: Dover.

Kahneman, D. (2011). *Thinking, fast and slow.* New York, NY: Macmillan.

Kendall, P. C., & Hollon, S. D. (1989). Anxious self-talk: Development of the anxious self-statement questionnaire (ASSQ). *Cognitive Therapy and Research, 13,* 81–93. doi:10.1007/BF01178491

Keysar, B., Barr, D., Balin, J., & Brauner, J. (2000). Taking perspective in conversation: the role of mutual knowledge in comprehension. *Psychological Science, 11,* 32–38.

Keysar, B., Lin, S., & Barr, D. (2003). Limits on theory of mind use in adults. *Cognition, 89,* 25–41.

Khodayarifard, M., Brinthaupt, T., Zardkhaneh, S., & Azar, G. (2014). The psychometric properties of the self-talk scale among Iranian university students. *Psychology, 5,* 119–126.

Kidd, C., Palmeri, H., & Aslin, R. (2013). Rational snacking: Young children's decision-making on the marshmallow task is moderated by beliefs about environmental reliability. *Cognition, 126,* 109–114.

Kim, H., & Sasaki, J. (2014). Cultural neuroscience: Biology of the mind in cultural contexts. *Annual Review of Psychology, 65,* 487–514.

Kinnucan, C., & Kuebli, J. (2013). Understanding explanatory talk through Vygotsky's theory of self-regulation. In B. Sokol, M. Grouzet, & U. Muller (Eds.), *Self-regulation and autonomy: Social and developmental dimensions of human conduct* (pp. 231–252). New York, NY: Cambridge University Press.

Kohn, A. (2008). Why self-discipline is overrated. The troubling theory and practice of control from within. *Phi Delta Kappa, 90,* 168–176.

Lagattuta, K. (2014). Linking past, present, and future: Child ability to connect mental states and emotions. *Child Development Perspectives, 8,* 90–95.

Lagattuta, K. H., Nucci, L., & Bosacki, S. L. (2010). Bridging theory of mind and the personal domain: Children's reasoning about resistance to parental control. *Child Development, 81,* 616–635. doi:10. 1111/j.1467-8624.2009.01419.x

Lagattuta, K. H., & Weller, D. (2014). Interrelations between theory of mind and morality: A developmental perspective. In M. Killen & J. Smetana (Eds.), *Handbook of moral development* (2nd ed., pp. 385–407). New York, NY: Psychology Press.

Lane, J., Wellman, H., Olson, S, Miller, A., Wang, L., & Tardif, T. (2013). Relations between temperament and theory of mind development in the United States and China: Biological and behavioral correlates of preschoolers' false-belief understanding. *Developmental Psychology, 49,* 825–836.

Larson, R. (2011). Positive development in a disorderly world. *Journal of Research in Adolescence, 21,* 317. doi:10.1111/j.1532-7795.2010.00707.x

Lecce, S., Caputi, M., & Hughes, C. (2011). Does sensitivity to criticism mediate the relationship between theory of mind and academic achievement. *Journal of Experimental Child Psychology, 110,* 313–331.

Lecce, S., Caputi, M., & Pagnin, A. (2014). Long-term effect of theory of mind on school achievement: The role of sensitivity to criticism. *European Journal of Developmental Psychology, 11*(3), 305–318. doi:10.1080/17405629.2013.821944

Lecce, S., Caputi, M., & Pagnin, E. (2015). False-belief understanding at age 5 predicts beliefs about learning in year 3 of primary school. *European Journal of Developmental Psychology, 12,* 40–53.

Lee, S. W. F. (2011). Exploring seven- to eight-year-olds' use of self-talk strategies. *Early Child Development and Care, 181*(6), 847–856.

Lee, S., McDonough, A., & Bird, J. (2014). Investigating eight-to nine-year-olds' self-regulatory self-talk in the context of their classroom tasks. *Early Child Development and Care, 184,* 1661–1676.

Leeves, S., & Banerjee, R. (2014). Childhood social anxiety and social support-seeking: Distinctive links with perceived support from teachers. *European Journal of Psychology of Education, 29,* 43–62.

Lockl, K., & Schneider, W. (2007). Knowledge about the mind: Links between theory of mind and later metamemory. *Child Development, 78*(1), 148–167. doi:10.1111/j.1467-8624.2007.00990

Mahy, C., Moses, L., & Pfeifer, J. (2014). How and where: Theory-of-mind in the brain. *Developmental Cognitive Neuroscience, 9,* 68–81.

Mahy, C. E. V., Vetter, N. C., Kühn-Popp, N., Löcher, C., Krautschuk, S., & Kliegel, M. (2014). The influence of inhibitory processes on affective theory of mind in young and old adults. *Aging, Neuropsychology, and Cognition, 21,* 129–145.

Marsh, H. W., & Perry, C. (2005). Does a positive self-concept contribute to winning gold medals in elite swimming? The causal ordering of elite athlete self-concept and championship performances. *Journal of Sport and Exercise Psychology, 27,* 71–91.

Marshall, S., Parker, P., Ciarrochi, J., & Heaven, P. (2014). Is self-esteem a cause or consequence of social support: A 4-year longitudinal study. *Child Development, 85,* 1275–1291.

Marton, K., Abramoff, B., & Rosenzweig, S. (2005). Social cognition and language in children with specific language impairment (SLI). *Journal of Communication Disorders, 38*(2), 143–162. doi:10.1016/j.jcomdis.2004.06.003

Masten, A. (2014). *Ordinary magic: Resilience in development.* New York, NY: Guilford.

Mead, G. (1934). *Mind, self, and society.* Chicago, IL: University of Chicago Press.

Miller, S. (2009). Children's understanding of second-order mental states. *Psychological Bulletin, 135*(5), 749–773. doi: 10.1037/a0016854

Milligan, K., Astington, J. W., & Dack, L. A. (2007). Language and theory of mind: Metaanalysis of the relation between language ability and false-belief understanding. *Child Development, 78*(2), 622–646. doi:10.1111/j.1467-8624.2007.01018.x

Mills, K. L., Lalonde, F., Clasen, L., Giedd, J. N., & Blakemore, S.-J. (2014). Developmental changes in the structure of the social brain in late childhood and adolescence. *Social Cognitive and Affective Neuroscience, 9,* 123–131.

Mink, D., Henning, A., & Aschersleben, G. (2014). Infant shy temperament predicts preschoolers theory of mind. *Infant and Child Behavior, 37,* 66–75.

Mischel, W. (2014). *The marshmallow test: Mastering self-control.* New York, NY: Little, Brown.

Morin, A. (2005). Possible links between self-awareness and inner speech: Theoretical background, underlying mechanisms, and empirical evidence. *Journal of Consciousness Studies, 12,* 115–134.

Nagel, T. (1986). *The view from nowhere.* New York, NY: Oxford University Press.

Neff, K. D. (2011). Self-compassion, self-esteem, and well-being. *Social and Personality Psychological Compass, 5,* 1–12. doi:10.111 1/j.1751-9004.2010.00330

O'Brien S., & Bierman K. (1988). Conceptions and perceived influence of peer groups: Interviews with preadolescents and adolescents. *Child Development, 59,* 1360–1365.

Orth, U., & Robins, R. W. (2014). The development of self-esteem. *Current Directions in Psychological Science, 23,* 381–387. doi:10.1177/0963721414547414

Overton, W. F. (2013). A new paradigm for developmental science: Relationism and relational-developmental systems. *Applied Developmental Science, 17,* 94–107. doi:10.10 80/10888691.2013.778717

Rochat, P. (2009). *Others in mind: Social origins of self-consciousness.* Cambridge, England: Cambridge University Press.

Roeder, K., Keneisher, S., Dukewich, T., Preacher, K., Felton, J., Jacky, A., & Tilghman-Osburne, C. (2014). Sensitive periods for the effect of peer victimization on self-cognition: Moderation by age and gender. *Development and Psychopathology, 26,* 1035–1048.

Rosenberg, M. (1965). *Society and the adolescent self-image.* Princeton, NJ: Princeton University Press.

Ruffman, T. (2014). To belief or not belief. *Developmental Review, 34,* 265–293.

Rutherford, H. J. V., Wareham, J. D., Vrouva, I., Mayes, L. C., Fonagy, P., & Potenza, M. N. (2012). Sex differences moderate the relationship between adolescent language and mentalization. *Personality Disorders, 3*(4), 393–405. doi:10.1037/a0028938

Sanchez, J. A., Alarcon, D., & De la Mata, M. L. (2009). Private speech beyond childhood: Testing the developmental hypothesis. In A. Winsler, C. Fernyhough, & I. Montero (Eds.), *Private speech, executive functioning, and the development of verbal self-regulation* (pp. 188–197). New York, NY: Cambridge University Press.

Schacter, D. L., Addis, D. R., & Buckner, R. L. (2007). Remembering the past to imagine the future: The prospective brain. *Nature Reviews Neuroscience, 8*, 657–661. doi:10.1038/nrn2213

Schaffer, R. (1996). *Social development*. Oxford, England: Blackwell.

Schall, J. V. (2001). *On the unseriousness of human affairs: Teaching, writing, playing, believing, lecturing, philosophizing, singing, dancing*. Wilmington, DE: ISI Books.

Sebastian, C., Viding, E., Williams, K., & Blakemore, S.-J. (2010). Social brain development and the affective consequences of ostracism in adolescence. *Brain Cognition, 72*, 134–145.

Seligman, M. (2011). *Flourish*. London: Nicholas Brealey.

Selman, R. L. (1980). *The growth of interpersonal understanding: Developmental and clinical analyses*. New York, NY: Academic Press.

Siegel, D. (2013). *Brainstorm: The power and purpose of the teenage brain*. New York, NY: Jeremy Tarcher/Penguin.

Steinberg, L. (2011). Demystifying the adolescent brain. *Educational Leadership, 68*, 42–26.

Sternberg, R. (2014). The development of adaptive competence: Why cultural psychology is necessary and not just nice. *Developmental Review, 34*, 208–224.

Suddendorf, T., & Corballis, M. C. (2007). Mental time travel across the disciplines: The future looks bright. *Behavioral and Brain Sciences, 30*, 335–351. doi:10.1017/S0140525X0700221X

Tan, L., & Martin, G. (2012). Mind full or mindful: A report on mindfulness and psychological health in healthy adolescents. *International Journal of Adolescence and Youth*, 1–11.

Tomasello, M. (1999). *The cultural origins of human cognition*. Cambridge, MA: Harvard University Press.

Tomasello, M. (2014a). *A natural history of human thinking*. Cambridge, MA: Harvard University Press.

Tomasello, M. (2014b). The ultra-social animal. *European Journal of Social Psychology, 44*, 187–194.

Van Dijk, W. W., Van Dillen, L. F., Seip, E. C., & Rotteveel, M. (2012). Emotional time travel: Emotion regulation and the overestimation of future anger and sadness. *European Journal of Social Psychology, 42*(3), 308–313.

Verschueren, K., Buyck, P., & Marooen, A. (2001). Self-representations and emotional competence in young children: A 3-year longitudinal study. *Developmental Psychology, 37*, 126–134.

Vinden, P. (1999). Children's understanding of mind and emotion: A multi-culture study. *Cognition and Emotion, 13*, 1948.

Vygotsky, L. S. (1978). Interaction between learning and development. In M. Cole, V. John-Steiner, S. Scribner, & E. Souberman (Eds.), *Readings on the development of children* (2nd ed., pp. 71–91). Cambridge, MA: Harvard University Press.

Vygotsky, L. S. (1986/1934). *Thought and language*. Cambridge, MA: MIT Press.

Wellman, H. (2014). *Making minds: How theory of mind develops*. Oxford, England: Oxford University Press.

Wigelsworth, M., Humphrey, N., Kalambouka, A., & Lendrum, A. (2010). A review of key issues in the measurement of children's social and emotional skills. *Educational Psychology in Practice, 26*(2), 173–186.

Wilson, T., & Gilbert, D. (2005). Affective forecasting: Knowing what to want. *Current Directions in Psychological Science, 14*(3), 131–134.

Winsler, A. (2009). Still talking to ourselves after all these years: A review of current research on private speech. In A. Winsler, C. Fernyhough, & I. Montero (Eds.), *Private speech, executive functioning, and the development of verbal self-regulation* (pp. 3–41). New York, NY: Cambridge University Press.

4

The Emotional Self
Self-Development and Emotional Regulation

"I shall take the heart," returned the Wooden Tin Man, *"for brains do not make one happy."* (Baum, 1900/1984, p. 47)

Introduction

This chapter will continue to focus on the self; whereas Chapter 3 focused on the cognitive aspect of the self, the following chapter will discuss the emotional self. More specifically, this chapter will explore the role of emotions in self-development and developing emotionality within emerging adolescents.

Research: Emotions and Self

The role of the emotions in the mind has long been a question among psychologists and educators; as Bridges (1925, p. 333) stated, "If we know something about 'thinking' and 'doing,' we know next to nothing about 'feeling.'" Given the various theories that currently aim to describe the connections between emotion, thought, and behavior, more recently a developmental relational, psychocultural systems approach to emotional self-knowledge has been found to be useful. That is, given the complexity surrounding emotions and self, this relational developmental systems approach tends to focus on the young individual's ability to recognize themselves, and other people, as psychological and emotional beings (Overton, 2013).

Social Cognition in Middle Childhood and Adolescence: Integrating the Personal, Social, and Educational Lives of Young People, First Edition. S. L. Bosacki.
© 2016 John Wiley & Sons, Ltd. Published 2016 by John Wiley & Sons, Ltd.

As mentioned earlier, this transdisciplinary approach draws on various social cognitive, ecological, and epistemological theories and research (Bronfenbrenner, 1977; Overton, 2013; Selman, 1980). Thus, such an approach may shed some light on the wealth of findings from psychosocial studies that show conceptual and emotional changes in self-worth, and an increase in reflection and self-conscious emotions during the transition from later childhood to early adolescence (ages 8 to 12 years approximately) (Harter, 1999; Rochat, 2009).

Similarly, there is substantial evidence of decline in academic motivation, and emotional attachment or engagement in school and academic achievement, across the later childhood and early adolescence years (Eccles & Roeser, 2003; Greenspan & Deardorff, 2014; Simmons & Blyth, 1987). Such educational experiences may have a direct influence on young people's feelings about themselves, and how they choose to express themselves and learn within the classroom. That is, the emotional atmosphere of the school, and teacher–student relationships may play a role in a young student's decision to either "voice," or express their thoughts and emotions with others, or to remain silent (Bosacki, 2005).

As described in the previous chapter, the cognitive representation of the self and self-language continues to develop through later childhood and early adolescence in tandem with other aspects of the self, such as the emotional self. Although the foundations of "I" are created in infancy through the interactions of the child and the caregiver (Harter, 1999), later childhood and early adolescence signifies a second individuation (Blos, 1979), when one must re-establish a sense of autonomy or distinctiveness from others. Cognitively, the young person experiences an intrapsychic restructuring that occurs through the development of abstract conceptual abilities such as the integration of self-reflection and perspective coordination (Selman, 1980; Siegel, 2013).

However, given the multidimensional and developing nature of the self, during the transition to adolescence, a child's cognitive sense of self may not necessarily develop in tandem with other aspects of the self such as the physical, social, emotional, moral, and spiritual. This lack of synchronicity in the rates of cognitive, physical, and emotional development may create emotional tension which, in turn, may lead to self-concept and social relational challenges. Such difficulties may be accompanied by negative emotions such as anxiety and nervousness, and feelings of inferiority and self-doubt (Dabrowski, 1967; Silverman, 1989).

Similar to Erikson's psychosocial approach to identity formation, where society plays an important role in assisting shaping of the adolescent, Dabrowski (1967) claims that self-development during later childhood and adolescence is due to the combined factors of both internal and interpersonal conflict. Corresponding with Blos's (1979) notion of adolescence as a second individuation, Dabrowksi states that adolescence is a period of "disintegration" or the reorganization and recreation of the self-structure. This recreation provides the ground for the birth and development of a more emotionally balanced and cognitively advanced sense of self.

In particular, Dabrowski's (1967) emphasis on the emotional effects of this disintegration process holds special relevance for self-concept and emotional development during later childhood and emerging adolescence. Dabrowski claimed that feelings of anxiety, nervousness, inferiority, shame, and guilt play an integral role in the disintegration process, and may be experienced to a greater extent by children who appear more "sensitive" or "overexcitable." Compared to children who appear more calm, and less excitable and sensitive, following Dabrowski's theory, children who are the most sensitive to these personal and social conflicts may experience emotional challenges. Thus, the extent to which a child learns to resolve her inner conflict and eventually achieve self-actualization is partially dependent upon her ability to transcend cultural ideals. That is, according to Dabrowski (1967), a child strives to eventually fuse her vision of her "ideal" self (what she ought to be according to others), with her "real" self (what she is in reality) (Dabrowski, 1967).

Given the relatively unexplored terrains of the mental, emotional, moral, and social worlds of the young person, to date, there fails to exist one, all-encompassing metatheory that can solve all of the psychosocial and emotional challenges of emerging adolescents. An interactionist, social constructivist theory is needed, or one that incorporates the dynamic interplay between biological and sociocultural factors, such as Overton's (2013) relational developmental systems approach that builds on Bronfenbrenner and others. Similar to Levitt and Selman's (1996) psychosocial notion of personal meaning that explains the development of the self in terms of multiple emotional and social context, Dabrowski's (1967) "third factor" included all aspects of the self-structure including self-awareness, self-control, and self-criticism. In particular, Dabrowski's third factor could serve as a cognitive lens through which individuals select and confirm/disconfirm various dynamics of internal experiences and influences of external environments. Such a personal organizer may help theorists and educators in their attempts to work with youth and to understand young people's identity formation.

As discussed in the previous chapter on cognition and the self, throughout childhood and adolescence language also plays a role in how children make sense of self and their emotions, particularly the complex social or moral emotions. Given the complex intertwined and interdependent concepts of a culture's emotional universe and emotional lexicon, Wierzbicka (2006) reminds us that a careful and thoughtful investigation is necessary. Thus, researchers need to address the instrumental role that language plays in the conceptualization and expression of emotions across cultures, and the implications this has for self and social understandings in young people.

Emotional regulation development

As children develop and approach adolescence, their ability to manage and negotiate their emotions becomes increasingly important and is referred to as the process of emotional regulation. As I described briefly in Chapter 2, this ability to "regulate" or manage emotions is a complex social cognitive ability that connects emotional awareness and understanding with appropriate behaviors. Research suggests that individual differences in later children's and adolescent emotional behavior changes are domain specific and vary in intensity.

Recent advances in neuroscience research grounded in an evolutionary developmental perspective suggest that the arousal in early adolescence is met with regulatory and coping behaviors carved from individual experiences and attachment relations. Such behaviors help to produce unique manifestations in each adolescent (Waters & Tucker, 2013). That is, research suggests that individual differences in the duration and intensity of transitions in emotional arousal during later childhood and adolescence are functionally modulated by emotional self-regulation skills and intimate relationships with others. The topic of autonomy and attachment within the family context will be further elaborated in Chapter 7 when I discuss the role of family relationships in self-development during emerging adolescence.

Regarding the ability to regulate our emotions, research suggests that, although we are born with biological mechanisms of emotional arousal, the ability to regulate and manage our emotions is gained through experience. In other words, according to recent neuroscience research findings (Lewis, 2015; Siegel, 2013), arousal is experience expectant, but regulation is experience dependent. This is perhaps exemplified most clearly in current models of normative adolescent emotional development (Casey, Getz, & Galvan, 2008; Siegel, 2013). In these models, the onset of adolescence is characterized by rapid changes in mechanisms of arousal, notably in the subcortical limbic system and ventral regions of the cortex. In contrast, the more cognitive mechanisms of executive control and self-regulation develop gradually and linearly across later childhood and adolescence.

This contrast of arousal and regulation is an oversimplified, but valuable, heuristic for later childhood and adolescent emotional development. The core assertion of these models is that there is a period of time during which older children's and adolescents' faculties for arousal exceed their capacities for regulating that arousal. Although the typical time span and degree of this discrepancy is not yet known, research suggests that there is interindividual variability in the duration and intensity of this discrepancy (Del Giudice, 2014).

For example, a young person faced with peer rejection may respond through social withdrawal, aggression, or may choose to invest more emotional energy in developing caring and supportive relationships with family or peers. Given that later childhood and adolescence often involves interpersonal and emotionally challenging events (Del Giudice, Ellis, & Shirtcliff, 2011; Larson, 2011), these experiences are often met with some regulatory compensation. Importantly, this regulatory compensation is more mature than in later childhood but also manifests in relatively unique ways across individuals.

More specifically, each individual has a domain, or range of domains, of adolescent change that is most prominent. Adolescent-typical behaviors occur in innumerable possible combinations, and researchers need to take less compartmentalized and more person-centered approaches to adolescent development to help promote positive aspects of psychological development (Rose, 2014). Research that focuses exclusively on a particular variable, such as aggressive behavior, may thus necessarily neglect social anxiety, and vice versa.

Furthermore, due to a combination of societal urgency and funding priorities, adolescent research has predominantly focused on problems and pathology at the expense of the understanding of normative development (Blakemore & Mills, 2014). As such, there remains a lack of evidence for, or against, the storm-and-stress hypothesis in the general population. The second, related, observation is that the intensity of an adolescent's aggression, depressive symptoms, and so forth is a within-individual experience, a relative change. In this case, between-subjects comparisons are biased toward the interpretation of only extreme cases in any particular domain.

Research suggests that most educators often care less about the occasionally aggressive youth as compared to the frequently aggressive (Siegel, 2013), and tend to focus more on the physical or sexual risk-takers than on the academic or social risk-takers. As a result, Larson

(2011) and others conclude that storm and stress is probable but not inevitable. From the theoretical perspective of modeling adolescent change, however, comparisons cannot be interindividual but rather should be intraindividual (Blakemore & Mills, 2014). The comparison case for any individual adolescent is not the aggregate, but her or his former and future selves. Thus, researchers need to consider relative intraindividual changes across all possible domains as the criteria for the assessment of adolescent development patterns.

Compared to young children and adults, emerging adolescents have been found to express more negative and fewer positive emotions (Larson, 2011), and to be more emotionally volatile (Siegel, 2013). This change in the quality and intensity of emotions may influence relationships, academic achievement, and psychosocial adjustment (Saarikallio, 2011; Siegel, 2013). Given that there are no relatively new emotional states that emerge in adolescence (Kim & Sasaki, 2014), the reason for these developmentally typical emotional changes may be due to adolescents' ability to regulate or manage emotions (Waters & Tucker, 2013). That is, more critical than *what* adolescents are feeling is *how* they regulate and manage those feelings.

Despite the prominence of emotion regulation (ER) within models of emotional, social, and cognitive development, understanding of typical ER in adolescence is remarkably poor, for several reasons. First, the dominant perspective of adolescence is mainly pathological, and focuses on mental health challenges or dangerous behavior at the expense of understanding the norm from which they deviate (Siegel, 2013). Second, theory and research about ER in late childhood through adolescence is a mere fraction of ER research compared with that on infancy, early childhood, and emerging adulthood (through a reliance on university undergraduate samples).

Third, late childhood and early adolescence are often defined by dramatic intraindividual changes that vary as a function of individual differences such as temperament. That is, the age at which normative transitions occur, and rates at which these changes occur, need to be explored over time, yet research continues to focus on cross-sectional/between-subject designs during this age period (Hollenstein & Lougheed, 2013). Finally, experimental-designed studies of adolescent ER are relatively limited as researchers rarely create studies with measures that activate or initiate emotion among youth (Siegel, 2013). Such experimental studies could demonstrate changes in emotion regulatory processes as these studies are often considered one of the optimal measures of ER.

Developing emotions

In the past 20 years, there has been a surge of interest in the development of emotion understanding among children and adolescents (Saarni, 1999). Transcultural research shows that, across the globe, most children begin talking about emotions around 2 to 3 years of age (Denham et al., 2014). Recent research has shown that, beginning in the preschool years, emotional lives become quite complex (see Denham, 1998). For example, research has shown that, between the ages of 2 and 4, children learn to label emotions accurately and begin to understand that certain situations are linked to certain emotions (see Denham, 1998; Harris, 1989). In addition, most typically developing young children show substantial ability to use emotion-descriptive adjectives, understand these terms in conversations with adults, and begin to employ emotion language to meet their own emotional needs. However, despite the increasing interest in children's and adolescents' emotional development, much remains to be learned about the complex processes involved.

Research on the development of social cognition has shown that most children first begin to talk about the simple or basic emotions (e.g., happy, sad) (Denham, 1998). That is, such emotions have been claimed to be innate and exist transculturally. Interestingly, the more complex, or social and moral emotions, also sometimes referred to as secondary emotions, involve more complex reasoning and cognitive development. Emotions such as pride and embarrassment require the child to reflect upon their self-concept and to imagine the value judgment of others.

Despite the important role of emotions in language and social development, the complex, or self-conscious, emotions have remained somewhat neglected within the study of children's and adolescents' emotion understanding. The majority of emotion research on children and adolescents has focused almost exclusively on the "simple" or primary and basic emotions (i.e., emotions linked to underlying physiology) such as happy and sad. In contrast, complex or "self-conscious" emotions such as pride and embarrassment that involve the ability to self-evaluate against internalized standards of behavior have received considerably less attention (Saarni, 1999). Thus, although a strong theoretical link exists among complex emotions, sense of self, and social relations, little is known about how such a nexus develops and differs in older children and adolescents.

As discussed earlier, higher-order mentalizing abilities help youth to understand and express complex and self-conscious or social moral emotions. In contrast to the simple or basic emotions (e.g., happy, sad), to understand complex emotions (e.g., pride, embarrassment), children must hold in mind two separate pieces of information: other people's and larger society's normal standards (Saarni, 1999). That is, children must imagine what others think of their behavior and self-evaluate against internalized behavioral standards. Given that higher-order social reasoning may help youth to understand the ambiguous nature of personal and social silences (Bosacki, 2008, 2013), past research suggests that higher-order reasoning is also in part fundamental to children's and adolescents' understanding of moral and spiritual beliefs, self-conscious moral emotions (e.g., embarrassment, pride), their sense of self and other persons, and social interactions.

Complex or self-conscious emotions

Recent evidence suggests that emotional understanding continues to develop during late childhood and early adolescence, particularly the understanding of complex and ambiguous emotions (Pons, Harris, & de Rosnay, 2004; Pons, Lawson, Harris, & de Rosnay, 2003). Young people may also begin to imagine how others judge their actions, and may self-evaluate their behavior against internalized or self-imposed behavioral standards. Thus, the moral imperatives derived from spiritual beliefs (e.g., honesty, beneficence) may impact their attitudes and behaviors that could lead to positive or negative self-adjustment. Although complex emotion understanding may also hinge on cognitive abilities such as second-order sociomoral reasoning and self-evaluation, future studies need to investigate the links between these social and emotional abilities during late childhood and early adolescence (Larson, 2011).

Given the lack of research on this area, the few studies on social emotions in children reveal contradictory findings. For example, compared to boys, girls have been found to exhibit a greater expression of pride (i.e., girls showed more positive expressions after success than boys) (Bosacki, 2008), and express greater emotional regulation and displays of shame and guilt (Roos, Hodges, & Salmivalli, 2013). In contrast, some studies have failed to find such gender differences among emotions of pride, shame, and guilt (Bosacki & Moore, 2004). Accordingly, given the complex interrelations among emotion expression, emotion regulation, and emotion understanding (Denham, 1998), future research needs to explore individual differences in children's and adolescents' self-conscious emotion understanding and the connections to other social cognitive abilities.

For example, although complex or self-conscious emotion understanding (e.g., pride, shame, envy, schadenfreude, revenge) may depend in part on linguistic and cognitive abilities such as higher-order ToM and self-evaluation, few studies have investigated the links between these three concepts among youth. Despite the growing interest in the links between ToM and emotion understanding, past studies have focused mainly on preschoolers' first-order ToM understanding and basic emotions such as happy and sad (Denham et al., 2014). Research on the links among self-concept, higher level ToM, and complex emotion understanding in youth remains in its infancy (Hughes, 2011), and future researchers will need to explore these relations longitudinally, and include sociocultural factors such as gender and culture, which I will return to in Chapter 8.

Moral emotions

In terms of complex emotions, recent research on adolescents' experiences of shame and guilt within social relationships may help researchers to understand the role emotional experiences may play in narcissism in personal and social ways. That is, as Morf and Rhodewalt (2001) claim, concomitant feelings of rage and shame in response to threats to one's self-esteem or public image play a central role in the conceptualization of how narcissism can impair social functioning. Therefore, attention-seeking behaviors and displays of grandiosity and vanity may perhaps be necessary for some youth, but not sufficient, for connecting narcissism with problematic behaviors such as aggression and negative emotional states such as anxiety and depression (Kluger, 2014).

To further explore the adaptive qualities of nonpathological narcissists, researchers could borrow from studies on the role of self-conscious or moral emotions in self-regulation and peer relationships. For example, research on the developmental changes in emotion–behavior connections may help to explain the inconsistent findings of differential behavioral correlates of dispositional guilt and shame. That is, sometimes guilt and shame have been found to be positively associated with both approach and avoidance tendencies among children (Roos et al., 2013). However, guilt and shame differentially influence children's social behaviors during early adolescence because the differential attributions that motivate behaviors begin to stabilize. For example, in response to guilt, early adolescents should be more motivated than younger children to engage in reparative actions because they may be more likely to attribute the cause of guilt to controllable behaviors rather than to nonintentional actions such as accidents (Roos et al., 2013).

Most recently, Roos et al. (2013) evaluated the degree to which guilt and shame explain individual differences in concurrent and subsequent changes in behaviors that have been shown to foster (i.e., prosocial behavior), or to limit (i.e., aggression, withdrawal) the development of positive peer relations. Similar research suggests that, compared with maladaptive shame, the adaptive nature of empathy-based guilt (Hoffman, 2000), is often based on the behavioral outcomes that these emotions are hypothesized to induce. In contrast, shame has a been found to have a tendency to be maladaptive and harmful as the emotion is focused on one's private self as opposed to social behavior.

Moreover, given that research shows that guilt is often aroused by the recognition of one's immoral act, the causal attributions involved are likely to be internal, specific, and fairly unstable. That is feelings of guilt are usually focused on "fixing" or amending a challenging situation, whereas feelings of shame may be focused on "avoiding" the situation (Tangney & Dearing, 2002). Thus, researchers often define guilt as a moral, interpersonal emotion that strengthens social bonds and attachments by arousing the desire to approach others. Given the focus on social interactions, guilt may be related to greater levels of prosocial behavior, and lower levels of aggression and withdrawal.

In contrast, compared with guilt, dispositional shame involves causal attributions that are internal, global, and stable, and may result in a more severe threat to the self (Tangney & Dearing, 2002). Although shame-proneness is often associated with the need for approval and acceptance, and thus with avoidance and withdrawal (Eisenberg, 2000; Roos, Salmivalli, & Hodges, 2011), it can also lead to various types of aggression (e.g., relational, physical). High, yet fragile, self-esteem tends to be associated with sensitivity to ego threats and negative events, as indicated by studies on narcissism (Bushman & Baumeister, 1998: Kluger, 2014). The insulted person may then enact aggressive moves against the source of insult, and thus reject the threat to the self as this process is mediated by shame. Thus, the maladaptive nature of dispositional shame may be reflected in either aggressive or avoidant (e.g., withdrawn) behavioral responses and fewer prosocial acts.

Inconsistencies in the behavioral correlates of dispositional guilt and shame are also likely due to methodological limitations. More specifically, dispositional guilt and shame, as well as social behaviors, have usually either all been assessed from a similar source, such as self-reports, or have been examined in studies without controls for the other emotion in evaluations of emotion–behavior associations. A few studies have managed to overcome one, but never both, of the aforementioned limitations. In studies that have avoided shared method variance, children's self-reported guilt-proneness and shame-proneness have been related both to their adult-reported internalizing symptoms, including withdrawal, as well as to externalizing responses, such as aggressive behavior (Cairns, Cairns, Neckerman, Ferguson, & Gariepy, 1989; Jambon & Smetana, 2014). In addition, past research shows that, compared to prosocial children, when children's roles in bullying have been identified with peer nominations, bullies report less guilt and shame (Roos et al., 2013).

However, the failure to find differential behavioral correlates of guilt and shame in these studies may have been due to the failure to control for the overlapping variance among guilt and shame. Given that, to date, no longitudinal study has controlled for either the initial levels of the outcome, or the overlap of the two dispositional emotions, there remains ambiguity concerning the direction and the uniqueness of the effects between emotions and adjustment (Aldwin, Park, Jeong, & Nath, 2014; Roos et al., 2013). Overall, although emerging literature is beginning to shed light on the behavioral correlates of guilt and shame, several prevalent methodological limitations have hampered further progress.

As mentioned earlier, Roos et al. (2013) evaluated, concurrently and longitudinally, the relations of dispositional guilt and shame to three social behaviors, while avoiding shared method variance. They hypothesized that early adolescents' self-reported guilt- and shame-proneness would differentially predict concurrent peer-reported aggressive, prosocial, and withdrawn behaviors, as well as changes in such behaviors. Dispositional guilt was expected to be an adaptive emotion increasing the likelihood of prosocial behavior and inhibiting aggression and withdrawal, whereas dispositional shame was expected to inhibit prosocial behavior and increase the likelihood of engaging in aggression and withdrawal.

Specifically, Roos et al. (2013) studied 395 Finnish fifth and sixth graders to evaluate whether dispositional guilt and shame differentially predicted prosocial, withdrawn, and aggressive behaviors in theoretically expected ways. Their results suggested that distinctiveness of dispositional guilt and shame was supported by their different associations with peer-reported social behaviors. Results of this study indicated that dispositional guilt had an adaptive nature with links to prosocial behavior. In contrast, dispositional shame was found to be a more maladaptive emotion, as it predicted prospective decreases in prosocial behavior.

Although in Roos et al.'s (2013) study, guilt-proneness did not predict decreases in aggression over time, it may have served to maintain low levels of aggression as it was found to be uniquely correlated with lower levels of aggression at each time point. Thus, their study supported that guilt-proneness supported reparative actions and reduced the likelihood of engagement in maladaptive behavior, whereas shame-proneness suggested more negative prospects through the reduction of prosocial behavior (Tangney & Dearing, 2002).

As Roos et al. (2013) and others suggest, given the complex connections among self-esteem, moral emotions, and interpersonal relationships during emerging adolescence, researchers need to explore the role of personal characteristics such as perfectionism and (trait) emotional intelligence (Flett & Hewitt, 2014). More specifically, researchers could explore the question of how these "traits" may influence young people's conceptual and emotional sense of self and social relationships, particularly within prosocial interactions (Kashdan, Weeks, & Savostyanova, 2011). I will return to the moral and social meanings of guilt and shame later on in the book, within the context of the moral self, peer networks, and friendships.

Counterfactual emotions

In addition to the social moral emotions such as pride, embarrassment, guilt, and shame, another subset of complex or secondary self-conscious emotions refers to counterfactual emotions. Counterfactual reasoning and emotions is often defined as the ability to understand that there are two or more interpretations of, and emotional responses to, the same piece of information. Counterfactual emotions, such as regret, remorse, and relief, are considered important in daily life choice behavior, learning, and emotion regulation. Interestingly, despite the various studies on counterfactual reasoning (Burns, Riggs, & Beck, 2012), researchers have just begun to investigate the development of children's understanding of counterfactual emotions such as regret and relief. Future research needs to continue to explore how such emotions develop and affect our ability to make decisions and engage in future thinking and planning, as well as the ability to understand counterintuitive claims (Lane, Harris, Gelman, & Wellman, 2015; Lane et al., 2013; O'Connor, McCormack, & Feeney, 2014; Van Dijk, Van Dillen, Seip, & Rotteveel, 2012; Weisberg & Beck, 2012).

Regret and relief are counterfactual emotions that rely on the comparison between an existing reality and an alternative reality that "could have been," or "what might be or happen." Counterfactual emotions are often thought to be powerful motivators of choice behavior, in which we aim to minimize regret, and rely on counterfactual information to make better decisions. In addition to the association with affective forecasting, decision-making, and learning, counterfactual emotions may also be beneficial because they serve an emotional and behavioral regulatory function (Baumeister, Vohs, DeWall, & Zhang, 2007; Wilson & Gilbert, 2005). The ability to reflect upon what could have been, as well as what could be, is thus an adaptive but complex skill that may have implications for emotional regulation as well as for the ability to trust in counterintuitive claims or claims that defy perceptions (Lane et al., 2013). Thus, similar to the development of the more basic emotions such as happiness, sadness, anger, or fear, the development of relief and regret may play an important role in young people's emotional and moral regulation, and overall mental health.

The ability to think counterfactually or understand that an alternative reality may exist, is shown to develop early in childhood, from at least 5 years or even earlier (Beck & Guthrie, 2011; Beck, Robinson, Carroll, & Apperly, 2006). However, several studies have shown a delayed onset of counterfactual emotions, such as regret and relief. Compared to counterfactual reasoning, the relatively late development of counterfactual emotions has been explained by the executive demands of holding in mind, and comparing two representations of reality with different kinds of associated emotions. That is, the individual needs to think about what could have happened and the possible emotions that they might have experienced (counterfactual reality), and what actually happened and which emotions they actually did experience (actual reality).

In addition to the cognitive tasks, the two realities (real and imagined) are also connected with emotions that may be mixed. Some studies showed that counterfactual emotions arise, as mentioned above, at approximately age 5 (Weisberg & Beck, 2010, 2012), whereas others indicated that they only can be observed from age 7 to about 9 or 10 (McCormack & Feeney, 2015; O'Connor et al., 2014; Rafetseder & Perner, 2012). Some of these studies have found that regret develops before relief (Guttentag & Ferrell, 2004; McCormack & Feeney, 2015; Weisberg & Beck, 2010); whereas others observed no lag (Weisberg & Beck, 2012), or focused only on regret (O'Connor, McCormack, & Feeney, 2012, 2014). These mixed findings suggest substantial individual differences in the experience of counterfactual emotions within age groups, and the developmental trajectory remains unclear.

Given that past research with traditional analysis (e.g., logistic regression) suggests that regret and relief are present from ages 7 to 8 (Weisberg & Beck, 2012), Van Duijvenoorde, Huizenga, and Jansen (2014) applied latent-class analyses (LCA) to the understanding of counterfactual emotions such as relief and regret. Compared to traditional analysis that treats trials separately or as a composite measure, LCA creates subgroups of scores, and investigates an individual's response pattern across trials, and, therefore, a general tendency to change ratings is likely to show up as a separate group.

In general, Van Duijvenoorde found that experiences of regret and relief appeared in all age groups across childhood (ages 5 to 13), although regret and relief understanding increased with age. Moreover, analyses indicated that higher cognitive reasoning scores increased the probability to belong to regret and relief subgroups. Van Duijvenvoorde et al.'s (2014) research suggested that an individual difference approach can advance insight into emotional development. That is, future research needs to explore the individual differences and developmental patterns of counterfactual reasoning across later childhood and adolescence such as remorse, nostalgia, and moral elation. Future research also needs to explore the possible influence of additional cognitive tasks such as executive functioning skills (e.g., inhibition), emotional time travel and forecasting (Van Dijk et al., 2012), and working memory, as past research shows mixed results (Burns et al., 2012).

Language and Emotions

Given the important role that talking about emotions plays in children's and adolescents' understanding of mind, emotion, and school behavior (de Rosnay & Hughes, 2006; de Rosnay, Fink, Begeer, Slaughter, & Peterson, 2014), researchers need to explore how these discourse experiences foster growth in social cognitive abilities such as self-conception and peer relationships. For example, in some of our ongoing research on advanced ToM, self-concept, and peer relations in Canadian school-aged children, we found evidence for relations among children's self-perceptions, advanced ToM, and the use of self-conscious emotion vocabulary (Bosacki, 2013). More specifically, we found that some children who reported relatively low personal self-worth also scored relatively highly on the advanced ToM measures. Moreover, we also found that their ToM explanations included a higher use of complex emotion terms such as jealousy, pride, gratefulness, embarrassment, guilt. Such results suggest the need for further research on emerging adolescents' understanding of morally complex emotions including gratefulness (Watkins, Uhder, & Pichinevskiy, 2015), reverence, remorse, spitefulness, and obligation.

As mentioned above, the literature suggests that a substantial part of children's emotion understanding is mediated through language processes—in particular, in cultural settings such as parent–child conversations in the home, or in peer conversations during school time and free play (Bosacki, 2013; Kitayama & Markus, 1994). A psychocultural approach to social cognitive and emotional development assumes that the development of language and emotion is interdependent, and is based on social interactions with more skilled partners (Gutiereez & Rogoff, 2003; Vygotsky, 1978). Many researchers claim that emotion words or labels play a large role in the young person's development of emotion conceptualization (Saarni, 1999; Wierzbicka, 2006). Past studies illustrate the importance of language abilities in young people's understanding of emotions, and suggest that the links are complex, especially when gender and cultural context are considered (Hughes, 2011).

Despite the potential to shed light on young people's developing emotional worlds, few studies have investigated children's and adolescents' understanding of complex emotions from a psychocultural perspective (for exceptions, see Kitayama & Markus, 1994; Kuppens, Ceulemans, Timmerman, Diener, & Kim-Prieto, 2006). Given Hyde's (2014) conceptualization of gender as a culture, a psychocultural approach to the study of self-conscious or moral emotions may help to unpack the links among language, gender-role socialization, and emotion understanding. Extant literature on emotional expression and understanding among youth and adults suggests that some girls and women exhibit a higher level of self-conscious emotion understanding and experiences than some boys or men. However, this finding is mixed and contingent upon age and social-cultural context (Bosacki & Moore, 2004; Hyde, 2014). I will return to the influence of gender and culture on emotions in more detail in Chapter 8.

Given that emotions represent a social phenomenon that is shaped by the sociocultural context in which they occur (Mesquita & Leu, 2007), culture may also help drive how emotions are understood (Mesquita & Leu, 2007). While emotions have been described as internal states or personal reactions, they can also be viewed as interpersonal exchanges that are inseparable from the larger social context (Kitayama & Markus, 1994). Indeed, within interdependent cultures, emotions have been shown to be more grounded in interpersonal relationships, while in independent cultures emotions primarily implicate the self or one's private experience (Uchida, Townsend, Markus, & Bergsieker, 2009).

Regarding the role of cultural context and relationships in adolescents' emotional development, Koh, Scollon, and Wirtz (2014) studied the influence of interdependent and independent culture on adolescents' emotional understandings. Koh et al. (2014) found that there were important cultural differences in the ways in which youth represented emotions cognitively. Specifically, compared to American youth (independent culture), they found stronger associations of emotions within close friendships among youth living in Singapore (interdependent culture).

Furthermore, their studies demonstrated a link between individuals' emotional consistency levels and their cognitive representation of emotions across cultures. More specifically, a significant inverse correlation was found between levels of emotional consistency across different relationships and tightness of representation of emotions around those relationships. People who were less emotionally consistent across relationships had stronger associations of their emotions within each relationship. Emotional consistency across relationships was found to fully mediate the observed cultural differences in emotion representations.

Koh et al.'s study (2014) examined the impact of cross-cultural differences in the nature of emotions as contextual, or belonging to the self at a cognitive level. Future research should extend their paradigm and look at different relationships including siblings, extended family, authority figures such as teachers, coaches, as well as romantic partners. As Koh et al. focused on the differences between Singaporean and American school settings, future research needs to explore if replication is possible within additional cultural contexts. For example, some research suggests that inter- and intracultural differences may exist among East Asian, North American, and European countries (Bosacki, Bialecka-Pikul, & Spzak, 2015; Kashima et al., 2004; Shahaeian, Nielsen, Peterson, & Slaughter, 2014).

To examine differences between samples and individuals on this cultural attitude factor, future researchers could also include a specific measure of cultural attitudes of independence and interdependence.

Koh et al.'s (2014) results support existing research that has shown that interdependent cultures tend to conceptualize emotions within the context of interpersonal relationships. Their study was the first to examine the impact of cross-cultural differences in cognitive representations of emotions on individual recollections of emotions as part of one's relations or as part of one's self. While previous studies have examined cultural differences in attention and eye gaze patterns, Koh et al.'s study examined cultural differences in the cognitive networks of emotions within the context of individual difference in the emotional memory.

Koh et al.'s (2014) study results also extend existing research that demonstrate individual traits within relationships retain robust stability despite the fact that such traits may vary across contexts. In contrast to other studies that compared differences in the consistency of self-reported personality descriptors across relationships (Gutiereez & Rogoff, 2003), Koh et al.'s study focused on computerized tasks that measured emotional experiences across relationships. Future research could incorporate a multimethod longitudinal design to capture the subtleties of cultural influence on young people's emotions within the context of social relationships (Bjorklund & Ellis, 2014; Slaughter & Perez-Zapata, 2014).

Although children and youth frequently talk about emotion in natural conversations with peers and family members (Bosacki, 2013), reference to emotion is often made in oblique terms, and not often with specific descriptors or labels. Emotional labels, by virtue of their rarity, are a powerful statement of value, and it would seem, are seldom applied in a value-neutral way. The act of emotion labeling is similar to the evaluation of emotional experience or behavior on dimensions such as controllability and intensity. Although new research initiatives in this area continue to develop (Lagattuta, 2014), as mentioned above, few researchers have explored young people's emotion talk in everyday conversation.

Building on previous work on the emotional context of peer and family conversations in older children and adolescents, our longitudinal study with Canadian youth on ToM and their conversational experiences found that young adolescents referred to mental state terms including emotion and cognition words in their self-descriptions and conversations about talking with, and listening to, their family and friends (Bosacki, 2013). Our findings showed that most participants reported that they experienced mainly positive emotions such as happiness and excitement during everyday conversations with their peers and family.

Interestingly, the majority of participants in our study reported feelings of mixed (e.g., happy and sad) and ambiguous emotions (e.g., boredom, nervousness, anxiety), during experiences of silence. Further, the complex emotional experiences of silence remained the same irrespective of the role that the participants played in the conversation. That is, participants reported similar emotional experiences across roles as either the recipient of the silence, or the creator. Thus, further research on young people's interpretations of socially ambiguous interactions is necessary as such research will help educators to understand the role emotions play in youth's ability to make sense of everyday social talk with friends and family.

As I have discussed elsewhere (Bosacki, 2005, 2008), given these subtleties and lack of studies in the field of emotions, conversations, and social silences, further research needs to explore the role of ToM and emotions in everyday life and school experiences of young people. For example, researchers need to explore why some young people choose to talk (or remain silent) about particular emotions over others, and how this preference differs across gender, ethnicity, and social class. The role of gender and culture diversity within social cognitive research will be further discussed in terms of cultural context in Chapter 8.

Self as Personal Fable: Self-Esteem and Narcissism

Given the complexities surrounding the adolescent experience (both personal and social), the adolescent personal fable has often been discussed in negative terms because of its potentially dangerous consequences. That is, given that adolescents often believe that problems afflicting others will not happen to them (e.g., Elkind, 1967), they may disregard certain natural limitations, sometimes even the permanence of death. Such beliefs of infallibility may lead to the engagement of risk-taking behaviors (e.g., driving while inebriated, extreme risk sports). The personal fable, however, may also have protective value against suicidal and depressive behavior.

For example, Cole (1989) found that adolescents who endorsed optimistic views of the future and life-affirming values were less likely to resort to suicidal thoughts or behavior. Cole speculated that adolescents who have a strong sense of their own invulnerability, and hence who do not see themselves as possible targets for silencing, nor feel the need to silence their own voices, will likely see themselves as capable of coping and handling life's problems. Thus, consistent with other researchers, Cole supports the idea that the positive and supportive aspects of the adolescent personal fable may act as a buffer in conjunction with supportive family and peer relationships against suicidal thoughts and behavior.

In contrast, sometimes impulsivity, fueled by feelings of invincibility and coupled with a failure to recognize one's own limitations, can lead the adolescent to feel alienated from parent, family, and peers. Such alienated youth may develop self-harmful thoughts and perhaps attempt self-harmful behaviors such as suicide (Hawton, Saunders, & O'Connor, 2012). The report on adolescent suicide formulated by the Group for the Advancement of Psychiatry (1996) suggests that the changes that characterize adolescence leave some young people at risk.

A heightened sense of self-consciousness, fluctuating levels of self-esteem, and a degree of impulsivity may place particular adolescents at a heightened risk for inappropriate response to stress under the best circumstances. Even a relatively minor perceived loss or rejection or disappointment in oneself has the potential to trigger self-destructive urges and thoughts, which can lead to self-silencing and self-alienation (Callan, Kay, & Dawtry, 2014).

As mentioned earlier, emerging adolescence is also a special time when many youth establish a degree of autonomy from their family and take significant steps in personal identity formation. At the same time, moving from parental relationships, peer relationships become increasingly important during the adolescent years. Concerning issues of voice and silence, situations with family and peers may have positive and negative consequences. For example, when adolescents do not feel comfortable to voice their own opinions, they may distance themselves from their friends and families. Also, given North America's relatively age-stratified society, adolescents and their peers may undertake these transitions simultaneously, and may produce an unsupportive social milieu (Muehlenkamp, Claes, Havertape, & Plener, 2012; Robbins, 1998). Thus, an adolescent may feel silenced by his or her family or peers, which in turn may lead to greater self-silencing, and consequent depression, inner conflict, and so on.

Moral emotions, self, and relationships: Narcissism and neuroticism

To a large extent, emotional processes help to guide young people's social interactions and relationships, and are needed to help create constructive solutions in personally and socially challenging situations. That is, the multidimensional process of self-image negotiation and co-construction with others helps to shape our social, cognitive, and emotional worlds (Rochat, 2009). One piece of this self-creation puzzle involves the development of emerging adolescents' self-recognition and a sense of self-worth and relationships within the context of narcissism (Kluger, 2014; Rochat, 2009).

The paradoxical balance between a fragile, vulnerable sense of self and grandiosity create what researchers have referred to as a psychodynamic mask (Kohut, 1966). This psychodynamic mask model of narcissism suggests that the notion of grandiosity masks or provides a façade that conceals one's underlying feelings of inferiority and vulnerability (Zeigler-Hill & Besser, 2013). Recent research shows that, while some forms of narcissism might be adaptive for adolescents based on the demands of that developmental period (Hill & Lapsley, 2011), others are more closely associated with maladjustment as indicated by higher levels of delinquency, aggression, contingent self-worth, anxiety, and impaired relationships with others.

In particular, Lapsley and colleagues noted that the demands of adolescence, such as separation-individuation, engenders the benefits of a sense of omnipotence, self-sufficiency, and assertiveness during that time (Hill & Lapsley, 2011). Given that some level of narcissism may be considered normative in adolescence, such as the nonpathological type, individual differences in narcissism during adolescence appear to provide meaningful information on a variety of behavioral, emotional, and social constructs (Barry & Kauten, 2014). However, the literature to date is limited in that it fails to provide a clear, developmental framework of narcissism. That is, a theory is needed to help researchers to distinguish between narcissistic tendencies that serve appropriate developmental roles for youth, and those that are indicative of self-development challenges, and restraint from antisocial behavior (e.g., aggression, delinquency).

To explore the role of narcissism in young people's relationships, Barry and Kauten (2014) studied narcissism and peer- and self-related reports of aggression in adolescents. According to Barry and Kauten, common notions of narcissism often include an individual who acts conceited. In reality, the concept is much more complex and is marked by specific behavioral, motivational, and cognitive tendencies. The narcissistic individual expects to be considered as superior by others and may become aggressive if this recognition or admiration is not received. Special regard is typically desired without reason, as individuals with narcissistic tendencies feel entitled to their needs and tend to exploit and manipulate others to achieve their personal social goals (Kluger, 2014).

Barry and Kauten's (2014) study examined the links among narcissism, prosocial behavior, and aggression in adolescents. The multi-informant aspect (i.e., self and peer report) of this study delineated the ways in which adolescents with narcissistic tendencies might behave from the vantage point of others rather than only considering their own perspective. The focus on later childhood and early adolescence is of particular importance, as adolescence represents a distinct period of personality development and emphasis on peer relationships. Researchers need to continue to explore the connections between adolescent self-perception and personality and the strategies used to reach social goals. Such research may inform educational efforts to prevent the internalizing and externalizing behaviors associated with narcissism, and provide a basis to promote more positive behaviors toward self and others (Ziegler-Hill & Jordan, 2011).

Recent empirical evidence has emerged regarding so-called pathological narcissism which includes a vulnerable element whereby self-esteem is contingent on others' opinions and perceptions (Roeder et al., 2014), and a grandiose element characterized by a desire to portray oneself as superior to others (Pincus et al., 2009). The dependency on positive feedback from others is thought to be tied to a fragile and generally low global self-esteem (Marshall, Parker, Ciarrochi, & Heaven, 2014). Although narcissism is usually associated with a sometimes gregarious and self-assured presentation (Kluger, 2014), it may also be indicative of the inability to create social connections, and of a fragile sense of self-worth.

Individuals characterized by pathological narcissism have been found to often exploit and devalue others to meet their own needs. Also, the pathologically narcissistic individual often reports a tendency to hide their true self for fear that others may recognize their faults (Pincus et al., 2009). However, to engender favorable views from others, they may present themselves in a helpful, self-deprecating manner while maintaining a secret mindset of (desired) superiority over others.

These patterns of manipulation by virtue of both gallant and avoidant behaviors are exemplified by the "self-sacrificing self-enhancement" and "hiding the self" elements of pathological narcissism, respectively (Pincus et al., 2009). Thus, some aspects of pathological narcissism may be associated with a tendency to engage in prosocial behaviors. However, it appears that individuals with high levels of narcissism also aggress reactively to protect their fragile ego, and proactively to assert dominance and perceived superiority in peer groups.

For individuals with narcissistic tendencies, aggressive or prosocial behavior could be chosen to meet social needs (e.g., affirmation, dominance). Prosocial and aggressive behaviors are not necessarily mutually exclusive, as an individual might carefully determine which behavior would be most self-serving in a given situation. As narcissism has been found to be connected to concerns of social control and self-importance, it shares characteristics with Machiavellianism. Thus, it remains possible that narcissistic individuals may maintain aggressive and prosocial interpersonal strategies that have been described for Machiavellianism. Within interpersonal relationships, narcissism tends to be associated with charisma, as Kluger (2014) describes the narcissist's interpersonal style as exuding confidence and charm.

Individual with high levels of narcissism have also been found to manipulate other individuals to feed their desires related to esteem and status, and to fail to reciprocate acts of praise and admiration (Kluger, 2014). Many researchers note that narcissists often approach relationships in a pragmatic or selfish way, aiming to gain maximum personal gains to the detriment of others (Zeigler-Hill & Besser, 2013). In addition, they suggest that peers are privileged only to the outward behaviors in which the narcissistic individual may engage, and are not privy to the potentially undesirable motivations behind the behaviors. Thus, some aspects of narcissism aim to attract others, and entice or persuade them to engage in interactions. The charm and grandiosity of individuals with narcissistic tendencies predicts positive short-term relationships, but the selfish approach to relationships may lead the relationships to break down in the long term (Kluger, 2014).

Self-reported pathological narcissism has been associated with self-reported aggression in adolescents and adults (Barry & Kauten, 2014; Kluger, 2014; Pincus et al., 2009). Such research indicates that individuals with high levels of narcissism may not be concerned about portraying themselves as aggressive, and/or do not recognize aggression as necessarily maladaptive. Additionally, past research suggests that adolescents who self-report relatively high levels of narcissism are more likely to be perceived as relationally or covertly aggressive by their peers (Twenge, 2011).

For example, narcissistic youth may assert their superiority in peer groups by spreading rumors about peers whom they dislike. Thus, prosocial behavior may not always be viewed as the most advantageous interpersonal strategy, as such a finding has also been made with socially anxious-withdrawn children (Bowker & Raja, 2011; Kashdan et al., 2011). It is also possible that peers may not only perceive those with narcissistic tendencies as aggressive, but also as less prosocial.

Barry and Kauten (2014) found that the association between narcissism and aggression has been empirically supported in adults and adolescents, but it is unclear whether narcissism might also be related to prosocial behavior. They investigated this issue in 183 adolescents aged 16–19 (159 males, 24 females; 64.5% Caucasian). Of these participants, 126 (104 males, 22 females) also had peer-reported data available. Results suggested that self-reported pathological narcissism was positively correlated with self-reports of both prosocial behavior and aggression, but it was not associated with peer nominations of either type of behavior. These findings indicated that adolescents with high levels of narcissism may have attempted to bolster their social status by reporting engagement in both prosocial behavior and aggression. Thus, the results suggest there was a disconnect between self-perceived narcissists' self-perceptions and peer perceptions of prosocial behavior.

Barry and Kauten's (2014) study provides questions for future research on self-reported narcissism and prosocial and adaptive social cognitive abilities. For example, future studies could help to explain the context-dependent nature of narcissism's association with socially desirable behaviors such as leadership abilities and healthy coping strategies. Longitudinal future research should investigate how the participants' gender and cultural background and their friendship history may play a role in the development of narcissistic behaviors across later childhood and adolescence. Future study of developmental relations among narcissism, social cognitive abilities, and prosocial behavior may help educators and researchers working with youth who experience social cognitive and peer relation challenges.

For example, constructs such as ToM may moderate the relation between self-perceived narcissism and prosocial behavior. That is, adolescents with narcissistic tendencies may be more likely to (report) engagement in prosocial behavior if they also have an elevated level of ToM. A more advanced ability to understand the thoughts and emotions of self and other may render youth acutely aware of the influence of their own behaviors on their relationships with others.

Past research shows that individuals characterized by narcissism are aware that others do not necessarily perceive them as positively as they perceive themselves (Bushman & Baumeister, 1988). It is possible that this interpersonal awareness, combined with a desire to self-present favorably, may motivate the individual to alter his or her behaviors to generate more favorable reactions. Finally, future research may also consider relationships with family, authority figures, and peers within the connection between adolescent narcissism and interpersonal behaviors.

Perfectionism

Similar to narcissism, which has been found to be negatively related to emotion understanding and well-being (Kluger, 2014; Pincus et al., 2009), an additional higher order personality characteristic that is associated with emotional understanding is the notion of perfectionism (Lyman & Luthar, 2014). In general, perfectionistic traits have been found to be positively related to a variety of emotional health challenges and self-harmful behaviors such as higher rates of suicide, body dissatisfaction and disordered eating, anxiety, and depression among young people (see Flett & Hewitt, 2014 for a review). For example, past research has found that young people with high perfectionistic concerns reported overly negative reactions to perceived failures, nagging self-doubts, and excessive concerns over others' criticisms and expectations (Brose, Schmiedek, Koval, & Kuppens, 2015; Flett & Hewitt, 2014).

Past research suggests that perfectionism may influence one's propensity to strive for flawlessness, set excessively high standards, and experience disappointment or dissatisfaction with anything falling short of perfection (Frost, Marten, Lahart, & Rosenblate, 1990). There is currently a broad consensus that perfectionism is comprised of two higher order dimensions: perfectionistic strivings and perfectionistic concerns. Individuals with high perfectionistic strivings rigidly and ceaselessly demand perfection of the self and hold unrealistically high personal standards. In contrast, individuals with high perfectionistic concerns have overly negative reactions to perceived failures, excessive concerns over others' expectations, and nagging self-doubts. Moreover, individuals with high perfectionistic concerns describe themselves as easily discouraged, eager to quit, unprepared, inept, cynical, sad, hopeless, and prone to anger and frustration (Flett & Hewitt, 2014).

As noted above, a wealth of research indicates neuroticism and self-harmful behaviors and attitudes are robustly associated with both types of perfectionism, as well as maladaptive perfectionism (Frost et al., 1990; Lyman & Luthar, 2014), and more research is needed on the subtle distinctions within the various dimensions of perfectionism and implications for young people's emotional health and social cognitive development (Flett & Hewitt, 2014). Thus, major gaps continue to exist in researchers' understanding of the neuroticism–perfectionistic concerns and the larger connections between social cognitive development and the development of perfectionistic tendencies in young people.

To further understand the developmental trajectory of the neuroticism–perfectionistic concerns link, and how it develops during later childhood and adolescence, researchers need to understand more about the factors involved in the origins of neuroticism within a social cognitive and emotional framework. Neuroticism has been defined as a higher-order domain of personality that involves negative emotions such as anxiety, sadness, and irritability (Saucier, 1994). As a basic tendency or personality trait, neuroticism has been found to be moderately stable from childhood to early adulthood, and substantially heritable (Caspi et al., 2003; Frost et al., 1990).

Overall, among young adults, research shows that 50–60% of the variance in neuroticism scores is attributable to genetic factors (Flett & Hewitt, 2014). Theory and evidence suggest neuroticism underlies and predisposes lower-order facets of personality, including perfectionism and trait emotional intelligence (Petrides, Frederickson, & Furnham, 2004). Finally, the importance of neuroticism as a core personality trait is underscored by its inclusion in the vast majority of personality models.

Thus, research suggests perfectionistic concerns are clearly distinguishable from neuroticism (Flett & Hewitt, 2014), although both are connected to larger areas of social cognitive and emotional abilities such as emotional regulation and understanding. As Flett and Hewitt (2014) suggest, future research needs to explore the social cognitive and emotional roots of perfectionism and resilience. Such research would lead to educational programs aimed to promote the emotional well-being of youth.

Emotional intelligence and neuroticism—perfectionistic concerns.   In addition to perfectionism and neuroticism, the research area of trait emotional intelligence (TEI) and how it influences young people's ability to regulate one's emotions and navigate their relationships is important to social cognitive development. Emotional trait intelligence is a lower-order personality trait comprised of a constellation of emotion-related self-perceptions. Specifically, TEI offers a comprehensive operationalization of the affective aspects of personality and has been found to have incremental validity over the Big Five, the Giant Three, and other personality variables.

In addition, TEI is central to the development and implementation of successful coping strategies (Petrides et al., 2004). Research suggests that individuals with low TEI, compared to individuals with high TEI, more readily engaged in maladaptive coping when confronted with perceived stressors (Petrides et al., 2004). Furthermore, TEI is related to perceived social support (Austin, Sakflofske, & Egan, 2005), and people with low TEI may tend to feel excluded and unwanted. In addition, TEI measures self-perceived ability to establish satisfying relationships characterized by intimacy, as well as self-perceived ability to control emotions and impulses.

Based on past research, individuals with high perfectionistic concerns may be more likely than individuals with low perfectionistic concerns to have low TEI. More specifically, individuals with high perfectionistic concerns tend to engage in maladaptive coping (e.g., denial) when confronted with perceived stressors. Research also suggests that perfectionistic concerns are maintained and manifested via various insecure expressions within relationships such as intimacy avoidance, disengagement from decisions and actions, and suspiciousness (Flett & Hewitt, 2014). Thus TEI is expected to have a negative relation with perfectionistic concerns.

Both TEI and perfectionistic concerns have been found to show a positive association with neuroticism and anxiety challenges (Mayer, Salovey, & Caruso, 2009; Petrides et al., 2004). Given that the higher-order personality trait of neuroticism may be underlain by TEI and perfectionistic concerns, future researchers should explore how TEI may influence the associations among neuroticism and perfectionistic concerns and conscientiousness, and how it plays a role in young people's social cognitive development (Eisenberg, Duckworth, Sinrad, & Valiente, 2014; Mayer et al., 2009). Overall, to prevent the development of perfectionism and to promote resilience, future researchers need to continue to explore the social cognitive architecture of the adolescent mind or mindset, and their emotional landscape within the school context.

Applications: So What?

The practical implications of research on the emotional aspect of self-development include a need for educators to focus on the prevention of the development of perfectionism and self-criticism, and to promote emotional well-being and resilience among emerging adolescents. More specifically, these programs could focus on how to develop caring and compassionate attitudes toward the self, including a growth mindset in terms of making mistakes as a learning process (Flett & Hewitt, 2014; Neff, 2011). Such programs could highlight the centrality of focusing on the adaptive nature of guilt, compared with the more maladaptive shame when, for instance, implementing prevention and intervention programs in schools. As I discussed earlier in this chapter, emotion processes guide emerging adolescents' social interactions and are needed for constructive solutions in challenging situations.

As Baumeister, Campbell, Krueger, and Vohs (2003) discussed, the majority of educational programs focus on boosting young people's self-esteem and sense of self-worth, irrespective of appropriate behavior. In support of Baumeister's suggestions, past research that focuses on the heterogeneity of self-concept will help researchers and educators to determine which sources of self-worth to focus on. Some of our past research findings on older children's and young adolescents' self-perceptions show that differential components of self-worth play different roles in a young person's emotional health and social cognitive development (Bosacki, 2008).

For example, we found that positive associations existed between a child's ToM ability, a general sense of well-being or happiness (global self-worth), and their moral self, or how well behaved they perceive themselves to be (Bosacki, 2015). That is, the more well behaved children perceived themselves to be, or the more likely to follow the rules, the more likely they were to score high on ToM tasks and to report positive or good feelings about their overall sense of self. In contrast, we found that self-perceived social and academic competence was only marginally associated, or not at all, with a global or general sense of well-being and did not play a role in a child's ToM ability or social competence.

As Baumeister et al. (2003) suggest, such research holds important implications for practice. Given the differential influences of various subtypes of self-esteem across the lifespan (Orth, Maes, & Manfred, 2015), educational programs need to focus on specific types of self-esteem and more on the sources of self-worth as compared to a global sense of high regard, irrespective of one's moral and ethical behavior. Baumeister et al. (2003) suggested that using self-esteem as a reward rather than an entitlement seemed more appropriate. That is, they found that educators need to help youth to determine what the most adaptive amount of self-esteem is for them.

For example, for some youth high self-esteem may allow them to feel "good enough," and to foster initiative (Orth et al., 2015; Rosenberg, 1965). High self-esteem may still prove a useful tool to promote success and virtue, and should be clearly and explicitly linked to desirable moral behavior. For example, Baumeister et al. (2003) failed to find data that showed educators should indiscriminately promote self-esteem in today's children or adults, just for being themselves. Thus, Baumeister et al. support the notion that a more appropriate strategy could involve attempts to try to boost people's self-esteem as a reward for ethical behavior and worthy achievements.

Past research suggests that educators could be encouraged to relate self-esteem to young people's learning and improvement. Studies have shown that learning contingent upon current academic performance may be considered most effective when one receives praise and criticism. The praise-only regimen of the self-esteem movement may ultimately be no more effective for learning than the criticism-only regimen of past educational programs. However, affective implications for praise-only would be much more pleasant than the criticism-only plan.

As Baumeister et al. (2003) and others note, praise that bolsters self-esteem in recognition of good performance could be a useful tool to facilitate learning and further improve performance. In contrast, praise for all youth for being themselves may devalue praise, and confuse young people as to what the legitimate standards are. In the long term, if such indiscriminate praise has any effect on self-esteem, as noted earlier, it may contribute more to narcissism or other forms of inflated self-esteem than to the kind of self-esteem that will be best for the individual and for society.

Thus, a focus on improvement may allow young people to self-compare so that they can refrain from gaining self-confidence at the expense of others. Self-improvement and learning could be considered one of the ideal conditions for boosting self-esteem. That is, as a person performs or behaves better, self-esteem is encouraged to rise, and the net effect will be to reinforce both good behavior and improvement. Those outcomes are conducive both to the happiness of the individual and the betterment of society.

Future Questions

Future longitudinal research should explore the developmental emergence of the various dimensions and facets of self-esteem, and the connection to narcissism and social cognitive and emotional abilities within emerging adolescence. Further, researchers should explore societal attitudes toward particular features of narcissism as some features may be associated with maladjustment contingent upon the cultural context. Theoretical and empirical evidence suggests that particular features of narcissism (e.g., autonomy, feelings of superiority) might be encouraged within individualistic societies as these forms might both serve self-regulatory functions (Kluger, 2014; Lilienfeld, Watts, & Francis-Smith, 2015;

Twenge, 2011; Zeigler-Hill & Besser, 2013). Therefore, further research should continue to consider the potential positive correlates of narcissism including different types of self-esteem and prosocial behavior, in addition to social cognitive abilities such as ToM and coping strategies.

Future research is needed on the development of self-consciousness and interpersonal processes such as attachment and separation anxiety for caregivers and authority figures. Future studies should also explore peer relationships within adolescence, as such relationships may play a role in how narcissistic features are self-perceived as well as perceived by others within a school setting (Kluger, 2014; Lilienfeld et al., 2015; Rochat, 2009). Empirical investigations of self-perceptions and narcissism and their correlates can also inform efforts to reinforce young people's moral behavior and academic achievement. Such studies may also prevent the development of narcissism and its negative consequences. As many researchers and educators suggest (Kim & Sasaki, 2014; Overton, 2013), the field of epigenetics aims to account for reciprocal transactions between biology and environment. Such research may then serve as one of the primary mechanisms that can move the field of social cognition and the emotional self away from the dominance of unidirectional explanations toward more parsimonious models.

Summary

Given the complex relations among emotion understanding, ToM, and self-perceptions, further research is necessary on the social cognitive development of youth. In particular, the connections between moral understanding and ToM and other social cognitive abilities remain lacking in research and are in need of further study. The next chapter will focus on the role of moral understanding and reasoning within the larger framework of social cognition among emerging adolescents.

References

Aldwin, C. M., Park, C. L., Jeong, Y.-J., & Nath, R. (2014). Differing pathways between religiousness, spirituality, and health: A self-regulation perspective. *Psychology of Religion and Spirituality, 6*(1), 9–21.

Austin, E., Sakflofske, D., & Egan, V. (2005). Personality, well-being and health correlates of trait emotional intelligence. *Personality and Individual Differences, 38,* 547–558.

Barry, C., & Kauten, R. (2014). Nonpathological and pathological narcissism: Which self-reported characteristics are most problematic in adolescents? *Journal of Personality Assessment, 96,* 212–219.

Baum, F. (1984/1900). *The wonderful wizard of Oz.* New York, NY: Signet Classic.

Baumeister, R., Campbell, J., Krueger, J., & Vohs, V. (2003). Does high self-esteem cause better performance, interpersonal success happiness, or health? *Psychological Science in the Public Interest, 4,* 1–44.

Baumeister, R. F., Vohs, K. D., DeWall, C. N., & Zhang, L. (2007). How emotion shapes behavior: Feedback, anticipation, and reflection, rather than direct causation. *Personality and Social Psychology Review, 11,* 167–203. doi:10.1177/1088868307301033

Beck, S., & Guthrie, C. (2011). Almost thinking counterfactually: Children's understanding of close counterfactuals. *Child Development, 82,* 1189–1198. doi:10.1111/j.1467-8624.2011.01590

Beck, S., Robinson, E., Carroll, D., & Apperly, I. (2006). Children's thinking about counterfactuals and future hypotheticals as possibilities. *Child Development, 77,* 413–426. doi:10.1111/j.1467-8624.2006.00879

Bjorklund, D., & Ellis, B. (2014). Children, childhood and development in evolutionary perspective. *Developmental Review, 34,* 225–264.

Blakemore, S.-J., & Mills, K. (2014). Is adolescence a sensitive period for sociocultural processing? *Annual Review of Psychology, 65,* 187–207.

Blos, J. (1979). *The adolescent passage: Developmental issues.* New York, NY: International Universities Press.

Bosacki, S. (2005). *Culture of classroom silence.* New York, NY: Peter Lang.

Bosacki, S. (2008). *Children's emotional lives: Sensitive shadows in the classroom.* New York, NY: Peter Lang.

Bosacki, S. (2013). Theory of mind understanding and conversational patterns in early adolescence. *Journal of Genetic Psychology, 174,* 170–191.

Bosacki, S., Bialecka-Pikul, M., & Spzak, M. (2015). Theory of mind and self-concept in Canadian and Polish youth. *International Journal of Youth and Adolescence, 20*(4), 457–469. doi:10.1080/02673843.2013.804423

Bosacki, S., & Moore, C. (2004). Preschoolers' understanding of simple and complex emotions: Links with gender and language. *Sex Roles: A Journal of Research, 50,* 659–675.

Bowker, J. C., & Raja, R. (2011). Social withdrawal subtypes during early adolescence in India. *Journal of Abnormal Child Psychology, 39,* 201–212. doi:10.1007/s10802-010-9461-7

Bridges, J. (1925). A reconciliation of current theories of emotion. *The Journal of Abnormal Psychology and Social Psychology, 19,* 333–340.

Bronfenbrenner, U. (1977). Toward an experimental ecology of human development. *American Psychologist, 32,* 513–531.

Brose, A., Schmiedek, F., Koval, P., & Kuppens, P. (2015). Emotional inertia contributes to depressive symptoms beyone perseverative thinking. *Cognition and Emotion, 29,* 527–538.

Burns, P., Riggs, K. J., & Beck, S. R. (2012). Executive control and the experience of regret. *Journal of Experimental Child Psychology, 111,* 501–515. doi:10.1016/j.jecp.2011.10.003

Bushman, B. J., & Baumeister, R. F. (1998). Threatened egotism, narcissism, self-esteem, and direct and displaced aggression: Does self-love or self-hate lead to violence? *Journal of Personality and Social Psychology, 75,* 219–229.

Cairns, R., Cairns, B., Neckerman, H., Ferguson, L., & Gariepy, J. (1989). Growth and aggression: Childhood to early adolescence. *Developmental Psychology, 23,* 320–330.

Callan, M., Kay, A., & Dawtry, R. (2014). Making sense of misfortune: Deservingness, self-esteem, and patterns. *Journal of Personality and Social Psychology, 107,* 142–162.

Casey, B., Getz, S., & Galvan, A. (2008). The adolescent brain. *Developmental Review, 28,* 62–77.

Caspi, A., Harrington, H. L., Milne, B., Amell, J. W., Theodore, R. F., & Moffitt, T. E. (2003). Children's behavioral styles at age 3 are linked to their adult personality traits at age 26. *Journal of Personality, 71,* 495–513. doi:10.1111/1467-6494.7104001

Cole, D. (1989). Validation of the reasons for living inventory in general and delinquent adolescent samples. *Journal of Abnormal Child Psychology, 17,* 13–27.

Dabrowski, K. (1967). *Personality shaping through positive disintegration.* Boston, MA: Little, Brown.

Del Giudice, M. (2014). Middle childhood: An evolutionary-developmental synthesis. *Child Development Perspectives, 4,* 193–2000.

Del Giudice, M., Ellis, B. J., & Shirtcliff, E. A. (2011). The adaptive calibration model of stress responsivity. *Neuroscience & Biobehavioral Reviews, 35,* 1562–1592. doi:10.1016/j.neubiorev.2010.11.007

Denham. S. (1998). *Emotional development in young children*. New York, NY: Guilford.

Denham, S., Bassett, H., Way, E., Kalb, S., Warren-Khot, H., & Zinsser, K. (2014). "How would you feel? What would you do?" Development and underpinnings of preschoolers' social information processing. *Journal of Research in Childhood Education, 28*, 128–202.

de Rosnay, M., Fink, E., Begeer, S., Slaughter, V., & Peterson, C. (2014). Talking theory of mind talk: Young school-aged children's everyday conversation and understanding of mind and emotion. *Journal of Child Language, 4*, 1179–1193.

de Rosnay, M., & Hughes, C. (2006). Conversation and theory of mind: Do children talk their way to socio-cognitive understanding? *British Journal of Developmental Psychology, 24*, 7–37.

Eccles, J., & Roeser, R. (2003). Schools as developmental contexts. In G. Adams & M. Berzonsky (Eds.), *Blackwell handbook of adolescence* (pp. 129–148). Malden, MA: Blackwell.

Eisenberg, N., Duckworth, A., Sinrad, R., & Valiente, C. (2014). Conscientiousness: Origins in childhood? *Developmental Psychology, 50*, 1331–1349.

Elkind, D. (1967). Egocentrism in adolescence. *Child Development, 38*, 1025–1034. doi:10.2307/1127100

Flett, G., & Hewitt, I. (2014). A proposed framework for preventing perfectionism and promoting resilience and mental health among vulnerable children and adolescents. *Psychology in the Schools, 51*, 899–912.

Frost, R. O., Marten, P., Lahart, C., & Rosenblate, R. (1990). The dimensions of perfectionism. *Cognitive Therapy and Research, 14*, 449–468.

Geronimi, E., & Woodruff-Borden, J. (2015). The language of worry: Examining linguistic worry models. *Cognition & Emotion, 29*, 311–318.

Greenspan, L., & Deardorff, J. (2014). *The new puberty: How to navigate early development in today's girls*. New York, NY: Rodale.

Group for the Advancement of Psychiatry, Committee on Adolescents (1996). *Adolescent suicide (Report no. 140)*. Washington, DC: American Psychiatric Press.

Gutiereez, K., & Rogoff, B. (2003). Cultural ways of learning: Individual traits or repertoires of practice. *Educational Researcher, 32*, 19–25.

Guttentag, R. E., & Ferrell, J. M. (2004). Reality compared with its alternatives: Age differences in judgments of regret and relief. *Developmental Psychology, 40*, 764–775. doi:10.1037/0012-1649.40. 5.764

Harris, P. (1989). *Children and emotion: The development of psychological understanding*. Oxford, England: Blackwell.

Harter, S. (1999). *The construction of the self: A developmental perspective*. New York, NY: Guilford.

Hawton, K., Saunders, K. E. A., & O'Connor, R. C. (2012). Self-harm and suicide in adolescents. *The Lancet, 379*, 2373–2382. doi:10.1016/S0140-6736(12)60322-5

Hill, P. L., & Lapsley, D. K. (2011). Adaptive and maladaptive narcissism in adolescent development. In C. T. Barry, P. K. Kerig, K. K. Stellwagen, & T. D. Barry (Eds.), *Narcissism and Machiavellianism in youth: Implications for the development of adaptive and maladaptive behavior* (pp. 89–106). Washington, DC: American Psychological Association.

Hoffman, M. L. (2000). *Empathy and moral development: Implications for caring and justice*. New York, NY: Cambridge University Press.

Hollenstein, T. & Lougheed, J. P. (2013). Beyond storm and stress: Typicality, transactions, timing, and temperament to account for adolescent change. *American Psychologist, 68*(6), 444–454. doi: 10.1037/a0033586

Hughes, C. (2011). *Social understanding and social lives: From toddlerhood through to the transition to school*. New York, NY: Psychology Press.

Hyde, J. (2014). Gender similarities and differences. *Annual Review of Psychology, 65*, 373–398.

Jambon, M., & Smetana, J. G. (2014). Moral complexity in middle childhood: Children's evaluations of necessary harm. *Developmental Psychology, 50*, 22–33. doi:10.1037/a0032992

Kashdan, T. B., Weeks, J. W., & Savostyanova, A. A. (2011). Whether, how, and when social anxiety shapes positive experiences and events: A self-regulatory framework and treatment implications. *Clinical Psychology Review, 31*, 786–799.

Kashima, Y., Kashima, E., Farsides, T., Kim, U., Strack, F., Werth, L., & Yuki, M. (2004). Culture and context-sensitive self: The amount and meaning of context-sensitivity of phenomenal self differ across cultures. *Self and Identity, 3*, 125–141. doi:10.1080/13576500342000095

Kim, H., & Sasaki, J. (2014). Cultural neuroscience: Biology of the mind in cultural contexts. *Annual Review of Psychology, 65*, 487–514.

Kitayama, S., & Markus, H. R. (Eds.). (1994). *Emotion and culture: Empirical studies of mutual influence.* Washington, DC: American Psychological Association.

Kluger, J. (2014). *The narcissist next door: Understanding the monster in your family, in your office, in your bed—in your world.* New York, NY: Riverhead Books.

Koh, S., Scollon, C., & Wirtz, D. (2014). The role of social relationships and culture in cognitive representations of emotions. *Cognition and Emotion, 28*, 507–519.

Kohut, H. (1966). Forms and transformations of narcissism. *Journal of the American Psychoanalytic Association, 14*, 243–272.

Kuppens, P., Ceulemans, E., Timmerman, M. E., Diener, E., & Kim-Prieto, C. (2006). Universal intracultural and intercultural dimensions of the recalled frequency of emotional experience. *Journal of Cross-Cultural Psychology, 37*, 491–515. doi:10.1177/0022022106290474

Lagattuta, K. (2014). Linking past, present, and future: Child ability to connect mental states and emotions. *Child Development Perspectives, 8*, 90–95.

Lane, J., Harris, P., Gelman, S., & Wellman, H. (2015). More than meets the eye: Young children's trust in claims that defy their perceptions. *Developmental Psychology, 50*, 865–871.

Lane, J., Wellman, H., Olson, S, Miller, A., Wang, L., & Tardif, T. (2013). Relations between temperament and theory of mind development in the United States and China: Biological and behavioral correlates of preschoolers' false-belief understanding. *Developmental Psychology, 49*, 825–836.

Larson, R. (2011). Positive development in a disorderly world. *Journal of Research in Adolescence, 21*, 317. doi:10.1111/j.1532-7795.2010.00707.x

Levitt, M., & Selman, R. (1996). The personal meaning of risk behavior. In G. Noam & W. Fischer (Eds.), *Development and vulnerability in close relationships* (pp. 201–233). Hillsdale, NJ: Erlbaum.

Lewis, M. (2015). *The biology of desire: Why addiction is not a disease.* New York, NY: Perseus Book Group.

Lilienfeld, S., Watts, A., & Francis-Smith, S. (2015). Successful psychopathology: A scientific status report. *Current Directions in Psychological Science, 24*, 298–303.

Lyman, E., & Luthar, S. (2014). Further evidence on the "costs of privilege": Perfectionism in high-achieving youth at socioeconomic extremes. *Psychology in the Schools, 51*, 91–93.

Marshall, S., Parker, P., Ciarrochi, J., & Heaven, P. (2014). Is self-esteem a cause or consequence of social support: A 4-year longitudinal study. *Child Development, 85*, 1275–1291.

Mayer, J., Salovey, P., & Caruso, D. (2009). Trait emotional intelligence: New ability or eclectic traits? *American Psychologist, 63*, 503–517.

McCormack, T., & Feeney, A. (2015). The development of the experience and anticipation of regret. *Cognition and Emotion, 29*, 266–280.

Mesquita, B., & Leu, J. (2007). The cultural psychology of emotion. In S. Kitayama, & D. Cohen (Eds.), *Handbook of cultural psychology* (pp. 734–759). New York, NY: Guilford.

Morf, C., & Rhodewalt, F. (2001). Unraveling the paradoxes of narcissism: A dynamic self-regulatory processing model. *Psychological Inquiry, 12*, 177–196.

Muehlenkamp, J. J., Claes, L., Havertape, L., & Plener, P. L. (2012). International prevalence of adolescent non-suicidal self-injury and deliberate self-harm. *Child and Adolescent Psychiatry and Mental Health, 6*(10). Retrieved from http://www.capmh.com/content/6/1/10

Mueller, M. (2014). Is human–animal interaction (HAI) linked to positive youth development? Initial answers. *Applied Developmental Science, 18*, 5–16.

Neff, K. D. (2011). Self-compassion, self-esteem, and well-being. *Social and Personality Psychological Compass, 5*, 1–12. doi:10.1111/j.1751-9004.2010.00330

O'Connor, E., McCormack, T., & Feeney, A. (2012). The development of regret. *Journal of Experimental Child Psychology, 111*, 120–127. doi:10.1016/j.jecp. 2011.07.002

O'Connor, E., McCormack, T., & Feeney, A. (2014). Do children who experience regret make better decisions? A developmental study of the behavioral consequences of regret. *Child Development, 85*, 1195–2010.

Orth, U., Maes, J., & Manfred, S. (2015). Self-esteem development across the life span: A longitudinal study with a large sample from Germany. *Developmental Psychology, 51*, 248–259.

Overton, W. F. (2013). A new paradigm for developmental science: Relationism and relational-developmental systems. *Applied Developmental Science, 17*, 94–107. doi:10.1080/10888691.2013.778717

Petrides, K., Frederickson, N. & Furnham, A. (2004). The role of trait emotional intelligence in academic performance and deviant behavior at school. *Personality and Individual Differences, 36*, 277–293.

Pincus, A. L., Ansell, E. B., Pimentel, C. A., Cain, N. M., Wright, A. G. C., & Levy, K. N. (2009). Initial construction and validation of the Pathological Narcissism Inventory. *Psychological Assessment, 21*, 365–379.

Pons, F., Harris, P. L., & de Rosnay, M. (2004). Emotion comprehension between 3 and 11 years: Developmental periods and hierarchical organization. *European Journal of Developmental Psychology, 2*(1), 127–152.

Pons, F., Lawson, J., Harris, P. L., & de Rosnay, M. (2003). Individual differences in children's emotion understanding: Effects of age and language. *Scandinavian Journal of Psychology, 44*, 347–411.

Rafetseder, E., & Perner, J. (2012). When the alternative would have been better: Counterfactual reasoning and the emergence of regret. *Cognition & Emotion, 25*, 800–819. doi:10.1080/02699931.2011.619744

Robbins, P. (1998). *Adolescent suicide*. Jefferson, NC: McFarland.

Rochat, P. (2009). *Others in mind: Social origins of self-consciousness*. Cambridge, England: Cambridge University Press.

Roeder, K., Keneisher, S., Dukewich, T., Preacher, K., & Felton, J., Jacky, A., & Tilghman-Osburne, C. (2014). Sensitive periods for the effect of peer victimization on self-cognition: Moderation by age and gender. *Development and Psychopathology, 26*, 1035–1048.

Roos, S., Hodges, E., & Salmivalli, C. (2013). Do guilt- and shame-proneness differentially predict prosocial, aggressive, and withdrawn behaviors during early adolescence. *Developmental Psychology, 50*, 941–946.

Roos, S., Salmivalli, C., & Hodges, E. V. E. (2011). Person context effects on anticipated moral emotions following aggression. *Social Development, 20*, 685–702. doi:10.1111/j.1467-9507.2011.00603.x

Rose, R. (2014). Self-guided multimedia stress management and resilience training. *The Journal of Positive Psychology, 9*, 489–493.

Rosenberg, M. (1965). *Society and the adolescent self-image*. Princeton, NJ: Princeton University Press.

Saarikallio, S. (2011). Music as emotional self-regulation throughout adulthood. *Psychology of Music, 39*, 307–327.

Saarni, C. (1999). *The development of emotional competence*. New York, NY: Guilford.

Selman, R. L. (1980). *The growth of interpersonal understanding: Developmental and clinical analyses.* New York, NY: Academic Press.

Shahaeian, A., Nielsen, M., Peterson, C. C., & Slaughter, V. (2014). Cultural and family influences on children's theory of mind development: A comparison of Australian and Iranian school-age children. *Journal of Cross-Cultural Psychology*, *45*, 555–568. doi:10.1177/0022022113513921

Siegel, D. (2013). *Brainstorm: The power and purpose of the teenage brain.* New York, NY: Jeremy Tarcher/Penguin.

Silverman, L. (1989). Invisible gifts, invisible handicaps. *Roeper Review*, *12*, 37–42.

Simmons, E., & Blyth, D. (1987*). Moving into adolescence: The impact of pubertal change and the school context.* Hawthorn, NY: Aldine de Gruyter.

Slaughter, V., & Perez-Zapata, D. (2014). Cultural variations in the development of mind reading. *Child Development Perspectives*, *8*, 237–241.

Tangney, J. P., & Dearing, R. L. (2002). Gender differences in morality. In R. F. Bornstein & M. Masling (Eds.), *Empirical studies in psychoanalytic theories: Vol. 10. The psychodynamics of gender and gender role* (pp. 251–269). Washington, DC: American Psychological Association.

Twenge, J. (2011). Narcissism and culture. In W. K. Campbell & J. D. Miller (Eds.), *The handbook of narcissism and narcissistic personality disorder* (pp. 202–209). Hoboken, NJ: Wiley.

Uchida, Y., Townsend, S. S. M., Markus, H. R., & Bergsieker, H. B. (2009). Emotions as within or between people? Lay theory of emotion expression and emotion inference across cultures. *Personality and Social Psychology Bulletin*, *35*, 1427–1439. doi:10.1177/0146167209347322

Van Dijk, W. W., Van Dillen, L. F., Seip, E. C., & Rotteveel, M. (2012). Emotional time travel: Emotion regulation and the overestimation of future anger and sadness. *European Journal of Social Psychology*, *42*(3), 308–313.

Van Duijvenvoorde, A., Huizenga, H., & Jansen, B. (2014). What is and what could have been: Experiencing regret and relief across childhood. *Cognition and Emotion*, *28*, 926–935.

Vygotsky, L. S. (1978). *Mind in society: The development of higher psychological processes.* Cambridge, MA: Harvard University Press.

Waters, A., & Tucker, D. (2013). Social regulation of neural development. In B. Sokol, M. Grouzet, & U. Muller (Eds.), *Self-regulation and autonomy: Social and developmental dimensions of human conduct* (pp. 279–296). New York, NY: Cambridge University Press.

Watkins, P., Uhder, J., & Pichinevskiy, S. (2015). Grateful recounting enhances subjective well-being: The importance of grateful processing. *The Journal of Positive Psychology*, *10*, 91–98.

Weisberg, D. P., & Beck, S. R. (2010). Children's thinking about their own and others' regret and relief. *Journal of Experimental Child Psychology*, *106*, 184–191. doi:10.1016/j.jecp.2010.02.005

Weisberg, D. P., & Beck, S. R. (2012). The development of children's regret and relief. *Cognition & Emotion*, *26*, 820–835. doi:10.1080/02699931.2011. 621933

Wierzbicka, A. (2006). *Emotions across languages and cultures: Diversity and universals.* Cambridge, England: Cambridge University Press.

Wilson, T., & Gilbert, D. (2005). Affective forecasting: Knowing what to want. *Current Directions in Psychological Science*, *14*(3), 131–134.

Zeigler-Hill, V., & Besser, A. (2013). A glimpse behind the mask: Facets of narcissism and feelings of self-worth. *Journal of Personality Assessment*, *95*, 249–260.

Zeigler-Hill, V., & Jordan, C. H. (2011). Behind the mask: Narcissism and implicit self-esteem. In W. K. Campbell & J. Miller (Eds.), *Handbook of narcissism and narcissistic personality disorder: Theoretical approaches, empirical findings, and treatment* (pp. 101–115). Hoboken, NJ: Wiley.

5

The Moral Self
Morality, Spirituality, and Self-Development

"...for my life is simply unbearable without a bit of courage." (Baum, 1900/1984, p. 55)

Introduction

Chapter 5 continues to focus on self-development, with a particular focus on morality. That is, this chapter will explore the role of moral reasoning and spirituality within the personal context of the young person.

Research

Moral understandings within social cognition

Within the social cognitive domain theory of moral development (Bandura, 1991), concepts about personal issues are distinguished from conceptions of morality (fairness and human welfare), and social convention (consensually determined arbitrary norms for social organizations). Understandings about personal issues are part of arbitrary norms for social organization, and play an integral role in the psychological development of conceptions about self, personhood, and identity (Nucci, 2013). Claims to a personal area coexist with young people's construction of morality and their understandings of the conventions of society. That is, the boundaries of the personal are framed in relation to the person's understandings of the interpersonal moral obligation, and the societal guidelines of cultural convention and legal regulation (Nucci, 2013).

Social Cognition in Middle Childhood and Adolescence: Integrating the Personal, Social, and Educational Lives of Young People, First Edition. S. L. Bosacki.
© 2016 John Wiley & Sons, Ltd. Published 2016 by John Wiley & Sons, Ltd.

Researchers also explore individual differences in how youth understand social conventions such as those that reflect concerns for justice and care (Linkins, Niemiec, Gillham, & Mayerson, 2015; Peterson & Seligman, 2004). In particular, social responsibility refers to one's sense of civic duty and obligation toward endorsing public interest over self-interest by helping others without the expectation of reciprocation (Crocetti, Jahromi, & Meeus, 2012). In addition, social responsibility has also been described as a natural human occurrence and a learned social behavior (Bloom, 2013; Witt, 2001). Such theories also support the evolutionary-developmental approach that predicts that individuals who possess higher levels of social responsibility and collective intentionality tend to place affiliation with, and concern for, others above their self-interests (Bloom, 2013; Del Giudice, 2014; Peterson & Seligman, 2004; Tomasello, 2014a).

Such youth may be motivated by feelings of altruism, and aim to merge their identity with feelings of empathy, sympathy, and compassion for others (Batson, 1988; Bloom, 2013). Developmental research shows that, as children approach early adolescence, they develop from self-oriented to other-oriented behavior (Siegel, 2013). That is, their moral behavior becomes increasingly associated with higher levels of social responsibility, a sense of moral care and justice, and empathy and compassion-related responses (Eisenberg, Martin, & Fabes, 1996; Jambon & Smetana, 2014).

When a young person makes a moral judgment about an individual's action, she needs to recruit and integrate information about the intent and the consequence of the action (Bloom, 2009; Piaget, 1981; Turiel, 2006). Building on past research on Piaget's theories about intentions and outcomes in early social judgments, there has been increased recognition that reasoning about intentions and beliefs, which is referred to as Theory of Mind (ToM) understanding, may be interrelated with moral judgments (Lagattuta, Nucci, & Bosacki, 2010). Such studies suggest that a more advanced understanding of others' mental states is necessary for more mature or advanced moral judgments. However, little research has tested this hypothesis directly, or examined how development in ToM understanding contributes to the development of moral judgment, or vice versa, in older children and emerging adolescents.

As children mature, they become better able to use intention information in a more social and collective manner, and begin to consider both outcomes and intentions when making moral judgments (Bloom, 2013; Tomasello, 2014a). With increased age, children show greater reliance on mental state information in their judgments of the wrongfulness of acts than in their judgment of deserved punishment (Bloom, 2013; Cushman, Sheketoff, Wharton, & Carey, 2013). A small number of studies have investigated the developmental relations of moral judgments and mental state understanding (Smetana, Jambon, Conry-Murray, & Sturge-Apple, 2012). Thus, most typically developing children often find the integration of the transgressor's intentions into moral judgment particularly challenging.

In particular, Smetana et al. (2012) measured the two abilities separately and found that advanced ToM abilities were associated with children's judgments of moral transgressions as more wrong, independent of authority, less permissible, and less independent of rules. The moral judgments investigated in their study, however, did not involve the task of providing explanations for the wrongdoer's intentions, or the transgressor's and victim's desires. Thus, the role of children's developing ToM in their constructions of moral judgments of intention–action for self and other conflicts remains unclear and in need of further study (Lagattuta et al., 2010).

Recently, researchers have started to explore the relation between young people's advanced ToM and their moral judgments. As described earlier, reasoning about a second-order mental state focuses on the understanding that one person's mental states can be embedded within mental states such as "He thinks that she thinks that …" (Perner & Wimmer, 1985; for reviews, see Miller, 2009, 2012). Several empirical studies have found that second-order ToM understanding may be involved in children's judgments about responsibility for an accident (Hughes, 2011); acts of commission and omission with negative outcomes; promising, secret-keeping, and lying (Gordon, Lyon, & Lee, 2014; Maas, 2008); and children's evaluative judgments attributed to an observer (Bloom, 2013).

Regarding ToM and moral behavior and attitude within the school context, Baird and Astington (2004) found that children's scores on the second-order false-belief tasks significantly correlated with their teachers' reports of their actual moral behaviors at school. Similarly, in some of our research with Canadian youth, we found positive associations between young adolescents' advanced ToM understanding and their perceptions of their moral selves (e.g., how well behaved do you think you are, how well do you follow the rules in school, etc.) (Bosacki, 2008, 2012). Such results suggest that positive associations may exist between young people's ability to think about mental states in self and others and teacher and self-perceptions of their moral behavior. Given the complex school environment of social and moral actions, further research is needed to continue to explore the role of ToM in moral and social competencies within emerging adolescence.

To date, there remains a dearth in studies that directly examine the role of second-order ToM understanding in children's and adolescents' moral beliefs regarding accidental transgressors. Past findings have shown that, around the age of 8 years, children begin to understand that the actions of the mover are not wrong (e.g., because the classroom helper who discarded the bag with the sandwich inside did not know the contents of the bag; Lagattuta & Weller, 2014). To achieve such understanding, the intention of the transgressor and also the second-order mental state of the victim's understanding about the transgressor's belief needs to be involved. For example, if the owner thinks that the mover thinks there is trash inside the bag, then the transgression should be judged as less negative than the case where the owner thinks the mover knows there is a sandwich inside the bag.

Recently, Fu, Xiao, Killen, and Lee (2014) tested first and second-order ToM in Chinese 4- to 7-year-olds and found a relation between ToM tasks and moral reasoning. More specifically, Fu et al. (2014) found that, above and beyond age, children's first-order ToM and second-order ToM each significantly and uniquely contributed to their moral evaluations of accidental transgression intentions. Moreover, Fu et al. (2014) found that, irrespective of age, and first-order ToM, children's second-order ToM was significantly related to their moral evaluations of the accidental transgressor's intention. That is, children with higher second-order ToM scores were more likely to judge the intention of the transgressor less negatively. This finds support in other studies that show that children can attribute responsibility or blame in a morally relevant context (Hayashi, 2007). Further research should be conducted to examine these potential connections in emerging adolescents' social and moral cognition. Overall, Fu et al.'s (2014) findings highlight the important role that ToM plays in children's ability to make appropriate moral judgments based on an actor's intention within a complex and morally ambiguous social situation.

Spiritual and moral development

Within the classroom setting, moral imperatives derived from spiritual beliefs (e.g., honesty, beneficence, compassion) have also been found to have an impact on adolescents' moral and ethical attitudes (Bussing, Föller-Mancini, Gidley, & Heusser, 2014; De Souza, 2014). That is, spirituality or an "attitude of search for meaning in life" (Bussing et al., 2014, p. 28) has the potential to influence a young person's moral and ethical development, including their self-regulation and peer relations. In addition, these moral imperatives could lead to the development of greater compassion, and an increased sense of accountability and social responsibility. However, extreme and fundamental positions on moral imperatives could also induce feelings of self-guilt, or could lead to a moral/religious intolerance for others (Jeynes, 2002).

Although religiosity, spirituality, and faith development play a role within the larger social cognitive realm (Aldwin, Park, Jeong, & Nath, 2014), research on spirituality in relation to adolescents' moral emotions (empathy, shame, guilt), and the personal moral domain remains understudied (Bussing, 2010). An increasing number of developmentalists have recently found evidence to support the claim that social cognitive research includes many aspects of development including social, emotional, and spiritual as well as moral (Bussing et al., 2014). Although morality and spirituality may share many conceptual commonalities, such as beliefs and values about human behavior (De Souza, 2014), compared to research on spirituality and religiosity, research on young people's moral reasoning development is more frequent (Bloom, 2013; Bussing et al., 2014; Moore, Talwar, & Bosacki, 2012).

A few studies exist, such as our recent research on the contributions of spiritual growth to young people's emotional, social, and moral development (Bosacki, Moore, Talwar, & Park-Saltzman, 2011), and findings that show spiritual knowledge can help to provide youth with "key organizing principles" and "inner resources." Despite these findings, emerging adolescents' perceptions of spirituality remain beyond the scope of most studies in social cognition (Aldwin et al., 2014; Moore et al., 2012).

However, to date, there remains a lack of developmental research on emerging adolescents' conceptions of morality, and spirituality within the context of social cognition especially regarding ToM and self-regulation (Aldwin et al., 2014; Bosacki, Harwood, & Sumaway, 2012). Regarding self-knowledge, morality, and spirituality, studies have shown that some adolescents reported an awareness of spirituality as faith in oneself and others within the framework of self-agency and autonomy (Aldwin et al., 2014; Bosacki et al., 2011; De Souza, 2014). In addition, recent research has shown that some adolescents also perceive spirituality as the representation of intentional moral actions such as generosity and compassion with others (Bussing et al., 2014).

Social cognitive research also considers morality and spirituality as integral components of young people's ability to understand the inner lives of self and others (Aldwin et al., 2014; Larson, 2011). Given that past research has found that some young children have ideas about the nature of the divine, faith, and the meaning of prayer (Coles, 1990; Harris, 2000), few studies explore social cognitive abilities and the spiritual understanding of self and other among older children and adolescents. Spiritual beliefs may influence emerging adolescents' sense of responsibility and commitment to their academic, social-emotional development. For instance, to achieve the life goal of becoming a physician, a young person may believe that a medical career demonstrates a higher power's love for others, which in turn may motivate a student to excel academically.

Spiritual beliefs may also be connected to moral, cognitive, and socioemotional development throughout childhood and adolescence, although empirical findings remain mixed and contradictory (Bloom, 2013; Bussing et al., 2014; Regnerus, 2003). Fowler (1981) claims that spiritual faith begins in early childhood and develops from an initial poetic-conventional stage in which young children believe there are multiple pathways to learning the truth and meaning in life. According to Fowler, as children approach adolescence, they develop a more individuating reflective faith, in which they rely less on their parents' beliefs, and develop a more personal faith based on their own experiences. Related to Fowler's developmental theory, recent ToM research has explored children's and adolescents' under-standings of metaphysics, spirituality, the magical and supernatural and suggests that further longitudinal research with young people is needed (Kim & Harris, 2014a, 2014b; Harris, 2000; Woolley, 2014).

For example, past studies report a modest relation between measures of religiosity and self-esteem, or a sense of moral self-worth (Johnston & Krettenauer, 2011). Related cross-cultural research has reported positive associations between young people's religious involvement and self-esteem across numerous countries and has found that, for adolescents living in religious rural midwestern US communities, their religious involvement was positively associated with self-confidence (Aldwin et al., 2014; Bosacki et al., 2011). Finally, past research has found that perfectionism was more prevalent in adolescents who perceived themselves to be religious, and who exhibited idealistic tendencies and dichotomous thinking (Flett & Hewitt, 2014).

In contrast, past studies have found little relation found little relation between spirituality and self-esteem, and suggest that such a relation may exist only in contexts where religious involvement is associated with well-being and adjustment (Moore et al., 2012). Regarding the role of self-regulation and agency, in some of our past studies, we found that Canadian young adolescents' responses to self-agency questions (e.g., How did you get to be the kind of person you are?) reflected a larger number of references to spirituality compared to self, parents, or teachers (Bosacki et al., 2011). In sum, the majority of past studies on spiritual development have tended to focus on adults and older adolescents, whereas emerging adolescents' perceptions of religiosity and spirituality, although growing, remains largely unexplored. Moreover, the majority of past research on spirituality and religiosity has relied mainly upon measures of church attendance, and thus calls for future studies that also explore young people's religious and spiritual beliefs and perceptions of one's self and emotions (Bloom, 2013; Bussing et al., 2014; Koenig, McCullough, & Larson, 2012).

Moral sensitivities among youth

Research on emotional and moral sensitivities among gifted children may also help us to understand the social-emotional and moral correlates of social behavior in typically developing youth. As Davis and Rimm (1998) discussed, giftedness involves the four psychological concepts of self-awareness, perspective-taking, emotional experience, and empathy—although a person's experience of sensitivity is not necessarily expressed directly to others. Similarly, studies on sensitivity, emotional intensity, and social cognitive ability may help researchers to further explore the complex connections that exist between socioemotional competence and social moral communicative acts (Sternberg, Jarvin, & Grigorenki, 2011).

Researchers have also found that, the more developed or advanced a child's general cognitive ability, the earlier moral concerns develop and the more profound effect they have on the child. Interestingly, many researchers claim that it usually takes cognitive maturity before a young person learns to translate moral and emotional sensitivity into consistent moral action (Baudson & Preckel, 2013; Gardner, Csikszentmihalyi, & Damon, 2001). Thus, this ability to become cognizant of other's evaluations and social standards and conventions may be heightened among youth who are more sensitive to such social cues.

Similarly, as mentioned earlier, the ability to understand and experience self-conscious emotions such as pride, shame, guilt, and embarrassment has developmental origins around the second birthday. Such a claim is further supported by evidence that an additional founding factor of self-conscious emotions—the acceptance of others' standards for oneself—also begins to emerge at this time. That is, toward the end of the second year, toddlers become personally sensitive to normative standards and expectations for achievement and behavior.

For example, Kagan (1981) reported that, during toddlerhood, children become visibly concerned when standards of intactness and wholeness have been violated, such as when they notice missing puzzle pieces, broken toys, misplaced objects, torn book pages, misplaced objects, and so on (Lamb, 2002). These examples may illustrate an emerging moral sense because each event violates the implicit norms or standards that are typically enforced by caregivers (teachers, family members, etc.) through sanctions on damaged or broken objects (Kagan, 2005). Similarly, Kochanska and Kim's (2013) study on the social and moral development of young children showed that early responses to mishaps, incompleteness, or damage may reflect an emerging system of internal standards about right and wrong.

As discussed in Chapter 1, given the parallel social cognitive developmental events that occur between the transition times of early toddlerhood and emerging adolescence (Blakemore & Mills, 2014; Siegel, 2013), future research needs to explore if young adolescents are also more sensitive to societal conventions and moral and ethical violations. Moreover, an advanced social cognitive moral sensitivity may lead to social and emotional consequences for older children and adolescents labeled as gifted, and such youth may develop an exceptional sensitivity to such self-conscious and moral emotions (Dabrowski, 1967; Lagattuta et al., 2010). I will explore the emotional consequences of this learning exceptionality in Chapter 10.

Gender, emotionality, and social cognition

As mentioned in Chapter 1, there is a large body of research on gender differences in moral or self-conscious emotions and behaviors. Given the importance of the moral emotions in middle childhood and adolescence, in this section I will briefly outline selected past literature regarding gender differences found in moral emotion understanding and related behaviors. Further research on the role gender plays in social cognitive development will be explored in more detail in Chapter 8. In general, Hyde (2014) claims that there remain deeply ingrained cultural expectations for interpersonal moral behavior in young females as compared to males. Overall, compared to males, research has found that young females seem to learn earlier, and more completely, the messages that it is important to be compassionate and caring toward others, that it is wrong to hurt others, and, more generally, that it matters how people feel (Bussing et al., 2014; Hyde, 2014).

However, as mentioned in Chapter 4 on the emotional self, research on emotion understanding in childhood and youth remains mixed and contradictory, and may change over the course of development (Hughes, 2011). For example, Thompson and Voyer's (2014) recent meta-analysis of 551 studies on gender differences in emotion understanding studies showed a small overall advantage for females over males ($d = .19$), although the results changed with age. In particular, the gender differences were the smallest before the age of 13, and increased with age while leveling off in late development. Thompson and Voyer (2014) found that the effects were the most significant for the negative emotions (anger, sadness, fear), particularly anger.

Furthermore, evidence for a lack of gendered associations between moral emotions and ToM development builds on research by Cutting and Dunn (2002). As I mentioned in Chapter 3, Cutting and Dunn investigated whether having an earlier, more advanced understanding of mind might lead to greater sensitivity to criticism. That is, the more a child was aware of, and knew about what others might be thinking and believing, the more cognizant a child might also be that she or he could also be the subject of negative judgement and evaluation. Cutting and Dunn's findings showed that irrespective of gender, compared to kindergarteners with low false-belief understanding in preschool, 3- and 4-year-olds who demonstrated advanced false-belief understanding were more likely as kindergarteners to lower their evaluation of a "student" puppet's performance after it received negative remarks by the "teacher" puppet.

Further research to support gender similarity in children's emotional competence include Dunn's (1995) study that demonstrated children's ability to pass a false-belief task at 40 months predicted greater sensitivity to teacher criticism of their own work. Similarly, Lecce, Caputi, and Hughes (2011; Lecce, Caputi, & Pagnin, 2014) found that sensitivity to criticism played a mediating role between ToM and academic achievement among older children. Relatedly, our recent work on ToM and social cognition in middle childhood showed that high ToM scores in 6-year-olds predicted higher teacher ratings of social withdrawal in 8-year-olds (Bosacki, 2012). That is, children who had a sophisticated ToM ability at 6 years of age were more likely to be rated as socially withdrawn by their teachers two years later, but high teacher ratings of social withdrawal at 6 years did not predict high ToM at 8 years.

Thus, as I have noted previously (Bosacki, 2000, 2005, 2008), given the differences in physiological and social cultural experiences of female and male adolescents (Hyde, 2014), gendered connections may exist between young people's ToM development and the emergence of a "looking glass self" (Cooley, 1912), or self-knowledge that incorporates other's evaluations. Given the malleable fragility of the self during later childhood and early adolescence (Blakemore & Mills, 2014; Greenspan & Deardorff, 2014), when personal standards are not met, such a fragile sense of self could result in increased vulnerability to feelings of shame, guilt, and embarrassment. Such a connection may lead to inter- and intrapersonal relational challenges, and may develop more frequently in children and emerging adolescents labeled as sensitive, or socially withdrawn.

Given these contradictory results in gender-related differences in social cognition, especially ToM and moral emotion competence, many researchers call for the need for further longitudinal research (Hyde, 2014; Thompson & Voyer, 2014). I will return to the development of gender, emotional understanding, ToM, and self-knowledge in Chapter 8 when I discuss gender differences in social cognition. Such research will also be discussed in Chapter 10 when I explore the social cognitive development of socially withdrawn and unsociable children.

Neuroscience research and empathy

Although empathy or the capacity to take another person's perspective and understand their emotion has received much attention in childhood (Denham, 1998), surprisingly little research exists on individual differences in empathy, compassion, and moral reasoning development during emerging adolescence. Given that this ability is thought to increase throughout adolescence with advances in cognition and emotion, some evidence suggests that emerging adolescents diverge in their tendency to empathize. More specifically, as young people progress through adolescence, compared to boys, girls have been found to report a greater understanding of empathy and compassion, as well as engage in more empathic behaviors (Bussing et al., 2014; Saarni, 1999). To date, the limited research on individual differences and patterns of empathy and compassion development during adolescence reflects mainly group comparisons and short multiyear samples, with mixed findings (Bloom, 2013).

A relatively new area of research that explores the understanding and experience of empathy is the fields of evolutionary developmental science and neurocognitive research that explore the role of mirror neurons in moral and spiritual development (De Souza, 2014; Tomasello, 2014a; Waters & Tucker, 2013). Discovered by Rizzolatti and his colleagues in the mid-1990s (Rizzolatti & Fabbri-Destro, 2008), mirror neurons refer to a group of neurons, or a brain network, that respond or "mirror" another person's emotional experience to understand other people through their actions (Iacoboni & Dapretto, 2008). That is, in general, mirror neurons refer to areas of the brain that are activated when an individual observes a particular behavior and then mimics or mirrors the same behavior and emotions (Amodio & Ratner, 2013).

Past research suggests that the areas of the brain that may be implicated in this network include the premotor cortex, inferior frontal cortex, superior temporal sulcus, anterior insula, amygdala, and possibly others. However, this emerging research area continues to suffer from a lack of consensus (Wellman, 2014), and is explored in terms of additional social cognitive skills in emerging adolescents such as self-control (Amodio & Ratner, 2013; Bloom, 2013; Iacoboni & Dapretto, 2006; Mischel, 2014).

Given that this ability to mimic or "mirror" another person's emotional experience reflects a dynamic interplay of signals from frontal inhibitory circuits (De Souza, 2014), these mirror neurons (frontal and parietal), and null signals from receptors, allow us to enjoy reciprocity with others, while simultaneously maintaining our subjective experience

(Ramachandran, 2011). For example, recent research shows that when we observe another person's emotional experience such as anger, we experience the emotions of the other as reflected by their neurological activity and physiological responses (Keysers, 2011). However, mirror neuron research may not be sufficient to help researchers to understand the complex connections among language, and emotional and social reasoning within the context of peer relationships (Bloom, 2013).

To illustrate the complexity involving emotional reasoning and relationships, Laghi et al. (2014) found that, in a recent study of 111 Italian speaking 6-year-olds, children who reported having a reciprocal best friend scored higher on emotion understanding when compared to children who did not report such friendships. Thus, mirror neurons may not be sufficient to explain how the role of friendship and the quality of relationship between two people may influence one's ability to understand another's emotions, and perhaps act in altruistic and reciprocal ways (Banerjee, Watling, & Caputi, 2011; Betts & Stiller, 2014; Bosacki, 2015; Caputi, Lecce, Pagnin, & Banerjee, 2012; Fink, Begeer, Hunt, & de Rosnay 2014; Fink, Begeer, Peterson, Slaughter, & de Rosnay, 2015).

In sum, given the complexity of social interactions and the developing state of the brain during emerging adolescence, more research is needed to further explore the possible role mirror neurons play in young people's ability to use their social cognitive abilities such as ToM and empathy. Such research may help researchers to learn more about how youth use their ToM abilities to help negotiate their friendships and peer relations during emerging adolescence (Banerjee et al., 2011).

Neuroscience and evolutionary developmental research could also help us to understand how and why individual differences develop in young people's ability to understand moral reasoning and related actions and relationships (Busso, 2014; Waters & Tucker, 2013). For example, some studies show gender-related differences in young people's reports of morally disengaged reasoning strategies, and the experience of moral emotions (Paciello, Fida, Tramontano, Lupinetti, & Caprara, 2008; Tangney & Dearing, 2002). In particular, recent studies show young females demonstrated higher levels of moral reasoning and social responsibility than males (Bussing et al., 2014; Malti, Killen, & Gasser, 2012; Niemi, Hepburn, & Chapman, 2000; Sosik, Jung, & Dinger, 2009).

In contrast, research findings on gender-related differences in moral disengagement and moral development remain mixed (Vikan, Camino, & Biaggio, 2005). For example, some studies indicate that, compared to males, many young females may face social inequality in various countries across the globe and could possibly be sensitized toward moral issues depending upon the cultural context (Malti et al., 2012; Masten, 2014b). As I will further discuss in Chapter 8, the role of gender and culture in young people's social, moral, and cognitive development remains in need of further study, particularly in terms of neuroscience and evolutionary developmental science.

Neurocognitive developmental research suggests that changes in the brain that accompany puberty may underlie advances in empathy (Greenspan & Deardorff, 2014; Siegel, 2013; Waters & Tucker, 2013). Specifically, the areas of the brain responsible for perspective-taking mature and become more active during adolescence (Crone & Dahl, 2012). Neurological and hormonal changes also underlie shifts in adolescents' emotional processing, which in turn may lead them to experience emotions more intensely (Blakemore & Mills, 2014).

Despite these findings that link pubertal timing with cognitive and affective change, to date, researchers have failed to investigate the role of the endocrine systems in social cognitive development, or more specifically, the relation of pubertal development to empathy during emerging adolescence (Amodio & Ratner, 2013).

A recent related study on empathy in 12- to 13-year-old students within Chilean schools showed that individual differences in ToM levels among adolescents were partially attributable to sex, empathy, and fluid intelligence variability (Ibanez et al., 2013). In particular, Ibanez et al. found that female sex alone did not guarantee greater accuracy in ToM scores; a high level of empathy was also necessary. That is, compared to male adolescents, female adolescents with a relatively high level of empathy scored higher on ToM tasks. Such findings raise considerations for clinical and educational research, as well as ToM's theoretical models of domain specificity.

Positive moral emotions: Moral elation

Interestingly, the majority of the studies on empathy in young people tend to focus mainly on other people's negative emotions and pain compared to understanding how others experience positive emotions (Decety, 2011; Quoidbach, Berry, Hansenne, & Mikolajczak, 2010). Research on what is referred to as "moral elevation" focuses on how young people understand feelings of elation and extreme positive affect in others, or witnessing acts of moral beauty (Carter, 2014). Studies that have measured behavioral and neural changes as a function of "witnessing acts of moral beauty" in others shows that experiencing "other praising emotions," including admiration, gratitude, and elevation, can be accompanied by a novel set of experiences and emotional responses (Harbaugh & Vasey, 2014).

Such emotions or moral elation have been differentiated experimentally from more conventional positive emotions such as the more basic emotions of joy and amusement (Algoe & Haidt, 2009). For example, psychobiological research has shown that the biological basis of moral elevation may be derived from the phenomenology of this behavior, which includes autonomic shifts such as stomach flutters or "butterflies," chills, or tearing/crying (Carter, 2014).

Given that most humans gain pleasure from working together, share the emotions of others and experience emotional contagion (Harbaugh & Vasey, 2014), most emerging adolescents have the ability to experience emotional elation through the observation of the triumphs of others in different contexts such as the classroom or playground. Further, the experience of the physical and emotional consequences of the feelings of others may encourage youth to emulate the virtuous behavior of others, including the expression of prosocial behaviors and social cohesion (Bowker & Raja, 2011; Kob & Fredrickson, 2010; Quoidbach et al., 2010). Given the important implications research on moral elation has for social relationships within the classroom, future research needs to continue to explore the ability of youth to experience and understand positive moral emotions.

In Chapter 8, I will further discuss the role of gender and culture in young people's moral reasoning and experiences and understanding of moral emotions. As the ability to empathize is crucial to learning to engage in prosocial behavior, emerging adolescents continue to develop an awareness of the rules of social convention and communication, including the subtlety of manners and acts of kindness and compassion. In the next section, I will explore the process of social communicative acts within the context of politeness and social convention, and how young people learn to navigate increasingly complex social situations as they approach adolescence.

Applications: So What?

As I have argued throughout this book, and in agreement with many others (Bosacki, 2005; Noddings, 2003; Overton, 2013), a relational developmental social ecological systems learning model that connects education to therapy provides a useful foundation within which to develop constructivist, developmentally appropriate educational models. As Bridges reminded us over 90 years ago when he stated, "The inadequacy of psychology has also been brought home to us by educationists who seek assistance in their aim to train feelings and sentiments as well as behavior and intellect" (1925, p. 333), present-day research findings from developmental social cognitive science, resilience, and positive psychology could help to create developmentally appropriate educational and clinical programs (Donaldson, Dollwet, & Rao, 2015; Watkins, Uhder, & Pichinevskiy, 2015).

For example, findings from ToM research with young people can be used to help create a developmentally appropriate curriculum for emerging adolescents that aims to promote social and personal competence. Relatedly, as I will discuss further throughout this book, online positive psychology programs (OPP) have also recently been found to promote aspects of well-being and resilience among youth (Parks, 2014; Rose, 2014).

Another example of an empirically based educational program is the field of developmental discipline, which aims to establish trust within classrooms, and enlist young people's intrinsic motivations of autonomy and social connection to help students engage in personally motivated moral conduct (Nucci, 2013). This developmental discipline approach grounded in attachment theory shares similarities with preschool classroom management practices based on social cognitive theories of moral development (Grossman et al., 2002; Kerns, 2008). Developmental approaches to attachment and social cognition integrate affective warmth from caring adults with an emphasis on personal connection and relationships, and include moral discourse and reflection as tools for emotional growth and behavioral change (Marchetti, Castelli, Sanvito, & Massaro, 2014). Such approaches would be helpful for emerging adolescents as they highlight how emotional competence requires understandings of fairness and compassion, and moves beyond blind compliance to adult norms and values.

The learning process often includes the ability to accept counterintuitive claims in that a counterintuitive claim may indicate a truly counterintuitive state of the world (e.g., complex scientific concepts like gravity, and religious concepts like deities). Alternatively, counterintuitive phenomena that defies our perceptions may alternatively reflect the informant's ignorance, incompetence, or misperception (Lane, Harris, Gelman, & Wellman, 2015). Accordingly, such a process also entails that the learner trusts or believes the informant or teacher, as well as emotional safety, as trust is associated with aspects of care, regulated by moral and emotional reciprocity, and continuity (Noddings, 2003; Nucci, 2013).

As Noddings (2003) advocates, an "ethics of care" is an essential component of moral education. Consistent with the ability to care for and understand the emotional needs of others, Noddings (2003) suggests that schools need to promote the notion of moral interdependence. That is, according to Noddings, teachers and students need to listen to one another's values, beliefs, and emotional experiences, and to share responsibility for treating each other with respect and kindness. In general, researchers and educators need to ask how they can best contribute to the ethical, emotional, and moral development of the young person within an engaging and supportive learning community.

Recent attempts to apply some of the empirical findings on moral emotions to education suggest ways in which school practices might foster the emotional component of moral functioning (Nucci, 2013). Unfortunately some research maintains the misconception that cognition and affect operate independently (Nucci, 2013). For example, critics state that emotivist models claim people's responses to moral events are directed by a set of inborn affective triggers, and that moral reasoning occurs after explaining our personal emotional reactions to ourselves (Bloom, 2013). Others claim that such emotivist models fail to adequately account for the ways in which cognitions influence affect regulation. That is, the final cognitive appraisal of a social situation that would help children to navigate their social and emotional worlds depends upon our thoughts and emotions. Such emotivist theories may possibly misrepresent the ways in which cognition and affect are reciprocally mutual and interrelated, and more research is necessary to determine the implications of such emotion theories (Damasio, 2010).

In contrast to the emotivist approaches, more integrative and comprehensive theories of how affect plays a role in young people's moral, emotional, and social development are gaining momentum within the educational field. Such contextual-based emotional models suggest that children associate different feelings with different domains of social events. Issues of social conventions generally elicit "cool" or neutral affect on the part of children (Denham, 1998).

Such models may also suggest why some children choose to comply as well as to transgress (Johnston & Krettenauer, 2011). For example, when children experience "hot" emotions, adults who occasionally respond with anger to children's conventional transgressions help to shape children's moral development. Issues of morality, however, are often viewed by children within the classroom as filled with "hot" emotions of anger, fear, and sadness among victims of transgressions, and experiences of happiness occur mainly among all parties where moral situations turn out fairly.

Another example of a developmental educational program that promotes social, emotional, and moral growth through social and emotional interactions is the extension of school-based social experiences to include community service activities. While efforts to promote youth engagement in community service within North America can be traced to William James (Nucci, 2013), community service is currently most often linked to the school curriculum in the form of mandated requirements it is labeled as "service learning." Moreover, "civil education" also aims to promote social responsibility and civility such as courteous and polite behaviors (Keyes, 2002; Malin, 2011).

Programs for service learning are diverse and include a range of activities, from tutoring or coaching youth sports to working in a local hospital, community soup kitchen, or a community shelter for the homeless. Based on the diversities of such activities, the impact of service learning has been difficult to evaluate empirically. However, some research suggests that effective service-learning programs have the potential to lead to an increased level of civic engagement, and an increase in positive action and a decrease in rates of delinquent behaviors (Youniss, McLellan, & Yates, 1999).

Past research suggests that service learning and civility education may positively impact students' social and emotional growth as it provides the learner with the opportunity to have a degree of choice for the activity. Past research shows positive relations between the ability to make choices to engage in personally meaningful activities and self-motivation and a healthy self-development among youth (Damon, 2008). Although in the past, the majority of service-learning programs have been a part of secondary schools (Malin, 2011), service-learning programs that promote emotional and social connection with others could be integrated into grade school classrooms through the implementation of routine field trips to hospitals, community centers, pen pal clubs with children or the elderly in a long-term care facility, animal rescue shelters, and so on. Therefore, service-learning programs within a caring and civil learning environment could promote interpersonal competence and growth, as well as an emotionally healthy sense of self among youth.

A second critical factor is that service-learning activity may also provide an opportunity for children to develop the ability to be mindful and critically reflective (Coholic, 2011). The degree of reflection varies from program to program from activities such as writing a one-page reflection paper or song, a poem, painting or drawing, or keeping a daily journal. As noted by cognitive literacy researchers (Donaldson, 1992; Olson, 1994), critical reflection is an important social cognitive skill in that it affords learners the opportunity to share and discuss their thoughts and emotional experiences, and to connect those experiences to their personal values and sense of self.

As discussed earlier, some researchers suggest that emotions are stored as part of the co-construction of social cognitive representations (Saarni, 1999), and repeated experiences may help children to form generalized social and emotional scripts (Saarni, 1999). As outlined in this chapter, through the use of psychoeducational programs, educators and developmental neurocognitivists can work together to create evidence-based educational activities combined with emotional coaching that encourage emotional awareness and coping skills in youth, and may be especially useful for all young people who experience shyness, social anxiety, and other emotional and social cognitive challenges in the classroom (Banerjee et al., 2011; Leeves & Banerjee, 2014).

Given the possible valuable research tools of various psychoeducational programs that incorporate mental state or ToM language, how do we use such language tools to promote emotional health in children and to help promote children to become wise and caring listeners within the North American and increasingly global cultural mosaic? How do we as educators and developmentalists address the universality as well as the unique diversity of human emotion and the emotion language across the North American cultural landscape?

For example, given the increasing diversity in the school population within Canada, how feasible will it be for government and policymakers to integrate language programs to represent all ethnicities in schools? Who will decide which language becomes part of the official or explicit curriculum? If linguistic universals such as concepts of "good" and "bad" exist (Wierzbicka, 2006), how can educators incorporate the use of such universals in the classroom to promote effective and caring social communication within a culturally competent and supportive classroom?

Further educational implications of the study of moral and emotional development include recent trends that emphasize the integration of social responsibility and civility in high school and collegiate educational institutions. Consistent with Just Community Theory (Powers, Higgins, & Kohlberg, 1989), are service-learning programs in US schools (Billig, 2000; Malin, 2011), emerging resilience development programs (Masten, 2014b; Rose, 2014), and the Compassionate Heart Scholars Program in China (Luo et al., 2011). Such findings may support the notion that "when one wants to improve moral behavior, one has to improve the contextual moral atmosphere in which the behavior occurs" (Host, Brugman, Tavecchio, & Beem, 1998, p. 48). Past studies indicate higher levels of social responsibility for older adolescents enrolled in education and nursing programs compared to students enrolled in economics, engineering, and fine arts programs (Host et al., 1998).

Building on prior studies (Malin, 2011), future research needs to identify ways to raise students' level of social responsibility and collective intentionality. For example, moral education courses in later elementary and high school may help to address the increasing demand of adult professions and organizations for a more socially responsible and ethical workforce (Crocetti et al., 2012; Killinger, 2008; Melo & Galan, 2011). Moreover, future studies should examine the contextual elements of the school's moral atmosphere or climate, and other specific aspects of the curriculum that are conducive to students' moral development in countries across the globe.

It is essential that the fields of education and social sciences (psychology, anthropology, sociology, etc.) continue to work collaboratively toward a dialectical educational approach. Such an approach would advance dialogue (inter- and intrapersonal) through pedagogical practice. These practices would promote engagement and critical inquiry through mutuality, reciprocity, and care rather than detachment and distance. Consistent with a relational developmental approach to development and education (Bruner, 1996; Overton, 2013), educational programs need to promote critical reflection and discussion that may lead to social cognitive competence.

To promote the creation of a connected classroom that encourages emerging adolescents to become courageous, reflective, and creative, teachers need to foster the development and use of the moral and spiritual voice (De Souza, 2014). Given the link between arts and language-based holistic teaching activities and social cognitive development (e.g., Coplan, Bullock, Archbell, & Bosacki, 2015; Donaldson, 1992), teachers can also implement a variety of teaching activities to foster moral and emotional learning. For instance, the use of activities that promote both critical reflection and self-expression, such as bibliotherapy, journal writing, psychodrama, and meditation, have the potential to foster the connection between intellect and morals, values, and ethics.

Educational activities that are ambiguous and open ended may also have the potential to encourage youth to take risks and be creative by expressing their moral voice (Damon, 2008). Thus, such activities promote imagination and divergent thinking, and encourage learners to seek patterns of self-discovery by learning to listen to and integrate their inner voices with their schooling experiences. Further examples of such pedagogy and learning activities will be discussed in more detail in Chapter 11.

Young people's understanding of self, others, and society supports their developing ability to consider other's rights and needs. That is, their growing sense of morality, or the general set of standards about right and wrong including such traits as honesty, compassion, and respect for other people's rights and needs, is in part dependent upon their social cognitive understanding (Nucci, 2013; Talwar, Arruda, & Yachison, 2015). As Noddings (2003) claims, if happiness is connected to moral goodness, exactly how do children learn this "moral goodness?" Thus, how do schools and youth workers promote this aspect of humanity in learners without over accentuating perfectionism or virtuousness?

As Noddings (2003) claims, one of the most challenging educational tasks is to encourage students to tolerate ambiguity, in that uncertainty will not lead to psychological paralysis and the prevention of social commitments. Given that educational programs, such as "character education" or Values in Action (VIA) programs aim to help our youth become and remain "happy," how can such programs also fulfill government mandates to promote academic excellence and superior performance across standardized tests? As educators and youth workers both struggle to answer the question of how to encourage youth to be "caring scholars," the challenge to balance ethics with academic excellence is relevant to schools across the globe (Gardner et al., 2001; Masten, 2014a).

As many moral educators suggest (Ferragut, Blanda, & Oritz-Tallo, 2014; Linkins et al., 2015), how can moral educators promote what researchers refer to as "good character," including the six key virtues or character capacities of wisdom, courage, humanity, transcendence, temperance, and justice? As Linkins et al. note, the majority of the VIA programs' broad dimensions of strength often fail to recognize all of the virtues or competencies. The range of traits endorsed by most character education programs usually fall within just three of the six VIA virtue clusters: courage, justice, and humanity. The many strengths within the wisdom, temperance, and transcendence virtue clusters largely fall outside of the traditional scope of character education. Thus, a more holistic and inclusive VIA-based approach into the classroom may serve to illustrate, and validate, a wider range of personal competencies.

As I mentioned in Chapter 2, researchers and educators continue to address cultural and moral diversity through the inclusion of diverse faith orientations within educational programs. Aside from addressing the rich tapestry of various religious faiths, educators also need to further the discussion concerning Catholic schools, given that it remains a controversy, particularly in Canada and larger North America. For example, within Canada, differences within Christian, Jewish, and Muslim, among other faith communities, are rarely addressed, for example, the distinction between Roman and Ukrainian Catholics. Thus, the creation of a developmentally appropriate curriculum that is sensitive to the diverse ethnicities and faiths of emergent adolescent learners and teachers will remain a challenge for future educators and researchers working within culturally diverse populations.

Although many researcher educators aim to raise awareness in parents and educators in spirituality and education, effective, evidence-based practical implications remain to be seen. For example, schools require feasible recommendations that may develop policies to foster a healthy pluralism in a morally diverse and complex society. Future curriculum needs to promote the theme of diversity in moral and spiritual realms, and foster moral and spiritual development and related social cognitive skills within the classroom.

During the writing of this book, I envisioned a future volume that would include research from a greater number of countries, including developing and technologically advanced countries from all across the globe. To reflect the importance of cultural diversity, and to ensure that everyone has the opportunity to share their spiritual/educational experiences, future work in social cognitive development should aim to include the multiple voices from around the globe.

Many social cognitive researchers suggest that, as industrialized countries become more diverse and pluralistic, there is a need for a coherent educational policy regarding religion and spirituality in the classroom (Hoechsmann, 2009; Masten, 2014b). To promote "meaningful and inclusive" pluralism, such a policy needs to include the partnerships of various people in the community: educators, parents, social science researchers, among others. Educational guidelines need to focus on the promotion of intellectual competencies, as well as to provide opportunities to foster critical thinking and reflective skills that enable learners to create new questions as opposed to "the answer."

Future Questions

Given the conceptual links between spirituality and morality, within a developmental social cognitive framework, how can researchers explore the question of how moral and spiritual reasoning develops throughout childhood and adolescence? From a psychological perspective, as previously discussed, early adolescence (approximately 8 to 13 years) is recognized as a pivotal time in all aspects of development including cognitive reflexivity (Piaget, 1981; Siegel, 2013), self-concept formation (Greenspan & Deardorff, 2014; Harter, 1999), and interpersonal relations (Rosenberg, 1965; Selman, 1980). Despite recognition of this complex and multifaceted developmental milestone, a transdisciplinary, relational approach that explores the links between self and social understanding, and the development of morality and spirituality remains to be taken. Thus, further research is necessary to explore children's and adolescents' perspectives of complex concepts such as mental worlds of self and other within a moral and spiritual context.

Despite the large literature base regarding bullying and moral actions, such as how does one decide whether or not to either help or harm others (Volk, Dane, & Marini, 2014), very little research exists on the complex process of helping within a social cognitive context. Thus, future research needs to explore how young people's reasoning about how cooperative behaviors such as helping and compromising relate to their sociocognitive development. Future work should consider a heterogeneous sample and a longitudinal design to study developments over time. To increase our understanding about children's reasoning about the refusal to help, future research could also examine related social cognitive abilities to social perspective-taking, such as empathy and multiple classification ability. Research also suggests that it is important to distinguish between different forms of prosocial behavior (for an overview, see Paulus, 2014; Paulus & Moore, 2012), and future work could focus on the influence of social and emotional costs and benefits in situations of sharing and comforting behavior.

As many writers provide neurophilosophical and biological explanations of morality (Bloom, 2009, 2013; DeWaal, 2009; Tomasello, 2014b), social cognitive developmentalists need to ask how brain-based science can help us to understand how our neurobiology and our interpersonal interactions help to guide our moral compasses? Similarly, what role does neuroscience research play in the study of how people learn and choose to be cruel, and the origins of empathy and the concept of "evil" among humanity (Bloom, 2013). As researchers and educators work together to promote positive emotional and mental health, neurosociobiological research of social skills and the nature of the capacity to attribute mental states to others may help us to understand the emotional, social, and moral worlds of adolescence.

Summary

Given that education is a moral and spiritual enterprise (Coles, 1990), the main task for future educators will be to continue to combine the study of how the mind is created and used (developmental cognitive neuroscience) within the educational practice. Perhaps the combined efforts of neuroscientists with developmentalists and moral educators who share the goal of understanding the inner worlds of our youth may help to develop research and educational programs that encourage youth to become caring and compassionate learners within the context of a socially responsible and civil community. Thus, I return to the theme with which this chapter began, educators need to re-examine and redefine the current frames of social cognitive development, education, and the moral learner as we aim to create an interdisciplinary research area that attempts to unite all three.

Ultimately, the goal of humanistic, social constructivist developmentalists is to encourage youth to develop a sense of direction, vision, and a caring and compassionate mind, which in turn will assist in lifelong learning and the motivation to search for meaning (Spiel, Schober, Wagner, & Finsterwald, 2012). Eventually, such a vision of "schooling" will help to weave the moral fabric that will encourage learners to develop the courage to wonder why silences, ambiguities, and contradictions exist and how to glean meaning from them. As I have discussed in depth elsewhere (Bosacki, 2005, 2012), such silences and ambiguities should be explored and celebrated within a caring and connected classroom. Given that this chapter outlined moral learning within the context of social cognitive development, in the next chapter, I will discuss how social cognition and moral action develop within the context of peer relations.

References

Aldwin, C. M., Park, C. L., Jeong, Y.-J., & Nath, R. (2014). Differing pathways between religiousness, spirituality, and health: A self-regulation perspective. *Psychology of Religion and Spirituality, 6*(1), 9–21.

Algoe, S., & Haidt, J. (2009). Witnessing excellence in action: The "other-praising" emotions of elevation, gratitude and admiration. *Journal of Positive Psychology, 4*, 105–127.

Amodio, D., & Ratner, K. (2013). The neuroscience of social cognition. In M. Anderson & S. Della Sala (Eds.), *Neuroscience in education: The good, the bad, and the ugly* (pp. 702–728). Oxford, England: Oxford University Press.

Baird, J. A., & Astington, J. W. (2004). The role of mental state understanding in the development of moral cognition and moral action. In J. Baird & B. W. Sokol (Eds.), *Connections between theory of mind and sociomoral development* (New Directions for Child and Adolescent Development No. 103, pp. 37–49). San Francisco, CA: Jossey-Bass.

Bandura, A. (1991). Social cognitive theory of moral thought and action. In W. Kurtines & J. Gewirtz (Eds.), *Handbook of moral behavior and development* (Vol. 1, pp. 45–103). Hillsdale, NJ: Erlbaum.

Banerjee, R., Watling, D., & Caputi, M. (2011). Peer relations and the understanding of faux pas: Longitudinal evidence for bidirectional associations. *Child Development*, *82*, 1887–1905. doi: 10.1111/j.1467-8624.2011.01669.x

Batson, C. D. (1998). Altruism and prosocial behavior. In D.T. Gilbert, S.T. Fiske, & G. Lindzey (Eds.), *The handbook of social psychology* (Vol. 2, 4th ed., pp. 282–316). Boston, MA: McGraw Hill.

Baudson, T., & Preckel, F. (2013). Teachers' implicit personality theories about the gifted: An experimental approach. *School Psychology*, *28*(1), 37–46.

Betts, L., & Stiller, J. (2014). Centrality in children's best-friend networks: The role of social behaviour. *British Journal of Developmental Psychology*, *32*, 34–49.

Billig, S. H. (2000, May). Research on K-12 school based service learning: The evidence builds. *Phi Delta Kappan*, 658–664.

Blakemore, S.-J., & Mills, K. (2014). Is adolescence a sensitive period for sociocultural processing. *Annual Review of Psychology*, *65*, 187–207.

Bloom, P. (2009). *Descartes' baby*. New York, NY: Basic Books.

Bloom, P. (2013). *Just babies: The origins of good and evil*. New York, NY: Random House.

Bosacki, S. (2000). Theory of mind and self-concept in preadolescents: Links with gender and language. *Journal of Educational Psychology*, *92*, 709–717.

Bosacki, S. (2005). *Culture of classroom silence*. New York, NY: Peter Lang.

Bosacki, S. (2008). *Children's emotional lives: Sensitive shadows in the classroom*. New York, NY: Peter Lang.

Bosacki, S. (2012). Socioemotional competence, self-perceptions, and receptive vocabulary in shy Canadian children. *International Electronic Journal of Elementary Education*, *4*(3), 573–591.

Bosacki, S. (2015). Children's theory of mind, self-perceptions, and peer relations: A longitudinal study. *Infant and Child Development*, *24*, 175–188. doi: 10.1002/icd.1878

Bosacki, S., Harwood, D., & Sumaway, C. (2012). Being mean: Children's gendered perceptions of peer teasing within the classroom. *Journal of Moral Education*, *41*, 473–489. doi: 10.1080/03057240.2012.690728

Bosacki, S., Moore, K., Talwar, V., & Park-Saltzman, J. (2011). Preadolescents' gendered spiritual identities and self-regulation. *Journal of Beliefs and Values*, *32*(3), 303–316. doi:10.1080/136172/2011.627679

Bowker, J. C., & Raja, R. (2011). Social withdrawal subtypes during early adolescence in India. *Journal of Abnormal Child Psychology*, *39*, 201–212. doi:10.1007/s10802-010-9461-7

Bridges, J. (1925). A reconciliation of current theories of emotion. *The Journal of Abnormal Psychology and Social Psychology*, *19*, 333–340.

Bruner, J. (1996). *The culture of education*. Cambridge, MA: Harvard University Press.

Bussing, A. (2010). Aspects of spirituality, God images, and the "self-centredness" in 17 year old adolescents attending religious education at high school. *Research on Steiner Education*, *1*, 70–79.

Bussing, A., Föller-Mancini, A., Gidley, & Heusser, P. (2014). Aspects of spirituality in adolescents. *International Journal of Children's Spirituality*, *15*, 25–44.

Busso, D. (2014). Neurobiological processes of risk and resilience in adolescence: Implications for policy and prevention science. *Mind, Brain, and Education*, *8*, 34–43.

Caputi, M., Lecce, S., Pagnin, A., & Banerjee, R. (2012). Longitudinal effects of theory of mind on later peer relations: The role of prosocial behavior. *Developmental Psychology*, *48*(1), 257–270. doi/abs/10.1080/17405629.2013.821944

Carter, S. (2014). Oxytocin pathways and the evolution of human behavior. *Annual Review of Psychology*, *65*, 17–39.

Coholic, D. (2011). Exploring the feasibility and benefits of arts-based mindfulness-based practices with young people in need: Aiming to improve aspects of self- awareness and resilience. *Child and Youth Care Forum*, *40*(4), 303–317.

Coles, R. (1990). *The spiritual life of children*. Boston, MA: Houghton Mifflin.

Cooley, C. (1912). *Human nature and social order*. New York, NY: Scribner.

Coplan, R. J., Bullock, A., Archbell, K. A., & Bosacki, S. (2015). Preschool teachers' attitudes, beliefs, and emotional reactions to young children's peer group behaviors. *Early Childhood Research Quarterly*, *30*, 117–127. doi:10.1016/j.ecresq.2014.09.005

Crocetti, E., Jahromi, P., & Meeus, W. (2012). Identity and civic engagement in adolescence. *Journal of Adolescence*, *35*, 521–532.

Crone, E. A., & Dahl, R. E. (2012). Understanding adolescence as a period of social-affective engagement and goal flexibility. *Nature Reviews Neuroscience*, *13*, 636–650. doi:10.1038/nrn3313

Cushman, F., Sheketoff, R., Wharton, S., & Carey, S. (2013). The development of intent-based moral judgment. *Cognition*, *127*, 6–21. doi:10.1016/j.cognition.2012.11.008

Cutting, A., & Dunn, J. (2002). The cost of understanding other people: Social cognition predicts young children's sensitivity to criticism. *Journal of Child Psychology and Psychiatry*, *43*, 849–860.

Dabrowski, K. (1967). *Personality shaping through positive disintegration*. Boston, MA: Little, Brown.

Damasio, A. (2010). *Self comes to mind: Constructing the conscious brain*. New York, NY: Pantheon Books.

Damon, W. (2008). *The path to purpose: How young people find their calling in life*. New York, NY: Simon & Schuster.

Davis, G., & Rimm, S. (1998). *Education of the gifted and talented* (4th ed.). Needham Heights, MA: Allyn & Bacon.

Decety, J. (2011). The neuroevolution of empathy. *Annual New York Academy of Science*, *1231*, 3–45.

Del Giudice, M. (2014). Middle childhood: An evolutionary-developmental synthesis. *Child Development Perspectives*, *4*, 193–2000.

Denham, S. (1998). *Emotional development in young children*. New York, NY: Guilford.

De Souza, M. (2014). The empathetic mind: The essence of human spirituality. *International Journal of Children's Spirituality*, *19*, 45–54.

DeWaal, F. (2009). Bodies talking to bodies. In *The age of empathy: Nature's lessons for a kinder society* (pp. 46–83). New York, NY: Three Rivers Press.

Donaldson, M. (1992). *Human minds: An exploration*. Harmondsworth, England: Allen Lane.

Donaldson, S., Dollwet, M., & Rao, M. (2015). Happiness, excellence, and optimal human functioning revisited: Examining the peer-reviewed literature linked to positive psychology. *The Journal of Positive Psychology*, *10*, 185–195.

Dunn, J. (1995). Children as psychologists: The later correlates of individual differences in understanding of emotions and other minds. *Cognition and Emotion*, *9*, 187–201.

Eisenberg, N., Martin, C. L., & Fabes, R. A. (1996). Gender development and gender effects. In D. C. Berliner & R. C. Calfee (Eds.), *Handbook of educational psychology* (pp. 358–396). New York, NY: Macmillan.

Ferragut, M., Blanda, M., & Oritz-Tallo, M. (2014). Psychological virtues during adolescence: A longitudinal study of gender difference. *European Journal of Developmental Psychology*, *11*, 521–531. doi:10.1080/17405629.2013.876403

Fink, E., Begeer, S., Hunt, C., & de Rosnay, P. (2014). False-belief understanding and social preference over the first 2 years of school: A longitudinal study. *Child Development*, *85*, 2389–2403.

Fink, E., Begeer, S., Peterson, C., Slaughter, V., & de Rosnay, P. (2015). Friendlessness and theory of mind: A prospective longitudinal study. *British Journal of Developmental Psychology, 33*, 1–17.

Flett, G., & Hewitt, I. (2014). A proposed framework for preventing perfectionism and promoting resilience and mental health among vulnerable children and adolescents. *Psychology in the Schools, 51*, 899–912.

Fowler, J. (1981). *Stages of faith: The psychology of human development and the quest for meaning.* New York, NY: Harper and Row.

Fu, G., Xiao, W. S., Killen, M., & Lee, K. (2014). Moral judgment and its relation to second-order theory of mind. *Developmental Psychology, 50*, 2085–2092.

Gardner, H., Csikszentmihalyi, M., & Damon, W. (2001). *Good work: When excellence and ethics meet.* New York, NY: Basic Books.

Gordon, H., Lyon, T., & Lee, K. (2014). Social and cognitive factors associated with children's secret-keeping for a parent. *Child Development, 85*, 2374–2388.

Greenspan, L., & Deardorff, J. (2014). *The new puberty: How to navigate early development in today's girls.* New York, NY: Rodale.

Grossmann, K., Grossmann, K. E., Fremmer-Bombik, E., Kindler, H., Scheuerer-Englisch, H., & Zimmermann, P. (2002). The uniqueness of the child–father attachment relationship: Fathers' sensitive and challenging play as a pivotal variable in a 16-year longitudinal study. *Social Development, 11*, 307–331.

Harbaugh, C., & Vasey, M. (2014). When do people benefit from gratitude practice? *Journal of Positive Psychology, 9*, 535–546.

Harris, P. (2000). On not falling down to earth: Children's metaphysical questions. In K. Rosengren, C. Johnson, & P. Harris (Eds.), *Imagining the impossible: The development of magical, scientific, and religious thinking in contemporary society* (pp. 157–178). Cambridge, England: Cambridge University Press.

Harter, S. (1999). *The construction of the self: A developmental perspective.* New York, NY: Guilford.

Hayashi, H. (2007). Children's moral judgments of commission and omission based on their understanding of second-order mental states. *Japanese Psychological Research, 49*, 261–274. doi:10.1111/j.1468-5884.2007.00352.x

Hoechsmann, M. (2009). Convertoons? Veggie tales for young souls. In S. Steinberg & J. Kincheloe (Eds.), *Christotainment: Selling Jesus through popular culture* (pp. 117–130). Boulder, CO: Westview Press.

Host, K., Brugman, D., Tavecchio, L., & Beem, L. (1998). Students' perception of moral atmosphere in secondary school and the relationship between moral competence and moral atmosphere. *Journal of Moral Education, 27*(1), 47–70.

Hughes, C. (2011). *Social understanding and social lives: From toddlerhood through to the transition to school.* New York, NY: Psychology Press.

Hyde, J. (2014). Gender similarities and differences. *Annual Review of Psychology, 65*, 373–398.

Iacoboni, M., & Dapretto, M. (2006). The mirror neuron system and the consequences of its dysfunction. *Nature Review Neuroscience, 7*, 942–951.

Ibanez, A., Huepe, D., Gemp, R., Gutierrez, V., Riveria-Rei, A., & Toledo, M. (2013). Empathy, sex and fluid intelligence. *Personality and Individual Differences, 54*, 616–621.

Jambon, M., & Smetana, J. G. (2014). Moral complexity in middle childhood: Children's evaluations of necessary harm. *Developmental Psychology, 50*, 22–33. doi:10.1037/a0032992

Jeynes, W. (2002). A meta-analysis of the effects of attending religious schools and religiosity on black and Hispanic academic achievement. *Education and Urban Society, 35*, 27–49.

Johnston, M., & Krettenauer, J. (2011). Moral self and moral emotion expectancies as predictors of anti- and prosocial behavior in adolescence: A case for mediation? *European Journal of Developmental Psychology, 8*, 228–243.

Kagan, J. (1981). *The second year: The emergence of self-awareness.* Cambridge, MA: Harvard University Press.

Kagan, J. (2005). Human morality and temperament. In G. Carlo (Ed.), *Moral motivation through the lifespan. Nebraska Symposium on Motivation* (Vol. 15). Lincoln, NE: University of Nebraska Press.

Kerns, K. A. (2008). Attachment in middle childhood. In J. Cassidy & P. Shaver (Eds.), *Handbook of attachment* (2nd ed., pp. 366–382). New York, NY: Guilford.

Keyes, C. L. (2002). Social civility in the United States. *Sociological Inquiry, 72*, 393-408.

Keysers, C. (2011). *The empathetic brain: How the discovery of mirror neurons changes our understanding of human nature.* Lexington, KY: Social Brain Press.

Killinger, B. (2008). *Integrity: Doing the right thing for the right reason.* Montreal, Canada: McGill-Queen's University Press.

Kim, S., & Harris, P. L. (2014a). Belief in magic predicts children's selective trust in informants. *Journal of Cognition and Development, 15*, 181–196.

Kim, S., & Harris, P. L. (2014b). Children prefer to learn from mind-readers. *British Journal of Developmental Psychology, 32*, 375–387. doi:10.1111/bjdp.12044

Kob, B., & Fredrickson B. (2010). Upward spirals of the heart: Autonomic flexibility, as indexed by vagal tone, reciprocally and prospectively predicts positive emotions and social connectedness. *Biological Psychology, 85*, 432–436.

Kochanska, G., & Kim, S. (2013). Early attachment organization with both parents and future behavior problems: From infancy to middle childhood. *Child Development, 84*, 283-296. doi:10.1111/j.1467-8624.2012.01852.x

Koenig, H. G., McCullough, M. E., & Larson, D. B. (2012). *Handbook of religion and health.* New York, NY: Oxford University Press.

Lagattuta, K. H., Nucci, L., & Bosacki, S. L. (2010). Bridging theory of mind and the personal domain: Children's reasoning about resistance to parental control. *Child Development, 81*, 616–635. doi:10. 1111/j.1467-8624. 2009.01419.x

Lagattuta, K. H., & Weller, D. (2014). Interrelations between theory of mind and morality: A developmental perspective. In M. Killen & J. Smetana (Eds.), *Handbook of moral development* (2nd ed., pp. 385–407). New York, NY: Psychology Press.

Laghi, F., Baiocco, R., Di Norcia, A., Cannoni, E. Baumgartner, E., & Bombi, A. (2014). Emotion understanding, pictorial representations of friendship, and reciprocity in school-aged children. *Cognition and Emotion, 28*, 1338–1346.

Lamb, M. E. (2002). Father involvement and child development: Section preface. In C. S. Tamis-LeMonda & N. Cabrera (Eds.), *Handbook of father involvement: Multidisciplinary perspectives* (pp. 91–92). Mahwah, NJ: Erlbaum.

Lane, J., Harris, P., Gelman, S., & Wellman, H. (2015). More than meets the eye: Young children's trust in claims that defy their perceptions. *Developmental Psychology, 50*, 865–871.

Larson, R. (2011). Positive development in a disorderly world. *Journal of Research in Adolescence, 21*, 317. doi:10.1111/j.1532-7795. 2010.00707.x

Lecce, S., Caputi, M., & Hughes, C. (2011). Does sensitivity to criticism mediate the relationship between theory of mind and academic achievement. *Journal of Experimental Child Psychology, 110*, 313–331.

Lecce, S., Caputi, M., & Pagnin, A. (2014). Long-term effect of theory of mind on school achievement: The role of sensitivity to criticism. *European Journal of Developmental Psychology, 11*(3), 305–318. doi/abs/10.1080/ 17405629.2013.821944

Leeves, S., & Banerjee, R. (2014). Childhood social anxiety and social support-seeking: Distinctive links with perceived support from teachers. *European Journal of Psychology of Education, 29*, 43–62.

Linkins, M., Niemiec, R., Gillham, J., & Mayerson, J. (2015). Through the lens of strength: A framework for educating the heart. *The Journal of Positive Psychology, 10*, 64–68.

Luo, R., Shi, Y., Zhang, L., Liu, C., Li, H., Rozelle, S., & Sharbono, B. (2011). Community service, educational performance and social responsibility in northwest China. *Journal of Moral Education, 40*(2), 181–202.

Maas, F. K. (2008). Children's understanding of promising, lying, and false belief. *Journal of General Psychology, 135,* 301–322. doi:10.3200/GENP.135.3.301-322

Malin, H. (2011). American identity development and citizenship education: A summary of perspectives and call for new research. *Applied Developmental Sciences, 15,* 111–116.

Malti, T., Killen, M., & Gasser, L. (2012). Social judgments and emotion attributions about exclusion in Switzerland. *Child Development, 83,* 697–711.

Marchetti, A., Castelli, I., Sanvito, L., & Massaro, D. (2014). Is a bird in the hand worth two in the future? Intertemporal choice, attachment and theory of mind in school-aged children. *Frontiers in Psychology, 5,* 483–493.

Masten, A. (2014a). Global perspectives on resilience in children and youth. *Child Development, 85,* 6–20.

Masten, A. (2014b). *Ordinary magic: Resilience in development.* New York, NY: Guilford.

Melo, T., & Galan, J. I. (2011). Effects of corporate social responsibility on brand value. *Journal of Brand Management, 18,* 423–437.

Miller, S. (2009). Children's understanding of second-order mental states. *Psychological Bulletin, 135*(5), 749–773. doi:10.1037/a0016854

Miller, S. A. (2012). *Theory of mind: Beyond the preschool years.* New York, NY: Psychology Press.

Mischel, W. (2014). *The marshmallow test: Mastering self-control.* New York, NY: Little, Brown.

Moore, K., Talwar, V., & Bosacki, S. (2012). Diverse voices: Children's perceptions of spirituality. *International Journal of Children's Spirituality, 17,* 217–234. doi:10.1080/1364436X.2012.742040

Niemi, R. G., Hepburn, M., & Chapman, C. (2000). Community service by high school students: A cure for civic ills? *Political Behavior, 21,* 45–69.

Noddings N. (2003). *Happiness and education.* Cambridge, England: Cambridge University Press.

Nucci, L. (2013). It's a part of life to do what you want. The role of personal choice in social development. In B. Sokol, M. Grouzet, & U. Muller (Eds.), *Self-regulation and autonomy: Social and developmental dimensions of human conduct* (pp. 165–188). New York, NY: Cambridge University Press.

Overton, W. F. (2013). A new paradigm for developmental science: Relationism and relational-developmental systems. *Applied Developmental Science, 17,* 94–107. doi:10.1080/10888691.2013.778717

Paciello, M., Fida, R., Tramontano, C., Lupinetti, C., & Caprara, G. V. (2008). Stability and change of moral disengagement and its impact on aggression and violence in late adolescence. *Child Development, 79*(5), 1288–1309.

Parks, A. (2014). A case for the advancement and design of online positive psychological interventions. *The Journal of Positive Psychology, 9,* 502–508.

Paulus, M. (2014). The emergence of prosocial behavior: Why do infants and toddlers help, comfort, and share? *Child Development Perspectives, 8,* 77–81.

Paulus, M., & Moore, C. (2012). Producing and understanding prosocial actions in early childhood. In J. B. Benson (Ed.), *Advances in child development and behavior* (pp. 271–305). London, England: Academic Press.

Perner, J., & Wimmer, H. (1985). "John thinks that Mary thinks that…": Attribution of second-order beliefs by 5- to 10-year-old children. *Journal of Experimental Child Psychology, 39,* 437–471. doi:10.1016/0022-0965(85)90051-7

Peterson, C., & Seligman, M. E. P. (2004). *Character strengths and virtues: A handbook and classification.* Washington, DC: American Psychological Association.

Piaget, J. (1981). *Intelligence and affectivity: Their relationship during children's development.* Palo Alto, CA: Annual Reviews.

Powers, F. C., Higgins, A., & Kohlberg, L. (1989). *Lawrence Kohlberg's approach to moral education*. New York, NY: Columbia University Press.

Quoidbach, J., Berry, E. V., Hansenne, M., & Mikolajczak, M. (2010). Positive emotion regulation and well-being: Comparing the impact of eight savoring and dampening strategies. *Personality and Individual Differences, 49*(5), 368–373.

Ramachandran, V. (2011). *The tell-tale brain: Unlocking the mystery of human nature*. London, England: Heinemann.

Regnerus, M. (2003). Religion and positive adolescent outcomes: A review of research and theory. *Review of Religious Research, 44*, 394–413.

Rizzolatti, G., & Fabbri-Destro, M. (2008). The mirror system and its role in social cognition. *Current Opinion in Neurobiology, 28*, 179–184.

Rose, R. (2014). Self-guided multimedia stress management and resilience training. *Journal of Positive Psychology, 9*, 489–493.

Rosenberg, M. (1965). *Society and the adolescent self-image*. Princeton, NJ: Princeton University Press.

Saarni, C. (1999). *The development of emotional competence*. New York, NY: Guilford.

Selman, R.L. (1980). *The growth of interpersonal understanding: Developmental and clinical analyses*. New York, NY: Academic Press.

Siegel, D. (2013). *Brainstorm: The power and purpose of the teenage brain*. New York, NY: Jeremy Tarcher/Penguin.

Smetana, J. G., Jambon, M., Conry-Murray, C., & Sturge-Apple, M. L. (2012). Reciprocal associations between young children's developing moral judgments and theory of mind. *Developmental Psychology, 48*, 1144–1155. doi:10.1037/a0025891

Sosik, J. J., Jung, D. I., & Dinger, S. L. (2009). Values in authentic action: Examining the roots and rewards of altruistic leadership. *Group & Organization Management, 34*(4), 395–431.

Spiel, C., Schober, B., Wagner, P., & Finsterwald, M. (2012). Assuring successful life-long learning: Can neuroscience provde the key? In M. Anderson & S. Della Sala (Eds.), *Neuroscience in education: The good, the bad, and the ugly* (pp. 286–289). Oxford, England: Oxford University Press.

Sternberg, R., Jarvin, L., & Grigorenki, E. (2011). *Explorations in giftedness*. New York, NY: Cambridge University Press.

Talwar, V., Arruda, C., & Yachison, S. (2015). The effects of punishment and appeals for honesty in children's truth-telling behavior. *Journal of Experimental Child Psychology, 130*, 209–217.

Tangney, J. P., & Dearing, R. L. (2002). Gender differences in morality. In R. F. Bornstein & M. Masling (Eds.), *Empirical studies in psychoanalytic theories: Vol. 10. The psychodynamics of gender and gender role* (pp. 251–269). Washington, DC: American Psychological Association.

Thompson, A., & Voyer, D. (2014). Sex differences in the ability to recognize non-verbal displays of emotion. *Cognition and Emotion, 28*, 1164–1195.

Tomasello, M. (2014a). *A natural history of human thinking*. Cambridge, MA: Harvard University Press.

Tomasello, M. (2014b). The ultra-social animal. *European Journal of Social Psychology, 44*, 187–194.

Vikan, A., Camino, C., & Biaggio, A. (2005). Note on a cross-cultural test of Gilligan's ethic of care. *Journal of Moral Education, 34*(1), 107–111.

Volk, A. Dane, A., & Marini, Z. (2014). What is bullying? A redefinition. *Developmental Review, 34*, 327–343.

Waters, A., & Tucker, D. (2013). Social regulation of neural development. In B. Sokol, M. Grouzet, & U. Muller (Eds.), *Self-regulation and autonomy: Social and developmental dimensions of human conduct* (pp. 279–296). New York, NY: Cambridge University Press.

Watkins, P., Uhder, J., & Pichinevskiy, S. (2015). Grateful recounting enhances subjective well-being: The importance of grateful processing. *The Journal of Positive Psychology, 10*, 91–98.

Wellman, H. (2014). *Making minds: How theory of mind develops*. Oxford, England: Oxford University Press.

Wierzbicka, A. (2006). *Emotions across languages and cultures: Diversity and universals.* Cambridge, England: Cambridge University Press.

Witt, A. L. (2001). Person-situation effects and gender differences in the prediction of social responsibility. *The Journal of Social Psychology, 130,* 543–553.

Woolley, J. (2014). Commentary: What do mind readers know and what do we know about mind readers? *British Journal of Developmental Psychology, 32,* 388–390.

Youniss, J., McLellan, J., & Yates, M. (1999). Religion, community service, and identity in American youth. *Journal of Adolescence, 22,* 243–253.

Part III

Social Cognitive Educational and Developmental Research
Social

"*Happiness is a hard master—particularly other people's happiness.*" (Huxley, 1932, p. 200)

Section Overview

Building on Marshall, Parker, Ciarrochi, and Heaven's (2014) claim that how young people view themselves helps to shape the way they interact with others, the next section will provide a critical overview of innovative research that explores the social worlds of the young person and how this may affect their sense of self and social cognitions. In particular, the next three chapters will focus on various social contexts that may influence social cognitive development in youth, specifically peers (Chapter 6), family (Chapter 7), and society including gender, ethnicity, and social class (Chapter 8).

Social Cognition in Middle Childhood and Adolescence: Integrating the Personal, Social, and Educational Lives of Young People, First Edition. S. L. Bosacki.
© 2016 John Wiley & Sons, Ltd. Published 2016 by John Wiley & Sons, Ltd.

6

Peer Relationships

"I desire the company of a man who could sympathise with me; whose eyes would reply to mine." (Shelley, 1969/1818, p. 19)

Introduction

Chapter 6 details past research on the social worlds of the young person involving their peer relationships. In particular, the chapter will focus on the language and verbal and nonverbal communication that occurs during peer conversations and social exchanges.

Research

Language, communication, and social relations

As mentioned by past theorists and researchers (Blos, 1979; Lerner, Lerner, Von Eye, Bowers, & Lewin-Bizan, 2011), emerging adolescence is considered a stage of reindividuation, when the child reorganizes and differentiates the self-concept. Given that the sense of self is derived from our social experience (Bruner, 1996), young people's social experiences with their peers play a significant role in the development of their self-concept (Selman, 1980; Sullivan, 1953). Accordingly, a relational developmental systems approach to social cognition in adolescence may assist in the investigation of the links between cognitive representations of self and other and social communication within peer relationships (Lerner et al., 2011). That is, intentional elements of social understanding or Theory of

Social Cognition in Middle Childhood and Adolescence: Integrating the Personal, Social, and Educational Lives of Young People, First Edition. S. L. Bosacki.
© 2016 John Wiley & Sons, Ltd. Published 2016 by John Wiley & Sons, Ltd.

Mind (ToM) suggest that higher order mental states are necessary for effective social interactions (Hughes, 2011; Miller, 2012; Selman, 1980).

According to folk psychology, social interaction is an interaction of minds that consists of mental states that are expressed through speech acts. That is, social interaction does not proceed directly via the interaction of these mental states, it proceeds indirectly by way of language (Astington, 1993). This notion is expressed in various speech-act theorists' claims that communication relies on both speaker and listener. Participants engaged in conversation take into account each other's knowledge and intentions (Grice, 1957) and, over time, young people develop varying levels of communicative competence (Donaldson, 1992).

In relation to the emerging adolescent's cognitive development, as previously noted, by early adolescence (ages 10 to 12 years), children are capable of abstract, recursive thought (Piaget, 1981). Research shows that, by this time, children's increased processing abilities (i.e., central conceptual structures) enable the integration of multiple perspectives to create coherent, meaningful messages. Within the context of narrative thought, studies on narrative complexity and cognitive competence have shown that the structural complexity of children's narratives increases with age, and that this increase may be attributed to information-processing capacity (Bruner, 1996).

Research on young people's mental states, language, and social interaction has found that the understanding of mental states in others is reflected by the use of metacognitive (e.g., believe, think, know), and metalinguistic verbs (e.g., assert, say, concede). Each set of verbs represent mental states and speech acts respectively (Rochat, 2009). The use of such mental state verbs has implications for higher-order interpersonal relations in that it represents one's own stance or position toward another person's mental states (Laing, 1961; Tomasello, 2014a). For example, the statement "she claims that she is hungry" implies that she believes it is true that she is hungry, but the speaker may not share her belief. Thus, the expression of mental states in speech acts facilitates interpersonal communication and truth-sharing in that it provides the basis for the ability to "read each other."

Emerging adolescents' ability to relate to their peers may also be partly influenced by their ability to understand mental states in others as expressed through their speech acts. However, peer relations are often excluded from studies that investigate psycholinguistic and pragmatic issues. For example, past research has shown connections between communicative ability and ToM in young adolescents in terms of speech acts such as the understanding of irony, promising, and gesture (Astington, 1993; Filippova & Astington, 2008; Goldin-Meadow, 2014). However, within emerging adolescents, related areas of social cognition including social competence, secret-keeping, peer networks, and friendship histories have yet to be approached from a ToM perspective (Banerjee, Watling, & Caputi, 2011; Betts & Stiller, 2014; Bosacki, 2013; Devine & Hughes, 2013; Fink, Begeer, Hunt, & de Rosnay, 2014; Gordon, Lyon, & Lee, 2014).

Research on emerging adolescents' ToM and their acquisition of mental state verbs may assist in the investigation of how young people come to understand intentional relations within the peer milieux (Bosacki, 2008). For example, past ToM research on relations between preschoolers' ToM and social behaviors, as well as intentional attribution, supports the claim that emerging adolescents draw on the intentional element of social understanding within social relations (Hughes, 2011). In sum, to understand some aspects of the emerging adolescent mind within the context of peer relationships, the next few sections will outline the research on ToM understanding, self-concept, and social relations. Such research, then, may provide a rich data base for the exploration of the developing matrix of social cognition and peer relations within later childhood and adolescence.

Social cognition and peer relations

A vast amount of research exists on young people's social cognitive abilities and peer relations, including studies that have demonstrated a link between self-cognitions and social behavior. In brief, the majority of studies show that positive feelings of self-worth are related to positive social experiences and prosocial behavior (Kashdan, Weeks, & Savostyanova, 2011; Roeder et al., 2014; Schaffer, 1996). More specifically, such studies have shown a positive relation between young people's self-concept and social competence (Bosacki, 2008; Harter, 1999), self-concept and peer acceptance and victimization (Blakemore & Mills, 2014; Roeder et al., 2014), and self-concept and attachment (Bosacki, Bialecka-Pikul, & Szpak, 2014).

Although peer relations play a large role in young people's social cognitive and affective development (Bosacki, 2015; Sullivan, 1953), teachers have also been found to affect the emerging adolescent's inner world. For example, recent research shows that although family, peers, and teachers had a cumulative positive influence on young people's general and academic self-concept, teachers had the most significant influence (Duckworth & Carlson, 2013). In addition to teachers and peers, sociocultural factors such as family structure (i.e., birth order, number of siblings) (Dunn, 2002; Kluger, 2011; Sulloway, 1996), cultural background (Rivas-Drake et al., 2014), and media exposure have also been suggested to influence social cognitive thought and behavior (Turkle, 2011, 2015).

Related research findings on social cognitive abilities and social relations in emerging adolescents remain contradictory and inconclusive. Social cognitive processes such as ToM, empathetic sensitivity, and person perception have all been found to be related to teacher and peer ratings of positive social behavior ratings and peer acceptance (Hughes, 2011). In contrast, some studies have failed to find any relations between various social cognitive abilities and sociometric status and peer relations. In particular, some past studies on 11–12-year-olds have failed to find significant associations between components of social reasoning such as referential communication and means–ends problem-solving and peer popularity (Bosacki, 2000). Similarly, in a sample of 11–13-year-olds, Salmivalli and Isaacs (2005) failed to find any significant relations between peer victimization and self-perception. Thus, the lack of consistent findings concerning social cognitive skills and peer ratings highlights the need for further study.

Ambiguities of social exclusion, silences, and ostracism

Young people's abilities to communicate effectively with others depend partly upon social cognitive knowledge and skills that may have little or nothing to do with language per se. As outlined in the previous chapter, social conventions that govern appropriate verbal interaction are referred to as sociolinguistic behaviors (Nucci, 2013). For example, students learn that they may have to greet others, and that conversations usually end with some form of a sign-off or signal of finality. Such behaviors fall within the broader domain of pragmatics, which includes learning the rules of conversational etiquette, such as turn-taking in conversations, stating goodbye when leaving, as well as strategies for initiating conversations, changing the topic of conversation, storytelling, and the ability to persuade others (Grice, 1975; Kołodziejczyki & Bosacki, 2015; Slaughter, Peterson, & Moore, 2013).

Building on this idea of social rule lessons, children and adolescents continue to refine their pragmatic skills and sociolinguistic conventions throughout the preschool years and elementary grades (Miller, 2009). However, this development is affected by the cultural differences in social communication (Masten, 2014). That is, through family and peer interactions, children from divergent cultures often learn different social conventions, particularly within the area of social etiquette. How then, do these cultural ways of treating others regarding social etiquette continue to develop during later childhood and into adolescence?

For example, psycholinguistic research explores how gender and ethnicity influence how youth learn effective communication through the subtleties of social language rules such as politeness and manners (Grice, 1975). As I explore further in Chapter 11, how can we help youth to learn how to cultivate the art of delicate social conversation and gesture, and to speak and act with discretion, respect, and kindness, and interpret the ambiguity of conversational silences? Also, regarding the increasingly diverse cultural landscape of North America, is the development of such a skill as "tact" or social discretion feasible within the context of political correctness? Such questions need to be addressed by future research, and I will describe some examples below regarding the increasing subtleties of "microaggressions" and cultural teasing.

One situation commonly found among older children and adolescents includes the multiple forms of social withdrawal such as shyness, social avoidance, unsociability, and regulated withdrawal (Coplan, 2014; Ding et al., 2015; Özdemir, Cheah, & Coplan, 2015; Rubin, Burgess, & Coplan, 2002). Within this framework, silence and social withdrawal have the potential to reflect negative social experiences and emotions, and may carry different psychological meanings. These experiences of silence may be especially pronounced during social group situations, where verbal expression is often equated with confidence, popularity, and social status. Such situations occur frequently within the social hierarchies of youth, when a peer with high social status may hold psychological power over another peer.

That is, such a peer may harass or psychologically damage a peer with lower social status through social silence or negative nonverbal communication (i.e., looks or gestures of disgust at the targeted individual, mocking actions). A popular adolescent may choose not to speak to another peer or to ignore social requests. This "silent treatment" may be interpreted as a form of psychological harassment or rejection, particularly if the recipient of the silence experiences emotional harm.

Alternatively, as discussed earlier, some emerging adolescents find it stressful to join social groups, or are so painfully shy that they may decide to remain silent in a group situation to avoid the negative feelings that may arise from possible rejection (Blote,

Bokhorst, Miers, & Westenberg, 2012; Rubin et al., 2002). That is, a young person may wish to talk with another peer, but future-oriented thought including rejection, social judgment, and/or ridicule may prevent them from taking the risk to express their thoughts. Negative forecasting may thus inhibit some youth to contribute to the conversation as they feel incapable of speaking due to fear. This process of self-silencing enables the youth to decide to either remain silent or to withdraw from the social situation.

In contrast, individuals who are verbally and socially competent may experience feelings of control and powerfulness, as they may be aware of their ability to influence another person's behavior. However, such youth may also decide to remain silent in that they are socially disinterested. They may lack the motivation to approach others while at the same time not necessarily having the motivation to avoid others. That is, when such individuals, sometimes referred to as "unsociable," are approached by others, they will not remain reticent and retreat and may not experience wariness and anxiety (Arbeau & Coplan, 2007; Rubin, Coplan, & Bowker, 2009). Shyness and unsociability will be further discussed in Chapter 10 on social cognition in atypical populations.

As I have discussed in my previous work on silences and social ambiguities (Bosacki, 2005, 2012), examples of social and personal ambiguity include social exclusion and ostracism, which often contain experiences of silence as feeling ostracized or ignored by the other in that one is "being silenced" by others. The experience of "feeling invisible," of being excluded from the social interactions of those around you, is discussed in more detail later on in the book. Moreover, silence will also be discussed in relation to forms of psychological and emotional harassment, bullying, and teasing, in virtual and real worlds.

Given that the peer group plays a large role in psychosocial, spiritual, and emotional health (Lightfoot, 1997; Twenge, 2011), the act of silencing someone else, or the "silent treatment," has significant ramifications for emerging adolescents' sense of self and their social relationships. As researchers have noted (Harter, 1999), engagement in some risk-taking behaviors may sometimes be due to the need to belong, and to avoid ostracism and rejection (Finy, Bresin, Korol, & Verona, 2014; Williams, 2001).

Given that many older children may experience increased self-consciousness and sensitivity as they approach adolescence, targeted youth may wonder why they are being excluded and how could they have provoked this treatment (Rochat, 2009). For example, the private script of the sensitive student may include questions like: "Why am I being left out and ignored?" "What don't they like about me?" "Am I a bad person and that's why they don't want to be my friend?" As I will explain further in Chapter 11 on educational implications, educators need to work with such youth who appear sensitive to such subtle cues of social exclusion, as such hostile internal dialogue could lead to deleterious effects on one's sense of self.

Ambiguity surrounding ostracism may lead some adolescents to develop social anxiety, gelotophobia, self-doubt, lowered self-esteem, and other related emotional health challenges. Developmental psychologists have documented the use of shunning and exclusion behaviors in children as a form of peer rejection (Asher & Coie, 1990; Gazelle, 2013; Gazelle & Ladd, 2003). For example, Barner-Barry (1986) described a case where a preschool class systematically ostracized a bully (i.e., ignored him, excluded him from conversations and playing) without adult prompting. Such a case suggests that the use of ostracism as a means of controlling the behavior of other is both adaptive and innate.

Research with adolescents suggests that, compared to males, some young females may choose ostracism as a favored strategy during conflicts, or as a form of psychosocial aggression, described as "the manipulation of group acceptance through alienation, ostracism, or character defamation" (Cairns, Cairns, Neckerman, Ferguson, & Gariepy, 1989, p. 323). In contrast to females, Cairns et al. (1989) found that adolescent males preferred to resort to physical violence as a means of conflict resolution.

According to Underwood (2002), ostracism may be viewed as another form of social aggression, That is, in contrast to direct aggression, to ostracize someone, individuals direct aggression toward damaging another's self-esteem and/or social status. Additional direct forms consist of negative facial expressions, body movements, and verbal rejections, and/or social rumors. Ostracism may also be considered a form of relational and psychological aggression, which includes behaviors aimed at harming others through the purposeful manipulation and damage of their peer relationships and self-worth.

Related research on sociometric and social competence, including peer popularity and social acceptance, has also examined young people's experiences of social silence or peer exclusion (Recchia, Brehl, & Wainryb, 2012; Schuster, 1996). For example, Schuster found that rejected children or those disliked by their peers, and neglected children or those not noticed by their peers, experienced victimization. In particular, rejected adolescents were more likely to experience victimization, whereas neglected children were not. Both types of adolescents claimed to have felt victimized, although in different ways, in that rejected adolescents experienced more direct acts of rejection and social silencing. In the next section, I will discuss the role silence and ambiguity plays in bullying, victimization, teasing, and deception among older children and young adolescents.

Deception, teasing, and psychological bullying within emerging adolescence

Negative moral behaviors: microaggression and deception   Microaggressions could also be considered within the context of subtle psychosocial teasing among peers—and this "teasing" usually focuses on the target's cultural background and gender. Recent research suggests that microaggressions including microinsults, microassaults, and microinvalidations have increased during adolescence, and may have inimical influences on a young person's mental and emotional well-being. Emerging research suggests that the sociolinguistic skill of effective microaggression production may be partially dependent upon one's intentions to emotionally harm another person (Casanova et al., 2014; McWhorter, 2014).

The process of microaggressions within emerging adolescence will be explored further in Chapter 8 when I discuss the roles gender and culture play in adolescents' social cognitive development. As Henry Louis Gates, Jr. stated, researchers and educators need to address this newly evolved social communication regarding cultural and gender-based issues among all ethnicities as this will be "the only way that you can produce a multicultural, ethnically diverse environment" (Gates, cited in Vega, 2014, A14).

Teasing and microaggressions   Microaggressions and teasing research has shown that such hostile actions may have a deleterious influence on a youth's psychological state and identity (Casanova et al., 2014). For example, Gleason, Alexander, and Somers (2000) found that older adolescents reacted to different types of teasing, and that early experiences of teasing had negative influences on their self-esteem. They examined the extent to which three types of childhood teasing experiences (competency, weight, and appearance) predicted adolescents' perceived self-worth and body image. Furthermore, the pattern of relations for each gender was explored in a groups of 89 female and 75 male undergraduates from two midwestern universities, with a mean age of 20. Results showed that more frequent teasing in childhood was significantly predictive of lower self-esteem and poorer body image among adolescent females and males. More specifically, teasing type and participant gender influenced whether or not teasing was related to self-esteem and body image.

Future research should also explore the links among relational aggression, teasing, and microaggressions in terms of young people's ToM and understanding of irony and sarcasm (see Chapter 3). The cognitive and linguistic approaches to harmful or hostile social inter-actions need to be explored and combined with the social, emotional, and moral approaches. Such approaches would have important implications for educators, especially the development of social-emotional learning (SEL) programs that include activities that pro-mote compassionate, kind, respectful, and peaceful language directed toward the self and others. Educational programs that promote personal and social compassion and peace will be elaborated on in Chapter 11 within the framework of intervention implications.

As I will discuss further in Chapter 9, on the role technology plays in social cognitive development, research on social withdrawal and the need to be alone becomes further complicated when we consider technology and the virtual world. Which social, emotional, and moral factors guide young people's choices to avoid face-to-face communication or private telephone calls, but to connect with others virtually? How do young people's self-cognitions and social experiences differ according to their choice of mode of communication in a virtual, electronic world, or a physical world? We will explore these questions further in Chapter 9 on the digital world and social media.

The issue of virtual versus real life also complicates the experiences of ostracism and social exclusion during later childhood and adolescence. To what extent do experiences of online social exclusion differ from experiences of in-person social exclusion? How do we know if these two different experiences create the same level and intensity of emotions? Why should we be concerned? Past research on face-to-face (FtF) and virtual ostracism encourages us to investigate the role technology plays in social relations (Turkle, 2011; Williams, 2001). That is, past research suggests that given that the Internet has the potential to be an effective and powerful communicative tool to harm or help others, some young people decide to use the Internet as a psychological weapon to hurt others and/or themselves, while some use technology to help and support others.

Given the ambiguous and complex social context of the emerging adolescent's leisure life and classroom, as children approach adolescence, some may learn how to hone their social cognitive abilities, including ToM understanding, to help them to navigate the sometimes perhaps tumultuous landscape of adolescence (Hughes, 2011; Tomasello, 2014b). That is, sophisticated social cognitive abilities may help youth to understand the social ambiguities among their peers which in turn may encourage them to help as opposed to hurt others within social situations (Bosacki, 2012).

Research on deception and social interactions across the lifespan is wide and varied (Fu, Xiao, Killen, & Lee, 2014). Research on deception and young adults suggests that a form of lying or deception involves the ability to misrepresent reality in the absence of a literal falsity. According to Schauer and Zeckhauser (2009), paltering or actions of insincerity involve the use of meaningless pieces of truth to create a false impression or illusion. That is, the process of paltering involves the intentional creation of a wrong impression through deliberate action. In other words, paltering is a deliberate attempt to create a misimpression in someone by means other than uttering a literal falsehood.

As outlined by Schauer and Zeckhauser (2009), paltering includes the ability to understand other's mental states in that one must understand that another person may hold a false belief that the palterer intends to create. However, in contrast to a literal falsity, the palterer may use alternative, more indirect and subtle means to create a false sense of belief in the other or the person who is deceived. To illustrate the process of paltering within an emerging adolescent social context, imagine a scenario that involves a teenaged female who wants her friends to believe that she is also friends with a particular male in her class. Although the girl (palterer) knows that she does not know this particular male, she could refer to the male by his first name to create the illusion to her friends that she knows this particular male and that perhaps they are friends.

Overall, this act of paltering includes a deliberate action to create a wrong impression in her friends rather than uttering a literal falsehood. That is, the palterer does not state directly that she is friends with this particular male as this would be a literal falsity and thus a lie. In contrast, by referring to the male by his first name, the palterer creates a context of pretense or illusion in which only she is aware of the deception involved, unbeknownst to her friends. That is, her actions deliberately lead her friends to believe that she (the palterer) is already friends with the particular male classmate.

Given this challenge to detect the subtle and ambiguous nature of misrepresentation, the process of paltering and social deception in emerging adolescence and how it relates to advanced ToM abilities also requires further study (Devine & Hughes, 2013; Hughes, 2011). Future research could also explore individual differences in young people's ToM and their deception choices either through direct lying, or a version of paltering. For example, recent research found that the sophistication of 8–16-year-olds' lies was significantly related to executive functioning abilities such as working memory, inhibitory control, and planning skills (Evans & Lee, 2011).

Interestingly, Evans and Lee (2011) found that the participants' reasons or motivations to lie were not necessarily related to their social cognitive skills. Thus, their data suggest that there is a need for future research on deception and social cognitive abilities such as advanced ToM and affective time travel or forecasting in older children and adolescents. Moreover, future research could explore the ambiguity of adolescents' deception choices, especially regarding socially ambiguous contexts when the moral choice is not always clear.

Building on Evans and Lee's study (2011), future research could explore how adolescents understand social ambiguities by investigating the connections between indirect lying or paltering and young people's ToM ability and self-concept. Also, to what extent are adolescents' motivation to palter to others related to the process of self-paltering (and vice versa), and does this relation differ according to the level of deception? What are the emotional experiences and thoughts of the palterer before, during, and after the event, and how does this differ in terms of individuals? Furthermore, how does the experience of paltering compare to the experiences of liars and various levels of deception—and across various modes of communication (e.g., virtual, FtF). I will return to such questions regarding the role of technology in deception in Chapter 9 when I discuss the role digital technologies play in adolescents' understanding of digital social ambiguity and self-representation.

Friendship in emerging adolescence: Social cognition and peer teasing   As paltering is a particular type or level of lying, teasing also falls on a moral continuum, as it is defined more as a mode of play than a form of bullying (Keltner, Capps, Kring, Young, & Heerey, 2001). Similar to paltering, psychological bullying and relayed forms of teasing are more psychological and subtle and, thus, more difficult for educators to identify as an inimical and possibly destructive behavior (Volk, Dane, & Marini, 2014). Within the ambiguous context of play and friendship in older childhood and emerging adolescence, teasing is sometimes referred to as an example of playful aggression. That is, the ambiguous act of teasing may increase as players learn how to navigate the ambiguities of living within the higher levels of school classrooms such as social hierarchies, friendships, and romantic relationships, social norms and social conflicts. Thus, teasing could be defined as a form of aggression as well as a mode of play with the intent to provoke others (Bosacki et al., 2012).

Teasing often occurs within the paradoxical context of relationships involving a continuum of friendships and is situated somewhere on that emotional continuum, ranging from a tease being a "playful nip" to being a full-fledged bullying statement or threat. Such ambiguous interactions make it difficult for the "teasee" (recipient or target of the tease) to determine which element of the interaction (verbal, nonverbal) deserves a response. Thus, the element or component of the teasing interaction that the teasee chooses to focus on may influence their emotional response.

When an individual is engaged in the process of teasing, Shapiro, Baumeister, and Kessler (1991) explain that "the target must decode an ambiguous message to arrive at an attribution of the teaser's true intention" (p. 466). That is, the target needs to recognize whether "he or she is being insulted or is being engaged in play" (p. 466). According to Boxer and Cortés-Conde (1997) "as with all talk, much depends on the identification of context, and indeed the exact message cannot be interpreted without encoding/decoding the metamessage" (p. 279). Within the scope of contextual information, in addition to pre-existing relationships between those involved and linguistic and paralinguistic cues, it is important to be aware of the intent of the teaser and the interpretation by the target.

However, although there are cues to aid interpretation, a recipient of teasing cannot always be expected to interpret teasing as a humorous event. That is, whether or not a comment or "tease" that is meant to be "funny" by the teaser is considered funny or hurtful is dependent upon the emotional response of the recipient. For instance, Eder's (1993) research on teasing in adolescent females defines teasing as "any playful remark aimed at another person, which can include mock challenges, commands, and threats, as well as imitating and exaggerating someone's behavior in a playful way" (p. 17).

Keltner et al.'s (2001) research shows that the ability to tease improves with age or social cognitive development. During late childhood, anywhere between ages 8 and 11, most typically developing children become more sophisticated in their abilities to interpret contradictory propositions about objects in the world. That is, most children at this age begin to move from either/or, absolute reasoning to a more interpretive and complex understanding of the world. Such an ability parallels children's ability to understand humor, sarcasm, and irony as well as gesture, as described earlier (Bosacki, 2013; Goldin-Meadow, 2014; O'Reilly, Peterson, & Wellman, 2014), and also allows the child to learn how to palter or misrepresent the truth without stating a literal falsity (i.e., the production of an insincere statement). Thus, given the connections between Keltner's work on teasing and literature on verbal deception, future research needs to investigate how adolescents interpret ambiguous contexts such as teasing and deception within friendships, and how they manage and cope with their emotional experiences.

Ambiguities in adolescent friendships: Prosocial behaviors and the role of the bystander and bully-victims

Given the paradoxical context of play and friendship that involves negative and positive emotions and social interactions (Rubin et al., 2009; Sullivan, 1953), ambiguity plays a role in situations that involve an emergency or psychological and emotional crisis. A major determinant of helplessness may be the characteristics of the stimulus for help. Research shows that ambiguous cues may result in fewer attempts to help, while distress cues that indicate greater rather than less need for assistance may lead to more help.

Ambiguity may also give rise to concern that a helpful act may be considered inappropriate, or appear foolish and thus may activate an approval goal. Darley and Latané (1968) emphasized that ambiguity often surrounds an emergency in that when a person faces the distress of a peer the nature or source of the other's distress is often unknown or unclear. For example, within the context of emerging adolescence, ambiguity and uncertainty often surround social situations that contain a level of risk such as within friendship, as well as bullying situations.

Ambiguity and uncertainty about a peer's need for help, and about the type of action one should take, may increase the observer's or bystander's anxiety and emotional discomfort. Thus, a youth may decide to reduce the probability that she will approach the victim, bully, or bully-victim. Ambiguity may also enable a peer to interpret the emotional distress cues of another peer in alternative ways.

Helping and altruistic behavior   Recent evidence on helping behavior and altruism from developmental evolutionary psychology with primates and much younger children may help researchers understand emerging adolescents' bystander and helping behavior within peer bullying scenarios (Tomasello, 2014b). To illustrate, Hepach, Vaish, and Tomasello (2013) found that young children's intrinsically motivated helping behavior develops from sympathetic concern for the other person. When 18-month-old children showed sympathetic concern for someone as measured in their facial expressions—for example, because a girl just had her toy destroyed—they subsequently helped her more often than in a neutral condition. Thus, the amount of sympathetic concern shown for the victim correlated positively across individuals with their tendency to help as revealed in a direct physiological measure of arousal such as pupil dilation.

Hepach et al. (2013) found that young children were equally satisfied when they helped someone in need and when they witnessed that person being helped by a third party. Further, they were also more satisfied in both of these cases than when the person was not being helped at all. Young children's motivation may not have been so much to help, but to witness the other helped. That is, given that research suggests that to benefit one's reputation, one has to perform the act oneself, Hepach et al.'s study suggested that a concern for self-reputation and reciprocity is probably not one of the main motivations for young children's helping behavior.

Overall, past research shows that even young children seem intrinsically motivated to help others in various situations. The evolutionary basis of this prosocial behavior might represent the interdependence of individuals who need one another for foraging success, and so are naturally concerned with each other's welfare (Bloom, 2013; Paulus, 2014; Tomasello, 2014b). The proximate, psychological motivation of individuals, however, seemingly does not involve considerations of this type; it may be simply intrinsically motivating and emotionally satisfying to help others.

Bystanders play an important role in the process of bullying and victimization as they are witnesses to a situation that contains emotional distress and an imbalance of power (Rigby & Johnson, 2006; Salmivalli & Isaacs, 2005; Staub, 1971; Voeten, Poskiparta, & Salmivalli, 2011). Past research shows that the majority of students in middle childhood and adolescence report they often choose to serve as a bystander within the bullying process. More specifically, the role of a bystander is diverse, as they could serve as a defender, comforter, reinforcer, passive observer, or assistant or follower of the bully, depending on the strategy they enact (Voeten et al., 2011). However, the level of helping behavior and the chosen strategy may differ according to the bystander's past or present relationship with the bully and victim. In addition, the gender and cultural background of the young people involved in the bullying scenario may also have an influence on the bystander's behavior.

For example, if a girl witnesses another peer being teased by two other girls, at which point of the interaction will the bystander (or witness) chose to intervene, and if she decides to help, to what extent? That is, a girl who observes another girl being teased by two others has the opportunity to make some decisions. She could act in the following ways: (1) ask the two girls to stop teasing the victim, (2) befriend the victim and ask her to join her and leave the situation, or (3) leave the scene of the teasing and seek assistance from a guardian such as a teacher or older student. Alternatively, the girl could choose to join the two girls and tease the victim or target, or leave the scene without mentioning the incident to anyone. In addition to the level of familiarity the bystander has with the bullies and victim, the bystander's behavior may differ according the gender and cultural backgrounds of the participants in the bullying scenario. Thus, the ambiguity of the situation provides the bystander with the opportunity to interpret the situation, and then decide which action to take (either harmful or helpful).

The scenario described above illustrates the complex process of bullying within the context of friendship and shows the integration of goal-directed power imbalance and harm. Given that few studies exist on the role of bully-victims and bystanders within children's friendships (Marini, Dane, Bosacki, & YLC-CURA, 2006; Özdemir & Stattin, 2011; Volk et al., 2014), future studies could explore peer experiences of bullying and friendship within later children and early adolescence. For example, what defines a "true" bully, victim, bystander, bully-victim, and how do these definitions differ from a "true" friend? Moreover, given diverse contexts and relationships during later childhood and early adolescence, what is the likelihood that these roles are interchangeable?

More specifically, researchers have studied the role of bystanders in emergency situations, or situations that include violence or harm to another individual (Darley & Latané, 1968; Nucci, 2013). Research has demonstrated that, under various conditions, individuals will choose to engage in prosocial bystander behaviors such as empathy and civility (Barlinska, Szuster, & Winiewski, 2013; Marini, 2009; Volk et al., 2014). More recently, interest has grown in intervention research aimed to prevent interpersonal violence in communities and bullying in schools, with a focus on the role of the bystander (Boulton, Hardcastle, Down, Fowles, & Simmonds, 2013; Voeten et al., 2011).

To date, little research exists on the role ambiguity plays in cases of interpersonal emotional and psychological violence, and how this ambiguity influences the behavior of the bully, victim, and bystander within the bullying scenario. For example, how does the ambiguous interpretation of teasing and hazing influence bystanders' decisions to either intervene and help, join in and help the bully, or ignore and leave the situation (Bosacki et al., 2012; Keltner et al., 2001). Past studies of the correlates of bystander behavior suggest that the level of ambiguity regarding whether or not someone is in distress may influence the extent to which bystanders help with the situation (Staub, 1971; Voeten et al., 2011).

In contrast to the vast amount of research on how children evaluate and reason about negative peer behaviors, such as exclusion, bullying, and discrimination (Killen & Turiel, 1998), social cognitive research on children's views about the refusal to help is scarce (Paulus & Moore, 2012; Sierksma, Thijs, Verkuyten, & Komter, 2014). Past research suggests that there is a strong social norm to help those in need (Barlinska et al., 2013), and research with adults shows that the level of the recipient's emotional need for help, as well as the personal costs of helping, influence the bystander's perceived obligation to help (Darley & Latané, 1968; Piliavin et al., 1981). Less is known about how children and adolescents morally reason about the obligation to help and act in a kind and caring way to others, although the meaning that children attribute to helping behavior is important for understanding and facilitating prosocial behavior (Hay, 1990; Janoff-Bulman, Sheikh, & Hepp, 2009).

Most recently, Sierksma et al. (2014) interviewed children (aged 8–13) about helping situations that systematically varied in terms of the recipient's need or help and the costs for the helper. They examined whether children's judgments of help reflected moral considerations and ToM abilities, and to what extent these considerations were overpowered. Sierksma et al. (2014) found that when children helped a peer that involved high costs, this overpowered the perceived obligation to help, but only in situations that involved low need, and when consistent with reciprocity. When both need and costs were high, younger children expressed stronger moral indignation or anger about unfairness, while older children were less negative and reasoned in terms of other solutions. Furthermore, stronger moral indignation was related to more advanced social perspective-taking skills when need and costs were high.

Sierksma et al.'s (2014) study further supports the important role moral obligation plays in helping behaviors, and suggest that this sense of obligation may be more powerful than the lack of reciprocity. Future research needs to explore the emotional and social cognitive factors involved within the helping or intervention process of social situations during emerging adolescence. In particular, researchers need to explore the role ToM and moral reasoning play in helping behaviors, and which factors, such as quality of friendship, may motivate young people's helping behaviors within diverse social situations.

Regarding the personal costs of helping or not helping, social cognitive domain research has typically focused on violations involving physical and psychological harm (Smetana, 2006). Children's moral reasoning about the refusal to help might differ from that of harming others because it may involve prescriptive morality rather than proscriptive moral rules (Janoff-Bulman et al., 2009). Compared to the latter, the former is less structured or rigid, and more commendatory, flexible, and lenient. For instance, choosing to harm another is usually explicit and proscriptive, whereas the refusal to help others is more subtle and less prescriptive (Janoff-Bulman et al., 2009; Kahn, 1992). Thus, compared to harm doing, the refusal to help is typically evaluated in more flexible terms, and might depend on a variety of personal and moral considerations.

Further, the ambiguity of the quality or status of the peer relationships involved within a bullying scene may also influence the bystander's behavior (Turkle, 2011; Weller & Lagattuta, 2012). For example, if a boy who observes two peers hazing or teasing one of his friends feels uncertain about their quality of friendship, he may decide to either help or not help his peer as he is victimized by teasing/hazing. Additional social and cultural factors such as gender and ethnic identity may also influence young people's willingness to help in terms of intervention and cooperation. Building on this research, future longitudinal studies could investigate factors such as age, gender, cultural background, and so on that may influence the bystander's decision to either help or harm a victim in need of help.

As mentioned earlier, recent evidence from evolutionary developmental psychology suggests that children's willingness to act in caring and cooperative ways may be deep rooted (De Waal, 2009; Tomasello, 2014b; Volk, Camilleri, Dane, & Marini, 2012; Volk et al., 2014). For example, recent evidence shows that children as young as 3 years old begin to show aspects of wanting to conform to others, and to understand helping and cooperative behavior. Related studies showed that 5-year-old children were more prosocial and less antisocial when they were being watched as compared to when they were alone. A related recent study showed that children of this same age were more concerned with their reputation with in-group members than with out-group members (Engelmann, Over, Herrmann, & Tomasello, 2013).

In addition to how children learn how to follow social norms, they also learn around 3 years of age to enforce social norms on others. This developmental moral cognition research remains difficult to interpret as researchers have not yet found prudential reasons for children's actions, and enforcing social norms can be risky if the person whose behavior is being corrected objects or retaliates. However, studies have found that when children around 3 years of age observed someone acting in harmful ways to others, such as damaging another person's property, or threatening to steal someone's possessions, most children attempted to intervene and appeared emotionally distressed (Bloom, 2013; Vaish, Missana, & Tomasello, 2011). Furthermore, past research shows that some children may object and intervene when someone begins playing a novel game in a way that does not conform to the rules as the child knows them (Rakoczy, Warneken, & Tomasello, 2008).

Further research on children's understanding of social norms found that 3-year-olds even engaged in the defense of other individual's entitlements (Schmidt, Rakoczy, & Tomasello, 2013). That is, when one person was authorized to behave in a certain way, and a second person objected that she could not perform that action, the child intervened against that second person's objection. This kind of second-order norm enforcement shows how some young children may have the potential to "stand up" for, or defend the rights of, another person by objecting to an illegitimate objection. Such evidence of early development of complex moral reasoning may help researchers to understand the developmental roots of puzzling bystander and bullying behaviors within emerging adolescents in school settings. Thus, such studies of young children's social and moral lives highlight the need for researchers to expand their approaches and investigate moral peer behavior among youth.

Regarding the moral sense of self, another characteristic of social norms is how and why a young person learns to apply moral rules to themselves. This application of personal, moral rules is especially interesting as such rules can become internalized into feelings of guilt and shame. Evolutionarily, guilt and shame could be defined as self-conscious or moral emotions that help an individual to avoid potentially punishable future behavior by punishing it internally now. As I discussed in Chapter 4, as complex and moral emotions, displays of guilt and shame have different functions (Tangney & Dearing, 2002). That is, guilt and shame are complex, moral emotions that may serve to prevent others from punishing on the spot because they feel sympathy for how bad the guilty person is feeling, and/ or judge them to be either ignorant or disrespectful of the social norm they are breaking.

Guilt and shame displays in young people may thus serve as an appeasement, and an affiliative function. For example, research on guilt and shame in children has found that children and adults judge people differently when they did or did not display guilt after a transgression. That is, research has found that children show more positive evaluations of those who express regret or remorse for harm (Ferguson, Stegge, & Damhuis, 2001). As previously mentioned, future research on the development of complex, moral emotions such as shame, pride, relief, remorse, regret, spitefulness, gratitude, among others may be necessary to help researchers to make better sense of the moral and emotional lives of emerging adolescents (Marcus, Mercer, Zeigler-Hill, & Alyssa, 2014).

Most recently, researchers have also started to explore the ambiguous role of the bystander and helping behavior within the virtual or digital world. More specifically, researchers have started to explore the intra- and interpersonal dynamics involved in cyberbullying. Cyberbullying has been defined as a set of behaviors performed by individuals or groups through digital media that repeatedly communicate aggressive or hostile messages with the intention to inflict discomfort or harm on others (Smith et al., 2008; Tokunaga, 2010). Research on cyberteasing and cyberbullying continues to escalate, as evidenced by the growth of and studies on the particular roles individuals play within the online school culture

(Brown, Demaray, & Secord, 2014; Kowalski, Schroeder, Giumetti, & Lattanner, 2014; Price, Chin, Higa-McMillan, Kim, & Frueh, 2013; Wade & Beran, 2011). I will return to the topic of virtual social ambiguities in Chapter 9 within the context of cyberbullying and social media, as well as in Chapter 11, when educational implications will be discussed.

Applications: So What?

In addition to young people, research shows that teachers play an important role in the bullying/victimization process in schools. For example, Veenstra, Lindenberg, Huitsing, Sainjo, & Salmivalli's (2014) study on 2,776 Finnish grade school (ages 9 to 12 years) students' perceptions of their teachers' efficacy regarding bullying programs showed that the level of bullying was lowest in classes in which the teacher was perceived to show high efficacy in bullying intervention, and low effort in bullying reduction. Students' perceptions of their teacher's effort in bullying intervention was related to a reduction in bullying over time. That is, in classes where teachers were perceived by the students as ineffective and exerted high effort in bullying intervention, students with pro-bullying attitudes and without antibullying effort reported the highest level of bullying.

Given that teachers need to be perceived by students and parents as significant leaders within bullying prevention and intervention programs (Yoon & Bauman, 2014), the larger school community is responsible for the co-creation of an inclusive and supportive climate in which bullying is unacceptable, and in which bullying is associated with low status and low affection. Veenstra et al.'s (2014) results suggest that students and teachers have the potential to work together to prevent harmful social behaviors and promote peace in the schools. Such student–teacher partnerships can help to solve the problem of each party shifting responsibility to the other. That is, students expect teachers to ensure their safety against peer victimization, whereas teachers expect students to deal with bullies by themselves. In sum, to encourage the development of cooperative bullying prevention programs, teachers need to be viewed as important supporters of bullying prevention and antibullying interventions (Hong, Lee, Lee, Lee, & Garbarino, 2014).

Given that emerging adolescents' beliefs about helpful and harmful social relations affect their actions at home, at school, and in the community, these are some suggestions to foster young people's understandings of peaceful, civil, and prosocial actions:

- Clarify which social behaviors are acceptable or "the right thing to do," and which are not, and help youth understand the reasons for various school regulations and prohibitions.
- Expose youth to a culturally diverse selection of models of moral behavior and social etiquette through modeling respectful and supportive moral and prosocial behavior.
- Encourage critical dialogue and inquiry on friendships and peer relations through group discussion and critical viewing of popular media (newspapers, tv news shows, social media, etc.).
- Encourage mixed aged and culturally diverse learning contexts that will challenge learners' social and moral reasoning with slightly more cognitively advanced reasoning and expose them to culturally diverse views about moral issues.

- Critically discuss the universality or global application of friendship and morality (i.e., universal definition of a "friend")—what does this mean, and is a culture-free definition possible? If so, how would a global moral landscape affect our identity and peer relationships?
- Encourage youth to understand their peers' perspectives and justifications regarding the choice to follow a moral, virtuous life, and to understand the perspectives of those who choose to lead a lifestyle with moral boundaries that divert from society guidelines. For example, learners could be encouraged to question why some people who are educated and deemed intelligent choose to perform acts of violence and hatred toward their friends and loved ones.

Although such exercises may be emotionally sensitive, emerging adolescents need to be encouraged to try to imagine the perspectives of a wide range of individuals, those who wish to follow their personal moral friendship codes or compasses, and those who do not, and set out to intentionally harm others. In sum, friendship and morality is complex and requires critical reflection and discussion. As many developmentalists agree, young people need to develop the ability to recognize the complexity and ambiguity of issues such as moral dilemmas within peer relationships.

During emerging adolescence, friendship and peer relations may help youth to understand the perspectives of others. Such social dilemmas could provide guided questions to encourage them to contemplate moral and social decision-making at a deeper level. For example, as mentioned in the previous chapter, educational programs that provide activities to promote the understanding of complex social moral concepts such as loyalty, gratitude, vengeance, remorsefulness, and forgiveness could help youth to think through moral issues and reflect upon their thoughts and feelings in light of others.

Future Questions

Ding et al. (2015) recommend that future research needs to explore the influence chronic peer rejection has on aggressive and socially withdrawn youth. That is, chronic social rejection may help youth to form internal working models (IWMs) of peer relations (adaptive and maladaptive). Gazelle and Ladd's (2003) research suggests that, compared to aggressive adolescents, chronic peer rejection may have a stronger influence on socially withdrawn adolescents' IWM of friendship. They consequently may be more vulnerable to the formation of friendship models that focus on peer rejection and exclusion.

Maladaptive models of peer relationships may place some youth at risk for long-term internalizing challenges such as feelings of anxiety and depression. Thus, researchers and educators need to work with such youth to provide ways in which to create healthy, adaptive mental models of peer relations. Given that the majority of typically developing youth possess a propensity to imagine how others perceive and possibly judge them, future studies are needed with socially challenged youth across the globe. Such studies may help to illustrate how all youth, irrespective of their friendship and cultural histories, process social information and reason about social ambiguities within peer relationships.

Summary

In sum, the literature discussed in this chapter highlights the importance of research on the social cognitive processes involved in peer relations among older children and adolescents. As children approach adolescence, their relationships with their peers and classmates grow in significance to their developing sense of self, their self-worth contingencies, and how they think of themselves in the eyes of their friends. In addition to the need to be accepted by and affiliated with others, the fear of rejection and anxiety around being abandoned and ostracized also shapes how youth develop their self-awareness and identity. As this fear of rejection and separation from others is also shaped by their family interactions, the next chapter will focus on the role family relationships play in young people's social cognitive development.

References

Arbeau, K. A., & Coplan, R. J. (2007). Kindergarten teachers' beliefs and responses to hypothetical prosocial, asocial, and antisocial children. *Merrill-Palmer Quarterly, 53*, 291–318. doi:10.1353/mpq.2007.0007

Asher, S., & Coie, J. (Eds.). (1990). *Peer rejection in childhood*. New York, NY: Cambridge University Press.

Astington, J. (1993). *The child's discovery of the mind*. Cambridge, MA: Harvard University Press.

Banerjee, R., Watling, D., & Caputi, M. (2011). Peer relations and the understanding of faux pas: Longitudinal evidence for bidirectional associations. *Child Development, 82*, 1887–1905. doi:10.1111/j.1467-8624.2011.01669.x

Barlinska, J., Szuster, A., & Winiewski, M. (2013). Cyberbullying among adolescent bystanders: Role of the communication medium, form of violence, and empathy. *Journal of Community & Applied Social Psychology, 23*, 37–51. doi:10.1002/casp.2137

Barner-Barry, C. (1986). Rob: Children's tacit use of peer ostracism to control aggressive behavior. *Ethology and Sociobiology, 7*, 281–293.

Betts, L., & Stiller, J. (2014). Centrality in children's best-friend networks: The role of social behaviour. *British Journal of Developmental Psychology, 32*, 34–49.

Blakemore, S.-J., & Mills, K. (2014). Is adolescence a sensitive period for sociocultural processing? *Annual Review of Psychology, 65*, 187–207.

Bloom, P. (2013). *Just babies: The origins of good and evil*. New York, NY: Random House.

Blos, J. (1979). *The adolescent passage: Developmental issues*. New York, NY: International Universities Press.

Blote, A. W., Bokhorst, C. L., Miers, A. C., & Westenberg, P. M. (2012). Why are socially anxious adolescents rejected by peers? The role of subject-group similarity characteristics. *Journal of Research on Adolescence, 22*, 123–134. doi:10.1111/j.1532-7795.2011.00768.x

Bosacki, S. (2000). Theory of mind and self-concept in preadolescents: Links with gender and language. *Journal of Educational Psychology, 92*, 709–717.

Bosacki, S. (2005). *Culture of classroom silence*. New York, NY: Peter Lang.

Bosacki, S. (2008). *Children's emotional lives: Sensitive shadows in the classroom*. New York, NY: Peter Lang.

Bosacki, S. (2012). Socioemotional competence, self-perceptions, and receptive vocabulary in shy Canadian children. *International Electronic Journal of Elementary Education, 4*(3), 573–591.

Bosacki, S. (2013). Theory of mind understanding and conversational patterns in early adolescence. *Journal of Genetic Psychology, 174*, 170–191.

Bosacki, S. (2015). Children's theory of mind, self-perceptions, and peer relations: A longitudinal study. *Infant and Child Development, 24,* 175–188. doi:10.1002/icd.1878

Bosacki, S., Bialecka-Pikul, M., & Szpak, M. (March, 2014). *Attachment, self-concept, and theory of mind in Polish adolescents: Does gender play a role?* Poster presented at the biennial meeting of the Society for Research in Adolescence, Austin, TX.

Bosacki, S., Harwood, D., & Sumaway, C. (2012). Being mean: Children's gendered perceptions of peer teasing. *Journal of Moral Education, 41*(4), 473–489. doi:10.1080/0305 7240.2012.690728

Boulton, M. J., Hardcastle, K., Down, J., Fowles, J., & Simmonds, J. (2013). A comparison of preservice teachers' responses to cyber versus traditional bullying scenarios: Similarities and differences and implications for practice. *Journal of Teacher Education, 65*(2), 145–155. doi:10.1177/0022487113511496

Boxer, D., & Cortés-Conde, F. (1997). From bonding to biting: Conversational joking and identity display. *Journal of Pragmatics, 27,* 275–294.

Brown, C., Demaray, M., & Secord, S. (2014). Cybervictimization in middle school and social emotional outcomes. *Computers in Human Behavior, 35,* 12–21.

Bruner, J. (1996). *The culture of education.* Cambridge, MA: Harvard University Press.

Cairns, R., Cairns, B., Neckerman, H., Ferguson, L., & Gariepy, J. (1989). Growth and aggression: 1. Childhood to early adolescence. *Developmental Psychology, 23,* 320–330.

Casanova, S., Martin, M., Suarez-Orozco, C., Cuellar, V., Smith, N., Dias, S., & Katsiafica, D. (2014). *Bias in the classroom: Interpersonal microaggressions in community colleges.* Poster presented at the biennial conference of the Society for Research in Adolescence, Austin, TX.

Coplan, R. (2014). The A, B, C's of recent work on shyness and social withdrawal: Assessment, biology, and context. *Infant Child and Development, 23,* 217–219.

Darley, J. M., & Latané, B. (1968). Group inhibition of bystander intervention in emergencies. *Journal of Personality and Social Psychology, 10,* 215–221.

Devine, R., & Hughes, C. (2013). Silent films and strange stories: Theory of mind, gender, and social experiences in middle childhood. *Child Development, 84,* 989–1003.

De Waal, F. B. M. (2009). *The age of empathy: Nature's lessons for a kinder society.* New York, NY: Harmony Books.

Ding, X., Coplan, R., Sang, B., Liu, J., Pan, T., & Cheng, C. (2015). Young Chinese children's beliefs about the implications of subtypes of social withdrawal: A first look at social avoidance. *British Journal of Developmental Psychology, 33,* 159–173.

Donaldson, M. (1992). *Human minds: An exploration.* Harmondsworth, England: Allen Lane.

Duckworth, A., & Carlson, S. (2013). Self-regulation and school success. In B. Sokol, M. Grouzet, & U. Muller (Eds.), *Self-regulation and autonomy: Social and developmental dimensions of human conduct* (pp. 208–230). New York, NY: Cambridge University Press.

Dunn, J. (2002). Mindreading, emotion understanding, and relationships. In W. W. Hartup, & R. K. Silbereisen (Eds.), *Growing points in developmental science: An introduction* (pp. 167–176). New York, NY: Psychology Press.

Eder, D. (1993). "Go get ya a french!" Romantic and sexual teasing among adolescent girls. In D. Tannen (Ed.), *Gender and conversational interaction* (pp. 17–31). New York, NY: Oxford University Press.

Engelmann, J., Over, H., Herrmann, E., & Tomasello, M. (2013). Young children care more about their reputation with ingroup members and possible reciprocators. *Developmental Science, 16,* 552–558.

Evans, A., & Lee, K. (2011). Verbal deceptions from late childhood to middle adolescence and its relation to executive functioning skills. *Developmental Psychology, 47*(4), 39–49.

Ferguson, T. J., Stegge, H., & Damhuis, I. (1991). Children's understanding of guilt and shame.

Child Development, 62, 827–839. doi:10.2307/ 1131180

Filippova, E., & Astington, J. W. (2008). Further development in social reasoning revealed in discourse irony understanding. *Child Development, 79*, 126–138.

Fink, E., Begeer, S., Hunt, C., & de Rosnay, P. (2014). False-belief understanding and social preference over the first 2 years of school: A longitudinal study. *Child Development, 85*, 2389–2403.

Finy, M., Bresin, K., Korol, D., & Verona, E. (2014). Impulsivity, risk-taking, and cortisol reactivity as a function of psychosocial stress and personality in adolescents. *Development and Psychopathology, 26*, 1093–1111.

Fu, G., Xiao, W. S., Killen, M., & Lee, K. (2014). Moral judgment and its relation to second-order theory of mind. *Developmental Psychology, 50*, 2085–2092.

Gazelle, H. (2013). Is social anxiety in the child or in the anxiety-provoking nature of the child's interpersonal environment? *Child Development Perspectives, 7*, 221–226.

Gazelle, H., & Ladd, G. W. (2003). Anxious solitude and peer exclusion: A diathesis-stress model of internalizing trajectories in childhood. *Child Development, 74*, 257–278. doi:10.1111/1467-8624.00534

Gleason, J., Alexander, A., & Somers, C. (2000). Later adolescents' reactions to three types of childhood teasing: Relations with self-esteem and body image. *Social Behaviour and Personality: An International Journal, 28*, 471–479.

Goldin-Meadow, S. (2014). How gesture works to change our minds. *Trends in Neuroscience and Education, 3*, 4–6.

Gordon, H., Lyon, T., & Lee, K. (2014). Social and cognitive factors associated with children's secret-keeping for a parent. *Child Development, 85*, 2374–2388.

Grice, H. (1957). Meaning. *Philosophical Review, 66*, 377–388.

Grice, H. (1975). Logic and conversation. In P. Cole & J. Morgan (Eds.), *Syntax and symantics* (Vol. 3, pp. 41–58). New York, NY: Academic Press.

Harter, S. (1999). *The construction of the self: A developmental perspective*. New York, NY: Guilford.

Hay, D. (1990). *Religious experiences today*. London, England: Fount.

Hepach, R., Vaish, A., & Tomasello, M. (2013). A new look at children's prosocial motivation. *Infancy, 18*(1), 67–90.

Hong, J., Lee, C., Lee, J., Lee, N., & Garbarino, J. (2014). A review of bullying prevention and intervention in South Korean schools: An application of the socio-ecological framework. *Child Psychiatry and Human Development, 45*, 433–442.

Hughes, C. (2011). *Social understanding and social lives: From toddlerhood through to the transition to school*. New York, NY: Psychology Press.

Huxley, A. (1932). *Brave new world*. London, England: Vintage.

Janoff-Bulman, R., Sheikh, S., & Hepp, S. (2009). Proscriptive versus prescriptive morality: Two faces of moral regulation. *Journal of Personality and Social Psychology, 96*, 521–537. doi:10.1037/a0013779

Kahn, P. H., Jr. (1992). Children's obligatory and discretionary moral judgments. *Child Development, 63*, 416–430. doi:10.2307/ 1131489

Kashdan, T. B., Weeks, J. W., & Savostyanova, A. A. (2011). Whether, how, and when social anxiety shapes positive experiences and events: A self-regulatory framework and treatment implications. *Clinical Psychology Review, 31*, 786–799.

Keltner, D., Capps, L., Kring, A. M., Young, R. C., & Heerey, E. A. (2001). Just teasing: A conceptual analysis and empirical review. *Psychological Bulletin, 127*, 229–248. doi:10.1037/0033-2909.127.2.229

Killen, M., & Turiel, E. (1998). Adolescents' and young adults' evaluations of helping and sacrificing for others. *Journal of Research on Adolescence, 8*, 355–375. doi:10.1207/ s15327795jra0803_4

Kluger, J. (2011). *The sibling effect*. New York, NY: Rainman.

Kołodziejczyk, A. M., & Bosacki, S. L. (2015). Children's understandings of characters' beliefs in persuasive arguments: Links with gender and theory of mind. *Early Child Development and Care*, *185*(4), 562–577. doi: 10.1080/03004430.2014.940930

Kowalski, R., Schroeder, A., Giumetti, G., & Lattanner, M. (2014). Bullying in the digital age: A critical review and meta-analysis of cyberbullying research. *Psychological Bulletin*, *140*, 1073–1137.

Laing, D. (1961). *The divided self*. London, England: Penguin.

Lerner, R. M., Lerner, J. V., Von Eye, A., Bowers, E. P., & Lewin-Bizan, S. (2011). Individual and contextual bases of thriving in adolescence: A view of the issues. *Journal of Adolescence*, *34*(6), 1107–1114.

Lightfoot, C. (1997). *The culture of adolescent risk-taking*. New York, NY: Guilford.

Marcus, D., Mercer, S., Zeigler-Hill, V., & Alyssa, N. (2014). The psychology of spite and the measurement of spitefulness. *Psychological Assessment*, *26*, 564–574.

Marini, Z. A. (2009). The thin line between civility and incivility: Fostering reflection and self-awareness to create a civil learning environment. *Collected Essays on Learning and Teaching*, *2*, 61-67.

Marini, Z. A., Dane, A. V., Bosacki, S., & YLC-CURA (2006). Direct and indirect bully-victims: Differential psychosocial risk factors associated with adolescents involved in bullying and victimization. *Aggressive Behavior*, *32*, 551–569.

Marshall, S., Parker, P., Ciarrochi, J., & Heaven, P. (2014). Is self-esteem a cause or consequence of social support: A 4-year longitudinal study. *Child Development*, *85*, 1275–1291.

Masten, A. (2014). *Ordinary magic: Resilience in development*. New York, NY: Guilford.

McWhorter, J. (2014, March 21) "Microaggression" is the new racism on campus. *Time Magazine*.

Miller, S. (2009). Children's understanding of second-order mental states. *Psychological Bulletin*, *135*(5), 749–773. doi:10.1037/a0016854

Miller, S. A. (2012). *Theory of mind: Beyond the preschool years*. New York, NY: Psychology Press.

Nucci, L. (2013). It's a part of life to do what you want. The role of personal choice in social development. In B. Sokol, M. Grouzet, & U. Muller (Eds.), *Self-regulation and autonomy: Social and developmental dimensions of human conduct* (pp. 165–188). New York, NY: Cambridge University Press.

O'Reilly, K., Peterson, C., & Wellman, H. (2014). Sarcasm and advanced theory of mind understanding in children and adults with prelingual deafness. *Developmental Psychology*, *50*(7), 1862–1877.

Özdemir, B., Cheah, C., & Coplan, R. (2015). Conceptualization and assessment of multiple forms of social withdrawal in Turkey. *Social Development*, *24*, 142–165.

Özdemir, M., & Stattin, H. (2011). Bullies, victims, and bully-victims: A longitudinal examination of the effects of bullying victimization experiences on youth well-being. *Journal of Aggression, Conflict and Peace Research*, *3*, 97–102.

Paulus, M. (2014). The emergence of prosocial behavior: Why do infants and toddlers help, comfort, and share? *Child Development Perspectives*, *8*, 77–81.

Paulus, M., & Moore, C. (2012). Producing and understanding prosocial actions in early childhood. In J. B. Benson (Ed.), *Advances in child development and behavior* (pp. 271–305). London, England: Academic Press.

Piaget, J. (1981). *Intelligence and affectivity: Their relationship during children's development*. Palo Alto, CA: Annual Reviews.

Price, M., Chin, M. A., Higa-McMillan, C., Kim, S., & Frueh, B. C. (2013). Prevalence and internalizing problems of ethnoracially diverse victims of traditional and cyber bullying. *School Mental Health*, *5*(4), 183–191. doi:10.1007/s12310-013-9104-6

Rakoczy, H., Warneken, F., & Tomasello, M. (2008). The sources of normativity: Young children's awareness of the normative structure of games. *Developmental Psychology*, *44*(3), 875–881.

Recchia, H., Brehl, B., & Wainryb, C. (2012). Children's and adolescents' reasons for socially excluding others. *Cognitive Development*, *27*, 195–203. doi:10.1016/j.cogdev.2012.02.005

Rigby, K., & Johnson, B. (2006). Expressed readiness of Australian schoolchildren to act as bystanders in support of children who are being bullied. *Educational Psychology, 26*, 425–440. doi:10.1080/01443410500342047

Rivas-Drake, D., Seaton, K., Markstrom, S., Quintana, S., French, S. Syed, M., … Yip, T. (2014). Feeling good, happy, and proud: A meta-analysis of positive ethnic–racial affect and adjustment. *Child Development, 85*, 77–102.

Rochat, P. (2009). *Others in mind: Social origins of self-consciousness.* Cambridge, England: Cambridge University Press.

Roeder, K., Keneisher, S., Dukewich, T., Preacher, K., Felton, J., Jacky, A., & Tilghman-Osburne, C. (2014). Sensitive periods for the effect of peer victimization on self-cognition: Moderation by age and gender. *Development and Psychopathology, 26*, 1035–1048.

Rubin, K., Burgess, K., & Coplan, R. (2002). Social withdrawal and shyness. In P. Smith & C. Hart (Eds.), *Blackwell handbook of childhood social development* (pp. 329–352). Oxford, England: Blackwell.

Rubin, K. H., Coplan, R. J., & Bowker, J. (2009). Social withdrawal in childhood. *Annual Review of Psychology, 60*, 141–171.

Salmivalli, C., & Isaacs, J. (2005). Prospective relations among victimization, rejection, friendlessness, and children's self- and peer-perceptions. *Child Development, 76*, 1161–1171.

Schaffer, R. (1996). *Social development.* Oxford, England: Blackwell.

Schauer, F., & Zeckhauser, R. (2009). Paltering. In B. Harrington (Ed.), *Deception from ancient empires to Internet dating* (pp. 38–73). Stanford, CA: Stanford University Press.

Schmidt, M. F. H., Rakoczy, H., & Tomasello, M. (2013). Young children understand and defend the entitlements of others. *Journal of Experimental Child Psychology, 116*(4), 930–944.

Schuster, B. (1996). Rejection, exclusion, and harassment at work and in schools: An integration of results from research on mobbing, bullying, and peer rejection. *European Psychologist, 1*, 293–317.

Selman, R. L. (1980). *The growth of interpersonal understanding: Developmental and clinical analyses.* New York, NY: Academic Press.

Shapiro, J. P., Baumeister, R. G., & Kessler, J. W. (1991). A three-component model of children's teasing: Aggression, humor and ambiguity. *Journal of Social and Clinical Psychology, 10*(4), 459–472.

Shelley, M. (1969/1818). *Frankenstein.* Oxford, England: Oxford University Press.

Sierksma, J., Thijs, J., Verkuyten, M., & Komter, S. (2014). Children's reasoning about the refusal to help: The role of need, costs, and social perspective taking. *Child Development, 85*, 1134–1149.

Slaughter, V., Peterson, C., & Moore, C. (2013). I can talk you into it: Theory of mind and persuasion behavior in young children. *Developmental Psychology, 49*, 227–231.

Smetana, J. G. (2006). Social cognitive domain theory: Consistencies and variations in children's moral and social judgments. In M. Killen & J. G. Smetana (Eds.), *Handbook of moral development* (pp. 119–154). Mahwah, NJ: Erlbaum.

Smith, P. K., Mahdavi, J., Carvalho, M., Fisher, S., Russell, S., & Tippett, N. (2008). Cyberbullying: Its nature and impact in secondary school pupils. *Journal of Child Psychology and Psychiatry, and Allied Disciplines, 49*(4), 376–385. doi:10.1111/j.1469-7610.2007.01846.x

Staub, E. (1971). The use of role-playing and induction in children's learning of helping and sharing behaviors. *Child Development, 42*, 805–816.

Staub. E. (2003). *The psychology of good and evil: Why children, adults, and groups help and harm others.* Boston, MA: Cambridge University Press.

Sullivan, H. (1953). *The interpersonal theory of psychiatry.* New York, NY: Norton.

Sulloway, F. (1996). *Born to rebel: Birth order, family dynamics and creative lives.* New York, NY: Vintage Books.

Tangney, J. P., & Dearing, R. L. (2002). Gender differences in morality. In R. F. Bornstein & M. Masling (Eds.), *Empirical studies in psychoanalytic theories: Vol. 10. The psycho-dynamics of gender and gender role* (pp. 251–269). Washington, DC: American Psychological Association.

Tokunaga, R. S. (2010). Following you home from school: A critical review and synthesis of research on cyberbullying victimization. *Computers in Human Behavior, 26,* 277–287.

Tomasello, M. (2014a). *A natural history of human thinking.* Cambridge, MA: Harvard University Press.

Tomasello, M. (2014b). The ultra-social animal. *European Journal of Social Psychology, 44,* 187–194.

Turkle, S. (2011). *Alone together: Why we expect more from technology and less from each other.* New York, NY: Basic Books.

Turkle, S. (2015). *Reclaiming conversation: The power of talk in a digital age.* New York, NY: Penguin.

Twenge, J. (2011). Narcissism and culture. In W. K. Campbell & J. D. Miller (Eds.), *The handbook of narcissism and narcissistic personality disorder* (pp. 202–209). Hoboken, NJ: Wiley.

Underwood, M. (2002). Sticks and stones and social exclusion: Aggression among boys and girls. In P. Smith & C. Hart (Eds.), *Blackwell handbook of childhood social development* (pp. 533–548). Oxford, England: Blackwell.

Vaish, A., Missana, M., & Tomasello, M. (2011). Three-year-old children intervene in third-party moral transgressions. *British Journal of Developmental Psychology, 29,* 124–130. doi: 10.1348/026151010X532888

Vega, T. (2014, March 22). Students see many slights as racial "microaggressions." *New York Times,* A1, A14.

Veenstra, R., Lindenberg, S., Huitsing, G., Sainjo, M., & Salmivalli, C. (2014). The role of teachers in bullying: The relation between antibullying attitudes, efficacy, and efforts to reduce bullying. *Journal of Educational Psychology, 106,* 1135–1143.

Voeten, M., Poskiparta, E., & Salmivalli, C. (2011). Bystander matter: Associations between reinforcing, defending and the frequency of bullying behavior in classrooms. *Journal of Clinical Child & Adolescent Psychology, 40,* 668–676. doi:10.1080/15374416.2011.597090

Volk, A., Camilleri, J., Dane, A., & Marini, Z. (2012). Is adolescent bullying an evolutionary adaptation? *Aggressive Behavior, 38,* 222–238. doi:10.1002/ab.21418

Volk, A., Dane, A., & Marini, Z. (2014). What is bullying? A redefinition. *Developmental Review, 34,* 327–343.

Wade, A., & Beran, T. (2011). Cyberbullying: The new era of bullying. *Canadian Journal of School Psychology, 26,* 44–61. doi:10.1177/0829573510396318

Weller, D., & Lagattuta, K. H. (2012). Helping the in-group feels better: Children's judg-ments and emotion attributions in response to prosocial dilemmas. *Child Development, 84,* 253–268. doi:10.1111/j.1467-8624.2012.01837.x

Williams, K. (2001). *Ostracism: The power of silence.* New York, NY: Guilford.

Yoon, J., & Bauman, S. (2014). Teachers: A critical but overlooked component of bully-ing prevention and intervention. *Theory into Practice, 53,* 308–314.

7

Family Relationships

"there is nothing higher, or stronger, or sounder, or more useful afterwords in life than some good memory, especially a memory from childhood, from the parental home." (Dostoevsky, 1990/1880, p. 774)

Introduction

Given that Part III details past research on the social worlds of the young person, this chapter will focus on the role of family and companion animal relationships in young people's social cognitive development. Overall, this chapter will concentrate on the role of attachment theory and research in emerging adolescents' social cognitive development and relationships, particularly within the family context—especially parents and siblings. Implications for research and practice will be addressed, as well as future questions for research.

Research

Attachment and theory of mind in childhood and adolescence

According to the theory of attachment (Bowlby, 1973), humans are characterized by a universal need to create and maintain a deep emotional relationship with their caregivers. The aim of the attachment system is the experimentation of security, which in turn acts as a regulator of the emotional experience. One of the seminal research paradigms devised to

Social Cognition in Middle Childhood and Adolescence: Integrating the Personal, Social, and Educational Lives of Young People, First Edition. S. L. Bosacki.
© 2016 John Wiley & Sons, Ltd. Published 2016 by John Wiley & Sons, Ltd.

evaluate attachment is that of the Strange Situation that has enabled researchers to identity at least three styles of attachment, that is, secure, insecure-avoidant, and insecure-ambivalent (Ainsworth, 1989), followed by the disorganized style identified later by Main and Solomon (1990).

Past research has shown that the type of attachment is crucial for subsequent child social and emotional development. More specifically, attachment is based on the quality of the relationship with the primary caregiver where the child co-constructs an "Internal Working Model" with the main caregiver (Bowlby, 1973). That is, the child socially co-constructs a flexible, cognitive representational structure that is linked to the conception of the self as worthy of receiving care, to the conception of one's own self-efficacy, and to the overall basis of self-confidence. The latter is rooted in the trustful relationships that children develop with their primary caregivers in the early years of life.

Although attachments emerge in the first year of life, they are important for healthy development across the life span (Ainsworth, 1989; Mahler, Pine, & Bergman, 1997), and parents continue to function as primary attachment figures for children at least through early adolescence and possibly across the adolescent years (Lecompte, Moss, Cyr, & Pascuzzo, 2014; Seibert & Kerns, 2009; Solomon, 2012). A major tenet of attachment theory is the competence hypothesis, which suggests that the formation of a secure attachment in childhood with caregivers who are emotionally available helps to prepare a child for future social and emotional challenges such as finding a place in the peer group and developing future relationships with significant others (Fonagy & Target, 1997). Thus, secure attachment with an emotionally responsive and sensitive primary caregiver may provide a young person with social and emotional skills that may serve as "emotional armor," or emotional immunization against life adversities (Carpendale & Lewis, 2004; Licata et al., 2016). That is, such emotional competencies may act as protective factors to help cope with life challenges, and may thus place the individual on a more positive developmental trajectory (Weinfield, Sroufe, Egeland, & Carlson, 2008).

Consistent with the competence hypothesis, compared to children who develop insecure attachment and have nonemotionally responsive or insensitive caregivers, children who are securely attached to emotionally sensitive and involved parents are likely to form more positive relationships with peers, cooperate more with adults, and regulate their emotions more effectively (Kerns, 2008; Thompson, 2008; Weinfield et al., 2008). In addition, as already mentioned, relationships with peers may also contribute to children's social and emotional development in that they help them to create positive mental schemas for how to negotiate personal relationships and self-perceptions (Kerns & Brumariu, 2014). That is, securely attached children have been found to be more cooperative, academically competent, and self-confident (Duchesne & Ratelle, 2010), better liked by peers, and to form more supportive friendships than insecurely attached children (Booth-LaForce & Kerns, 2009).

In contrast, past research has shown that children who fail to form secure attachments with their primary caregiver may be more likely to develop internalizing and anxiety problems (Kerns & Brumariu, 2014). Recent research has explored the role disorganized attachment plays in adolescents' internalizing behaviors and self-esteem (Lecompte et al., 2014; Obsuth, Hennighausen, Brumariu, & Lyons-Ruth, 2014). In general, the term disorganized refers to the lack of a consistent, organized, and coherent attachment response to the parent when under stress. This disorganized or incoherent response style is reflected by particular combinations or patterns of disorganized behaviors observed in infancy that tend to be idiosyncratic from child to child. For example, this may include apprehensive, depressed, or helpless behaviors; unexpected alternations of approach and avoidance toward the attachment figure; and other marked conflict behaviors, such as lengthy stilling or freezing, or slowed movements as if one attempts to move underwater (Main & Solomon, 1990).

Given the complex categorization of disorganized behavior within attachment relations, many attachment researchers recommend that future research needs to consider a conceptual continuum to describe disoriented and punitive caring versus caregiving/role-confused attachment behaviors in emerging adolescence (Hsiao, Koren-Karie, Bailey, & Moran, 2015). Research could then draw from this continuum to study the relations between controlling–punitive and controlling–caring behaviors and various social cognitive and emotional competences such as perceived self-worth and Theory of Mind (ToM).

Overall, research that examines associations between patterns of early attachment and later anxiety and depression remains inconclusive, and highlights the need for further longitudinal research (Ge, Natsuaki, Neiderhiser, & Reiss, 2009). The few existing longitudinal studies show that children who exhibit disorganized attachment style behaviors with primary caregivers may experience low self-esteem and internalizing challenges such as depression and anxiety as young adolescents (Kerns & Brumariu, 2014; Lecompte et al., 2014). Research on the role of attachment in emerging adolescents' maladaptive social cognitive reasoning and emotional dysregulation continues to explore these complex relations. For example, future studies could examine factors such as peer difficulties, self-perceptions, and academic competencies as possible additional mediators because of their association with early disorganization and later difficulties (Moss & St-Laurent, 2001). I will return to this topic of attachment and psychopathological development in Chapter 10 when I discuss social cognitive and emotional challenges among youth.

Regarding the connections between attachment and social cognitive development, although attachment was not studied directly, Mischel (1958, 1961) found that 7- to 9-year-old Trinidadian children from a two-parent family were more likely to delay self-gratification compared to children from a single-mother family. Such findings suggest that the family cultural context and parent–child relationship may have an influence on a child's ability to inhibit or control one's behaviors.

Several decades later, Moore and Symons (2005) explored the relations between the quality of the child–main caregiver attachment relationship at 3½ years of age and various social cognitive competencies at 4 years of age. In particular, Moore and Symons explored children's ToM, prosociality, and intertemporal choice. Specifically, intertemporal choice or decision-making was measured with two modified versions of the delayed choice paradigm: two stickers for you now versus two stickers to be shared now; two stickers for you now versus two stickers to be shared in the future. The executive control ability of behavioral inhibition was measured by the gift delay paradigm where the child could receive a gift only if she turned to face the wall and not peek while the gift was being wrapped.

Moore and Symons found that secure attachment, in addition to being linked to ToM (Meins, Fernyhough, Arnott, Leekam, & de Rosnay, 2013), was related to the intertemporal choice and to behavioral inhibitory control. Given that no links between attachment and prosociality were found, they suggested future exploration of this topic, especially concerning the measurement of social relations and friendships.

More recently, Marchetti, Castelli, Sanvito, and Massaro's (2014) study of 6- to 10-year-old children suggested that attachment style with the family caregiver, but not with the school caregiver, had a similar result to that of Moore and Symons (2005). This finding supports the notion that the primary caregiver plays a crucial role in shaping a trustful relationship, which in turn may be a prerequisite for self-confidence. However, despite the important role attachment plays in the delay of self-gratification process, attachment alone did not explain the age variability. Thus, according to Marchetti et al. (2014), although attachment may partly help to explain children's ability in intertemporal choice, it is not sufficient to account for the entire process.

Marchetti et al. (2014) found that only first-order ToM influenced the two components of intertemporal choice (i.e., the tolerance to the waiting time and the sensitivity to the outcome increase). This result supports past literature (Moore, Barresi, & Thompson, 1998; Moore & Symons, 2005), and is interesting given the type of task Marchetti et al. (2014) devised to study the two components of intertemporal choice separately. Marchetti et al. suggested that such a complex level of representation may probably not be necessary to manage the task of temporal choice and that perhaps first-order belief understanding was sufficient.

Interestingly, no correlations were found between second-order ToM and attachment style, which suggests the need for future research in this area. For example, some of our ongoing longitudinal cross-cultural studies with emerging adolescents in Poland and Canada explore the developmental links between ToM and self-perceived attachment relations with siblings and family members, as well as peers within a school or social setting (Bosacki, Bialecka-Pikul, & Szpak, 2014). In addition to ToM, additional social cognitive tasks such as self-perceptions, emotional forecasting and regulation, and the ability to understand persuasion and deception may also prove to be interesting areas of research in connection with attachment relations among emerging adolescents (Kołodziejczyk & Bosacki, 2015).

Parental attachment from childhood to adolescence: Implications for social cognition

Attachment relations, or the way in which we interact with our main caregiver, influences our social, cognitive, and emotional development throughout life (Bowlby, 1973). Research shows that an individual's attachment style, or how one relates or connects in an emotionally intimate way to another (Licata, Kristen, & Soldian, 2016), may strongly impact one's mental and physical health (Scharfe & Eldredge, 2001), and social cognitive abilities including the ability to cope with stress (Licata et al., 2016; Rose, 2014). Research findings suggest that, compared to young people who report secure attachments with others, some insecurely attached individuals may experience more health-related challenges (Scharfe & Eldredge, 2001), respond to stress poorly, and cope in unhealthy ways such as self-harming behavior (Callan, Kay, & Dawtry, 2014; Muehlenkamp, Claes, Havertape, & Plener, 2012).

Numerous studies of infants and younger children support the theoretical assertion that positive qualities in parent–child relationships promote positive adjustment by protecting against the deleterious effects of stressors (Hsiao et al., 2015). However, significant changes in parent–child relationships may have a considerable impact on the ability of parents to buffer against stressful events as children age. As children begin to transition into adolescence, relationships with parents undergo a period of adjustment in response to youth maturational changes.

Specifically, during adolescence, parents and children experience more intense conflict (Kochanska & Kim, 2013; Nucci, Araki, Smetana, Nakaue, & Comer, 2014), express less physical affection, spend less time with each other, and have less intimacy in their relationships with one another (Larson, 2011). In addition, compared to early childhood, positive parenting, parental warmth, and overall relationship quality with parents decrease across the transition into adolescence (Bosacki, 2013).

At the same time, other studies have highlighted that, as parent–child relationships change they may remain an important source of influence (Siegel, 2013). Importantly, research shows that adolescents who have more supportive, positive relationships with parents experience lower levels of later depressive symptoms (Ge et al., 2009), and are at decreased risk for developing clinical levels of depression (Luthar & Latendresse, 2005b). In contrast, research shows that youth exposed to low levels of support and having poor relationships with parents are at greater risk for depression (Leussis & Anderson, 2008).

Given the many changes that occur in parent–child relationships during adolescence, research suggests that there are two competing possibilities about the role of parents in stressor protection as youth transition into adolescence. One possibility is that the parental relationship influence usually declines during adolescence, and thus may lead some parents to be less effective at buffering against rising peer stressors (Greenspan & Deardorff, 2014).

An alternative possibility is that relationships with parents continue to be important for adolescents despite normative shifts that occur within the parent– child dyad (Furman & Buhrmester, 1985). Thus, it is possible that positive, supportive relationships with parents may continue to serve as protective factors against the impact of stressors or negative life events for adolescents (Rose, 2014). To explore this possibility, Hazel, Oppenheimer, Young, Technow, and Hankin (2014) evaluated whether positive relationships with parents could buffer the effects of youth stressors on depressive symptoms despite the considerable changes that occur within parent–child relationships from middle childhood to adolescence.

Although social support has been repeatedly shown to buffer against the deleterious effects of stress in adults and young children, findings among adolescents have been mixed (Ge et al., 2009). However, Hazel et al. (2014) found clear, robust support for the stress-buffering hypothesis, which was consistent across parental and youth's reports of average relationship quality with mothers and fathers, and this effect was similar across grades (Grade 3 to 9). Across each model, whereas peer stress was positively correlated with prospective increases in depressive symptoms, the association was stronger among youth who experienced lower levels of relationship quality with parents. Their follow-up analysis also demonstrated that the main findings were obtained among youth before and throughout the adolescent transition. Overall, Hazel et al.'s results suggest that low levels of parent relationship quality leave youth particularly vulnerable to the deleterious effects of peer stressors from childhood through adolescence.

As Hazel et al. (2014) suggest, future research needs to pinpoint which specific parent behaviors serve as protective factors from life stressors among older children and adolescents. As I discuss in Chapter 11, similar research findings on teacher–child attachment relations suggest that the quality of early child–teacher relationships have the potential to foreshadow later success and failure at school (Spilt, Koomen, & Harrison, 2015). Thus, future research needs to continue to explore how attachment theory may help researchers understand how youth create mental working models of their relationships with their teachers (Sabol & Pianta, 2012), and then apply these working models to help shape their schooling experiences and peer relationships (Sette, Baumgartner, & Schneider, 2014).

Concurrent and longitudinal research shows that positive child–teacher relationships are also correlated with positive peer interactions and healthy functioning for children with externalizing and internalizing problems (Sabol & Pianta, 2012). For example, Mitchell-Copeland, Denham, and DeMulder (1997) found that children who have warm and secure relationships with their teachers may use teachers as resources for other social experiences, especially peer relationships. Additionally, as Hazel et al. (2014) focused on positive relationship qualities, it is also possible that negative relationship qualities such as conflict and dependency may influence the impact of stressors on depressive and other internalizing challenges.

For example, Sette et al. (2014) found that, in a sample of Italian young school children and teachers, relationship qualities of closeness, conflict, and dependence in the child–teacher relationship moderated the links between child shyness and teacher reports of preschool social competence and maladjustment. More specifically, at very high levels of teacher–student dependence, Sette et al. found that there was a negative relation between teacher ratings of student shyness and social competence. The findings suggest that perhaps positive, supportive student–teacher relationships may be a protective factor for social maladjustment during emerging adolescence. In Chapters 11 and 12 I will return to discuss how future researchers could examine how parent–child relationships, combined with exposure to various teacher and peer stressors, may influence the etiology of depressive and other internalizing symptoms among youth during the transition into adolescence.

Moral development and parent–youth relations across cultures

Given that research on young people's self-regulation, moral reasoning, and self-concept in diverse cultures remains limited, many questions remain, including what are the antecedents and consequences of social-moral reasoning and inhibitory control among adolescents across cultures? For instance, the studies mentioned above have interesting implications for the development of moral reasoning, ToM, and identity among youth across cultures. Based on these past transcultural studies, how do young people of mixed heritage learn to express greater respect for their parents and self within a culturally and morally diverse environment? How does this parental respect and complaints about parental control influence youth's social-emotional experiences and their need for self-expression?

For example, future research could explore how youth from diverse cultures learn to make personal choices within the constraints of parental control and social-cultural expectations? Further, as I have mentioned elsewhere (Bosacki, 2005, 2013), we need to explore the processes of how young people's varied levels of moral reasoning, ToM, and self-identity affect their notions of personal decisions regarding privacy and discretion. In other words, how do emerging adolescents learn to keep their thoughts and feelings to themselves, and decide to comply with parental rules and social-cultural norms? Alternatively, how do they learn to share their thoughts and feelings with others, and commit to noncomply or go against parental rules to follow their personal rules?

Also, given that parental control plays a role in youth's social cognitive development, researchers and educators need to ask questions such as: To what extent do parental rules influence a young person's personal rules, and within which contexts of privacy and discretion? How and why do some adolescents learn to question rather than to adapt to societal expectations to fit their personal voice and personal code of conduct? Finally, to what extent does parental control become integrated into the young person's developing sense of self and self-control?

To explore some of these questions within a particular cultural context, Nucci et al. (2014) studied adolescents' management of disclosure and information to parents in a sample of Japanese teenagers. Overall, Nucci and his colleagues found that Japanese adolescents felt most obligated to disclose prudential issues such as comfort, safety, and self-harm, but disclosed most about personal issues including privacy, control over the body, and personal preferences. Nondisclosure was mainly justified with claims to personal choice and for prudential issues as well as concerns with parental disapproval. Overall, youth rarely lied, and mostly told parents if asked or avoided the issue.

Findings revealed consistencies with prior work on disclosure with European and US adolescents, as well as patterns specific to the Japanese cultural setting. Gender-related differences revealed that Japanese youth chose to mainly disclose to same-sex parents. For example, Japanese females were more likely to disclose to their mother, whereas Japanese males were more likely to disclose to their father. Such research affirms the importance of exploring the interactions between culture and gender regarding areas of adolescent–parent attachment, disclosure, and moral development.

Role of parents in economically advantaged families

Luthar, Barkin, and Crossman (2013) emphasized that affluent parents as a group are neither neglectful nor disparaging (Luthar & Barkin, 2012; Luthar & Latendresse, 2005a). Research on the role of parents in young people's psychosocial development suggests that it is not family wealth per se, but rather living in the cultural context of affluence, that connotes risks (Chaplin, Hill, & John, 2014; Coren & Luthar, 2014). On average, research shows that most affluent youth often do not feel closer to their parents than very low-income youth (Luthar & Latendresse, 2005b). For example, across various dimensions, suburban sixth graders from affluent, mostly two-parent Caucasian families rated parent–child relationships no more positively than did their low socioeconomic status (SES) counterparts generally from single-parent, ethnic minority households, and living in harsh conditions of poverty.

Similar to some children within the low-income community, some affluent children reported feeling quite emotionally distant from their parents. Beyond emotional closeness or connectedness to parents, researchers have tried to capture "contextually salient" family processes in their programmatic work with affluent youth. That is, researchers examine factors that are (a) potent in, and (b) largely unique to the subculture of affluence. Findings have shown that laissez-faire monitoring may often serve as a particularly powerful predictor.

For example, middle school youth who routinely had no adult supervision after school (i.e., almost 50% of seventh-grade boys, and 25% of girls) were among the most vulnerable, reporting high substance use, delinquency, and depressive/anxiety symptoms (Luthar & Barkin, 2012). Of parallel importance in high school was parents' knowledge of their children's whereabouts outside school. For instance, regarding substance abuse, the single most robust predictor was found to be low parent containment. That is, US high schoolers who anticipated inadequate consequences from their parents were among the heaviest substance users (Luthar & Barkin, 2012).

Luthar and Goldstein (2008) also measured two constructs that captured the predicament of these high SES families and their youth with highly demanding work lives. The first construct was perceived parental "commitment," or the parent's belief that the child is her parents' primary priority, over and above their careers and other pursuits. The second was children's perceived parental values. For example, when children believed that their parents disproportionately valued their financial successes such as their future careers over their personal integrity, such as viewing their children as competent, moral, and adaptive persons, they show elevated internalizing symptoms (Luthar & Barkin, 2012). For these particular children, their perceived parental pride, and thus their perceived self-worth, was measured by or depended largely on the achievement or maintenance of their "star status" in various areas of a their lives (social, academic, athletic, physical appearance) (Lyman & Luthar, 2014).

In terms of powerful, discrete parenting behaviors, research on resilience shows that "bad is stronger than good" (Baumeister, Bratslavsky, Finkenauer, & Vohs, 2001). That is, negative or aversive interactions within the parent–child relationship has been found to have long-term developmental consequences for future communication and emotional regulatory problems (Repetti, Taylor, & Seeman, 2002). Social psychologists have established that disparaging and negative judgmental words from self-reported perfectionistic parents can have much stronger effects than words of praise or affection, by as much as a factor of three (Lyman & Luthar, 2014; Smith, Saklofeske, & Nordstokke, 2014). Consistent with this claim, Luthar and Barkin (2012) also found that perceived parent criticism showed stronger links with diverse adjustment indices as compared to positive family adjustment indices such as such as secure and robust child–parent attachment. Given the lack of research on youth and their families and peers within a "culture of affluence," future research needs to continue to explore the social, cognitive, and moral lives of these children of the financially privileged (Chaplin et al., 2014).

Some recent examples of research with affluent youth show that, compared to impoverished youth, affluent teens had a higher sense of self-worth, and were less likely to place high value on material objects such as money and clothes, cars, and so on (Chaplin et al., 2014). Relatedly, recent studies demonstrated a positive connection between perfectionism, emotional distress, and lower interpersonal functioning among affluent youth, particularly those from coeducational independent schools (Coren & Luthar, 2014; Lyman & Luthar, 2014).

Building on past research with young children's parental attachment and ToM (Licata et al., 2016), future research could explore connections between patterns of child–parent and sibling attachment relations in high-income families and young people's social cognitive development, emotional well-being, and self-perceptions, as well as their schooling experiences and their leisure and consumer habits. Such studies could prove useful to developmentalists and educators as they highlight the complex social and cultural factors found within the family culture that may influence young people's social cognitive development. I will return to the research on materialism, economic family structure, and social cognitive and emotional implications for youth in Chapters 8 and 12 as such topics remain in need of further research.

Theory of mind, executive function, and family relationships

Over the past two decades, researchers have explored the connections between children's social cognitive development and family structure. However, the vast amount of research has revealed mixed findings regarding the relation between ToM and children's family relationships including parents, siblings, and extended family. Moreover, few studies explore the links between ToM and family relations in middle childhood and emerging adolescence. In particular, siblings may be of specific interest as they often blur the lines between family and peers (Cicirelli, 1995). Research suggests that siblings may serve as significant attachment figures for other family members and may help to guide future attachment relationships with others (Ruffman, Perner, Naito, Parkin, & Clements, 1998; Sulloway, 1996). For example, past research has demonstrated that young people have similar working models of attachment with parents, peers, and romantic partners (Lippman & Campbell, 2014).

Over the lifespan, sibling relationships are presumed to have important implications for the development of young people's social cognitive skills and social relationships. To date, researchers have explored the uniqueness of sibling relationships throughout history and duration across the lifespan (Kluger, 2011), as well as the influence of sibling relationships on the dynamics of other family and peer relationships (Stocker et al., 1997). Although researchers have examined sibling attachment in infancy and childhood, few have explored this distinctive relationship in emerging adolescents and in relation to social cognitive development such as ToM (Hughes, 2011).

To illustrate, several studies have documented that children with more siblings, especially older siblings, have been found to demonstrate superior ToM performance compared to children with fewer or no siblings (Brown, Donelan-McCall, & Dunn, 1996; Ruffman et al., 1998). Researchers have interpreted these data to suggest that siblings provide opportunities to engage in social interactions that may improve children's mental state understanding. Older siblings may be particularly advantageous because older children may be more developmentally advanced, and thus can serve as a social mentor to the younger "apprentice" (Perner, Ruffman, & Leekam, 1994). Most recently, researchers have shown growing interest in questions that explore the relations among ToM, sibling composition, and attachment (with parents and siblings) in emerging adolescence.

For example, past research with middle-school children has shown that, when controlling for age and executive function, children with a greater number of older siblings, or with more same-sex siblings, demonstrated stronger ToM. That is, compared to the participants that had a smaller number of older siblings or fewer same-sex siblings, this particular group of participants provided more elaborate predictions and explanations that people with different past experiences can have diverse interpretations of ambiguous stimuli (Perner et al., 1994; Ruffman et al., 1998). Such data provide evidence for the potential influence of sibling constellations on young people's individual differences in ToM and suggest the need for future studies with older adolescents.

Sibling relationships and social cognitive development in childhood   There are several reasons to predict that the associations between siblings and ToM may differ in older as opposed to younger children (Miller, 2012). When children enter school, around the age of 5 to 6 years, many socialization practices shift. More specifically, the transition from home to grade school may influence most children to begin to spend significantly more time outside of the home with nonfamilial peers, as the number of peer contact hours has often been found to increase over childhood into adolescence (Larson, 2011).

The frequency of mental state talk with peers—talk about emotions, desires, beliefs, thoughts, intentions—may in part predict individual differences in ToM (Clark & Symons, 2009). For example, past studies have shown that most school-age children engage in more mental state talk with friends than with siblings, as evidenced by associations between children's peer relations and ToM throughout childhood (Brown et al., 1996; Cassidy, Werner, Rourke, Zubernis, & Balaraman, 2003). Given the relative drop in time spent with siblings, and the growing prominence of peers during the elementary school years, future research needs to examine how peer and sibling relations influence ToM development in older children and emerging adolescents.

Miller (2012) recently examined whether the number of siblings predicted 5- to 8-year-olds' reasoning about ToM second-order false-belief tasks or children's ability to reason about a person's belief about another person's belief or emotion. Results showed no relation between sibling composition and ToM performance. However, Miller acknowledged that this null finding may have been due to high performance and limited sibling variability.

Studies on ToM and sibling relationships with older children from atypical populations, including 4- to 12-year-olds with autism spectrum disorder (ASD) (O'Brien, Slaughter, & Peterson, 2011), and 4- to 8-year-olds with hearing impairments (Brinton & Fujiki, 2002), have revealed mixed results. Whereas hearing-impaired children were found to benefit from older siblings, children with ASDs who had older siblings exhibited impaired ToM. Such mixed findings suggest that more studies are needed to build a stronger research base on individual differences in ToM during middle childhood and adolescence, including potential relations to sibling composition.

To address this issue, as I mentioned in Chapter 2, recent studies on typically developing children have used an advanced test of ToM also referred to as an *Interpretive Theory of Mind* (IToM). Lalonde and Chandler (2002) defined IToM as the capacity to recognize that the same situation can be open to multiple legitimate interpretations. A typical task involves a researcher who shows the participant a complete drawing, and then covers the majority of the drawing with blank paper but leaves one small, ambiguous section of the drawing uncovered (e.g., a curved line) The participant then predicts and explains the interpretations of other people who have or who have not had prior access to the full drawing.

Prior research has shown that children start to exhibit knowledge that different people can interpret the same situation in several different ways, especially ambiguous situations, between the ages of 5 and 7 (Lagattuta et al., 2015), with further development between 7 and 12 years of age and into adulthood (Bosacki, 2013). In contrast to false-belief tasks, where researchers look for participants to provide a single, predefined "false" versus "true" belief (Wellman, 2014), IToM and advanced ToM tasks test children's reasoning that there can be many ways to interpret a situation, and that prior experience can shape their psychological reactions.

Although several studies have documented significant relations between sibling composition and ToM during early childhood, researchers remain divided with regard to whether or not an "ideal" composition of siblings best predicts more advanced ToM understandings. That is, does having a large number of siblings in one's family benefit ToM development more than a small number or being an only child (McAlister & Peterson, 2013)? Further, is it possible that having more older siblings has more social cognitive benefits compared to having younger siblings (Kluger, 2011; Ruffman et al., 1998)? To explore related questions, a subset of studies have found that preschoolers with siblings who are diverse in gender or age demonstrate the most advanced ToM. However, disagreement remains about whether children's ToM development benefits more from either older or younger siblings (Peterson, 2000), or opposite-sex siblings (Carlson & Moses, 2001; Cassidy, Fineberg, Brown, & Perkins, 2005; Ruffman et al., 1998).

Other researchers have documented no significant correlations between any kind of sibling composition and ToM performance (Cutting & Dunn, 2002). Exposure to a greater number of sibling perspectives has been found to possibly benefit children's understanding of mental diversity by providing more frequent opportunities to interact with children whose views differ from their own (see also Dunn, Slomkowski, & Beardsall, 1994; Licata et al., 2016). Older siblings may be especially advantageous in that children have the opportunity to learn from direct interactions with developmentally more advanced children (e.g., Ruffman et al., 1998), as well as from observations of their siblings' behaviors and listening to their siblings' conversations with others (Hughes, White, & Ensor, 2014).

Opposite-sex siblings may help children to learn more about diversity in psychological states due to the possible exposure to differences in preferences and play styles that may follow gender-role stereotypes (Bosacki, 2013; Hyde, 2014). Alternatively, same-sex siblings have been found to show more shared interests and greater warmth and intimacy in their relationships than opposite-sex siblings (Dunn et al., 1994; Furman & Buhrmester, 1985); which in turn may potentially promote more advanced social cognition. Gender of siblings may also play a role in that some research has shown that having female siblings is associated with closer, more prosocial, and less conflictual sibling relationships (Dunn, 2002; Erwin, 1995).

Given that prior studies on sibling–ToM relations have focused nearly exclusively on children 3 to 6 years of age, sibling chronological age has been confounded with relative age (older vs. younger status). That is, in most studies "older siblings" were, by default, at least 4 to 5 years of age—the age when most typically developing Western children pass the benchmark false-belief task (Wellman, 2014). Perhaps it is not having a greater number of older siblings that helps ToM (*apprenticeship model*), but rather having more siblings who have reached a certain age threshold, and thus a certain level of social and cognitive skills (*age threshold model*). Future longitudinal research needs to examine whether ToM performance varies by diversity in sibling age (having both older and younger siblings), or gender (having both male and female siblings).

Individual differences in executive function (EF) have been found to reliably predict ToM in preschool-aged children even when language skills have been controlled (Carlson, 2011; Devine & Hughes, 2014; Hughes, 1998). Recent work has found positive relations between EF and more advanced ToM in middle childhood and adulthood (German & Hehman, 2006; Lagattuta, Nucci, & Bosacki, 2010; Lagattuta et al., 2015). Despite this strong base of research on EF–ToM relations, only a few studies on the relations between sibling composition and ToM have controlled for EF. To illustrate, with EF controlled, Hughes and Ensor (2005) reported significant relations between sibling relationship quality and ToM in a sample of 2-year-olds. Similarly, with EF accounted for, McAlister and Peterson (2013) found that the number of siblings independently predicted ToM in 3- to 5-year-olds, as well as 12 months later (McAlister & Peterson, 2013). Finally, O'Brien et al. (2011) showed that number of older siblings and EF independently predicted ToM in children with ASDs.

Further extensions of the siblings–ToM research base can also be gleaned from our ongoing work on ToM and social cognition in young people (Bosacki, 2015). In particular, we have found positive associations between children's higher number siblings (younger and older) and their advanced ToM. In contrast, we found negative associations between sibling number and children's self-understanding and self-perceived moral behavior. Our current research also explores if sibling composition independently predicts advanced ToM performance and self-perceptions of social and moral behavior in emerging adolescents. Future research needs to expand to include EF tasks in adolescents such as verbal working memory and inhibitory control—because performance on these measures correlates significantly to ToM performance in younger and older children (Carlson & Moses, 2001; Lagattuta et al., 2010).

In summary, past research addresses significant gaps in the literature on sibling composition and ToM through the exploration of young people on advanced measures of mental state understanding that include predictions and explanations. Future research needs to assess whether sibling composition independently predicts advanced ToM performance in middle childhood above and beyond contributions of EF. Studies could also investigate if sibling–ToM connections exist in emerging adulthood, an age period largely untested in prior work.

The inclusion of older school-age children can provide a stringent test of the apprenticeship model (older siblings matter for ToM because they are more developmentally advanced than the target child) by comparing it against an age threshold model. This age threshold model predicts that having siblings of a certain age influences ToM irrespective of whether they are older or younger than the target child. Finally, cross-cultural longitudinal studies will also allow for a more detailed analysis of the relations among different types of sibling composition and advanced ToM across ages and families and explore variables such as sibling gender and cultural diversity.

Such research may support an apprenticeship model of sociocognitive learning in the family, as past research has found that a greater number of older siblings may foster the development of an interpretive ToM (Perner et al., 1994). That is, children with a greater number of older siblings may accurately predict how two people would interpret ambiguous stimuli, and may also be better able to explain this mental diversity in relation to differences in their past experiences. The sex composition and gender orientation of the siblings may also be of interest to future researchers as same-sex siblings, regardless of whether they are older or younger, as it may also be a predictor of ToM and other social cognitive abilities in emerging adolescents. Thus, in a field dominated by a focus on ToM in infancy and early childhood (see Miller, 2012), future research may offer new insights into sources of individual differences in social cognition among emerging adolescents.

Results of past studies support an apprenticeship model and support prior work that has showed the beneficial effects of interacting with developmentally advanced others for social cognitive development (Perner et al., 1994; Vygotsky, 1978). The possibility of having older siblings, or being an only child, may afford children more opportunities to converse about mental states in a more cognitively advanced manner, potentially improving their ability to consider multiple perspectives (Bosacki, 2013). Children with older siblings may also benefit from more sophisticated levels of play and conversation, which have also been shown to be associated with ToM development (Hughes et al., 2014). Overhearing more advanced conversations between older siblings and peers or parents may also provide useful linguistic and sociocognitive information.

Studies have shown that, as early as 2 years of age, children learn from overhearing or eavesdropping on conversations (Brinton & Fujiki, 2002), and, by 3 years of age, they begin to intrude on and participate in these discussions (Brown et al., 1996). Children have also been found to admire and more frequently imitate parents and older versus younger siblings (Dunn, 2002), perhaps suggesting a stronger preference to observe and gather information from parents and older siblings. In addition, conflict situations that involve moral dilemmas—especially disputes about who is at fault and why—hold the potential to provide salient contexts for learning about siblings' divergent perspectives and psychological states (Brown et al., 1996).

The positive relation between having a greater number of older siblings and higher performance on advanced ToM tasks may also be explained by research that shows older siblings frequently act as teachers or mentors and caregivers for their younger siblings. For example, older siblings often instruct and manage their younger siblings in play and didactic contexts (Kluger, 2011). Some older siblings may assume the role of a caregiver in that they may help younger siblings in their daily routines (e.g., eating, getting dressed), and comfort them in times of distress and anxiety, such as during a separation from parents (Dunn, 2002). These interaction patterns likely provide younger children with access to emotionally valuable play, conversation, and learning environments that may aid in their social cognitive and emotional growth.

Some studies have also found that advanced ToM may be differentially influenced by same- and opposite-sex siblings. Specifically, research suggests that children with more same-sex siblings may outperform those with fewer or no same-sex siblings on social cognitive measures (Dunn et al., 1994). As Kim, McHale, Osgood, and Crouter (2006) suggest, perhaps this same-sex sibling ToM superiority during emerging adolescence may be a result of more emotionally and psychologically intense sibling relationships that include elaborate mental state vocabulary and social interactions. In contrast, previous studies have shown that 3- to 5-year-olds who have at least one opposite-sex sibling perform better on false-belief tasks than children without an opposite-sex sibling (Carlson & Moses, 2001; Cassidy et al., 2005).

Research on sibling relationship quality provides an informative perspective on the current findings. For instance, same-sex (versus opposite sex) siblings may have more prosocial and intimate relationships, more frequent and imaginative play and conversations, and more opportunities to imitate and learn from each other (Furman & Buhrmester, 1985). Emotionally closer sibling relationships may elicit a deeper sharing of perspectives, beliefs, and emotions, which in turn may facilitate superior skills in the recognition and interpretation of mental and emotional diversity. Many studies have shown that higher sibling relationship quality predicts better performance on ToM tasks in young children (Brown et al., 1996; Hughes & Ensor, 2005; Hughes et al., 2014). During middle childhood and early adolescence, same-sex siblings maintain closeness and intimacy, whereas opposite-sex siblings show a significant decline (Kim et al., 2006). Thus, potential benefits for learning about psychological states from play, conversation, and sibling interactions may be maximized across emerging adolescence in families with same-sex siblings.

The application of a lifespan approach to social cognitive development may encourage future researchers to investigate if sibling diversity may not only be predictive of ToM during early childhood (as has been tested in previous research), but also may reduce in significance during middle childhood and emerging adolescence. During such a time of increased peer relations, children may experience greater opportunities for exposure to peers from diverse social groups outside of the home. However, beyond adolescence and into emerging adulthood, sibling relationships that were previously emotionally distant may change in intensity and become more supportive. In contrast, perhaps some siblings remain emotionally connected throughout adolescence, and such a supportive relationship may continue to help youth develop an advanced ToM and additional social cognitive abilities.

Related research on sibling attachment shows secure sibling relationships may influence emotional well-being and cooperation in young adults (Tibbetts & Scharfe, 2014). ToM researchers can build on such findings to explore the connections among sibling attachment, ToM, and other social cognitive and emotional abilities such as empathy and emotional well-being in emerging adolescents. Future research also needs to assess young people's definition of "family" as this may change throughout adolescence. That is, youth may perceive the concept of "family" as including a broader array of friends and family, such as close friends and romantic partners, extended family (cousins), grandparents, aunts, uncles. In addition, new research on human–animal interactions (HAI) suggest that some youth may perceive their pets or animal companions as valuable family members (Endenburg, van Lith, & Kirpensteijn, 2014; Melson, 2013).

The limited number of studies that show positive connections between companion animal relationships and social cognitive abilities such as empathy (Daly & Suggs, 2010; Daly, Taylor, & Signal, 2014; Endenburg et al., 2014; Mueller, 2014), often explore animal-assisted learning therapies that investigate therapy animals, such as therapy dogs who work with children with learning exceptionalities. Given that research is relatively nascent in the area of youth human–animal interactions and ToM (Mueller, 2014), a few previous studies, including our ongoing research with middle childhood learners and their relationships with companion animals, have provided some preliminary findings that suggest a positive relation between companion animal emotional attachment, ToM, and empathy scores (Tardif-Williams, Bosacki, & Huizinga, 2013; Melson, 2013; Mueller, 2014).

Applications: So What?

In general, research on attachment relations with family and peers in emerging adolescence holds important implications for educational practice. As mentioned earlier, past research has suggested that adolescents' attachment figures also have important implications for motivation in the academic domain (Duchesne & Larose, 2007; Duchesne & Ratelle, 2010). The transition to adolescence is a highly opportune time to investigate goal processes and their contextual determinants, as past studies have demonstrated that students' school interest and motivation to learn and become engaged decrease during this period (see Eccles & Roeser, 2003), and that goal intensity fluctuates from elementary to middle and secondary schools (Damon, 2008). However, to date, researchers have yet to examine how attachment security to parents and siblings contributes to achievement goal orientation and school engagement, especially during the transition to adolescence.

In addition, the role of gender in family attachment also needs to be explored and has significant implications for learning. That is, the majority of past studies focus on the role the mother–child attachment plays in children's learning. In contrast, few studies examine the role of the father, or of male family role models such as older brothers, cousins, uncles, and grandfathers, on young people's social cognitive learning. For example, the few existing studies have shown that children with a secure attachment to their father reported greater self-confidence (Grossmann et al., 2002; Lamb, 2002; Lamb & Lewis, 2004), engaged more in exploratory play (Grossman et al., 2002), were more engaged in their schoolwork (Nord, Brimhall, & West, 1997), and demonstrated stronger academic performance (Wagner & Phillips, 1992). Further research is thus needed to explore the contribution of fathers, grandfathers, uncles, brothers, and other male family members to achievement goal orientations.

In addition, secure child–caregiver attachments have also been found to increase one's feelings of self-worth, as well as academic engagement (Learner & Kruger, 1997). Research demonstrates a positive link between anxiety and attachment; previous findings showed that attachment security to the mother predicted fewer anxiety symptoms in children and adolescents (Duchesne & Ratelle, 2010; Zimmermann, Mohr, & Spangler, 2009). That is, past findings suggest that daily experiences of interactions (verbal and nonverbal) that promote security and comfort by the main caregiver may nurture youth's communication within that relationship. These interactions may enable caregivers to be more responsive to their child's negative emotions such as worry, guilt, shame, anger, and sadness (Geronimi & Woodruff-Borden, 2015). Such an awareness of their child's emotional states may also help the parent to support their child in the regulation of these emotions, which would limit the formation and development of anxiety symptoms (Duchesne & Ratelle, 2010).

Attachment, coping, and school engagement: A case for self-regulation

Past research shows attachment relations with family members and peers may influence how youth engage with their school work in terms of social cognitive abilities such as work attitude (e.g., cynicism, optimism), attention, and self-regulation (Moss & St-Laurent, 2001; Pintrich, 2000). That is, during the childhood to adolescence transition, research suggests that attachment relations with others may play a role in the reduction of children's self-perceived competencies (Harter, 1999). Such a decline may also be linked to pubertal changes that have the potential to have a negative impact on body image (Gleason, Alexander, & Somers, 2000; Greenspan & Deardorff, 2014), as well as on the academic transition from grade school to high school, which involves more academically challenging and socially complex contexts.

When young people experience a school transition, it is important for parents to be made aware of their positive contribution, through the establishment of a secure relationship with their child. Within the context of a secure attachment relationship, through responsive, caring, and nonjudgmental interactions, parents could create conditions that may help their children to learn how to cope with stress and develop effective social problem-solving and emotional regulation skills (Ge et al., 2009; Moss & St-Laurent, 2001). Consequently, as children develop these social cognitive skills, they may also construct a competent, caring, and compassionate self-view, which in turn may foster learning intentions that are oriented toward success and the development of social cognitive and emotional competencies. Thus, through compassion, kind acceptance, and supportive communication, parents can help their emerging adolescents to cope with the inevitable fears and worries that may arise during this major transition (Duchesne & Ratelle, 2010; Margolin, Ramos, Timmons, Miller, & Han, 2016).

In addition, many studies found that students' perceptions of academic competence and the presence of anxiety symptoms are influenced by classroom contextual factors, particularly teachers' implicit theories of personality, pedagogical, and assessment methods (Coplan, Bullock, Archbell, & Bosacki, 2015; Sternberg, 2014). These studies have illustrated that individualized teaching practices that value student cooperation and autonomy contribute to students' perceptions of academic competence. In contrast, teachers' beliefs and teaching practices based more on performance, social comparison, and competition have the potential to possibly undermine student competence and psychological well-being.

Past research suggests that young people could benefit from creating learning partnerships with teachers who employ inclusive and collaborative pedagogical practices. That is, such practices would aim to promote students' perceptions of social cognitive and emotional competencies including self-regulation and mastery goal orientation (Duckworth & Carlson, 2013). Moreover, given that many students may share feelings of anxiety and worry during emerging adolescence and related academic school transitions (Larson, 2011; Lecce, Bianco, Demichelli, & Cavallini, 2014; Lecce, Caputi, & Hughes, 2011; Lecce, Caputi, & Pagnin 2014; Letcher, Sanson, Smart, & Toumbourou, 2012), collaborative teaching and assessment practices could also be considered as a universal preventive measure for students' emotional health as they endure school transition stress.

Regarding insecure attachment, particularly disorganized attachment, some young people who show disorganized attachment may be more likely to develop a negative or distorted perception of the self. Such a negative or incoherent self-concept may compromise learning opportunities and the capacity to orient attention on personal success and self-regulation (Deci & Ryan, 2013; Ryan, Deci, Grolsnick, & LaGuardia, 2006). As such children may need to focus their emotional and cognitive energies on self-protection from their attachment figure, and they may experience challenges in the development of efficient emotion regulation and executive functioning strategies.

The accumulation of emotional challenges, increased academic and social responsibilities, and diminished self-esteem may heighten once children reach adolescence (Lyons-Ruth, Alpern, & Repacholi, 1993; Moss & St-Laurent, 2001). Further consequences of disorganized attachment for emerging adolescents may include the development of self-harming behaviors and self-sabotage, such as an increase in cruel and judgmental self-talk during learning situations and contexts (Baetens et al., 2014; Callan et al., 2014; Urdan, Midgley, & Anderman, 1998; Urdan, Ryan, Anderman, & Gheen, 2002).

In contrast, supportive and secure attachments with parents may help to immunize youth from the development of self-harmful coping behaviors such as nonsuicidal self-harming injuries (Hawton, Saunders, & O'Connor, 2012; Nock, 2009). Such findings could lead to the development of educational and clinical programs that aim to foster emotional self-regulation through peer and family-based interventions that promote supportive and caring relationships. For example, past research shows that a trusting and safe school environment has the potential to play a strong preventive role in self-harming behaviors among youth, and promote supportive and collaborative relationships (Fett et al., 2014).

Attachment theory may hold implications for emerging adolescence in that, according to traditional attachment theory (Bowlby, 1973), our primary relationships with our parents help to guide our subsequent relationships with others throughout our lifetime including our siblings, peers, and romantic partners (Margolin et al., 2016). To illustrate the long-term implications of parental attachment, LaGuardia, Ryan, Couchman, and Deci (2000) studied a group of late adolescents' connections between the security of their initial parental attachments and their current attachment relationships with their romantic partners and best friends. Results showed that one-third of the variance in attachment security was explained by the between-person level suggesting consistency across attachment security across relationships. In particular, LaGuardia et al. (2000) found that the need for autonomy and competence within a relationship predicted attachment security. Such a finding supports the notion that a strong sense of self is necessary for secure attachment relationships and vice versa (Deci & Ryan, 2013).

Within the conceptual framework of attachment, teacher–student relationships might be especially important during the transition to adolescence when motivation, engagement, and achievement may be vulnerable to decline. Research from a stage–environment fit perspective has shown that the nature of change in students' engagement during the transition to adolescence depends largely on the emotional climate of the school and classroom environment such as the inclusion of information and digital technologies

(Parisi, 2013). For example, past research shows that when students move into an inviting and supportive school environment, they do not show the same declines as compared to students who are exposed to a competitive and nonsupportive climate and may thus not enjoy their learning context (Turkle, 2015).

As I will discuss in more detail in Chapter 9 on communication, digital technologies, and social cognition, few studies explore how aspects of the classroom context such as the use of digital learning tools relate to peer relationships and social cognitive development (Parks, 2014; Turkle, 2011, 2015). To this date, researchers have yet to follow students' digital media habits and histories, attachment relations, and their social cognitive development across the transition from middle grade school to high school. Given the significant changes that take place in classroom contexts and peer groups, such a context provides a unique window for future researchers to examine the interplay among context, peer relationships, and academic, social, and emotional adjustment.

Attachment and mental health within schools

Given that research has found job burnout and stress to be associated with health problems (Schaufeli, Martinez, Pinto, Salanova, & Bakker, 2002) and unhealthy coping strategies (Scharfe & Eldredge, 2001; Siegel, 2013), attachment theory could be a useful framework to explore school burnout, anxiety, and stress. Recent research with Canadian emerging adults showed that positive associations exist between secure attachment relations with parents and peers and their school engagement and mental health (Bumbacco & Scharfe, 2014). More specifically, Bumbacco and Scharfe reported preliminary findings from a pilot study to support the hypothesis that school burnout and schoolwork engagement may be influenced by interpersonal relationships.

In particular, Bumbacco and Scharfe's (2014) correlational analysis indicated that for each of three relationships (mother, father, and peer), preoccupied attachment was moderately associated with cynicism. Such a finding could suggest that preoccupied students may be prone to emotional burnout and less likely to become engaged or absorbed in their schoolwork. Compared to other forms of insecure attachment styles such as disorganized, fearful, and dismissing attachment, preoccupied, fearful students may become disengaged and bored with their academic work.

Furthermore, Bumbacco and Scharfe (2014) found that, compared to mother and peer attachment, the strongest positive relations were found between school work engagement and father attachment. Such findings also support recent longitudinal research with younger children that suggest, compared to mother attachment, stronger associations were found between 2-year-olds' father attachment and school behavioral competencies six years later (Boldt, Kochanska, Yoon, & Nordling, 2014). As others suggest (Bretherton, 2010; Kochanska & Kim, 2013; Tibbett & Scharfe, 2015), future longitudinal studies need to explore the links between social cognitive development and relationships with fathers, mothers, and siblings in older children and adolescents. For example, studies that follow young people's attachment style throughout their academic journey from grade school to university or college could help educators and researchers identify students who are at risk for emotional burnout and disengagement in their studies. Thus, such studies have implications for creating educational interventions for academically or emotionally challenged students based on their attachment style with parents and peers, as well as siblings (Duchesne & Ratelle, 2014).

Similar research with Chinese and US parents suggests that parenting differences in China and in the United States may have differential implications for children's academic and emotional functioning (Pomerantz, Ng, Cheung, & Qu, 2014). Pomerantz et al. discussed whether the Chinese style of learning-related parenting fosters children's academic functioning, which may contribute to the relatively higher scores in Chinese students' academic achievement found in past research. In addition, other researchers suggest Americans should adopt the Chinese style of learning-related parenting (Huntsinger, Jose, & Larson, 1998).

Given that past research has shown lower feelings of self-worth and happiness among Chinese youth (Diener & Suh, 1999), Pomerantz et al. (2014) highlighted the costs of the Chinese parenting style for children's emotional functioning. Overall, although Pomerantz et al.'s research focused on China and the United States, an approach to learning-related parenting that integrates aspects of all cultural styles is valuable, and could be applied to various culturally diverse societies across the globe.

Such proposals for more globally informed, holistic, and supportive parenting and teaching practices may help to further young people's social, emotional, and cognitive worlds and may be applicable to many culturally diverse communities. That is, such a multicultural and integrative approach suggests that, regardless of their ethnic heritage, socioeconomic status, or other attributes such as political views, parents and teachers are exposed in some ways to their country's mainstream cultural values via the media as well as other avenues (Sperber, 1996; Sternberg, 2014). However, within various multicultural countries that consist of many combinations of cultures, such as China and Canada, variability in the extent to which parents adopt such values leads to variability in their learning-related parenting and student mental health.

Past research on parenting assumes that the variability is nested within distributions of parenting in two countries that may in some ways overlap, but are also distinct (Muehlenkamp et al., 2012). Although within country variation is significant in that it creates differences in children's functioning within various countries, given the increasingly culturally diverse student population across the globe, researchers need to focus on differences in the social and emotional factors involved within parent–child and teacher–student relationships. Such research within culturally diverse countries will help researchers and educators to understand what underlies differences in emerging adolescents' social cognitive and emotional functioning.

As educators, we need to explore the emotional worlds of mixed heritage youth, and ways in which their learning experiences may differ from those youth who are raised in a uniethnic home. Given the increasing prevalence of multicultural families, a critical examination of the way in which race and ethnicity is taught in schools is necessary. Educational and research programs need to allow for fluidity and multiplicity regarding racial-ethnic identification. For example, within the educational context, universal standards for human rights and social justice need to be promoted (Masten, 2014). To provide a psychologically safe learning environment for learners of all ages, the implementation of "the golden rule" ("treat others the way you wish to be treated") is necessary to promote critical dialogue and enquiry among all students.

The school culture or climate also represents the nature of the interpersonal relationships (student–student, student–teacher, teacher–teacher/parent) that exist in the school and how involved parents are in daily activities and decision-making processes in the school. The emotional or psychological tone that is set in the school establishes expectations for standards of interpersonal relationships among the students beyond school walls. That is, to promote a larger culture of kindness, compassion, and empathy, the classroom and school need to reflect the larger community (and vice versa). Furthermore, educators and researchers need to collaborate to address emerging tensions between ethnic and school or academic identities within educational practice (Ellis et al., 2012; Price, Chin, Higa-McMillan, Kim, & Frueh, 2013).

Future Questions

Future research needs to continue to explore the patterns of attachment relations in terms of relationships with peers, family members (parents, siblings, extended family), as well as coaches and colleagues. The complexity of each relationship may be investigated longitudinally to document how social exchanges change over time, in relation to the development of self-perceptions as well as related social cognitive abilities such as perspective-taking, the understanding of nonverbal communication such as gestures, and empathic sensitivities.

Given that attachment research shows that the need for exploration and the drive to maintain closeness and proximity is at the juncture of many developmental transitions, including the development of self-consciousness and self-concept during the second year of life, this pattern requires further exploration within the context of adolescence. Of particular interest is the question of what motivates young people's drive to engage in risk-taking leisure activities (e.g., speed car racing, skydiving, etc.) (Bjork & Pardini, 2015), and the current need to document and share one's personal experiences with the use of personal mobile communication devices (e.g., the "selfie" syndrome via smartphones). Future research could explore if an adolescent's propensity to engage in such leisure activities relates to their attachment relations with parents, siblings, peers, and how such behaviors relate to identity and moral self-perceptions. As Rochat states (2009), the negotiation of the self-image with others is what drives most of psychological research—particularly social cognitive research.

An increasingly emerging area of literature as noted throughout this book is the area of applied cognitive social neuroscience or neuroeducation (Busso, 2014; Carter, 2014; Liszkowski, 2013; Mahy, Moses, & Pfeifer, 2014). That is, the combined efforts of neuroscientists and applied social cognitive developmentalists within learning contexts could lead to significant educational and clinical implications for practice. The development of attachment relations across the lifespan may particularly benefit from a marriage between developmental social cognitive research and neuroscience, particularly during the transition to adolescence from middle childhood.

For example, to explore the connections between the development of autonomy and attachment relations throughout adolescence, the combination of a neurodevelopmental and relational systems perspective may help researchers to make sense of the complex area of social cognitive development during emerging adolescence, particularly in terms of self-regulation, ToM, and attachment relations (Margolin et al., 2016; Overton, 2013). As noted by Waters and Tucker (2013), the development of autonomy and attachment can be described in cybernetic terms that describe the dynamics of the development of emotional self-regulatory mechanisms within the human brain. That is, the development of autonomy and attachment can be described as a dual processes as the impetus (impulse) and the artus (constraint) (Tucker & Luu, 2012). As social cognitive research suggests, cognitive development occurs within the context of social relations.

To illustrate, autonomy may represent a shift in the influence of the parent–child relationship from one aspect of the neurocybernetic module to the other (i.e., from impetus to artus). The attachment relation may then be retained as a necessary component for effective self-regulation. However, given the negotiation between genes and environment (Belsky & Pluess, 2009), the attachment relation may influence by various environmental demands, as well as internal drives and self-schema. As Waters and Tucker (2013) suggest, perhaps neurocognitive development proceeds within the context of the attachment–autonomy negotiation. Such a neurodevelopmental approach to studying the attachment–autonomy dynamic between two people could help researchers and educators to learn more about how emerging adolescents may develop relationships with others as well as a sense of identity, self-compassion, and self-regulation.

Future studies on family relationships and young people's social cognitive development also need to explore the question of how to piece together findings from cultural neuroscience research into an integrative framework. That is, integration is required at many levels of analysis. As attachment researchers suggest (Keller, 2013; Obsuth et al., 2014), there is evidence of a cultural influence on social cognitive and developmental neuroplasticity at multiple levels. That is, from the more macro level of biological evolution to the more micro levels of neural and genetic change. Similarly, Kim and Sasaki (2014) posit that a major challenge for researchers is to demonstrate how changes at one developmental level can lead to changes at another. For example, to better understand how family interactions affect social cognitive development, a gene–culture interaction model may help researchers to understand how neural and molecular mechanisms link cultural and genetic factors to culture-specific behavioral outcomes (Overton, 2013).

Studies that investigate gene–environment interactions may help to inform the mechanisms of the gene–culture interaction model within the family relationship. For example, past studies have shown how contextual factors may trigger changes in gene expression (Keller, 2013; Dobbs, 2009), and may implicate physiological responses in empathy and stress reactions (Rodrigues, Saslow, Garcia, John, & Keltner, 2009). Moreover, brain reactivity may explain psychological and biological outcomes of psychosocial challenges such as depression and anxiety that may be experienced by young people (Carter, 2014). Such new theories and the integration of genetic, physiological, and neural evidence may be necessary for cultural neuroscience to move toward a more holistic understanding of the mind, emotions, and relationships during emerging adolescence (Larson, 2011). Thus, there remains a need for innovative and integrative theoretical frameworks that will enable researchers to take advantage of the unique potential of neuroscientific methods and generate new research questions for social cognition in young people.

As mentioned earlier, future research on family relations also needs to explore emerging adolescents' experiences with companion animals, and how this relates to the young person's social cognitive and emotional competencies (Melson, 2014; Mueller, 2014). Drawing from the animal-assisted therapy and humane education programs (Baumgartner & Cho, 2014; Faver, 2010), many educational programs have been developed to help youth with social-emotional learning exceptionalities to develop a positive sense of self and effective life and interpersonal skills. Based on past studies that suggest caring relationships with companion animals have a positive influence on the mental and emotional health of young children and adults (Baumgartner & Cho, 2014; Endenburg et al., 2014; Mueller, 2014), there remains a lack of research on emerging adolescents and HAI, as well as their attachment relations with others and various social cognitive abilities such as ToM and self-regulation (Hurley, 2014; Mueller, 2014).

Thus, future researchers need to investigate the relation between typically developing emerging adolescents' perceptions of their HAI and their social cognitive competencies such as ToM, self-perceptions, and emotional understandings. As I will further explain in Chapters 10 and 11 on exceptional learning and developmental pedagogy, such a research program will promote the development of affective and moral educational programs that focus on the development of caring and compassionate relationships with all living beings including oneself.

Summary

Given the growth in diverse learning communities across the globe, how do we as educators and researchers work with parents to help young people to develop social cognitive competence, self-regulation, and emotional well-being (Pomerantz et al., 2014)? As discussed in this chapter, given that family relationships help to guide the negotiation between attachment and autonomy, secure attachment relations are viewed as crucial to the development of self-regulation and social cognitive competencies across childhood and adolescence. Future research needs to continue to explore the particular role parents, siblings, and extended family play, including the role of companion animals within the framework of attachment theory and social cognitive learning.

In addition, given societal growth, the definition of family needs continual revision and re-examination as this definition continues to change across time and cultures. Thus, the role of the family's cultural heritage and its multiple definitions requires further investigation as such factors have the potential to play a crucial role in young people's social cognitive development and self-regulation. In the next chapter, I will continue to explore the role culture plays in social cognitive development, particularly the role of gender and cultural ethnicity.

References

Ainsworth, M. D. S. (1989). Attachments beyond infancy. *American Psychologist, 44,* 709–716. doi:10.1037/0003-066X.44.4.709

Baetens, I., Claes, L., Onghena, P., Grietens, H., Van Leeuwen, K., Pieters, C., … Martin, G. (2014). Is non-suicidal self-injury associated with parenting and family factors? *Journal of Early Adolescence, 34,* 387–405.

Baumeister, R. F., Bratslavsky, E., Finkenauer, C., & Vohs, K. D. (2001). Bad is stronger than good. *Review of General Psychology, 5,* 323–370.

Baumgartner, E., & Cho, J. (2014). Animal-assisted activities for students with disabilities: Obtaining stakeholders' approval and planning strategies for teachers. *Childhood Education, 90,* 281–290.

Belsky, J., & Pluess, M. (2009). Beyond diathesis stress: Differential susceptibility to environmental influences. *Psychological Bulletin, 135,* 885–908.

Bjork, J., & Pardini, D. (2015). "Who are those risk-taking adolescents?" Individual differences in developmental neuroimaging. *Developmental Cognitive Neuroscience, 11,* 56–64.

Boldt, L., Kochanska, G., Yoon, J., & Nordling, J. (2014). Children's attachment to both parents from toddler age to middle childhood: Links to adaptive and maladaptive outcomes. *Attachment & Human Development, 16,* 211–229.

Booth-LaForce, C., & Kerns, K. A. (2009). Child-parent attachment relationships, peer relationships, and peer group functioning. In K. H. Rubin, W. Bukowski, & B. Laursen (Eds.), *Handbook of peer interactions, peer relationships, and peer group functioning* (pp. 490–507). New York, NY: Guilford.

Bosacki, S. (2005). *Culture of classroom silence.* New York, NY: Peter Lang.

Bosacki, S. (2013). Theory of mind understanding and conversational patterns in early adolescence. *Journal of Genetic Psychology, 174,* 170–191.

Bosacki, S. (2015). Children's theory of mind, self-perceptions, and peer relations: A longitudinal study. *Infant and Child Development, 24,* 175–188. doi:10.1002/icd.1878

Bosacki, S., Bialecka-Pikul, M., & Szpak, M. (March, 2014). *Attachment, self-concept, and Theory of Mind in Polish adolescents: Does gender play a role?* Poster presented at the biennial meeting of the Society for Research in Adolescence. Austin, Texas.

Bowlby, J. (1973). *Attachment and loss: Vol. 2. Separation.* New York, NY: Basic Books.

Bretherton, I. (2010). Fathers in attachment theory and research: A review. *Early Child Development and Care, 180*(1–2), 9–23.

Brinton, B., & Fujiki, M. (2002). Social development in children with specific language impairment and profound hearing loss. In P. Smith & C. Hart (Eds.), *Blackwell handbook of childhood social development* (pp. 588–603). Oxford, England: Blackwell.

Brown, J., Donelan-McCall, N., & Dunn, J. (1996). Why talk about mental states? The significance of children's conversations with friends, siblings, and mothers. *Child Development, 67,* 836–849. doi:10.1111/j.1467-8624.1996.tb01767.x

Bumbacco, C., & Scharfe, E. (2014). *"Time flies when I'm studying:" Attachment, school burnout, and schoolwork engagement.* Poster presented at the Development 2014 Meeting, Carlton University, Ottawa, ON, Canada.

Busso, D. (2014). Neurobiological processes of risk and resilience in adolescence: Implications for policy and prevention science. *Mind, Brain, and Education, 8,* 34–43.

Callan, M., Kay, A., & Dawtry, R. (2014). Making sense of misfortune: Deservingness, self-esteem, and patterns. *Journal of Personality and Social Psychology, 107,* 142–162.

Carlson, S. (2011). Introduction to the special issue: Executive function. *Journal of Experimental Child Psychology, 108,* 411–413.

Carlson, S. M., & Moses, L. J. (2001). Individual differences in inhibitory control and children's theory of mind. *Child Development, 72*(4), 1032–1053. doi:10.1111/1467.8624.00333

Carpendale, J. I. M., & Lewis, C. (2004). Constructing an understanding of mind: The development of children's understanding of mind within social interaction. *Behavioral and Brain Sciences, 27,* 79–150.

Carter, S. (2014). Oxytocin pathways and the evolution of human behavior. *Annual Review of Psychology, 65,* 17–39.

Cassidy, K. W., Fineberg, D. S., Brown, K., & Perkins, A. (2005). Theory of mind may be contagious, but you don't catch it from your twin. *Child Development, 76*(1), 97–106. doi:10.1111/j.1467-8624.2005.00832.x

Cassidy, K. W., Werner, R. S., Rourke, M., Zubernis, L. S., & Balaraman, G. (2003). The relationship between psychological under-standing and positive social behaviors. *Social Development, 12*(2), 198–221. doi:10.1111/1467-9507.00229

Chaplin, L., Hill, R., & John, D. (2014). Poverty and materialism: A look at impoverished versus affluent children. *Journal of Public Policy & Marketing, 33,* 78–92.

Cicirelli, V. G. (1995). *Sibling relationships across the life span.* New York, NY: Plenum.

Clark, S., & Symons, D. (2009). Representations of attachment relationships, the self, and significant others in 5 to 9 year old children. *Journal of the Canadian Academy of Child and Adolescent Psychiatry, 18,* 316–321.

Coplan, R. J., Bullock, A., Archbell, K. A., & Bosacki, S. (2015). Preschool teachers' atti-tudes, beliefs, and emotional reactions to young children's peer group behaviors. *Early Childhood Research Quarterly, 30,* 117–127. doi:10.1016/j.ecresq.2014.09.005

Coren, S., & Luthar, S. (2014). Pursuing perfec-tion: Distress and interpersonal functioning among adolescent boys in single-sex and co-educational independent schools. *Psychology in the Schools, 51,* 931–946.

Cutting, A., & Dunn, J. (2002). The cost of understanding other people: Social cognition predicts young children's sensitivity to criti-cism. *Journal of Child Psychology and Psychiatry, 43,* 849–860.

Daly, B., & Suggs, S. (2010). Teachers' experi-ences with humane education and animals in the elementary classroom: Implications for empathy development. *Journal of Moral Education, 39,* 101–112.

Daly, B., Taylor, N., & Signal, T. (2014). Pups and babes: Quantifying sources of difference in emotional and behavioral reactions to accounts of human and animal abuse. *Anthrozoos, 27,* 205–217.

Damon, W. (2008). *The path to purpose: How young people find their calling in life.* New York, NY: Simon & Schuster.

Deci, E., & Ryan, R. (2013). The importance of autonomy for development and well-being. In B. Sokol, M. Grouzet, & U. Muller (Eds.), *Self-regulation and autonomy: Social and developmental dimensions of human conduct* (pp. 19–46). New York, NY: Cambridge University Press.

Devine, R., & Hughes, C. (2014). Relations between false belief understanding and exec-utive function in early childhood: A meta-analysis. *Child Development, 85,* 1777–1794.

Diener, E., & Suh, E. M. (1999). National differ-ences in subjective wellbeing. In D. Kahneman, E. Diener, & N. Schwartz (Eds.), *Wellbeing: The foundations of hedonic psy-chology* (pp. 434–450). New York, NY: Russell Sage Foundation.

Dobbs, D. (2009). Orchid children. *The Atlantic, 1,* 51–60.

Dostoevsky, F. (1990/1880). *The brothers Karamazov* (R. Pevear & L. Volokhonsky Trans.). New York, NY: Farrar, Straus and Giroux.

Duchesne, S., & Larose, S. (2007). Adolescent parental attachment and academic motiva-tion and performance in early adolescence. *Journal of Applied Social Psychology, 37,* 1501–1521.

Duchesne, S., & Ratelle, C. F. (2010). Parental behaviors and adolescents' achievement goals at the beginning of middle school: Emotional problems as potential mediators. *Journal of Educational Psychology, 102,* 497–507.

Duchesne, S., & Ratelle, C. F. (2014). Attachment security to mothers and fathers and develop-mental trajectories of depressive symptoms in adolescence: Which parent for which trajectory? *Journal of Youth and Adolescence, 43*, 641–654.

Duckworth, A., & Carlson, S. (2013). Self-regulation and school success. In B. Sokol, M. Grouzet, & U. Muller (Eds.), *Self-regulation and autonomy: Social and developmental dimensions of human conduct* (pp. 208–230). New York, NY: Cambridge University Press.

Dunn, J. (2002). Mindreading, emotion understanding, and relationships. In W. W. Hartup & R. K. Silbereisen (Eds.), *Growing points in developmental science: An introduction* (pp. 167–176). New York, NY: Psychology Press.

Dunn, J., Slomkowski, C., & Beardsall, L. (1994). Sibling relationships from the preschool period through middle childhood and early adolescence. *Developmental Psychology, 30*(3), 315–324. doi:10.1037/0012-1649.30.3.315

Eccles, J. & Roeser, R. (2003). Schools as developmental contexts. In G. Adams & M. Berzonsky (Eds.), *Blackwell handbook of adolescence* (pp. 129–148). Malden, MA: Blackwell.

Ellis, B., Del Giudice, M., Dishion, T., Figueredo, A., Gray, P., Griskevicius, V., … Wilson, D. (2012). The evolutionary basis of risky adolescent behavior: Implications for science, policy, and practice. *Developmental Psycholology, 48*, 598–623.

Endenburg, N., van Lith, H. A., & Kirpensteijn, J. (2014). Longitudinal study of Dutch children's attachment to companion animals. *Society and Animals, 22*, 390–414.

Erwin, P. (1995). *Friendship and peer relations in children.* Chichester, England: Wiley.

Faver, C. A. (2010). School-based humane education as a strategy to prevent violence: Review and recommendations. *Children and Youth Services Review, 32*, 365–370.

Fett, K., Shergill, S., Gromann, P., Dumontheil, L., Blakemore, S., Yakub, F., & Krabbendam L. (2014). Trust and social reciprocity in adolescence—A matter of perspective taking. *Journal of Adolescence, 37*, 175–184.

Fonagy, P., & Target, M. (1997). Attachment and reflective function: Their role in self-organization. *Development and Psychopathology, 9*, 679–700.

Furman, W., & Buhrmester, D. (1985). Children's perceptions of the qualities of sibling relationships. *Child Development, 56*(2), 448–461. doi:10.2307/1129733

Ge, X., Natsuaki, M. N., Neiderhiser, J. M., & Reiss, D. (2009). The longitudinal effects of stressful life events on adolescent depression are buffered by parent–child closeness. *Development and Psychopathology, 21*, 621–635. doi:10.1017/S0954579409000339

German, T. P., & Hehman, J. A. (2006). Representational and executive selection resources in "theory of mind": Evidence from compromised belief-desire reasoning in old age. *Cognition, 101*, 129–152. doi:10.1016/j.cognition.2005.05.007

Geronimi, E., & Woodruff-Borden, J. (2015). The language of worry: Examining linguistic worry models. *Cognition & Emotion, 29*, 311–318.

Gleason, J., Alexander, A., & Somers, C. (2000). Later adolescents' reactions to three types of childhood teasing: Relations with self-esteem and body image. *Social Behaviour and Personality: An International Journal, 28*, 471–479.

Greenspan, L., & Deardorff, J. (2014). *The new puberty: How to navigate early development in today's girls.* New York, NY: Rodale.

Grossmann, K., Grossmann, K. E., Fremmer-Bombik, E., Kindler, H., Scheuerer-Englisch, H., & Zimmermann, P. (2002). The uniqueness of the child–father attachment relationship: Fathers' sensitive and challenging play as a pivotal variable in a 16-year longitudinal study. *Social Development, 11*, 307–331.

Harter, S. (1999). *The construction of the self: A developmental perspective.* New York, NY: Guilford.

Hawton, K., Saunders, K. E. A., & O'Connor, R. C. (2012). Self-harm and suicide in adolescents. *The Lancet, 379*, 2373–2382. doi:10.1016/S0140-6736(12)60322-5

Hazel, N., Oppenheimer, C., Young, J., Technow, J., & Hankin, B. (2014). Parent relationship quality buffers against the effect of peer stressors on depressive symptoms from middle childhood to adolescence. *Developmental Psychology, 50,* 2115–2123.

Hsiao, C., Koren-Karie, N., Bailey, H., & Moran, G. (2015). It takes two to talk: Longitudinal associations among infant–mother attachment, maternal attachment representations, and mother–child emotion dialogues. *Attachment and Human Development, 17,* 43–64.

Hughes, C. (1998). Executive function in preschoolers: Links with theory of mind and verbal ability. *British Journal of Developmental Psychology, 16*(2), 233–253. doi:10.1111/j.2044-835X.1998.tb00921.x

Hughes, C. (2011). *Social understanding and social lives: From toddlerhood through to the transition to school.* New York, NY: Psychology Press.

Hughes, C., & Ensor, R. (2005). Executive function and theory-of-mind in 2 year olds: A family affair? *Developmental neuropsychology, 28*(2), 645–668. doi:10.1207/s15326942dn2802_5

Hughes, C., White, N., & Ensor, R. (2014). How does talk about thoughts, desires, and feelings foster children's socio-cognitive development? Mediators, moderators, and implications for intervention. In K. H. Lagattuta (Ed.), *Children and emotion: New insights into developmental affective science* (pp. 95–105). Geneva, Switzerland: Karger Medical and Scientific Publishers.

Huntsinger, C. S., Jose, P. E., & Larson, S. L. (1998). Do parent practices to encourage academic competence influence the social adjustment of young European American and Chinese American children? *Developmental Psychology, 34,* 747–756. doi:10.1037/0012-1649.34.4.747

Hurley, K. (2014). Development and human–animal interaction: Commentary on Mueller. *Human Development, 57,* 50–54.

Hyde, J. (2014). Gender similarities and differences. *Annual Review of Psychology, 65,* 373–398.

Keller, M. (2013). Attachment and culture. *Journal of Cross-Cultural Psychology, 44,* 175–194.

Kerns, K. A. (2008). Attachment in middle childhood. In J. Cassidy & P. Shaver (Eds.), *Handbook of attachment* (2nd ed., pp. 366–382). New York, NY: Guilford.

Kerns, K., & Brumariu, L. (2014). Is insecure parent–child attachment a risk factor for the development of anxiety in childhood and adolescence? *Child Development Perspectives, 8,* 12–17.

Kim, J. Y., McHale, S. M., Osgood, D. W., & Crouter, A. C. (2006). Longitudinal course and family correlates of sibling relationships from childhood through adolescence. *Child Development, 77*(6), 1746–1761.

Kim, H., & Sasaki, J. (2014). Cultural neuroscience: Biology of the mind in cultural contexts. *Annual Review of Psychology, 65,* 487–514.

Kluger, J. (2011). *The sibling effect.* New York, NY: Rainman.

Kochanska, G., & Kim, S. (2013). Early attachment organization with both parents and future behavior problems: From infancy to middle childhood. *Child Development, 84,* 283–296. doi:10.1111/j.1467-8624.2012.01852.x

Kołodziejczyk, A. M., & Bosacki, S. L. (2015). Children's understandings of characters' beliefs in persuasive arguments: Links with gender and theory of mind. *Early Child Development and Care, 185*(4), 562–577. doi:10.1080/03004430.2014.940930

Lagattuta, K. H., Nucci, L., & Bosacki, S. L. (2010). Bridging theory of mind and the personal domain: Children's reasoning about resistance to parental control. *Child Development, 81,* 616–635. doi:10.1111/j.1467-8624.2009.01419.x

Lagattuta, K. H., Kramer, H. J., Kennedy, K., Hjortsvang, K., Goldfarb, D., & Tashjian, S. (2015). *Beyond Sally's missing marble: Further development in children's understanding of mind and emotion in middle childhood. Advances in child development and behavior* (Vol. 48). Oxford, England: Elsevier. doi:10.1016/bs.acdb.2014.11.005

LaGuardia, J., Ryan, R., Couchman, C., & Deci, E. (2000). Within-person variation in security of attachment: A self-determination theory perspective on attachment, need fulfillment, and well-being. *Journal of Personality and Social Psychology, 79,* 367–384.

Lalonde, C., & Chandler, M. (1995). False belief understanding goes to school: On the social-emotional consequences of coming early or late to a first theory of mind. *Cognition and Emotion, 9,* 167–185.

Lamb, M. E. (2002). Father involvement and child development: Section preface. In C. S. Tamis-LeMonda & N. Cabrera (Eds.), *Handbook of father involvement: Multidisciplinary perspectives* (pp. 91–92). Mahwah, NJ: Erlbaum.

Lamb, M. E., & Lewis, C. (2004). The development and significance of father–child relationships in two-parent families. In M. E. Lamb (Ed.), *The role of the father in child development* (4th ed.). New York, NY: Wiley.

Larson, R. (2011). Positive development in a disorderly world. *Journal of Research in Adolescence, 21,* 317. doi:10.1111/j.1532-7795.2010.00707.x

Learner, D., & Kruger, L. J. (1997). Attachment, self-concept, and academic motivation in high school students. *American Journal of Orthopsychiatry, 67,* 485–492.

Lecce, S., Bianco, F., Demichelli, P., & Cavallini, E. (2014). Training preschoolers on first-order false belief understanding: Transfer of advanced ToM skills and metamemory. *Child Development, 85,* 2404–2418.

Lecce, S., Caputi, M., & Hughes, C. (2011). Does sensitivity to criticism mediate the relationship between theory of mind and academic achievement? *Journal of Experimental Child Psychology, 110,* 313–331.

Lecce, S., Caputi, M., & Pagnin, A. (2014). Long-term effect of theory of mind on school achievement: The role of sensitivity to criticism. *European Journal of Developmental Psychology, 11*(3), 305–318. doi:10.1080/17405629.2013.821944

Lecompte, V., Moss, E., Cyr, C., & Pascuzzo, K. (2014). Preschool attachment, self-esteem and the development of preadolescent anxiety

and depression. *Attachment & Human Development, 16,* 242–260.

Letcher, P., Sanson, A., Smart, D., & Toumbourou, J. W. (2012). Precursors and correlates of anxiety trajectories from late childhood to late adolescence. *Journal of Clinical Child and Adolescent Psychology, 41,* 417–432.

Leussis, M., & Andersen, S. (2008). Is adolescence a sensitive period for depression? Behavioral and neuroanatomical findings from a social stress model. *Synapse, 6,* 22–30.

Licata, M., Kristen, S., & Soldian, B. (2016). Mother–child interaction as a cradle of theory of mind: The role of maternal emotional availability. *Social Development, 25,* 139–156.

Lippman, J., & Campbell, S. (2014). Damned if you do, damned if you don't … if you're a girl: Relational and normative contexts of adolescent sexting in the United States. *Journal of Children and Media, 8*(4), 371–386. doi:10.1080/17482798.2014.923009

Liszkowski, U. (2013). Using theory of mind. *Child Development Perspectives, 2,* 104–109.

Luppa, M., Sikorski, C., Luck, T., Ehreke, L., Konnopka, A, & Riedel-Heller, S. (2012). Age- and gender-specific prevalence of depression in latest-life—systematic review and meta-analysis. *Journal of Affective Disorders, 136,* 212–221.

Luthar, S., & Barkin, S. (2012). Are affluent youth truly "at risk"? Vulnerability and resilience across three diverse samples. *Development and Psychopathology, 24,* 429–449.

Luthar, S., Barkin, S., & Crossman, E. (2013). "I can, therefore I must": Fragility in the upper middle classes. *Development and Psychopathology, 4,* 1529–1549.

Luthar, S. S., & Goldstein, A. S. (2008). Substance use and related behaviors among suburban late adolescents: The importance of perceived parent containment. *Development and Psychopathology, 20,* 591–614.

Luthar, S., & Latendresse, S. J. (2005a). Children of the affluent: Challenges to well-being. *Current Directions in Psychological Science, 14,* 49–53.

Luthar, S., & Latendresse, S. (2005b). Comparable "risks" at the socioeconomic status extremes: Preadolescents' perceptions of parenting. *Development and Psychopathology, 17,* 207–230.

Lyman, E., & Luthar, S. (2014). Further evidence on the "costs of privilege": Perfectionism in high-achieving youth at socioeconomic extremes. *Psychology in the Schools, 51,* 91–930.

Lyons-Ruth, K., Alpern, L., & Repacholi, B. (1993). Disorganized infant attachment classification and maternal psychosocial problems as predictors of hostile-aggressive behavior in the preschool classroom. *Child Development, 64,* 572–585.

Mahler, M. S., Pine, F., & Bergman, A. (1975). *The psychological birth of the human infant: Symbiosis and individuation.* New York, NY: Basic Books.

Mahy, C., Moses, L., & Pfeifer, J. (2014). How and where: Theory-of-mind in the brain. *Developmental Cognitive Neuroscience, 9,* 68–81.

Main, M., & Solomon, J. (1990). Procedures for identifying infants as disorganized/disoriented during the Ainsworth Strange Situation. In M. T. Greenberg, D. Cicchetti, & E. M. Cummings (Eds.), *Attachment in the preschool years: Theory, research, and intervention* (pp. 121–160). Chicago, IL: University of Chicago Press.

Marchetti, A., Castelli, I., Sanvito, L., & Massaro, D. (2014). Is a bird in the hand worth two in the future? Intertemporal choice, attachment and theory of mind in school-aged children. *Frontiers in Psychology, 5,* 483–493.

Margolin, G., Ramos, M., Timmons, A., Miller, K., & Han, S. (2016). Intergenerational transmission of aggression: Physiological regulatory processes. *Child Development Perspectives, 10,* 15–21.

Masten, A. (2014). Global perspectives on resilience in children and youth. *Child Development, 85,* 6–20.

McAlister, A., & Peterson, C. (2013). Siblings, theory of mind, and executive functioning in children aged 3–6 years: New longitudinal evidence. *Child Development, 84,* 1442–1458.

Meins, E., Fernyhough, C., Arnott, B., Leekam, S., & de Rosnay, M. (2013). Mind-mindedness and theory of mind: Mediating roles of language and perspectival symbolic play. *Child Development, 84,* 1777–1790. doi:10.1111/cdev.12061

Melson, G. (2013). Children's ideas about the moral standing and social welfare of non-human species. *Journal of Sociology and Social Welfare, 60,* 81–106.

Miller, S. A. (2012). *Theory of mind: Beyond the preschool years.* New York, NY: Psychology Press.

Mischel, W. (1958). Preference for delayed reinforcement: An experimental study of a cultural observation. *Journal of Abnormal & Social Psychology, 56,* 57–61.

Mischel, W. (1961). Father absence and delay of gratification: A cross-cultural comparison. *Journal of Abnormal & Social Psychology, 63,* 116–124.

Mitchell-Copeland, J., Denham, S. A., & DeMulder, E. K. (1997). Q-sort assessment of child-teacher attachment relationships and social competence in the preschool. *Early Education & Development, 8,* 27–39. doi:10.1207/s15566935eed08013

Moore, C., Barresi, J., & Thompson, C. (1998). The cognitive basis of future-oriented prosocial behavior. *Social Development, 7,* 198–218. doi:10.1111/1467-9507.00062

Moore, C., & Symons, D. (2005). Attachment, theory of mind, and delay of gratification. In B. Homer and C. Tamis-LeMonda (Eds.), *The development of social cognition and communication* (pp. 181–199). Mahwah, NJ: Erlbaum.

Moss, E., & St-Laurent, D. (2001). Attachment at school age and academic performance. *Developmental Psychology, 37,* 863–874.

Muehlenkamp, J. J., Claes, L., Havertape, L., & Plener, P. L. (2012). International prevalence of adolescent non-suicidal self-injury and deliberate self-harm. *Child and Adolescent Psychiatry and Mental Health, 6,* 1–9. Retrieved from http://www.capmh.com/content/6/1/10

Mueller, M. (2014). Is human–animal interaction (HAI) linked to positive youth development? Initial answers. *Applied Developmental Science, 18,* 5–16.

Nock, M. K. (2009). Why do people hurt themselves? New insights into the nature of functions of self-injury. *Current Directions in Psychological Science, 18,* 78–83. doi:10.1111/j.1467-8721.2009.01613.x

Nord, C. W., Brimhall, D., & West, J. (1997). *Fathers' involvement in their children's schools.* NCES 98-091. Washington, DC: US Department of Education, National Center for Education Statistics.

Nucci, L., Araki, N., Smetana, J., Nakaue, M., & Comer, J. (2014). Japanese and adolescents' disclosure and information management with parents. *Child Development, 85,* 901–907.

O'Brien, K., Slaughter, V., & Peterson, C. C. (2011). Sibling influences on theory of mind development for children with ASD. *Journal of Child Psychology and Psychiatry, 52*(6), 713–719.

Obsuth, I., Hennighausen, K., Brumariu, L., & Lyons-Ruth, K. (2014). Disorganized behavior in adolescent–parent interaction: Relations to attachment state of mind, partner abuse, and psychopathology. *Child Development, 85,* 370–387.

Overton, W. F. (2013). A new paradigm for developmental science: Relationism and relational-developmental systems. *Applied Developmental Science, 17,* 94–107. doi:10.1080/10888691.2013.778717

Parisi, D. (2013). Schools and the new ecology of the mind. In M. Anderson & S. Della Sala (Eds.), *Neuroscience in education: The good, the bad, and the ugly* (pp. 312–318). Oxford, England: Oxford University Press.

Parks, A. (2014). A case for the advancement and design of online positive psychological interventions. *The Journal of Positive Psychology, 9,* 502–508.

Perner, J., Ruffman, T., & Leekam, S. R. (1994). Theory of mind is contagious: You catch it from your sibs. *Child Development, 65,* 1228–1238. doi:10.2307/1131316

Peterson, C. C. (2000). Kindred spirits: Influences of siblings' perspectives on theory of mind. *Cognitive Development, 15*(4), 435–455. doi:10.1016/S0085-2014(01)00040-5

Pintrich, P. R. (2000). The role of goal orientation in self-regulated learning. In M. Boekaerts, P. R. Pintrich, & M. Zeidner (Eds.), *Handbook of self-regulation: Theory, research, and applications* (pp. 451–502). San Diego, CA: Academic Press.

Pomerantz, E., Ng, F. F., Cheung, C., & Qu, Y. (2014). Raising happy children who succeed in school. Lessons from China and United States. *Child Development Perspectives, 8,* 71–76.

Price, M., Chin, M. A., Higa-McMillan, C., Kim, S., & Frueh, B. C. (2013). Prevalence and internalizing problems of ethnoracially diverse victims of traditional and cyber bullying. *School Mental Health, 5*(4), 183–191. doi:10.1007/s12310-013-9104-6

Repetti, R., Taylor, S., & Seeman, T. (2002). Risky families: Family social environments and the mental and physical health of offspring. *Psychological Bulletin, 128,* 330–366.

Rochat, P. (2009). *Others in mind: Social origins of self-consciousness.* Cambridge, England: Cambridge University Press.

Rodrigues, S., Saslow, L., Garcia, N., John, O., & Keltner, D. (2009). Oxytocin receptor genetic variation relates to empathy and stress reactivity in humans. *Proceedings of National Academy of Science USA, 106,* 21437–21441.

Rose, R. (2014). Self-guided multimedia stress management and resilience training. *Journal of Positive Psychology, 9,* 489–493.

Ruffman, T., Perner, J., Naito, M., Parkin, L. & Clements, W. (1998). Older (but not younger) siblings facilitate false belief understanding. *Developmental Psychology, 34,* 161–174. doi:10.1037/0012-1649.34.1.161

Ryan, R., Deci, E., Grolsnick, W., & LaGuardia, J. (2006). The significance of autonomy and autonomy support in psychological development and psychopathology. In D. Cicchetti and D. Cohen (Eds), *Developmental psychopathology: Vol 1. Theory and methods* (2nd ed., pp. 295–849). New York, NY: Wiley.

Sabol, T. J., & Pianta, R. C. (2012). Recent trends in research on teacher–child relationships.

Attachment & Human Development, 14, 213–231. doi:10.1080/14616734.2012.672262

Scharfe, E., & Eldredge, D. (2001). Associations between attachment representations and health behaviors in late adolescence. *Journal of Health Psychology, 6,* 295–307. doi:10.1177/135910530100600303

Schaufeli, W. B., Martinez, I. M., Pinto, A. M., Salanova, M., & Bakker, A. B. (2002). Burnout and engagement in university students: A cross-national study. *Journal of Cross-Cultural Psychology, 33,* 464–481. doi:10.1177/0022022102033005003

Seibert, A. C., & Kerns, K. A. (2009). Attachment figures in middle childhood. *International Journal of Behavioral Development, 33,* 347–355. doi:10.1177/0165025409103872

Sette, S., Baumgartner, E., & Schneider, B. (2014). Shyness, child–teacher relationships, and socio-emotional adjustment in a sample of Italian preschool-aged children. *Infant and Child Development, 23,* 323–332.

Siegel, D. (2013). *Brainstorm: The power and purpose of the teenage brain.* New York, NY: Jeremy Tarcher/Penguin.

Smith, M., Saklofeske, D., & Nordstokke, D. (2014). The link between neuroticism and perfectionistic concerns: The mediating effect of trait emotional intelligence. *Personality and Individual Differences, 61–62,* 97–100.

Solomon, A. (2012). *Far from the tree.* New York, NY: Scribner.

Sperber, D. (1996). *Explaining culture: A naturalistic approach.* Oxford, England: Blackwell.

Spilt, J., Koomen, M., & Harrison, L. (2015). Language development in the early school years: The importance of close relationships with teachers. *Developmental Psychology, 51,* 185–196.

Sternberg, R. (2014). The development of adaptive competence: Why cultural psychology is necessary and not just nice. *Developmental Review, 34,* 208–224.

Stocker, C. M., Lanthier, R. P., & Furman, W. (1997). Sibling relationships in early adulthood. *Journal of Family Psychology, 11,* 210–221. doi:10.1037/0893-3200.11.2.210

Sulloway, F. (1996). *Born to rebel: Birth order, family dynamics and creative lives.* New York, NY: Vintage Books.

Tardif-Williams, C., Bosacki, S., & Huizinga, T. (2013, April). *Children's summer camp experiences with companion animals and intra- and interpersonal competencies: Implications for humane education.* Poster presented at the biennial meeting of the Society for Research in Child Development, Seattle, WA.

Thompson, R. (2008). Early attachment and later development: Familiar questions, new answers. In J. Cassidy & P. R. Shaver (Eds.), *Handbook of attachment* (2nd ed., pp. 348–365). New York, NY: Guilford.

Tibbetts, E., & Scharfe, E. (2014, May). *War and peace: Attachment, conflict, and cooperation in adult sibling relationships.* Poster presented at the Development, 2014 Conference, Ottawa, ON.

Tibbetts, E., & Scharfe, E. (2015). Oh, Brother (or Sister)!: An examination of sibling attachment, conflict, and cooperation in emerging adulthood. *Journal of Relationships Research, 6,* 1–11.

Tucker, D., & Luu, P. (2012). *Cognition and neural development.* New York, NY: Oxford University Press.

Turkle, S. (2011). *Alone together: Why we expect more from technology and less from each other.* New York, NY: Basic Books.

Turkle, S. (2015). *Reclaiming conversation: The power of talk in a digital age.* New York, NY: Penguin.

Urdan, T., Midgley, C., & Anderman, E. M. (1998). Classroom influences on self-handicapping strategies. *American Educational Research Journal, 35,* 101–122.

Urdan, T., Ryan, A. M., Anderman, E. M., & Gheen, M. (2002). Goals, goal structures, and avoidance behaviors. In C. Midgley (Ed.), *Goals, goal structures, and patterns of adaptive learning* (pp. 55–83). Mahwah, NJ: Erlbaum.

Vygotsky, L. S. (1978). Interaction between learning and development. In M. Cole, V. John-Steiner, S. Scribner, & E. Souberman

(Eds.), *Readings on the development of children* (2nd ed., pp. 71–91). Cambridge, MA: Harvard University Press.

Wagner, B. M., & Phillips, D. A. (1992). Beyond beliefs: Parent and child behaviors and children's perceived academic competence. *Child Development, 63,* 1380–1391.

Waters, A., & Tucker, D. (2013). Social regulation of neural development. In B. Sokol, M. Grouzet, & U. Muller (Eds.), *Self-regulation and autonomy: Social and developmental dimensions of human conduct* (pp. 279–296). New York, NY: Cambridge University Press.

Weinfield, N. S., Sroufe, L. A., Egeland, B., & Carlson, E. (2008). Individual differences in infant–caregiver attachment: Conceptual and empirical aspects of security. In J. Cassidy & P. Shaver (Eds.), *Handbook of attachment* (2nd ed., pp. 78–101). New York, NY: Guilford.

Wellman, H. (2014). *Making minds: How theory of mind develops.* Oxford, England: Oxford University Press.

Zimmermann, P., Mohr, C., & Spangler, G. (2009). Genetic and attachment influences on adolescents' regulation of autonomy and aggressiveness. *Journal of Child Psychology and Psychiatry, 50,* 1339–1347.

8

Gender and Culture

"All animals are equal." (Orwell, 1945, p. 15)

Introduction

Within the larger social-cultural context, this chapter will explore issues of diversity in gender and culture. I will first focus on how gender shapes young people's identities and relationships in terms of social cognitive development. I will then address the role of cultural identity in self-development, as well as the interplay between gender and culture regarding self-knowledge and relationships. Finally, to encourage youth workers to be mindful and respectful of diversity, I will outline educational strategies that aim to promote a caring, compassionate, and inclusive learning community.

Research

Gender and social cognitive development

Most theorists agree that late childhood and early adolescence represents a pivotal time in the process of self-definition or identity formation. This is when the act of internal balancing and rebalancing of boundaries between self and other becomes heightened (Blakemore & Mills, 2014; Kroger, 1996). Although the ability to develop an "observing center of awareness" (also referred to as a sense of "I," "me," "ego," "identity," or "self") has been approached by various perspectives, past psychological theorists have concentrated on the developmental

Social Cognition in Middle Childhood and Adolescence: Integrating the Personal, Social, and Educational Lives of Young People, First Edition. S. L. Bosacki.
© 2016 John Wiley & Sons, Ltd. Published 2016 by John Wiley & Sons, Ltd.

view that focuses on intrapsychic restructuring (Blos, 1979; Erikson, 1968; Kegan, 1994). More recently, theorists have begun to integrate sociocultural factors such as societal norms and conditions into the self-definition process or identity formation (Hyde, 2014; Silverstein & Perlick, 1995).

From this relational and developmental social constructivist perspective, sociocultural and psychological developmental factors contribute to the cognitive and affective transformative processes (Overton, 2013). Such factors may assist in the recreation or reorganization of a sense of self during the second decade of life. Social and historical circumstances may accelerate, delay, or even impair the developmental transformation of the sense of self and consequent ways of filtering and making sense of one's life experience (Schaffer, 1996). Thus, the ambiguous and paradoxical cultural and gender role prescriptions of modern industrialized society, combined with the youth's mental and emotional conflict, may create a complicated task of self-definition within the societal milieu.

As mentioned earlier, most developmentalists agree that late childhood and early adolescence (approximately ages 8 to 13 years) is a pivotal time in social cognitive development, a time when girls and boys learn to define and understand their own sense of self and their sense of others and relationships, resulting in a sense of identity (Siegel, 2013). However, increasing evidence suggests that the challenge of identity formation in early adolescence may a particular challenge for young females who may be in danger of losing their sense of self or "voice" as they attempt to define themselves as individuals in relation to others (Greenspan & Deardorff, 2014; Hyde, 2014; Pipher, 1994).

The main claim of the aforementioned researchers is that conventional norms and values may help to strengthen the stereotypic male voice during early adolescence. In contrast, for girls who do not conform to stereotypic gender roles such as passiveness and dependence, their voices may be somewhat diminished. Research has shown that, compared to adolescent males, reports of identity and well-being challenges such as depression, eating disorders, and negative self-evaluations and less self-compassion are more prevalent among adolescent females (Bluth & Banton, 2015; Greenspan & Deardorff, 2014; Hyde, 2014). Thus, as young females approach early adolescence, they may face an impasse as they need to create a distinct sense of self but also remain connected to others in a society that continues to value the stereotypic male independence model.

As mentioned throughout this book, past research suggests that early adolescence is a time of particular cultural vulnerability (Fiske, Kitayama, Markus, & Nisbett, 1998). For example, research has shown that the impact of puberty on the brain may increase young people's sensitivity to their social environments (Blakemore & Mills, 2014; Crone & Dahl, 2012, Greenspan & Deardorff, 2014). For example, some adolescents may experience a period of social reorienting where the opinions of peers become more important than those of family members (Larson, 2011).

Moreover, adolescents aged 13 to 17 years reported that peer evaluations affected their feelings of social or personal worth, and that peer rejection indicated their unworthiness as an individual (O'Brien & Bierman, 1988). Although the adolescents and children aged 10 to 13 years similarly felt that peers provided companionship, stimulation, and support, the younger group did not indicate that peer acceptance impacted self-evaluation. O'Brien and Bierman (1988) suggested that a more advanced ability to create abstract representations, as well as an increase in motivation for peer acceptance, might have accounted for the influence of peers on self-evaluations in adolescence.

The past 20 years has witnessed an increase in the systematic study of young female and male psychosocial development, with more recent efforts concentrating on early adolescence. This recent interest in the young person's mind has also been paralleled by an increase in social cognitive developmental research that investigates the links between affect and cognition in the areas of inter- and intrapersonal understanding. The recent influx of studies on young adolescents' self-views and identity partially builds on research conducted during the 1980s and 1990s. This gender-focused research mainly suggested that, despite the major progress sociopolitical women's movements have made in the past (Belenky, Clinchy, Goldberger, & Tarule, 1986), psychosocially, adolescent females' social and emotional lives perhaps had not improved to the extent previously predicted (Greenspan & Deardorff, 2014; Silverstein & Perlick, 1995).

In contrast to researchers' and educators' predictions of the late 1960s and early 1970s, more recent research continues to show that the majority of young females and increasingly males continue to struggle to develop a positive, stronger sense of self (Hyde, 2014). For instance, cross-sectional studies and large survey studies show that, as girls and boys approach adolescence, their attitudes toward themselves and others continue to adhere to cultural stereotypes of femininity and masculinity, and may become increasingly negative (Fine, 2010; Kehler, 2009).

More specifically, emerging adolescent females' self-perceptions tend to focus on their physical and social attributes as opposed to their mental and moral competencies (Bosacki, 2013; Harter, 1999). In addition to their physical self and body image, adolescent females have been found to value social relationships more than other aspects of their life (Rogers, 1993). That is, research shows that compared to other self-concept domains such as academic or athletic competencies, adolescent females perceived social self-concept, or how they view themselves in social situations, to have a greater effect on their general sense of self-worth (Harter, 1999; Hyde, 2014). Similarly, studies drawn from the gifted or academically talented literature have also illustrated that, compared to their female counterparts, adolescent males are more likely to believe in themselves and feel more positive about themselves (Marsh & Perry, 2000). Thus, academic or intellectual competence may have the potential to have a deleterious influence on psychosocial development in young females, and may serve to hinder further self-definition and positive self-regard.

Based on the aforementioned self-formation theories, a possible explanation for the decrease in self-worth among young adolescent females (irrespective of academic achievement) is that a negative self-view may result from inner conflict regarding the ability to compare one's own image with those of others. According to some researchers (Dabrowski, 1967; Kerr, 1994), the ability to be sensitive to, and to ruminate over, the mental states and emotions of others may lead to increased internalizing difficulties and social comparisons. Such mental and emotional challenges may place some young people at risk for developing self-concept and emotional disorders such as depression and anxiety problems including disordered eating.

Specific sociocultural factors may play an influential role in self-concept development and gender-role awareness during emerging adolescence. The biosociocultural model maintains that current sociocultural standards of beauty emphasize the desirability of thinness and sexiness for women, and a lean, muscular build for men; these ideas are generally accepted and internalized by most women and men (Bronfenbrenner & Morris, 2006). This physical ideal is often transmitted and reinforced by a number of different social agents, including peers, family, and the mass media (Field, Camargo, Taylor, Berkey, & Colditz, 1999; Greenspan & Deardorff, 2014).

As discussed in the previous chapter, research suggests that parental and sibling influences often serve as salient sources of self-knowledge for children and young adolescents (Bosacki, 2013). However, many studies continue to focus on how only maternal comments and modeling influence young adolescent females' attitudes about self-image, including physical appearance and body image (Fine, 2010; Hyde, 2014). Thus, there remains a gap in the literature regarding studies on how fathers and siblings, including brothers, influence adolescents' sense of self, body image, and gender-role orientations.

Gender, culture, and emerging adolescents' self-concept

Recent research on self-esteem provides evidence that supports and contradicts the gender differences hypothesis regarding self-development. As Hyde (2014) asserts, the majority of popular media contend that most adolescent females experience many challenges as they strive to develop a positive sense of self. However, some adolescent males may also experience similar self-esteem challenges as females. For example, Kling, Hyde, Showers, and Buswell's (1999) meta-analysis of the self-esteem reports of female and male children, adolescents, and adults found that, averaged over all ages, the meta-analysis indicated a small difference ($d=0.21$) that favored males but not the large difference that they expected based on popular media reports. The effect size increased from 0.16 in elementary school to 0.23 in middle school and 0.33 in high school, but then declined to 0.18 among college students, and 0.10 among adults between the ages of 23 and 59. In sum, Kling et al. (1999) found that the gender difference was not large for any age group.

Kling et al. (1999) also conducted a meta-analysis by ethnicity for US samples and found that the magnitude of the gender difference was $d=0.20$ among whites, but −0.04 among blacks. That is, their meta-analysis suggested that the gender differences reported by the popular media may be found only among whites and not among ethnic minorities, as there were too few samples of other ethnic minorities available for analysis. Given the cultural complexities regarding the self-concept (Harter, 1999), future research needs to explore young people's development of their self-esteem with a focus on gender and culture (Hyde, 2014).

The meta-analysis described above synthesized studies that measured global self-esteem or one's feeling of overall self-worth. Another approach to the study of self-esteem is to measure domain-specific self-esteem or self-concept, including perceptions of academic competence such as language ability, and of athletic ability, physical appearance, and moral conduct (Harter, 1999). Gentile et al.'s (2009) meta-analysis examined studies on young adults' domain-specific self-esteem, and found that males scored higher than females on physical appearance ($d=0.35$), athletic self-esteem (0.41), and self-satisfaction (0.33). In contrast, females scored higher on behavioral conduct ($d=−0.17$), and moral-ethical (−0.38) self-esteem. For all other domains, gender similarities were found; effect sizes were close to 0 for academic, social, and family self-esteem.

Transcultural research on adolescents' self-esteem and body image perceptions suggests that those individuals with varied ethnic ancestry report diverse levels of body satisfaction. Given such findings, further studies need to explore how the complex interaction between gender and cultural background may influence a young person's sense of body image within Canada and the United States. For example, past research has shown that among ethnically diverse adolescent girls, there may exist differences in body-image satisfaction (Franko & Striegel-Moore, 2002). However, more research is needed with younger males and females as many inconsistencies across gender and culture exist.

As Hyde (2014) and others suggest (Fine, 2010), although some meta-analyses focus on longitudinal gender-related differences (see Quest, Hyde, & Linn, 2010), few gender meta-analyses investigate variations in the magnitude of the gender difference as a function of ethnicity or other potential moderators such as social class. Meta-analysis may provide a more stringent and conservative method for the analysis of the intersection of gender and ethnicity. Future gender meta-analyses could include ethnicity, social class, and their interactions as potential moderators.

However, such a complex approach may be affected by several factors. First, ethnic groups are somewhat specific to nations. That is, the examples given that the previous paragraphs were for US and Canadian samples, other nations have different relevant ethnic groups, with different meanings attached to membership in those groups. Thus, meta-analysts could consider ethnicity within Europe and North American samples, and examine this in emerging adolescents from other nations based on an inclusive understanding of relevant ethnic groups in those nations.

Second, although Canadian and American Psychological Association style guidelines mandate the reporting of the ethnicity of participants, few studies actually include this information in their publications. For example, in Hyde's (2014) meta-analysis of young people's mathematical abilities, 70 studies reported ethnicity and the remaining 184 did not. Moreover, in studies with samples that included multiple ethnicities, the data typically were not analyzed for gender differences by ethnicity. As Hyde (2014) recommends, to promote the potential of intersectional approaches in education and psychology, researchers must improve the documentation of the gender and ethnicity of their samples and, ideally, analyze gender X ethnicity X social class interactions. That is, given the increasingly global educational context, researchers need to explore young people's cultural competencies and affinity for their cultural, ethnic, and racial identity, and how such competencies influence their developing social and cognitive abilities.

Role of gender social cognitive development

Surprisingly, the exploration of gender-related differences in social cognitive abilities during late childhood and early adolescence continues to remain relatively unexplored. In general, research on gender-related differences in Theory of Mind (ToM) remains mixed and contradictory (Devine & Hughes, 2013). For example, controlling for general language ability, several ToM studies have found evidence to support a female advantage on ToM tasks

(Bosacki & Astington, 1999; Charman, Ruffman, & Clements, 2002; Devine & Hughes, 2013), whereas others have found no differences or a male advantage (Hughes, 2011; Ronald, Viding, Happé, & Plomin, 2006). In contrast, other studies have found either that boys possess higher levels of emotional understanding than girls (Laible & Thompson, 1998), or no gender differences (Astington & Jenkins, 1995).

Within late childhood and early adolescence, with general language ability controlled, some studies have found that girls tend to score higher than boys on advanced ToM tasks such as strange stories, socially ambiguous narratives (Bosacki, 2013; Devine & Hughes, 2013), and visual, nonverbal tasks such as the Silent Film Task (Devine & Hughes, 2013). Within adults, Baron-Cohen (2002) found significant gender effects on scores derived from an adult ToM-type task (Reading the Mind in the Eyes Task, RMET) designed to measure Baron-Cohen's (2003) notion of "the language of the eyes." Although general language ability was not controlled for, results showed that adult females scored significantly higher on the RMET task than males. That is, females inferred a greater number of mental states from photographs of human eyes.

Regarding social cognitive abilities, the mixed results on gender-related differences shows that boys score higher than girls on nonsocial spatial perspective-taking tasks (Hyde, 2014), whereas girls have been found to score higher than boys on social perspective-taking and empathy tasks (Bosacki & Astington, 1999; Ibanez et al., 2013; Kluger, 2014; Van der Graaff et al., 2014).

Overall, these gender-related findings support Baron-Cohen's (2002, 2003) claim that, within a model of autism, females are more likely to be "empathizers," as compared to males who are more likely to be "systemizers." However, given the overall mixed gender-related findings, researchers need to continue to further investigate gender-related differences in ToM. In particular, longitudinal and transcultural research is needed to explore if such differences occur across the lifespan and in various cultural contexts.

Related research suggests that girls who have been found to have a sensitivity to, or heightened awareness and understanding of, others' mental states and feelings may experience negative consequences for later psychoemotional functioning. For example, longitudinal studies on developmental models of depression have found that, as young girls, depressed adolescent females were more concerned with maintaining interpersonal relationships, more able to recognize the feelings of others, and more likely to include moral issues in their play patterns than boys (Hyde, 2014; Hyde, Mezulis, & Abramson, 2008). In addition, Bosacki (2000) found that early adolescent girls who scored relatively high on advanced ToM tasks were also more likely to report negative self-perceptions, whereas high ToM boys reported relatively more positive self-perceptions.

Evidence from the socialization of empathy and guilt suggests that high empathy levels and guilt experiences may serve as precursors for later depression in women (Leussis & Andersen, 2008; Luppa et al., 2012; Nolan-Hoeksema, 2001). Similarly, in a study of 115 young adolescent girls and boys (8 to 12 years old), Neff (2011) found that the most robust correlation between sensitivity and shame existed among the older girls (11–12-year-olds). In addition, recent research suggests that, compared to male adolescents, female adolescents may experience less self-compassion and greater self-judgment (Bluth & Banton, 2015). Such studies may support Dabrowski's (1967) view that interpersonally sensitive individuals may be very concerned with the psychological needs of others to the detriment of their own, which may eventually lead to challenges with self-definition. I will return to the topic of gender-related differences in depression and social cognition in Chapter 10 on atypical populations.

Gender-related differences in emotional understanding   The social cognitive-developmental framework conceptualizes adaptive development as the capacity for successful control or containment of emotion through self-understanding and the capacity for behavioral and emotional self-restraint. Hall (1986) stressed the significant role language plays in the child's successful development of self-control. Advocating that the child be encouraged to use regulatory private language to "master strong emotions," Hall inferred a progression from directly acting on the impulses generated by strong feelings of self-control, through clarifying, tolerating, and containing feelings through language.

Although Hall's (1986) work focused on preschoolers, the underlying concepts of his theory can be applied to all ages, including emerging adolescents. For example, strong sociocultural gender-typed messages are received by our youth regarding emotional display and/or experience based on gender. Across many cultures, according to gender-typed societal emotional rules, girls are expected mainly to comply and smile, and learn how to control and restrain some emotions such as anger and pride. In contrast, according to societal gender-role stereotypes, boys are often expected appear more self-reliant and somewhat less caring for others than girls, and to be free to express emotions such as anger and pride (Bosacki & Moore, 2004).

Else-Quest, Higgins, Allison, and Morton (2012) conducted a meta-analysis of gender-related differences in temperament (biologically based emotional and behavioral tendencies) in children aged 3 months to 13 years, and found that for the negative affectivity factor or negative emotions, there was no gender difference for negative affectivity ($d = -0.06$), sadness (-0.10), or emotionality (0.01). These findings are perhaps surprising given the power of negative affectivity to predict later depression, and that past research suggests females report higher incidences of depression as compared to males (Watson & Clark, 1984).

Despite recent investigations of gender differences in sociocognition (Hyde, 2014), empirical results and explanatory theories that attempt to interpret such findings continue to remain contradictory and inconclusive. Relatedly, some researchers suggest that gender differences need to be investigated in terms of interaction effects between biological sex and societal gender-role expectations (Doey, Coplan, & Kingsbury, 2014; Hyde, 2014). To support this view, results from some of our previous research with Canadian preschoolers showed parents' gender-role perceptions of stereotypic feminine behavior were related to high levels of emotion understanding in both girls and boys (Bosacki & Moore, 2004). Such links remain to be examined in middle-school-aged children and adolescents in relation to psychological understanding.

Although many cross-sectional studies explore gender-related differences in social cognitive development such as empathy and ToM and perspective-taking, few longitudinal studies explore adolescents' trajectories. Although cross-sectional studies often show conflicting results regarding the association between age and perspective-taking in adolescence (e.g., Halpern, 1992; Van der Graaff et al., 2014), results of the few available longitudinal studies reveal increases in adolescents' perspective-taking between the ages of 15 and 17 years (Epley, Caruso, & Bazerman, 2006) and between the ages of 15 and 25 years (Eisenberg, Cumberland, Guthrie, Murphy, & Shepard, 2005).

Theories on the development of emotional concern propose that, even though affective empathy is already evident in early childhood, advances in perspective-taking have the potential to enhance the ability to sympathize with others in adolescence and may thus result in increased empathic concern (Hoffman, 2000). However, although cognitive advances are expected to facilitate growth in empathic concern, changes in adolescents' affective processing might also play a role. For example, compared to self-focused distress, the cognitive ability of emotion regulation has been found to be important for the ability to respond to others' negative emotions with concern (Denham, 1998). Although emotion regulation develops in childhood, neurodevelopmental changes in affective processing might temporarily challenge emotion regulation in mid-adolescence (Crone & Dahl, 2012; Siegel, 2013), and thus could result in stagnated growth in empathic concern.

Results of empirical studies have yet to provide support for either an increase in empathic concern as a result of cognitive advances, or the stagnation of empathic concern development due to challenged emotion regulation. For example, cross-sectional studies have found no association between age and empathic concern among 8th and 11th graders (e.g., Karniol, Gabay, Ochion, & Harari, 1998). In contrast, other studies found a positive association for girls only in a sample of 13- to 16-year-olds (e.g., Olweus & Endresen, 1998).

Results of longitudinal studies have also been found to be inconsistent. Girls' and boys' empathic concern has been found to increase between ages 13 and 14 years (Mestre, Samper, Frías, & Tur, 2009). Increases in empathic concern have also been found in a 3-year longitudinal study, but only for adolescents from 9th to 10th grade (Davis & Franzoi, 1991). Finally, Eisenberg et al. (2005) failed to find any significant developmental changes in empathic concern between the ages of 15 and 25 years.

Given the inconsistencies in the theoretical and empirical literature, few studies have explored the gendered connections among pubertal maturation, ToM, and empathy development during later childhood and early adolescence. This silence in the literature is surprising given the conceptual reasons to expect that pubertal changes have the potential to affect adolescents' empathy, especially empathic concern (Greenspan & Deardorff, 2014). Hill and Lynch's (1983) gender intensification theory suggests that, as adolescents' bodies mature, gender-specific socialization pressures strengthen. These pressures have been found to result in an increased adherence to gender stereotypical behavior and, in turn, greater behavioral and psychological differences between boys and girls (Hyde, 2014). Whereas research suggests that girls are often encouraged to show emotional and caring behavior, boys are usually encouraged to inhibit these kinds of behaviors (Maccoby, 1998). In this way, during emerging adolescence, pubertal maturation might accompany increased empathic concern for females, but decreased empathic concern for males.

Consistent with research on empathic concern, Else-Quest et al.'s (2012) meta-analysis revealed an increase in gender differences in self-conscious emotions during adolescence. A neurophysiological explanation for this difference includes research that shows boys' testosterone levels increase dramatically between early and mid-adolescence (Greenspan & Deardorff, 2014). High levels of testosterone have been found to accompany behavior intended to assert dominance and to achieve power (Mazur & Booth, 1998), which, in turn, might reduce emotional empathy (Lanzetta & Englis, 1989). Results of correlational and experimental studies have suggested that testosterone relates negatively to empathy, although effect sizes were typically small (Yildirim & Derksen, 2012).

In conclusion, longitudinal research on gender similarities and differences in developmental trends in perspective-taking, ToM, and empathic concern is scarce and continues to reveal inconsistent results. Moreover, despite the conceptual reasons to expect associations between pubertal maturation and adolescents' social cognitive development, as Greenspan and Deardorff (2014) note, few researchers specifically explore the role of puberty in social cognition, especially empathy and perspective-taking. One exception is the recent longitudinal study by Van der Graaff et al. (2014) on 283 Dutch boys' and 214 girls' development of perspective-taking and empathic concern from ages 13 to 18 years and its associations with pubertal status. Their research found gender differences in perspective-taking emerged during adolescence, with girls' increases being steeper than those of the boys.

Girls also showed higher levels of empathic concern than did boys. Whereas girls' empathic concern remained stable across adolescence, boys showed a decrease from early to middle adolescence with a rebound to the initial level thereafter. Boys who were physically more mature also reported lower empathic concern than did their less physically developed peers. Their study supports theoretical notions that the links between cognitive abilities and perspective-taking develop differently for females and males during the transition to adolescence, and suggests that pubertal maturation plays a role in boys' development of empathic concern.

Van der Graaff et al. (2014) also suggest that perspective-taking increased during adolescence for both genders, although boys' perspective-taking increased only from the age of 15 years onward. In contrast, levels of empathic concern did not significantly increase across adolescence. That is, over the course of the 6 years (13 to 18), boys showed a temporary decline in empathic concern and girls showed relatively stable levels. Moreover, results suggested that pubertal processes might play a role in boys' development of empathic concern (but not perspective-taking) between early and mid-adolescence. The finding that perspective-taking showed an increase in adolescence for the entire sample supports previous longitudinal research findings on ToM and perspective-taking (Eisenberg et al., 2005). Such findings also support developmental theories that suggest that, throughout adolescence, youths develop the ability to simultaneously consider the perspectives of self and other (Selman, 1980).

Neurological studies that compared adolescents of different ages also suggest that perspective-taking increases during adolescence as a consequence of continued maturation in relevant brain regions (Crone & Dahl, 2012). Thus, Van der Graaff et al.'s (2014) findings of increased perspective-taking in adolescence converge with results from previous research, as well as broader theories on empathy development. Such results support past research on adolescent brain development that indicates how pubertal processes may influence emotional development (see Crone & Dahl, 2012). To explain the mechanisms underlying the diverging social cognitive development of youth as they approach adolescence, future researchers need to explore the role pubertal maturation plays in young people's gendered developmental patterns and the links among perspective-taking, ToM, and empathic concern.

Media, body image, and gender   Although theoretical biosociocultural models may apply to females and males, the majority of studies have focused on the role sociocultural factors such as the popular mass media play in adolescent females' and males' self-development and ideas of masculinity and femininity (Moore, 2010). Within the past few decades, research has found that the desire to develop muscularity and "perfectly fit" bodies has emerged as a central issue associated with male body image (Kehler, 2009), and the sociocultural pressure for the ideal muscular build has been increasingly evident in recent years in the greater muscular bulk of video game characters, male action toys, and magazine models (Martins, Williams, Ratan, & Harrison, 2011; Pope, 2001).

Related research shows that many youth often become sensitive to external gender stereotypic media images, which may have an influence on concepts of self, especially when individuals internalize these cultural appearance standards (Greenspan & Deardorff, 2014; Harter, 1999: Hill & Lynch, 1983). The internalized appearance ideals may play a significant role in young adolescents' developing sociomoral and cognitive repertoire of personal goals and standards against which to judge self and others (Cross & Madson, 1997). As such, some young people may internalize such media messages, and begin to integrate them into their developing sense of self. This integration into their own self-structure has been a critical mechanism accounting for the influence of the media on body image and self-concept (Harter, 1999).

Thus, given young people's cognitive ability to decode the cultural messages that portray stereotypic gender-role expectations, research suggests that some cognitively competent and emotionally sensitive youth may be at risk for the development of personal and social challenges. The topic of extreme sensitivity in terms of emotionality and social anxiety is further discussed in Chapter 10 when I review learning exceptionalities within social cognitive development. Regarding typically developing youth and those that are prone to social anxiety (Leeves & Banerjee, 2014), young people may need to develop emotional coping skills to help immunize themselves against the potentially harmful gender-role stereotypic media and social-cultural messages. Such cultural messages (i.e., magazines) tend to focus on physicality as compared to the psychological, social, and moral aspects of the self.

Summary of empirical evidence of gender research and gender similarity   Overall, based on the meta-analyses and research studies discussed throughout this part of the chapter, there appears to be much evidence in support of the gender similarities hypothesis. The research suggests that the topics in which gender differences are small (around $d = 0.20$), or trivial ($d \leq 0.10$), include a few personality dimensions such as conscientiousness and gregariousness, reward sensitivity, mathematics and verbal skills, negative affectivity, relational aggression, tentative speech, some aspects of sexuality (e.g., attitudes about sex, attitudes about masturbation), leadership effectiveness, self-esteem, and academic self-concept.

Nonetheless, as some gender researchers suggest (Fine, 2010; Hyde, 2014), the gender similarities hypothesis acknowledges outliers or exceptions to the general rule. Exceptions to gender similarities, examples of studies that found gender-related differences to be moderate ($d = 0.50$) or large ($d = 0.80$), include 3D mental rotation, sensation-seeking, interests in objects versus people, physical aggression, the personality dimension of agreeableness/tender-mindedness, some sexual behaviors (e.g., masturbation and pornography use), and attitudes about casual sex. Such research findings demonstrate evidence of the important role the cultural context plays in the creation or elimination of gender differences in social cognition and behavior.

To illustrate the role of culture, for example, deindividuation, which removes the influence of gender roles, may minimize the gender difference in physical aggression. Countries with greater gender equality have also been found to show much smaller gender gaps in mathematics performance and in mate preferences. Vast quantities of research have been conducted on psychological gender differences and have demonstrated the patterns of results described above. However, the developmental picture of young people is complicated and the exploration of gender factors needs to occur within a cultural context. In the section below, I will discuss the role of cultural context in young people's social cognitive development as well as suggesting which areas of research are the most important for future directions.

Culture, ethnicity, race, and social cognitive development

Despite the recent efforts of cultural psychology (Bruner, 1996; Rivas-Drake et al., 2014), social science researchers continue to renew conversations regarding the conceptualization and application of cultural differences including race and ethnicity from a cultural-historical perspective (Lee, 2003). Status variables including gender, ethnicity, and social class are often overlooked in developmental and religious/spiritual studies. The vast majority of research is conducted in North America and Western Europe, and researchers need to examine how cultural norms play a role in social cognitive development. That is, researchers need to examine the means by which such norms are socialized, and the developmental prognoses for children, who, while displaying normative behavior in one culture, may not conform to expected behavioral norms in their own country.

Recently, Tomasello (1999, 2014b) supports others before him (Mead, Vygotsky, Wittgenstein) who claim that human culture depends upon the fundamental social cognitive skills including the individual human being's ability and tendency to identify with other human beings. This capacity involving reflexive thinking reflects the ability to operate with symbols or signs. Social cognitive skills such as the understanding of false beliefs are similar to any complex social game such as chess in that they are products of historical and cultural developments that work with a variety of pre-existing human cognitive skills.

All human beings live in a world of cultural institutions such as language, government, science, and religion which are all composed of cultural conventions (Kincheloe, 2009). To add to this already complex puzzle, sociomoral and social cognition is also influenced by cultural influences in that different cultures may use mental state terms differently, which in turn may affect young people's social cognitive abilities. For example, universal social cognitive skills may include the ability to understand mental states in others; the more complex abilities such as collective intentionality and psychological reasoning are more likely to be influenced by others within the particular culture (Killinger, 2008; Lillard, 1998; Shahaeian, Nielsen, Peterson, and Slaughter, 2014; Slaughter & Perez-Zapata, 2014; Tomasello, 2014a).

Thus, once young people develop this possible universal social cognitive competence, they may develop more sophisticated abilities such as reflexive and self-conscious thought within their particular culture (Lillard, 1998; Rochat, 2009). To help to develop this foundation, researchers need to explore the multileveled, dynamic interdependency among socially appropriate behavior, the self, and emotion.

Theory of Mind within diverse cultural contexts   One of the most direct and convincing ways to understand the impact of cultural contexts is to examine the change in cultural environments and subsequent changes in behavior. Given the dynamic cultural contexts that engage young people, such context changes may influence how young people process social information (Kim & Markus 1999), experience emotion (De Leersnyder, Mesquita, & Ki, 2011), and interact with others (Taylor et al., 2004). Thus, young people's individual and group interactions are influenced by their own thoughts and emotions and also how they perceive thoughts or emotions in others.

As one mechanism to navigate social situations, ToM, or the ability to reason about beliefs, desires, and intentions, may help young people predict other people's mental states and their subsequent behaviors within diverse cultural contexts (Slaughter & Perez-Zapata, 2014; Tomasello, 2014a). For example, in some of our ongoing cross-cultural research on social cognitive development in Polish and Canadian young adolescents, we found differences across cultures regarding ToM and self-concept. More specifically, we found that, compared to Polish youth, Canadian youth's responses to advanced ToM tasks focused more on the role of self to help explain ToM. In contrast, Polish youth focused on the role of other (Bosacki, Bialecka-Pikul, & Spzak, 2015). Our current research builds on these findings as we continue to explore the role of self-perceived relationships and attachment among youth.

Recent neuroscience evidence has found culture-related differences in ToM processing. For example, a recent study showed that early adolescents (8 to 11 years), who read a ToM-relevant story and observed a ToM-relevant cartoon, showed particular activation in the ventral medial prefrontal cortex, which is associated with labeling stimuli as self-relevant regardless of cultural background (Saxe & Kanwisher, 2003). However, monolingual American children showed greater activation in the right temporo-parietal junction (TPJ), a region associated with mental state inference, compared with bilingual Japanese children (Kobayashi, Glover, & Temple, 2007).

Similarly, research with Japanese and American young adults demonstrated strong activation patterns for both groups in several brain regions that have been associated with ToM, including the right MPFC (medial prefrontal cortex), right anterior cingulate cortex, and bilateral TPJ. However, compared with bilingual Japanese, monolingual Americans also showed greater activation in other ToM-related brain areas (e.g., bilateral temporal pole, right insula, and right MPFC) (Kobayashi, Glover, & Temple, 2006). Similarly, Barrett et al. (2013) found that children performed identically on false-belief understanding across three traditional societies tested in Ecuador, Fiji, and China, with no differences in performance between these children and Western children tested previously. In contrast, Shahaeian et al. (2014) found that Iranian youth outperformed Australian youth on sarcasm understanding tasks, which have also been found to be related to advanced ToM ability.

Such studies suggest that there may be some components or systems of ToM that are processed similarly across cultures, whereas other components or levels may be more culture specific. For example, the two-systems approach to ToM claims ToM ability includes two levels—the first level is automaticity and efficiency and the second is cognitive flexibility (Apperly, 2012). Such cross-cultural differences may suggest that ToM may be potentially underpinned by different neural processes, and may be influenced by one's cultural experiences. However, given that many aspects of culture may influence social cognitive findings (e.g., languages, family structure and financial background, cultural attitudes such as individualism or collectivism), future research needs to continue to explore the role of culture and ethnicity in ToM development (Slaughter & Perez-Zapata, 2014).

A recent study on the ToM-related experience of empathy, or the process in which one feels vicariously what another person feels, found that, although European American and Korean young people showed greater activation in the left TPJ during the observation of the emotional pain of an in-group versus an out-group member, this effect was stronger for Koreans than European Americans (Cheon et al., 2011). Similarly, research on the experience of young people's empathy in response to anger expressions showed that when Chinese participants attempted to empathize with a person with an angry face, they showed greater activation in the left dorsolateral prefrontal cortex, a region associated with emotion regulation. In contrast, German participants showed stronger responses in the right TPJ, right inferior and superior temporal gyri, and left middle insula—regions typically involved in empathy and emotion processing (de Greck et al., 2012).

These findings demonstrate that the same information may be processed through different neural pathways in different cultures, which in turn may perhaps lead to different psychological responses (Sternberg, 2014). Thus, metacognitive abilities may be underpinned by a multitude of social cognitive processes, as reflected by different patterns of neural activation. Most importantly, the degree of neural response to ToM- or empathy-related tasks seem to vary according to cultural background. These divergences in neural activation suggest that the social cognitive and neural pathways for social interactions may differ across cultures and suggest the need for further research.

Cultural influences on self-regulation and language   Across most cultures, formal schooling begins between the ages of 5 to 7, and involves the ability to internalize explicit rules. That is, as children progress through childhood, they begin to develop the ability to remember particular rules without being told (self-regulation), and to engage in reflective discourse and to talk about their own mental reasoning to others and themselves (metacognition). For example, they begin to understand and use embedded mental state language such as "She thinks that I think that I am angry." As mentioned in Chapter 3 on the cognitive self, Vygotsky (1986/1934) suggested that the child begins to internalize the dialogue which first begins with the caregiver, then is learned, and becomes part of the child's private speech or self-talk, which plays an important role in self-regulatory behaviors.

Although the parental dialogue that children internalize may differ according to cultural dialect and syntax, the underlying message remains the same across all languages and is generally "learn how to control yourself." Thus, through the internalization of parent–child conversations or intersubjective dialogues concerning the regulation of behavioral conduct, children learn how to control themselves in the sense that they learn how to manage their emotions, thoughts, and behaviors.

Cultural differences in private speech and self-regulation across childhood and adolescence   As discussed in Chapter 3 on language and social cognitive development, empirical evidence supports the claim that private speech and self-talk continue to develop and remain used throughout adolescence and adulthood. However, research has also shown that due to children's increasing awareness of social conventions, private speech and self-talk may wane in frequency in older children. As noted by Goffman (1981), self-talk is considered to be a stigmatized or taboo topic in most adult societies, which may partly account for the drop in self-reported and observed private speech in young people and adults.

Interestingly, despite claims that self-regulation and private speech occurs universally, little research exists to discuss the accompanying emotions that children may experience as they talk to themselves and regulate their own behavior (Kinnucan & Kuebli, 2013; Mischel, 2014). Perspectives can perhaps be represented by "voices" in the mind; the internalization of parental rules and the regulation behaviors may be thought of as the internalization of parents' "voices." Similarly, past research findings on private speech support Vygotsky's general cultural-historical framework and his claim that human psychological processes become verbally mediated. Therefore, given that such a voice may also contain an emotional tone, the internalization of an instructional directive may have conceptual and moral components.

As noted in Chapter 3, limited research exists on cross-cultural studies of private speech in youth, as the majority of research is with younger children, and adults who are second language learners (L2). Further research is necessary to help researchers learn more about the use and application of private speech in children and adults. Such studies may help to describe how private speech reflects localized knowledge based on particular cultural experiences, and the mastery of particular cultural tools, such as literacy. For example, several studies have found that, when engaged in an academic task, children from different cultural backgrounds and socioeconomic strata used different frequencies of private speech (Winsler, 2009).

Furthermore, studies of L2 adults showed that L2 proficiency influenced the use of private speech (Alarcon-Rubio, Sanchez-Medina, & Winsler, 2013). Thus, some researchers hypothesize that adults' private speech changes as a temporary function of experiential conditions, such as task difficulty, context familiarity, and literacy proficiency. For example, Sanchez, Alarcon, and De la Mata (2009) examined private speech production among adults who varied in levels of literacy and related such findings to what is known about children's self-speech.

Relatedly, Alarcon-Rubio et al. (2013) investigated the private speech of 126 Spanish-speaking adults (82% women) who were enrolled in a literacy educational program.

Specifically, they asked whether the use of private speech in illiterate adults was related to their individual experiences with literacy and cognitive challenges during the completion of an academic task. Alarcon-Rubio et al. found that, similar to past research on children's self-talk, the frequency of private speech among the adults increased according to the participants' literacy level, as well as to the challenge level of the task in the illiterate group.

Most recently, as mentioned in Chapter 3, Khodayarifard, Brinthaupt, Zardkhaneh, and Azar (2014) conducted a study of private speech in Iranian youth. In particular, they investigated the psychometric properties of the Self-Talk Scale (STS) among Iranian university students. Six hundred and eight university students completed the STS and one of six self- and cognitive-related measures. The results of the exploratory and confirmatory factor analysis showed the same four factors (i.e., self-reinforcement, self-management, self-criticism, and social-assessment) in the STS-Iranian version. In sum, self-talk frequency scores were associated with personality measures and suggested self-talk plays a role in self-knowledge development. Thus, the results indicated that the STS could be viewed as an acceptable measure to assess self-talk frequency among Iranian youth and perhaps could be adapted for use in other cultures.

Cultural and moral implications of private speech and the personal domain in emerging adolescence   As Bruner (1996) suggests, when children start to internalize parental orders or rules, they will also need to interpret the "deontic" aspect of the message, which implies some kind of emotional or moral aspect to the message. Given this emotional dimension of moral injunctions such as "you should behave in this way," few studies explore connections between personal speech, deontic reasoning, and emotional experiences. Recent research has shown that children begin to apply their ToM skills to deontic judgements about social rules and their feelings related to compliance and noncompliance. Lagattuta et al.'s (2015) research on developmental changes in children's predictions and feelings about compliance/noncompliance to maternal moral rules has shown that older children are more likely to comply with a mother's moral rule and feel good about compliance and bad about noncompliance.

In a subsequent study on children's reasoning about resistance to maternal control, Lagattuta, Nucci, and Bosacki (2010) showed that older children had a greater understanding of their control over a personal domain of actions and their sense of self. It was their mother's rule against choices about the essential aspect of the self that lead to the most noncompliance. This research with children supports past studies that show older children and adolescents are more likely to justify their decisions regarding personal issues when choices are connected to their identity. As Nucci (2013) suggests, future research on older children and adolescents needs to further explore their justifications for making choices within areas of behavioral discretion and privacy. Future research needs to explore the connections between ToM and the personal domain, particularly how young people think and feel about their personal decisions, and how such decisions play a role in their self-knowledge and identity development.

Given the role social-cultural factors play in the development of personal choice and rules of privacy and discretion, future research needs to explore young people's justifications for their personal moral choices and their emotional experiences. As past studies suggest, parental control over the personal domain of privacy and discretion may influence youth's internalizing difficulties and emotional experiences. That is, the influence of parental control may differ according to the social-cultural context such as the roles of parental income and cultural heritage, and gender of the youth and parent (Smetana, 2006).

As Nucci suggests (2013), the area of justified or committed noncompliance regarding young people's responses to parental control over personal issues is one that requires further study. Such research may be particularly beneficial for our increasingly pluralistic global society where young people need to learn how to negotiate their decisions regarding cultural and personal rules. For example, parental control over their adolescent children regarding private issues such as physical appearance, diet, or personal relationships may lead to possible internalizing challenges and negative emotions such as anxiety. Further work on the role of gender is also needed, as the complex connection between cultural and gendered stereotypic expectations may influence how a youth makes personal choices and decisions.

Cultural influence on young people's self-conscious or moral emotions   As noted in Chapter 4, studies on social or secondary emotions or those that require self-reflection (e.g., pride, embarrassment, shame, guilt), suggest that such emotions start to develop around the 1-year mark, as evidenced by children acting shy and coy in front of other persons and mirrors (Lewis, Sullivan, Stanger, & Weiss, 1989). These self-conscious emotions continue to develop, and gradually emerge in most typically developing children around the same time as self-regulatory behaviors among 5- to 7-year-olds (Denham, 1998; Pons & Harris, 2005). However, very little transcultural research exists on the connections between self-regulatory behaviors and the role of inner dialogue and self-conscious emotions in middle childhood and adolescents.

Exceptions to the dearth in the research are Rochat (2009) and his colleagues' studies of young (2 to 7 years) rural Kenyan children's development of self-consciousness as reflected in the self-recognition mirror task. Overall, Rochat (2009) found that, compared to American children where the majority of children passed the self-recognition in the mirror task by approximately 2 years of age (Lewis et al., 1989), the majority of rural Kenyan children failed at the self-recognition task.

More specifically, Rochat (2009) and his colleagues observed that many Kenyan children appeared "frozen" or transfixed by their reflection. Such behaviors differed greatly from the North American studies that showed a variance across children in their reactions to their mirror image, ranging through varying affective responses (e.g., negative, positive, ambivalent, mixed). Although Rochat suggested various interpretations, in general, such studies reflect the young child's ability to see themselves in the mirror as others see them.

As discussed in Chapter 4 on emotions, research shows that, although emotions are often described as subjective mental states, they may also be influenced by the sociocultural context in which they occur as we learn how to express and understand emotions within interpersonal interactions (Kitayama & Markus, 1994; Mesquita & Leu, 2007). Within interdependent cultures, emotions have been shown to be more grounded in interpersonal relationships, while in independent cultures, emotions mainly implicate the self (Bosacki, Moore, Talwar, & Park-Saltzman, 2013; Uchida, Townsend, Markus, & Bergsieker, 2009). For example, an emotional experience sampling study by Oishi, Diener, Napa Scollon, and

Biswas-Diener (2004) found that the influence of the relationship context on an individual's self-report of emotions was larger for individuals from interdependent cultures (Hispanics, Indian, and Japanese) as compared to independent cultures (Americans). Experiences with friends increased positive affect across samples, but the effect was stronger for Japanese participants.

Thus, for individuals from countries that support interdependence and social conformity, emotions differed depending on whom one was with, whereas emotions were relatively less affected by the social context for independent individuals. Given the psychological implications of living in a particular cultural context, issues of social conformity and fear of rejection and loneliness in young people's developing sense of self will remain a puzzle for future researchers. That is, researchers need to continue to investigate how young individuals' self-consciousness develops within our personal relationships within our larger cultural frames (Rochat, 2009).

Culture also has been found to influence people's recollections of their emotional memories. Large cultural differences have been observed in retrospective reports of emotions that reference longer time frames (Scollon, Koh, & Au, 2011). In addition, past research showed that European Americans and Asian Americans differed in their retrospective accounts, but not in their online momentary reports of emotional experiences (Wirtz, Chiu, Diener, & Oishi, 2009). Further, a recent study showed that beliefs about ideal affect correlated less with online emotional reports and more with recalled reports that referenced longer time frames (Scollon, Howard, Caldwell, & Ito, 2009).

Taken together, cross- or transcultural studies provide evidence to support that emotions are more socially embedded in interdependent cultures than in independent ones, and that emotional memories are influenced by culture. Such findings suggest that future researchers need to explore the question of how emerging adolescents across different cultures may differ in their cognitive representation of their emotional memories. In addition to cross-cultural research, researchers need to explore emerging adolescents' emotional understanding in intracultural contexts, particularly given the ever-changing multicultural landscapes of various continents across the globe.

Personal choices regarding ethnicity/race and moral reasoning   Within the school context, cultural variations have also been found in young peoples' values and conceptions of the self as independent and autonomous. In these studies, identity was often differentiated as autonomous, independent, and individualistic, or agentic versus relational or collectivist (Markus & Kitayama, 1994). For example, Kashima et al. (1995) showed that adults' self-conceptions were placed on three dimensions (agentic and assertive), relational (self as a relational being), and collectivist (self as a member of a group with group needs taking priority over individual needs). Results demonstrated that adults in Australia, Japan, the United States, Korea, and Hawaii differed on independent and collectivist self-conceptions, but differed most significantly on independence. In other words, Hawaiian, Japanese, and Korean adults perceived themselves as less agentic and assertive than individuals in Australia and the United States.

Overall, consistent with the relational developmental systems approach to development (Overton, 2013), the metathemes gleaned from past transcultural studies on young people's moral reasoning regarding the personal domain suggest that our identities and moral decisions are dynamic and constantly changing, and may adapt to the particular context we live in. In particular, past findings suggest that the identification of a personal zone of privacy serves a psychological function (Nucci, 2013), and that control imposed either by self or a significant other may influence one's psychological well-being. That is, young people may constantly create and recreate themselves as they become responsive to change and create new personal rules and means of self-expression.

Research shows that most cultures differ in the extent to which particular forms of personal expression and behavior are partially determined by the individual within the confines of societal conventions (Masten, 2014a; Shweder, 1991). In contrast to the view of cultures as either individualistic or individual rights-based (Western), or collectivistic and duty-based (Smetana, 2006), a comprehensive meta-analysis found no consistent associations between culture and the individualism–collectivism dichotomy (Markus & Kitayama, 1994). Thus, as suggested by past research, a more accurate illustration of cultures may be that they are complex and heterogeneous with respect to self-expression and collectivist orientations (Bilewicz, Mikolajczak, Kumagai, & Castano, 2010; Masten, 2014b; Miller, 2000). That is, such zones of personal choice may be maintained by individuals across diverse cultures (Miller, 2000).

Moreover, current research suggests that many basic moral concepts about distinct moral issues, such as unprovoked harm, remain consistent over time, and that more complex moral situations, such as indirect harm or stealing, may tend to generate more complex reasoning (Ruedy, Moore, Gino, & Schweitzer, 2013). Moreover, the age at which youth show complex moral reasoning may somewhat be influenced by the salience of the moral action at different times throughout the lifespan and across different cultures. Given the increasing moral diversity and ambiguity within the global context, more longitudinal transcultural studies on young people's moral reasoning about complex moral situations are required.

Gender similarities, differences, and intersectionality

To this point, this chapter has described the evidence regarding gender and cultural differences and similarities in isolation. In contrast, other important social categories that may influence gender and culture, such as ethnicity and sexual orientation, remain relatively understudied. Intersectionality is an approach that simultaneously considers multiple categories of identity, difference, and privilege, such as gender, race, class, sexual orientation, disability, and faith orientations (Miller, 2000). Intersectionality states that gender-related influences must always be examined in context as compared to in isolation. That is, gender-related differences must be investigated within the context of ethnicity and other social identities and categories.

One implication of intersectionality is that researchers should avoid global statements about gender-related differences, referring to an entire nation, much less to cross-culturally universal differences. As an example, the sections below will describe in detail the intersection of gender and ethnicity within the social cognitive context among young people.

Many developmental researchers agree that meta-analysis provides a valuable method for the analysis of the intersection of gender and ethnicity (Hyde, 2014). For example, a meta-analysis of gender differences in self-conscious emotions within the United States found evidence of the intersection of gender and ethnicity (Else-Quest, 2012). More specifically, results showed a gender X ethnicity interaction for shame, $d = -0.32$ for whites (females scored higher than males), but -0.06 for nonwhites. That is, the overall finding of $d = -0.29$ for shame obscured variations in the magnitude of the gender-related difference across ethnic groups and, in particular, masked the absence of the difference among nonwhites. Despite this result, few gender meta-analyses have looked for such hidden variations in the magnitude of the gender-related difference as a function of ethnicity or other potential moderators such as social class.

Given the complexity among gender and cultural differences, future gender meta-analyses should routinely consider ethnicity and social class as potential moderators. Several factors have the potential to complicate this effort. First, ethnic groups are specific to nations. Nations other than those within multicultural, pluralistic societies such as North and South America, or Europe, among others have different relevant ethnic groups, with different meanings attached to membership in those groups. At the least, meta-analysts can consider ethnicity in such samples from multicultural societies (e.g., Canada), and examine data in samples from other nations based on an understanding of relevant ethnic groups in those nations.

Second, many researchers neglect to report the ethnicity of their samples, despite American Psychological Association style guidelines that mandate this reporting. For example, in a math meta-analysis, 70 studies reported ethnicity and the remaining 184 did not (Hyde, 2014). Moreover, in studies with samples covering multiple ethnicities, the data typically are not analyzed for gender differences separately by ethnicity. As Hyde (2014) suggests, given the potential of intersectional approaches in psychology and education, researchers need to provide accurate reports of the gender and ethnicity interactions found within their research samples and, ideally, analyze gender X ethnicity X social economic class interactions.

Hyde's (2014) plea to focus on the interplay between gender and cultural context is reiterated by Balliet, Macfarlan, Li, and Van Vugt (2011) in their meta-analysis of gender differences in cooperation among older adolescents and adults. Based on a meta-analysis of research with social dilemmas, Balliet et al. (2011) found that, in their response to social dilemmas, males and females did not differ significantly from each other. However, they found that when the context of the interactions were explored more closely, significant gendered patterns emerged. Specifically, in same gendered groups, males were more likely to cooperate (e.g., male–male) compared to females in all female groups (e.g., female–female). Females were more likely than males to cooperate in mixed sex groups (female–male), and in large groups.

Although Balliet et al. (2011) analyzed studies based mainly on a North American and European sample, they concluded that the social context in which the social interactions occurred must be considered when exploring gender-related differences in cooperation. From a lifespan developmentalist perspective, Baillet et al.'s (2011) findings are reminiscent of Maccoby's (1998) research that claimed that young girls are more likely to engage in stereotypic gender-role type behavior within a mixed-gender context (e.g., male–female) as compared to all female groups (female–female). The reverse was not found for young boys.

Thus, similar to Hyde (2014), and others, Baillet et al.'s (2011) research highlights the need for developmental social cognitivists to incorporate a relational, developmental systems approach with a biosocial-cultural focus (integration of sociocultural and evolutionary perspectives) to guide future gender-related difference research in the development of social cognition among youth.

Gender X culture within social cognition research among youth   The completeness of conventional accounts of emotional socialization are now being questioned by social constructivist or psychocultural views of development (Hyde, 2014; Shields, 2002). In general, consistent with a psychocultural approach to development, social constructivists claim that developmental progress is defined in terms of the child's approximation to and variation on culturally agreed upon norms of conduct. Developmental progress is defined in terms of a fixed, mature state. Research on the role of socialization in social cognition suggests that family and peer groups cultivate a "nice girl" orientation in girls (quiet and compliant) that deletes anger from the normal emotional script. In contrast, females are often encouraged to express (and understand) happiness, shame, fear, and warmth or friendliness. Boys, however, are encouraged to express (and understand) emotions that reflect a sense of entitlement, anger, contempt, pride, and so on, while other emotional expressions may be dampened (Fine, 2010).

Recent research shows that such gendered stereotypes are consistent with particular examples of emotional behavior among youth. Chaplin and Aldao's (2013) meta-analysis examined gender differences in emotion expression in children from birth to adolescence. Overall they found minimal gender differences for positive emotions ($d = -0.08$), internalizing emotions such as anxiety and sadness ($d = -0.10$), and externalizing emotions such as anger ($d = 0.09$). Interestingly, the magnitude of the gender differences varied as a function of age. For example, the gender gap in positive emotions grew larger with age ($d = -0.20$ in middle childhood and -0.28 in adolescence) and perhaps reflects increasing socialization pressure with age. The magnitude of gender differences also varied with context and social relationships. For example, when children were alone, the effect was less for internalizing emotions ($d = -0.03$), but $d = -0.16$ when the children were with adults. Such results highlight the importance of context in the development of gender-related differences in the emotional experiences of youth.

Similarly, Else-Quest and colleagues (2012) conducted a meta-analysis of gender differences in the self-conscious emotions, which as mentioned in Chapter 4, found that results supported gender-role stereotypes. In particular, their findings suggested that women were expected to experience more guilt, shame, and embarrassment, whereas men were expected to experience more pride. Their results indicated small differences favoring females for guilt ($d = -0.27$) and shame ($d = -0.29$) and, contrary to stereotypes, trivial differences for embarrassment ($d = -0.08$), authentic pride ($d = -0.01$), and hubristic pride ($d = -0.09$). Overall, consistent with Chaplin and Aldao's (2013) findings, although gender-role stereotypes portray women as emotional and cooperative individuals and hold that there were large gender differences in emotions such as fear and pride, the data, from children and adults, indicated that gender-related differences in emotional experience were mainly trivial.

Applications: So What?

Research on psychological gender and culture-related differences will continue for years to come (Hyde, 2014), given many scientists' firm beliefs that such differences exist and are large and the media's insatiable thirst for new findings of gender-related differences. What, then, are the best directions in which to take this research? According to Hyde (2014), two approaches seem especially promising: intersectional approaches and contextual approaches.

Intersectional approaches to the study of gender similarities and differences have the potential to investigate the intersections and interconnections among gender, ethnicity, and social class. Researchers need to go beyond studies that test for gender differences alone, as ethnicity and social class need to be taken into account. That is, researchers should chart the magnitude and direction of gender differences across different ethnic groups and social class. Thus, meta-analysts should routinely examine race and social class as moderators of the magnitude of gender differences, and vice versa. Similar to relational developmental system approaches (Overton, 2013), an intersectional approach to data analysis would promote a gender and culture inclusive approach to data interpretation and reports.

The identification of diverse contexts in which gender differences appear or disappear will continue to be an important strategy, in primary research and in meta-analyses. For example, Eagly and Crowley's (1986) meta-analysis of research on gender differences in helping behavior suggests future researchers should incorporate theoretically derived variables that should moderate the gender difference. To illustrate, gender-role stereotypes such as the stereotypic masculine role emphasize heroic and chivalrous helping, whereas the stereotypic feminine role emphasizes nurturant helping (Fine, 2010). Eagly and Crowley's literature analysis found that, when helping behavior was observed, such as encouraging heroic helping, the effect size for the gender difference (favoring males) was large, $d = 0.74$. In contrast, when the helping was not observed, there was no gender difference, $d = -0.02$. Thus, future work on gender differences in social cognition among youth should incorporate possible moderating factors of gender-role stereotypes.

As other have noted (Fine, 2010; Shields, 2002), large gender-related differences can be created and erased by the context. Situational variables such as the cultural and sociopolitical settings must be taken into account in meta-analyses. That is, more culturally and developmentally sensitive meta-analysis should warrant more primary research guided by theories such as relational developmental system models that encompass sociocultural theory, expectancy value theory, and cognitive social learning theory (Overton, 2013; Tomasello, 2014a).

Above all, given that all findings are contingent upon cultural context, researchers need to report the possibilities of gender differences and similarities, and interpret their findings with caution. Researchers need to avoid an overemphasis on gender and culture-related differences, as they have a responsibility to remain ethical and respectful of others' perspectives and experiences. A nonsignificant gender difference or similarity also needs to be reported, as such findings are equally interesting as a difference, and may provide a meaningful contribution to the discourse in social cognitive development across ages and diverse contexts.

In sum, what do the past gendered and cross-cultural findings on social cognition among young people tell us about their school experiences? Based on the findings described above, compared to males, adolescent females may be more likely to engage in solitary, social-relational activities that may affect their social and emotional experiences. Young females may also be more likely to engage in thinking about the inner worlds of others rather than their own, as well as helping others in distress situations. Thus, researchers need to explore the implications of gendered and cultured social cognition for exploring young people's classroom experiences and their mental health during the developmentally sensitive age of emergent adolescence.

Research that addresses the question of why identity formation and defining one's place in the societal milieu is a complex and difficult task for young people holds significant implications for the fields of psychology and education. Psychological studies that examine the personal experience of young people can help researchers and educators to better understand the mechanisms and processes of the emerging adolescent mind and consequently assist young people in their journey of self-discovery. However, the investigation of such a complex phenomenon of the mind and the self commands that researchers draw from an interdisciplinary conceptual foundation, and employ multimethodological techniques to accurately assess the perspective of the adolescent.

The application of a biopsychocultural relational developmental systems approach to the study of emerging adolescents (Bruner, 1996; Tomasello, 2014a), will help researchers to integrate psychological and socio cultural studies. Such an integrative approach combines feminist and cultural socioanthropological theory with psychological literature on the psychosocial aspects of identity formation. Modern research that speaks to the current issues of today's young people's social, cognitive, and emotional development should aim to combine feminist social science theories (Belenky et al., 1986), and cultural psychology (Bronfenbrenner, 1977; Bruner, 1996; Shweder, 1991; Sternberg, 2014; Tomasello, 2014b) into the works of past (Blos, 1979; Dabrowski, 1967; Erikson, 1968; Piaget, 1965/1932), and contemporary psychologists who investigate social cognitive development (Baumeister, Campbell, Krueger, & Vohs, 2003; Damon & Hart, 1988; Harter, 1999; Rochat, 2009).

Methodologically, a culturally sensitive approach to the psychosocial development of emerging adolescents involves the issue of research design. Although short-term, cross-section studies within one population are the most economically feasible, such studies provide culturally biased information and do not allow researchers to examine the development of attitudes over time. Given the strong sociocultural influences on emerging adolescent self-identity, future researchers could follow a group of youth and interview them periodically throughout childhood and adolescence concerning emotional and psychological issues that are most pertinent to the person.

Ideally, more cross-gender, culture, and class longitudinal studies on perceptions and emotions of social cognitive development would provide a much needed comprehensive sketch of how young people see, think of, and feel about themselves in various cultures and social classes. Multimethod approaches that incorporate questionnaires and interviews could be used with emerging adolescents, as well as the inclusion of peer, teacher, and parent reports of self-attitudes and perceptions and related social cognitive abilities (Tahiroglu et al., 2014).

Furthermore, if gender is defined as a culture or social category (Fine, 2010), to fully explore the uniqueness of psychological development across genders and cultures, research on social cognition and identity in emerging adolescence must continue to examine cognitive and affective processes in diverse populations of youth to ensure a well-distributed representation of multiple cultural backgrounds and gender-role orientations. As many theorists note (Hyde, 2014), future research needs to consider further definitions of gender such as one's belief in culturally defined gender-role expectations as opposed to the biological definition based on sex alone.

Educational implications for older children and adolescents within a culturally diverse school culture

Although psychological research can help young people to recognize their potential to share responsibility for their self-development, society must also share some responsibility for the emotional and moral guidance of young people. That is, cultural institutions such as schools, workplaces, healthcare settings, and others must also be accountable for the creation of learning communities that nurture, direct, and inspire optimal mental health and personal competence in young people. Drawing on recent work of educators and psychologists (Bruner, 1996; Gardner & Davis, 2013), school plays an important role in self-development, especially during emerging adolescence. Similar to psychologists, educational researchers need to draw on the classic theories of development (e.g., Blos, 1979; Piaget, 1965/1932), contemporary psychological integrative theories of identity construction (Damon & Hart, 1988; Selman, 1980), and gender development theories (Hyde, 2014), and apply their findings to an educational context that will help emerging adolescents to develop a coherent sense of self and healthy and supportive relationships.

As many researchers have noted (Blakemore & Mills, 2014; Bruner, 1996; Kroger, 1996), to fully benefit the psychological development of youth, the relation between psychology and education needs to be reciprocal and transactional. Those who work with young people within an educational context could also consider Dabrowski's (1967) notion of self-education or the process of working out one's inner dilemmas. Thus, educators and researchers need to support and work with youth in collaborative ways to remain sensitive to their social, cultural, and emotional needs during this pivotal time of social cognitive and identity development.

From a curricular perspective, inclusive, developmentally appropriate curriculum that include a balanced number of activities that address cognitive and emotional skills will benefit older children and adolescents. In particular, a developmentally appropriate and culturally sensitive curriculum needs to draw on holistic educational models such those inspired by Steiner (1976) and Miller (2000) that emphasize an education that promotes the fusion of body and mind, and focus on the development of an inner, spiritual curriculum. A holistic, developmentally appropriate curriculum would provide a warm, supportive, and psychologically safe environment (De Souza, 2014), where learners feel safe enough to use their voice and to critically discuss the cultural and societal messages portrayed in the media.

For example, young people need to be encouraged to critically analyze and discuss the media messages concerning gender and cultural expectations. To strengthen self-reliance, emotional coping skills, and resilience and perspective-taking, classroom activities could include a combination of mindful, self-reflective activities (e.g., yoga, meditation, journaling, visual arts), and critical analysis of television commercials, magazines, and films (Neff, 2011; Neff & Germer, 2013; Thompson & Gauntlett-Gilbert; Weare, 2013).

In addition, as I will discuss in more detail in Chapter 11, the technique of bibliotherapy integrates psychology and education to promote a positive sense of self through the encouragement of young people to read books on individuals' emotional experiences and peer relations and identity. Educators need to encourage such mindful reading for social cognitive development across all children. Thus, the use of the arts as a vehicle for self-exploration and self-development can help educators encourage young people to construct moral courage and an emotionally resilient, powerful sense of self.

Longitudinal developmental research on gender and cultural differences in social cognitive abilities continues to remain relatively scarce and reveal inconsistent results. Moreover, although there are conceptual reasons to expect pubertal maturation to be associated with adolescents' empathy (Van der Graaff et al., 2014), at the time of writing, the role of puberty in empathy development in youth across cultures remains relatively nascent (Greenspan & Deardorff, 2014). The majority of research discussed in this chapter suggests marked individual and developmental differences across later childhood and into adolescence. For example, as mentioned earlier, Van de Graaff et al. (2014) found significant gender differences in empathic concern from early adolescence onward and that these gender differences in perspective-taking strengthened between early- and mid-adolescence. Therefore, researchers need to continue to investigate young females' and males' pubertal status and their development of perspective-taking and empathic concern longitudinally and cross-culturally during adolescence.

Given our emotional responses to change, ambiguity, and contradiction, such a cultural school context may lead to feelings of ambivalence that may influence how youth develop personally as well as socially. As noted by Yon (2000), living with such contradictory positions and opposing multiple subjectivities may lead to ambivalence or feelings that are mixed and uncertain. In Chapter 9, I will describe related research that explores the personal and social-cultural ambiguities experienced by adolescents in the classroom, during play and leisure time regarding virtual games, social networking, and involvement in social media. Finally, in the remaining section of the book, I will discuss educational programs that promote this pathway to the culture of engagement.

Culturally sensitive education: Ethnic and racial identity (ERI)

As discussed earlier, given the complex web involving language, identity, cognition, and emotion within North American society today, how can education programs integrate young people's cultural and ethnic identities with the larger cultural landscape? Cultural researchers suggest that today's youth of mixed heritage often possess a particular "cultural competence" in that they express pride in being unique and thus have the potential to demonstrate social competence and the ability to appreciate multiple perspectives (Rivas-Drake et al., 2014). However, despite the advantages of identifying with multiple racial–ethnic identities, some researchers suggest that the power of psychological harassment, including derogatory comments (verbal or electronic) about ethnicity or race, may have a greater negative impact on an adolescents' emotional life compared to more physical acts of harassment (Crick et al. 2001; Turkle, 2011).

To further promote cultural competence, an increasing number of inclusive and developmentally appropriate music educational programs have been developed. These programs aim to promote young people's social cognitive development and emotional coping skills through the use of language and music (Bosacki & O'Neill, 2015; Miranda & Gaudreau, 2010; Rentfrow & McDonald, 2010). Given the past research that shows that music engagement plays an important role in young people's social and emotional development (Chin & Rickard, 2014), educational programs need to incorporate music into their curriculum to motivate emerging adolescents to engage in social cognitive and emotional learning activities (Bonneville-Roussy, Rentfrow, Xu, & Potter, 2013; Rentfrow, McDonald, & Oldmeadow, 2009; Saarikallio, 2011; ter Bogt, Keijsers, & Meeus, 2013). As illustrated in Table 11.1 in Chapter 11, various social cognitive abilities such as self-reflection, perspective-taking, and empathetic sensitivity could be developed through the integration of music into the classroom.

Given the importance of athletics and physical health to many youth, it is an environment where many spend their leisure time of their own accord and leisure activities play a role in their social, cognitive and emotional lives. An example of an integrated sports and life skills program includes the SUPER program (Sports United to Promote Education and Recreation) (Danish, Taylor, & Fazio, 2003). Overall, the SUPER program is a series of sports-based life skills that are taught within sports clinics. For example, sessions involve three sets of activities that focus on various competencies: physical skills (e.g., swimming), life skills such as social and emotional coping strategies, and social skills necessary to play the sport. Some of the life skills taught include how to convert imagined goals and dreams into feasible, reasonable goals, develop healthy coping and problem-solving skills, develop supportive peer relations, emotional regulation and resilience, and learning positive self-talk.

This SUPER program has also been adapted by Indigenous populations such as the Maori within New Zealand where it is entitled the Hokowhitu Program. Such a program is a culturally sensitive, life skills, sport-oriented drug and alcohol program designed by, and developed for, Maori (Heke, 2001). As Anderson (2000) and others claim (Bell, 2013), developmentally appropriate, culturally sensitive programs that incorporate the use of Indigenous literature have the potential to help youth develop cultural competence and self-knowledge through the learning process that includes resistance, reclamation, reconstruction, and action (Hadaway & Young, 2014; Thompson, Whitesell, Galliher, & Gfellner, 2012).

To further promote global access to such resilience training programs, recent positive psychology interventions (PPI) and resilience programs incorporate the use of digital technology to promote young people's well-being, cultural competence, and social awareness across languages and cultures (Parks, 2014; Redzic et al., 2014). I will return to how culturally sensitive education has the potential to help promote the social cognitive and emotional lives of youth in Chapter 11.

Future Questions

Cultural Neuroscience and Neuroeducation

As I mentioned in Chapter 3, although cultural neuroscience studies continue to demonstrate cultural diversity in neural functions, they may not necessarily show the process through which cultural factors influence them. Moreover, the causal role of cultural experiences in connection with gender remains unclear and often contradictory. Thus, there needs to be greater empirical efforts in cultural neuroscience research and neuroeducation to investigate the psychological and emotional consequences of cultural change (Busso, 2014; Kim & Sasaki, 2014). For instance, to understand the impact of dynamic, multicultural school contexts, researchers need to look at changes in all aspects of cultural environments (e.g., language, cultural values, economic and political landscape), and subsequent changes in behavior.

Given that young people are engaged in dynamic, ever-changing multicultural learning environments, the way they construe meanings may also change. The changing nature of the multicultural context may influence their social cognitive abilities, or the way they process and interpret information (Kim & Markus, 1999), experience emotion (De Leersnyder et al., 2011), and socially interact with others (Taylor et al., 2004). Moreover, culture-specific social cognitive processes are quite responsive to situational cues, such as cultural icons like popular culture, and religion (Hong, Morris, Chiu, & Benet-Martinez, 2000; Steinberg, 2009; Sternberg, 2014). Alternatively, the reverse may also be true, as culture could be thought of as a dependent variable and one that is influenced by other factors such as gender, and the adolescent's social cognitive ability. The study of culture as a dependent variable would enable researchers to explore how cultures develop, transform, and evolve.

Building on these studies, cultural neuroscience research and neuroeducation need to focus on youth who undergo cultural changes via acculturation and multicultural families and partnerships (Kim & Sasaki, 2014), or situational malleability, with methods such as experimental priming (Ng, Han, Mao, & Lai, 2010; Sasaki et al., 2013). Investigations of immediate situational shifts, as well as gradual, developmental long-term changes will complement each other and provide insight into cultural-biological malleability.

Summary

Overall, the data presented in this chapter supports the claim that identity holds sociohistorical relativity (Kroger, 1996; Larson, 2011), and that the transactional relation between culture and mind allows us to create our sense of selves through a process of personal meaning-making (Bruner, 1996). That is, from a developmental, relational systems perspective, this chapter addressed the question of why the task of the construction of a positive and coherent sense of self remains a challenge for today's emerging adolescent within an increasingly culturally and economically diverse world. This chapter's outline of developmental relational systems and neurobiological approaches to social cognitive development aims to encourage researchers and educators to make more effective social responses to emerging adolescents. Implications for educators will be discussed at length in Chapter 11, when pedagogical implications of social cognitive development will be described.

References

Alarcon-Rubio, A., Sanchez-Medina, J., & Winsler, A. (2013). Private speech in illiterate adults: Cognitive functions, task difficulty, and literacy. *Journal of Adult Development, 20*, 100–111.

Anderson, K. (2000). *A recognition of being: Reconstructing Native womanhood*. Toronto, ON, Canada: Second University Press.

Apperly, I. A. (2012). What is "theory of mind"? Concepts, cognitive processes and individual differences. *Quarterly Journal of Experimental Psychology, 65*, 825–839. doi:10.1080/174702 18.2012.676055

Astington, J., & Jenkins, J. (1995). Theory of mind development and social understanding. *Cognition and Emotion, 9*, 151–165.

Balliet, D., Macfarlan, S., Li, N., & Van Vugt, M. (2011). Sex differences in cooperation: A meta-analytic review of social dilemmas. *Psychological Bulletin, 137*, 881–909.

Baron-Cohen, S. (2002). The extreme male brain theory of autism. *Trends in Cognitive Sciences, 6*, 248–254.

Baron-Cohen, S. (2003). *The essential difference*. London, England: Penguin.

Barrett, H. C., Broesch, T., Scott, R. M., He, Z. J., Baillargeon, R., Wu, D., … Laurence, S. (2013). Early false-belief understanding in traditional non-Western societies. *Proceedings of the Royal Society B–Biological Sciences, 280*, 2012–2654. doi:10.1098/Rspb.2012.2654

Baumeister, R., Campbell, J., Krueger, J., & Vohs, V. (2003). Does high self-esteem cause better performance, interpersonal success happiness, or health? *Psychological Science in the Public Interest, 4*, 1–44.

Belenky, M., Clinchy, B., Goldberger, N., & Tarule, J. (1986). *Women's ways of knowing*. New York, NY: Basic Books.

Bell, N. (2013). Just do it: Anishinaabe culture-based education. *Canadian Journal of Native Education, 36*, 36–58.

Bilewicz, M., Mikolajczak, M., Kumagai, T., & Castano, E. (2010). Which emotions are uniquely human? Understanding of emotion words across three cultures. In B. Bokus (Ed.), *Studies in the psychology of language and communication* (pp. 275–285). Warsaw, Poland: Matrix.

Blakemore, S.-J., & Mills, K. (2014). Is adolescence a sensitive period for sociocultural processing? *Annual Review of Psychology, 65*, 187–207.

Blos, J. (1979). *The adolescent passage: Developmental issues*. New York, NY: International Universities Press.

Bluth, K., & Banton, P. (2015). The influence of self-compassion on emotional well-being among early and older adolescent males and females. *The Journal of Positive Psychology, 10*, 219–230.

Bonneville-Roussy, A., Rentfrow, P., Xu, M., & Potter, J. (2013). Music through the ages: Trends in musical engagement and preferences from adolescence through middle adulthood. *Journal of Personality and Social Psychology, 105*, 703–717.

Bosacki, S. (2000). Theory of mind and self-concept in preadolescents: Links with gender and language. *Journal of Educational Psychology, 92*, 709–717.

Bosacki, S. (2005). *Culture of classroom silence*. New York, NY: Peter Lang.

Bosacki, S. (2008). *Children's emotional lives: Sensitive shadows in the classroom*. New York, NY: Peter Lang.

Bosacki, S. (2013). Theory of mind understanding and conversational patterns in early adolescence. *Journal of Genetic Psychology, 174*, 170–191.

Bosacki, S. L., & Astington, J. W. (1999). Theory of mind in preadolescence: Relations between social understanding and social competence. *Social Development, 8*, 237–255.

Bosacki, S., Bialecka-Pikul, M., & Spzak, M. (2015). Theory of mind and self-concept in Canadian and Polish youth. *International Journal of Youth and Adolescence, 20*(4), 457–469. doi:10.1080/02673843.2013.804423

Bosacki, S., & Moore, C. (2004). Preschoolers' understanding of simple and complex emotions: Links with gender and language. *Sex Roles: A Journal of Research, 50*, 659–675.

Bosacki, S., Moore, K., Talwar, V., & Park-Saltzman, J. (2011). Preadolescents' gendered spiritual identities and self-regulation. *Journal of Beliefs and Values, 32*(3), 303–316. doi: 10.1080/136172/2011.627679

Bosacki, S., & O'Neill, S. (2015). Early adolescents' emotional perceptions and engagement with popular music activities in everyday life. *International Journal of Adolescence and Youth, 20*(2), 228–244. doi:10.1080/02673843.2013.785438

Bronfenbrenner, U. (1977). Toward an experimental ecology of human development. *American Psychologist, 32*, 513–531.

Bronfenbrenner, U., & Morris, P. (2006). The bioecological model of human development. In R. M. Lerner (Ed.), *Handbook of child psychology: Vol. 43. Theoretical models of human development* (pp. 793–828). Hoboken, NJ: Wiley.

Bruner, J. (1996). *The culture of education.* Cambridge, MA: Harvard University Press.

Busso, D. (2014). Neurobiological processes of risk and resilience in adolescence: Implications for policy and prevention science. *Mind, Brain, and Education, 8*, 34–43.

Charman, T., Ruffman, T., & Clements, W. (2002). Is there a gender difference in false belief development? *Social Development, 11*, 1–10.

Chaplin T. M., & Aldao A. (2013). Gender differences in emotion expression in children: A meta-analytic review. *Psycholological Bulletin, 139*, 735–765.

Cheon, B., Im, D., Harada, T., Kim J., Mathur V., Scimeca, J. M., & Chiao, J. Y. (2011). Cultural influences on neural basis of intergroup empathy. *NeuroImage, 5*, 642–650.

Chin, T., & Rickard, N. (2014). Emotion regulation strategy mediates both positive and negative relationships between music uses and well-being. *Psychology of Music, 42*, 692–713.

Crick, N., Nelson, D., Morales, J., Cullerton-Sen, C., Casas, J., & Hickman, S. (2001). Relational victimization in childhood and adolescence: I hurt you through the grapevine. In J. Juvonen & S. Graham (Eds.), *School-based peer harassment: The plight of the vulnerable and victimized* (pp. 196–214). New York, NY: Guilford.

Crone, E. A., & Dahl, R. E. (2012). Understanding adolescence as a period of social-affective engagement and goal flexibility. *Nature Reviews Neuroscience, 13*, 636–650. doi:10.1038/nrn3313

Cross, S. E., & Madson, L. (1997). Models of the self: Self-construals and gender. *Psychological Bulletin, 122*(1), 5–37.

Dabrowski, K. (1967). *Personality shaping through positive disintegration.* Boston, MA: Little, Brown.

Damon, W., & Hart, D. (1988). *Self-understanding in childhood and adolescence.* New York, NY: Cambridge University Press.

Danish, S., Taylor, T., & Fazio, R. (2003). Enhancing adolescent development through sports and leisure. In G. Adams, & M. Berzonsky (Eds.), *Blackwell handbook of adolescence* (pp. 129–148*).* Malden, MA: Blackwell.

Davis, M. H. (1983). Measuring individual differences in empathy: Evidence for a multidimensional approach. *Journal of Personality and Social Psychology, 44*, 113–126. doi:10.1037/0022-3514.44.1.113

Davis, M., & Franzoi, S. (1991). Stability and change in adolescent self-consciousness and empathy. *Journal of Research in Personality, 25*, 70–87.

de Greck, M., Shi, Z., Wang, G., Zuo, X., Yang X., Wang, X., … Han, S. (2012). Culture modulates brain activity during empathy with anger. *NeuroImage, 59*, 2871–2882.

De Leersnyder, J., Mesquita, B., & Ki, H. (2011). Where do my emotions belong? A study of immigrants' emotional acculturation. *Personality and Social Psychology Bulletin, 37*, 451–463.

Denham. S. (1998). *Emotional development in young children.* New York, NY: Guilford.

De Souza, M. (2014). The empathetic mind: The essence of human spirituality. *International Journal of Children's Spirituality, 19*, 45–54.

Devine, R., & Hughes, C. (2013). Silent films and strange stories: Theory of mind, gender, and social experiences in middle childhood. *Child Development, 84,* 989–1003.

Doey, L., Coplan, R. J., & Kingsbury, M. (2014). Bashful boys and coy girls: A review of gender differences in childhood shyness. *Sex Roles, 70,* 255–266. doi:10.1007/s11199-013-0317-9

Eagly, A., & Crowley, M. (1986). Gender and helping behavior: A meta-analytic review of the social psychological literature. *Psychological Bulletin, 100,* 283–308.

Eisenberg, N., Cumberland, A., Guthrie, I. K., Murphy, B. C., & Shepard, S. A. (2005). Age changes in prosocial responding and moral reasoning in adolescence and early adulthood. *Journal of Research on Adolescence, 15*(3), 235–260.

Ellis, B., Del Giudice, M., Dishion, T., Figueredo, A., Gray, P., Griskevicius, V., … Wilson, D. (2012). The evolutionary basis of risky adolescent behavior: Implications for science, policy, and practice. *Developmental Psycholology, 48,* 598–623.

Else-Quest, N. (2012). Gender differences in temperament. In M. Zentner & R. Shiner (Eds.), *Handbook of temperament* (pp. 479–496). New York, NY: Guilford.

Else-Quest, N. M., Higgins, A., Allison, C., & Morton, L. C. (2012). Gender differences in self-conscious emotional experience: A meta-analysis. *Psychological Bulletin, 138,* 947–981.

Epley, N., Caruso, E., & Bazerman, M. H. (2006). When perspective-taking increases taking: Reactive egoism in social interaction. *Journal of Personality and Social Psychology, 91*(5), 872–889.

Erikson, E. (1968). *Identity, youth, and crisis.* New York, NY: Norton.

Field, A., Camargo, C. Taylor, C., Berkey, C., & Colditz, G. (1999). Relation of peers and media influence to the development of purging behaviors among preadolescents and adolescent girls. *Archives of Pediatrics & Adolescent Medicine, 153,* 1184–1189.

Fine, C. (2010). *Delusions of gender: How our minds, gender, and neurosexism create difference.* New York, NY: Norton.

Fiske, A., Kitayama, S., Markus, H., & Nisbett, R. (1998). The cultural matrix of social psychology. In D. Gilbert, A. Fiske, & G. Lindzey (Eds.), *The handbook for social psychology* (Vol. 2, pp. 915–981). New York, NY: McGraw Hill.

Franko, D. L., & Striegel-Moore, R. H. (2002). The role of body dissatisfaction as a risk factor for depression in adolescent girls: Are the differences black and white? *Journal of Psychosomatic Research, 53,* 975–983. doi: 10.1016/S0022-3999(02)00490-7

Gardner, H., & Davis, K. (2013). *The App generation: How today's youth navigate identity, intimacy, and imagination in a digital world.* New Haven, CT: Yale University Press.

Gentile, B., Grabe, S., Dolan-Pascoe, B., Twenge, J., Wells, B., & Maitino, A. (2009). Gender differences in domain specific self-esteem: A meta-analysis. *Review of Genetic Psychology, 13,* 34–45.

Goffman, I. (1981). *Forms of speech.* New York, NY: Doubleday.

Greenspan, L., & Deardorff, J. (2014). *The new puberty: How to navigate early development in today's girls.* New York, NY: Rodale.

Hadaway, N., & Young, T. (2014). Preserving languages in the new millennium: Indigenous bilingual children's books. *Childhood Education, 90,* 358–364.

Hall, R. (1986). What nursery school teachers ask us about: Psychoanalytic consultations in preschools: Living with Spiderman et al.: Mastering aggression and excitement. *Emotions and Behavior Monographs, 5,* 89–99.

Halpern, D. (1992). *Sex differences in cognitive abilities* (2nd ed.). Hillsdale, NJ: Erlbaum.

Harter, S. (1999). *The construction of the self: A developmental perspective.* New York, NY: Guilford.

Heke, I. (2001). *The Hokowhitu Program: Designing a sporting intervention to address alcohol and substance abuse in adolescent Maori.* Manuscript, University of Otago, Dunedin, New Zealand.

Hill, J., & Lynch, M. (1983). The intensification of gender-related role expectations during early adolescence. In J. Brookes-Gunn & A. Peterson (Eds.), *Girls at puberty: Biological and psychosocial perspectives* (pp. 201–228). New York, NY: Plenum.

Hoffman, M. L. (2000). *Empathy and moral development: Implications for caring and justice.* New York, NY: Cambridge University Press.

Hong, Y., Morris, M., Chiu, C., & Benet-Martinez, V. (2000). Multicultural minds: A dynamic constructivist approach to culture and cognition. *American Psychologist, 55,* 709–720.

Hughes, C. (2011). *Social understanding and social lives: From toddlerhood through to the transition to school.* New York, NY: Psychology Press.

Hyde, J. (2014). Gender similarities and differences. *Annual Review of Psychology, 65,* 373–398.

Hyde, J., Mezulis, A., & Abramson, L. (2008). The ABCs of depression: Integrating affective, biological and cognitive models to explain the emergence of the gender difference in depression. *Psychological Review, 115,* 291–313.

Ibanez, A., Huepe, D., Gemp, R., Gutierrez, V., Riveria-Rei, A., & Toledo, M. (2013). Empathy, sex and fluid intelligence. *Personality and Individual Differences, 54,* 616–621.

Karniol, R., Gabay, R., Ochion, Y., & Harari, Y. (1998). Is gender or gender-role orientation a better predictor of empathy in adolescence? *Sex Roles, 39,* 45–59. doi:10.1023/A:1018825732154

Kashima, Y., Yamaguchi, S., Kim, U., Choi, S., Gelfand, M., & Yuki, M. (1995). Culture, gender, and self: A perspective from individualism-collectivism research. *Journal of Personality and Social Psychology, 69,* 925–937.

Kegan, J. (1994). *In over our heads: The mental demands of modern life.* Cambridge, MA: Harvard University Press.

Kehler, M. (2009). Boys, friendships, and knowing "it wouldn't be unreasonable to assume I am gay." In W. Martino, M. Kehler, & M. B. Weaver-Hightower (Eds.), *The problem with boys' education: Beyond the backlash* (pp. 198–223). New York, NY: Taylor & Francis.

Khodayarifard, M., Brinthaupt, T., Zardkhaneh, S., & Azar, G. (2014). The psychometric properties of the self-talk scale among Iranian university students. *Psychology, 5,* 119–126.

Killinger, B. (2008). *Integrity: Doing the right thing for the right reason.* Montreal, Canada: McGill-Queen's University Press.

Kim, H., & Markus, H. (1999). Deviance or uniqueness, harmony or conformity? A cultural analysis. *Journal of Personality and Social. Psychology, 77,* 785–800.

Kim, H., & Sasaki, J. (2014). Cultural neuroscience: Biology of the mind in cultural contexts. *Annual Review of Psychology, 65,* 487–514.

Kincheloe, J. (2009). Selling a new and improved Jesus: Christotainment and the power of political fundamentalism. In S. Steinberg & J. Kincheloe (Eds.), *Christotainment: Selling Jesus through popular culture* (pp. 1–22). Boulder, CO: Westview Press.

Kinnucan, C., & Kuebli, J. (2013). Understanding explanatory talk through Vygotsky's theory of self-regulation. In B. Sokol, M. Grouzet, & U. Muller (Eds.), *Self-regulation and autonomy: Social and developmental dimensions of human conduct* (pp. 231–252). New York, NY: Cambridge University Press.

Kitayama, S., & Markus, H. R. (Eds.). (1994). *Emotion and culture: Empirical studies of mutual influence.* Washington, DC: American Psychological Association.

Kling, K., Hyde, J., Showers, C., & Buswell, B. (1999). Gender differences in self-esteem: A meta-analysis. *Psychological Bulletin, 125,* 470–500.

Kluger, J. (2014). *The narcissist next door: Understanding the monster in your family, in your office, in your bed—in your world.* New York, NY: Riverhead Books.

Kobayashi, C., Glover, G., & Temple, E. (2006). Cultural and linguistic influence on neural bases of "theory of mind": An fMRI study with Japanese bilinguals. *Brain Language, 98,* 210–220.

Kobayashi, C., Glover, G., & Temple, E. (2007). Cultural and linguistic effects on neural bases of "theory of mind" in American and Japanese children. *Brain Research, 1164,* 95–107.

Kroger, J. (1996). *Identity in adolescence: The balance between self and other.* London, England: Routledge.

Laible, D., & Thompson, R. (1998). Attachment and emotion understanding in preschool. *Developmental Psychology, 34,* 1038–1045.

Lagattuta, K. H., Kramer, H. J., Kennedy, K., Hjortsvang, K., Goldfarb, D., & Tashjian, S. (2015). *Beyond Sally's missing marble: Further development in children's understanding of mind and emotion in middle childhood. Advances in child development and behavior* (Vol. 48). New York, NY: Elsevier.

Lagattuta, K. H., Nucci, L., & Bosacki, S. L. (2010). Bridging theory of mind and the personal domain: Children's reasoning about resistance to parental control. *Child Development, 81,* 616–635. doi:10.1111/j.1467-8624.2009.01419.x

Lanzetta, J. T., & Englis, B. G. (1989). Expectations of cooperation and competition and their effects on observers' vicarious emotional responses. *Journal of Personality and Social Psychology, 56,* 543–554.

Larson, R. (2011). Positive development in a disorderly world. *Journal of Research in Adolescence, 21,* 317. doi:10.1111/j.1532-7795.2010.00707.x

Lee, C. (2003). Why we need to re-think race and ethnicity in educational research. *Educational Researcher, 32,* 3–5.

Leeves, S., & Banerjee, R. (2014). Childhood social anxiety and social support-seeking: Distinctive links with perceived support from teachers. *European Journal of Psychology of Education, 29,* 43–62.

Leussis, M., & Andersen, S. (2008). Is adolescence a sensitive period for depression? Behavioral and neuroanatomical findings from a social stress model. *Synapse, 6,* 22–30.

Lewis, M., Sullivan, M., Stanger, C., & Weiss, M. (1989). Self-development and self-conscious emotions. *Child Development, 60,* 146–156.

Lillard, A. (1998). Ethnopsychologies: Cultural variations in theories of mind. *Psychological Bulletin, 123,* 3–32.

Luppa, M., Sikorski, C., Luck, T., Ehreke, L., Konnopka, A, & Riedel-Heller, S. (2012). Age- and gender-specific prevalence of depression in latest-life: Systematic review and meta-analysis. *Journal of Affective Disorders, 136,* 212–221.

Maccoby, E. (1998). Gender and relationships: A developmental account. *American Psychologist, 45,* 513–520.

Markus, H., & Kitayama, S. (1994). The cultural construction of self and emotion: Implications for social behavior. In S. Kitayama & H. Markus (Eds.), *Emotion and culture: Empirical studies of mutual influence* (pp. 89–132). Washington, DC: American Psychological Association.

Marsh, H. W., & Perry, C. (2005). Does a positive self-concept contribute to winning gold medals in elite swimming? The causal ordering of elite athlete self-concept and championship performances. *Journal of Sport and Exercise Psychology, 27,* 71–91.

Martins, N., Williams, D. C., Ratan, R. A., & Harrison, K. (2011). Virtual muscularity: A content analysis of male video game characters. *Body Image, 8*(1), 43–51. doi:10.1016/j.bodyim.2010.10.002

Masten, A. (2014a). Global perspectives on resilience in children and youth. *Child Development, 85,* 6–20.

Masten, A. (2014b). *Ordinary magic: Resilience in development.* New York, NY: Guilford.

Mazur, A., & Booth, A. (1998). Testosterone and dominance in men. *Behavioral and Brain Sciences, 21,* 353–397.

Mesquita, B., & Leu, J. (2007). The cultural psychology of emotion. In S. Kitayama & D. Cohen (Eds.), *Handbook of cultural psychology* (pp. 734–759). New York, NY: Guilford.

Mestre, M. V., Samper, P., Frías, M. D., & Tur, A. M. (2009). Are women more empathetic than men? A longitudinal study in adolescence. *Spanish Journal of Psychology, 12,* 76–83.

Retrieved from http://redalyc.uaemex.mx/redalyc/pdf/172/17213005008.pdf

Miller, J. (1993). *The holistic curriculum*. Toronto, ON, Canada: OISE Press.

Miller, J. (2000). *Education and the soul: Toward a spiritual curriculum*. New York, NY: State University of New York Press.

Miranda, D., & Gaudreau, P. (2011). Music listening and emotional well-being in adolescence: A person- and variable-oriented study. *European Review of Applied Psychology, 61,* 1–11.

Mischel, W. (2014). *The marshmallow test: Mastering self-control*. New York, NY: Little, Brown.

Moore, R. (2010). *Sells like teen spirit: Music, youth culture, and social crisis*. New York, NY: New York University Press.

Neff, K. D. (2011). Self-compassion, self-esteem, and well-being. *Social and Personality Psychological Compass, 5,* 1–12. doi:10.1111/j.1751-9004.2010.00330.

Neff, K., & Germer, G. (2013). A pilot study and randomized controlled trial of the Mindful Self-Compassion Program. *Journal of Clinical Psychology, 69,* 28–44.

Newman, D. L., Sontag, L. M., & Salvato, R. (2006). Psychosocial aspects of body mass and body image among rural American Indian adolescents. *Journal of Youth and Adolescence, 35,* 281–291.

Ng, S. H., Han, S., Mao, L., & Lai, J. C. L. (2010). Dynamic bicultural brains: A fMRI study of their flexible neural representation of self and significant others in response to culture priming. *Asian Journal of Social Psychology, 13,* 83–91

Nolen-Hoeksema, S. (2001). Gender differences in depression. *Current Directions in Psychological Science, 10,* 173–176.

Nucci, L. (2013). It's a part of life to do what you want. The role of personal choice in social development. In B. Sokol, M. Grouzet, & U. Muller (Eds.), *Self-regulation and autonomy: Social and developmental dimensions of human conduct* (pp. 165–188). New York, NY: Cambridge University Press.

O'Brien S., & Bierman K. (1988). Conceptions and perceived influence of peer groups: Interviews with preadolescents and adolescents. *Child Development, 59,* 1360–1365.

Offer, D., Ostrov, E., Howard, K., & Atkinson, R. (1988). *The teenage world: Adolescent self-image in ten countries*. New York, NY: Plenum Press.

Oishi, S., Diener, E., Napa Scollon, C., & Biswas-Diener, R. (2004). Cross-situational consistency of affective experiences across cultures. *Journal of Personality and Social Psychology, 86,* 460–472. doi:10.1037/0022-3514.86.3.460

Olweus, D., & Endresen, I. M. (1998). The importance of sex-of-stimulus object: Age trends and sex differences in empathic responsiveness. *Social Development, 7,* 370–388. doi:10.1111/1467-9507.00073

Overton, W. F. (2013). A new paradigm for developmental science: Relationism and relational-developmental systems. *Applied Developmental Science, 17,* 94–107. doi:10.1080/10888691.2013.778717

Parks, A. (2014). A case for the advancement and design of online positive psychological interventions. *The Journal of Positive Psychology, 9,* 502–508.

Piaget, J. (1965/1932). *The moral judgement of the child*. New York, NY: Free Press.

Pipher, M. (1994). *Reviving Ophelia: Saving the selves of adolescent girls*. New York, NY: Ballantine.

Pons, F., & Harris, P. (2005). Longitudinal change and longitudinal stability of individual differences in children's emotion understanding. *Cognition and Emotion, 19,* 1158–1174.

Pope, C. (2001). *"Doing school." How we are creating a generation of stressed out, materialistic, and miseducated students*. London, England: Yale University Press.

Quest, N., Hyde, J., & Linn, M. (2010). Cross-national patterns of gender differences in mathematics: A meta-analysis. *Psychological Bulletin, 136,* 103–127.

Redzic, N., Taylor, V., Chang, M., Trockel, M., Shorter, A., & Taylor, C. (2014). An Internet-based positive psychology program: Strategies to improve effectiveness and engagement. *Journal of Positive Psychology, 9,* 494–501.

Rentfrow, P. J., & McDonald, J. A. (2010). Preference, personality, and emotions. In P. N. Juslin & J. Sloboda (Eds.), *Handbook of music and emotions: Theory, research, applications* (pp. 669–695). New York, NY: Oxford University Press.

Rentfrow, P. J., McDonald, J. A., & Oldmeadow, J. A. (2009). You are what you listen to: Young people's stereotypes about music fans. *Group Processes & Intergroup Relations, 12,* 329–344. doi:10.1177/1368430209102845

Rivas-Drake, D., Seaton, S., Markstrom, C., Quintana, S., Syed, M., Lee, R., ... Ethnic and Racial Identity in the 21st Century Study Group. (2014). Ethnic and racial identity in adolescence: Implications for psychosocial, academic, and health outcomes. *Child Development, 85,* 40–57.

Rochat, P. (2009). *Others in mind: Social origins of self-consciousness.* Cambridge, England: Cambridge University Press.

Rogers, A. (1993). Voice, play, and practice of courage in girls' and women's lives. *Harvard Educational Review, 63,* 265–295.

Ronald, A., Viding, E., Happé, F., & Plomin, R. (2006). Individual differences in theory of mind ability in middle childhood and links with verbal ability and autistic traits: A twin study. *Social Neuroscience, 1,* 412–425.

Ruedy, N., Moore, C., Gino, F., & Schweitzer, M. (2013). Cheater's high? The unexpected affective benefits of unethical behavior. *Journal of Personality and Social Psychology, 105*(4), 531–548. doi:10.1037/a0034231

Saarikallio, S. (2011). Music as emotional self-regulation throughout adulthood. *Psychology of Music, 39,* 307–327.

Sanchez, J. A., Alarcon, D., & De la Mata, M. L. (2009). Private speech beyond childhood: Testing the developmental hypothesis. In A. Winsler, C. Fernyhough, & I. Montero (Eds.), *Private speech, executive functioning, and the development of verbal self-regulation* (pp. 188–197). New York, NY: Cambridge University Press.

Sasaki, J. Y., Kim, H. S., Mojaverian, T., Kelley, L. D., Park, I. Y., & Janušonis, S. (2013). Religion priming differentially increases prosocial behavior among variants of dopamine D4 receptor (DRD4) gene. *Social Cognitive Affective Neuroscience, 8,* 209–215.

Saxe, R., & Kanwisher, N. (2003). People thinking about thinking people: The role of the temporo-parietal junction in "theory of mind." *NeuroImage, 19,* 1835–1842.

Schaffer, R. (1996). *Social development.* Oxford, England: Blackwell.

Scollon, C. N., Howard, A. H., Caldwell, A. E., & Ito, S. (2009). The role of ideal affect in the experience and memory of emotions. *Journal of Happiness Studies, 10,* 257–269. doi:10.1007/s10902-007- 9079-9

Scollon, C. N., Koh, S., & Au, E. (2011). Cultural differences in the subjective experience of emotion: When and why they occur. *Personality and Social Psychology Compass, 5,* 853–864. doi:10.1111/j.1751- 9004.2011.00391.x

Selman, R. L. (1980). *The growth of interpersonal understanding: Developmental and clinical analyses.* New York, NY: Academic Press.

Shahaeian, A., Nielsen, M., Peterson, C. C., & Slaughter, V. (2014). Cultural and family influences on children's theory of mind development: A comparison of Australian and Iranian school-age children. *Journal of Cross-Cultural Psychology, 45,* 555–568. doi:10.1177/0022022113513921

Shields, S. (2002). *Speaking from the heart: Gender and the social meaning of emotion.* Cambridge, England: Cambridge University Press.

Shweder, R. (1991). *Thinking through cultures: Expeditions in cultural psychology.* Cambridge, England: Cambridge University Press.

Siegel, D. (2013). *Brainstorm: The power and purpose of the teenage brain.* New York, NY: Jeremy Tarcher/Penguin.

Silverstein, B., & Perlick, D. (1995). *The cost of competence: Why inequality causes depression, eating disorders, and illness in women.* New York, NY: Oxford University Press.

Slaughter, V., & Perez-Zapata, D. (2014). Cultural variations in the development of mind reading. *Child Development Perspectives, 8*, 237–241.

Smetana, J. G. (2006). Social cognitive domain theory: Consistencies and variations in children's moral and social judgments. In M. Killen & J. G. Smetana (Eds.), *Handbook of moral development* (pp. 119–154). Mahwah, NJ: Erlbaum.

Steinberg, S. (2009). Screening Jesus: Hollywood and christonormativity. In S. Steinberg & J. Kincheloe (Eds.), *Christotainment: Selling Jesus through popular culture* (pp. 131–152). Boulder, CO: Westview Press.

Steiner, R. (1976). *Education of the child in the light of anthroposophy.* (G. Adams & N. Adams, Trans.). London, England: Rudolph Steiner Press.

Sternberg, R. (2014). The development of adaptive competence: Why cultural psychology is necessary and not just nice. *Developmental Review, 34*, 208–224.

Tahiroglu, D., Carlson, S. Olofson, E., Moses, L., Mahy, C., & Sabbagh, M. (2014). The children's social understanding scale: Construction and validation of a parent-report measure for assessing individual differences in children's theories of mind. *Developmental Psychology, 50*, 2485–2497.

Taylor, S., Sherman, D., Kim, H., Jarcho, J., Takagi, K., & Dunagan, M. S. (2004). Culture and social support: Who seeks it and why? *Journal of Personality and Social Psychology, 87*, 354–362.

ter Bogt, T. F. M., Keijsers, L., & Meeus, W. H. J. (2013). Early adolescent music preferences and minor delinquency. *Pediatrics, 131*, e380–e389. doi:10.1542/peds.2012-0708

Thompson, M., & Gauntlett-Gilbert, J. (2008). Mindfulness with children and adolescents: Effective clinical application. *Clinical Child Psychology and Psychiatry, 13*(3), 395–407.

Thompson, N., Whitesell, N., Galliher, N., & Gfellner, B. (2012). Unique challenges of child development research in sovereign nations in the United States and Canada. *Child Development Perspectives, 6*, 61–65.

Tomasello, M. (1999). *The cultural origins of human cognition.* Cambridge, MA: Harvard University Press.

Tomasello, M. (2014a). *A natural history of human thinking.* Cambridge, MA: Harvard University Press.

Tomasello, M. (2014b). The ultra-social animal. *European Journal of Social Psychology, 44*, 187–194.

Turkle, S., (2011). *Alone together: Why we expect more from technology and less from each other.* New York, NY: Basic Books.

Turnage, B. F. (2004). Influences on adolescent African American females' global self-esteem: Body image and ethnic identity. *Journal of Ethnic and Cultural Diversity in Social Work, 13*, 27–45.

Uchida, Y., Townsend, S. S. M., Markus, H. R., & Bergsieker, H. B. (2009). Emotions as within or between people? Lay theory of emotion expression and emotion inference across cultures. *Personality and Social Psychology Bulletin, 35*, 1427–1439. doi:10.1177/0146167209347322

Van der Graaff, J., Branje, S., De Wied, M., Hawk, S., Van Lier, P., & Meeus, W. (2014). Perspective taking and empathic concern in adolescence: Gender differences in developmental changes. *Developmental Psychology, 3*, 881–888. doi:10.1037/a0034325

Vygotsky, L. S. (1986/1934). *Thought and language.* Cambridge, MA: MIT Press.

Watson, D., & Clark, L. (1984). Negative affectivity: The disposition to experience aversive emotional states. *Psychological Bulletin, 96*, 465–490.

Weare, K. (2013). Developing mindfulness with children and young people: A review of the evidence and policy context. *Journal of Children's Services, 8*(2), 141–153.

Winsler, A. (2009). Still talking to ourselves after all these years: A review of current research on private speech. In A. Winsler, C. Fernyhough, & I. Montero (Eds.), *Private speech, executive functioning, and the development of verbal self-regulation* (pp. 3–41). New York, NY: Cambridge University Press.

Wirtz, D., Chiu, C., Diener, E., & Oishi, S. (2009). What constitutes a good life? Cultural differences in the role of positive and negative affect in subjective well-being. *Journal of Personality, 77,* 1167–1196. doi:10.1111/j.1467-6494.2009.00578.x

Yildirim, B. O., & Derksen, J. J. L. (2012). A review on the relationship between testosterone and the interpersonal/affective facet of psychopathy. *Psychiatry Research, 197,* 181–198. doi:10.1016/j.psychres.2011.08016

Yon, D. (2000). *Elusive culture: Schooling, race, and identity in global times.* New York, NY: State of New York University Press.

Part IV

Ecologies of Social Cognitive Development

"… the pulpit leads the world … the world's a ship on its passage out, and not a voyage is complete; and the pulpit is its prow." (Melville, 1967/1851, p. 55)

Section Overview

Part IV explores how youth apply their social cognitive abilities to diverse social ecologies. That is, this section provides a critical overview of innovative research that explores the larger context surrounding the developing young person including the popular media, the larger community, and the digital world. Chapter 9 focuses on the importance of navigating the digital world and social media. Chapter 10 highlights the research on social cognition and various behavioral and emotional challenges experienced by some youth.

Social Cognition in Middle Childhood and Adolescence: Integrating the Personal, Social, and Educational Lives of Young People, First Edition. S. L. Bosacki.
© 2016 John Wiley & Sons, Ltd. Published 2016 by John Wiley & Sons, Ltd.

9

Digital Worlds and Social Media

"But people are never alone now … We make them hate solitude …" (Huxley, 1932, p. 207)

Introduction

This chapter focuses on the importance of young people's digital media habits and histories for their social cognitive development. Given the increasingly complex landscape of the digital world, a growing number of educators and researchers explore the role technology plays in young people's social communicative skills and identity development. The following sections will discuss the role technology plays in the educational worlds of the young person, and outline the thoughts of educators and researchers regarding how to help youth make sense of, and learn from, the often contradictory and ambiguous nature of the moral landscape of the Internet (Ahn, 2014; Spitzer, 2014; Turkle, 2011, 2015).

According to digital technology researchers (Boyd, 2014), the Internet has simultaneously enabled two contradictory influences on belief. First, the Internet reduces intellectual isolation by providing more opportunity for people to learn the diversity of opinion on any topic. Second, the Internet, especially social media, simultaneously allows others to share their beliefs—however valid or trustworthy their claims may be. How do we as adults learn to cope with the paradoxical messages the rapidly evolving technological landscape provides us with regarding the promise of freedom of speech, as well as the right to privacy and safety?

Moreover, how do we as researchers and educators reconcile these contradictions and ambiguities, and how does this complexity affect our youth today? As Turkle (2011) and others note, given that knowledge is increasingly becoming open source, how does this accessibility to information shape our thoughts, attitudes, and values? More importantly, this

Social Cognition in Middle Childhood and Adolescence: Integrating the Personal, Social, and Educational Lives of Young People, First Edition. S. L. Bosacki.
© 2016 John Wiley & Sons, Ltd. Published 2016 by John Wiley & Sons, Ltd.

chapter will outline the current literature on young people's digital media habits, and discuss the implications for the social cognitive development and emotional well-being of our youth.

Research

Psychological aspects of electronic communication

According to McKenna, Green, and Gleason (2002), there are four main psychological components of electronic communication that distinguish computer-mediated communication or CMC (e.g., Internet, e-mailing, texting), from face-to-face communication (FtF): (1) Greater anonymity, (2) decreased importance in physical appearance, (3) greater control over content of the text, and (4) capacity to find similar others. Such key psychological factors are suggested to play an important role in the connections between emerging adolescents' CMC skills and their social cognitive development.

The issue of virtual versus real life also complicates the experiences of ostracism and social exclusion during adolescence. For example, to what extent do CMC experiences of social exclusion and silence feel different from experiences of FtF social exclusion in terms of emotional intensity? More importantly, how do we study this further and why should we as researchers and educators of youth be concerned? Building on past research on FtF or in-person social ostracism Williams (2001), Turkle (2011), and others explore examples of virtual or CMC ostracism, and they encourage us to think critically about the role technology plays in social relations. Moreover, a growing amount of research suggests that, given that the Internet has the potential to be an effective and powerful communicative tool (Boyd, 2014), individual differences exist in whether adolescents decide to use the Internet as a psychological tool or weapon to either help or harm themselves and others (Turkle, 2011), and it may improve or impede learning (Spitzer, 2014).

Challenges of modern technologies for psychoeducators

The challenge for neuroscience researchers and educators for the next few decades will be for educators to apply research findings on how modern technology influences developing minds to the classroom setting. Researchers need to help youth find ways to make sense of the deluge of digital media in an adaptive way. By serving as master digital navigators, as mentors and role models, researchers and educators can help adolescents make healthy choices regarding their use of technological tools to promote their learning and development.

Within the current culture of personal and social ambiguity, many researchers claim that the constant flow of stimuli offered by digital technologies challenges our ability to focus our attention and learn (Boyd, 2014; Levitin, 2014; McKenna et al., 2002; Turkle, 2011). Developmentalists and educators need to ask how this abundant virtuality affects the human brain and the mind in terms of potential harms and benefits. As Spitzer (2014) warns policy makers and educators, contradictory research shows that the known risks and side effects of information technology stand in marked contrast to the often claimed but largely unproven possible benefits.

Benefits of virtuality include a diverse wealth of educational materials, and increased communication that eliminates travel costs (e.g., overseas communication). Despite such benefits, there remain limitations to this technological progress, such as speed of delivery, and the multiplexing of contents within the same time frame may affect the learner's ability to multitask and problem-solving skills (Levitin, 2014). For example, how does processing speed and divided attention affect memory retention in youth, and does it stifle the ability to imagine or to enhance information? What role do emotions play in young people's social cognitive processing while engaged with digital media? To answer such questions, future research is needed to enhance the educational benefits of such new technologies while minimizing the possible disadvantages.

Examples of potential risks and harms involve the harmful use of technology in peer relationships, including the process of cyberbullying. As discussed in Chapter 6 on peer relations, an increasing number of researchers focus on the social, moral, and emotional implications of cyberactivities, and the potential harms and benefits to social relationships and feelings of self-worth and identity (Dooley, Pyżalski, & Cross, 2009; Salmivalli, Sainio, & Hodges, 2013; Smith et al., 2008). For example, a recent meta-analysis of cyberbullying research with young people suggests the need for research on cyberbullying and the psychosocial and emotional implications for youth (Kowalski, Schroeder, Giumetti, & Lattanner, 2014), especially given the possible connections to other media habits such as violent videogame playing (Dittrick, Beran, Mishna, Hetherington, & Shariff, 2013). Such research encourages adults who work with youth to create healthy, adaptive critical multimedia educational programs that foster students' abilities to think and reflect critically as they engage in social networks and communicate through various technologies.

More specifically, Jean Twenge's (2006) discussion of North American youth as the "Me generation," and Turkle's (2011) caution regarding the decision to use CMC over FtF communication support recent media discussions of the psychological characteristics and technological expertise of the "Z generation" (children born after approximately 1995) (Kingston, 2014). Given this ongoing interest in our emerging adolescents within the Z generation, many researchers suggest adults need to encourage youth to limit their engagement time with social technologies and cyberactivities (Gardner & Davis, 2013). Thus, by serving as role models, when educators monitor and manage their personal media diets and digital decorum, their actions may encourage youth to think critically and reflect upon their CMC experiences, and to further engage in FtF social connections with their peers.

Technology and popular media influences   Given our technologically advanced society, and the important role media plays in the lives of young people via television, Internet and social media, film, radio, and so on, surprisingly little research exists on the link between media and digital technologies and adolescents' sociocognitive and psychosocial development (Gardner & Davis, 2013). As noted by many researchers, the number of people across the globe who are "online" or have access to either a computer or the Internet continues to grow exponentially (Boyd, 2014; Turkle, 2011).

Interestingly, in a 2012 Canadian Internet Use Survey from a sample of about 30,000 (Statistics Canada, 2013), 83% of those aged 16 and older living in Canadian households had access to the Internet at home compared with 80% in 2010, and 59% had access to the

Internet using wireless devices such as mobile phones compared with 24% in 2010. Further, the popularity of social media and the Internet as a communication tool increased from 2010 to 2012. Just over two-thirds (67%) of those Canadians who used the Internet visited social networking sites (e.g., Facebook or Twitter) in 2012, up from 58% in 2010.

In general, digital technologies have become an extension to our schools and larger social cognitive universe (Gardner & Davis, 2013; Turkle, 2011). On the Internet, particularly social media sites (e.g., Facebook, Twitter), young people participate in activities tradition-ally considered social, such as competition, shopping, gambling, conversation, meeting new acquaintances, and attending concerts. Unlike traditional media such as TV, film, radio, print, the Internet provides young people with access to a variety of content and more social interactions. Thus, the Internet has created a new dimension for researchers to examine the effects of problematic content (violence and sex) and educational electronic media content. Given that some researchers claim that the Internet is the most interactive and socially engaging media source (Fitton, Ahmedani, Harold, & Shifflet, 2013), empirical evidence suggests that the influence on social cognitive development and well-being could be stronger than those for television or other traditional media (Turkle, 2011).

To explore the role of information technology habits in young people's psychosocial development, Fitton et al. (2013) recently interviewed 128 young adolescents within the United States (13- and 14-year-olds) on their experiences of informational technologies (IT). Overall, findings showed that students perceived technology as integral to all aspects of their everyday life experience (Fitton et al., 2013). In particular, the participants understood the beneficial role technology played in the development of their cognitive and academic skills, and they referred to their need to have technology skills for their future careers. Some participants also reported how IT helped them to develop psychosocially, especially in terms of peer communication and friendship developments. Overall, throughout the interviews, these young adolescents expressed pleasure and pride in their self-reported high level of technoliteracy.

Social networking and mental health in youth   Since the beginning of social networking site (SNS) technologies, adolescents' use of these technologies has expanded, and they are now a primary way of communication and for the acquisition of information about others within their social network (Shapiro & Margolin, 2014). As Turkle (2011, 2015) and others discuss, although computers were initially developed for adults, children and adolescents have fully embraced these technologies for their own social purposes, and are often the family experts on how to use electronic media and social networking sites. Initially, adolescents and young adults dominated SNSs such as MySpace and Facebook, with parents often following their children's digital media habits.

Although perhaps an underestimation, recent data show that approximately 90% of American adolescents use the Internet (Pew, 2009), and 73% use social networking sites (Lenhart, 2009; Lenhart, Ling, Campbell, & Purcell, 2010). Moreover, statistical reports show the amount of time that adolescents and young adults spend using electronic media: on average, 11–18 year olds spend over 11 hours per day exposed to electronic media (Kaiser Family Foundation, 2010). In sum, the presence of SNS use in many adolescents' lives is thus indisputable; however, researchers have just started to explore the impact of SNS experiences on adolescents' social cognitive development and their social lives.

Recent research shows that, overall, adolescents and young adults' stated motivations for using SNSs are quite similar to more traditional forms of communication—to stay in touch with friends, make plans, get to know people better, and present oneself to others (Jiang & de Bruijn, 2014; Turkle, 2011). Social networking sites offer young people new opportunities and challenges for self-expression within a global context. For example, in one-on-one communications within SNSs (e.g., Facebook messages), adolescents can express their likes and dislikes as well as their worldviews and receive immediate feedback. Also, with SNSs, the recipients of this information include both known and unknown targets.

Although there has been variability over time in the specific format of SNS profiles, adolescents have the option of choosing which self-identifying information to provide (Shapiro & Margolin, 2014). Thus, with the beginning of SNSs, most adolescents will widely share, with varying degrees of honesty, accuracy, and openness, information that through more traditional modes of communication (e.g., telephone, FtF), would have been private or reserved for select individuals. Important questions for future researchers include when, how, and why some young people decide to portray their identities online, and how the use of SNSs might influence adolescents' identity and social cognitive development.

Such widespread use of media technologies has implications for the school classroom and the larger culture education. For example, "wireless classrooms" and "laptop schools" have become a growing phenomenon in North America and other modernized countries across the global educational landscape (Turkle, 2011). The recent educational movement has integrated laptop computers into elementary schools and high schools, where all students and faculty own and work on a laptop computer. Thus, the concept of a "wireless school" has the potential to change educational context for youth into a wireless Internet-access or digital zone (Kirschner & Karpinski, 2010).

For instance, all students at the Packer Collegiate Institute in Brooklyn, New York own a laptop computer that has access to the Internet because they are in constant high bandwidth contact with the wireless school and one another (Grossman, 2003). That is, the school created a cyber or virtual school campus that may not necessarily have reflected the societal rules and social processes within the real-life school context. Given the rapid growth of information technology, as I write this book, government and school policies and regulations continue to change as they attempt to provide legal and ethical boundaries for the rapid digital growth. Thus, the challenge for legislators, researchers, and educators is to study new social and moral life digital developments such as online cheating and cyber-crime, and to learn new ways to effectively cope with the legal, social, moral, and emotional consequences (Kirwan & Power, 2013; Ruedy, Moore, Gino, & Schweitzer, 2013).

At the university level, to avoid plagiarism, many North American professors request that their students submit their papers to websites such as Turnitin.com that ensure that their work is original and not a plagiarized copy of an existing published paper. Despite these measures to catch plagiarists and online cheating, academic cheating continues to take place and remains in need of systematic study. More specifically, as mentioned in Chapter 5 on the moral self, given the lack of research on the affective factors involved in unethical acts such as cheating (Ruedy et al., 2013), future research needs to focus on the role that social-moral, cognitive, and emotional factors play when a young person engages in a deceptive, online act (Ruedy et al., 2013; Talwar, Gomez-Garibello, & Shariff, 2014).

Another issue that arises from online learning concerns how most young people still prefer to have a personal space for "play" and "privacy" away from the eyes of educators and parents. Strategies such as videogames, downloading movies and music, texting, and the use of social media such as Facebook and Twitter, are ways in which some students may procrastinate and avoid school work (Turkle, 2011; 2015). To address such issues, many schools have installed computer monitoring devices to document students' media habits or have school policies that restrict the use of games and social media during school time.

Despite the benefits such as instant connections to others across the globe, and increased access for children with learning and physical challenges, a wireless society also holds significant moral and socioemotional implications for young people (Ruedy et al., 2013; Turkle, 2011). In addition, more challenging societal and psychological issues may also underly the immediate, surface-level benefits of a wireless school (Boyd, 2014). For example, to what extent are we really "connected" if youth consider digital texting to be synonymous with FtF talking? What kind of moral, social, and emotional lives will people have if they decide to engage in unethical or morally ambiguous digital behaviors? Does technological progress and social cognitive and moral growth develop in tandem, or independently of one another? For instance, what role do social cognitive abilities play in young people's decision-making processes about whether or not to send emotionally charged remarks, either supportive or disparaging, via text, telephone, or FtF?

To answer such questions, researchers have just started to explore some of the sociomoral and emotional consequences of technological progress and Internet habits (Kirwan & Power, 2013). Given the active and interactive use of CMC, Kraut and his colleagues (1998) found that individuals who made more use of the Internet for just a year or two were more likely to become lonely and depressed. As a result of frequent but often emotionally shallow interactions, Kraut et al. claimed that, as the quality of interaction decreased, feelings of loneliness and depression increased, and a sense of belonging decreased. Such results help to support the more recent findings that show a relation between young people's reported social and emotional challenges and increased digital technological use (Gardner & Davis, 2013; Ruedy et al., 2013; Turkle, 2011, 2015).

Unfortunately, given that the Internet has the potential to be an effective and powerful communicative tool, as mentioned in Chapter 6 on peer relations, some adolescents have chosen to use the Internet as a psychological weapon to harm others. Cyberbullying has become increasingly popular among adults and adolescents, using the Internet and e-mail as a way to psychologically harass others (e.g., sending an insulting or threatening e-mail; creating a Website with derogatory, personal comments about a particular individual, posting unflattering photos without permission on Websites; Brown, Demaray, & Secord, 2014; Talwar et al., 2014). Research shows that cyberostracism and electronic victimization are also on the increase (Salmivalli et al., 2013), as ignoring, or not responding to a text or e-mail correspondence may also have deleterious psychological ramifications on the sender and receiver (Kowalski et al., 2014; Williams, 2001).

Within an educational context, researchers and educators need to explore the question of how a wireless and virtual society may either help or hinder adolescents' ability to create meaning from an unlimited and continuous flow of information. Furthermore, is technology another tool that enables students to further their own learning by providing opportunities for youth to build on their thoughts and imagine alternate realities? Moreover, neuroscientists and educators have started to ask how digital media habits influence the structure of neural pathways and cortical brain development of youth and thus have an influence on how they think and feel (Fitton et al., 2013; Giedd et al., 1999; Siegel, 2013; Spitzer, 2014).

As discussed in Chapter 3 on the cognitive self, brain-imaging technology such as functional Magnetic Resonance Imaging (fMRI) studies of typically developing children shows an increase in cortical gray matter and synaptic overproduction in emerging adolescents (Blakemore & Mills, 2014; Giedd et al., 1999). That is, emerging adolescence is considered to be a critical time in development, when the learning experiences may guide selective synapse elimination (Giedd et al., 1999). In sum, given the highly experiential and pervasive nature of digital media use among emerging adolescents, future researchers need to explore the role electronic communication plays in cortical brain development and the direction of synaptic pruning during adolescence.

Gender-related differences in media habits   Recent research has begun to explore the process of texting and the cultural context involved regarding females and males in emerging adolescence (Ling, Baron, Lehart, & Campbell, 2014; Lippman & Campbell, 2014). Texting, as a social media process, is direct, person-to-person contact where young people can develop their gendered identity and also investigate romantic interactions.

Developmentally, the mobile or cell phone plays a crucial role in the development of social cognitive skills among youth, particularly social communicative skills, as well as self-regulatory skills in terms of self- and emotional expression (Campbell & Park, 2014). In particular, the process of texting may provide adolescents with a great sense of control over, and privacy in, their communications with peers, and thus is ideally suited to facilitate their gradual separation from their parents (Ling, 2005). Clearly, the mobile phone and texting fit well into teens' lives. That is, texting and mobile phones provide youth with access to one another (Ling, 2008), and their use and role in young people's social lives is not matched by other age groups (Ling et al., 2014).

Past research suggests gender-related differences occur in language use with digital media technologies that parallel FtF communication (Baron & Campbell, 2012; Hyde, 2014), including differences in conversation domination, vocabulary type, phatic interaction, courteous and status-laden language (Tannen, 1994). For example, research on information and communication technologies has found that, compared to males, females take longer turns using instant messaging and are more likely to use emoticons in their writing (Baron, 2004; Dresner & Herring, 2010). Women have been found to often use mediated communication for relationship maintenance, and are more likely to be courteous and follow social conventions of communication (Colley, Todd, White, & Turner-Moore, 2010). Girls have also been found to use emoticons to buffer and to moderate their language more often than boys (Baron & Campbell, 2012). Furthermore, compared with teen boys, teen girls have been shown to write lengthier texts and to use more "writing like" or cursive formulations (Herring & Zelenkauskaite, 2008).

Compared to adolescent females, studies show that adolescent males report greater knowledge about Internet technology, spend more time searching for information online and playing more videogames (Ohannessian, 2009). Empirical evidence also suggests that videogaming and watching television may act as a protective factor for boys, lowering anxiety (Ohannessian, 2009). Research shows that the majority of adolescent females use technology for communication, including more mobile phone air time than their male counterparts (Ohannessian, 2009). In addition to gender-related differences, for already socially engaged youth, research suggests that their interpersonal interactions may be enhanced by Internet use. In contrast, for socially isolated youth, Internet use may create social and emotional challenges such as feelings of loneliness and isolation (Turkle, 2011, 2015).

Research on gender-related differences in texting habits has found that some females are more likely to use texting for social purposes (Baron, 2004). In contrast, males have been found to be more likely to have an instrumental use (Baron & Campbell, 2012). The majority of research findings suggest that adolescent males have been found to appear more frank or direct in their texting with females (Herring, 1994); they have also been found to accommodate their style when interacting with females (Herring, 1994).

Past research suggests that males are more likely to accommodate their texting style to match those of females in an attempt to perhaps gain social acceptance (Baron & Campbell, 2012; Turkle, 2015). Regarding romantic relationships, research has shown that, when interacting with someone they were attracted to, respondents would realign their cues and utterances. Such gender-related differences in communication patterns of texting may play a role in social communication between female and male youth and lead to possible interpersonal and self-presentation challenges for some.

To explore the topic of texting and its importance for social communication in teens, Ling et al. (2014) examined the interaction strategies used by teenagers when texting with members of the opposite sex. They analyzed material from a series of nine focus groups from 2009 in four US cities and reported texting strategies, and the challenges encountered by the participants. They found that both genders showed the ability to make detailed interpretations of texts and interpret the meaning of punctuation and other paralinguistic devices. Ling et al. (2014) suggested that such texting etiquette perhaps illustrates how some teens engage with texting to negotiate their sense of gender within romantic online relationships.

A specific type of texting has emerged in recent years, the process of "sexting" or sending a photo or video involving the nudity of someone known to the sender and/or receiver with a mobile phone. This sexually focused communication has become an area of interest for researchers, especially given the implications for personal relationships and a sense of psychosexual and cultural identity (D'Antona, Kevorkian, & Russom, 2010; Lenhart, 2009; Lippman & Campbell, 2014). For example, a study of teens' sexting patterns found that 19% of teens in the United States (ages 13–19 years) reported sending nude or semi-nude pictures or videos of themselves to someone via electronic means, and 31% of teens have received such a message (National Campaign to Prevent Teen and Unplanned Pregnancy, 2008).

From a relational perspective, researchers suggest there may be several potential explanations to help understand why some adolescents engage within the process of sexting. Recent studies on sexting from a risk-taking behavior perspective examined the relations between sexting and risky, or negative, emotional health outcomes (Benotsch, Snipes, Martin, & Bull, 2012; Dake, Price, Maziarz, & Ward, 2012; Gordon-Messer, Bauermeister, Grodzinski, & Zimmerman, 2012). In general, past findings suggest that sexting is often associated with a greater likelihood of engaging in additional sexual behaviors (e.g., sexual intercourse), and having a higher level of sexual experience (e.g., number of sexual partners).

However, researchers continue to explore if these findings reflect the expression of sexual interest through sexual activity and sexting, as they may not be causally related to one another. Alternatively, some researchers suggest that the process of texting could provide an additional sociocommunicative pathway to increased levels of sexual activity and experience. Recent findings on the relation between sexting and mental health outcomes remain somewhat mixed and contradictory. That is, some studies suggest that the process of sexting is associated with negative emotional health outcomes such as depression and anxiety challenges (Dake et al., 2012). In contrast, research also suggests that emotional difficulties and sexting habits remain unrelated (Hasinoff, 2013).

Some researchers suggest that in contrast to the risk-taking approach (Benotsch et al., 2012), an initial, exploratory interest or curiosity may be viewed as a healthy aspect of adolescent development (Hyde, 2014). For example, Levine (2013) suggested that sexting could be viewed as a healthy means of self-exploration and social communication with the opposite sex as it promotes emotional and self-expression. Given that most adolescents often may not feel comfortable discussing sexual matters with adults (Greenspan & Deardorff, 2014), peers and popular media may serve as primary resources for adolescents as they try to make sense of their emerging sexual identity (Sutton, Brown, Wilson, & Klein, 2002).

Thus, popular media and peers often play a significant role in the development of emerging adolescents' sexual attitudes, beliefs, and expectancies. Digital media sources may contribute to the peer pressure some teens may feel to engage in particular sexual attitudes and behaviors that they may not feel comfortable with (Ward, 2003). The constant changing patterns of digital communication may also be explained in terms of emancipation from parents and adult authority figures (Campbell & Park, 2014). For example, recent research has found that sexting habits may be positively related with peer mobile communication, but negatively related to family communication.

Given the importance of sexting to social communication and sexual identity in youth, researchers are increasingly starting to explore the relational, normative and gendered developmental dynamics of emerging adolescent texting, presexting, and sexting (Lippman & Campbell, 2014; Talwar et al., 2014). For example, Lippman and Campbell (2014) found that older adolescents described sexting as taking place mainly within the context of romantic interactions or flirting. In contrast, younger adolescents reported "resexting" behaviors or those that involved the humorous exchange of sexually suggestive but non-nude photos with platonic friends.

Lippman and Campbell's (2014) study on the process of sexting among youth provides important implications and avenues for future research and educational practice. Regarding policy and practical implications, in addition to the creation of legislation to prevent underage and criminal intent texting (Calvert, 2009), educational campaigns may provide an effective means by which to minimize the harms associated with adolescent sexting. Rather than attempting to eliminate adolescent sexting entirely (an approach that may appear to be as (in)effective as abstinence-only education), these educational initiatives could instead focus on discouraging the unauthorized distribution of sexts (Hasinoff, 2013). This approach would treat breaches of consent, rather than sexual expression itself, as the problem in need of remedy.

As Myers (2000) notes, within technologically advanced countries, one of the greatest paradoxes of the twenty-first century is that we are spiritually hungry in a world that has access to a rich digital diet. As we continue to create our curriculum and schools for the twenty-first century and begin to think about the twenty-second, we need to ask if we wish to encourage students to be valuable members of society and excited to engage in "good work" or activities that combine ethics and excellence (Damon, 2008; Larson, 2011). How do developmentalists and researchers work together to provide a classroom culture that promotes intellectual excellence and passion, personal integrity, and cooperation as opposed to anxiety, deceit, and competition? In the next section I will outline some directions for educators to connect some of the current research on young people's digital worlds to the classroom.

Applications: So What?

In general, researchers need to explore the social cognitive and social-moral lives of the young adolescent immersed in the technological world (Fitton et al., 2013). To highlight the general human characteristic of adaptation and flexibility, and point to the role of digital experiences in the plasticity and sculpting of the human brain, researchers need to explore the voices of the youth engaged in CMC and SNS experiences (Ahn, Kwolek, & Bowman, 2015; Turkle, 2011, 2015). Overall, the breadth and depth of the interface between technology and adolescent social cognitive development raises a plethora of questions for educational policy, research, and practice, which I will outline below.

As noted above, with the increasing popularity of SMS sites such as Skype and FaceTime among youth (Ahn et al., 2015; Lippman & Campbell, 2014), long-distance communication now has the possibility to include live video feed. Compared to voice-only or text-only CMC, future researchers should explore how such live and instant video communication influences young people's interactive communication patterns and feelings of self-worth and value. Such software, with its live FtF format, has the potential to alter, and perhaps interfere with, the slow and more reflective dynamic of FtF or text-only communication which includes time to think and reflect.

Thus, as mentioned earlier in this chapter, such increased social demands of instant video communication may also lead to an increase in social awkwardness and perhaps anxiety in some children and adolescents, particularly those who question gender-role stereotypes and societal norms (Olson, Key, & Eaton, 2015). So helping children and adolescents to choose the technologies that best suit their interactive communication styles could be an important tool for social development. This also raises questions about the usefulness and effectiveness of online psychosocial therapy for adolescents who require lengthy periods of time to process relational, social-emotional interactions.

Given the importance of communication in family relations, such advanced technological abilities could create ambivalence and mixed emotions for young adolescents. Although some young people may feel pleasure and pride to have more technological skill than a parent, they may also reflect concern about parental lack of technological proficiency. As Fitton et al. (2013) found in their interviews with 13- and 14-year-olds on their experiences with instructional technologies, some of these students perceived their parents as unable to protect them from potential Internet harm. In addition, they found that some youth perceived their parents acting as mentors in proficient IT use to help them learn positive skill acquisition and maintenance.

As discussed in Chapter 7 on family relations, parents often depend on the power dynamics of the parent–child relationship to maintain order, discipline, and structure for children and emerging adolescents. Researchers will need to explore the social cognitive implications of when an adolescent is more knowledgeable than a parent or their siblings in such a meaningful and growing arena as technology. How do families navigate these digital waters when children become the experts and knowledge brokers? Such research topics will provide future assessment questions in family therapy.

Technology and psychobehavioral economics—persuasion and epistemic authority

Given the large amount of cognitive and emotional space that digital media engagement takes up within young people's lives, such experiences have educational implications. That is, many educators and researchers show interest in the connections between digital media habits and social cognitive development. For example, current research on persuasion and epistemic authority in young people claims that the source of influence is less important than how a young person interprets or processes the information (Grouzet, 2013). According to Kruglanski (1989), epistemic authority helps to explain how people process or make sense of the information (e.g., social norms, arguments, goals) and its source (e.g., teacher, parent, media), which holds a particular kind of authority or power and is considered to be valid and reliable. Thus, epistemic authority has implications for which types of sources may influence young people's minds as they process or interpret information.

In terms of persuasion, the potential a subtle message or "nudge" within a digital media setting has to influence a young person's thoughts and behaviors may be dependent upon the amount of epistemic authority the youth gives to that particular media source. That is, compared to an authority figure (parent, teacher) or a book, a piece of information from a digital source in terms of a persuasive text or advertisement may hold a stronger influence on how a young person interprets the information. Thus, a digital source may have a stronger influence on the youth's future decisions or behaviors (Sternberg, 2014).

As discussed earlier, neuroscientists and cognitive developmentalists have found that we have two systems of thinking—one is automated and somewhat influenced by our "hot" or basic emotions, such as joy and fear (Mischel, 2014), while the other is reflective and perhaps guided by the "cold" or morally complex emotions, such as pride and guilt (Levitin, 2014; Mischel, 2014). The automatic system is rapid, and is, or feels, instinctive, and it does not involve what we usually associate with thinking (e.g., smiling at a puppy). According to some neurocognitive scientists, the activities of the automatic system are associated with older parts of the brain (Tomasello, 2014), the parts we share with other animals, and is uncontrolled, effortless, associative, fast, unconscious, and skilled. In contrast, the reflective system is controlled, effortful, deductive, slow, self-aware, and rule following.

The application of such neuroscience research to the digital media habits of youth holds potential to be informative and useful for educators. For example, when young people need to make decisions to apply to a particular secondary school, join a social group, or create a language project for school or complete mathematical equations, they use the reflective system. In contrast, when youth speak in their home language they use the automated system, but use the reflective system to understand or learn a second language. Thus, when an individual learns another language and becomes bilingual, they gradually begin to use their automated learning system for both languages (Kobayashi, Glover, & Temple, 2007).

The use of emotional and cognitive frames, mindsets, or habits of mind may also influence young people's decision-making by framing question or problems in a particular manner (Kamins & Dweck, 1999) (e.g., particular mathematics questions). Thus, cognitive mindsets or frames are powerful cognitive and emotion "nudges," and may influence young people's social cognitive abilities and behaviors. Research shows that most neurotypical youth can create and adopt seemingly sensible rules of behavior that may sometimes lead them to engage in risky behavior (Larson, 2011; Turkle, 2011). Overall, youth are busy trying to cope emotionally in a complex world where they cannot afford to think deeply about every choice they have to make. I will return to the role of the development of a caring and resilient mindset directed toward self and other in future chapters.

Given that most young people live busy and often stressful lives and may experience somewhat fragmented attention (Blakemore & Mills, 2014), research on persuasion suggests that some youth are more likely to accept questions as posed rather than trying to determine whether their answers would vary under alternative formulations (Grouzet, 2013). Overall, past literature suggests that most developmentally typical youth are considered to be "nudgeable"—or able to be tricked or persuaded by others. Such a possibility has implications for FtF and CMC as to which modes of communication may have more persuasion power, and will most likely remain an area of interest for future researchers.

Behavioral and neuroeconomists have borrowed from perception and persuasion psychology research and suggest that our understanding of human behavior can be improved through the appreciation of how people systematically make cognitive errors or think incorrectly (Groopman, 2007; Levitin, 2014). To obtain that understanding, we need to explore some aspects of human thinking, as knowledge about the cognitive system allows others to discover systematic biases in the way we think and feel. Such research has implications for social behavior and moral decision-making in young people as they continue to increase their use of CMC and thus their exposure to online persuasive text.

Such research on persuasion and digital media may provide some insight for educators of youth to incorporate ways to influence young learners' thoughts and beliefs regarding various academic domains. For example, Langois, Blanchet-Cohen, and Beer's (2012) developmental evaluation was based on an action research study that involved a group of Canadian developmental evaluators in a three-year comprehensive community initiative on youth and community change. In their study, they found five practices that were central to the art of the nudge: (1) practice of servant leadership, (2) prediction of program energy, (3) supportive common spaces, (4) untying recursive cognitive knots, and

(5) attention to structure. Such practices can help developmental evaluators and educators to detect and support opportunities for learning and adaptation that may lead to appropriately timed feedback.

In recent years, similar to applied developmental research on persuasion, "nudge" theory has gained increasing attention for the creation of population-wide health interventions (Saghai, 2013). In general, researchers explore how nudging labels implicitly influence individuals' freedom of choice without engaging the influencees' cognitive capacities. Saghai argues for a preservation of freedom of choice in terms of choice-set preservation, and recommends we remain critical regarding our exposure to contexts of persuasion within learning contexts such as the healthcare field. Such a proposition has implications for the educational context in which nudges via CMC such as Internet advertising may have priority over more controlling influences. That is, such persuasive nudges have the potential to influence young people's social cognitive abilities and eventually their moral and social decisions.

Research on persuasion has implications for educational programs that apply the use of technology to perception and attention—particularly given the cognitive challenges associated with multitasking with multiple technologies. For example, research on the cognitive impact of multitasking remains somewhat mixed regarding whether the ability to multitask benefits or harms learning (Levitin, 2014; Lui & Wong, 2012; Ophir, Nass, & Wagner, 2009; Spitzer, 2014). These contradictory findings raise many research questions on focused attention and multitasking as they suggest changes in cognitive brain development, handedness, and dominance (Fitton et al., 2013).

More specifically, students' abilities to effectively use technology in everyday life and in educational pursuits indicate that these critical media literacy methods must be incorporated into learning environments and educational tools impacting educational policies (Boyd, 2014). Furthermore, as I will discuss further in Chapter 10, how does digital media influence those youth with emotional learning exceptionalities, especially given the potentially morally ambiguous nature of many technological devices?

Recent research on choice architecture—the cognitive structure and reasoning patterns for making choices or decisions—explores the process of when does a nudge or a gentle cognitive and emotional "push" or "whisper" become a "shove" or "shout." That is, a nudge is considered a gentle mental "push" that may slow people's thinking to allow them to take more time to make their own decision. Research on multitasking shows that when you have less time to focus on a decision—particularly if you feel stressed or fatigued, you are more likely to be "persuaded" or affected by the nudge (especially visual imagery) (Grouzet, 2013). In addition, findings from neuroscience show that the ability to make all types of decisions (e.g., to e-mail a friend, engage in a conversation during class), requires neural processing that consists of cognitive and emotional energy. Thus, this notion of decision fatigue may occur throughout the daily life of a young person due to multiple decisions occurring with the use of communication technologies (Levitin, 2014).

The application of research to an educational context leads to questions such as to what extent are youth covertly influenced or persuaded by subtle visual imagery and text within the digital world? More specifically, how do they interpret or make sense of this information within the digital world, and how does the context of digital media influence their everyday life decision-making? In addition, how can educators minimize this "decision fatigue," due to the amount of cognitive and emotional energy used within communication technologies to maximize the cognitive effort that is necessary for learning within an academic context? As many educators suggest, focused classroom time could be improved by limiting or banning the use of communicative technologies such as the Internet and social media. In addition, such digital media habits could be monitored by the classroom instructor and allowed within a particular time frame.

Critical media literacy: Promotion of caring, critical,
and creative thinking

Given the increasing violent and sexual content reflected in popular media within today's society (Strasburger & Wilson, 2002; Turkle, 2011), as mentioned earlier, many educators and researchers question the social, moral, and spiritual implications of our advanced technology (Gardner & Davis, 2013; Postman, 1999; Talwar et al., 2014). That is, many researchers suggest that future researchers need to study how communicative technologies and social media such as television, mobile phones, Internet, video games, and movies, influence children and adolescents' values, beliefs, and behaviors toward human beings (Bauerline, 2009; Spitzer, 2014).

Educators of youth need to promote the use of critical and creative thinking and encourage students to become critical consumers of popular media. To develop a healthy skepticism, educators can encourage students to ask questions and to engage in critical conversations regarding the moral, emotional, and ethical implications of various media sources such as TV shows, Websites including social media, and videogames. Within the framework of a critical media literacy program, to promote a sense of empathic sensitivity and conceptual role-taking, young people could be encouraged to ask questions around the experience of how particular individuals are silenced or marginalized. For example, educators can promote young people's social cognitive abilities by encouraging all youth to imagine the experiences of those from minority groups, physically challenged persons, exceptional learners, and others who feel marginalized from the accepted majority and thus feel "silenced" from the popular media (Bosacki, 2005).

More specifically, young people can learn how to critically consume and question digital media, such as what proportion of the population is portrayed by the majority of TV shows, films, magazines, SNSs, and why? In addition to critical thinking, to avoid information mental and emotional overload, and decision-making stress and anxiety, young people need to learn how to organize and make sense of the vast amounts of information in ways that are beneficial to their learning (Levitin, 2014; Turkle, 2011). The capacity to think in critical, imaginative, and insightful ways may also lead to more proactive actions to ensure a peaceful and safe classroom. To explore more specific educational applications, Chapter 11 describes in further detail pedagogical implications of research on social cognitive development among youth.

Future Questions

In sum, the key questions for future digital media researchers could focus on how to connect issues of diversity including moral, emotional, cultural, spiritual capacities, and the role of technology, particularly communicative technologies within the classroom. For example, researchers need to explore the underlying reasons why some youth may choose to engage in technology and digital media as opposed to engaging in alternative FtF learning activities? What role do family relationships and the peer group play in young people's social, emotional, and moral experiences with the digital media? As discussed by an increasing number of researchers (Redzic et al., 2014; Rose, 2014; Turkle, 2011), how can researchers and educators work together to investigate how digital learning tools and alternative learning activities such as outdoor physical activity may promote cultural and social competence, resilience, and well-being?

Future educational research also needs to explore how communicative technologies and digital social media influence young people's social cognitive, emotional and moral, as well as physiological, development. For example, the area of sleep architecture, or the mechanics of sleep, is a relatively unknown field, and is in need of research to explore adolescents' sleep experiences including sleep deprivation and how varied sleep habits relate to emotional and academic learning (Noone et al., 2014; Ribeiro & Stickgold, 2014). Given the increasingly important role technology and popular culture play in the majority of young people's lives, future research needs to explore how electronic media and popular culture influence young people's sense of selves, and their emotional lives and social relations.

More specifically, given the potential negative effects of IT, researchers need to explore the role of CMC in young people's social and emotional lives, such as threats to child safety and cyberbullying (Brown et al., 2014). Further research is needed on how exposure to inappropriate sexual and violent content, Internet "addiction," displacement of physical activity, social isolation, sleep disturbance (Ribeiro & Stickgold, 2014), vision problems, musculoskeletal problems, and obesity affects young people's social cognitive abilities (Ahn et al., 2015; Brown et al., 2014).

In contrast to inimical implications, digital media use has been shown to offer opportunities for children and adolescents to develop new and diverse learning skills. Some potential positive benefits of computer use include enhanced cognitive development, increased school achievement, and reduced barriers to social interaction (Ito et al., 2009; Straker, Pollock, & Maslen, 2009). Research also suggests that access to electronic communication and digital media allows children and adolescents to expand their worldviews and learning styles with immediate access to global information (Gardner & Davis, 2013). In addition, the use of CMC has also been found to extend social networks across distance and culture through increased communication technologies and skills (Ito et al., 2009; Jackson & McKibben, 2009).

For example, Schneider and Amichai-Hamburger (2010) suggest that future research needs to explore the influences of CMC on the stability and consistency of friendships though emerging adolescence and beyond. That is, to what extent does social media enhance friendships above and beyond FtF interactions, and are there any emotional costs to CMC engagement? The relations between CMC and youth identity also requires further exploration as the anonymous feature of CMC as well as the lack of focus on physical appearance may have implications for young people's developing sense of self-worth and identity. For example, as mentioned in Chapter 6 on peer relations and cyberbullying, future research studies need to explore the question of how the mode of communication influences harmful or malevolent social behaviors within peer groups.

Postman's (1999) warning from almost 20 years ago that suggested technology and popular culture might have an inimical impact on the spiritual and moral development of children is still relevant today. Such a claim supports more recent assertions regarding the connections between digital media habits and emotional health in youth (Gardner & Davis, 2013; Turkle, 2011, 2015). Furthermore, it remains imperative that educators and parents of youth remain up to date on the current status of the notion of emotionality and spirituality within the context of popular culture and the influence such media have on the mental and emotional worlds of youth (Kingston, 2014).

A growing number of educators and researchers are engaged in conversations regarding the social, moral, and emotional implications of our technologically advanced society (Myers, 2000; Parisi, 2012; Talwar et al., 2014; Turkle, 2011, 2015). As Noddings (2003) and others suggest, perhaps the digital overload may have a deleterious effect on our emotional and spiritual well-being. Given the complexities surrounding our interactions with digital media, researchers need to continue to ask why, if we are so efficient and productive, are an increasing number of children so unhappy, as illustrated by an increase in reported mental health challenges in youth within many technologically advanced societies such as North America (Fitton et al., 2013; Noddings, 2003; Pomerantz, Ng, Cheung, & Qu, 2014; Turkle, 2011, 2015)? Alternatively, is it possible that advanced technologies may help young people to develop and strengthen additional social cognitive skills and feel more emotionally secure? Such questions remain to be studied by future researchers, particularly within the context of emerging adolescents' social cognitive and moral development.

Given the increasing violent and sexual content reflected in popular media in today's society (Bauerlein, 2009), many educators and researchers question the social, moral, and religious implications of our experiences with advanced technology (Collins & Halverson, 2009; Jackson & McKibben, 2009; Postman, 1999; Turkle, 2011). More research is needed on how media such as television, Internet (including social media), electronic games, and movies influence young people's values, beliefs, and social communicative behaviors toward other human beings (Ream & Savin-Williams, 2003; Strasburger & Wilson, 2002; Talwar et al., 2014; Turkle, 2011, 2015).

As I discussed earlier, some positive psychology and social cognitive researchers recommend that educators and researchers remain critical and cautious of the promotion of programs that focus only on the maintenance of students' positive self-worth and self-esteem (Baumeister, Campbell, Krueger, & Vohs, 2003; Donaldson, Dollwet, & Rao, 2015; Flett & Hewitt, 2014; Marshall, Parker, Ciarrochi, & Heaven, 2014; Neff, 2011; Seligman, 2011). As Seligman notes, programs such as Baumeister, Vohs, DeWall, and Zhang's (2007), that involved the development of caring self-discipline and self-monitoring, encourage youth to develop a strong and positive sense of self-agency, responsibility, gratefulness, and accountability for their learning and personal development.

Educational programs that include social cognitive approaches such as self-regulation, self-caring and soothing, self-improvement, and self-compassion have the potential to help to promote emotional resilience and competencies in youth. Such programs aim to create healthy and effective coping and problem-solving strategies (cognitive and emotional) to help youth to make healthy lifestyle decisions and changes (Bluth & Banton, 2015; Damon, 2008; Neff, 2011; Tiger & McGuire, 2010). Further psychological and counseling support for youth in secondary school may also be used to help young people to make healthy lifestyle choices regarding digital media habits (Jackson & McKibben, 2009), as well as to increase support for families to become active in youth's learning process and emotional health. Such programs promote the need for collaborative and team-based approaches to youth's learning journey through the encouragement of partnerships among students, parents, peers, and educators within the larger community.

As psychoeducational researchers suggest (Spilt, van Lier, Leflot, Onghena, & Coplin, 2014; Wright & Mahfoud, 2014), future research is necessary to increase teachers' knowledge of digital technology habits. For example, digital instructional tools can be used to support positive teacher–student and peer FtF interactions that involve a combination of CMC and FtF conversation (Turkle, 2015). Such positive interpersonal teacher–child relationships may help to facilitate students' motivation, engagement, and achievement within the classroom (Sabol & Pianta, 2012; Spilt, Koomen, & Harrison, 2015). Researchers could also explore the extent to which teachers' digital media habits affect teacher–student and peer FtF interactions and relationship. More specifically, teachers could be encouraged to implement various management IT strategies such as seating assignments, discipline style, and classroom organization that promote effective CMC within the classroom.

Summary

The approach to adolescence is a challenging time for youth as they struggle to find a balance between autonomy and connectedness. The Internet, CMC, and SNSs provide a novel ever-changing and fluid "seascape" in that it provides fluid and transitory context for learning, experimenting, and reflecting upon new identities, skills, and also for establishing affiliations. Although Internet use and SNSs reflect a significant shift in the ways that adolescents communicate and spend their leisure time, CMC dovetails with, and may facilitate, and perhaps intensify in either beneficial or harmful ways, in terms of cyberbullying (Talwar et al., 2014), the psychosocial tasks of adolescent development. Overall, the recent literature points to several positive influences of SNSs on adolescents' psychosocial development, including enhanced peer relationships, widened opportunities to affiliate, and increased occasions for self-disclosure—all of which can enhance well-being. Importantly, evidence suggests that socially skilled adolescents, in particular, may benefit from SNS use.

In contrast, several potential psychosocial costs of CMC and SNS use have also emerged, including pressure for self-disclosure, potential for exposure to a large amount of negative feedback, increase in depression and internalizing symptoms (Ahn et al., 2015; Kraut et al., 1998), and the possibility of unhealthy social comparisons (Turkle, 2011, 2015). Similar to the advent of television, another powerful technological innovation that transformed society and changed the way that children and adolescents spend time and receive information (Turkle, 2011), the initial wave of research into CMC and SNS habits has focused on the identification of positive and negative, mainly cognitive, impacts. Given the concerns related to dangers inherent in SNS use (Kowalski et al., 2014), the next wave of research has the opportunity to further investigate SNSs' potential to foster adolescents' adaptive psychosocial development (Shapiro & Margolin, 2014).

In summary, how can we build on Grinder and Englund (1966)'s claim, which remains relevant almost 50 years later, that "Major and rapid social and technological changes, as aspects of cultural contact, are disrupting traditional generalizations about socializing experiences, personality traits, and cultural patterns" (p. 459). As I discuss in the remaining chapters, as educators and researchers, we need to continue to investigate these complexities in the hopes that developmental, social cognitive research may provide educational strategies to help youth develop a sense of personal well-being and social and emotional competence within an increasingly complicated and morally ambiguous cultural context.

Overall, this chapter reviewed the theory and research regarding the role of technology in young people's social cognitive development. As you will read in the next chapter, digital technology may continue to serve as an important aid to help young people cope with various social, behavioral, and emotional challenges that they may experience during their school life.

References

Ahn, J. (2014) It's complicated: The social lives of networked teens; The App generation: How today's youth navigate identity, intimacy, and imagination in a digital world, *Journal of Children and Media, 8*, 313–316. doi:10.1080/17482798.2014.923607

Ahn, H., Kwolek, E. & Bowman, N. (2015). Two faces of narcissism on SNS: The distinct effects of vulnerable and grandiose narcissism on SNS privacy control. *Computers in Human Behavior, 45*, 375–381.

Baron, N. (2004). See you online: Gender issues in American college student use of instant messaging. *Journal of Language and Social Psychology, 23*, 397–423.

Baron, N., & Campbell, E. (2012). Talking takes too long: Gender and cultural patterns in mobile telephony. *Language Sciences, 34*, 13–27.

Bauerlein, M. (2009). *The dumbest generation: How the digital age stupefies young Americans and jeopardizes our future.* London, England: Tarcher.

Baumeister, R., Campbell, J., Krueger, J., & Vohs, V. (2003). Does high self-esteem cause better performance, interpersonal success happiness, or health? *Psychological Science in the Public Interest, 4*, 1–44.

Baumeister, R. F., Vohs, K. D., DeWall, C. N., & Zhang, L. (2007). How emotion shapes behavior: Feedback, anticipation, and reflection, rather than direct causation. *Personality and Social Psychology Review, 11*, 167–203. doi:10.1177/1088868307301033

Benotsch, E. G., Snipes, D. J., Martin, A. M., & Bull, S. S. (2012). Sexting, substance use, and sexual risk behavior in young adults. *Journal of Adolescent Health, 52*, 307–313. doi:10.1016/j.jadohealth.2012.06.011

Blakemore, S.-J., & Mills, K. (2014). Is adolescence a sensitive period for sociocultural processing? *Annual Review of Psychology, 65*, 187–207.

Bluth, K., & Banton, P. (2015). The influence of self-compassion on emotional well-being among early and older adolescent males and females. *The Journal of Positive Psychology, 10*, 219–230.

Bosacki, S. (2005). *Culture of classroom silence.* New York, NY: Peter Lang.

Boyd, D. (2014). *It's complicated: The social lives of networked teens.* New Haven, CT: Yale University Press.

Brown, C., Demaray, M., & Secord, S. (2014). Cybervictimization in middle school and social emotional outcomes. *Computers in Human Behavior, 35*, 12–21.

Calvert, C. (2009). Sex, cell phones, privacy, and the first amendment: When children become child pornographers and the Lolita effect undermines the law. *CommLaw Conspectus*, *18*, 1–65.

Campbell, S. W., & Park, Y. J. (2014). Predictors of mobile sexting among teens: Toward a new explanatory framework. *Mobile Media and Communication*, *2*, 20–39. doi:10.1177/2050157913502645

Colley, A., Todd, Z., White, A., & Turner-Moore, T. (2010). Communication using camera phones among young men and women: Who sends what to whom? *Sex Roles*, *63*, 348–360.

Collins, A., & Halverson, R. (2009). *Rethinking education in the age of technology: The digital revolution and schooling in America*. New York, NY: Teachers College Press.

Dake, J. A., Price, J. H., Maziarz, L., & Ward, B. (2012). Prevalence and correlates of sexting behavior in adolescents. *American Journal of Sexuality Education*, *7*, 1–15. doi:10.1080/15546128. 2012.650959

Damon, W. (2008). *The path to purpose: How young people find their calling in life*. New York, NY: Simon & Schuster.

D'Antona, R., Kevorkian, M., & Russom, A. (2010). Sexting, texting, cyberbullying and keeping youth safe online. *Journal of Social Sciences*, *6*, 523–528. doi:10.3844/jssp.2010.523.528

Dittrick, C. J., Beran, T. N., Mishna, F., Hetherington, R., & Shariff, S. (2013). Do children who bully their peers also play violent video games? A Canadian national study. *Journal of School Violence*, *12*, 297–318. doi:10.1080/15388220.2013.803244

Donaldson, S., Dollwet, M., & Rao, M. (2015). Happiness, excellence, and optimal human functioning revisited: Examining the peer-reviewed literature linked to positive psychology. *The Journal of Positive Psychology*, *10*, 185–195.

Dooley, J. J., Pyżalski, J., & Cross, D. (2009). Cyberbullying versus face-to-face bullying. *Zeitschrift Für Psychologie/Journal of Psychology*, *217*(4), 182–188. doi:10.1027/0044-3409.217.4.182

Dresner, E., & Herring, S. C. (2010). Functions of the nonverbal in CMC: Emoticons and illocutionary force. *Communication Theory*, *20*, 249–268.

Fitton, V., Ahmedani, B., Harold, R., & Shifflet, E. (2013). The role of technology on young adolescent development: Implications for theory, research, and practice. *Child and Adolescent Social Work Journal*, *30*, 399–413.

Flett, G., & Hewitt, I. (2014). A proposed framework for preventing perfectionism and promoting resilience and mental health among vulnerable children and adolescents. *Psychology in the Schools*, *51*, 899–912.

Gardner, H., & Davis, K. (2013). *The App generation: How today's youth navigate identity, intimacy, and imagination in a digital world*. New Haven, CT: Yale University Press.

Giedd, J. N., Blumenthal, J., Jeffries, N. O., Castellanos, F. X., Liu, H., Zijdenbos, A., … Rapoport, J. L. (1999). Brain development during childhood and adolescence: A longitudinal MRI study. *Neuroscience*, *2*(10), 861–863.

Gordon-Messer, D., Bauermeister, J. A., Grodzinski, A., & Zimmerman, M. (2012). Sexting among young adults. *Journal of Adolescent Health*, *52*(3), 301–306. doi:10.1016/j.jadohealth.2012.05.013

Greenspan, L., & Deardorff, J. (2014). *The new puberty: How to navigate early development in today's girls*. New York, NY: Rodale.

Grinder, R., & Englund, D. (1966). Adolescents in other cultures. *Review of Educational Research*, *36*, 450–462.

Groopman, J. (2007). *How doctors think*. Boston, MA: Mariner.

Grossman, L. (2003, November, 24). Old school, new tricks, *Time Magazine* (Canadian ed.), pp. 36–40.

Grouzet, F. (2013). Self-regulation and autonomy: The dialectic between organismic and socio-cognitive valuing process. In B. Sokol, M. Grouzet, & U. Muller (Eds.), *Self-regulation and autonomy: Social and developmental dimensions of human conduct* (pp. 47–77). New York, NY: Cambridge University Press.

Hasinoff, A. A. (2013). Sexting as media production: Rethinking social media and sexuality.

New Media and Society, 15, 449–465. doi: 10.1177/1461444812459171

Herring, S. C. (1994). Politeness in computer culture: Why women thank and men flame. In *Cultural performances: Proceedings of the third Berkeley women and language conference* (pp. 278–294). Berkeley, CA: Berkeley Women and Language Group.

Herring, S. C., & Zelenkauskaite, A. (2008). Gendered typography: Abbreviation and insertion in Italian iTV SMS. In J. F. Siegel, T. C. Nagel, A. Laurent-Lapole, & J. Auger (Eds.), *IUWPL7: Gender in language: Classic questions, new contexts* (pp. 73–92). Bloomington, IN: Indiana University Linguistics Club.

Huxley, A. (1932). *Brave new world.* London, England: Vintage.

Hyde, J. (2014). Gender similarities and differences. *Annual Review of Psychology, 65*, 373–398.

Ito, M., Antin, J., Finn, M., Law, A., Manion, A., Mitnick, S., … Horst, H. A. (2009). *Hanging out, messing around, and geeking out: Kids living and learning with new media.* Cambridge, MA: MIT Press.

Jackson, M., & McKibben, B. (2009). *Distracted: The erosion of attention and the coming dark age.* Amherst, NY: Prometheus Books.

Jiang, Y., & de Bruijn, O. (2014). Facebook helps: A case study of cross-cultural social networking and social capital. *Information, Communication & Society, 17*(6), 732–749. doi:10.1080/1369118X.2013.830636

Kaiser Family Foundation (2010). Total media exposure, by age. *Media and Health.* Retrieved from http://facts.kff.org/chart.aspx?ch=1368

Kamins, M. L., & Dweck, C. S. (1999). Person versus process praise and criticism: Implications for contingent self-worth and coping. *Developmental Psychology, 35*, 835–847. doi:10.1037/0012-1649.35.3.835

Kingston, A. (2014, July 24). Get ready for generation Z. *Macclean's: Canada's National Magazine, 127*(28), 42–45.

Kirschner, P. A., and Karpinski, A. C. (2010). Facebook® and academic performance. *Computers in Human Behavior, 26*(6), 1237–1245. doi:10.1016/j.chb.2010.03.024

Kirwan, G., & Power, A. (2013). *Cybercrime: The psychology of online offenders.* Cambridge, England: Cambridge University Press.

Kobayashi, C., Glover, G., & Temple, E. (2007). Cultural and linguistic effects on neural bases of "theory of mind" in American and Japanese children. *Brain Research, 1164*, 95–107.

Kowalski, R., Schroeder, A., Giumetti, G., & Lattanner, M. (2014). Bullying in the digital age: A critical review and meta-analysis of cyberbullying research. *Psychological Bulletin, 140*, 1073–1137.

Kraut, R., Patterson, M., Lundmark, V., Kiesler, S., Mukopahdyay, T., & Scherlis, W. (1998). Internet paradox: A social technology that reduces social involvement and psychological well-being? *American Psychologist, 53*, 1017–1031.

Kruglanski, A. (1989). *Lay epistemics and human knowledge: Cognitive and motivational bases.* New York, NY: Plenum Press.

Langois, M., Blanchet-Cohen, N., & Beer, T. (2012). The art of the nudge: Five practices for developmental evaluators. *Canadian Journal of Program Evaluation, 27*(2), 39–59.

Larson, R. (2011). Positive development in a disorderly world. *Journal of Research in Adolescence, 21*, 317. doi:10.1111/j.1532-7795.2010.00707.x

Lenhart, A. (2009). *Teens and sexting: How and why minor teens are sending sexually suggestive nude or nearly nude images via text messaging.* Retrieved from http://www.pewinternet.org/Reports/2009/Teens-and-Sexting.aspx

Lenhart, A., Ling, R., Campbell, S. W., & Purcell, K. (2010). *Teens and mobile phones. A project of the Pew Research Center and the University of Michigan.* Retrieved from http://www.pewinternet.org/Reports/2010/Teens-and-Mobile-Phones.aspx

Levine, D. (2013). Sexting: A terrifying health risk … or the new normal for young adults? *Journal of Adolescent Health, 52*, 257–258. doi:10.1016/j.jadohealth.2013.01.003

Levitin, D. (2014). *The organized mind: Thinking straight in the age of information overload.* New York, NY: Dutton.

Ling, R. (2005). The socio-linguistics of SMS: An analysis of SMS use by a random sample of Norwegians. In R. Ling & P. Pedersen (Eds.), *Mobile communications: Renegotiation of the social sphere* (pp. 335–349). London, England: Springer.

Ling, R. (2008). *New tech, new ties.* Cambridge, MA: MIT Press.

Ling, R., Baron, N., Lehart, A., & Campbell, S. (2014). " Girls text really weird": Gender, texting, and identity among teens. *Journal of Children and Media, 8*(4), 423–439. doi:10.1080/17482798.2014.931290

Lippman, J., & Campbell, S. (2014). Damned if you do, damned if you don't … if you're a girl: Relational and normative contexts of adolescent sexting in the United States. *Journal of Children and Media, 8*(4), 371–386. doi:10.1080/17482798.2014.923009

Lui, K. F., & Wong, A. C. (2012). Does media multitasking always hurt? A positive correlation between multitasking and multisensory integration. *Psychological Bulletin Review, 19*(4), 647–653.

Marshall, S., Parker, P., Ciarrochi, J., & Heaven, P. (2014). Is self-esteem a cause or consequence of social support: A 4-year longitudinal study. *Child Development, 85,* 1275–1291.

McKenna, K., Green, A., & Gleason, M. (2002). Relationship formation on the Internet: What's the big attraction? *Journal of Social Sciences, 58,* 9–32.

Melville, H. (1967/1851). *Moby-Dick.* New York, NY: Random House.

Mischel, W. (2014). *The marshmallow test: Mastering self-control.* New York, NY: Little, Brown.

Myers, D. (2000). *The American paradox: Spiritual hunger in an age of plenty.* New Haven, CT: Yale University Press.

National Campaign to Prevent Teen and Unplanned Pregnancy. (2008). *Sex and tech: Results from a survey of teens and young adults.* Retrieved from http://www.thenationalcampaign.org/sextech/PDF/SexTech_Summary.pdf

Neff, K. D. (2011). Self-compassion, self-esteem, and well-being. *Social and Personality Psychological Compass, 5,* 1–12. doi:10.1111/j.1751-9004.2010.00330

Noddings, N. (2003). *Happiness and education.* Cambridge, England: Cambridge University Press.

Noone, D., Willis, T., Cox, J., Harkness, F., Ogilvie, J., Forbes, E., … Gregory, A. (2014). Catastrophizing and poor sleep quality in early adolescent females. *Behavioral Science Medicine, 12,* 41–52.

Ohannessian, C. M. (2009). Media use and adolescent psychological adjustment: An examination of gender differences. *Journal of Child and Family Studies, 18*(5), 582–594. doi:10.1007/s 10826-009-9261-2

Olson, K., Key, A., & Eaton, N. (2015). Gender cognition in transgender children. *Psychological Science, 26,* 467–474.

Ophir, E., Nass, N., & Wagner, A. (2009). Cognitive control in media multitaskers. *Proceedings of the National Academy of Sciences U.S.A., 106*(37), 15583–15587. doi:10.1073/pnas.0903620106

Parisi, D. (2013). Schools and the new ecology of the mind. In M. Anderson & S. Della Sala (Eds.), *Neuroscience in education: The good, the bad, and the ugly* (pp. 312–318). Oxford, England: Oxford University Press.

Pew (2009). *Home broadband adoption.* Paper presented at Pew Internet & American Life Project. Washington, DC. Retrieved from http://pewinternet.org/Reports/2009/10-Home-Broadband-Adoption-2009.aspx

Pomerantz, E., Ng, F., Cheung, C., & Qu, Y. (2014). Raising happy children who succeed in school: Lessons from China and United States. *Child Development Perspectives, 8,* 71–76.

Postman, N. (1999). *Building a bridge to the 18th century.* New York, NY: Vintage Books.

Ream, G., & Savin-Williams, R. (2003). Religious development in adolescence. In

G. Adams & M. Berzonsky (Eds.), *Blackwell handbook of adolescence* (pp. 51–59). Malden, MA: Blackwell.

Redzic, N., Taylor, V., Chang, M., Trockel, M., Shorter, A., & Taylor, C. (2014). An Internet-based positive psychology program: Strategies to improve effectiveness and engagement. *Journal of Positive Psychology, 9,* 494–501.

Ribeiro, S., & Stickgold, R. (2014). Sleep and school education. *Trends in Neuroscience and Education, 3,* 18–23.

Rose, R. (2014). Self-guided multimedia stress management and resilience training. *Journal of Positive Psychology, 9,* 489–493.

Ruedy, N., Moore, C., Gino, F., & Schweitzer, M. (2013). Cheater's high? The unexpected affective benefits of unethical behavior. *Journal of Personality and Social Psychology, 105*(4), 531–548. doi:10.1037/a0034231

Sabol, T. J., & Pianta, R. C. (2012). Recent trends in research on teacher–child relationships. *Attachment & Human Development, 14,* 213–231. doi:10.1080/14616734.2012.672262

Saghai, Y. (2013). Salvaging the concept of nudge. *Journal of Medical Ethics, 39,* 487–493. doi:10.1136/medethics-2012-100727

Salmivalli, C., Sainio, M., & Hodges, E. V. E. (2013). Electronic victimization: Correlates, antecedents, and consequences among elementary and middle school students. *Journal of Clinical Child and Adolescent Psychology, 42,* 442–453.

Schneider, B., & Amichai-Hamburger, Y. (2010). Electronic communication: Escape mechanism or relationship-building tool for shy, whithdrawn children and adolescents? In K. Rubin & R. Coplan (Eds.), *The development of shyness and social withdrawal* (pp. 236–261). New York, NY: Guilford.

Seligman, M. (2011). *Flourish.* London, England: Nicholas Brealey.

Shapiro, L., & Margolin, M. (2014). Growing up wired: Social networking sites and adolescent psychosocial development, *Clinical Child Family Psychology Review, 17,* 1–18.

Siegel, D. (2013). *Brainstorm: The power and purpose of the teenage brain.* New York, NY: Jeremy Tarcher/Penguin.

Smith, P. K., Mahdavi, J., Carvalho, M., Fisher, S., Russell, S., & Tippett, N. (2008). Cyber-bullying: Its nature and impact in secondary school pupils. *Journal of Child Psychology and Psychiatry, and Allied Disciplines, 49*(4), 376–385. doi:10.1111/j.1469-7610.2007.01846.x

Spilt, J., Koomen, M., & Harrison, L. (2015). Language development in the early school years: The importance of close relationships with teachers. *Developmental Psychology, 51,* 185–196.

Spilt, J., van Lier, P., Leflot, G., Onghena, P., & Coplin, H. (2014). Children's social self-concept and internalizing problems: The influence of teachers and peers. *Child Development, 85,* 1248–1256.

Spitzer, M. (2014). Information in technology: Risks and side effects. *Trends in Neuroscience and Education, 3,* 81–85.

Statistics Canada (2013, October 28). Individual internet use and e-commerce, 2012. *The Daily,* Ottawa, ON, Canada.

Sternberg, R. (2014). The development of adaptive competence: Why cultural psychology is necessary and not just nice. *Developmental Review, 34,* 208–224.

Straker, L., Pollock, C., & Maslen, B. (2009). Principles for the wise use of computers by children. *Ergonomics, 52*(11), 1386–1401.

Strasburger, V., & Wilson, B. (2002). *Children, adolescents, and the media.* Thousand Oaks, CA: Sage.

Strassberg, D. S., McKinnon, R. K., Sustaíta, M. A., & Rullo, J. (2013). Sexting by high school students: An exploratory and descriptive study. *Archives of Sexual Behavior, 42,* 15–21. doi: 10.1007/s10508-012-9969-8

Sutton, M. J., Brown, J. D., Wilson, K. M., & Klein, J. D. (2002). Shaking the tree of knowledge for forbidden fruit: Where adolescents learn about sexuality and contraception. In J. D. Brown, J. R. Steele, & K. Walsh-Childers (Eds.), *Sexual teens, sexual media: Investigating media's influence on adolescent sexuality* (pp. 25–55). Mahwah, NJ: Erlbaum.

Talwar, V., Gomez-Garibello, C., & Shariff, S. (2014). Adolescents' moral evaluations and ratings of cyberbullying: The veracity and intentionality behind the event. *Computers in Human Behavior, 36,* 122–128.

Tannen, D. (1994). *Gender and discourse.* New York, NY: Oxford University Press.

Tiger, L., & McGuire, M. (2010). *God's brain.* New York, NY: Prometheus Books.

Tomasello, M. (2014). *A natural history of human thinking.* Cambridge, MA: Harvard University Press.

Turkle, S. (2011). *Alone together: Why we expect more from technology and less from each other.* New York, NY: Basic Books.

Turkle, S. (2015). *Reclaiming conversation: The power of talk in a digital age.* New York, NY: Penguin.

Twenge, J. (2006). *Generation Me: Why today's young Americans are more confident, assertive, entitled—and more miserable than ever before.* New York, NY: Free Press.

Ward, L. M. (2003). Understanding the role of entertainment media in the sexual socialization of American youth: A review of empirical research. *Developmental Review, 23,* 347–388. doi:10.1016/s0273-2297(03)00013-3

Williams, K. (2001). *Ostracism: The power of silence.* New York, NY: Guilford.

Wright, B., & Mahfoud, J. (2014). Teacher-centered exploration of the relevance of social factors to theory of mind development. *Scandinavian Journal of Psychology, 55,* 17–25.

10

Social Cognition and Behavioral and Emotional Challenges

"Oh yes; I am anxious," returned the Scarecrow, "It is such an uncomfortable feeling to know one is a fool." (Baum, 1984/1900, p. 36)

Introduction

This chapter explores the various challenges some young people face in terms of social cognitive development and related behaviors. Overall, few young people have insight or awareness of their mental or emotional health challenges (Siegel, 2013). Insight is a multidimensional concept as it contains the awareness or recognition that one has a mental world including mental health exceptionalities with skills and challenges. Insight also includes the ability to attribute, or understand, the extent to which particular factors may influence one's mental health (Amador et al., 1993). This chapter outlines research that explores various psychological and environmental factors that may influence adolescents' mental health and behavioral challenges such as internalizing and externalizing challenges.

Given that past studies have shown that prolonged and untreated mental health challenges over time may negatively impact patients' neurocognitive functioning (Norman & Malla, 2001; Schneider, 2014; Shatkin, 2015; Wang, Berglund, Olfson, & Kessler, 2004), this chapter discusses the educational implications of past research on young people's social cognitive and behavioral challenges, and ends with ideas for future research. For example, the chapter outlines ideas for additional longitudinal studies that are required to further understand the nature of the role of insight in adolescents' experience of mental health challenges. Future research studies could also explore the association between insight and additional social cognitive variables such as coping and Theory of Mind (ToM), as well as the duration of untreated mental health challenges.

Social Cognition in Middle Childhood and Adolescence: Integrating the Personal, Social, and Educational Lives of Young People, First Edition. S. L. Bosacki.

Research

Social cognition and psychopathology

Mental health challenges often have an onset in later childhood and emerging adolescence with anxiety and impulse challenges emerging as early as ages 5 to 7, whereas mood and substance abuse emerge during early adolescence, followed by schizophrenia and other mental challenges in later adolescence (Kessler et al., 2005; Schneider, 2014; Shatkin, 2015). The heightened vulnerability to psychiatric conditions during adolescence has been suggested to relate to genetically preprogrammed neural development at the same time as new stresses and challenges emerge in the young person's environment (Kozina, 2014). During adolescence, stress exposure, including social stress, may be longer lasting and qualitatively different from stress exposure at other periods of life. This could be due to possible interactions between the developing hypothalamic-pituitary-adrenal (HPA) axis, which is a major part of the neuroendocrine system that helps to control our reactions to stress and regulates many body processes, and glucocorticoids, which are steroid hormones that are produced by the adrenal cortex (McCormick, Mathews, Thomas, & Waters, 2010).

One possible reason why adolescents show increased sensitivity to stress-induced levels of glucocorticoids is the increase in glucocorticoid regulation in the human prefrontal cortex (Perlman, Webster, Herman, Kleinman, & Weickert, 2007; Siegel, 2013). This neural change, which increases from infancy through childhood and adolescence, may increase adolescents' vulnerability to psychosocial challenges (Perlman et al., 2007). Comparative rodent studies indicate that social stress induced by isolation has the potential to have long-lasting impacts (McCormick et al., 2013).

Exposure to social isolation during later childhood and adolescence may thus increase the likelihood of depressive-like behaviors as well as alterations in the structure of the prefrontal cortex (Leussis & Andersen, 2008). The long-lasting effects of stress in adolescence include disrupted social and reproductive behavior. For example, male rats exposed to chronic social instability stress during adolescence were, in adulthood, more anxious and less socially interactive (Green, Barnes, & McCormick, 2012), showed deficits across many sexual behaviors (McCormick et al., 2013), and had lower plasma testosterone concentrations than rats not exposed to social stressors during adolescence (McCormick et al., 2013).

A recent study found that, compared to rats who were not isolated, rats socially isolated during early adolescence remembered drug-associated contextual stimuli at a faster rate (Whitaker, Degoulet, & Morikawa, 2013). The socially isolated rats showed enhanced synaptic plasticity in an area of the brain involved in reward-based learning and addictive behaviors, and their drug-associated memories took longer to extinguish (Whitaker et al., 2013). Moreover, later resocialization of the rats isolated during early adolescence did not reverse the neural changes.

Whitaker et al.'s (2013) study, as well as others on the activation of the dorsolateral prefrontal cortex (Lewis, 2015), may provide evidence for the suggestion that early adolescence may be a sensitive period for social signals (Siegel, 2013), and that social isolation during this time has the potential to change neural mechanisms involved in the acquisition and maintenance of drug-associated cues, possibly increasing vulnerability to addictive behaviors (Whitaker et al., 2013). Although this particular study involved rodents, the impact of social isolation on adolescent health and life trajectories may likely apply to humans. If so, the consequences of social exclusion can be so great that prosocial mechanisms and behaviors that promote peer acceptance may be considered adaptive.

Although, as Blakemore and Mills (2014) claim, much evidence for adolescence as a sensitive period for social processing may be gleaned from rodent studies, there is also evidence to suggest that ecological or environmental conditions experienced during human adolescence may have an influence on young people's attitudes toward health and reproduction. For example, Brumbach, Figueredo, and Ellis (2009) found that, in the short term, emerging adolescents within socially unpredictable and inconsistent environments experienced decreased physical and mental health. In addition, the results also showed that the participants adopted more impulsive, or less mindful, life history strategies in young adulthood, such as decreased health, less sexual restrictedness, and less resource-accruing potential. Further human research is needed to investigate whether the emerging adolescent brain is particularly sensitive to social environmental cues.

Developmental and learning challenges

In addition to the neurophysiological and environmental challenges during emerging adolescence, differences in learning abilities may also create challenges for the emerging adolescent. Interestingly, although the World Health Organization estimates that 10% of the world's population has some type of disability that interferes with social functioning and full community participation (World Health Organization, 1999), definitions of "disability" are constantly changing across communities and cultures (Diamond, 2002; Roe & Kravetz, 2003; Schneider, 2014). More specifically, given the prevalence of adolescents with exceptionalities within the current school system, surprisingly little research exists on the social cognitive abilities of emerging adolescents within the classroom setting (Wolfendale, 2000). One possible explanation for this lack of research is the definitional problem of inconsistency, and a lack of consensus surrounding terms such as "special needs" and "learning disabilities." For example, the term "intellectual disability" is the new term used in DSM-V (Diagnostic Statistics Manual) to replace "mental retardation" in DSM-IV (Schneider, 2014).

Such definitional issues are important for theoretical as well practical reasons, particularly for diagnosis issues. For instance, according to Swanson (2000), the number of students classified with learning disabilities has increased over the past 20 years. Research on the social experiences of exceptional adolescents also includes students whose neurodevelopmental exceptionalities include a range of challenges such as social behavioral disorders, attention deficit disorder, visual or hearing impairments, learning disabilities, autism, and neurodevelopmental delay (London, 2014; Schneider, 2014; Sternberg, Jarvin, & Grigorenko, 2011).

Normalized school experiences for adolescents with exceptionalities are contingent upon the cultural context, which includes cultural expectations of success and competence. For example, notions of equity in opportunity and treatment may reflect to some extent distinctly Western cultural values (Killinger, 2008; Kollerova, Janosova, & Rican, 2015). Also, because of the value Western industrialized societies place on independent living, much of the research on the social and self-competence of exceptional students has occurred within the context of Western Europe and North America. Thus, from a psychocultural perspective, as researchers and educators, we need to explore how adolescents with exceptionalities make sense of silence, and how their feelings of being silenced may differ according to their family's cultural background (Bosacki, 2005; Coplan, 2014).

In particular, special communicative needs may play a crucial role in how an adolescent communicates with teachers and peers. As I have mentioned throughout this book, emerging adolescence is an important time in self-development, and adolescents often experience an increase in self-consciousness (Harter, 1999; Rochat, 2009). Thus, any defining characteristic that the adolescent may have (e.g., hearing aid, glasses, teeth or body braces) that brings attention to any physical or cognitive special need may lead to either strategic (imposed by others), or structural (self-imposed) silence. Regarding strategic silence as a self-protection mechanism, adolescents with exceptional learning needs may silence themselves to avoid ridicule or ostracization from the social group.

Regarding structural silence, the classroom may be physically organized to silence the student (e.g., placing the desk in the back by a computer), or the student may be withdrawn from the regular class for a period of time to work with a specialist (e.g., speech pathologist). Similarly, the various challenges young people with exceptionalities experience in classroom and small-group interactions may extend to less-structured contexts. For example, students with learning exceptionalities are sometimes isolated at recess, or remain transitory as they move from playgroup to playgroup, or spend time alone.

For young people with exceptional learning needs, the ability to develop age-appropriate social behaviors to achieve successful participation with peers within the school and community context is an ongoing challenge (Sternberg et al., 2011). For example, research on peer relationships among adolescents with mild learning challenges shows that such youth experience social communication and sensory challenges (Erwin, 1995). Social competence challenges have also been found for adolescents with significant mental, physical, and behavioral exceptionalities (Sternberg et al., 2011), and chronic health problems (Laugeson, Ellingsen, Sanderson, Tucci, & Bates, 2014). Furthermore, youth with exceptional needs have been found to elicit a number of behavior patterns that make them vulnerable to poor social relationships including friendships (Coplan, 2014; Schneider, 2016). Compared to their typically developing peers, adolescents with exceptionalities reported forming significantly fewer friendships with school peers, within and outside of the school context.

Social-emotional development of youth with exceptional needs: Empirical evidence

Internalizing challenges   Given the developmental challenges all youth experience during later childhood and early adolescence (Blakemore & Mills, 2014), youth who experience extreme sensitivity to social situations may also experience what is referred to as internalizing or emotional challenges. Research on the links between social understanding and internalizing problems has shown that adolescents have an increased susceptibility to internalizing problems (Coplan, 2014; Coplan & Rudasill, 2016), and previous research has linked depression to enhanced social understanding (Harkness, Sabbagh, Jacobson, Chowdrey, & Chen, 2005). Some researchers suggest that this link between depression and enhanced social understanding skills may be in part due to the finding that depressed and socially withdrawn individuals may be more sensitive to social cues than nondepressed individuals (Harkness et al., 2005).

Given the high variability of young people's developmental emotional experiences (Blakemore & Mills, 2014; Hollenstein & Lougheed, 2013), researchers need to disentangle general developmental trajectories from trajectories of individual differences. For example, while there may be, on average, a temporary decline in adolescent social understanding, those who experience symptoms of depression may mature more quickly in social understanding. Such a link between depression and social understanding in adolescence would thus help to demonstrate the interconnectedness of emotion and cognitive processes.

Youth who are sensitive to social events are often known to exhibit shy behaviors such as inhibited behavior, social wariness, introversion, and social reticence (Coplan & Rubin, 2010). The construct of shyness is most often defined as wariness during novel social events, and/or the display of self-conscious behavior in situations where there is a perception of being socially judged (Coplan & Rubin, 2010). As discussed earlier, over the past 25 years, research has shown that there are different types of social withdrawal, characterized by different motivational and emotional underpinnings (Coplan & Rubin, 2010; Özdemir, Cheah, & Coplan, 2015).

For example, shy children are often reported as acting warily and reticent in social contexts. In addition, although they may be interested in social interactions (i.e., high social approach motivation), they may often refrain from peer interaction because of social fear and anxiety (i.e., high social avoidance motivation) (Coplan, 2014; Ding et al., 2015). Accordingly, although shy children may engage in solitary activities, they may not necessarily "prefer" to do so. Throughout childhood and early adolescence, shyness is often associated with socioemotional maladjustment, including internalizing problems (e.g., anxiety and loneliness), and peer relationship difficulties (exclusion and victimization) (Ding et al., 2015; Gazelle, 2008).

In contrast, some socially withdrawn youth may prefer to play alone. For example, unsociable children evidence a preference for solitude, but neither fear nor avoid peer interaction (i.e., low approach and low avoidance motivations) (Coplan, 2014). Compared to shyness, past research defines unsociability as a relatively "benign" form of social withdrawal or nonfearful preference for solitude, particularly in early childhood, where it has been largely unassociated with indices of socioemotional functioning (Coplan, 2014). However, a third group of withdrawn children, referred to as socially avoidant, has been found to show a high in preference for solitude and also actively avoid peer interaction (i.e., low approach and high avoidance motivations) (Ding et al., 2015). Little is known to date about this subtype of social withdrawal, although recent research suggests that socially avoidant youth may perhaps be at risk for chronic emotional and social adjustment challenges (Bowker & Raja, 2011; Ding et al., 2015).

In addition to social avoidance, recent research with young Turkish adolescents has revealed a newly discovered fourth type of social withdrawal referred to as "regulated withdrawal" (Özdemir et al., 2015). Although the authors did not investigate social avoidance, compared to shyness and unsociability, Özdemir et al. (2015) found a third subgroup of socially withdrawn children who behaved in controlled and over-regulated ways within social situations. Given that the findings are just emerging on different types of social withdrawal, further research is needed to untangle the relations among regulated control and the already existing subtypes of social withdrawal, particularly shyness and social avoidance. Moreover, as research suggests an increase in the focus on peer relations during emerging adolescence, further studies that explore social withdrawal and social cognitive development may hold significance for educational settings during the transition from later childhood to early adolescence.

Overall, there is widespread recognition of the psychological benefits of social interaction and prosocial behaviors (Coplan & Rudasill, 2016; Seligman, 2011). People are considered to be mainly social beings, whose fundamental need is to belong and to interact with others (Rochat, 2009). Based on this knowledge, research on solitude has mainly focused on its negative emotional consequences, such as loneliness and depression (see Rubin, Coplan, & Bowker, 2009 for a review). However, solitude can be a valued and intentionally aspired state that may serve different adaptive psychological functions. For instance, young people may seek solitude to engage in agentic and private activities such as self-reflection and contemplation, creative and artistic work, and seeking spiritual experiences or emotional renewal (Bosacki, 2005).

Upon the transition to adolescence, solitude often becomes more salient and may begin to have more conscious and deliberate functions (Larson, 2011), such as fostering identity formation (Goossens & Marcoen, 1999). However, some adolescents may differ in their attitudes toward solitude, and these attitudes are relatively stable individual characteristics (Goossens & Beyers, 2002). Numerous constructs have been used to describe the positive and negative significance individuals attribute to solitude (Goossens, 2014). Past research has distinguished between aversion to aloneness, or the experience of solitude as a time of boredom, unhappiness, and unease, and the affinity for aloneness. In contrast, the use of solitude could also be viewed as having a constructive and active purpose to gain emotional renewal, self-knowledge, or reflection (Ding et al., 2015). Both attitudes can be viewed as distinct constructs, instead of opposite poles on a single continuum (Kashdan, Weeks, & Savostyanova, 2011), and are predicted in part by different personality traits (Teppers et al., 2013).

Given that extended periods of solitude are viewed as mainly normative in adolescence (Larson, 2011), attitude toward aloneness might influence psychosocial adjustment and well-being (Goossens & Beyers, 2002). Previous studies adopted a variable-centered approach by focusing on separate aloneness attitudes and how they relate to adjustment. Mixed findings show that the affinity for aloneness is typically associated with better adjustment in late rather than in mid-adolescence. More specifically, affinity for aloneness was related to unsatisfactory interpersonal relations in early adolescence, but not in late adolescence.

Similarly, preference for solitude has been found to be associated more strongly with emotional adjustment challenges (e.g., greater depression and less social competence) in early adolescence rather than in late adolescence (Wang et al., 2013). Stronger aversion to aloneness has been associated with more satisfactory peer relations in early and late adolescence, but with greater loneliness in mid-adolescence (Teppers et al., 2013). These mixed findings suggest the need for a more detailed, longitudinal investigation of associations between preferences for aloneness and psychosocial functioning across the transition from childhood to adolescence.

Most recently, Teppers et al. (2013) found that three attitudes (affinity, aversion, and indifference) toward aloneness were related to various psychosocial outcomes in a group of adolescents and emerging adults. More specifically, Teppers et al. found that the indifferent group showed the most optimal profile of psychological adjustment. They used the least passive coping strategies, such as avoidance and depressive reaction patterns. Furthermore, the indifferent group experienced greater self-esteem, less depressive symptoms, and lower loneliness as compared to the other two groups. Future research needs to explore the characteristics, relationships, and lifestyle behaviors of those youth who report feeling "indifferent" to being alone. Such findings would provide some clues as to how youth can learn how to cope and self-comfort when they feel challenged by spending time alone.

Despite the lack of clear research findings, recent studies on solitude in adolescence demonstrated that three specific constellations of attitudes toward aloneness were uniquely associated with perceptions of loneliness, coping, and adjustment. Overall, such findings on the internalizing or emotional challenges of youth with learning exceptionalities could allow researchers to develop intervention efforts tailored to the needs of these vulnerable youth. As I will discuss later within this chapter, to promote effective coping skills and emotional well-being and resilience in youth, educators of young people should aim to encourage youth of all learning abilities to strive for a balance between time alone and time spent with others.

Depression among youth   Regarding emotional experiences and mental health across the lifespan, compared to research with adults that show twice as many women as men are depressed (Kessler, McGonagle, Swartz, Blazer, & Nelson, 1993), few gender differences have been found in childhood depression (Hyde, 2014). Of the few studies that exist, more girls have been found to be depressed than boys by the ages 13 to 15 (Kessler et al. 1993), Given the contradictory evidence regarding gender differences in depression and negative emotional experiences, two specific meta-analyses have been conducted.

The first was conducted by Twenge and Nolen-Hoeksema (2002) of studies that had used the Children's Depression Inventory (CDI) and found that, between the ages of 8 and 12, the gender-related difference was a relatively minimal at $d = 0.04$, whereas between ages 13 and 16, the gender difference was somewhat larger ($d = -0.16$). However, as this gender difference in adolescence was not considered to be large, it contradicted past findings that suggest a 2:1 ratio of depressed females to depressed males.

The authors claimed that the discrepancy in effect sizes between adolescents and adults may have been caused by mean differences in community samples, whereas the statistics on depression examined scores at the extreme end of the distribution. Moreover, the CDI is a self-report survey that measures perceived symptoms of depression, whereas most studies that found the 2:1 female to male ratio assessed psychological diagnoses of depression by a mental healthcare specialist. Regarding developmental trends, Twenge and Nolen-Hoeksema's (2002) research also showed boys' CDI scores remained relatively constant from younger to older ages, whereas girls' scores increased, so that $d = -0.22$ by age 14.

A more recent meta-analysis explored gender differences in depression at the other end of the lifespan, among those 75 and older (Luppa et al., 2012). Gender ratios for prevalence rates ranged between $d = 1.4$ and 2.2, and suggested that the preponderance of women with depression continues throughout the lifespan. Given the multidimensional complexity of depression, a comprehensive theoretical model to help explain gender difference in depression and why it emerges in adolescence remains to be developed. To attempt to synthesize past studies and theoretical models, Hyde, Mezulis, and Abramson (2008) proposed the ABC model of gender differences in depression. According to their model, affective, biological, and cognitive factors converge to create an overall vulnerability to depression.

Drawing on a vulnerability-stress approach, Hyde et al.'s (2008) model states that negative life events interact with depressogenic vulnerability, and produce increased levels of depression in some adolescents, particularly females. Biological factors include genetic factors such as 5-HTTLPR polymorphism, as well as pubertal hormones and pubertal timing (early, on time, or late). The affective factors include numerous dimensions of temperament including, especially, negative affectivity. Finally, the model includes three types of cognitive vulnerability: hopelessness theory of depression (Abramson, Metalsky, & Alloy, 1989); objectified body consciousness, that is, a cognitive process in which individuals become observers and critics of their bodies and appearance (Fredrickson & Roberts, 1997; McKinley & Hyde, 1996); and rumination, or the tendency to perseverate or think repetitively and passively about the negative emotions elicited by negative events (Brose, Schmiedek, Koval, & Kuppens, 2015; Nolen-Hoeksema, 2001, 2004).

Rumination and emotional inertia in adolescence increases in importance because, as mentioned in previous chapters, during this stage of life adolescent egocentrism emerges (Brose et al., 2015), which, according to Elkind (1967), enables adolescents' increased ability for metacognition, including self-reflection and self-consciousness. Additionally, adolescents experience social, academic, and biological changes that may provide opportunities for rumination (Blakemore & Mills, 2014). Finally, rumination may be a risk factor for depression, rates of which increase dramatically around mid-adolescence, approximately ages 14–15, and gender differences in depression often emerge at this time, in addition to self-compassion (Hyde, 2014; Kuppens et al., 2012).

Recent research suggests there are two subtypes of rumination—brooding and reflection—as both have been empirically established in adolescent and adult samples (Burwell & Shirk, 2007; Treynor, Gonzalez, & Nolen-Hoeksema, 2003). Studies have shown brooding rumination (i.e., passively dwelling on one's experiences) confers risk for negative outcomes such as depression, maladaptive disengagement coping, and negative affectivity (López, Driscoll, & Kistner, 2009; Mezulis, Simonson, McCauley, & Vander Stoep, 2011; Treynor et al., 2003). Whereas reflective rumination (i.e., attempting to understand one's experiences) is linked with more active and adaptive coping (Burwell & Shirk, 2007).

According to the ABC model, multiple factors may contribute to the gender difference in depression. That is, given the tumultuous time during emerging adolescence, females and males may differ in how they cope with intrapersonal stress such as physiological and hormonal pubertal changes and body image, including objectified body consciousness. Moreover, gender differences have also been found in children and adolescents regarding their preferences for social withdrawal and experiences of interpersonal stress such as contentious peer relations, including bullying and teasing, academic experiences, and family relationships (Doey, Coplan, & Kingsbury, 2014).

Regarding coping mechanisms of social stress, some researchers may claim that young people's tendency to ruminate or think to excess or obsess about a particular issue such as one's body image, or how others perceive one's behavior, plays a prominent role in mental health. For example, Rood, Roelofs, Bogels, Nolen-Hoeksema, and Schouten's (2009) meta-analysis showed that emerging gender differences in in rumination widened from childhood ($d = -0.14$) to adolescence ($d = -0.36$), and thus paralleled the gender differences in depression. Thus, future research needs to continue to explore the developmental process of rumination, and how this cognitive ability relates to emotional health and possibly affects one's sense of self and personal relationships within adolescence.

Perception and externalizing challenges   In addition to problems with mentalizing and emotional challenges, youth with learning exceptionalities may experience greater social relational challenges such as interpersonal interactions. Within the peer realm, as mentioned briefly in Chapter 6, there is evidence to suggest that adolescents with mild cognitive deficits may sometimes be perceived by others as less popular and more likely to be rejected and neglected than their typically developing peers (Ochoa & Palmer, 1995). Furthermore, research on inclusive playgroups has consistently demonstrated that children with exceptionalities are included in social interactions with their peers much less than neurotypical youth.

 Some youth with various learning exceptionalities may also experience disruptive behavior challenges such as oppositional defiant disorder (ODD) or conduct disorder (CD). Although such behavioral difficulties have been found to be related (Schneider, 2014), many researchers suggest that these are two separate disruptive behavior challenges as children are often diagnosed with CD before the age of 10, and it tends to dissipate by adulthood. In contrast, behaviors related to ODD usually do not present themselves until later in adolescence, but before 18 years, and may be related to adult delinquency and antisocial personality challenges (Moffitt, 2006). Given that both CD and ODD focus on disruptive behavior, younger youth who experience difficulty with rules at school and/or home are often diagnosed with conduct difficulties and impulse control challenges by their teacher and/or parent.

In relation to educational implications, research suggests that disruptive behavior disorders are one of the most frequent reason for referrals of children and adolescents to mental health professionals in North America and Western Europe (Schneider, 2014), with a higher prevalence among males for CD and ODD (Moffitt, 2006). Young people's disruptive behaviors may also be connected to social cognitive challenges such as impulse control and attention deficit challenges. Consequently, such behavioral challenges may lead to learning and social relational difficulties within the classroom. Given the complexity and increasing prevalence of disruptive behavioral challenges among youth, future research needs to continue to explore the role gender and culture play in the development of such challenges.

In the next chapter, I will discuss various youth learning programs that aim to address practical implications that focus on the development of prevention and intervention models regarding disruptive behavior within school and at home.

Language proficiency and peer interaction   In addition to behavioral challenges, some youth may experience various perceptual difficulties such as impairment of hearing and language. Besides severe hearing impairments, adolescents may also suffer from specific language impairment (SLI). Unlike adolescents with profound hearing loss, youth with SLI are impaired in language ability, yet they hear normally, score at age-appropriate levels on tests of nonverbal intelligence, and usually show no neurological disease or damage (Leonard, 2014). Also, in contrast to youth with profound hearing loss, adolescents with SLI often find it difficult to find a viable alternative to spoken language, and membership in a cultural community that is compassionate and supportive toward youth with language impairment. For example, an adolescent who has profound hearing loss may be fluent in American Sign Language (ASL) and may find connection and engage in social interactions with other members of the hard of hearing culture. In contrast, for a young person with SLI, growing up in a society that values verbal fluency, there is no equivalent community to that of ASL.

The isolation that adolescents with SLI may feel at school and the difficulty they may experience with classroom social tasks could be expected to affect the way they are viewed by their peers. Although studies on the personal and social experiences of ASL children are rare, extant literature suggests that, compared to typically developing adolescents, SLI adolescents experience greater loneliness, and as early as preschool are perceived by their peers as lacking in desirability as playmates (Leonard, 2014).

Overall, research on the social and emotional lives of young people with profound and specific hearing loss has been complicated by a myriad of factors that influence social cognitive development. For example, adolescents with profound hearing loss demonstrate varying levels of language development, a wide range of communicative opportunities within the home, and different opportunities to interact with peers who share the same language system (Brinton & Fujiki, 2002). In general, future studies need to systematically control for the possible confounding factors such as working and short-term memory, executive function, and other social and cognitive abilities (Wellman, 2014). Young people's social and emotional experiences within diverse learning contexts also require further study and suggest that need for more multimethod, cross-linguistic, and longitudinal studies (Leonard, 2014).

Given the complex social and emotional lives of young people, in addition to language ability, a variety of other factors also play a crucial role in social and emotional functioning. For example, visual or physical impairments may also influence adolescents' social interactions and self-perceptions. Compared to other research on adolescents with exceptionalities, little research exists on the social and personal experiences of adolescents who are visually impaired (VI) (Sacks, 2012). Loeb and Sarigiani (1986) studied children and adolescents with hearing loss and compared them to hearing peers as well as to peers with visual impairments. Teachers perceived the students with hearing loss as being shyer and having lower self-esteem than other groups. Furthermore, compared to students with visual impairments, students with hearing losses perceived themselves as less popular and shyer.

Results also suggest that adolescents with visual impairments may find themselves to be more isolated from peer interaction, have more frequent contacts with adults, and participate in more solitary activity than do their sighted peers (Warren, 1994). Given that visually impaired youth may be less active and engage in fewer physical activities with their peers, a recent study with Brazilian and Italian VI youth (Greguol, Gobbi, & Carraro, 2014) found that most of the VI youth experienced more negative perceptions of body image. Greguol et al. (2014) suggested that youth with VI should be encouraged to increase physical activity, which in turn may lower Body Mass Index (BMI) and increase positive body image.

In addition to visual impairments, research involving adolescents with chronic illnesses and physical challenges have also shown that adolescents who experience these syndromes may appear vulnerable to peer relationship problems (Laugeson et al., 2014). This, in part, may be caused by the limited opportunities for social interactions due to absenteeism from school, physical limitations, and parents' concerns. Research that examines specific cognitive processes and social development such as ToM skills in adolescents with autistic spectrum disorders have found that these adolescents may experience challenges in interpersonal perception and empathy and social communication (Mathersul, McDonald, & Rushby, 2013). In turn, this challenge may interfere with the adolescent's ability to understand that their peers may play important roles in the social learning community of the classroom.

Consistent with Guralnick's (1999) model, adolescents with autistic spectrum disorders show deficits in cognitive foundation processes (including emotion regulation and psychological understanding) which are critical for socially competent behavior (Mathersul et al., 2013). For example, Lord and Magill-Evans (1995) found that autistic adolescents produced significantly fewer initiations with peers than did children with language impairments or typically developing children. Similar to past learning exceptionality research, researchers are just beginning to examine the personal and social experiences of young people who experience physical and chronic learning exceptionalities. More recently, research with young people diagnosed with autism and similar developmental social cognitive challenges have begun to focus on the connections between affective and cognitive processes (Ibanez et al., 2013; Rueda, Fernandez-Berrocal, & Baron-Cohen, 2015). Such studies may be particularly helpful to those interested in exploring the complex inner worlds and silences experienced by exceptional learners.

In sum, emerging adolescents with exceptionalities may experience particular classroom social cognitive experiences that are different from their typically developing peers. The results of recent studies suggest that characteristics of the social setting, including the availability of typically developing peers, and supportive adults, are important in the development of young people's social skills (Hughes, 2011). Guralnick's (1999) general model of social competence suggests that abnormalities in social cognitive skills may also be associated with deficits in other areas of social development. More frequent interactions and higher levels of social competence have been reported for adolescents when they participate in activities with typically developing peers. Researchers have recently started to examine the role of adults, peers, and companion animals, as well as child and setting characteristics in the social cognitive and emotional development of adolescents with learning exceptionalities (Hurley, 2014; Melson, 2013; Mueller, 2014).

Recent research that examines social cognitive processes such as ToM in adolescents with autism is working to understand the ways in which adolescents with specific social and emotional competencies interact within social relationships (Ibanez et al., 2013; Rueda et al., 2015). In addition to discrete dimensions of behaviors or neurocircuity (London, 2014), researchers also need to understand which characteristics of the social context play a supportive role in the social interactions of adolescents with learning exceptionalities. Finally, evidence suggests that typically developing adolescents may benefit from interactions with peers with exceptionalities (Seligman, 2011). Research that examines the ways in which these interactions foster the development of socially desirable characteristics such as altruism, gratitude, and compassion in both neurotypical and clinical samples provides an important focus for future research.

For example, for youth with language loss, SLI educational programs have wisely targeted language development as a major objective. However, a stronger educational emphasis on social and emotional functioning is warranted. Educators need to look for more effective, efficient ways to facilitate multiple language and social skills simultaneously. Many researchers agree that we need to help adolescents bridge the gap between exceptional and typically developing young people. That is, researchers and practitioners need to work together to help those learners with exceptional needs emerge successfully into the adolescent social world.

Given that the incidence of abuse and peer harassment with youth with learning exceptionalities exceeds the incidence of victimization within the general population (Cappadocia, Weiss, & Peplar, 2012), researchers and educators need to explore the social and personal experiences of these youth and their experiences of feeling marginalized. Sobsey and Mansell (1997) claim that for meaningful change to take place, educators and researchers must find ways of empowering young people with exceptionalities so that they can develop a sense of agency and engagement within learning experiences. For example, as part of an empowerment strategy, as mentioned in Chapter 6, researchers need to explore how young people play a role in the victimization process (bully, victim, bystander, bully-victim), and how these behaviors can best be identified. As Volk, Camilleri, Dane, and Marini (2012) suggest, the multidimensional approach to the identification of bullying provides the opportunity to develop targeted preventative strategies that could aim to develop abilities of "resistance" to peer harassment in adolescents with exceptionalities.

Challenges of giftedness in emerging adolescence   Furthermore, a relational developmental, social ecological systems approach to social cognitive development in emerging adolescents may help to demonstrate that the dynamics of social cognition differ for youth who experience learning challenges (Bronfenbrenner, 1977; Overton, 2013). In relation to giftedness, an explicit understanding of the emerging adolescent mind may also help to illustrate that advanced social cognitive ability may have different consequences for gifted or exceptionally talented females and males (Dabrowski, 1967; Sternberg et al., 2011). Such an understanding may encourage educators to recognize both the social-emotional and cognitive needs and sensitivities of exceptional students.

Research on emotional intensity and sensitivity among gifted children may help researchers to understand the social-emotional and moral correlates of social behavior in typically developing youth. Building on Dabrowski's (1967) idea of "overexcitabilities," Mendaglio (1995) defined giftedness in terms of sensitivities to intrapersonal competencies. That is, some children were found to be extremely sensitive to intrapersonal experiences such as self-awareness and emotional experiences, as well as interpersonal competencies such as perspective-taking, and empathetic sensitivity. Similarly, literature on emotional intensity and sensitivities, and social cognitive ability, may help researchers to further explore the complex connections that exist between socioemotional competence and social-moral communicative acts.

The early leaders in the field recognized the moral component of giftedness. For example, Lewis Terman in 1925 studied the emotional stability, social adjustment, and moral character of gifted learners to demonstrate that these developmental facets were all interwoven with advanced cognition. The importance of understanding the complex inner lives, early ethical concerns, and heightened awareness of the world of the gifted population also connects to recent research on psychopathology (Francis, Hawes, & Abbott, 2015). For example, recent researchers continue to investigate the benefits and challenges of advanced moral reasoning among intellectually gifted youth (Francis et al., 2015; Sternberg et al., 2011).

Researchers of the psychological development of gifted youth have noted the moral and emotional sensitivity of gifted learners, as many are considered to be exceptionally sensitive to moral issues (Francis et al., 2015; Sternberg et al., 2011). According to Silverman's clinical reports, many parents have reported that their gifted children seemed to have an innate sense of right and wrong, and empathetic sensitivity to others.

For example, multiple documented cases of gifted children showed that such children were more likely than their typically developing peers to fight injustice, befriend and protect handicapped children, respond to others' emotional needs, become emotionally distraught if a classmate was humiliated, become vegetarian in meat-eating families, cry at the violence in cartoons, become perplexed at why their classmates were pushed in line, and refuse to fight back when attacked. Many children considered all forms of violence, including self-defense, morally wrong, and often wrote poems of anguish at the cruelty in the world.

As discussed in Chapter 5, given Dabrowski's (1967) theory of "overexcitabilities" that includes self-awareness and self-control, such factors may also be related to increased self-scrutiny and self-criticism. For example, compared to boys, some girls in later childhood and early adolescence may score higher on ToM tasks, and thus reflect more advanced understanding of mental states and emotions in both themselves and others (Bosacki, 2013). Compared to boys, some girls were also more likely to think of others in psychological terms as opposed to more behavioral or physical terms (Hughes, 2011), as well as more likely to experience self-criticism and inner conflict (Harter, 1999).

Such feelings of low self-worth may lead to a feeling of inadequacy, as some girls in later childhood and early adolescence may begin to compare various aspects of themselves to cultural ideals (Fine, 2010). Taken together, such studies suggest that, although many girls in later childhood and adolescence develop the cognitive ability to compare themselves to others, they may also find it a challenge to develop effective coping skills to deal with the possible negative emotions that may result from such social comparisons.

Similarly, as briefly mentioned in Chapter 5, Kochanska and Kim (2013) found that young children who showed a developmentally earlier emotional reaction to mishaps and incompleteness might possess an emerging system of internal standards about right and wrong. Such an early developing and advanced moral understanding may thus lead to further emotional implications in later adolescence (Cross, Coleman, & Terhaar-Yonkers, 2014; Dabrowski, 1967). For example, past research has shown that many youth who are labeled as academically gifted are also more likely than their typically developing peers to experience anxiety, insomnia, and additional emotional challenges (Francis et al., 2015; Gagne & Gagnier, 2003; Mendaglio, 1995; Tokarz, 2003).

Related research has shown that some gifted individuals may have tendencies toward perfectionism and depression (Flett & Hewitt, 2014; Lyman & Luthar, 2014), and experience fear and anxiety more often, or more intensely than their nongifted peers. As explained by Dabrowski (1967), such experiences may be due to asynchronous development of the social cognitive and emotional areas of development. That is, some studies suggest that although some gifted individuals cognitively understand complex concepts such as moral dilemmas, they may still experience challenges as they attempt to manage their emotions and cope in emotionally healthy and productive ways.

Educational implications for gifted students   Due to the lack of empirical work on the relations between young people's advanced ToM skills and their schooling experiences (Bosacki, 2008; Hughes, 2011; Walker & Shore, 2011), as noted in previous chapters, researchers continue to explore the possibilities of educational programs that prevent perfectionism and promote resilience. That is, such educational programs aim to help youth cope with more sophisticated ToM abilities in healthy, adaptive ways within a caring and compassionate social learning classroom community. Given the growing number of studies that suggest that there may exist connections between ToM and schooling, including the relations among ToM development, self-concept, and social competence (Bosacki, 2008; Hughes, 2011), such findings may have implications for social behavior of all youth within the classroom.

Drawing on the past empirical evidence as outlined in this chapter, given the ambiguity and complexities surrounding perceptual and behavioral challenges regarding disruptive behavior and specific language impairment, more research is needed on how exceptional adolescents see themselves, their thoughts on classroom silences, and how they think they are accepted by their peers. Although interventions are helpful and essential, manifestations of disruptive behaviors, impulse control challenges, and language impairment may be likely to persist into adulthood (Schneider, 2014). For example, some longitudinal studies have shown that the social adjustment of some young males with SLI may be influenced in negative ways later on in their personal and social lives (Leonard, 2014). More recently, Conti-Ramsden and Botting (2008) found that compared to normally hearing adolescents, those with SLI reported higher rates of depression and anxiety.

Overall, many adolescents with learning exceptionalities share common challenges in social cognitive and emotional development. Their experiences with their peers in the classroom often entails exclusion, and educators need to provide caring and supportive learning environments to encourage learners to feel valued and cared for, to ensure the establishment and maintenance of self and other compassion and resilience within supportive and caring relationships. As mentioned earlier, language ability plays a crucial role in young people's social cognitive development, the interaction of impaired language with other cognitive, social, emotional, and behavioral processes is complex and may vary across learners.

Given these challenges, what can educators do to maintain an inclusive classroom that promotes a culture of acceptance for students with learning exceptionalities? How can educators and researchers help exceptional youth to cope with their emotional experiences? As I will describe below, as well as in more detail in Chapter 11, educators could consider a more holistic, inclusive approach to education, which in turn may help emerging adolescents with learning exceptionalities to cope effectively with their social-emotional experiences.

Applications: So What?

The next sections will outline various strategies that can be implemented into programs for exceptional learners' personal and social lives. Past research shows that the majority of youth with learning exceptionalities often find themselves challenged with barriers to optimal social cognitive learning. That is, as learners, they may have limited instructional diversity, and teachers with inadequate knowledge of effective pedagogical practices for teaching students with learning exceptionalities. One particular educational approach that is gaining recognition includes the use of technology in learning or Universal Design for Learning (UDL) (Mastropieri et al., 2006). Such strategies that include the use of video-games in instructional design are increasingly being used by educators to promote learning in youth with learning disabilities (LD) (Marino et al., 2011).

A recent review of literature by Young et al. (2012) showed that the high degree of variability in current videogame designs contributed to inconclusive findings in efficacy studies across educational contexts. Many researchers of the digital culture note that, although videogames can be valuable educational assets, there is often a disconnect between the efficacy of the games and their effectiveness in the classroom (Miller, 2011; Turkle, 2011, 2015). In addition, researchers note that many educational videogames lack clearly defined learning objectives and outcomes. Therefore, it is often difficult to examine how these games contribute to students' cognitive and social-emotional, moral, and spiritual development (Marino, Basham, & Beecher, 2011; Yust, 2014).

UDL provides curriculum developers and teachers with guidelines for designing and implementing instruction in a flexible manner that meets the needs of diverse learners (Rose, Meyer, & Hitchcock, 2005). For example, a recent study by Marino et al. (2014) showed that adolescent students reported an appreciation for curricular materials that met students' preferences and learning needs. Their study supported the notion that UDL-aligned curricula that incorporates videogames can increase knowledge transfer between virtual and classroom learning.

Thus, such UDL-aligned technologies should be included to the greatest extent possible in classrooms with exceptional learners. In addition, as others have noted (Miller, 2011), educational videogames have the potential to promote collaborative learning and engagement. Finally, as compared to many existing games that lack such collaborative attributes (Young et al., 2012), Marino et al.'s (2014) study articulated educational objectives that aligned with North American national educational benchmarks.

Authentic assessment of learning exceptionalities

Overall, as Marino et al. (2014) noted, authentic assessment is a critical component of the teaching and learning cycle. Marino et al.'s research indicated that a focus on UDL principles in standards, instruction, and assessment has the potential to result in enhanced accessibility for expanded groups of all users including those with learning exceptionalities. Marino et al. also found that traditional paper-based assessments failed to yield significant differences between UDL-aligned and traditional environments. However, more meaningful assessment results may emerge with alternative assessment methods that correlate with the qualitative data.

For example, modeling methods have the potential to capture different dimensions of student responses, and have the ability to dynamically adapt the assessment instrument to the individual ability of specific students (Timms et al., 2012). Other assessment options include the documentation of students' learning progressions and trajectories across various subjects, developmental continuums or learning maps in reading and the arts, as well as social cognitive skills and emotion regulation and coping (Gower et al., 2014; Özdemir et al., 2015; Polan, Sieving, & McMorris, 2013). Overall, educators are encouraged to identify a diverse range of highly correlated assessments during the curriculum development and implementation cycle.

As discussed earlier, based on Dabrowski's (1967) and Levitt and Selman's (1996) psychosocial theory, very sensitive and "overexcitable" young people could learn to work with educators, as such practitioners could assist youth to integrate and resolve internal experience with potentially damaging external influences. In addition, recent work on self-compassion and resilience addresses this dilemma for young adolescents, and suggests youth need to develop compassion for others, but also for themselves, to prevent perfectionistic tendencies such as over control and self-harming behaviors, and to develop psychological and emotional resilience and well-being (Bluth & Banton, 2015; Flett & Hewitt, 2014; Neff, 2011; Rose, 2014).

Social cognitive training programs for youth with chronic social cognitive learning challenges

An important target for early intervention for learning exceptionalities is the domain of social cognition or the mental operations that underlie understanding, interpretation, and perception of social information (Green & Harvey, 2014). Severe social cognition deficits, often comparable to those seen in chronic developmentally challenged persons, have been repeatedly documented in early-phase schizophrenia during later adolescence (Bertrand, Sutton, Achim, Malla, & Lepage, 2007; Green, Hellemann, Horan, Lee, & Wynn, 2012). These social cognitive challenges can span the domains of affect perception (Green, Hellemann, et al., 2012), social cue perception (including gaze perception, ToM and attributional style (Bertrand et al., 2007).

Importantly, social cognitive challenges have been strongly associated with poor social functional outcome in schizophrenia (Fett et al., 2010). Specifically, affect recognition and social perception have each been linked with community functioning, social problem-solving, and social skills (see Homer, Halkitis, Moeller, & Solomon, 2012). ToM, as well as affect perception and social perception, has been found to mediate the relationship between neurocognition and social functional outcome (Cross et al., 2014). Surprisingly, however, to date, only a few studies have examined the direct effects of social cognition training in youth or early psychosis patients (Shatkin, 2015), and none have evaluated a computerized intervention. Intervention studies have shown that cognitive enhancement therapy, computer-based cognitive training with group-based social skills training, may have a positive influence on neurocognitive, social cognitive, and functional outcome measures among participants (Combs et al., 2007). Moreover, application of these intervention studies to the classroom may be difficult given the invested time, personnel, and research ethics demands within a school setting.

Given these challenges, computer-based training has the potential to enable individualized educational programs to perform from the classroom or home, and at considerable cost savings (see Homer et al., 2012; Ventura, Wilson, Wood, & Hellemann, 2013). Recent studies tested computerized training of facial affect recognition and mental state decoding in chronic mentally challenged emerging adults (Hooker et al., 2012; Sacks et al., 2013). Results showed improvement in emotion perception and management, and social functioning (Kurtz & Richardson, 2012). Such results suggest that improvements in social cognition and social skills with an individual, computer-based intervention is feasible and potentially beneficial. However, it remains unclear whether younger students within a classroom setting would comply with computerized social cognitive training, and with the requirement to individually train from home for several hours each week over a several-week-long psychoeducational program.

Most recently, Nahum, Lee, and Merzenich (2013) examined the feasibility and initial efficacy of a new, online social cognitive training program (SocialVille created by Brain Plasticity Institute of Posit Science), in older adolescents with schizophrenia. SocialVille aims to treat social cognition impairments with the principles of neuroplasticity-based learning (Nahum et al., 2013).

In particular, the impaired brain systems underlying social cognition are targeted, rather than the impaired social behaviors per se that are usually targeted by social skills training. The rationale behind this approach was successfully applied to address general cognitive deficits in chronic schizophrenia (Fisher et al., 2009; Subramaniam et al., 2012). That is, this social cognitive approach aims to directly strengthen the accuracy of representations of socially relevant information in the brain and thus, should improve an individual's social behavior.

The SocialVille activities employ psychophysical principles of learning, especially implicit learning mechanisms. That is, contingent upon the student's performance, the activities increasingly adapt in difficulty. This online program was designed to treat social cognition deficits in schizophrenia, and consisted of 19 computerized exercises that targeted speed and accuracy of neural functions dedicated to social information processing (Nahum et al., 2013). Specifically, the SocialVille exercises targeted the social cognitive domains of affect perception (both visual and vocal), social cue perception, ToM, and self-referential processing.

The SocialVille exercises aimed to improve efficiency of stimulus representation and processing speed in the specific neural systems that underlie social cognition, and have been shown to function abnormally in schizophrenia (e.g., Nahum et al., 2013). The user began gradually to learn through tasks that involve many socially relevant stimulus examples while being given feedback on correct and incorrect discriminations. These neuroplasticity-based principles provided the foundation for the construction of SocialVille (see Fett et al., 2010 for full details).

Regarding the success of the program, Nahum et al. (2014) found that participants who completed the SocialVille task improved in their social cognitive abilities. In particular, following training, participants improved on motivation and reward sensitivity, and showed decreased behavioral inhibition and increased drive, as well as increased anticipatory pleasure. Nahum et al. (2014) claimed that their study was one of the first demonstrations of motivation changes following cognitive training in early schizophrenia.

Furthermore, motivation is generally considered a stable trait in typically developing individuals and not subject to change. Recent reports have shown that motivation plays a significant and mediating role between neurocognition, social cognition, and behavioral outcome (Cross et al., 2014; Green, Hellemann, et al., 2012). Nahum et al.'s (2014) finding that motivation can be perhaps enhanced with social cognitive training provides strong support for this mediation model, and suggests future research should target social cognition as well as different dimensions of motivation such as moral motivation in youth with chronic mental and social-emotional challenges (Kollerova et al., 2015).

Based on past research, SocialVille is considered by some researchers to be a promising intervention that may result in initial positive outcomes in social cognition, social functioning, and motivation in young individuals with schizophrenia. Given the importance of early intervention, and the lack of effective social cognitive educational programs, there is a clear need for additional effective and scalable psychotherapeutic programs. Future randomized controlled trials and intervention studies within the classroom will help to determine whether Nahum et al.'s (2014) findings are replicable to youth with additional learning exceptionalities. If such findings are replicated, researchers may be able to discover the "active ingredients" of beneficial learning, which would enable such learning to transfer to everyday functioning. Such a program could also be adapted for use with those youth who experience other chronic social cognitive and emotional challenges such as depression, social anxiety, and eating disorders.

In addition to social cognitive programs, educational programs that focus on mindfulness and stress and anxiety reduction may also be applied to help youth with a variety of learning exceptionalities. Similarity, humane education programs that incorporate animal-assisted living to help children with social cognitive and emotional impairments may also help to promote emotional health in youth with learning exceptionalities (Baumgartner & Cho, 2014; Tardif-Williams & Bosacki, 2015).

Given that many youth with learning exceptionalities experience stress, anxiety, and other negative emotions (Sternberg et al., 2011), programs that focus on mindfulness, meditation, and self-regulation may help young people to cope with stress, anxiety, and worry (Geronimi & Woodruff-Borden, 2015), and develop self-comforting strategies. For instance, teaching children to develop positive, calming self-talk may help them to learn adaptive coping mechanisms and regulation, and ways in which to acquire greater self-knowledge and self-directed compassion and acceptance (Coplan & Rudasill, 2016; Kuypers, 2011; Neff, 2011). As Wall (2005) and others suggest, the integration of social neuroscience with more mindful practices of holistic, educational programs may help to create a more inclusive learning environment that promotes social cognition and emotional health.

For example, integrative, multidisciplinary programs that combine self-regulation strategies with collaborative, nonjudgmental community activities to promote self-worth and social peer relations will help youth with sometimes chronic social cognitive and emotional challenges (Lewis, 2015). For example, youth with callous-unemotional (CU) traits (see Herpers, Scheepers, Bons, Buitelaar, & Rommelse, 2014 for a review), as well as youth with autism spectrum disorders (ASDs) may benefit from such programs as the PEERS-UCLA program (Laugeson et al., 2014). Further, as Gower et al. (2014) note, to help youth with sociability challenges, as mentioned in Chapter 6, research findings provide support for interventions that seek to build young people's stress management skills and personal responsibility to reduce aggressive and violent behaviors. There is growing evidence for the effectiveness of school-based social-emotional learning interventions on multiple indicators of social adjustment and academic performance (Durlak, Weissberg, Dymnicki, Taylor, & Schellinger, 2011). In the next chapter, I will discuss in more detail a variety of psycho-educational programs that aim to promote the healthy development of the social, cognitive, and emotional lives of youth.

Future Questions

Overall, given the increasing number of social cognitive intervention programs undergoing development, future research needs to include evaluation studies that test for their effectiveness. Given that many social cognitive intervention studies often fail to control for general cognitive ability, language abilities of the student, or quality of instruction, results of such intervention studies may be limited. For example, it could be possible that improvements in students' learning are driven by nonspecific effects of training such as the participants' increased attention span or generally improved processing speed. Still, results from several recent studies imply that nonsocial cognitive training may not improve social cognition and social function (Sacks et al., 2013).

Currently, there remains a lack of consensus on the optimal social cognition outcome measures to be used in social cognitive intervention studies for youth (Lecce, Bianco, Demichelli, & Cavallini, 2014; Nahum et al., 2014), as many of them are considered to have poor psychometric characteristics. As I will discuss further in the next chapter on developmental pedagogy, future studies on social cognitive educational programs should consider the application of additional or different outcome measures, given new psychometric information on outcome measures (Green et al., 2013; Kern et al., 2013).

Given the past research on the social cognitive and emotional lives of the adolescent exceptional learner, research on internalizing challenges and learning exceptionalities, particularly behavioral inhibition (BI), suggests that, to date, it remains unclear why, compared to BI, anxiety is only predicted by behavior-dependent negative life events (Broeren, Newall,

Dodd, Locker, & Hudson, 2013). One possibility is that anxiety and negative-dependent life events may be influenced by the same shared source, for example, genetics or a vulnerable temperament, negative or harmful family environment, parental modeling, or an adverse social environment. Although more research is needed to clarify the process by which negative dependent life events precipitate anxiety in young people, Broeren et al.'s (2013) study suggests that the temperamental trait of BI is unlikely to be the shared cause. That is, BI was not linked to negative life events in Broeren's study, as illustrated by the lack of differences found between children categorized as BI and behaviorally uninhibited (BUI) at baseline in subsequent negative life events.

However, positive life events may act as a protective factor in the development of BI challenges. That is, past research suggests that when children experience more positive behavior-independent life events, their risk of being diagnosed with an anxiety challenge may decrease (Gower et al., 2014). This suggests that theoretical models on childhood and youth anxiety should include negative behavior-dependent life events as well as positive life events and relationships in the youth's mental and emotional lives (Masten, 2014; Schneider, 2016).

In sum, future research should examine whether specific events and stressors (e.g., social, nonsocial) are most important in the development of social cognitive including anxiety problems in young people with learning exceptionalities. Such studies would provide important clues on the qualitative and relative contribution of negative life events, and their possible relation to temperament in predicting anxiety and mood disorders in youth. For example, Broeren et al. (2013) and others suggest that, to promote healthy mental and emotional development, researchers and educators need to focus on the influence of positive life events on the development of anxiety, and help youth to develop effective emotional and social coping skills to negotiate negative life events that occur in school, home, and community (Kuyper, 2011; Shatkin, 2015).

Overall, given the diverse and complex array of social learning exceptionalities discussed in this chapter, future applied cognitive neuroscience research within the educational context will be most helpful. As current research suggests, the rapid emergence of social and affective neuroscience is now a main influence in developmental social cognitive research and neuroeducation (Busso, 2014; Ochsner, 2008). These domains of inquiry focus on the neural substrates of social and emotional processes in healthy and impaired populations. For example, there has been research on the patterns of neural activation during identification of facial emotion in schizophrenia (Taylor et al., 2004). Given the prominence of social processing and affective impairments in developmental and affective exceptionalities such as ASDs and schizophrenia, this research direction can help to identify underlying neural abnormalities that give possible rise to social and emotional functioning.

As I will discuss further in Chapter 12, future research needs to examine the dynamic interplay between cognition and emotion. That is, such research can explore how emotion dysregulation is associated with young people's self-regulation challenges; the cognitive impact of negative or traumatic emotional experiences; and the relations between individual differences in emotional reactivity and cognitive ability. In addition, examination of underlying commonalities and differences in brain activation during emotional and cognitive tasks could inform treatments jointly aimed at emotional factors and cognitive impairments. Overall, the expansion of social and affective neuroscience within applied developmental social science or neuroeducation will shed light on the neural basis of social cognitive and emotional challenges associated with emerging adolescence (Busso, 2014; Green et al., 2013).

Summary

Drawing on the vast array of social cognitive literature outlined in the above chapter, empirical findings are mixed concerning the dynamic interplay among social understanding, self-concept, and social relations within emerging adolescents challenged by learning exceptionalities. Although there exists a large number of studies on social cognition in younger children and older adolescents with learning challenges (Laugeson et al., 2014), few examine specific components of social cognition and social relations, or the interrelations between these two constructs during the transition from childhood to adolescence within neurotypical and clinical samples. Furthermore, the relatively new set of existing studies now focus on the role positive life events and resilience play in the prevention of mental and emotional health challenges among vulnerable youth (Broeren et al., 2013; Gower et al., 2014; Rose, 2014; Seligman, 2011).

In sum, this chapter provided a critical analysis of a diverse collection of research studies on social cognition and social relations in emerging adolescents with learning exceptionalities. Such studies may also have many educational implications for all typically developing or neurotypical youth. Thus, based on this literature, the next chapter aims to provide some more explicit educational ideas and strategies that may encourage educators and researchers who work with youth to continue to explore and address social and emotional experiences within the classroom.

References

Abramson, L. Y., Metalsky, G., & Alloy, L. (1989). Hopelessness depression: A theory-based subtype of depression. *Psychological Review, 96*, 358–372.

Amador, X., Strauss, D., Yale, S., Flaum, M., Endicott, J., & Gorman, J. (1993). Assessment of insight in psychosis. *American Journal of Psychiatry, 150*, 873–879.

Baum, F. (1984/1900). *The wonderful wizard of Oz*. New York, NY: Signet Classic.

Baumgartner, E., & Cho, J. (2014). Animal-assisted activities for students with disabilities: Obtaining stakeholders' approval and planning strategies for teachers. *Childhood Education, 90*(4), 281–290.

Bertrand, M. C., Sutton, H., Achim, A. M., Malla, A. K., & Lepage, M. (2007). Social cognitive impairments in first episode psychosis. *Schizophrenia Research, 95*, 124–133.

Blakemore, S.-J., & Mills, K. (2014). Is adolescence a sensitive period for sociocultural processing? *Annual Review of Psychology, 65*, 187–207.

Bluth, K., & Banton, P. (2015). The influence of self-compassion on emotional well-being among early and older adolescent males and females. *The Journal of Positive Psychology, 10*, 219–230.

Bosacki, S. (2005). *Culture of classroom silence*. New York, NY: Peter Lang.

Bosacki, S. (2008). *Children's emotional lives: Sensitive shadows in the classroom.* New York, NY: Peter Lang.

Bosacki, S. (2013). Theory of mind understanding and conversational patterns in early adolescence. *Journal of Genetic Psychology, 174,* 170–191.

Bowker, J. C., & Raja, R. (2011). Social withdrawal subtypes during early adolescence in India. *Journal of Abnormal Child Psychology, 39,* 201–212. doi:10.1007/s10802-010-9461-7

Brinton, B., & Fujiki, M. (2002). Social development in children with specific language impairment and profound hearing loss. In P. Smith & C. Hart (Eds.), *Blackwell handbook of childhood social development* (pp. 588–603). Oxford, England: Blackwell.

Broeren, S., Newall, C., Dodd, H., Locker, H., & Hudson, J. (2013). Longitudinal investigation of the role of temperament and stressful life events in chidhood anxiety. *Development and Psychopathology, 26,* 437–449.

Bronfenbrenner, U. (1977). Toward an experimental ecology of human development. *American Psychologist, 32,* 513–531.

Brose, A., Schmiedek, F., Koval, P., & Kuppens, P. (2015). Emotional inertia contributes to depressive symptoms beyond perseverative thinking. *Cognition and Emotion, 29,* 527–538.

Brumbach, B., Figueredo, A., & Ellis, B. (2009). Effects of harsh and unpredictable environments in adolescence on development of life history strategies: A longitudinal test of an evolutionary model. *Human Nature, 20,* 25–51.

Burwell, R. A., & Shirk, S. R. (2007). Subtypes of rumination in adolescence: Associations between brooding, reflection, depressive symptoms, and coping. *Journal of Clinical Child and Adolescent Psychology, 36,* 56–65. doi:10.1207/s15374424jccp3601_6

Busso, D. (2014). Neurobiological processes of risk and resilience in adolescence: Implications for policy and prevention science. *Mind, Brain, and Education, 8,* 34–43.

Cappadocia, C., Weiss, J., & Peplar, D. (2012). Bullying experiences among children and youth with autism spectrum disorders. *Journal of Austism and Development Disorders, 42,* 266–277.

Combs, D. R., Adams, S. D., Penn, D. L., Roberts, D., Tiegreen, J., & Stem, P. (2007). Social Cognition and Interaction Training (SCIT) for inpatients with schizophrenia spectrum disorders: Preliminary findings. *Schizophrenia Research, 91,* 112–116.

Conti-Ramsden, G., & Botting, N. (2008). Emotional health in adolescents with and without a history of specific learning impairment. *Journal of Child Psychology and Psychiatry, 49,* 516–525.

Coplan, R. (2014). The A, B, C's of recent work on shyness and social withdrawal: Assessment, biology, and context. *Infant Child and Development, 23,* 217–219.

Coplan, R. J., & Rubin, K. H. (2010). Social withdrawal and shyness in childhood: History, theories, definitions, and assessments. In R. Coplan & K. Rubin (Eds.), *The development of shyness and social withdrawal* (pp. 3–20). New York, NY: Guilford.

Coplan, R. J., & Rudasill, K. (2016). *Quiet at school: An educator's guide to shy children.* New York, NY: Teachers College Press.

Cross, T., Coleman, L., & Terhaar-Yonkers, M. (2014). The social cognition of gifted adolescents in schools: Managing the stigma of giftedness. *Journal for the Education of the Gitfted, 37,* 30–39.

Dabrowski, K. (1967). *Personality shaping through positive disintegration.* Boston, MA: Little, Brown.

Diamond, K. (2002). The development of social competence in children with disabilities. In P. Smith & C. Hart (Eds.), *Blackwell handbook of childhood social development* (pp. 571–587). Oxford, England: Blackwell.

Ding, X., Coplan, R., Sang, B., Liu, J., Pan, T., & Cheng, C. (2015). Young Chinese children's beliefs about the implications of subtypes of social withdrawal: A first look at social avoidance. *British Journal of Developmental Psychology, 33,* 159–173.

Doey, L., Coplan, R. J., & Kingsbury, M. (2014). Bashful boys and coy girls: A review of gender differences in childhood shyness. *Sex Roles, 70*, 255–266. doi:10.1007/s11199-013-0317-9

Durlak, J. A., Weissberg, R. P., Dymnicki, A. B., Taylor, R. D., & Schellinger, K. B. (2011). The impact of enhancing students' social and emotional learning: A meta-analysis of school-based universal interventions. *Child Development, 82*(1), 405–432.

Elkind, D. (1967). Egocentrism in adolescence. *Child Development, 38*, 1025–1034. doi:10.2307/1127100

Erwin, P. (1995). *Friendship and peer relations in children*. Chichester, England: Wiley.

Fett, A. K., Viechtbauer, W., Dominguez, M. D., Penn, D. L., van Os, J., & Krabbendam, L. (2010). The relationship between neurocognition and social cognition with functional outcomes in schizophrenia: A meta-analysis. *Neuroscience Biobehavioural Review, 35*, 573–588.

Fine, C. (2010). *Delusions of gender: How our minds, gender, and neurosexism create difference*. New York, NY: Norton.

Flett, G., & Hewitt, I. (2014). A proposed framework for preventing perfectionism and promoting resilience and mental health among vulnerable children and adolescents. *Psychology in the Schools, 51*, 899–912.

Francis, R., Hawes, D., & Abbott, M. (2015). Intellectual giftedness and psychopathology in children and adolescents. *Exceptional Children, 82*, 279–802.

Fredrickson, B., & Roberts, T. (1997). Objectification theory: Toward understanding women's lived experiences and mental health risks. *Psychology of Women Quarterly, 21*, 173–206.

Gagné, F., & Gagnier, N. (2003). The socio-affective and academic impact of early entrance to school. *Roeper Review, 26*(3), 128–138.

Gazelle, H. (2008). Behavioral profiles of anxious solitary children and heterogeneity in peer relations. *Developmental Psychology, 44*, 1604–1634. doi:10.1037/a0013303

Geronimi, E., & Woodruff-Borden, J. (2015). The language of worry: Examining linguistic worry models. *Cognition & Emotion, 29*, 311–318.

Goossens, L. (2014). Affinity for aloneness and preference for solitude in childhood: Linking two research traditions. In R. J. Coplan & J. Bowker (Eds.), *Handbook of solitude: Psychological perspectives on social isolation, social withdrawal, and being alone* (pp. 150–166). Malden, MA: Wiley Blackwell.

Goossens, L., & Beyers, W. (2002). Comparing measures of childhood loneliness: Internal consistency and confirmatory factor analysis. *Journal of Clinical Child and Adolescent Psychology, 31*, 252–262. doi:10.1207/153744202753604520

Goossens, L., & Marcoen, A. (1999). Adolescent loneliness, self-reflection, and identity: From individual differences to developmental processes. In K. J. Rotenberg & S. Hymel (Eds.), *Loneliness in childhood and adolescence* (pp. 225–243). New York, NY: Cambridge University Press.

Gower, A., Shlafer, R., Polan, J., McMorris, B., Pettingell, S., & Sieving, R. (2014). Brief report: Associations between adolescent girls' social-emotional intelligence and violence perpetration. *Journal of Adolescence, 37*, 67–71.

Green, M., Barnes, B., & McCormick, C. (2012). Social instability stress in adolescence increases anxiety and reduces social interactions in adulthood in male Long-Evans rats. *Developmental Psychobiology, 55*, 849–859. doi:10.1002/dev.21077

Green, M., & Harvey, (2014). Cognition in schizophrenia: Past, present, and future. *Schizophrenic Research: Cognition, 1*, e1–e9.

Green, M. F., Hellemann, G., Horan, W. P., Lee, J., & Wynn, J. K. (2012). From perceptions functional outcome in schizophrenia: Modeling the role of ability and motivation. *Archive of Genetic Psychiatry, 69*, 1216–1224.

Green, M. F., Lee, J., & Ochsner, K. (2013). Adapting social neuroscience measures for schizophrenia clinical trials, part 1: Ferrying paradigms across perilous waters. *Schizophrenic Bulletin, 39*, 1192–1200.

Greguol, M., Gobbi, E., & Carraro, A. (2014). Physical activity practice, body image and visual impairment: A comparison between

Brazilian and Italian children and adolescents. *Research in Developmental Disabilities*, 35, 21–26.

Guralnick, M. (1999). Family and child influences on the peer-related social competence of young children with developmental delays. *Mental Retardation and Developmental Disabilities Research Reviews*, 5, 31–29.

Harkness, K. L., Sabbagh, M. A., Jacobson, J. A., Chowdrey, N. K., & Chen, T. (2005). Enhanced accuracy of mental state decoding in dysphoric college students. *Cognition and Emotion*, 19(7), 999–1025.

Harter, S. (1999). *The construction of the self: A developmental perspective*. New York, NY: Guilford.

Herpers, P., Scheepers, F., Bons, D., Buitelaar, J., & Rommelse, J. (2014). The cognitive and neural correlates of psychopathy and especially callous–unemotional traits in youths: A systematic review of the evidence. *Development and Psychopathology*, 26, 245–273.

Hollenstein, T., & Lougheed, J. P. (2013). Beyond storm and stress: Typicality, transactions, timing, and temperament to account for adolescent change. *American Psychologist*, 68(6), 444–454. doi:10.1037/a0033586

Homer, B., Halkitis, P., Moeller, R., & Solomon, T. (2012). Methamphetamine use and HIV use in relation to social cognition. *Journal of Health Psychology*, 18, 900–910.

Hooker, C. I., Bruce, L., Fisher, M., Verosky, S. C., Miyakawa, A., & Vinogradov, S. (2012). Neural activity during emotion recognition after combined cognitive plus social cognitive training in schizophrenia. *Schizophrenia Research*, 139, 53–59. doi:10.1016/j.schres.2012.05.009

Hughes, C. (2011). *Social understanding and social lives: From toddlerhood through to the transition to school*. New York, NY: Psychology Press.

Hurley, K. (2014). Development and human–animal interaction: Commentary on Mueller. *Human Development*, 57, 50–54.

Hyde, J. (2014). Gender similarities and differences. *Annual Review of Psychology*, 65, 373–398.

Hyde, J., Mezulis, A., & Abramson, L. (2008). The ABCs of depression: Integrating affective, biological and cognitive models to explain the emergence of the gender difference in depression. *Psychological Review*, 115, 291–313.

Ibanez, A., Huepe, D., Gemp, R., Gutierrez, V., Riveria-Rei, A., & Toledo, M. (2013). Empathy, sex and fluid intelligence. *Personality and Individual Differences*, 54, 616–621.

Kashdan, T. B., Weeks, J. W., & Savostyanova, A. A. (2011). Whether, how, and when social anxiety shapes positive experiences and events: A self-regulatory framework and treatment implications. *Clinical Psychology Review*, 31, 786–799.

Kern, R. S., Penn, D. L., Lee, J., Horan, W. P., Reise, S. P., Ochsner, K. N., … Green, M. F. (2013). Adapting social neuroscience measures for schizophrenia clinical trials, part 2: Trolling the depths of psychometric properties. *Schizophrenic Bulletin*, 39(6), 1201–1210.

Kessler, R., Berglund, P., Demler, O., Jin, R., Merikangas, K., & Walters, E. (2005). Lifetime prevalence and age-of-onset distributions of DSM-IV disorders in the National Comorbidity Survey Replication. *Archives of Genetic Psychiatry*, 62, 593–602.

Kessler, R., McGonagle, K., Swartz, M., Blazer, D., & Nelson, C. (1993). Sex and depression in the National Comorbidity Survey: I. Lifetime prevalence, chronicity and recurrence. *Journal of Affective Disorders*, 29, 85–96,

Killinger, B. (2008). *Integrity: Doing the right thing for the right reason*. Montreal, Canada: McGill-Queen's University Press.

Kochanska, G., & Kim, S. (2013). Early attachment organization with both parents and future behavior problems: From infancy to middle childhood. *Child Development*, 84, 283–296. doi:10.1111/j.1467-8624.2012.01852.x

Kollerova, L., Janosova, P., & Rican, P., (2015). Moral motivation in defending classmates victimized by bullying. *European Journal of Developmental Psychology*, 12, 297–309.

Kozina, A. (2014) Developmental and time-related trends of anxiety from childhood to early adolescence: Two-wave cohort study. *European Journal of Developmental Psychology*, *11*, 546–559. doi:10.1080/1740562 9.2014.881284

Kuppens, P., Sheeber, L. B., Yap, M. B. H., Whittle, S., Simmons, J. G., & Allen, N. B. (2012). Emotional inertia prospectively predicts the onset of depressive disorder in adolescence. *Emotion*, *12*, 283–289. doi:10.1037/a0025046

Kurtz, M. M., & Richardson, C. L. (2012). Social cognitive training for schizophrenia: A meta-analytic investigation of controlled research. *Schizophrenia Bulletin*, *38*, 1092–1104.

Kuypers, L. (2011). *The zones of regulation: A curriculum designed to foster self-regulation and emotional control*. San Jose, CA: Think Social Publishing.

Larson, R. (2011). Positive development in a disorderly world. *Journal of Research in Adolescence*, *21*, 317. doi:10.1111/j.1532-7795.2010.00707.x

Laugeson, E., Ellingsen, R., Sanderson, J., Tucci, L., & Bates, S. (2014). The ABC's of teaching social skills to adolescents with autism spectrum disorder in the classroom: The UCLA PEERS program. *Journal of Autism Developmental Disorders*, *44*, 2244–2256.

Lecce, S., Bianco, F., Demichelli, P., & Cavallini, E. (2014). Training preschoolers on first-order false belief understanding: Transfer of advanced ToM skills and metamemory. *Child Development*, *85*, 2404–2418.

Leonard, L. (2014). Specific language impairment across languages. *Child Development Perspectives*, *8*, 1–5.

Leussis, M., & Andersen, S. (2008). Is adolescence a sensitive period for depression? Behavioral and neuroanatomical findings from a social stress model. *Synapse*, *6*, 22–30.

Levitt, M., & Selman, R. (1996). The personal meaning of risk behavior. In G. Noam & W. Fischer (Eds.), *Development and vulnerability in close relationships* (pp. 201–233). Hillside, NJ: Erlbaum.

Lewis, M. (2015). *The biology of desire: Why addiction is not a disease*. New York, NY: Perseus Book Group.

Loeb, R., & Sarigiani, P. (1986). The impact of hearing impairment on self-perceptions of children. *The Volta Review*, *88*, 89–100.

London, E. (2014). Categorical diagnosis: A fatal flaw for autism research? *Trends in Neurosciences*, *37*, 683–686.

Lopez, C. M., Driscoll, K. A. & Kistner, J. A. (2009). Sex differences and response styles: Subtypes of rumination and associations with depressive symptoms. *Journal of Clinical Child and Adolescent Psychology*, *38*, 27–35. doi:10.1080/15374410802575412

Lord, C., & Magill-Evans, J. (1995). Peer interactions of autistic children and adolescents. *Development and Psychopathology*, *7*, 611–626.

Luppa, M., Sikorski, C., Luck, T., Ehreke, L., Konnopka, A., & Riedel-Heller, S. (2012). Age- and gender-specific prevalence of depression in latest-life—systematic review and meta-analysis. *Journal of Affective Disorders*, *136*, 212–221.

Lyman, E., & Luthar, S. (2014). Further evidence on the "costs of privilege": Perfectionism in high-achieving youth at socioeconomic extremes. *Psychology in the Schools*, *51*, 91–930.

Marino, M. T., Basham, J. D., & Beecher, C. C. (2011). Using video games as an alternative science assessment for students with disabilities and at-risk learners. *Science Scope*, *34*(5), 36–41.

Marino, M., Gotch, C., Isreael, M., Vasquez, E., Basham, J., & Beht, K. (2014). UDL in the middle school science classroom: Can video games and alternative text heighten engagement and learning heighten engagement and learning for students with learning disabilities? *Learning Disabilities Quarterly*, *37*(2), 87–99. doi:10.1177/0731948713503963

Masten, A. (2014). Global perspectives on resilience in children and youth. *Child Development*, *85*, 6–20.

Mastropieri, M. A., Scruggs, T. E., Norland, J. J., Berkely, S., McDuffie, K., Tornquist, E. H., &

Berkeley, S. (2006). Differentiated curriculum enhancement in inclusive middle school science: Effects on classroom and high-stakes tests. *Journal of Special Education, 40*, 130–137.

Mathersul, D., McDonald, S., & Rushby, J. (2013). Understanding advanced theory of mind and empathy in high-functioning adults with autism spectrum disorder. *Journal of Clinical Experimental Neuropsychology, 35*, 655–668.

McCormick, C., Green, M., Cameron, N., Nixon, F., Levy, M., & Clark, R. (2013). Deficits in male sexual behavior in adulthood after social instability stress in adolescence in rats. *Hormone Behavior, 63*, 5–12.

McCormick, C., Mathews, I., Thomas, C., & Waters, P. (2010). Investigations of HPA function and the enduring consequences of stressors in adolescence in animal models. *Brain Cogition, 72*, 73–85.

McKinley, N., & Hyde, J. (1996). The Objectified Body Consciousness Scale: Development and validation. *Psychology of Women Quarterly, 20*, 181–215.

Melson, G. (2013). Children's ideas about the moral standing and social welfare of non-human species. *Journal of Sociology and Social Welfare, 60*, 81–106.

Mendaglio, S. (1995). Sensitivity among gifted persons: A multi-faceted perspective. *Roeper Review, 17*, 169–172.

Mezulis, A., Simonson, J., McCauley, E., & Vander Stoep, A. (2011). The association between temperament and depressive symptoms in adolescence: Brooding and reflection as potential mediators. *Cognition & Emotion, 25*, 1460–1470. doi:10.1080/02699931.2010.543642

Miller, V. (2011). *Understanding digital culture.* Los Angeles, CA: Sage.

Moffitt, T. (2006). Life-course persistent versus adolescent-limited antisocial behaviors. In D. Cicchetti and D. Cohen (Eds.), *Developmental psychopathology* (Vol. III, pp. 57–98). New York, NY: Wiley.

Mueller, M. (2014). Is human–animal interaction (HAI) linked to positive youth development? Initial answers. *Applied Developmental Science, 18*, 5–16.

Nahum, M., Fisher, M., Loewy, M., Poelke, G., Ventur, J., Nuechterlein, K., … Vinogradov, S. (2014). A novel, online social cognitive training program for young adults with schizophrenia: A pilot study. *Schizophrenia Research: Cognition, 1*, e11–e10.

Nahum, M., Lee, H., & Merzenich, M. M. (2013). Principles of neuroplasticity-based rehabilitation. *Program of Brain Research, 207*, 141–171.

Neff, K. D. (2011). Self-compassion, self-esteem, and well-being. *Social and Personality Psychological Compass, 5*, 1–12. doi:10.1111/j.1751-9004.2010.00330

Nolen-Hoeksema, S. (2001). Gender differences in depression. *Current Directions in Psychological Science, 10*, 173–176.

Nolen-Hoeksema, S. (2004). The response styles theory. In C. Papageorgiou & A. Wells (Eds.), *Depressive rumination: Nature, theory and treatment* (pp. 107–123). Chichester, England: Wiley.

Norman, R. M., & Malla, A. K. (2001). Duration of untreated psychosis: A critical examination of the concept and its importance. *Psychological Medicine, 31*, 381–400.

Ochoa, S. H., & Palmer, D. J. (1995). Comparison of the peer status of Mexican-Amercian students with learning disabilities and non-disabled low-achieving students. *Learning Disability Quarterly, 18*, 57–63.

Ochsner, K. N. (2008). The social-emotional processing stream: Five core constructs and their translational potential for schizophrenia and beyond. *Biological Psychiatry, 64*, 48–61.

Overton, W. F. (2013). A new paradigm for developmental science: Relationism and relational-developmental systems. *Applied Developmental Science, 17*, 94–107. doi:10.1080/10888691.2013.778717

Özdemir, M., Cheah, C., & Coplan, R. (2015). Conceptualization and assessment of multiple forms of social withdrawal in Turkey. *Social Development, 24*, 142–165.

Perlman, W., Webster, M., Herman, M., Kleinman, J., & Weickert, C. (2007). Age-related differences in glucocorticoid receptor mRNA levels in the human brain. *Neurobiological Aging, 28,* 447–458.

Polan, J. C., Sieving, R. E., & McMorris, B. J. (2013). Are young adolescents' social and emotional skills protective against involvement in violence and bullying behaviors? *Health Promotion Practice, 14,* 599–606. doi:10.1177/1524839912462392

Rochat, P. (2009). *Others in mind: Social origins of self-consciousness.* Cambridge, England: Cambridge University Press.

Roe, D., & Kravetz, S., 2003. Different ways of being aware of a psychiatric disability: A multifunctional narrative approach to insight into mental disorder. *The Journal of Nervous and Mental Disease, 191,* 417–424.

Rood, L., Roelofs, J., Bogels, S., Nolen-Hoeksema, S., & Schouten, E. (2009). The influence of emotion-focused rumination and distraction on depressive symptoms in non-clinical youth: A meta-analytic review. *Clinical Psychololgical Review, 29,* 607–616.

Rose, D. H., Meyer, A., & Hitchcock, C. (2005). *The universally designed classroom. Accessible curriculum and digital technologies.* Boston, MA: Harvard Education Press.

Rose, R. (2014). Self-guided multimedia stress management and resilience training. *Journal of Positive Psychology, 9,* 489–493.

Rubin, K. H., Coplan, R. J., & Bowker, J. (2009). Social withdrawal in childhood. *Annual Review of Psychology, 60,* 141–171.

Rueda, P., Fernandez-Berrocal, P., & Baron-Cohen, S. (2015). Dissociation between cognitive and affective empathy in youth with Asperger Syndrome. *European Journal of Developmental Psychology, 12,* 85–98.

Sacks, O. (2012). *Hallucinations.* New York, NY: Knopf.

Sacks, S., Fisher, M., Garrett, C., Alexander, P., Holland, C., Rose, D., … Vinogradov, S. (2013). Combining computerized social cognitive training with neuroplasticity-based auditory training in schizophrenia. *Clinical Schizophrenic Relational Psychoses, 7*(2), 78A–86A.

Schneider, B. (2014). *Child psycholopathology: From infancy to adolescence.* Cambridge, England: Cambridge University Press.

Schneider, B. (2016). *Childhood friendships and peer relations: Friends and enemies* (2nd ed.). New York, NY: Routledge.

Seligman, M. (2011). *Flourish.* London, England: Nicholas Brealey.

Shatkin, J. (2015). *Child and adolescent mental health: A practical all-in-one guide.* New York, NY: Norton.

Siegel, D. (2013). *Brainstorm: The power and purpose of the teenage brain.* New York, NY: Jeremy Tarcher/Penguin.

Silverman, L. (1989). Invisible gifts, invisible handicaps. *Roeper Review, 12,* 37–42.

Sobsey, D., & Mansell, S. (1997). Teaching people with disabilities to be abused and exploited: The special educator as accomplice. *Developmental Disabilities Bulletin, 25,* 77–93.

Sternberg, R., Jarvin, L., & Grigorenko, E. (2011). *Explorations in giftedness.* New York, NY: Cambridge University Press.

Swanson, H. (2000). Issues facing the field of learning disabilities. *Learning Disabilities Quarterly, 23,* 37–49.

Tardif-Williams, C. Y., & Bosacki, S. L. (2015). Evaluating the impact of a humane education summer camp program on school-aged children's relationships with companion animals. *Anthrozoös, 28,* 587–600.

Taylor, S., Sherman, D., Kim, H., Jarcho, J., Takagi, K., & Dunagan, M. S. (2004). Culture and social support: Who seeks it and why? *Journal of Personality and Social Psychology, 87,* 354–362.

Teppers, E., Klimstra, T. A., Van Damme, C., Luyckx, K., Vanhalst, J., & Goossens, L. (2013). Personality traits, loneliness, and attitudes toward aloneness in adolescence. *Journal of Social and Personal Relationships, 30,* 1045–1063. doi:10.1177/0265407513481445

Timms, M., Clements, D. H., Gobert, J., Ketelhut, D. J., Lester, J., Reese, D. D., & Wiebe, E. (2012). *New measurement paradigms.* Newton, MA: Community for Advancing Discovery Research in Education.

Tokarz, A. (2003). Procedures for stimulating motivational mechanisms in the development of creative abilities and attitudes at school. In F. Mönks & H. Wagner (Eds.), *Proceedings of the 8th ECHA Conference "Development of Human Potential: Investment into our Future"* (pp. 165–167). Bad Honnef, Germany: K. H. Bock.

Treynor, W., Gonzalez, W., & Nolen-Hoeksema, S. (2003). Rumination reconsidered: A psychometric analysis. *Cognitive Therapy and Research*, *27*, 247–259. doi:10.1023/A: 1023910315561

Turkle, S. (2011). *Alone together: Why we expect more from technology and less from each other*. New York, NY: Basic Books.

Turkle, S. (2015). *Reclaiming conversation: The power of talk in a digital age*. New York, NY: Penguin.

Twenge, J., & Nolen-Hoeksema, S. (2002). Age, gender, race, socioeconomic status, and birth cohort differences on the Children's Depression Inventory: A meta-analysis. *Journal of Abnormal Psychology*, *111*, 78–88.

Ventura, J., Wilson, S. A., Wood, R. C., & Hellemann, G. S. (2013). Cognitive training at home in schizophrenia is feasible. *Schizophrenia Research*, *143*, 397–398.

Volk, A., Camilleri, J., Dane, A., & Marini, Z. (2012). Is adolescent bullying an evolutionary adaptation? *Aggressive Behavior*, *38*, 222–238. doi:10.1002/ab.21418

Walker, W., & Shore, B. (2011). Theory of mind and giftedness: New connections. *Journal for the Education of the Gifted*. *34*, 644–668.

Wall, R. B. (2005). Tai chi and mindfulness-based stress reduction in a Boston public middle school. *Journal of Pediatric Health Care*, *19*(4), 230–237.

Wang, P., Berglund, P., Olfson, M., & Kessler, R. (2004). Delays in initial treatment contact after first onset of a mental disorder. *Health Services Research*, *39*, 393–415.

Warren, D. (1994). *Blindness and children: An individual differences approach*. New York, NY: Cambridge University Press.

Wellman, H. (2014). *Making minds: How theory of mind develops*. Oxford, England: Oxford University Press.

Whitaker, L., Degoulet, M., & Morikawa, H. (2013). Social deprivation enhances VTA synaptic plasticity and drug-induced contextual learning. *Neuron*, *77*, 335–345.

Wolfendale, S. (Ed.). (2000). *Special needs in the early years: Snapshots of practice*. New York, NY: Routledge Falmer.

World Health Organization (1999). *WHO statistical information system*. Geneva, Switzerland: Author.

Young, M. F., Slota, S., Cutter, A. B., Jalette, G., Mullin, G., Lai, B., … Yukhymenko, M. (2012). Our princess is in another castle: A review of trends in serious gaming for education. *Review of Educational Research*, *82*, 61–89.

Yust, K.-M. (2014). Digital power: Exploring the effects of social media on children's spirituality. *International Journal of Children's Spirituality*, *19*, 133–143.

Part V

Future Questions and Implications for Practice
Helping Young People to Move Forward

"Nothing is so painful to the human mind as a great and sudden change." (Shelley, 1969/1818, p. 197)

Section Overview

Part V focuses on future questions and implications for practice aimed to help young people to move forward towards a healthy and balanced life. This section will address key future questions for researchers and practitioners, such as how to work with youth to promote the importance of becoming a wise, compassionate, and caring young person within the global cultural mosaic. Further, how we can help young people to develop a healthy sense of self and relationships, and to cope in healthy ways with growing diversity and technology. Chapter 11 expands on the connections between social cognitive developmental research and pedagogy including social cognitive and emotional learning programs that promote emotional and social cognitive learning.

Chapter 12 introduces topics that move beyond the category of social cognition through the exploration of less-researched related, but emerging, topics. Such topics include the emerging field of social or interpersonal neuroscience, and young people's understanding of the supernatural, magic, spirituality, and complex moral emotions for self and other including self-consciousness, compassion, moral elation, remorse, revenge, schadenfreude, moral and personal disgust, social robots, humor, persuasion, artistic learning, emotional sensitivities, and internalizing challenges (unsociability, callous-unemotional personality), and so on.

11

Developmental Social Cognitive Pedagogy

"Experience is the only thing that brings knowledge, and the longer you are on the earth the more you experience you are sure to get." (Baum, 1984/1900, p. 160)

Introduction

In this chapter I will expand on the connections between social cognitive and emotional developmental research and pedagogy, and discuss social cognitive and emotional learning programs that promote emotional and social cognitive learning. This chapter builds on the previous sections of the book, as I will examine how current research findings help to further advance developmental theory regarding the personal and social lives of young learners. That is, how do the theories and empirical evidence findings discussed in previous chapters further the discourse in current educational and developmental literature? Further, how do such theories help to develop programs that aim to foster social, cognitive, and emotional competencies in young people?

In particular, this chapter describes current social cognitive developmental research on the importance of self-regulation, as well as relationships in the classroom, and how such research may be applied to the classroom in terms of curricula. It describes various multi-faceted, holistic approaches that aim to integrate all aspects of a young person's sense of self. Such self-integration may help to prepare young people for the complex increasingly global and rapidly technologically advancing century that lies ahead. Thus, as I will discuss later in this chapter, through the implementation of learning activities that promote balance, inclusion, and relationships within a supportive, compassionate, and caring environment,

Social Cognition in Middle Childhood and Adolescence: Integrating the Personal, Social, and Educational Lives of Young People, First Edition. S. L. Bosacki.
© 2016 John Wiley & Sons, Ltd. Published 2016 by John Wiley & Sons, Ltd.

young people may learn to develop a positive sense of self and to form trusting, secure relationships with themselves and others.

Given that researchers in the educational field and developmental sciences have tended to work independently of one another in the past, the utilization of diverse methodologies from multiple disciplines creates the challenge to build a coherent body of knowledge about the educational and personal life of the emerging adolescent. In the following chapter, through the lens of a relational developmental, psychocultural systems approach (Overton, 2013), I will outline various ways in which researchers and educators may consider how various aspects of the school experience may influence the young person's sense of self and social cognitive abilities. I will also suggest numerous educational strategies to promote the development of social cognitive and emotional factors in learning.

Pedagogical Directions: Creation of a Caring Curriculum to Promote Connectivity

As educators and researchers become increasingly concerned with the promotion of young people's psychological and emotional health, we need to focus on programs and activities that promote healthy and adaptive self-regulatory abilities, such as mindfulness and positive self-cognitions and self-talk. Programs that combine cognitive with emotional needs could include strategies that may help young people to learn how to cope and manage their personal and social worlds in healthy ways (Schonert-Reichl et al., 2015). That is, we need to draw from emotional and cognitive psychology, as well as psychotherapeutic contexts that include strategies to promote self-management and self-compassion.

For example, programs could integrate self-comforting strategies into daily classwork, such as relaxation techniques, visualization, art therapy, play therapy, psychodrama, and animal-assisted learning. Researchers, educators, and youth workers need to provide positive role models for learners to aspire to. More specifically, educational leaders who aim to present themselves as caring, courageous, and mindful teachers interested in self-understanding and social moral awareness may inspire learners to do the same.

A relational developmental psychocultural and social ecological approach to development and education cannot be reduced to any single technique as it includes the art of the cultivation of meaningful human relationships. The focus is on dialogue, connection, and the mutual co-creation of meaning. For example, given the need for further emerging research in developmental research with Indigenous youth (Thompson, Whitesell, Galliher, & Gfellner, 2012), educators and developmentalists can co-create evidence-based programs for all cultures and borrow and expand upon existing culture-based programs that aim to promote learning in various Indigenous cultures across the globe (Bell, 2013). Such a transformative approach to education includes all partners across generations and cultures (children, teacher–researchers, community members, parents) as valued members of the learning community (Bell, 2013; Hadaway & Young, 2014; Sternberg, 2014).

Thus, researchers and educators who aim to promote a psychocultural and social ecological approach could promote developmentally and culturally sensitive educational programs that will allow us to share our expertise with others (Bronfenbrenner, 1997). Though respect, compassion, and openmindedness may begin as an inner, personal discipline (Neff, 2011), they also have the potential to evolve into a dynamic, interactive experience. Developmentally and culturally sensitive learning communities can help teachers and young learners within culturally diverse populations to learn together the practices of compassionate openmindedness, awareness, tolerance, respect, and kindness (Linkins, Mark Niemiec, Gillham, & Mayerson, 2015).

Consistent with past educational research discussed throughout this book (e.g., Bruner, 1996), educators and young learners are responsible in part for their learning and exploration of their social cognitive experiences. Thus, the teacher and students share the role of learner and co-constructor of knowledge. The research mentioned in this book, especially regarding the development of self-regulation, may also encourage teachers and students to think of themselves as collaborators and co-learning partners.

Such relational perspectives to education may help young people to realize that they have an equal opportunity to co-learn and to co-create knowledge. In addition, the focus on relationships may help to prevent potential teacher–student power struggles that are common to late childhood and adolescent classrooms (Noddings, 2003; Sette, Baumgartner, & Schneider, 2014). A caring and collaborative classroom thus encourages the teacher and the learner to work as partners toward the shared goal of becoming reflective and caring learners and practitioners.

For example, the inclusion of opportunities for emerging youth to participate in the collaborative development of a social cognitive curriculum with their peers and teachers may provide students with a sense of personal power and agency (Sternberg, 2014). That is, through their shared contributions to the school curriculum, students may learn to envision themselves as valued and engaged learners who are active participants in the construction of their academic knowledge (Goldberger, 1996). Furthermore, given the elimination of traditional teacher and student roles, young people may develop a greater sense of agency and self-control based on a greater belief in their social cognitive abilities, which in turn may lead to greater competence in all areas of school (Coplan & Rudasill, 2016; Duckworth & Carlson, 2013; Kuypers, 2011).

Within a holistic psycho- and neuroeducational framework, the use of narrative or story is one way to promote young people's social cognitive development. Cultural and social narratives may influence our social cognitive abilities, such as empathetic sensitivity and Theory of Mind (ToM), and define all aspects of humanity, including who we are and the various roles we play in life (Bruner, 1996). Thus, through the use of verbal and written forms of storying and dramatic or visual arts, psychoeducators need to encourage emerging adolescents to explore their sense of selves (Goldstein & Winner, 2012). In the next section, I will outline various strategies for teachers and learners to co-learn how to become caring, compassionate, and mindful individuals in society.

Setting the Stage: Communication Facilitates Psychological Comfort

Drawing on various works from psychoeducation and applied social cognitive neuroscience, neuroeducational programs need to encourage educators and students to learn from each other, and thus support the holistic principle that claims teaching and learning are mutually reinforcing processes. Based on psychoeducational literature (Hyde, 2014; Larson, 2011), educational programs situated within a psychocultural foundation view the group facilitator/teacher and the participants as co-learners who come to share beliefs, goals, and intentions to subsequently form a culture or a caring community of learners. Thus, some learners may need encouragement to engage in a collaborative, dialogical relationship as each co-learner is a knowledgeable individual of her or his own situation.

To create a psychosocial curriculum that incorporates aspects of mindfulness, self-reflection, and other related metacognitive skills, educators first must learn to view curriculum from a psychocultural and relational perspective. A psychocultural curriculum would also pro- mote aspects of social cognitive and communicative skills such as empathetic sensitivity and ToM (Bosacki, 2013; Hughes, 2011). Educational activities that focus on mindfulness and critical discussion may also help to promote critical consciousness and social awareness among young people (Lau & Hue, 2014; Masten, 2014a). However, despite the social cognitive benefits of reflexive thought and mindfulness, as mentioned earlier, the majority of critical reasoning curriculum continues to remain mainly within the domain of gifted education (Sternberg et al., 2011).

In addition, given claims that language plays a critical role in social cognition and self-development (Bosacki, 2013; Hughes, 2011), language activities are crucial for the development of young people's self-regulation and self-knowledge. Past research sug- gests that narrative and metacognition is necessary for a comprehensive social cognitive curriculum for young people (Bruner, 1996; Olson, 1994). According to narrative theory (Bruner, 1996), people learn to make sense of their social world as they acquire the ability to tell stories about their experiences. The process of writing and reading stories can also help emerging adolescents to develop the ability to understand multiple per- spectives. That is, young people can use narratives to integrate what they and others think, feel, and do.

To incorporate the role of narrative in the classroom, educators of young people need to encourage silent reading, book sharing, and "story-time" with books that focus on the private, subjective experiences of the emerging adolescent. For example, Markus Zusak's (2005) *The Book Thief* and Judy Blume's (1974) *Blubber* are illustrative examples of contem- porary novels that explore the complex inner world of emerging adolescents respectively. Classic novels such as *Animal Farm* (1945) by George Orwell, and *Frankenstein* (1818) by Mary Shelley are additional examples of books that may encourage critical thought about the role of emotions, power, and identity within relationships. Thus, through the critical examination of a fictional novel's characters' thoughts and emotions, emerging adolescents may learn to clarify and develop a critical worldview, in addition to honing their ToM skills.

As I have discussed earlier, researchers claim that the value of language activities is in part that they encourage dialogical reasoning and critical reflection, as well as promoting interpretive understanding and intentional creativity (Goldstein, 2009; Goldstein & Winner, 2012). For example, consistent with claims that metacognitive and mindful activ- ities require further integration into the classroom (Paley, 1999; Zelazo & Lyons, 2012), activities that utilize metacognitive and reflective abilities, such as journal writing, biblio- therapy, and psychodrama, may encourage youth to develop self-awareness and a greater understanding of their own mind and emotions and social relations. Thus, the relatively recent interest in mindfulness within the area of developmental social cognitive science can help educators to apply cutting-edge research findings to the classroom (Lau & Hue, 2014; Tan & Martin, 2016), and provide the opportunity for all classroom learners to engage in mindful activities.

Related findings from social cognitive research suggest that metacognitive understanding may be linked to aspects of social and self-understanding. Thus, based on past research, which has shown that exposure to metacognitive and metalinguistic verbs is associated with a greater understanding of mental states or ToM (Bosacki, 2013; Wellman, 2014), educators and curriculum designers should also be encouraged to increase their use of metacognitive or mental-state language in classroom talk and curriculum materials. Within a relational developmental educational framework, educators can increase their usage of metacognitive and psychological language by sharing their thought processes and emotions. Thus, by making their implicit psychological self-talk more explicit, educators may foster the growth of metacognitive understanding in their students (Bosacki, 2008). The use of mental state self-language or private speech, then, may help to promote individual growth and a collaborative, inclusive classroom consciousness focused on respect, caring, and compassion.

Past research on ToM development in youth (Bosacki, 2000; Mink, Henning, & Aschersleben, 2014), suggests that some females with an advanced ToM, and males with a relatively less advanced ToM, may experience social-emotional challenges such as social anxiety and other internalizing challenges. In addition, as discussed in Chapter 8 on gender, Devine and Hughes (2013) found that in a group of children and early adolescents, females who scored low on ToM tasks reported greater feelings of loneliness, whereas males reported feelings of peer rejection. Such findings support the view that the core educational issue remains the child's perceived value as a person, and programs that strive to increase this perceived self-worth need to be a classroom priority.

Thus, drawing on relevant psychoeducational programs that aim to foster self-knowledge and regulation (Kuypers, 2011), various activities can be used to increase young people's social cognitive competencies and self-confidence. For example, a developmentally appropriate arts-based program that focuses on self-expression and understanding through multiple art mediums such as music, drama, visual arts, and poetry could be used to foster a coherent sense of self and effective emotional coping skills (Bonneville-Roussy, Rentfrow, Xu, & Potter, 2013; Bosacki & O'Neill, 2015; Chin & Rickard, 2014).

Consistent with recent research on personal and emotional intelligences (Gardner & Davis, 2013; Goleman, 1995), empirical evidence from social cognitive research lays the groundwork for a developmental and relational educational program that focuses on the metacognitive abilities of social and self-understanding. Drawing on inclusive psychocultural educational principles and goals (Miller, 1993), and borrowing from various affective educational programs and curriculum documents (Schonert-Reichl., et al., 2015; Seligman, Ernst, Gillham, Reivich, & Linkins, 2009), over the years I have developed a flexible framework for a metacognitive, social cognitive curriculum for young people (approximately ages 6 to 12 years) (Bosacki, 2005, 2008). Building on these past frameworks, I adapted my previous frameworks to one that focuses more on the advanced social cognitive abilities of the emerging adolescent (12 years and beyond, see Table 11.1).

Table 11.1 Curriculum framework for the social cognitive and moral lives of older children and emerging adolescents (8 to 13 years)

Overall learning goals: (1) to advance the critical understanding, care and compassion of self and other as psychological beings within the global context; (2) to promote personal, social, and transcultural competence; (3) to foster the social cognitive abilities that underlie the ability to critically understand one's personal, social worlds, and cultural worlds (i.e., encourage critical emotional and cultural competencies).

Social cognitive skill	Learning goals	Learning activities
I. Social and global connections		
Learning question: What are others thinking? Why?		
• interpersonal understanding	• develop ability to attribute mental states to others mental states within transcultural context	• critically read, reflect, and respond to novels that focus on the attribute psycho emotional aspect of interpersonal and global relationships (peers, family, teachers, animals, environment/nature)
1. Perspective-taking	• understand multiple perspectives or points of view • understand the beliefs and intentions of others	• dramatic role-playing • painting and writing • critical dialogue, debate co-operative games, peer teaching and learning
Learning question: What are others feeling? Why?		
2. Empathetic sensitivity	• understand others' emotional experiences	• dramatic role-playing • creative writing (short stories, poems, novels, etc.)
3. Person perception	• to view others as psychological, emotional beings (i.e., understand personality traits)	• creative writing/film, TV, Internet, music • critical bibliotherapy (emotions) • painting human portraits • create comics, characters
Learning question: Is there another way to think about this?		
4. Divergent thinking	• imaginative problem-solving • promotes cognitive flexibility	• critical media analysis (TV, radio, magazines, Internet/ websites)
II. Self connections		
Learning question: What am I thinking? Why?		
• intrapersonal understanding	• develop ability to attribute mental states to self	• read and reflect on novels, poetry with a bio-psychosocial focus

Table 11.1 *(Continued)*

Social cognitive skill	Learning goals	Learning activities
Learning question: What am I feeling? Why?		
1. Affective	• develop ability to trust, care, and accept oneself	• guided imagery focused on body–mind–world connection • guided meditation/mindfulness • self-portrait of face/body • eurhythmy, dancing • yoga
2. Cognitive	• understand mental world (thinking process and creation of mental scripts)	• critical bibliotherapy • journaling, dream work • self-portrait of the mind • self-narrative/dialogue and autobiographical writing and music writing, video creation

Notes: Activities within each domain (social and self respectively) are interchangeable. Learning activities can be applied to a variety of psychocultural themes to reflect multiple sources of diversity (e.g., gender, ethnicity, class, race), and may serve as individual and/or cooperative group assignments. Mixed gender and age groups are recommended (Ellis et al., 2012).
Adapted from Bosacki, 2005, p. 131, 2008, p. 142.

In general, the main goal of this educational framework is to foster personal and social growth through arts-based activities designed to improve young people's social cognitive skills and mindfulness. The activities listed in Table 11.1 aim to provide young people with an understanding of the social world; to help them recognize the diverse beliefs, desires, and feelings that different people can bring to the same situations. Based on the concepts of ToM and self-management and knowledge, Table 11.1 includes the corresponding social cognitive skills followed by the educational goals and suggested learning activities.

Although space does not permit the discussion of all of the suggested activities within Table 11.1, I will describe two activities that may hold specific relevance to social cognitive development in emerging adolescence. First, Steiner's (1976) concept/method of eurhythmy or "music and speech expressed in bodily movement" is an educational method that may especially help youth to develop emotionally balanced attitudes toward the body–mind connection. An integral part of Waldorf Education, this form of arts-based movement education, as well as others, such as forms of visual arts and ballet schools for learning exceptionalities, may help youth to focus on social cognitive learning and self-development through rhythmic experience by moving to music (Hyde et al., 2009; Limont, 2012; Richards, 1980).

Building on this arts-based movement, activities could integrate additional art forms other than dance alone, as some young people may not feel comfortable dancing within a group setting. The incorporation of music into learning activities would provide emerging adolescents with a personal sense of mastery by enabling them to create rhythmic movement as well as other art forms such as drama, visual art, video, and poetry through modes of multimedia technology. Through music engagement and self-expression, young people can develop a sense of competence that may help them to cope with self-concept challenges and doubts and develop emotional regulation and coping skills as well as resilience (Bonneville-Roussy et al., 2013; Bosacki & O'Neill, 2013; Limont, 2012; Saarikallio, 2011).

The second activity involves the process of guided imagery and group meditation that promotes the concept of mindfulness, or the ability to be aware of mind and body in the present (Kabat-Zinn, 2003; Miller, 1993; Neff & McGeehee, 2010). In such activities, the teacher asks the learner to imagine a particular scenario; one that is comforting and has personal meaning for the learner, or a body scan, which consists of a guided movement of attention throughout the body from the head to the toes while sitting or lying down. The goal of visualization or guided imagery is to develop young people's awareness of their thoughts, physical sensations, and emotions simultaneously.

Activities that focus on mindfulness can promote connections within all realms of the self, including body–mind, thought–emotion, and logic–intuition. Furthermore, such activities could also serve as stress-reduction and relaxation techniques to help young people develop regulatory emotional and cognitive strategies. These social cognitive abilities may also serve as coping mechanisms to deal with real-life emotional stress experienced by some young people, including academic-related and social anxiety, as well as gelotophobia, that is, the fear of being laughed at during a challenging task or social situation (Ruch, 2009).

As illustrated in Table 11.1, empirical evidence from social cognitive and evolutionary psychological research could help educators to create activities from the language arts to promote moral and social development. For example, evidence gleaned from evolutionary psychology suggests that mismatches between environmental and ancestral environments may lead to risky behavior during adolescence (Ellis et al., 2012).

School classrooms provide influential social contexts for the emergence of peer networks to develop positive peer relationships that have the potential for positive developmental outcomes (Betts & Stiller, 2014; Fabes, Hanish, Martin, Moss, & Reesing, 2012). However, very little research exists on the role social cognitive factors play in emerging adolescents' prosocial actions with peers and friendships.

To promote prosocial relations and less risky, self-harmful behaviors, educators should be encouraged to provide mixed-age settings and peer environments, as they may help reduce aggression and self-harm. Similarly, research from a developmental evolutionary psychology approach suggests that the gender ratio of the group may influence aggression and risky behavior in youth. As such, educators should promote mixed-gender groups and remain mindful of the male–female ratio within group activities.

For example, regarding racial and ethnicity issues, an increasing number of books have been included in classrooms to promote young people's understanding of multiple perspectives and emotions across various cultures (Hadaway & Young, 2014). Books such as *First Person, First Peoples* by Garrod and Larimore, and *We Feel Good Out Here* (2008) by Andre and Willett are examples of books that will encourage youth to think about the perspectives of people from diverse cultures and to understand issues such as prejudice, power, marginalization, and cultural identity. Books by Toni Morrison, such as *The Bluest Eye* (1994), and

Ann Martin's *Rain Reign* (2014) may also add social cognitive value to the emergent adolescent classroom library.

Some young children's books also may also serve as an effective way to help young people learn about emotions and "life lessons" that need to be addressed in the school social curriculum for emerging adolescents. For example, young children's books that remain relevant to older children and adolescents include Witek's *In My Heart: A Book of Feelings* (2013), Young's *The 7 Blind Mice and the Elephant* (1992), Freymann and Elffers' *How Are You Peeling: Foods with Moods?* (1999), and Lionni's *Fish Is Fish* (1970). Such books have the potential to promote human values of respect, compassion, kindness, and the notion that we need to "read beyond the cover." That is, these and other books of fiction may help youth to learn the importance of tolerance and compassion directed towards other human beings, irrespective of physical appearance, abilities, or cultural values (Goldstein & Winner, 2012; Mar et al., 2006).

Further exploration of young people's social cognitive abilities and their socioemotional consequences suggests the need for useful assessment tools and interventions to benefit teachers of youth. Given past research that shows positive associations between social cognitive competencies and school experiences (Astington, 1993; Bosacki, 2008; Hughes, 2011), educators could learn to teach "psychological language" to adolescents that would focus on social cognitive abilities such as self-regulation and interpersonal understanding. Educators could learn to encourage youth to develop a mental-state vocabulary of the self and others. Such initiatives would provide support for educators of youth who advocate the importance of social cognition and metacognition in education.

The narrative process of writing and reading stories enables young people to develop their ability to integrate multiple perspectives (Bruner, 1996). Curriculum development that utilizes narrative may thus enhance young people's ability to understand self and other in a psychological sense. Books that describe people's psychoemotional worlds can be used in the later elementary and secondary grades to encourage emerging adolescents' mental-state understanding. For instance, excerpts from Judy Blume's *Deenie* (1973), Marthe Jocelyn's *What We Hide* (2014), and Sylvia McNicoll's *Revenge on the Fly* (2014) could be used within the classroom to illustrate the landscape of adolescents' private worlds and inner voices. Future research on the emotional experiences of youth's reading, and their interpretations of such psychological novels could thus provide empirical evidence for the development of holistic educational framework aimed to foster both inter- and intrapersonal competencies.

In sum, through the integration of ideas from social cognitive research (metacognitive and mindful activities), and inclusive curriculum models (art-based and compassion-focused activities), a developmentally appropriate psychocultural educational program may provide a valuable contribution to education. Such an educational program could be used to enhance school curricula in that it could contribute affective and cognitive activities. However, it should be noted that, due to the self-exploratory nature of some of the activities, although such an inclusive program is not intended to provide psychotherapy for serious emotional challenges, the activities could be integrated into a relevant psychoeducational program. As I discussed in Chapter 10, educators would thus need to be aware of exceptional learners and to provide them with the proper psychological resource if need be.

A Caring and Connected Curriculum: Psychocultural Educational Strategies

The concept of balance or the ability to maintain various energies and qualities in the correct proportion underlies all aspects of holistic education (Miller, 1993; Steiner, 1976). This "education of balance" strives to assist children in their self-development by the integration of body, mind, and soul. From this view, the intellectual development of the learner is kept in appropriate relation to their social, emotional, physical, and moral development. Thus, holistic education views mind and body as connected and interrelated, and advocates a balance between cognition and emotion and, more specifically, between the use of rational/logical scientific and intuitive/narrative thought.

Young people living in the 2020s and beyond may be especially susceptible to this dichotomous way of thinking through their exposure to conflicting sociocultural messages. Researchers claim that, during the ages of approximately 8 to 14 or 15 years, many early adolescents may experience an increase in societal pressure to conform to gender-role stereotypes of the stereotypic "perfect body" (Hyde, 2014). For example, although the majority of schools support a mainly cognitive-based education that values the intellect; in contrast, messages from the media (i.e., TV, magazines, films) value the physical body and physical appearance.

Such mixed messages have the potential to encourage self-criticism and perfectionism, as many of the key themes in a recent issue of *Seventeen* magazine focus on the importance of fashion, beauty, and body to confidence. Thus, traditional models of education may contribute to the recent research findings that show an increase in self-regulation and emotional challenges among young people today (Schneider, 2014). Accordingly, holistic programs that incorporate personal integration and social awareness need to be implemented in young people to promote a body/mind unity. Such programs have the potential to provide emerging adolescents with adaptive coping strategies that can be used to combat possibly harmful contradictory sociocultural messages.

Classroom strategies to foster emotional strength, resilience, and sensitivity

The theories and research findings reviewed in the previous chapters have implications for those who work with young people within an educational context. Once educators become aware of their assumptions and experiences concerning young people's social cognitive abilities, they may then become actively engaged in the creation of educational activities for youth aimed to promote affective and cognitive competencies. Given that the majority of young people spend much of their mental energy engaged in social cognition, or thinking about people (including themselves) and society, the sections below offer some suggestions that may help to develop adolescents' "social cognitive sensibilities." Such activities may encourage emerging adolescents to engage in critical enquiry and dialogue regarding complex and sensitive issues such as morality, spirituality, and religiosity.

To bridge the divide between theory and practice, drawing on the use of arts education, I will outline some suggestions in the sections below for inclusive educational activities aimed to develop emerging adolescents' social cognitive development. More specifically, I will group the classroom activities based on personal connections and social awareness of the larger community and world.

Personal connections   Drawing on holistic and inclusive curriculum models (Bruner, 1996; Miller, 1993), the individual person is at the source of learning, and participates in a cyclic journey of self-growth. For example, an inclusive psychoeducational program could encourage youth to provide a personal definition of learning by outlining the goals and commitments that meet their individual learning needs. Such an activity encourages the student to take ownership and responsibility for her or his own learning. As Bruner (1996) suggests, we cannot force another person to learn, the motivation and appetite for learning must begin from within, although it may be "sparked" by outside sources.

Consistent with educators who work with youth (Bosacki & O'Neill, 2015; Larson, 2011; Linkins et al., 2015), an arts-based, holistic program designed for young people can help foster the development of a positive relation between body and mind. In particular, the use of narrative or storytelling, visual arts, music, dance, movement, drama, and journaling can be used as a vehicle to foster self-expression, to develop a greater self-understanding in both a psychoclinical (nonschool) and school context. For instance, emerging adolescent learners could participate in role-playing or video and music production activities that describe scenarios that include a student who feels silenced, or marginalized/ostracized from the classroom learning community. The reason for the marginalization could reflect particular themes relevant to the class at the time (e.g., social class, ethnicity), as the key is that the learner believes and feels themselves to be marginalized. Once this role is established, students could be asked to play the role of the "ostracizers" or "silencers" and dramatize a scenario to illustrate issues of power and control among various group members.

Dramatic and music arts could also help to promote a positive sense of self by promoting self-expression and self-knowledge. In addition to drama, the use of music, drawing, sculpture, and so forth could also be used to promote self-expression. Within a school context, the use of art and music could encourage emerging adolescents to explore different aspects of their personalities, which in turn could help to develop their artistic learning competencies (Bosacki & O'Neill, 2015; Miranda & Gaudreau, 2011).

Building on applications of narrative research to the classroom (e.g., Bruner, 1996; Noddings, 2003; Richards, 1980; Steiner, 1976), as discussed earlier, the use of personal storytelling and self-narration (i.e., journal writing) could be a valuable vehicle to self-regulation and identity development in young people. Thus, conceived as a metanarrative (Mar et al., 2006), art forms such as stories, songs, poems, and drawings could help emerging adolescents to examine past and current patterns in both their values, beliefs, and behaviors. Thus, a narrative approach to learning can help adolescents to create a personal guide or inner curriculum focused on self-acceptance and personal integration.

Self-awareness and knowledge can be further strengthened through mindfulness practice or the ability to be aware in the present in the classroom. Mindfulness is a core meditation skill that originated from India over 2,500 years ago, practiced in both monastic and lay communities in Theravada Buddhist traditions in parts of South Asia. To promote positive emotions and emotional growth, proponents of mindfulness claim the application of mindfulness practice to our daily activities aims to cultivate wholesome thoughts, speech, and actions with compassion, joy, and lovingkindness (Langer, 2000; Palmo, 2002; Shonin, Van Gordon, & Griffiths, 2013).

In recently developed secular mindfulness programs, mindfulness is often referred to as a level of consciousness with nonreactive awareness and openhearted acceptance at the present moment (Kabat-Zinn, 2003). Most mindfulness educational and clinical programs aim to cultivate a mental state with a flexible moment-to-moment attention, awareness, and acceptance of an object in mind and body, such as feelings, sensations, and thoughts (Kabat-Zinn, 2003; Neff, 2011; Shonin et al., 2013; Tan & Martin, 2016). Applied to school settings, mindfulness can be cultivated in daily school life activities such as mindful walking, standing, sitting, lying down, and eating, either individually or with a group.

There has been a recent growing interest in the exploration of the effects of mindfulness-based training with children and adolescents in North American and European academic and public discourses, such as recent national Canadian magazine *MacLean's* (Lunau, 2014). Past research has shown positive effects of mindfulness training with neurotypical (Broderick & Metz, 2009; Metz et al., 2013; Napoli, Krech, & Holly, 2005), and nonclinical children and adolescents with attention-deficit disorder, ADHD, and aggressive behavior patterns (Beauchemin, Hutchins, & Patterson, 2008; Hassed, Lisle, Sullivan, & Pier, 2009; Singh et al., 2007; Zylowska et al., 2008). Such studies often implement the use of mindfulness activities including guided imagery exercises to help young people with social and emotional challenges to understand the powerful emotions often connected to the process of marginalization or social exclusion.

As previously noted, the concept and practice of mindfulness may encourage youth to be appreciative of their current surroundings, including their physical selves. A growing number of educators and researchers suggest that such mindful experiences are adaptable to either individual/personal or social/common activities (Lau & Hue, 2014). For example, to promote the virtues of caring, collaboration, personal integrity, and responsibility, group activities could be planned to promote the caretaking of nature (gardening, animal caretaking), followed by personal reflection or contemplation time (journal writing, music writing, sculpture, painting, etc.). Furthermore, as Lunau (2014) recently outlined, the notion of applying the techniques of mindfulness to the grade school classroom has raised the interest of the general public, particularly school boards and parents.

Given that mindful activities are considered a combination of social and personal experiences, opportunities to reflect upon such events are critical in that all individuals will respond differently to each activity (Zelazo & Lyons, 2012). For example, two adolescents may participate in a flower-planting ceremony although each youth may experience the event differently as each learner will develop their own personal meaning of the experience and preferences for self-expression. That is, some learners may wish to write about the flower-planting in their journal, whereas others may prefer to paint or draw a picture, make a video, and so on. The common element to such mindful activities is that they all include a concentrated amount of time and silence, or a lack of verbal expression and a focus on "listening," as silence may encourage learners to listen to their bodies and mind.

To promote mindfulness with the use of guided imagery, educators could ask students to imagine a scenario where they are deliberately ignored or left out of a social group that they would like to belong to, and to ask them to become aware of what they are thinking and how they are feeling (emotionally and physically). Students could then apply this skill to imagining the experience of a peer who has been marginalized or ostracized, which in turn could help develop empathic sensitivity and compassion. This use of visualization or guided imagery could easily be adapted to other uses in the classroom where teacher-guided visualizations could include themes of diversity and social status.

Building on Steiner's (1976) educational model that integrates mind, body, and spirit, imagery and visualization could help to develop adolescents' awareness of their thoughts, physical sensations, and emotions simultaneously. Thus, the use of visualization or guided imagery describes activities that promote connections within all realms of the self including body–mind, thought–emotion, and logic–intuition. Furthermore, teaching strategies that promote relaxation and mindfulness techniques may help young people to develop social cognitive strategies that can be used as a coping strategy to deal with real-life emotional stress, anxiety, and other internalizing challenges (Neff & McGeehee, 2010; Schonert-Reichl & Lawlor, 2010; Schonert-Reichl et al., 2015).

A relational and developmental approach to education for youth needs to include activities that inspires all learners to both challenge and escape the tyranny of societal expectations that value linear, dichotomous thinking. Similar to approaches used in cognitive neuroscience programs (Anderson & Della Sala, 2013), educators of adolescents can provide activities that encourage their students to replace dualistic thinking with a more healthy, global, and holistic perspective that enables them to view concepts on a continuum. In particular, programs such as Acceptance and Commitment Therapy (ACT) that teaches people to create distance from and to let go of potentially harmful negative self-concepts may help to promote adaptive social and self-development in youth (Ciarrochi & Bailey, 2008; Marshall, Parker, Ciarrochi, & Heaven, 2014).

Given emerging adolescents' developing metacognitive abilities, the ability to think about thinking (Gardner & Davis, 2013), classroom discussions that encourage students to critically discuss dichotomous terms such as masculine/feminine, fat/thin, good/bad may prove to be beneficial to students in that they may foster their development of interpersonal and intrapersonal understanding. Thus, the integration of ideas from cognitive psychology and neuroscience (metacognitive development, neuroplasticity), together with holistic curriculum models (mindfulness, guided imagery), can contribute to a holistic neuroeducational approach that is developmentally appropriate for emerging adolescents (Busso, 2014; Goswami, 2012).

Self and social understandings   To further promote the development of self-knowledge and the awareness of mental states in both self and others, educators can engage in the following strategies:

- Through dialogue and inquiry, encourage critical discussion about psychological and philosophical phenomena and other people's perspectives.
- Include a rich repertoire of mental state references and psychological language (thoughts, feelings, intentions, imagination) in daily classroom conversations.

- Provide learning opportunities to encounter multiple perspectives, and encourage learners to share their perspectives with others.
- Pay special attention to the interpretations of children with cognitive and social-emotional challenges (see Chapter 10).
- Provide opportunities for "play" or unstructured activities, which are not formally evaluated, such as an artists' (music, visual) or authors' corner in the classroom, with accompanying materials.
- Include opportunities for drama where costumes and scripts can be created and/or developed.

Societal and cultural understandings   Young people's abilities to navigate effectively in their social world depend on their understanding of themselves as valued partners with other community members (DiBiase, Gibbs, & Potter, 2005; Ramey & Rose-Krasnor, 2015), as well as their understanding of their role within global society. Listed below are some suggestions to foster young people's conceptions of social institutions and social groups across the globe.

- Encourage youth to visit the world of the professional adult workplace including retail, commerce, government, academia, trades, among others.
- Encourage community–school partnerships by inviting community leaders from diverse cultural backgrounds into the classroom.
- Critically examine society's inequities concerning "status variables" such as gender, ethnicity, and social class.
- Provide opportunities to volunteer and visit the larger community and encourage youth to care for and show compassion for others through action within the community.
- Address prejudice and cultural and gender-role stereotypes through critical analysis of media messages from TV, film, radio, magazines, Internet, and social media.
- Encourage the critical consumption of popular media and examine how other countries are represented on the radio, Internet (social media), in newspaper articles, and live and videotaped television news programs from around the globe.

Global connections: Toward a more psychocultural approach to adolescent education

Community connections   The adaptation of the ecological, psychological, and also the evolutionary perspective toward the self and education could help to strengthen emerging adolescents' connections to the community (Ellis et al., 2012). Building on the principles of developmental eco-spiritualism and the ecology of the mind (Caine, 2003; Parisi, 2013), perhaps educators of youth can encourage adolescents to direct their thoughts, feelings, and actions towards the big picture or the web of life, including the digital world (Capra, 1996). Such an integrative approach incorporates genetic, social, psychological, and ecological factors in learning and development and advocates for the development of psychological and ecological understandings (Gardner & Davis, 2013; Goleman, 1995; Damon, Menon, & Bronk, 2003; Masten, 2014b).

According to researchers who explore the ecological factors in human growth (Cajete, 1994; Koizumi, 2013), eco-spirituality subsumes any conception of a higher power of creation within all living beings such as plants, animals, humans, earth, rocks, water, and other elements. Eco-spirituality celebrates our connection with nature, and asks us to embrace a connection with all other species. An ecological approach to mind and education (Schonert-Reichl, 2015; Schonert-Reichl et al., 2015; Tolan, Guerra, & Kendall, 1995), combined with Bronbenbrenner's (1977) concept of ecological self, is a perspective that emphasizes humans as part of nature and our communality with all living things, and encourages young people to develop a positive relationship with their minds and their bodies. This framework may motivate adolescents to examine their connections to our global society, and how various sociocultural factors influence their thoughts, emotions, and behaviors.

Regarding applications to practice, an example classroom activity for emerging adolescents could involve critical analysis and discussion regarding various popular magazine advertisements and television commercials that perpetuate cultural and gender-role stereotypes (i.e., ethnicity, body types), compared to more contemporary, progressive advertisements that promote more humanist values (i.e., all women must have a university education; caring, sensitive stay-at-home father). Thus, a holistic educational approach encourages learners to engage in critical discussion regarding contradictory media messages, and hypothesize about why such stereotypes exist, and also how such a learning experience makes them think and feel. Such an activity encourages youth to critically question and reflect upon paradoxical messages found in the media regarding stereotypical body images and the portrayal of woman and men.

World connections   From a global perspective, an emphasis on a "world core curriculum" (Masten, 2014a) and corresponding universal themes such as respect for the earth, and caring and compassion for all living beings may encourage emerging adolescents to view themselves within a larger global picture, and to develop a sense of connection to the global family. More specifically, various activities used in Waldorf Education, such as physical activities with the environment (i.e., gardening and cooking with organic foods), may encourage youth to see themselves within the larger framework of the ecosystem and nature (Miller, 1993). As Caine (2003) suggests, eco-spiritual education encourages educators to extend curricula beyond the classroom, and integrate our experiences of nature and the environment into the classroom. For example, learners could be asked to share their perception of, and critically discuss, the ethics and practices of vegetarianism/veganism, eco-tourism, free -trade, sustainable fishing, humane agricultural techniques, and so forth.

Similarly, the integration of Indigenous people's literature, such as the Indigenous concept of the Medicine Wheel, could provide the basis for various discussions on other intergenerational "cultural stories," and encourage more culture-based education (Bell, 2013; Hadaway & Young, 2014). Exposure to the cultural stories of their peers could help learners to co-create and adapt their own, new, personal stories by recognizing the numerous global stories that exist around the world. For example, youth could be encouraged to discuss North America and Europe's emphasis on materialistic consumption and aesthetic perfection, and then questioned about why, compared to our Westernized culture, emotional, anxiety, and internalizing challenges are less likely to be found in developing and economically challenged countries.

Related discussions could include why, compared to developing countries, economically advantaged societies may value different aspects of physical appearance and moral behavior, including self-control and resilience as signs of personal success, power, and social status (Masten, 2014a, 2014b; Rose, 2014). Discussions involving different cultural perspectives have the potential to provide students with the opportunity to broaden their worldviews, and realize that emotional sensitivities may be largely due to sociocultural factors. In general, the development of a more holistic and caring attitude toward other cultures and environmental issues may help to de-emphasize the egocentrism that may develop during adolescence (Larson, 2011; Shatkin, 2015). Consequently, as emerging adolescents learn to develop a more holistic world view or perspective, they may learn to view themselves and others through a more tolerant, inclusive, and accepting lens.

Regarding the link between psychology and education, as I was researching for this book, I was surprised to find few examples of developmental models of social cognitive research that explore topics regarding adolescents' language development, religiosity, and spirituality within an educational context. A comprehensive discussion of social cognitive development needs to include examples of psychological research from areas such as epistemology, self-concept, morality, and identity formation, ToM. For instance, we need to draw on works of researchers and educators who focus on broader views of social cognition including the integration of morality and spirituality (Aldwin, Park, Jeong, & Nath, 2014; Coles, 1990), or other works that explore links between holistic education and young people's spiritual, emotional, and moral development within the classroom (Donaldson, 1992; Miller, 1993).

As I discussed in Chapter 9, future work also needs to include elaborate discussion of the influence of technology and the media on young people's development. Given the increasingly important role technology and popular media culture plays in the majority of young people's lives, research needs to explore these issues. For example, Turkle (2015) warns that technology and popular culture might have an adverse influence on the spiritual and moral development of children. Furthermore, it is imperative that educators and parents of youth remain well versed on how popular culture may influence the social cognitive development of youth (Turkle, 2015).

The contemplation of meaning and self-identity, including philosophical enquiry and dialogue, can also provide a sense of connection, trust, and belonging with others, nature, and also oneself (Bronfenbrenner & Morris, 2006). To help adolescents develop and maintain such connections, schools need to encourage them to develop a mindful vocabulary, which in turn may help older children and adolescents to build a repertoire of contemplative or mindful activities (Roeser & Eccles, 2015). Such activities may encourage emerging adolescents to develop self-awareness and concentrate on the present as compared to the past or future.

Culturally inclusive peace education

What does the "connected and caring classroom" mean in today's increasingly multiethnic, multilingual, and technologically advanced world (Noddings, 2003)? A psychologically safe and sacred place is necessary for children and adolescents to explore and learn. They cannot be "afraid" to be silent and/or to articulate their questions. As research shows, negative affect, including negative self-beliefs and self-talk, may have a deleterious effect on learning (Conroy & Metzler, 2004; Harter, 1999). Also, as Lopez (2003) asks, what does it mean for those youth who are considered to be of "mixed" racial or ethnic heritage to identify as such, as North American society is different today compared to previous times in history?

Humane education and animal-assisted learning

As mentioned in Chapter 7, a growing body of research indicates that children's emotional attachments and relationships with companion animals (CAs) are associated with many positive physical, cognitive, and socioemotional outcomes (Daly & Suggs, 2010; Daly, Taylor, & Signal, 2014; Endenburg, van Lith, & Kirpensteijn, 2014; Mueller, 2014). As discussed in the previous chapter on learning exceptionalities, studies have also documented the social cognitive and emotional benefits of CAs for children with learning exceptionalities (Baumgartner & Cho, 2014; Greenspan & Deardorff, 2014; Melson, 2013), severe emotional difficulties or maltreatment (Faver, 2010; Solomon, 2010), physical challenges (Greenspan & Deardorff, 2014), as well as able-bodied and neurotypical children experiencing emotional stressors or undergoing a medical/dental procedure (Daly & Suggs, 2010). In addition, strong child–animal bonds have been linked to children's expression of empathy toward other children (Melson, 2013), and researchers have also found connections among youth, conduct disorder, and animal violence within different cultural contexts (Pagani, Robustelli, & Ascione, 2008).

Humane Education Programs (HEP) for Youth

Humane education programs (HEP) are typically conducted by animal shelter workers during in-class visits with children and youth (neurotypical and exceptional learners) (Baumgartner & Cho, 2014), and recent evidence suggests they have the potential to promote children's feelings of empathy and positive attitudes towards animals (Daly & Suggs, 2010; Melson, 2013). For example, studies of young people engaged in HEP programs have shown significant improvements in empathic understanding, cognitive development, and perspective-taking (Rule & Zhbanova, 2012; Wagoner & Jensen, 2010). Regarding the promotion of prosocial behavior, recent research has shown that HEP programs help children to learn about kindness, respect, and compassion toward animals with the potential to transfer to human relations (Daly et al., 2014; Mueller, 2014). Thus, such programs may serve as a successful educational strategy for youth with exceptional learning challenges to help prevent peer victimization and school violence (Faver, 2010).

Although the research to date suggests that HEP may help children to develop feelings of empathy and more positive attitudes toward animals and humans, their overall effectiveness requires further empirical study (Endenburg et al., 2014; Hurley, 2014). There is a need for more research to encourage and validate the efforts of educators, and to understand the influence of various methods and contexts used to deliver humane education to children and youth (Bexell, Jarrett, Ping, & Xi, 2009). Future research is needed to explore the impact of program length, format, materials, and the contexts used to deliver humane education on young people's social cognitive abilities.

In addition to schools, educationally based camp programs for children and youth often represent distinct, yet equally meaningful, types of learning communities. Camp-based programs for school-aged youth that incorporate CAs are becoming increasingly popular, and represent unique environments as they encourage and nurture direct contact between young people and animals (Bexell, Jarrett, Ping, & Xi, 2009; Melson, 2013). However, further empirical evidence of the educational influence of summer camp experiences is necessary, particularly including studies with adolescents who experience learning challenges in social cognitive areas such as empathy and ToM.

Psychoeducational implications: Ethical concerns and cautions

To address social cognitive and emotional learning in youth, adults need to take time to explore their inner worlds, and reflect upon their mental states, including thinking and feeling. Given the complex combination of cognitive and emotional states, for some learners this skill may take time to develop and require cautious guiding by adult educators. For example, for some individuals, mindful activities that promote introspection may be associated with negative emotions and have a possibly deleterious influence on their learning in the classroom (Davidson et al., 2012). Accordingly, adults who work with youth need to take the time to develop a trusting and respectful relationship.

Similar to the highschool classroom, the educational therapist aims to work with the adolescent in a respectful, open, and curiously compassionate atmosphere (Griffith & Griffith, 1994). Therapists and educators need to develop a trusting, authentic relationship with the adolescent to create a nonjudgmental atmosphere that can help to eliminate negative emotions and promote the self-confidence of therapists and adolescents. Given that issues involving learning challenges are likely to be emotional and sensitive, educators and researchers need to proceed with caution when working with adolescents. Similar to researchers, therapists and clinicians must also be aware of ethical issues when working with adolescents, such as confidentiality and the risk of psychological and emotional harm. The psychological and emotional safety of the adolescent must be ensured at all times.

For example, as described earlier, activities that involve self-disclosure such as bibliotherapy may be educational and therapeutic. Similar to narrative therapy, the educational activity of bibliotherapy can be applied to both a classroom and a therapist's office. Although a high school teacher may have specific curriculum objectives to achieve, educators and therapists aim to promote the development of a healthy self-concept in the adolescent. That is, both the educator and therapist require the young learner to engage in a conversation about their emotional and social experiences. Such learning activities (irrespective of whether or not implemented within the therapeutic or educational context), require a trusting and respectful relationship between the learner and the adult worker (therapist, teacher, etc.).

To promote a healthy overall psychological and emotional state in adolescents, we need to focus on programs and activities that promote positive self-thoughts, and adaptive coping techniques. Such strategies may help young people to cope with sometimes anxiety-producing social and academic experiences in a healthy and constructive manner. Borrowing strategies from the spiritual and clinical psychotherapy, activities that promote self-comfort and self-acceptance, such as relaxation techniques, visualization, art therapy, play therapy, psychodrama, may help adolescents to explore their inner worlds and develop a caring and compassionate inner dialogue.

According to various holistic educators (Kessler, 2000; Miller, 1993; Weare, 2013), the use of literature and art serve as effective teaching strategies as the structural organization of literature mirrors adolescents' spontaneous cognitive processes. Thus, this interpretive process enables the adolescent to access unconscious knowledge that can offer creative ways to resolve problems and enhance growth (Weare, 2013). Given that adolescents' social cognitive abilities may help to promote creative healing, such abilities may also help to unfold the unconscious resources. For instance, as already noted, bibliotherapy can serve as a therapeutic vehicle in that the literature offers material in a context and form that allows the adolescent learner to further develop their social cognitive abilities.

In a similar vein, another example of an educational and therapeutic activity that addresses social cognitive abilities involves dream work. In addition to collaborative group discussions, young people's dreams can be explored through similar concepts with the use of visual art, drama, narrative and metaphor, and music. Given the importance dreams play in psychological development (Noone et al., 2014; Ribeiro & Stickgold, 2014), neuro-psychoeducational activities that help to promote adolescents' understandings of dreams may also lead to further growth in self-development and self-knowledge (Nielsen & Kuiken, 2013).

The development of an understanding of one's dream experiences can aid in the growth in self-knowledge, which is crucial for mental and emotional health (Nadorff et al., 2014). In sum, further educational neuroscience research is needed to explore the functions of dreams in cognitive and emotional abilities such as memory and empathy (Ribeiro & Stickgold, 2014). Building on this research, through the use of dream-work incorporated into the classroom, youth can learn how to imagine hypothetical scenarios, and reflect critically on their dreams. Such activities may help youth to further develop self-knowledge and effective social coping and problem-solving skills to negotiate their school life experiences.

Future Questions: Global Educational Neuroscience

Building on the framework of relational developmental science (Overton, 2013), educational programs that share the goal of emotional health promotion and well-being in young people need to take a global, translational approach (Ribeiro & Stickgold, 2014). Children from across the globe share the personal need for acceptance and lovingkindness, and have the right to a safe and peaceful learning environment. Through collaborative research from areas of resilience neuroscience, positive psychology, social-emotional learning, with the help of instructional digital tools (Donaldson, Dollwet, & Rao, 2015; Parks, 2014; Pincham et al., 2014; Redzic et al., 2014), a global approach to developmental social cognitive neuroscience may eventually be feasible.

Similar to developmental resilience science (Masten, 2014a), developmental social cognition as well as developmental contemplative science combines mindfulness and compassion to reflect a more dynamic process as compared to a static entity (Neff, 2011; Roeser & Eccles, 2015). Such a conceptualization reflects a movement of social cognitivists to begin to embrace a broader systems transformation in developmental science (Lerner, Lerner, Von Eye, Bowers, & Lewin-Bizan, 2011; Zelazo & Lyons, 2012). According to Overton (2013), this relational developmental systems framework integrates ideas from developmental systems theory (Lerner et al., 2005, 2011), ecological systems theory (Bronfenbrenner & Morris, 2006), family systems theory (Kluger, 2011), biological systems (Busso, 2014), evolutionary perspectives (Ellis et al., 2012), and developmental psychopathology (Schneider, 2014).

More specifically, research programs that combine neuroscience and education will continue to be a main avenue for future researchers. Although I have described a selected few examples of research from educational neuroscience throughout this book (Pincham et al., 2014; Zelazo & Lyons, 2012), a more thorough and critical discussion regarding the role of educational neuroscience in understanding learning and social cognitive development is beyond the scope of this book. Based on the multitude of researchers exploring the human mind, the field of applied neurocognitive science remains relatively new and will most likely be one of the main avenues for future research to explore the neurobiological foundations of social cognitive development.

For example, as I mentioned earlier, the field of epigenetics explores the theory of "vantage or differential sensitivity." This theory suggests that learners experience varied positive responses to beneficial exposure and experiences of mental health educational programs (Gazelle, 2013; Pluess & Belsky, 2013). Such research may help educators and researchers to learn why, after experiencing a particular educational program such as Roots of Empathy (Gordon, 2005; Schonert-Reichl, Smith, Zaidman-Zait, & Hertzman, 2012), some individual learners may respond more positively to the program than others.

Given such information, educators and researchers may begin to focus more on the endogenous or genetic determinants of variation in response to assumed beneficial learning experiences (Ellis et al., 2012). In particular, past research suggests that genetic vantage or differential-sensitivity factors or potential "plasticity genes" may include markers such as the dopamine receptor D4 gene (DRD4-7R) and 5-HTTLPR. A larger proportion of Genetic X Environment research is gleaned from genetic variants in the serotonergic system, with the majority on the serotonin-transporter-linked polymorphic region (5-HTTLPR).

Past research shows that those children carrying at least one short allele have been associated with reduced expression of the serotonin transporter module. This module is involved in the reuptake of serotonin from the synaptic cleft and thus considered to be related to depression. A recent meta-analysis of research on 2,276 Caucasian children showed that those participants with one or two short alleles benefited more from positive environmental exposures than children without the short alleles (van IJzendoorn, Belsky, & Bakermans-Kranenburg, 2012).

Similar studies have illustrated the vantage-sensitivity character of 5-HTTLPR in young children's exposure to varied maternal responsiveness (Kochanska, Kim, Barry, & Philibert,

2011) and high-quality foster care (Drury et al., 2012). In addition, a study with young adults showed that participants with the short allele, compared to those with the long allele, scored significantly higher on life satisfaction and lower in neuroticism if they experienced a preponderance of positive life events (Donaldson et al., 2015). In sum, such recent work highlights the possibility that some learners may be more susceptible to a multitude of environmental "nutrients" than others. However, more research is needed before any educational implications and conclusions can be suggested.

Future research should also address whether there are psychological, physical, or neurobiological mechanisms that are specific to vantage sensitivity for various psychoeducational programs. Researchers could explore whether vantage sensitivity can be directly influenced through intervention as mentioned above, past research has shown that some vantage-sensitivity factors are shaped by early environmental influences such as prosocial interactions (Kashdan, Weeks, & Savostyanova, 2011; van IJzendoorn et al., 2012). If this is possible, the efficacy of existing psychoeducational programs and services might be increased significantly by interventions that target the promotion of vantage sensitivity. Thus, educators with this new knowledge may begin to work with individual learners to co-develop educational programs that provide optimal learning opportunities for all engaged.

In conclusion, vantage sensitivity provides a relatively new explanation for why individuals differ generally in their response to positive experiences. Applications of a vantage-sensitivity approach to development may enhance the person–environment fit for a variety of psychoeducational programs that aim to foster social cognitive competencies in young learners.

Global learning programs for developmental scientists

An increasing number of developmental scientists claim there is a growing need for educators and developmentalists to engage in global activities that foster the well-being and resilience of young people (Masten, 2014a, 2014b; Rose, 2014). Researchers and educators need to partner with global governmental and nongovernmental organizations to create empirically based, developmentally and culturally appropriate educational programs that promote social cognitive and cultural competence. As developmentalists and educators, Masten claims that it is our responsibility to provide empirically sound evidence, and communicate our science across fields and cultures.

Collaborations between developmental scientists and educators who are committed to the application of empirical research to practice may help to improve the well-being of youth globally and ultimately the future well-being of global health and human development. Such a global, relational, and developmental approach to research and education in social cognition among youth will capture the efforts of various other programs such as social-emotional learning (SEL) (Humphrey, 2013; Humphrey et al., 2011), and social-emotional and character development (SECD) (Schonert-Reichl et al., 2015). These programs will encourage the development of future programs that aim to promote the social, emotional, and cognitive well-being of youth across the globe.

As discussed in Chapter 2, consistent with the relational developmental approach to development and learning, Allred's social-emotional educational program (2014) is a recent example of research aimed to collaborate and share the SECDS with others as the self-report scale is intended to assess each of the overlapping facets of SECD (i.e., prosocial behavior, honesty, self-development, self-control, and respect for rules and expectations for appropriate behavior both at school and in the home). These different facets of skill and behavior were conceptualized as being subsumed under a more global construct of overall SECD. The SECDS uses a self-report format and was designed for use with children as young as 3rd grade. The broader goal was to contribute an instrument to the literature that would be of value both in the evaluation of SEL/SECD/PYD programs and in research on the development and etiology of social-emotional skills and character among elementary school-age children.

Given Allred et al.'s (2014) goal to promote resilience and social cognitive development in youth, such a global, holistic program could incorporate all areas of SEL, SECD, PYD, and more developmental social cognitive programs that focus on emotional and cognitive well-being, including those that foster contemplative practices such as mindfulness and compassion training (Mueller, 2014; Zelazo & Lyons, 2012). In addition, it could involve others from the exceptionality learning areas, such as art and music psychoeducational programs and therapies, and companion-animal assisted programs, such as AAI, to help children deal with emotional and behavioral difficulties (Hurley, 2014).

Summary

Overall, this chapter explored some of the pragmatic issues of the application of current research on social cognitive development to educational practice. It described some ways in which educators and researchers can encourage learners to develop their understanding of their inner world, as well as the psychological world of others. Thus, this chapter aimed to provide educators and researchers with helpful pedagogical and empirical directions that may encourage social cognitive and emotional learning to remain an important aspect of the curriculum.

References

Aldwin, C. M., Park, C. L., Jeong, Y.-J., & Nath, R. (2014). Differing pathways between religiousness, spirituality, and health: A self-regulation perspective. *Psychology of Religion and Spirituality, 6*(1), 9–21.

Allred, C. G. (2014). *Effects of a social-emotional and character development (SECD) program on character and distal manifestations of character such as positive and negative health* behaviors, emotional/mental health, and academics. Paper presented at Can Virtue Be Measured? The Second Annual Conference of the Jubilee Centre for Character and Values, University of Birmingham, Oriel College, University of Oxford.

Anderson, M., & Della Sala, S. (2013). Neuroscience in education: An (opinionated) introduction. In M. Anderson & S. Della Sala

(Eds.), *Neuroscience in education: The good, the bad, and the ugly* (pp. 3–12). Oxford, England: Oxford University Press.

Astington, J. (1993). *The child's discovery of the mind.* Cambridge, MA: Harvard University Press.

Baum, F. (1984/1900). *The wonderful wizard of Oz.* New York, NY: Signet Classic.

Baumgartner, E., & Cho, J. (2014). Animal-assisted activities for students with disabilities: Obtaining stakeholders' approval and planning strategies for teachers. *Childhood Education,* 281–290.

Beauchemin, J., Hutchins, T., & Patterson, F. (2008). Mindfulness meditation may lessen anxiety, promote social skills, and improve academic performance among adolescents with learning disabilities. *Complementary Health Practice Review, 13,* 34–35.

Bell, N. (2013). Just do it: Anishinaabe culture-based education. *Canadian Journal of Native Education, 36,* 36–58.

Betts, L., & Stiller, J. (2014). Centrality in children's best-friend networks: The role of social behaviour. *British Journal of Developmental Psychology, 32,* 34–49.

Bexell, S. M., Jarrett, O. S., Ping, X., & Xi, F. R. (2009). Fostering humane attitudes towards animals: An educational camp experience in China. *Encounter, 22*(4), 25–27.

Bonneville-Roussy, A., Rentfrow, P., Xu, M., & Potter, J. (2013). Music through the ages: Trends in musical engagement and preferences from adolesence through middle adulthood. *Journal of Personality and Social Psychology, 105,* 703–717.

Bosacki, S. (2000). Theory of mind and self-concept in preadolescents: Links with gender and language. *Journal of Educational Psychology, 92,* 709–717.

Bosacki, S. (2005). *Culture of classroom silence.* New York, NY: Peter Lang.

Bosacki, S. (2008). *Children's emotional lives: Sensitive shadows in the classroom.* New York, NY: Peter Lang.

Bosacki, S. (2013). Theory of mind understanding and conversational patterns in early adolescence. *Journal of Genetic Psychology, 174,* 170–191.

Bosacki, S., & O'Neill, S. (2015). Early adolescents' emotional perceptions and engagement with popular music activities in everyday life. *International Journal of Adolescence and Youth, 20*(2), 228–244. doi:10.1080/02673843.2013.785438

Broderick, P., & Metz, S. (2009). Learning to BREATHE: A pilot trial of a mindfulness curriculum for adolescents. *Advances in School Mental Health Promotion, 2,* 35–46.

Bronfenbrenner, U. (1977). Toward an experimental ecology of human development. *American Psychologist, 32,* 513–531.

Bronfenbrenner, U., & Morris, P. (2006). The bio-ecological model of human development. In R. M. Lerner (Ed.), *Handbook of child psychology: Vol. 43. Theoretical models of human development* (pp. 793–828). Hoboken, NJ: Wiley.

Bruner, J. (1996). *The culture of education.* Cambridge, MA: Harvard University Press.

Busso, D. (2014). Neurobiological processes of risk and resilience in adolescence: Implications for policy and prevention science. *Mind, Brain, and Education, 8,* 34–43.

Caine, R. (2003). Eco-spirituality. *Encounter: Education for meaning and social justice, 16,* 48–51.

Cajete, G. (1994). *Look to the mountain: An ecology of indigenous education.* Skyland, NC: Kivaki Press.

Capra, F. (1996). *The web of life.* New York, NY: Anchor.

Chin, T., & Rickard, N. (2014). Emotion regulation strategy mediates both positive and negative relationships between music uses and well-being. *Psychology of Music, 42,* 692–713.

Ciarrochi, J., & Bailey, A. (2008). *A CBT-practitioner's guide to ACT: How to bridge the gap between cognitive behavioral therapy and acceptance and commitment therapy.* Oakland, CA: New Harbinger.

Coles, R. (1990). *The spiritual life of children.* Boston, MA: Houghton Mifflin.

Conroy, D. E., & Metzler, J. N. (2004). Patterns of self-talk associated with different forms of competitive anxiety. *Journal of Sport and Exercise Psychology, 26,* 69–89.

Coplan, R. J., & Rudasill, K. (2016). *Quiet at school: An educator's guide to shy children.* New York, NY: Teachers College Press.

Daly, B., & Suggs, S. (2010). Teachers' experiences with humane education and animals in the elementary classroom: Implications for empathy development. *Journal of Moral Education, 39,* 101–112.

Daly, B., Taylor, N., & Signal, T. (2014). Pups and babes: Quantifying sources of difference in emotional and behavioral reactions to accounts of human and animal abuse *Anthrozoos, 27,* 205–217.

Damon, W., Menon, J. M., & Bronk, K. C. (2003). The development of purpose during adolescence. *Applied Developmental Science, 7,* 119–128.

Davidson, R., Dunne, J., Eccles, J., Engle, A., Greenberg, M., Jennings, P., … Vago, D. (2012). Contemplative practices and mental training: Prospects for American education. *Child Development Perspectives, 6*(2), 146–153.

Devine, R., & Hughes, C. (2013). Silent films and strange stories: Theory of mind, gender, and social experiences in middle childhood. *Child Development, 84,* 989–1003.

DiBiase, A., Gibbs, J., & Potter, G. (2005). *EQUIP for educators: Teaching youth (Grades 5–8) to think and act responsibly.* Champaign, IL: Research Press.

Donaldson, M. (1992). *Human minds: An exploration.* Harmondsworth, England: Allen Lane.

Donaldson, S., Dollwet, M., & Rao, M. (2015). Happiness, excellence, and optimal human functioning revisited: Examining the peer-reviewed literature linked to positive psychology. *The Journal of Positive Psychology, 10,* 185–195.

Drury, S. S., Gleason, M. M., Theall, K. P., Smyke, A. T., Nelson, C. A., Fox, N. A., & Zeanah, H. (2012). Genetic sensitivity to the caregiving context: The influence of 5HTTLPR and BDNF VAL66MET on indiscriminate social behavior. *Physiology &*

Behavior, 106, 728–735. doi:10.1016/j.physbeh.2011.11.014

Duckworth, A., & Carlson, S. (2013). Self-regulation and school success. In B. Sokol, M. Grouzet, & U. Muller (Eds.), *Self-regulation and autonomy: Social and developmental dimensions of human conduct* (pp. 208–230). New York, NY: Cambridge University Press.

Ellis, B., Del Giudice, M., Dishion, T., Figueredo, A., Gray, P., Griskevicius, V., … Wilson, D. (2012). The evolutionary basis of risky adolescent behavior: Implications for science, policy, and practice. *Developmental Psychology, 48,* 598–623.

Endenburg, N., van Lith, H. A., & Kirpensteijn, J. (2014). Longitudinal study of Dutch children's attachment to companion animals. *Society and Animals, 22,* 390–414.

Fabes, R. A., Hanish, L. D., Martin, C. L., Moss, A., & Reesing, A. (2012). The effects of young children's affiliations with prosocial peers on subsequent emotionality in peer interactions. *British Journal of Developmental Psychology, 30,* 569–585. doi:10.1111/j.2044-835X.2011.02073.x

Faver, C. A. (2010). School-based humane education as a strategy to prevent violence: Review and recommendations. *Children and Youth Services Review, 32,* 365–370.

Gardner, H., & Davis, K. (2013). *The App generation: How today's youth navigate identity, intimacy, and imagination in a digital world.* New Haven, CT: Yale University Press.

Gazelle, H. (2013). Is social anxiety in the child or in the anxiety-provoking nature of the child's interpersonal environment? *Child Development Perspectives, 7,* 221–226.

Goldberger, N. (1996). Cultural imperatives and diversity in ways of knowing. In N. Goldberger, J. Tarule, B. Clinchy, & M. Belenky (Eds.), *Knowledge, differences, and power: Essays inspired by women's ways of knowing* (pp. 335–371). New York, NY: Basic Books.

Goldstein, T. R. (2009). The pleasure of pure unadulterated sadness: Experiencing sorrow in fiction, nonfiction, and in our own lives.

Psychology of Aesthetics, Creativity, and the Arts, 3, 232–237.

Goldstein, T., & Winner, E. (2012). Enhancing empathy and theory of mind. *Journal of Cognition and Development, 13*, 19–37.

Goleman, D. (1995). *Emotional intelligence.* New York, NY: Bantam Books.

Gordon, M. (Ed.). (2005). *The roots of empathy: Changing the world child by child.* Toronto, ON, Canada: Thomas Allen.

Goswami, U. (2012). Principles of learning, implications for teaching? Cognitive neuroscience and the classroom. In M. Anderson & S. Della Sala (Eds.), *Neuroscience in education: The good, the bad, and the ugly* (pp. 47–60). Oxford, England: Oxford University Press.

Greenspan, L., & Deardorff, J. (2014). *The new puberty: How to navigate early development in today's girls.* New York, NY: Rodale.

Griffith, J., & Griffith, M. (1994). *The body speaks: Therapeutic dialogues for mind–body problems.* New York, NY: Basic Books.

Hadaway, N., & Young, T. (2014). Preserving languages in the new millennium: Indigenous bilingual children's books. *Childhood Education, 90*, 358–364.

Harter, S. (1999). *The construction of the self: A developmental perspective.* New York, NY: Guilford.

Hassed, C., Lisle, G., Sullivan, G., & Pier, C. (2009). Enhancing the health of medical students: Outcomes of an integrated mindfulness and lifestyle program. *Advances in Health Science Education, 14*, 387–398.

Hughes, C. (2011) *Social understanding and social lives: From toddlerhood through to the transition to school.* New York, NY: Psychology Press.

Humphrey, N. (2013). *Social-emotional learning: A critical appraisal.* London, England: Sage.

Humphrey, N., Kalambouka, A., Wigelsworth, M., Lendrum, A., Deighton, J., & Wolpert, M. (2011). Measures of social and emotional skills for children and young people: A systematic review. *Educational and Psychological Measurement, 71*(4), 617–637.

Hurley, K. (2014). Development and human–animal interaction: Commentary on Mueller. *Human Development, 57*, 50–54.

Hyde, J. (2014). Gender similarities and differences. *Annual Review of Psychology, 65*, 373–398.

Hyde, K., Lerch, J., Norton, A. C., Forgeard, M., Winner, E., Evans, A., & Schlaug, G. (2009). Music training shapes structural brain development. *Journal of Neuroscience, 29*, 3019–3025.

Kabat-Zinn, J. (2003). Mindfulness-based intervention in context: Past, present, and future. *Clinical Psychology-Science and Practice, 10*(2), 144–156.

Kashdan, T. B., Weeks, J. W., & Savostyanova, A. A. (2011). Whether, how, and when social anxiety shapes positive experiences and events: A self-regulatory framework and treatment implications. *Clinical Psychology Review, 31*, 786–799.

Kessler, R. (2000). *The soul of education: Helping students find connection, compassion, and character at school.* Alexandria, VA: ASCD.

Kluger, J. (2011). *The sibling effect.* New York, NY: Rainman.

Kochanska, G., Kim, S., Barry, R. A., & Philibert, R. A. (2011). Children's genotypes interact with maternal responsive care in predicting children's competence: Diathesis-stress or differential susceptibility? *Development and Psychopathology, 23*, 605–616. doi:10.1017/S0954579411000071

Kuypers, L. (2011). *The zones of regulation: A curriculum designed to foster self-regulation and emotional control.* San Jose, CA: Think Social Publishing.

Langer, E. (2000). Mindful learning. *Current Directions in Psychology Science, 9*, 220–223.

Larson, R. (2011). Positive development in a disorderly world. *Journal of Research in Adolescence, 21*, 317. doi:10.1111/j.1532-7795.2010.00707.x

Lau, N., & Hue, M. (2014). Preliminary outcomes of a mindfulness-based programme for Hong Kong adolescents in schools: Well-being, stress, and depressive symptoms. *International Journal of Children's Spirituality, 16*, 315–330. doi:10.1080/1364436X.2011.639747

Lerner, R. M., Lerner, J. V., Almerigi, J. B., Theokas, C., Phelps, E., Gestsdottir, S., ... von Eye, A. (2005). Positive youth development, participation in community youth development programs, and community contributions of fifth-grade adolescents: Findings from the first wave of the 4-H Study of Positive Youth Development. *Journal of Early Adolescence, 25*(1), 17–71.

Lerner, R. M., Lerner, J. V., Von Eye, A., Bowers, E. P., & Lewin-Bizan, S. (2011). Individual and contextual bases of thriving in adolescence: A view of the issues. *Journal of Adolescence, 34*(6), 1107–1114.

Limont, W. (2012). Support and education of gifted students in Poland. *Journal for the Education of the Gifted, 36,* 66–83.

Linkins, M., Mark Niemiec, R., Gillham, J., & Mayerson, D. (2015). Through the lens of strength: A framework for educating the heart. *Journal of Positive Psychology, 10,* 64–68.

Lopez, A. (2003). Mixed-race school age children: A summary of census 2000 data. *Educational Researcher, 32,* 25–37.

Lunau, K. (2014, June 15). Bringing mindfulness to the school curriculum. *Macleans, 2014,* pp. 1–5.

Machnik, S., & Martinez-Conde, S. (2010). *Sleights of mind: What the neuroscience of magic reveals about our everyday deceptions.* New York, NY: Henry Holt.

Mar, R. A., Oatley, K., Hirsh, J., dela Paz, J., & Peterson, J. B. (2006). Bookworms versus nerds: Exposure to fiction versus nonfiction, divergent associations with social ability, and the simulation of fictional worlds. *Journal of Research in Personality, 40,* 694–712.

Marshall, S., Parker, P., Ciarrochi, J., & Heaven, P. (2014). Is self-esteem a cause or consequence of social support: A 4-year longitudinal study. *Child Development, 85,* 1275–1291.

Masten, A. (2014a). Global perspectives on resilience in children and youth. *Child Development, 85,* 6–20.

Masten, A. (2014b). *Ordinary magic: Resilience in development.* New York, NY: Guilford.

Melson, G. (2013). Children's ideas about the moral standing and social welfare of non-human species. *Journal of Sociology and Social Welfare, 60,* 81–106.

Metz, S., Frank, J., Reibel, D., Cantrell, T., Sanders, R., & Broderick, P. (2013). The effectiveness of the learning to BREATHE program on adolescent emotion regulation. *Research in Human Development, 10,* 252–272.

Miller, J. (1993). *The holistic curriculum.* Toronto, ON, Canada: OISE Press.

Mink, D., Henning, A., & Aschersleben, G. (2014). Infant shy temperament predicts preschoolers theory of mind. *Infant and Child Behavior, 37,* 66–75.

Miranda, D., & Gaudreau, P. (2011). Music listening and emotional well-being in adolescence: A person and variable-oriented study. *European Review of Applied Psychology, 61,* 1–11.

Mueller, M. (2014). Is human–animal interaction (HAI) linked to positive youth development? Initial answers. *Applied Developmental Science, 18,* 5–16.

Nadorff, M., Porter, B., Rhoades, H., Greisinger, J., Kunik, M., & Stanley, M. (2014). Bad dream frequency in older adults with generalized anxiety disorder: Prevalence, correlates, and effect of cognitive behavioral treatment for anxiety. *Behavioral Sleep Medicine, 12,* 28–40.

Napoli, M., Krech, P., & Holly, L. (2005). Mindfulness training for elementary school students: The attention academy. *Journal of Applied School Psychology, 2,* 99–125.

Neff, K. D. (2011). Self-compassion, self-esteem, and well-being. *Social and Personality Psychological Compass, 5,* 1–12. doi:10.111 1/j.1751-9004.2010.00330

Neff, K. D., & McGeehee, P. (2010). Self-compassion and psychological resilience among adolescents and young adults. *Self and Identity, 9,* 255–240.

Nielsen, T., & Kuiken, D. (2013). Relationships between non-pathological dream-enactment and mirror behaviors. *Consciousness and Cognition, 22,* 975–986.

Noddings, N. (2003). *Happiness and education.* Cambridge, England: Cambridge University Press.

Noone, D., Willis, T., Cox, J., Harkness, F., Ogilvie, J., Forbes, E., … Gregory, A. (2014). Catastrophizing and poor sleep quality in early adolescent females. *Behavioral Science Medicine, 12,* 41–52.

Olson, D. (1994). *The world on paper.* New York, NY: Cambridge University Press.

Overton, W. F. (2013). A new paradigm for developmental science: Relationism and relational-developmental systems. *Applied Developmental Science, 17,* 94–107. doi:10.10 80/10888691.2013.778717

Pagani, C., Robustelli, F., & Ascione, F. R. (2008). Animal abuse experiences described by Italian school-aged children. In F. R. Ascione (Ed.), *The international handbook of animal abuse and cruelty: Theory, research, and application* (pp. 247–268). West Lafayette, IN: Purdue University Press.

Paley, V. (1999). *The kindness of children.* Cambridge, MA: Harvard University Press.

Palmo, T. (2002). *Reflections on a mountain lake: Teachings on practical Buddhism.* New York, NY: Snow Lion.

Parks, A. (2014). A case for the advancement and design of online positive psychological interventions. *The Journal of Positive Psychology, 9,* 502–508.

Pincham, H., Matejko, A., Obersteiner, A., Killikelly, C., Abrahao, K., Benavides-Varela, S., … Vuillier, L. (2014). Forging a new path for educational neuroscience: An international young-researcher perspective on combining neuroscience and educational practices. *Trends in Neuroscience and Education, 3,* 28–31.

Pluess, M., & Belsky, J. (2013). Vantage sensitivity: Individual differences in response to positive experiences. *Psychological Bulletin, 139*(4), 901–916. doi:10.1037/a0030196

Ramey, H., & Rose-Krasnor, L. (2015). The new mentality: Youth-adult partnerships in community mental health promotion. *Children and Youth Services Review, 50,* 28–37.

Redzic, N., Taylor, V., Chang, M., Trockel, M., Shorter, A., & Taylor, C. (2014). An Internet-based positive psychology program: Strategies to improve effectiveness and engagement. *Journal of Positive Psychology, 9,* 494–501.

Ribeiro, S., & Stickgold, R. (2014). Sleep and school education. *Trends in Neuroscience and Education, 3,* 18–23.

Richards, M. (1980). *Toward wholeness: Rudolf Steiner education in America.* Middletown, CT: Wesleyan University.

Roeser, R., & Eccles, J. (2015). Mindfulness and compassion in human development: Introduction to the special issue. *Developmental Psychology, 51,* 1–6.

Rose, R. (2014). Self-guided multimedia stress management and resilience training. *Journal of Positive Psychology, 9,* 489–493.

Ruch, W. (2009). Fearing humor? Gelotophobia: The fear of being laughed at. Introduction and overview. *Humor: International Journal of Humor Research, 22,* 1–25. doi:10.1515/ HUMR.2009.001

Rule, A. C., & Zhbanova, K. S. (2012). Changing perceptions of unpopular animals through facts, poetry, crafts, and puppet plays. *Early Childhood Education Journal, 40*(4), 223–230.

Saarikallio, S. (2011). Music as emotional self-regulation throughout adulthood. *Psychology of Music, 39,* 307–327.

Schneider, B. (2014). *Child psychopathology: From infancy to adolescence.* Cambridge, England: Cambridge University Press.

Schonert-Reichl, K., & Lawlor, M. (2010). The effects of a mindfulness-based education program on pre- and early adolescents' well being and social and emotional competence. *Mindfulness, 1,* 137–151.

Schonert-Reichl, K., Oberle, K., Lawlor, M., Abbott, D., Thomson, K., Oberlander, T., & Diamond. A. (2015). Enhancing cognitive and social–emotional development through a simple-to-administer mindfulness-based school program for elementary school children: A randomized controlled trial. *Developmental Psychology, 51,* 52–66.

Schonert-Reichl, K., Smith, V., Zaidman-Zait, A., & Hertzman, C. (2012). Promoting children's prosocial behaviors in school: Impact of the "Roots of Empathy" program on the social and emotional competence of school-aged children. *School Mental Health, 4*, 1–21. doi: 10.1007/s12310-011-9064

Sette, S., Baumgartner, E., & Schneider, B. (2014). Shyness, child–teacher relationships, and socio-emotional adjustment in a sample of Italian preschool-aged children. *Infant and Child Development, 23*, 323–332.

Seligman, M. E. P., Ernst, R. M., Gillham, J., Reivich, K., & Linkins, M. (2009). Positive education: Positive psychology and classroom interventions. *Oxford Review of Education, 35*, 293–311.

Shatkin, J. (2015). *Child and adolescent mental health: A practical all-in-one guide*. New York, NY: Norton.

Shonin, E., Van Gordon, W., & Griffiths, M. D. (2013). Buddhist philosophy for the treatment of problem gambling. *Journal of Behavioral Addictions, 2*, 63–71.

Singh, N., Lancioni, S., Joy, A., Winton, M., Sabaawi, R., Wahler, G., & Singh, J. (2007). Adolescents with conduct disorder can be mindful of their aggressive behavior. *Journal of Emotional and Behavioral Disorders, 15*, 56–63.

Solomon, O. (2010). What a dog can do: Children with autism and therapy dogs in social interaction. *Journal of the Society for Psychological Anthropology, 38*(1), 143–166.

Steiner, R. (1976). *Education of the child in the light of anthroposophy* (G. Adams & N. Adams, Trans.). London, England: Rudolph Steiner Press.

Sternberg, R. (2014). The development of adaptive competence: Why cultural psychology is necessary and not just nice. *Developmental Review, 34*, 208–224.

Sternberg, R., Jarvin, L., & Grigorenko, E. (2011). *Explorations in giftedness*. New York, NY: Cambridge University Press.

Tan, L., & Martin, G. (2016). Mind full or mindful: A report on mindfulness and psychological health in healthy adolescents.

International Journal of Adolescence and Youth, 21, 64–74.

Thompson, N., Whitesell, N., Galliher, N., & Gfellner, B. (2012). Unique challenges of child development research in sovereign nations in the United States and Canada. *Child Development Perspectives, 6*, 61–65.

Tolan, P. H., Guerra, N. G., & Kendall, P. C. (1995). A developmental-ecological perspective on antisocial behavior in children and adolescents: Toward a unified risk and intervention framework. Special Section: Prediction and prevention of child and adolescent antisocial behavior. *Journal of Consulting and Clinical Psychology, 63*, 579–584.

Turkle, S. (2015). *Reclaiming conversation: The power of talk in a digital age*. New York, NY: Penguin.

van IJzendoorn, M. H., Belsky, J., & Bakermans-Kranenburg, M. J. (2012). Serotonin transporter genotype 5HTTLPR as a marker of differential susceptibility? A meta-analysis of child and adolescent gene-by environment studies. *Translational Psychiatry, 2*, e147. doi:10.1038/tp.2012.73

Wagoner, B., & Jensen, E. (2010). Science learning at the zoo: Evaluating children's developing understanding of animals and their habitats. *Psychology and Society, 3*(1), 65–76.

Weare, K. (2013). Developing mindfulness with children and young people: A review of the evidence and policy context. *Journal of Children's Services, 8*(2), 141–153.

Wellman, H. (2014). *Making minds: How theory of mind develops*. Oxford, England: Oxford University Press.

Zelazo, P., & Lyons, K. (2012). The potential benefits of mindfulness training in early childhood: A developmental social cognitive neuroscience perspective. *Child Development Perspectives, 6*(2), 154–160.

Zylowska, L., Ackerman, M. H., Yang, J. L., Futrell, N., Horton, N., Hale, T., … Smalley, S. (2008). Mindfulness meditation training in adults and adolescents with ADHD: A feasibility study. *Journal of Attention Disorders, 11*, 737–746.

12

Beyond Social Cognition

"My spirit will sleep in peace, or if it thinks, it will not surely think thus. Farewell."
(Shelley, 1969/1818, p. 223)

Introduction

The following chapter introduces topics that move beyond the category of social cognition through the exploration of nascent yet promising areas of research such the neuroscience of social cognition, social or interpersonal neuroscience, and young people's understanding of the supernatural, magic, and spirituality. In addition, this chapter explores research possibilities regarding new aspects of complex moral emotions including self-consciousness, compassion, moral elation, remorse, revenge, schadenfreude, and moral and personal disgust. Research areas regarding persuasion, secret-keeping, trust and deception, artistic learning, emotional sensitivities and internalizing challenges (unsociability, callous-unemotional personality) are also relatively unexplored and will be mentioned briefly as well.

Research

Future directions of developmental neuroscience of social cognition

Given that the social neurosciences are one of the fastest growing areas within the biomedical, psychological, and educational fields (Amodio & Ratner, 2013; De Souza, 2014), these scientific advances will continue to influence developmental social cognition and

Social Cognition in Middle Childhood and Adolescence: Integrating the Personal, Social, and Educational Lives of Young People, First Edition. S. L. Bosacki.
© 2016 John Wiley & Sons, Ltd. Published 2016 by John Wiley & Sons, Ltd.

educational applications such as developmental contemplative practices for years to come. Outlined below is a selected overview of some of the cutting-edge trends in social neuroscience and education.

Hyperscanning (fMRI) of interpersonal and intergroup interactions   To explore the complex dynamics of interpersonal communication, researchers have started to apply multiple fMRIs to explore how the self is created within the context of others' minds (Rochat, 2009). For example, a novel and promising research technology has been developed to scan multiple brains during social interactions (Montague et al., 2002). This emerging research area is referred to as collaborative brain science or affective social neuroscience, and will continue to advance in the upcoming decades and support the claim that the mind develops and works in concert with other minds (Kim & Sasaki, 2014). Thus, affective social neuroscience and evolutionary developmental research will help to inform educators and researchers about how the emerging adolescent's mind is affected by complex social and emotional processes.

Modeling of neural networks and microsystems: Role of oxytocin in social behavior   Recent research on the role that neurotransmitters and hormones play in social interactions has also received increased attention over the past decade (Kim & Sasaki, 2014). That is, researchers have started to investigate more mechanistic roles of biological measures in sociocultural and sociocognitive processes. In particular, many studies investigate oxytocin, which is a neuropeptide produced in the hypothalamus that functions as a neurotransmitter and hormone (Carter, 2014). A range of prosocial tendencies, such as trust, cooperation, affiliation, attachment, and positive communication, have been found to be associated with oxytocin, examined as plasma oxytocin (Carter, 2014), and as exogenously administered oxytocin in animals and humans (see Meyer-Lindenberg, Domes, Kirsch, & Heinrichs, 2011 for a review).

Yet recent research suggests that, in addition to promoting prosociality, oxytocin may increase sensitivity to significant social cues (Miller, 2013). That is, some studies suggest that complex social interactions and social bonds could not have evolved without the physiological and behavioral functions of oxytocin (Carter, 2014). Given the complex process of exploring the role of hormones and neurotransmitters in emerging adolescents' social cognitive abilities, prosocial actions, and social relationships, the recent multitude of findings remain relatively mixed and require further research (Devine & Hughes, 2013).

For example, to further explore the past findings that suggested a positive association among social relations, social cognition, and oxytocin levels, Anagnostou et al. (2014) found that intranasal oxytocin treatment of individuals with autism spectrum disorders (ASDs) made them more likely to respond positively to others in social interactions. Similarly, research on social cognitive abilities such as joint attention, empathy, and self-recognition revealed that oxytocin increased the ability to accurately attribute the emotions and mental states of 18-month-olds as well as adults (Bartz et al., 2010, Wade, Hoffman, Wigg, & Jenkins, 2014).

Empirical evidence from studies with rodents shows that oxytocin has been found to increase the ability to accurately detect disease-infected others with the use of oxytocin-gene-knockout rodents (Kavaliers et al., 2004; see Kavaliers & Choleris, 2011 for a review). Recently, Calcagnoli et al. (2014) showed that local oxytocin expression and receptor binding in the male rat brain was associated with aggressiveness. They found that excessively aggressive rats showed diminished levels of oxytocin and enhanced OXTR (oxytocin receptor gene) binding capacities in targeted nodes of the social behavioral brain circuitry. Calcagnoli et al. (2014) suggested that their data on the neurobiology of abnormal aggressive male rats supported findings from human studies where pathological and excessive forms of aggression, impulsivity, irritability, and disrupted self-control have been associated with hypo-OXTergic function, as well as low plasma levels of testosterone (Albers, 2012; McCormick et al., 2013).

Regarding the role of neurotransmitters and hormones within in-group situations, past studies have shown that oxytocin may increase in-group bias among humans. That is, with the administration of the experimental method of intranasal oxytocin spray, a study found that oxytocin increased the degree to which participants favored in-group others and derogated and increased prejudice toward out-group others (De Dreu, 2012; see Bartz et al., 2010; Meyer-Lindenberg et al., 2011; Miller, 2013 for reviews).

Ethnocentrism, in which people favor familiar in-group others over unfamiliar out-group others, is a basic part of human sociality. This tendency may first be implicated in sociocultural processes in that psychological closedness in ethnocentrism would serve to maintain and strengthen culture-specific behaviors. Moreover, it may play a role in helping to shape particular aspects of cultural diversity that may be useful for schools and those who work with youth within an increasing culturally diverse student population. For example, research shows that regions with higher pathogen prevalence tend to develop collectivistic cultures that foster stronger in-group biases than do regions with lower pathogen prevalence (Miller, 2013). Thus, oxytocin may play an important role in the emergence and maintenance of sociocultural systems.

Although research suggests that there are likely other neurotransmitters and hormones that are associated with additional social behaviors, such as vasopressin (Carter, 2014), oxytocin provides one example of how neurotransmitters may play important functions in larger collective and social processes. The genetically related and structurally similar peptide vasopressin has been found to influence oxytocin, and is related to anxiety, mobilization, and defensive behaviors but also the formation of selective social bonds (Young, Gobrogge, Liu, & Wang, 2011). Given that the connections between oxytocin and vasopressin are complex, researchers have yet to unpack the links, which remain under current investigation (Carter, 2014). For research on emerging adolescents, oxytocin and vasopressin studies can also help to illustrate how Theory of Mind (ToM) and culture can incorporate biological processes within the explanatory framework of social behavior. That is, ToM research can serve as a valuable area of future study for researchers and educators to explore environmental and genetic contributions to emerging adolescents' cognitive and socioemotional functioning.

In sum, given the emergent status of research on oxytocin, vasopressin, social cognition, and social behavior among youth, current mixed findings suggest that oxytocin is a double-edged sword. That is, high levels of oxytocin and vasopressin may promote bonds with familiar individuals, but, at the same time, may promote unfriendly behavior toward strangers. As Miller (2013) suggests, oxytocin may increase the desire to connect and heighten attention to social cues, and may promote bonding within an established pair (or group) at the expense of outsiders. Future research needs to continue to explore the role of genetic and neurobiological factors associated with social cognitive development and especially prosocial behavior with emerging adolescents. Collaborations with educators, neurobiologists, and neuroscientists will also be necessary for the development of psycho-educational programs that incorporate biological, psychological, and social factors in social cognitive development (Bates, 2012; Carter, 2014).

Neuroeducation: Educational neurosocial cognitive and evolutionary developmental applied psychology

As mentioned in previous chapters, current research on developmental social cognition shows that inhibitory control may continue to develop throughout childhood and into adulthood (Mischel, 2014). For example, recent studies on the lifespan development of executive functioning, such as inhibitory control (IC), used an eye-tracking task to measure inhibitory control in children and adults (Kindt & van den Hout, 2001; Seefeldt, Kramer, Tuschen-Caffier, & Heinrichs, 2014). Results showed that, while there were improvements within childhood and between childhood and adulthood, even adults were not at ceiling. Thus, their study revealed another measure of IC that can be adapted for use across the lifespan.

A more developmentally appropriate research test battery will further elucidate the development of IC and its relation to cognitive, social, and emotional competence. As mentioned earlier, ongoing studies that incorporate the use of fMRI, EEG, and electrophysiological measures such as event-related potentials (ERP) in brain research may also help researchers to explore how emerging adolescents' social cognitive abilities are co-developed within the company of others (Carter, 2014; Mischel, 2014; Rochat, 2009). For example, recent research that suggests sleep plays an important role within adolescents' social and emotional functioning implies the need to continue to explore the development of neurobiological and psychological factors within adolescents' social communication processes (Rochat, Serra, Fadiga, & Gallese, 2008). Overall, given the lack of research on developmentally appropriate measures of inhibited control, research needs to continue in this area—especially within the context of adolescence.

Within this field of neurosocialcognitive research and neuroeducation (Busso, 2014), emerging evidence suggests that medial-frontal negativities (MFNs) generated from midline structures (e.g., the anterior cingulate cortex) are particularly correlated with levels of shyness, self-concept, and other psychosocial variables. According to research (Lackner, Santesso, Dywan, Wade, & Segalowitz, 2014), MFNs are a collection of ERPs including the inhibitory (or Nogo) N2, the error-related negativity (ERN), and the feedback-related negativity (FRN) that are thought to reflect the need for controlled attention and/or conflict detection (Bartholow et al., 2005; van Noordt & Segalowitz, 2012), especially under conditions of potential reward or punishment (Yu, Zhou, & Zhou, 2011).

Most recently, Lackner et al. (2014) found that, compared to low-shy youth, high-shy 12- to 14-year-olds were found to be hyperattentive to environmental cues about forthcoming behavioral requirements, and feedback from the environment about their behavior.

The authors also suggest that, given that past research shows correlations between anxiety and shyness (Coplan, 2014), future work should explore MFNs, shyness, and self-concept in terms of anxiety levels.

Moreover, as discussed in Chapter 7, given the role of neural development in self-regulation (Waters & Tucker, 2013), the motivational mechanisms of the impetus (e.g., anxiety, hostility, fear, and overall negative affect) may be integral to the negativism of autonomy strivings at key developmental life stages. That is, to what extent do emotionally meaningful transitions (e.g., birth of a child, death of a loved one) influence the self-regulation of a 2- or 3-year-old, an emerging adolescent, or an adult later in life? Thus, as discussed in Chapter 4, given the significant role emotions play in development, a neurodevelopmental approach to self-conscious emotions and self-regulation could help researchers and educators understand how, and why, adolescents interpret social, emotional, and moral events. Furthermore, such a research agenda could help educators learn how to help young people to develop strong self-regulatory and coping mechanisms, and make healthy life choices, as well as to form and maintain supportive and caring relationships with others.

Theory of mind and prosocial behavior (verbal and nonverbal)

Given that prosocial behavior has consistently been found to have inverse links with aggressive and externalizing behavior, especially beyond early childhood (see Eisenberg, Cumberland, Guthrie, Murphy, & Shepard, 2005 for a review), recent research suggests that some children who demonstrate high levels of prosocial behavior might demonstrate quite different patterns of social reasoning than nonprosocial children. These prosocial children may have a greater propensity to accurately code social cues and thus may demonstrate a benign or positive and kind attribution bias (rather than a hostile attribution bias). Such children may then be more likely to select relational and affiliative goals, and generate and evaluate positively socially competent strategies for achieving those goals, than nonprosocial children (Moore et al., 2012).

Future researchers could focus on the development of new measures of social cognitive processing that might tap into emerging adolescents' prosocial or socially competent biases. Also, as the majority of study designs are correlational and although the cross-lagged design provides a test of the direction of effects, experimental and intervention studies are needed to more confidently determine causal relations. Prevention and intervention programs aimed to improve social information-processing, emotional regulations including positive talk, and prosocial relations (verbal and nonverbal such as gestures of care and kindness) may help to support the links between social information-processing and aggressive behavior and socially anxious–withdrawn youth (Goldin-Meadow, 2014).

However, analogous research on prosocial behavior, including the development of friendships and social cognitive abilities such as ToM, self-conception, and inhibitory control, remains to be examined. In addition, past research supports the notion that peer experiences and friendships may help to shape young people's social cognition and social-emotional adjustment (Banerjee, Watling, & Caputi, 2011; Betts & Stiller, 2014; Bosacki, 2015; Caputi, Lecce, Pagnin, & Banerjee, 2012; Fink, Begeer, Hunt, & de Rosnay, 2014; Fink, Begeer, Peterson, Slaughter, & de Rosnay, 2015; Laible, McGinley, Carlo, Augustine, &

Murphy, 2014; Schneider, 2016). More work, however, is needed on the role of prosocial behavior (verbal and nonverbal, including gesture, humor) and positive and friendly peer experiences in social cognition.

Overall, these recent research findings on prosocial behaviors and social cognition have important implications for research and intervention. First, researchers need to examine bidirectional links between prosocial behavior and social information-processing longitudinally to better understand children's prosocial development. Second, recent findings add to the mounting evidence on the relevance of social information processing and ToM models in understanding socially competent and emotionally resilient behaviors, such as self-compassion and prosociality (Bluth & Banton, 2015; Neff, 2011; Masten, 2014a). And third, this book suggests future research directions to examine the possible protective roles social cognition and prosocial behavior may play in the development of hostile attribution biases and harmful behaviors directed at self and others. Such research could point to the importance of positive self-language and socially competent behaviors in the development and maintenance of supportive and caring friendships, well-being, and the reduction of internalizing and aggressive and externalizing behaviors (Fink et al., 2015; Leeves & Banerjee, 2014).

Social cognitive development research and the culture of affluence   Given that the study of influence of neighborhood and family income on social cognitive development has increased within Europe and North America over the past decade (Brattbakk & Wessel, 2013), the focus remains on low-income neighborhoods and families. Compared to research on the influence of low income and poverty on child and adolescent mental health and social cognitive development, the influence of high income of families on these same issues remains surprisingly unexplored. Although to date, few researchers have explored the influence of high-income families on the social cognitive development of youth (Lyman & Luthar, 2014), a nascent but promising area of research has started to explore how the social composition of the neighborhood and financial cultural landscape affect the social, cognitive, and emotional lives of youth.

As discussed in previous chapters, recent evidence based on studies with extremely impoverished or very affluent youth show group differences in social cognitive and emotional factors such as self-esteem and emotional well-being (Coren & Luthar, 2014). Future longitudinal research needs to explore how the social and cultural composition of a neighborhood community affect the young person's socioeconomic status, social cognitive development, and emotional well-being later in life. Finally, the results of such research could guard against negative cultural stereotypes and begin to disentangle and address the powerful ecosystemic forces that help to establish economically advantaged parents and youth (Bronfenbrenner, 1977; Lyman & Luthar, 2014; Masten, 2014b; Masten et al., 2014).

Applications: So What?

As discussed earlier, recent neuroscience research on mirror neurons may also have important educational implications for educational programs to promote social cognitive development among youth. According to De Souza (2014), educators need to utilize and empathize with the rich wisdom and heritage of diverse cultural traditions that compose our pluralistic, globalized world. Arts-based activities discussed earlier such as story-sharing and dramatic role-playing may help students activate their mirror neurons and promote empathy and compassion toward self and others.

Given that social cognitive, moral and emotional difficulties connected with high-income families may occur during later childhood and early adolescence, to develop collaborative family patterns in communication and shared activities, implications for preventative practice need to include dissemination efforts to encourage affluent parents. Given the focus on the mother in most developmental research, and especially the mainly absent role of the majority of the fathers in extreme low- and high-income levels, it is imperative that both parents be made equally aware of (a) the long-term risks to their children of the high influence and value of achievements (which often begins in preschool), and (b) the critical importance, for families, of shared leisure time, open and consistent communication and monitoring, as well as firm and consistent limit-setting.

Members of the upper and upper-middle class are disproportionately the shapers and standard-bearers of most literate cultures (Luthar, Barkin, & Crossman, 2013). Early trajectories of "gaming the system" often end up in serious crime later in life, with white-collar crimes such as Ponzi schemes having enormous negative repercussions for society as a whole. High envy among these youth has also been related to perfectionistic tendencies, and has the potential to lead to ego depletion or eroded personal resources and self-control (Lyman & Luthar, 2014). Such self-inhibition challenges may eventually begin to undermine mental energy for everyday tasks (Hill & Lapsley, 2011), and also decrease altruism toward others (Mischel, 2014). Aside from dishonesty, emotional distress can also have considerable long-term costs (Schneider, 2014, 2016). At a societal level, unhappiness and loneliness can accentuate personal acquisitiveness as opposed to philanthropy (Diener, Lucas, & Scollon, 2006). At an individual level, serious depressive episodes during adolescence may connote an elevated risk for recurrent episodes later in life (Seligman, 2011).

Why are these affluent youth, as a group, driven to make risky and often self-harming choices to excess? According to Lyman and Luthar (2014), Deresiewicz (2014), and others, the single largest factor is societal-cultural pressure: a common credo is "Work hard, play hard!" These youngsters may be at risk to develop extremely high or perfectionistic self-expectations to excel at school and extracurricular activities and also in their social lives. Affluent cultural messages promote that high-achievement performance is translated into leisure time, often with accompanying alcohol and drug use.

In addition to self-harmful behaviors and substance abuse, research on affluent young people also explores the area of consumerism and materialist values (Chaplin, Hill, & John, 2014). Research has shown that concerns about materialism have become a public policy issue, with consumer activists and social scientists calling for restrictions on youth marketing and advertising procedures. A recent UNICEF report on the welfare of children suggests that those from low- as well as high-income families may be particularly vulnerable to marketing efforts.

To explore the consumer values of impoverished and affluent children, Chaplin et al. conducted interviews with 177 children and adolescents from impoverished and affluent families to reveal differences in materialistic values. Although younger children (ages 8–10 years) from poor families exhibited similar levels of materialism to their more affluent peers, when they reach adolescence (ages 11–13 years) and beyond (ages 16–17 years), impoverished youth were more materialistic than their wealthier counterparts. Further analysis showed that this difference was also associated with lower self-esteem among impoverished teens. The authors suggested that implications of their findings include public policy solutions aimed to help reduce young people's vulnerability to developing materialistic values that undermine their well-being, and to promote resilience to such detrimental consumer habits.

More recently, Lyman and Luthar (2014) studied two groups of academically gifted 11th and 12th grade youth at the socioeconomic status (SES) extremes; one from an exclusive private, affluent school, and the other from a target school with low-income students. Results found that, compared to the impoverished youth, the affluent youth were at a relative disadvantage, with substantially higher substance use and peer envy. Affluent girls seemed particularly vulnerable, with pronounced elevations in perfectionistic tendencies and peer envy, as well as body dissatisfaction. Examination of risk and protective processes showed that relationships with mothers were associated with students' emotional distress, as well as positive adjustment. Additionally, findings showed links between (a) envy of peers and multiple outcomes (among high SES girls in particular), (b) dimensions of perfectionism in relation to internalizing symptoms, and (c) high extrinsic versus intrinsic values in relation to externalizing symptoms.

Coren and Luthar (2014) extended past findings of heightened social and emotional problems among affluent youth by examining adjustment patterns among boys in two academically elite, independent high schools: one for boys only and the other coeducational. Findings showed disproportionately high rates of internalizing and externalizing symptoms, but only the coeducational boys showed elevations in substance use. However, boys from all schools reported a relatively high incidence of exhibitionistic narcissistic characteristics, which is also an area that is largely understudied. Further findings showed that parent criticism—a defining feature of youths' maladaptive perfectionism—and perceived maternal depression also emerged as major vulnerability factors for both samples in relation to high levels of social and emotional challenges.

In addition, boys in the single-sex school reported a higher sensitivity to feelings of alienation from their fathers and perceived paternal depression. Envy of peers' physical attractiveness was associated with adolescent distress in both samples, but appeared to be especially critical for coeducational boys. Coren and Luthar's (2014) results have implications for future research and practice regarding the social cognitive and emotional costs and benefits of boys' attendance at a single-sex versus coeducational school, along with implications for practice and future research. For example, a similar study could be explored for females and additional social cognitive and emotional measures could be included, such as body dissatisfaction, self and other compassion, and additional internalizing challenges as mentioned in Chapter 10.

Given this recent data, researchers have started to question why affluent youth might experience so much stress and pressure (intrinsic and extrinsic). Luthar suggests that researchers consider the web of factors that collectively present in youth who are considered to be "privileged but pressured," that is, those factors that can demonstrate social equality (Cicchetti & Rogosch, 1996; Masten et al., 2014). Moreover, in upwardly mobile communities, the cultural ethos emphasizes perfection and stellar all-round school success and achievements. As Deresiewicz (2014) suggests, for financially advantaged children and parents alike, it is difficult to ignore the ubiquitous, pervasive message that is perpetuated from their early years onward: there is one path to ultimate happiness and personal success—financial gain—that in turn may derive from the attendance of prestigious colleges.

Surprisingly, researchers found that time in extracurricular activities was not necessarily a major risk factor in itself (Luthar & Latendresse, 2005). The critical issue remains the sense of pressure, criticism, and overly high expectations from adults. Thus, the sheer number of hours involved in extracurricular activities may be correlated with loneliness or distress. Such reports of parental pressure and lack of attachment was also found among extremely overextended high school juniors and seniors (Luthar & Barkin, 2012).

Pressures to succeed and excel may not originate from the parents alone, but may also come from within oneself, as well as outside the family. For example, coaches and teachers may be highly invested in the performer's star status, setting exacting and sometimes extreme standards in quests for their team's distinction. Peer group comparisons also contribute, because teens rank themselves against each other in extracurriculars as in academics, but also for physical attractiveness (especially in females, Luthar & Barkin, 2012), and sexual promiscuity (especially in males; Chase, 2008). In contrast to external pressure, self-pressure may also affect how teens perform in extracurricular activities and feel about themselves. Given these complex associations between self and other pressure to succeed, further research is needed.

Research suggests that peer aggression may also be connected to high peer status among these youth. Luthar and Barkin (2012) found significant peer admiration for girls also rated by peers as aggressive toward others. Such a finding supports the notion of the social dominance of "mean girls" (LaFontana & Cillessen, 2002). Parallel associations among boys were found but they were not as pronounced. In addition, among males, it was physical rather than relational aggression that was linked with peers' admiration. Such findings may encourage future researchers to consider the factors of family economic history as well as cultural backgrounds when studying bullying and victimization within peer relations among young people. More specifically, researchers need to explore the process of risk and resilience for youth who live in the extremes of the economic continuum such as affluent as well as impoverished families, including the homeless (Chaplin et al., 2014; Masten et al., 2014).

Future Questions

Faith development in social cognition among youth

As discussed in previous chapters, little research exists on the role language plays in the connections among faith development, self-cognitions, and emotional experiences (De Souza, 2014). This lack of research on young people's religious concepts is surprising, but most psychologists focus on the externals of religion such as explicit claims to belief and religiosity scales and frequency of church attendance (Bloom, 2013). Given this gap, researchers are becoming increasingly interested in adolescents' perceptions of spirituality and the role that social cognition plays in these experiences (Aldwin, Park, Jeong, & Nath,

2014; Moore, Talwar, & Bosacki, 2012). Thus, the question remains for researchers and educators of how to study the social cognitive connection to spirituality among youth and subsequently intervene to create educational programs that foster a spiritual dimension. In what ways does conventional schooling encourage adolescents to be silent about their "hunches" and hide their inner life? How can we as educators truly believe that this will foster a sense of well-being and fulfillment later on in life?

To answer the question of how schooling, teachers, and books have become separated or disengaged from spiritual awareness, a fruitful area for future research includes a focus on emerging adolescents' spiritual experiences and social cognitive abilities. How then, can researchers apply this construct of a spirituality of caring to explore the development of moral and spiritual reasoning among youth? From a psychological perspective, as discussed throughout this book, emergent adolescence (8–9 to 13–14 years) is recognized as a pivotal time in all aspects of development including cognitive reflexivity (e.g., Piaget, 1981), self-concept formation (e.g., Harter, 1999), and interpersonal relations (e.g., Rosenberg, 1965; Selman, 1980). Despite recognition of this complex and multifaceted developmental milestone, a holistic, social cognitive approach to investigating the links among self, social, and spiritual understanding remains to be taken (Bosacki, 2005; Bosacki, Harwood, & Sumaway, 2012; Moore et al., 2012).

As discussed briefly in Chapter 5 on the moral self, another area of research that has begun to investigate spiritual development in children and youth is ToM research within the discipline of cognitive science (e.g., Coles, 1990; Gardner, Csikszentmihalyi, & Damon, 2001; Harris, 2000; Taylor & Carlson, 2001). Following the cognitive revolution of the 1970s and early 1980s (see Bruner, 1996), a research area that investigated mental state understanding in children and adults emerged in the mid-1980s exploring children's understandings of false belief in both self and other. That is, to what extent do children understand that other people have thoughts, intentions, beliefs, desires, and emotions, as well as themselves (see Astington, 1993 for a brief history).

The majority of cognitive science studies borrow from Piaget's work on children's cognitive and moral development. These studies are consistent with the notion that concepts organize experiences, including spiritual and religious experience. Barrett, Richert, and Driesenga (2001) claims that challenges to the standard Piagetian developmental theme may be applied to the case of the spiritual and religion. In short, Barrett and colleagues believe that differences between measures used with children and adults have inaccurately maintained the anthropomorphic to abstract shift observed in god concepts. Barrett argues that contextual cognitive demands determine in part how anthropomorphic an agent concept is, both for children and for adults.

Given that the concept of prayer involves mentalistic elements of thought and belief (Harris, 2000), the studies on youth's understanding of religion support related ToM research. Studies from this burgeoning field of child social cognitive development document that, by 3 to 5 years of age, children clearly differentiate between mental and physical entities, and fantasy and reality (Kim & Harris, 2014a, 2014b; Woolley, 2014). Similarly, false-belief tasks demonstrate that young children have the ability to attribute mental states to self and others. That is, by age 5, children are able to understand that other people have mental states such as beliefs and intentions that influence our behavior (see Wellman, 2014).

Such studies of children's spiritual and religious experiences suggest that children have religious and spiritual representations in the minimal sense that they think and talk about matters that belong to the metaphysical and religious (Braun-Lewensohn & Sagy, 2010; De Souza, 2014). Therefore, young people's emotional experiences may provide the opportunity for adolescents to develop higher-order thinking skills such as ToM, as well as divergent and imaginative thinking skills regarding the concepts of the supernatural and consciousness (Devine & Hughes, 2013; Humphrey, 2011; Woolley, 2014).

Overall, given the roles that social cognitive abilities play in the complex relation between spirituality/religiosity and mental health, spirituality/religiosity may have an empirically demonstrable influence on mental health in that is it is broadly compatible with mental health coping and adjustment (Aldwin et al., 2014; Harris, 2000), critics notwithstanding (Ellis, 1980). Regarding educational contexts, school and educational psychologists agree that spirituality and religiosity may act as a developmental asset, both in the lives of the individual youth and in their communities (De Souza, 2014; Lantieri, 2001; Youniss, McLellan, & Yates, 1999). That is, various factors that relate to religiosity in adolescents may also help to serve as building blocks of adaptive development that assist youth to make wise decisions about their learning and health. Such factors include religious involvement, service to others, caring values, personal or self integrity, and honesty. These factors have found to have a significant positive influence on youth's lives, and help to protect them from engaging in self-harming and unhealthy behaviors and choices ranging from drug abuse to depression and attempted suicide (Keltner, 2009; Lantieri, 2001; Lewis, 2015).

In sum, although studies on religiosity/spirituality and mental health do not explicitly explore the connections between social cognition and mental health, many religious and spiritual activities such as church services, individual praying, and so on may involve opportunities for silence and mindfulness and contemplation. Thus, such findings may suggest that silence experiences within the context of some spiritual and religious events may help to strengthen adolescents' connections with themselves, their families, peers, teachers, and the larger community.

Developmental positive psychology and resilience science

Given the more contemporary, broader concepts of morality and spirituality, the concept of happiness and subjective well-being may also provide researchers with some answers to the inner world of the emerging adolescent. As discussed throughout this book, research on developmental positive psychology, especially self-compassion (Bluth & Banton, 2015), may provide some insight into adolescents' social cognitive and emotional experiences in the classroom (Parks, 2014; Rose, 2014). The theme of this inclusive and multidimensional approach to adolescent development focuses on the positive aspects of our character and our relationships.

Seligman and Csikszentmihalyi (2000) described the movement as a response to psychology's history of focusing on pathology and health challenges. In contrast to this negative focus, positive psychology aims to examine the positive features of human life that make our life meaningful, including the study of such topics as future mindedness, gratefulness, hope, wisdom, creativity, and spirituality, responsibility, and perseverance amongst others (Donaldson, Dollwet, & Rao, 2015; Watkins, Uhder, & Pichinevskiy, 2015). Given that spirituality is listed in the mandate for this new research movement in psychology, the focus on initiative (individualism, autonomy), resiliences, and social connectedness could help to promote further research on adolescents' social cognitive development, and may extend to research on leisure, play, and flow (Csikszentmihalyi, 1990; Seligman, 2011).

Positive psychology may also help to illuminate the connection between social cognitive experiences and emotional health in adolescents, and includes studies on the concept of flow, positive private speech, and resilience (Donaldson et al., 2015; Park, 2014; Watkins et al., 2015). Csikszentmihalyi's (1990) research on flow, or what the humanist psychologist Maslow (1971) referred to as peak experiences, may also provide an area for collaboration regarding social cognition and spiritual experiences. This field of research draws on the claims of some neuroscientists who claim that flow may be an altered state of consciousness, and this positive emotional state may have a neurological basis (De Souza, 2014). This concept of flow has been studied in adolescents and past research has shown that adolescents who report experiences of flow are more likely to experience a greater sense of psychological well-being and successful academic achievement (Csikszentmihalyi, 1990; Humphrey, 2011; Seligman, 2011).

Further, research on emotional experiences and subjective well-being may also provide researchers with some answers to the inner, spiritual world of adolescents. For example, Ben-Zur (2003) investigated the internal and social influences on subjective well-being (SWB) in university students and middle adolescents (15 to 17 years of age). In general, the results found that mastery, optimism, and positive adolescent–parent relationships helped to contribute to the overall health of adolescents. Thus, the field of positive psychology and studies on emotional well-being and health is an area for future research that may help to illustrate the complex links between adolescents' social cognitive experiences and mental health issues (Bluth & Banton, 2015; Donaldson et al., 2015; Schneider, 2014, 2016; Seligman, 2011; Seligman & Csikszentmihalyi, 2000; Siegel, 2013; Watkins et al., 2015).

Summary

As discussed in this chapter, within social cognitive developmental research—especially resilience research—once a broad risk factor has been identified, we aim to disentangle questions of "why or how." Accordingly, future research needs to explore the social cognitive and emotional processes within contexts of diversity including issues of financial (dis)advantage, cultural and ethnic backgrounds, and many others, as they might pose challenges for youth today. Research on little-studied groups urges us to consider not just well-known risks that affect all youth, such as alienation from parents, but also subculture-specific ones, such as the discrimination of ethnic minority youth, that operate in addition to the usual social and emotional challenges of adolescence. Those who work with youth must work to change the salient vulnerability and protective processes that may influence young people's social cognitive and emotional lives.

References

Albers, H. (2012). The regulation of social recognition, social communication and aggression: Vasopressin in the social behavior neural network. *Hormones and Behavior, 61,* 283–292.

Aldwin, C. M., Park, C. L., Jeong, Y.-J., & Nath, R. (2014). Differing pathways between religiousness, spirituality, and health: A self-regulation perspective. *Psychology of Religion and Spirituality, 6*(1), 9–21.

Amodio, D., & Ratner, K. (2013). The neuroscience of social cognition. In M. Anderson & S. Della Sala (Eds.), *Neuroscience in education: The good, the bad, and the ugly* (pp. 702–728). Oxford, England: Oxford University Press.

Anagnostou, E., Soorya, L., Brian, J., Dupuis, A., Mankad, D., Smile, S., & Suma, J. (2014). Intranasal oxytocin in the treatment of autism spectrum disorders: A review of literature and early safety and efficacy data in youth. *Brain Research, 1580,* 188–198.

Astington, J. (1993). *The child's discovery of the mind.* Cambridge, MA: Harvard University Press.

Banerjee, R., Watling, D., & Caputi, M. (2011). Peer relations and the understanding of faux pas: Longitudinal evidence for bidirectional associations. *Child Development, 82,* 1887–1905. doi:10.1111/j.1467-8624.2011.01669.x

Barrett, J. L., Richert, R. A., & Driesenga, A. (2001). God's beliefs versus mother's: The development of non-human agent concepts. *Child Development, 72,* 50–65. doi:10.1111/1467-8624.00265

Bartholow, B. D., Pearson, M. A., Dickter, C. L., Sher, K. J., Fabiani, M., & Gratton, G. (2005). Strategic control and medial frontal negativity: Beyond errors and response conflict. *Psychophysiology, 42*(1), 33–42. doi:10.1111/j.1469-8986.2005.00258.x

Bartz, J. A., Zaki, J., Bolger, N., Hollander, E., Ludwig, N.N., Kolevson, A., & Ochsner, K. N. (2010). Oxytocin selectively improves empathic accuracy. *Psychological Science, 21,* 1426–1428.

Bates, T. (2012). Education 2.0: Genetically-informed models for school and teaching. In M. Anderson & S. Della Sala (Eds.), *Neuroscience in education: The good, the bad, and the ugly* (pp. 188–212). Oxford, England: Oxford University Press.

Ben-Zur, H. (2003). Happy adolescents: The link between subjective well-being, internal resources, and parental factors. *Journal of Youth and Adolescence, 32,* 67–79.

Betts, L., & Stiller, J. (2014). Centrality in children's best-friend networks: The role of social behaviour. *British Journal of Developmental Psychology, 32,* 34–49.

Bloom, P. (2013). *Just babies: The origins of good and evil.* New York, NY: Random House.

Bluth, K., & Banton, P. (2015). The influence of self-compassion on emotional well-being among early and older adolescent males and females. *The Journal of Positive Psychology, 10,* 219–230.

Bosacki, S. (2005). *Culture of classroom silence.* New York, NY: Peter Lang.

Bosacki, S. (2015). Children's theory of mind, self-perceptions, and peer relations: A longitudinal study. *Infant and Child Development, 24,* 175–188. doi:10.1002/icd.1878

Bosacki, S., Harwood, D., & Sumaway, C. (2012). Being mean: Children's gendered perceptions of peer teasing within the classroom. *Journal of Moral Education, 41,* 473–489. doi:10.1080/03057240.2012.690728.

Brattbakk, I., & Wessel, T. (2013). Long-term neighbourhood effects on education, income and employment among adolescents in Oslo. *Urban Studies, 50*(2), 391–406.

Braun-Lewensohn, O., & Sagy, S. (2010). Sense of coherence, hope and values among adolescents under missile attacks: A longitudinal study. *International Journal of Children's Spirituality, 15,* 247–260.

Bronfenbrenner, U. (1977). Toward an experimental ecology of human development. *American Psychologist, 32,* 513–531.

Bruner, J. (1996). *The culture of education.* Cambridge, MA: Harvard University Press.

Busso, D. (2014). Neurobiological processes of risk and resilience in adolescence: Implications for policy and prevention science. *Mind, Brain, and Education, 8,* 34–43.

Calcagnoli, F., de Boer, S., Beiderbeck, D., Althaus, M., Koolhass, J., & Neuman, I. (2014). Local oxytocin expression and oxytocin receptor binding in the male rat brain is associated with aggressiveness. *Behavioural Brain Research, 261,* 315–322.

Caputi, M., Lecce, S., Pagnin, A., & Banerjee, R. (2012). Longitudinal effects of theory of mind on later peer relations: The role of prosocial behavior. *Developmental Psychology, 48*(1), 257–270. doi:10.1080/17405629.2013.821944

Carter, S. (2014). Oxytocin pathways and the evolution of human behavior. *Annual Review of Psychology, 65,* 17–39.

Chaplin, L., Hill, R., & John, D. (2014). Poverty and materialism: A look at impoverished versus affluent children. *Journal of Public Policy & Marketing, 33,* 78–92.

Chase, S. A. (2008). *Perfectly prep: Gender extremes at a New England prep school.* New York, NY: Oxford University Press.

Cicchetti, D., & Rogosch, F. A. (1996). Equifinality and multifinality in developmental psychopathology. *Development and Psychopathology, 8,* 597–600.

Coles, R. (1990). *The spiritual life of children.* Boston, MA: Houghton Mifflin.

Coplan, R. (2014). The A, B, C's of recent work on shyness and social withdrawal: Assessment, biology, and context. *Infant Child and Development, 23,* 217–219.

Coren, S., & Luthar, S. (2014). Pursuing perfection: Distress and interpersonal functioning among adolescent boys in single-sex and co-educational independent schools. *Psychology in the Schools, 51,* 931–946.

Csikszentmihalyi, M. (1990). *Flow.* New York, NY: Harper and Row.

De Dreu, C. K. (2012). Oxytocin modulates cooperation within and competition between groups: An integrative review and research agenda. *Hormone Behavior, 61,* 419–428.

Deresiewicz, W. (2014). *Excellent sheep: The miseducation of the American elite and the way to a meaningful life.* New York, NY: Free Press.

De Souza, M. (2014). The empathetic mind: The essence of human spirituality. *International Journal of Children's Spirituality, 19,* 45–54.

Devine, R., & Hughes, C. (2013). Silent films and strange stories: Theory of mind, gender, and social experiences in middle childhood. *Child Development, 84,* 989–1003.

Diener, E., Lucas, R. E., & Scollon, C. N. (2006). Beyond the hedonic treadmill: Revising the adaptation theory of well-being. *American Psychologist, 61,* 305.

Donaldson, S., Dollwet, M., & Rao, M. (2015). Happiness, excellence, and optimal human functioning revisited: Examining the peer-reviewed literature linked to positive psychology. *The Journal of Positive Psychology, 10,* 185–195.

Eisenberg, N., Cumberland, A., Guthrie, I. K., Murphy, B. C., & Shepard, S. A. (2005). Age changes in prosocial responding and moral reasoning in adolescence and early adulthood. *Journal of Research on Adolescence, 15*(3), 235–260.

Ellis, A. (1980). Psychotherapy and asthetic values: A response to A. E. Bergins "psychotherapy and religions values." *Journal of Consulting and Clinical Psychology, 48,* 635–639.

Fink, E., Begeer, S., Hunt, C., & de Rosnay, P. (2014). False-belief understanding and social preference over the first 2 years of school: A longitudinal study. *Child Development, 85,* 2389–2403.

Fink, E., Begeer, S., Peterson, C., Slaughter, V., & de Rosnay, P. (2015). Friendlessness and theory of mind: A prospective longitudinal study. *British Journal of Developmental Psychology, 33*(1), 1–17.

Gardner, H., Csikszentmihalyi, M., & Damon, W. (2001). *Good work: When excellence and ethics meet.* New York, NY: Basic Books.

Goldin-Meadow, S. (2014). How gesture works to change our minds. *Trends in Neuroscience and Education, 3,* 4–6.

Harris, P. (2000). On not falling down to earth: Children's metaphysical questions. In K. Rosengren, C. Johnson, & P. Harris (Eds.), *Imagining the impossible: The development of magical, scientific, and religious thinking in contemporary society* (pp. 157–178). Cambridge, England: Cambridge University Press.

Harter, S. (1999). *The construction of the self: A developmental perspective*. New York, NY: Guilford.

Hill, P. L., & Lapsley, D. K. (2011). Adaptive and maladaptive narcissism in adolescent development. In C. T. Barry, P. K. Kerig, K. K. Stellwagen, & T. D. Barry (Eds.), *Narcissism and Machiavellianism in youth: Implications for the development of adaptive and maladaptive behavior* (pp. 89–106). Washington, DC: American Psychological Association.

Humphrey, N. (2011). *Soul dust: The magic of consciousness*. Princeton, NJ: Princeton University Press.

Kavaliers, M., Agmo, A., Choleris, E., Gustafson, J. A., Korach, K. S., Muglia, L. J., … Ogawa, S. (2004). Oxytocin and estrogen receptor α and β knockout mice provide discriminably different odor cues in behavioral assays. *Genes, Brain, and Behavior, 3*, 189–195.

Kavaliers, M., & Choleris, E. (2011). Sociality, pathogen avoidance, and the neuropeptides oxytocin and arginine vasopressin. *Psychological Science, 22*, 1367–1374.

Keltner, D. (2009). *Born to be good. The science of a meaningful life*. New York, NY: Norton.

Kim, S., & Harris, P. L. (2014a). Belief in magic predicts children's selective trust in informants. *Journal of Cognition and Development, 15*, 181–196.

Kim, S., & Harris, P. L. (2014b). Children prefer to learn from mind-readers. *British Journal of Developmental Psychology, 32*, 375–387. doi:10.1111/bjdp.12044

Kim, H., & Sasaki, J. (2014). Cultural neuroscience: Biology of the mind in cultural contexts. *Annual Review of Psychology, 65*, 487–514.

Kindt, M., & van den Hout, M. (2001). Selective attention and anxiety: A perspective on developmental issues and the causal status.

Journal of Psychopathology and Behavioral Assessment, 23(3), 193–202.

Lackner, C., Santesso, D., Dywan, J., Wade, T., & Segalowitz, S. (2014). Event-related potentials elicited to performance feedback in high-shy and low-shy adolescents. *Infant and Child Development, 23*, 283–294.

LaFontana, K. M., & Cillessen, A. H. (2002). Children's perceptions of popular and unpopular peers: A multimethod assessment. *Developmental Psychology, 38*, 635–647.

Laible, D., McGinley, M., Carlo, G., Augustine, M., & Murphy, T. (2014). Does engaging in prosocial behavior make children see the world through rose-colored glasses? *Developmental Psychology, 50*, 872–880.

Lantieri, L. (2001). A vision of schools with spirit. In L. Lantieri (Ed.), *Schools with spirit: Nurturing the inner lives of children and teachers* (pp. 7–20). Boston, MA: Beacon Press.

Leeves, S., & Banerjee, R. (2014). Childhood social anxiety and social support-seeking: Distinctive links with perceived support from teachers. *European Journal of Psychology of Education, 29*, 43–62.

Lewis, M. (2015). *The biology of desire: Why addiction is not a disease*. New York, NY: Perseus Book Group.

Luthar, S., & Barkin, S. (2012). Are affluent youth truly "at risk"? Vulnerability and resilience across three diverse samples. *Development and Psychopathology, 24*, 429–449.

Luthar, S., Barkin, S., & Crossman, E. (2013). "I can, therefore I must": Fragility in the upper middle classes. *Development and Psychopathology, 4*, 1529–1549.

Luthar, S., & Latendresse, S. J. (2005a). Children of the affluent: Challenges to well-being. *Current Directions in Psychological Science, 14*, 49–53.

Lyman, E., & Luthar, S. (2014). Further evidence on the "costs of privilege": Perfectionism in high-achieving youth at socioeconomic extremes. *Psychology in the Schools, 51*, 91–930.

Maslow, A. (1971). *The farther reaches of human nature*. New York, NY: Viking.

Masten, A. (2014a). Global perspectives on resilience in children and youth. *Child Development, 85,* 6–20.

Masten, A. (2014b). *Ordinary magic: Resilience in development.* New York, NY: Guilford.

Masten, A., Cutuli, J., Herbers, J. Hinz, E., Obradovi, J., & Wentzl, W. (2014). Academic risk and resilience in the context of homelessness. *Child Development Perspectives, 8,* 201–206.

McCormick, C., Green, M., Cameron, N., Nixon, F., Levy, M., & Clark, R. (2013). Deficits in male sexual behavior in adulthood after social instability stress in adolescence in rats. *Hormone Behavior, 63,* 5–12.

Meyer-Lindenberg, A., Domes, G., Kirsch, P., & Heinrichs, M. (2011). Oxytocin and vasopressin in the human brain: Social neuropeptides for translational medicine. *National Review of Neuroscience, 12,* 524–538.

Miller, G. (2013). The promise and perils of oxytocin. *Science, 339,* 267–269.

Mischel, W. (2014). *The marshmallow test: Mastering self-control.* New York, NY: Little, Brown.

Montague, P. R., Berns, G. S., Cohen, J. D., McClure, S. M., Pagnoni, G., Dhamala, G. M., … Fisher, R. E. (2002). Hyperscanning: Simultaneous fMRI during linked social interactions. *Neuroimage, 16,* 1159–1164.

Moore, K., Talwar, V., & Bosacki, S. (2012). Diverse voices: Children's perceptions of spirituality. *International Journal of Children's Spirituality, 17,* 217–234. doi:10.1080/1364436X.2012.742040

Neff, K. D. (2011). Self-compassion, self-esteem, and well-being. *Social and Personality Psychological Compass, 5,* 1–12. doi:10.1111/j.1751-9004.2010.00330

Parks, A. (2014). A case for the advancement and design of online positive psychological interventions. *The Journal of Positive Psychology, 9,* 502–508.

Piaget, J. (1981). *Intelligence and affectivity: Their relationship during children's development.* Palo Alto, CA: Annual Reviews.

Rochat, P. (2009). *Others in mind: Social origins of self-consciousness.* Cambridge, England: Cambridge University Press.

Rochat, M., Serra, L., Fadiga, J., & Gallese, V. (2008). The evolution of social cognition: Goal familiarity shapes monkeys' action understanding. *Current Biology, 18,* 227–232.

Rose, R. (2014). Self-guided multimedia stress management and resilience training. *Journal of Positive Psychology, 9,* 489–493.

Rosenberg, M. (1965). *Society and the adolescent self-image.* Princeton, NJ: Princeton University Press.

Schneider, B. (2014). *Child psychopathology: From infancy to adolescence.* Cambridge, England: Cambridge University Press.

Schneider, B. (2016). *Childhood friendships and peer relations: Friends and enemies* (2nd ed.). New York, NY: Routledge.

Seefeldt, W., Kramer, M., Tuschen-Caffier, B., & Heinrichs, N. (2014). Hyper vigilance and avoidance in visual attention in children with social phobia. *Journal of Behavior Therapy and Experimental Psychiatry, 45,* 105–112.

Seligman, M. (2011). *Flourish.* London, England: Nicholas Brealey.

Seligman, M. E. P., & Csikszentmihalyi, M. (2000). Positive psychology: An introduction. *American Psychologist, 55*(1), 5–14. doi: 10.1037/0003-066X.55.1.5

Selman, R. L. (1980). *The growth of interpersonal understanding: Developmental and clinical analyses.* New York, NY: Academic Press.

Shelley, M. (1969/1818). *Frankenstein.* Oxford, England: Oxford University Press.

Siegel, D. (2013). *Brainstorm: The power and purpose of the teenage brain.* New York, NY: Jeremy Tarcher/Penguin.

Taylor, M., & Carlson, S. (2001). The influence of religious beliefs on parental attitudes about children's fantasy behavior. In K. Rosengren, C. Johnson, & P. Harris (Eds.), *Imagining the impossible: The development of magical, scientific, and religious thinking in contemporary society* (pp. 247–268). Cambridge, England: Cambridge University Press.

van Noordt, S. J., & Segalowitz, S. J. (2012). Performance monitoring and the medial prefrontal cortex: A review of individual differences and context effects as a window on self-regulation. *Frontiers in Human Neuroscience, 6,* 197. doi: 10.3389/fnhum.2012.00197

Wade, M., Hoffman, T., Wigg, K., & Jenkins, J. (2014). Association between the oxytocin receptor (OXTR) gender and children's social cognition at 18 months. *Genes, Brain, and Behavior, 13*(7), 603–610. doi:10.1111/gbb.12148

Waters, A., & Tucker, D. (2013). Social regulation of neural development. In B. Sokol, M. Grouzet, & U. Muller (Eds.), *Self-regulation and autonomy: Social and developmental dimensions of human conduct* (pp. 279–296). New York, NY: Cambridge University Press.

Watkins, P., Uhder, J., & Pichinevskiy, S. (2015). Grateful recounting enhances subjective well-being: The importance of grateful processing. *Journal of Positive Psychology, 10*, 91–98.

Wellman, H. (2014). *Making minds: How theory of mind develops.* Oxford, England: Oxford University Press.

Woolley, J. (2014). Commentary: What do mind readers know and what do we know about mind readers? *British Journal of Developmental Psychology, 32*, 388–390.

Young, K., Gobrogge, K., Liu, Y., & Wang, Z. (2011). The neurobiology of pair bonding: Insights from a socially monogamous rodent. *Frontiers of Neuroendocrinology, 32*, 53–69.

Youniss, J., McLellan, J., & Yates, M. (1999). Religion, community service, and identity in American youth. *Journal of Adolescence, 22*, 243–253.

Yu, R., Zhou, W., & Zhou, X. (2011). Rapid processing of both reward probability and reward uncertainty in the human anterior cingulate cortex. *PLOS ONE, 6*(12), e29633. doi:10.1371/journal.pone.0029633

Conclusion
Closing Thoughts and New Questions

"Ending is better than mending ..." (Huxley, 1932, p. 43)

Overall, educational programs that are developmental, relational, and responsive to young learners' developmental and cultural needs are required. The approach must also be developmentally and culturally sensitive in that it considers the physical, cognitive, emotional, and spiritual changes that young people experience as they develop their own sense of identities within the school world. Given the power of psychological language, educators need to redefine existing cultural classification schemes and create programs that reconceptualize diversity within educational research and practice (Lee, 2003).

Through the implementation of a curriculum that includes a balance of affective and cognitive components within a "psychologically safe" classroom climate, educators could work with researchers to develop a learning environment that will maximize the growth of both intra- and interpersonal functioning. As I have argued throughout this book, a relational developmental systems model of social and self-understanding for older children and adolescents may help to strengthen the relations between the fields of education and social cognitive research. In the end, the aim of this book is to deepen educators' and researchers' awareness of the different ways in which girls and boys interpret and understand social and self-knowledge, thus furthering the discourse in social cognitive psychology and education.

Although research continues to grow in the area of adolescent mental health, two promising areas of psychological research may offer exciting novel possibilities to help explore researchers investigate older children and adolescents' psychological experiences within the classroom. In particular, the research areas of developmental social cognitive science, and the positive psychology movement may promote the creation of new questions about the psychological and social lives of the young person.

Social Cognition in Middle Childhood and Adolescence: Integrating the Personal, Social, and Educational Lives of Young People, First Edition. S. L. Bosacki.
© 2016 John Wiley & Sons, Ltd. Published 2016 by John Wiley & Sons, Ltd.

Regarding the social cognitive neurosciences, the particular focus of Theory of Mind (ToM) research suggests promising links between spiritual, moral, emotional, and social development and cognitive growth. As mentioned earlier, ToM researchers have started to explore children's and adolescents' understandings of metaphysics, spirituality, religiosity, the magical and the supernatural, and future longitudinal research will need to explore these topics with emerging adolescents (Kim & Harris, 2014a, 2014b). Issues of spirituality, morality, religiosity can also be explored with the context of older children's and emerging adolescents' play, particularly imaginative or make-believe play, in real life as well as digital worlds (see Taylor & Carlson, 2001, discussed earlier).

ToM research within the broader frames of developmental social cognitive psychology and neuroscience research (Mahy, Moses, & Pfeifer, 2014; Tomasello, 2014b; Wellman, 2014), may provide particular insight into the social cognitive experiences of adolescents. As explained throughout this book, developmental social cognitive neuroscience research such as neurobiology may help educators and researchers to understand the social cognitive and neural processes that underlie the development of young people's personal knowledge and social understanding. Such research may help us to learn more about how specific brain processes may influence how young people develop their thinking in ways that are in tune with ourselves, others, nature, and beyond.

Research in visual neuroscience is another emerging area and may help us to make sense of how young people interpret and understand ambiguous interpersonal interactions. A newly developed area of research that stems from perception and neuroscience is that of neuromagic. This area of research studies visual illusions and how we interpret ambiguous and incomplete information such as social exchanges that involve persuasion and deception (Kołodziejczyk & Bosacki, 2015).

For example, Machnik and Martinez-Conde (2010) explored the neuroscience of magic and enchantment and revealed how we make sense of everyday deceptions. Machnik and Martinez-Conde (2010) aimed to understand how our minds understand the process of magic and illusion, and suggested that we can better understand how similar cognitive tricks function in persuasive strategies and interpersonal relations. This field of research also relates to recent research on the development of young individuals' understandings of unexplained phenomena such as near death experiences, halluciations, and the supernatural or mystical (Parnia, 2013; Sacks, 2012; Wellman, 2014). Such unexplored territories of research may help us to understand how understanding of the process of "magic" works in the mind of the young person, and may help researchers and neuroeducators to uncover the neural bases of consciousness and the concept of the self, including the brain, consciousness, and soul.

The second main area for future research concerns the recent movement of positive psychology and resilience neuroscience and explores the themes of relatively new approaches to child and adolescent development including prosociality and moral motivations, resilience, persuasion, and emotional and self-regulation within our personal and social worlds (Donaldson, Dollwet, & Rao, 2015; Kollerova, Janosova, & Rican, 2015; Kołodziejczyk & Bosacki, 2015; Masten, 2014a, 2014b; Parks, 2014; Rose, 2014; Seligman, 2011). These recent movements have been viewed as a response to psychology's past practice, which has been mainly dominated by a clinically oriented pathological framework that emphasized the emergence of mental health challenges and deviant behavior (Seligman, 2011).

In contrast to the focus on maladaptive development, positive psychology and resilience science examine the positive aspects of human life that make our life meaningful, including the study of future mindedness, hope, wisdom, creativity, spirituality, responsibility, perseverance, and resilience (Broeren, Newall, Dodd, Locker, & Hudson, 2013; Donaldson et al., 2015; Masten, 2014a, 2014b; Rose, 2014). Accordingly, there remains a dearth of literature on normative, typically developing youth. Such an initiative promotes aspects of individualism, autonomy, and collective intentionality, which could help to promote social cognitive development in youth, and may extend research on play, flow, and learning within the arts (Csikszentmihalyi, 1990; Larson, 2011; Tomasello, 2014a).

The application of the new areas of research mentioned above includes multidisciplinary, inclusive, and developmentally appropriate therapeutic and educational programs that draw on other cultures for their sources of expertise. An inclusive, relational developmental learning model that connects research to practice could provide a useful foundation within which educational and therapeutic programs could be developed. Research findings from developmental cognitive science and positive psychology could be used to help create developmentally appropriate educational and clinical programs. For example, findings on ToM with youth within fields of neuroeducation and applied developmental cognitive science could be used to help create a developmentally appropriate curriculum for children in the classroom that aims to promote interpersonal and intrapersonal competence.

As I began this book, I realized my main goal was to provide material that will encourage researchers and educators to continue to question and explore the complex social cognitive dimensions of adolescents' private and public worlds. Research on developmental social cognition will continue as our global society moves further to develop in moral complexity and diversity. Throughout this book, I aimed to highlight possible issues surrounding the development of social cognition within emerging adolescence, and noted that the connections among these constructs have yet to be made in any coherent manner. It is my hope that after reading this book, the reader will leave with a sense of optimism for the future of our youth, as I hope to provide some new questions that may lead to new research agendas. Educational programs that promote the development of social cognitive skills such as mindfulness and emotional regulation may help to ensure that the young people of today develop into caring and compassionate resilient adults.

As we delve further into the twenty-first century and look toward the twenty-second, the need is great for educators and social cognitive researchers to co-create a "curriculum of caring and compassion" that encourages youth to value interiority over materialism, and to embrace ambiguity and complexity within a community of learners. As many researchers suggest, we need to promote the development of mindful moral courage and compassion, intellectual curiosity, and passionate creativity in our youth of today. Recent findings from developmental social cognitive research support the need for developmentalists and educators to work collaboratively toward fostering young people's emotional well-being within a context of critical inquiry and dialogue. In the end, if the reader finishes my book with a renewed interest in the connections between social cognition and emotional health during emerging adolescence, then my task has been accomplished.

References

Broeren, S., Newall, C., Dodd, H., Locker, H., & Hudson, J. (2013). Longitudinal investigation of the role of temperament and stressful life events in childhood anxiety. *Development and Psychopathology, 26*, 437–449.

Csikszentmihalyi, M. (1990). *Flow.* New York, NY: Harper and Row.

Donaldson, S., Dollwet, M., & Rao, M. (2015). Happiness, excellence, and optimal human functioning revisited: Examining the peer-reviewed literature linked to positive psychology. *The Journal of Positive Psychology, 10*, 185–195.

Huxley, A. (1932). *Brave new world.* London, England: Vintage.

Kim, S., & Harris, P. L. (2014a). Belief in magic predicts children's selective trust in informants. *Journal of Cognition and Development, 15*, 181–196.

Kim, S., & Harris, P. L. (2014b). Children prefer to learn from mind-readers. *British Journal of Developmental Psychology, 32*, 375–387. doi:10.1111/bjdp.12044

Kollerova, L., Janosova, P., & Rican, P., (2015). Moral motivation in defending classmates victimized by bullying. *European Journal of Developmental Psychology, 12*, 297–309.

Kołodziejczyk, A. M., & Bosacki, S. L. (2015). Children's understandings of characters' beliefs in persuasive arguments: Links with gender and theory of mind. *Early Child Development and Care, 185*(4), 562–577. doi: 10.1080/03004430.2014.940930

Larson, R. (2011). Positive development in a disorderly world. *Journal of Research in Adolescence, 21*, 317. doi:10.1111/j.1532-7795.2010.00707.x

Lee, C. (2003). Why we need to re-think race and ethnicity in educational research. *Educational Researcher, 32*, 3–5.

Machnik, S., & Martinez-Conde, S. (2010). *Sleights of mind: What the neuroscience of magic reveals about our everyday deceptions.* New York, NY: Henry Holt.

Mahy, C., Moses, L., & Pfeifer, J. (2014). How and where: Theory-of-mind in the brain. *Developmental Cognitive Neuroscience, 9*, 68–81.

Masten, A. (2014a). Global perspectives on resilience in children and youth. *Child Development, 85*, 6–20.

Masten, A. (2014b). *Ordinary magic: Resilience in development.* New York, NY: Guilford.

Parks, A. (2014). A case for the advancement and design of online positive psychological interventions. *The Journal of Positive Psychology, 9*, 502–508.

Parnia, S. (2013). *Erasing death: The science that is rewriting the boundaries between life and death.* New York, NY: Harper Collins.

Rose, R. (2014). Self-guided multimedia stress management and resilience training. *The Journal of Positive Psychology, 9*, 489–493.

Sacks, O. (2012). *Hallucinations.* New York, NY: Knopf.

Seligman, M. (2011). *Flourish.* London, England: Nicholas Brealey.

Taylor, M., & Carlson, S. (2001). The influence of religious beliefs on parental attitudes about children's fantasy behavior. In K. Rosengren, C. Johnson, & P. Harris (Eds.), *Imagining the impossible: The development of magical, scientific, and religious thinking in contemporary society* (pp. 247–268). Cambridge, England: Cambridge University Press.

Tomasello, M. (2014a). *A natural history of human thinking.* Cambridge, MA: Harvard University Press.

Tomasello, M. (2014b). The ultra-social animal. *European Journal of Social Psychology, 44*, 187–194.

Waters, F., Collerton, D., Ffytche, D. H., Jardri, R., Pins, D., Dudley, R., … Larøi, F. (2014). Visual hallucinations in the psychosis spectrum and comparative information from neurodegenerative disorders and eye disease. *Schizophrenia Bulletin, 40* suppl, S233–S245.

Wellman, H. (2014). *Making minds: How theory of mind develops.* Oxford, England: Oxford University Press.

Index

This index has been prepared using letter-by-letter alphabetization

ABC model 255–256
academic achievement
  cognitive self 66, 71, 73
  developmental positive psychology
    and resilience science 318
  emotional self 83, 86, 103
  family relationships 172–174, 175
  gender and culture 175, 190
  moral self 115
Acceptance and Commitment
    Therapy (ACT) 291
age threshold model 167–168
aggression
  emotional self 85–86, 89–90, 96–98
  peer relationships 140–143
aloneness 253–254
altruism 110, 117, 144–149
ambiguous emotions 94
American Sign Language (ASL) 257
androgens 4
animal-assisted learning 295
anxiety
  cognitive self 63, 65

emotional self 83, 85, 88, 96,
    99–101
family relationships 158–159,
    169–174, 177
gender and culture 189, 190, 197,
    203, 207
moral self 121
neuroeducation 311
peer relationships 139, 144, 150–151
Apperly, I. 38–39, 200
apprenticeship model of sociocognitive
    learning 165, 167–169
arts 283, 285–286, 288–289, 297
ASD see autism spectrum disorders
ASL see American Sign Language
Asperger's Syndrome 36
Astington, J. 20–23, 60, 111, 316
attachment theory
  competence hypothesis 158
  coping and school engagement
    172–174
  disorganized attachment 158–159,
    173, 174

economically advantaged families
    163–165
family relationships 157–165,
    172–178
mental health within schools
    174–176, 177–178
self-regulation 172–174
social cognition 160–162
Theory of Mind 157–160
attention
  cognitive self 58–59
  digital and social media 227
  emotional self 94
  school engagement 172–174,
    229–230, 237–238
  shared intentionality and joint
    attention 58–59
audiovisual-based ToM tasks 38–41
autism spectrum disorders
    (ASD) 266–267
  family relationships 166
  neural networks 308
  Theory of Mind 36, 39–40

*Social Cognition in Middle Childhood and Adolescence: Integrating the Personal, Social,
and Educational Lives of Young People*, First Edition. S. L. Bosacki.
© 2016 John Wiley & Sons, Ltd. Published 2016 by John Wiley & Sons, Ltd.

autonomy
  cognitive self 71
  digital and social media 241
  emotional self 83, 85, 95
  family relationships 19, 172–173,
    177–178
  moral self 112, 119
avoidance
  behavioral and emotional challenges
    252–253
  emotional self 89–90, 95–96
  peer relationships 138, 141
Awareness of Social Inference Test,
  The (TASIT) 40

behavioral inhibition (BI) 266–267
belief-desire model of rational
    action 58
BI *see* behavioral inhibition
bibliotherapy 122, 211, 282, 284–285,
    296–297
biopsychocultural relational
    developmental systems 209
body image
  behavioral and emotional challenges
    256, 258
  gender 190–192, 197
  peer relationships 141
Bronfenbrenner, U. 84, 280
brooding 255–256
Bruner, J. 8, 18–19, 135–136, 202,
    287, 289
bullying
  ambiguities of social exclusion,
    silence, and ostracism 137–140
  culture of affluence 315
  cyberbullying 148–149, 227,
    230, 239
  deception, teasing, and
    psychological bullying 140–144
  emotional self 89
  helping and altruistic behavior
    144–149
  peer relationships 137–151
  prosocial behavior, bystanders and
    bully-victims 144–149
bully-victims 144–149

burnout 174–175
bystanders 144–149

catastrophic life events 16–17
CD *see* conduct disorder
Children's Depression Inventory (CDI)
    254–255
choice architecture 237
civil education 120
cognitive self 57–81
  across time and emotion 69–70
  applications 70–74
  concepts and definitions 57–58
  development of ToM, self-
    knowledge, and private speech
    61–67
  educational programs 73–74
  executive functions 69
  family and peer relationships
    60–61, 65–67
  future directions 75
  language 59–67
  perspective-taking 59, 60, 67–68
  research 58–70
  self-conception and self-
    understanding 63–67
  shared intentionality and joint
    attention 58–59
  social brain network research 68
  social cognitive development
    59–61, 67–68
  social cognitive research 5
  Theory of Mind 59–67, 69
communication
  cognitive self 58–59, 67, 69
  developmental social cognitive
    pedagogy 281–287
  digital and social media 225–247
  family relationships 171
  peer relationships 135–137, 141
  Theory of Mind 21–22, 36
companion animals 170–171,
    178, 295
compassion
  behavioral and emotional
    challenges 257, 259, 261–263
  cognitive self 63

developmental social cognitive
    pedagogy 280–281, 283–287,
    290–298
  emotional self 101, 312–314
  family relationships 172, 176–178
  gender and culture 189, 193
  moral self 110, 112, 115–119, 123
  peer relationships 141
competence hypothesis 158
complex emotions 87–88, 92, 114–116,
    148, 193–197, 203–204, 207
conceptual role-taking 25–26
conduct disorder (CD) 256–257
consumerism 313
coping strategies
  behavioral and emotional
    challenges 260, 266
  developmental social cognitive
    pedagogy 291
  emotional regulation 42, 84
  emotional self 95, 98–102
  family relationships 172–174
  moral self 121
counterfactual emotions 90–92
counterintuitive phenomena 119
creativity
  behavioral and emotional
    challenges 253
  cognitive self 71
  developmental social cognitive
    pedagogy 283, 285–286
  digital and social media 238
  moral self 122, 123–124
critical media literacy 237, 238
critical thinking
  developmental social cognitive
    pedagogy 282–283
  digital and social media 238
  moral self 124
culturally inclusive peace education
    294–295
cultural neuroscience 213
*Cultural Origins of Human Cognition,
  The* (Tomasello) 58
culture
  applications 208–212
  cognitive self 63, 65

culture (*cont'd*)
  concepts and definitions 188–222
  cultural diversity and school
    culture 210–211
  developmental social cognitive
    pedagogy 286–287, 292,
    294–295
  educational implications 210–212
  emotional self 92–94, 98, 203–204,
    207–212
  ethnicity, race, and social cognitive
    development 191–192, 198–205
  family relationships 162–163, 168,
    175–178
  future directions 213
  gender 190–192, 205–207
  intersectionality 205–207
  language 200–203
  moral self 115–116, 117, 202–205
  neural networks 309
  peer relationships 138, 145, 147
  personal choices and moral
    reasoning 204–205
  research 188–207
  self-regulation 200–202
  social cognitive research 6, 207
  Theory of Mind 199–200, 202–203
culture of affluence 163–165, 312,
  313–315
cyberbullying 148–149, 227, 230, 239

deception 140–144
decision fatigue 237–238
dehydroepiandrosterone (DHEA) 4
delayed self-gratification 73, 159–160
delinquency 96
depression
  behavioral and emotional
    challenges 252–256, 261, 265
  cognitive self 63
  digital and social media 230,
    233, 241
  emotional self 88, 96, 99
  family relationships 159–161, 177
  gender and culture 189, 190,
    193–194
  peer relationships 150

developmental discipline 119
developmental psychology 2
developmental relational systems
  approach 59–60
developmental shift-points 23–24
developmental social cognition 34–53
  applications 42–47
  concepts and definitions 1–2, 34
  emotional regulation 42
  future directions 47, 307–310
  measure development and
    rationale 43–46
  measurement issues 43–47
  measurement of social cognition
    35–42
  methodological issues 46–47
  online and nonverbal tasks
    35–38
  relational developmental systems
    theory 45–46
  research methodologies 35–42
  social-emotional character
    development 43–47
  social-emotional learning 43–47
  text- and audiovisual-based
    measure development 38–41
  Theory of Mind 34, 35–42
  see also social cognitive
    development
developmental social cognitive
  pedagogy
  animal-assisted learning 295
  caring and connected curriculum
    288–295
  co-learning and co-creating
    knowledge 281–282
  communication facilitates
    psychological comfort 281–287
  community connections 292–293
  concepts and definitions 279–280
  creation of a caring curriculum to
    promote connectivity 280–281
  culturally inclusive peace education
    294–295
  curriculum framework 284–285
  emotional strength, resilience, and
    sensitivity 288–292

ethical concerns and cautions
  296–297
future directions 298–300
global connections 292–294
global educational neuroscience
  297–300
global learning programs for
  developmental scientists 299–300
holistic educational approach
  281–282, 287–294, 297
humane education programs
  295–298
personal connections 289–291
positive psychology and resilience
  education 297–298
psychocultural and social ecological
  approach 280–281
psychocultural educational
  strategies 288–295
self and social understandings
  291–292
societal and cultural
  understandings 292
developmental theory 1–2
DHEA *see* dehydroepiandrosterone
Diagnostic Statistics Manual
  (DSM) 250
digital and social media 225–247
  applications 234–238
  caring, critical, and creative
    thinking 238
  challenges for psychoeducators
    226–234
  computer-mediated versus face-to-
    face communication 226–227,
    229–230, 236, 238–239
  concepts and definitions 225–226
  critical media literacy 237, 238
  cyberbullying 148–149, 227, 230, 239
  future directions 238–242
  gender 231–234
  persuasion and epistemic authority
    235–238
  psychobehavioral economics
    235–238
  psychological aspects of electronic
    communication 226

research 226–234
risks and harms 226–227, 239
school engagement 229–230
sexting 232–234
social networking and mental
  health in youth 228–231
technology and popular media
  influences 227–228
discrimination, peer relationships 146
disintegration 83–84
diversity *see* culture; gender
dramatic arts 283, 285–286, 289, 297
DSM *see* Diagnostic Statistics Manual
Dunn, J. 115, 169

eating disorders 189, 190
ecological self 292–293
eco-spirituality 292–293
education
  animal-assisted learning 295
  behavioral and emotional challenges
    261–266
  caring and connected curriculum
    288–295
  cognitive self 73–74
  co-learning and co-creating
    knowledge 281–282
  communication facilitates
    psychological comfort 281–287
  community connections 292–293
  concepts and definitions 279–280
  creation of a caring curriculum to
    promote connectivity 280–281
  culturally inclusive peace education
    294–295
  culture 210–212
  curriculum framework 284–285
  developmental social cognitive
    pedagogy 279–306
  digital and social media 226–234,
    237–241
  emotional strength, resilience, and
    sensitivity 288–292
  ethical concerns and cautions
    296–297
  future directions 298–300
  gender 210–211

global connections 292–294
global educational neuroscience
  297–300
global learning programs for
  developmental scientists
  299–300
holistic educational approach
  281–282, 287–294, 297
humane education programs
  295–298
moral self 119–123
personal connections 289–291
positive psychology and resilience
  education 297–298
psychocultural and social ecological
  approach 280–281
psychocultural educational
  strategies 288–295
self and social understandings
  291–292
social cognitive research 7–8
societal and cultural
  understandings 292
educational neurosocial cognitive
  psychology 310–311
educational psychology 2
EF *see* executive function
electronic communication *see* digital
  and social media
emotional arousal 84–85
emotional intelligence 90, 100–101, 283
emotional regulation (ER)
  cognitive self 61, 69–70
  concepts and definitions 1–2
  development in the emotional
    self 84–86, 90–91
  social cognitive research 5
  Theory of Mind 42
emotional self 82–108
  age and sociocultural context 93
  applications 101–103
  behavioral and emotional challenges
    248–275
  complex or self-conscious emotions
    87–88, 92, 114–116, 148,
    193–197, 203–204, 207
  concepts and definitions 82–83

counterfactual emotions 90–92
culture 203–204, 207–212
culture of affluence 312, 313–315
depression among youth 254–256
developing emotions 86–87
developmental positive psychology
  and resilience science 317–318
developmental social cognitive
  pedagogy 287–292, 296–297
digital and social media 231, 233,
  239–240
disintegration process 83–84
educational implications for gifted
  students 261–262
emotional consistency across
  relationships 93
emotional intelligence and
  neuroticism 100–101
emotional regulation
  development 84–86, 90–91
family relationships 163–164, 170,
  171, 173–175
future directions 103
gender and culture 92–94, 98,
  193–197, 207–211
giftedness 259–262
internalizing challenges 251–254
language and emotions 86–87,
  92–95
language proficiency and peer
  interaction 257–259
mixed and ambiguous emotions 94
moral emotions 88–90, 96–99,
  114–119, 148, 203–204
moral self 101–102, 114–120
narcissism and neuroticism 88, 89,
  96–99, 102–103
perception and externalizing
  challenges 256–257
perfectionism and neuroticism 90,
  99–101
research on emotions and self 82–92
self as personal fable 95–101
self-esteem 95, 97–98, 101–102
social-emotional development of
  youth with exceptional
  needs 251–268

emotional self (*cont'd*)
  Theory of Mind 35–36, 38–40, 88, 92–95, 98–99, 101
  training programs for youth with chronic learning challenges 263–266
empathy/empathetic sensitivity
  behavioral and emotional challenges 260
  culture 200, 211
  developmental social cognitive pedagogy 281
  gender 193–194, 195–197, 211
  moral self 116–118
  peer relationships 137, 146
  Theory of Mind 26
epistemic authority 235–238
ER *see* emotional regulation
ERI *see* ethnic and racial identity
ERN *see* error-related negativity
ERP *see* event-related potentials
error-related negativity (ERN) 310
ethics 46, 296–297
ethnic and racial identity (ERI) 211–212
ethnocentrism 309
etiquette 138
eurhythmy 285–286, 291
event-related potentials (ERP) 310
evolutionary development
  emotional self 84–85
  juvenile transition 3–4
  moral self 110
  social cognitive research 16
evolutionary developmental applied psychology 310–311
evolutionary developmental psychology 147
evolutionary psychology 58, 60
executive function (EF) 69, 159, 165–171
extracurricular activities 315
eye gaze patterns 94

factor analysis 44
fairness judgments 67, 146–147
false belief 21–22, 35, 38–39, 111, 115

family relationships 157–187
  applications 171–176
  apprenticeship/age threshold models of sociocognitive learning 165, 167–169
  attachment theory 157–165, 172–178
  cognitive self 60–61
  concepts and definitions 157
  coping and school engagement 172–174
  economically advantaged families 163–165
  emotional self 85, 94–96
  executive function 159, 165–171
  future directions 176–178
  human–animal interactions 170–171, 178
  mental health within schools 171, 174–176, 177–178
  moral development and parent–youth relations across cultures 162–163
  parenting styles 175
  parent–child relationship 159, 160–162, 174–175
  research 157–171
  self-regulation 172–174
  sibling relationships 165–171
  social cognition and parental attachment 160–162
  social cognitive research 19
  Theory of Mind 157–160, 162–163, 165–171
feedback-based learning 69
feedback-related negativity (FRN) 310
FI *see* fluid intelligence
first-order beliefs 21–22, 38–39
flirting 233
fluid intelligence (FI) 35
fMRI *see* functional magnetic resonance imaging
folk psychology 20
FRN *see* feedback-related negativity
functional magnetic resonance imaging (fMRI) 47, 69, 231, 307

gender
  applications 208–212
  behavioral and emotional challenges 254–256
  body image 190–192, 197
  cognitive self 61, 65
  concepts and definitions 188–222
  culture 190–192, 205–207
  digital and social media 231–234
  educational implications 210–211
  emotional self 92–93, 98, 193–197, 207–211
  family relationships 163, 167, 169–170, 171
  future directions 213
  intersectionality 205–207
  moral self 114–116, 117–118
  peer relationships 138, 140–141, 145, 147, 189–190
  perspective-taking 194–197
  research 188–207
  self-conception 190–192
  social cognitive development 188–205
  social cognitive research 6, 17, 27, 207
  stereotyping and media representations 189, 190–191, 194, 197, 206–208
  Theory of Mind 193–197
gene–culture interactions 177–178
gene–environment interactions 177–178
giftedness 259–262
global educational neuroscience 297–300
guilt
  emotional self 83, 88–90
  gender 193–194, 207
  moral self 114–116
  peer relationships 148

HAI *see* human–animal interactions
hearing impairment 257
helping behavior 144–149
HEP *see* humane education programs
holistic educational approach 281–282, 287–294, 297

hormones 4, 195–196, 308–310
Hughes, C. 27, 40–41, 165
humane education programs
    (HEP) 295–298
human–animal interactions
    (HAI) 170–171, 178, 295

IC *see* inhibitory control
identity
    cognitive self 64, 72
    culture 204–205
    digital and social media 227, 239
    emotional self 83, 95–96
    family relationships 162–163
    gender 188–190
    moral self 110
    social cognitive research 5–6, 19
impulsivity 18–19, 95
individual differences
    behavioral and emotional
        challenges 253
    moral self 109–110, 118
    peer relationships 142
individualism–collectivism 205
inhibitory control (IC) 310
inner speech 61
intention 58–59, 110, 135–136
interdependence–independence 204
intergroup interactions 307
interpersonal relationships
    cognitive self 65
    culture 203–204
    digital and social media 232–233
    emotional self 90, 92–94, 97–98
    family relationships 167, 174–176
    gender 193
    see also family relationships; peer
        relationships
interpersonal understanding 25
interpretive Theory of Mind
    (IToM) 166–169
intersectionality 205–207
intertemporal choice 159–160
IToM *see* interpretive Theory of Mind

joint attention 58–59
juvenile transition 3–4

labeling 94
language
    behavioral and emotional challenges
        257–259
    cognitive self 59–67
    culture 200–203
    developmental social cognitive
        pedagogy 282–283, 287
    digital and social media 231, 236
    emotional self 86–87, 92–95
    family relationships 169
    moral self 121–122
    peer relationships 135–137
    semantic and syntactic language 60
    Theory of Mind 35, 39
    see also private speech
latent-class analysis (LCA) 91–92
learning exceptionalities
    applications 262–266
    assessment of learning
        exceptionalities 263
    behavioral and emotional challenges
        248–275
    concepts and definitions 248
    depression among youth 254–256
    developmental and learning
        challenges 250–251, 262–266
    educational implications for gifted
        students 261–262
    future directions 266–268
    giftedness 259–262
    internalizing challenges 251–254
    language proficiency and peer
        interaction 257–259
    perception and externalizing
        challenges 256–257
    psychopathology and social
        cognition 249–250
    research 249–262
    social cognitive development
        248–275
    social-emotional development of
        youth with exceptional
        needs 251–268
    training programs for youth with
        chronic learning challenges
        263–266

literature 282, 286–287
loneliness 253–254
lying 140–144

Machiavellianism 97
manipulative behavior 97–98, 140
Marshmallow Test 73
Masten, A. 71, 175, 299
materialism 313
MCII *see* mental contrasting with
    implementation intentions
Mead, G. 59
medial-frontal negativities
    (MFN) 310–311
media representations
    developmental social cognitive
        pedagogy 293
    gender 191, 194, 197
    technology and popular media
        influences 227–228, 240
    see also digital and social media
memory retention 227
mental contrasting with implementation
    intentions (MCII) 73–74
mental health
    behavioral and emotional challenges
        248–275
    depression among youth with
        learning exceptionalities
        254–256
    developmental and learning
        challenges 250–251, 262–266
    digital and social media
        228–231
    family relationships 171, 174–176,
        177–178
    gender 189, 190, 193–194
    giftedness 259–262
    internalizing challenges
        251–254
    language proficiency and peer
        interaction 257–259
    perception and externalizing
        challenges 256–257
    psychopathology and social
        cognition 249–250
    see also anxiety; depression

mentalization
    behavioral and emotional
        challenges 256
    cognitive self 68
    emotional self 87
    Theory of Mind 20, 36, 39
metacognition 136, 283
metalinguistics 136
metamemory 35
MFN *see* medial-frontal negativities
microaggression
    deception 140
    peer relationships 140–143
    teasing 140–144
microsystems 308–310
Miller, S. 166, 310
mindfulness 282–283, 286,
        289–291, 317
mirror neurons 116–117, 312–313
mixed emotions 94
moral emotions 88–90, 96–99,
        114–119, 148, 203–204
moral obligation 146–147
moral self 109–132
    applications 119–124
    behavioral and emotional challenges
        259–261
    culture 202–205
    developmental social cognitive
        pedagogy 286
    educational programs 119–123
    emotional self 101–102, 114–120
    faith development in social
        cognition among youth 315–317
    family relationships 162–163
    future directions 124–125
    gender, emotionality, and social
        cognition 114–116, 117–118
    judgments of intention–
        action 110–111
    language 121–122
    moral sensitivities among
        youth 113–114
    moral understandings within social
        cognition 109–111
    neuroscience research and
        empathy 116–118

peer relationships 140–143,
        146–148, 150
    positive moral emotions and moral
        elation 118–119
    research 109–119
    self-esteem 113
    social cognitive research 5
    social responsibility 109–110,
        120–122
    spiritual and moral
        development 112–113
    Theory of Mind 110–112, 115–118
motivation 265
multitasking 237
music 283, 285–286, 297

narcissism 88, 89, 96–99, 102–103
narrative 282, 287, 297
neural networks 308–310
neuroeducation
    culture 213
    developmental social cognitive
        pedagogy 281–282
    family relationships 176
    future directions 310–311
neuroimaging
    cognitive self 68, 69
    digital and social media 231
    future directions 47, 308, 310
    visuo-spatial processing 37
neuroscience
    behavioral and emotional challenges
        248–250, 255
    cognitive self 68, 71, 73
    culture 199–200, 213
    digital and social media 235–236
    family relationships 176–178
    future directions 307–310,
        312–313
    global educational neuroscience
        297–300
    hyperscanning and intergroup
        interactions 308
    moral self 116–118
    neural networks, microsystems,
        and oxytocin 308–310
    social cognitive research 15–16

neuroticism
    emotional intelligence 100–101
    emotional self 96–103
    narcissism 96–99, 102–103
    perfectionism 99–101
neurotransmitters 308–310
nonverbal ToM tasks 35–38
Nucci, L. 109, 119–120, 163, 202–203
nudge theory 235–237

ODD *see* oppositional defiant
        disorder
online positive psychology programs
        (OPP) 119
online ToM tasks 35–38
OPP *see* online positive psychology
        programs
oppositional defiant disorder
        (ODD) 256–257
ostracism 137–140, 141, 289
other-understanding 65–66
oxytocin 308–310

PA *see* Positive Action
paltering 142–143
parenting styles 175
pathological narcissism 97–98
peer envy 314
peer relationships 135–156
    ambiguities of social exclusion,
        silence, and ostracism
        137–140, 141
    applications 149–150
    behavioral and emotional challenges
        257–259
    cognitive self 60–61, 65–67
    concepts and definitions 2
    deception, teasing, and
        psychological bullying 140–144
    digital and social media 238–239
    emotional self 88, 94–98
    family relationships 162
    friendship 143–150
    future directions 150–151
    gender 189–190
    helping and altruistic
        behavior 144–149

language, communication, and
  social relations 135–137, 141
microaggression and deception
  140–143
moral self 140–143, 146–148, 150
negative moral behaviors 140–143
prosocial behavior 137, 144–149
research 135–149
social cognition and peer relations
  137, 143–144
social cognitive research 5–6, 19
Theory of Mind 135–137, 141–143
perfectionism
  culture of affluence 314
  emotional self 90, 99–101
  family relationships 164
personal fable
  emotional self 95–101
  narcissism and neuroticism 96–99
  perfectionism and neuroticism
    99–101
  social cognitive research 18
person perception 26–27
perspective-taking
  behavioral and emotional
    challenges 260
  cognitive self 59, 60, 67–68
  culture 211
  gender 194–197, 211
  peer relationships 147
  Theory of Mind 25, 36–38
persuasion 235–238
Piaget, Jean 58–59, 110, 316
plagiarism 229
Positive Action (PA) program 45
positive private speech (PPS) 72
positive psychology
  developmental positive psychology
    and resilience science 317–318
  developmental social cognitive
    pedagogy 297–298
  digital and social media 240
  gender and culture 212
power imbalances 145–146
PPS *see* positive private speech
pragmatics 136, 138
private speech

behavioral and emotional challenges
  265–266
cognitive self 61–67, 72
developmental social cognitive
  pedagogy 283
gender and culture 201–203
prosocial behavior
  behavioral and emotional
    challenges 253
  developmental social cognitive
    pedagogy 286
  emotional self 89–90, 97–99, 102
  family relationships 159–160
  peer relationships 137, 144–149
  Theory of Mind 309, 311–312
psychobehavioral economics
  235–238
psychocultural approach 17–18,
  19–20, 280–281, 288–295
psychoeducation
  developmental social cognitive
    pedagogy 281–283, 296–297
  digital and social media 226, 241
  moral self 121
  social cognitive research 17
psycholinguistics 59, 136, 138
psychological bullying 140–144
psychological understanding 2

RDST *see* relational developmental
  systems theory
reading 282, 286–287
Reading the Mind's Eye Test
  (RMET) 35–36, 39, 193
reciprocity
  emotional self 97–98
  moral self 110, 117, 119
  peer relationships 146–147
  Theory of Mind 38
reflection
  behavioral and emotional challenges
    255–256
  developmental social cognitive
    pedagogy 282
  moral self 121
regret 90–92
regulated withdrawal 252–253

relational developmental systems
  theory (RDST)
  gender and culture 208
  social cognitive research 16, 18
  social-emotional character
    development 45–46
relativism 23
reliability 45
relief 90–92
religion 112–113, 123, 315–317
remorse 90, 92
research ethics 46
resilience
  culture 212
  developmental positive psychology
    and resilience science
    317–318
  developmental social cognitive
    pedagogy 288–292, 297–298
  family relationships 164
  social cognitive research 16–17
risk-taking
  cognitive self 71
  culture of affluence 313
  digital and social media
    232–233, 236
  emotional self 85–86, 95
  social cognitive research 18
RMET *see* Reading the Mind's
  Eye Test
rumination 255

schizophrenia 267
school culture
  cultural diversity 210–211
  family relationships 173–174, 176
  social cognitive research 18
school engagement 172–174,
  229–230, 237–238
SCL *see* social cognitive learning
SECD *see* social-emotional character
  development
second-order beliefs 22, 38–39, 111,
  115
Second Step program 74
SEL *see* social-emotional learning
self-awareness 289–290

self-conception
    cognitive self 63–67
    concepts and definitions 2
    developmental social cognitive
        pedagogy 296
    emotional self 87
    family relationships 158
    gender 190–192
    peer relationships 135, 137,
        142–143
    Theory of Mind 21–24
self-confidence 158, 160, 171
self-conscious emotions 87–88, 92,
    114–116, 148, 193–197,
    203–204, 207
self-definition process 188–189
self-development 1–2, 83–84
self-disclosure 163, 241, 296
self-esteem
    behavioral and emotional
        challenges 254
    emotional self 95, 97–98, 101–102
    family relationships 158–159, 173
    gender 191–192
    moral self 113
    peer relationships 140, 141
self-expression 231–233, 283,
    285–286, 289–290
self-harm *see* suicidality and self-
    harm
self-knowledge 61–67
self-recognition mirror task 203
self-regulation
    behavioral and emotional
        challenges 265–266
    cognitive self 58, 61–62, 70–74
    culture 200–202
    developmental social cognitive
        pedagogy 281, 282
    emotional self 88
    family relationships 172–174
    moral self 112
    neuroeducation 311
    Theory of Mind 26
self-report measures
    behavioral and emotional
        challenges 254–255

emotional self 94, 96, 98
    social-emotional character
        development 44, 45
self-silencing 95–96, 251
self-talk *see* private speech
Self-Talk Scale (STS) 202
self-understanding 63–67
self-worth
    behavioral and emotional
        challenges 260
    cognitive self 65
    digital and social media 227, 239
    emotional self 83, 92, 96–97,
        101–102
    family relationships 159, 164, 171
    moral self 113
    peer relationships 140, 141
    Theory of Mind 23
Selman's model of interpersonal
    understanding 25
Selman's theory of social cognitive
    development 59–60
semantic language 60
service learning 120–122
sexting 232–234
sexual behavior
    culture of affluence 315
    emotional self 85–86
    gender 198
shame
    emotional self 83, 88–90
    gender 193–194, 207
    moral self 114–116
    peer relationships 148
shared intentionality hypothesis 58–59
shyness
    behavioral and emotional
        challenges 252
    family relationships 162
    neuroeducation 310–311
    peer relationships 138–139
silence
    behavioral and emotional
        challenges 251
    developmental social cognitive
        pedagogy 289
    peer relationships 137–140

silent films task 40–41
SLI *see* specific language impairment
SNS *see* social networking sites
social brain network 68
social class 192
social cognition, definition 3
social cognitive development
    applications 262–266
    assessment of learning
        exceptionalities 263
    behavioral and emotional
        challenges 248–275
    cognitive self 59–61, 67–68
    concepts and definitions 248
    culture, ethnicity, and race 191–192,
        198–205
    culture of affluence 312
    depression among youth 254–256
    developmental and learning
        challenges 250–251, 262–266
    diversity 6
    educational implications 7–8
    educational implications for gifted
        students 261–262
    future directions 266–268
    gender 188–205
    giftedness 259–262
    internalizing challenges 251–254
    language proficiency and peer
        interaction 257–259
    learning exceptionalities 248–275
    perception and externalizing
        challenges 256–257
    psychopathology and social
        cognition 249–250
    research 249–262
    social cognitive research 6–8,
        17–19
    social-emotional development of
        youth with exceptional
        needs 251–268
    training programs for youth with
        chronic learning challenges
        263–266
social cognitive learning (SCL) 74
social cognitive research
    applications 27–28

complexity 21–27
conceptual role-taking 25–26
diversity and social cognitive development 6
educational implications 7–8
empathetic sensitivity 26
family and peer relationships 19
future directions 28
gender X culture intersectionality 207
historical development 15–17
identity and relationships 5–6
integrative, multilateral approach 23–24
juvenile transition 3–4
mind, spirit, emotion, and morals 5
personal fable 18
person perception 26–27
resilience 16–17
risk-taking and impulsivity 18–19
social cognitive abilities and school experiences 15–33
social cognitive development 6–8, 17–19
Theory of Mind 19–28
social construction
cognitive self 58–59, 66
family relationships 164
gender 189
social development, definition 1–2
social ecological approach 280–281
social-emotional character development (SECD)
developmental social cognitive pedagogy 299–300
measure development and rationale 43–46
measurement issues 43–47
methodological issues 46–47
relational developmental systems theory 45–46
validity and reliability 44–45
social-emotional learning (SEL)
behavioral and emotional challenges 266
cognitive self 74

developmental social cognitive pedagogy 299–300
educational implications 8
family relationships 178
measure development and rationale 43–46
measurement issues 43–47
methodological issues 46–47
peer relationships 141
social exclusion 137–140, 141
social media *see* digital and social media
social networking sites (SNS) 228–231, 234, 241
social norms 147–148
social responsibility 109–110, 120–122
social stigma 62–63
SocialVille 264–265
socioeconomic status (SES) 163–165, 312, 313–315
sociolinguistic behavior 137–138
specific language impairment (SLI) 257, 259, 261
spirituality
eco-spirituality 292–293
faith development in social cognition among youth 315–317
moral self 112–113
social cognitive research 5
Steiner, Rudolf 285–286, 291
stereotyping
gender 189, 190–191, 194, 197, 206–208
social cognitive research 17
storm and stress hypothesis 85
Strange Situation paradigm 158
strange stories task 39, 41
stress 160–162, 255, 314–315
STS *see* Self-Talk Scale
subjectivity 46
substance abuse 313–314, 317
suicidality and self-harm
culture of affluence 313, 317
emotional self 95, 99
family relationships 160, 173
social cognitive research 18

SUPER program 212
sympathetic concern 144–145
syntactic language 60

TASIT *see* Awareness of Social Inference Test, The (TASIT)
teacher criticism 66, 115
teacher–student relationship 83, 162, 173–175
teasing 140–144
TEI *see* trait emotional intelligence
terministic screens 17
testosterone 196
text-based ToM tasks 38–41
Theory of Mind (ToM)
applications 27–28
apprenticeship/age threshold models of sociocognitive learning 165, 167–169
attachment theory 157–160
behavioral and emotional challenges 258–261, 264
cognitive self 59–67, 69
complexity 21–27, 40
concepts and definitions 2
conceptual role-taking 25–26
culture 199–200, 202–203
developmental social cognition 34, 35–42
developmental social cognitive pedagogy 281, 283
development of ToM, self-knowledge, and private speech 61–67
educational implications 7–8
emotional regulation 42
emotional self 88, 92–95, 98–99, 101
empathetic sensitivity 26
executive function and sibling relationships 165–171
executive functions 69
family relationships 157–160, 162–163, 165–171
first- and second-order beliefs 21–23, 38–39, 111, 115
future directions 309, 311–312
gender 193–197

Theory of Mind (ToM) (*cont'd*)
  integrative, multilateral
    approach 23–24
  measurement of social cognition
    35–42
  moral development and parent–
    youth relations across cultures
    162–163
  moral self 110–112, 115–118
  neural networks 309
  online and nonverbal tasks 35–38
  peer relationships 135–137, 141–143
  person perception 26–27
  prosocial behavior 309, 311–312
  self-conception and self-
    understanding 63–67
  social cognitive research 5–8, 19–28
  text- and audiovisual-based
    measure development 38–41
theory-theory of the self 64, 66
ToM *see* Theory of Mind

Tomasello, M. 58–59, 68, 144–145,
  198–199
trait emotional intelligence (TEI) 90,
  100–101
trust 37–38
trust game 37
Turkle, S. 225, 227, 294

Universal Design for Learning
  (UDL) 262–263

validity 44, 45
Values in Action (VIA) programs 123
vantage or differential sensitivity
  298–299
vasopressin 309–310
VIA *see* Values in Action
victimization 137–140, 145, 315
violence
  behavioral and emotional
    challenges 260

digital and social media 227–228,
  238–240
  social cognitive research 16
visual impairment 258
visuo-spatial processing 37
vulnerability-stress approach 255
Vygotsky's theory of cognitive
  development 61–62

Waldorf Education 285–286
withdrawal
  behavioral and emotional
    challenges 252–253
  emotional self 89–90,
    95–96
  peer relationships 138, 141
Wittgenstein, Ludwig 59, 198
writing 282

youth positive development
  (YPD) 34, 45, 48